新世纪全国高等中医
Chinese-English Bilingual New Century Innovation Textbook
for International Students of Chinese TCM Institutions

经络腧穴学
（汉英对照）
Meridians and Acupoints
（Chinese – English）

主编（译） （Compiler and Translator – in – Chief）
郑美凤（Zheng Meifeng）

副 主 编 （Vice Compiler – in – Chief）
吴 强（Wu Qiang）

编（译）委 （Compiling and Translating Committee）
（按姓氏笔画排序）
（Listed in the order of strokes of their Chinese surname）

纪 峰（Ji Feng） 李来泽（Li Laize）
吴 强（Wu Qiang） 吴追乐（Wu Zhuile）
何芙蓉（He Furong） 张学君（Zhang Xuejun）
陈采益（Chen Caiyi） 林 栋（Lin Dong）
林 莺（Lin Ying） 郑美凤（Zheng Meifeng）
郑雪峰（Zheng Xuefeng）

主编单位 （Editors' Unit）
福建中医药大学（Fujian University of TCM）

中国中医药出版社
China Press of Traditional Chinese Medicine
·北 京·
· Beijing ·

图书在版编目（CIP）数据

经络腧穴学：汉英对照/郑美凤主编（译）．—北京：中国中医药出版社，(2013.8 重印)
ISBN 978－7－5132－0582－5

Ⅰ．①经…　Ⅱ．①郑…　Ⅲ．①经络－双语教学－高等学校－教材－汉、英　②俞穴（五腧）－双语教学－高等学校－教材－汉、英　Ⅳ．①R224

中国版本图书馆 CIP 数据核字（2011）第 186479 号

中国中医药出版社出版
北京市朝阳区北三环东路 28 号易亨大厦 16 层
邮政编码　100013
传真　010 64405750
北京泰锐印刷有限公司印刷
各地新华书店经销
*
开本 850×1168　1/16　印张 31.25　字数 977 千字
2012 年 3 月第 1 版　2013 年 8 月第 2 次印刷
书　号　ISBN 978－7－5132－0582－5
*
定价　45.00 元
网址　www.cptcm.com

如有印装质量问题请与本社出版部调换

社长热线　010 64405720
购书热线　010 64065415　010 64065413
书店网址　csln.net/qksd/

编写说明

《经络腧穴学》（汉英对照）是“新世纪全国高等中医药院校创新教材”。

本教材分为绪言、总论、各论及附篇。绪言主要介绍了经络腧穴的起源和发展史。总论第一章阐述经络的概念、组成、作用、临床应用及其经络的纵横关系，便于学生了解经络的含义和经络系统的概况。第二章介绍腧穴的概念、分类、命名、作用和主治规律、定位方法和特定穴的概念等，使学生理解腧穴的定义，了解腧穴理论的基本内容及其临床意义。各论第三章到第十四章为十二经脉及其相应的腧穴内容，论述了十二经脉、络脉、经筋的循行分布及其腧穴的含义、定位、解剖、功用、主治和刺灸方法等，使学生能重点掌握各个经络和腧穴理论及其临床应用。第十五章介绍奇经八脉的循行分布、功能和病候，其中第一、二节任、督脉腧穴和第十六章经外奇穴的介绍与十二经脉的腧穴体例相同，便于学生定位腧穴、理解含义、记忆主治，为临床选穴应用打下基础。附篇为经络腧穴的现代研究。

本教材的编写和翻译工作均由编译委员会分工完成，其中主编译统审中英文稿。在整个编译过程中，委员会各成员做了很多努力，但编写中医汉英双语教材是一项繁重的工作，也因为我们经验不足，水平有限，编译中难免存在一些问题，敬请提出宝贵意见，便于进一步改进、完善。谢谢！

编译委员会
2012 年 1 月

Prefer

This is one of the Chinese – English Bilingual Innovation Textbooks for international students of Chinese TCM institutions.

First of all, introduction gives a brief outline about the origination and development of the meridians and acupuncture points. Part one, general introduction of the meridians and collaterals and acupuncture points. In which, chapter 1 explains definitions of the meridian and collateral, the main components of the meridian system, the functions of the meridians, collaterals, the clinical applications and their vertical – horizontal relationships. It provides an overview of the basic concepts of meridian, collateral and the system for the students. Chapter 2 introduces the definition, the classification and nomenclature of points, locations, functions and regular patterns of the indications, and needling techniques of the points. It also introduces the concepts of specific points, etc. This will help students to understand the basic contents of acupuncture point and their clinical applications. Part 2 introduces the details of meridians and acupoints. From chapter 3 to chapter 14, it discusses the twelve regular meridians, collaterals and tendon regions and their points including the distributions, point meaning records, locations, regional anatomy, properties, indications, needling and moxibustion methods. Chapter 15 introduces the distributions, functions and manifestations of the eight extra meridians. Chapter 16 introduces extra points. The stylistic rules and layout in the section 1 and 2 of chapter 15, the governor vessel and conception vessel, and chapter 16 are the same as the presentations of the twelve regular meridian in chapter 3 to chapter 14 before. Appendix introduces the achievements of modern studies of meridians and collaterals.

This book is complied by editors and translators respectively. Due to our limitation in compiling experience and knowledge and the hard work to publish such a bilingual textbook, we apologize if there are any flaws in the book. Welcome your further suggestion to improve our work. Thank you!

Compiling and Translation Committee of Meridian and Acupoint
Jan. 2012

目 录
Contents

经络腧穴各论
Meridians and Collaterals, Acupoints

附篇 经络腧穴现代研究
Appendix Modern Research on Meridians and Acupoints

绪　言
Introduction

经络腧穴学是针灸学的基础理论和核心内容，是学习针灸的入门课程。针灸的历史非常悠久，针法起源于古代的砭石，灸法起源于古代的生活用火。由于针法、灸法的应用，产生了对人体经络腧穴的认识，并逐渐形成了独立的理论体系。经络腧穴的起源和发展与针灸疗法的应用密切相关，故绪言部分将结合针灸的起源、形成和发展进行总体介绍。

Science of meridian and acupoint, as the basic and key theory of science of acupuncture and moxibustion, is an introductory course for learning acupuncture and moxibustion. Acupuncture and moxibustion are known to have a long history. Acupuncture therapy originated from ancient bian – stone therapy, while moxibustion therapy from ancient application of fire for life. With the application of acupuncture and moxibustion therapy, the meridians, collaterals and acupoints of human body were discovered and gradually formed separate theory. Since origination and development of meridians, collaterals and acupoints were closely related to the application of acupuncture and moxibustion therapy, the following will give an overall introduction of its origin and development combined with the origination, formation and development of acupuncture and moxibustion.

针灸学是以中医理论为指导，运用经络、腧穴理论和刺灸方法以防治疾病的一门学科。针灸学是中医学的重要组成部分，其主要内容包括经络、腧穴、刺灸和临床治疗等部分。针灸历史悠久，在长期的医疗实践中积累了丰富的经验，具有适应证广、疗效明显、操作方便、经济安全等特点，深受人们欢迎，为中华民族数千年的繁衍昌盛作出了巨大的贡献，并正在为世界人民的医疗保健事业发挥着越来越大的作用。

Science of acupuncture and moxibustion is a discipline within the framework of Traditional Chinese Medicine (TCM) concerning prevention and treatment of diseases with acupuncture and moxibustion therapy according to the theory of meridians, collaterals and acupoints.

As an important component of TCM, acupuncture and moxibustion mainly consist of four parts: meridians and collaterals, points, techniques of acupuncture and moxibustion, and clinical application of acupuncture and moxibustion. Acupuncture and moxibustion have been used for a long time for the treatment of diseases, thus abundant empirical experience have been accumulated. It has now been established that acupuncture and moxibustion are suitable for a wide range of applications, have good therapeutic efficacy, are inexpensive and easy to perform, and most importantly, have an excellent safety profile. Over the centuries, they have always been well accepted by the general public as safe and efficacious therapies. Moreover, these methods have made great contributions to the popularization and prosperity of the Chinese nation for thousands of years, and are playing an increasingly important role in medical and health care all over the world today.

一、起源
Origin of Meridians, Collaterals and Acupoints

关于针刺疗法起源的传说可追溯到原始社会的氏族公社时期。皇甫谧《帝王世纪》有伏羲"尝味百草而制九针"的记载。罗泌《路史》又说"伏羲尝草制砭，以治民疾"。针法起源于古代的砭石，而针刺疗法真正的产生时间应是砭石应用相当长一段时期后的新石器时代。在内蒙古多伦县的新石器时代遗址中及山东日照市的新石器时代墓葬里发现的砭石实物，为针刺起源于新石器时代之说提供了证据。早在石器时代，先民们就将不同形状的石块磨制成各种医用器具。尖锐的用来刺血、排脓，刀形的可用来切割，棒形、圆形的用于按摩和热熨。其中尖锐者最为常用，故《说文解字》说："砭，以石刺病也。"《山海经·东山经》称之为箴石，"高氏之山，其上多玉，其下多箴石"。砭石是针具的雏形和前身，其后还出现骨针和竹针。人类进入青铜器时代和铁器时代时，随着冶金技术的发展，铜质、铁质的金属针才开始出现，之后又有金质、银质针的应用。

The legends about the origin of acupuncture therapy can be traced back to clan commune period of the primitive Chinese society. It was recorded in *Di Wang Shi Ji* written by Huang Fumi that Fuxi tasted hundreds of herbs and made the nine kinds of metal needles. And *Lu Shi* written by Luo Mi says Fuxi tasted hundreds of herbs and made bian - stone needles to treat diseases. Acupuncture therapy originated from ancient bian - stone therapy and developed in the Neolithic Age, a considerable length of time after the application of bian - stone therapy. Bian - stone needles were found as funerary objects in tombs of the Neolithic Age in the Neolithic sites in Inner Mongolia Autonomous Region and in the city of Rizhao located in Shandong province, which provided evidence that the origin of acupuncture can be traced back to the Neolithic Age. As early as in Stone Age, people ground different shapes of stones into medical instruments, among which the sharp was used for bloodletting and removing pus, while the lancet - shaped was used to create incisions, and the club or round shaped were used for massage and heat application. As the sharp was most commonly used, it was recorded in *Shuo Wen Jie Zi* (an analytical dictionary of characters) that Bian, means treating diseases with stones puncturing. Bian - stone had another name of zhen - stone in *Shan Hai Jing* (the Classic of Mountains and Seas), and there is a paragraph in the Volume of Dongshan saying: "Gaoshi mountain was riched in jade on the upper level and zhen - stone on the lower level." Therefore, Bian - stone needles is the predecessor of acupuncture instruments. There were bone needles and bamboo needles subsequently. Furthermore, with the development of metallurgy, metal needles such as copper needles, iron needles, gold needles and silver needles gradually used as therapeutic tools.

灸法的起源也可追溯到原始社会的氏族公社时期。灸法的应用是在人类发明用火之后开始的，来源于我国北部以畜牧为生的民族。灸法的发明与寒冷的生活环境有密切联系。人们发现某些寒性病痛在烤火取暖后可以缓解或解除，经过长期的经验积累，发明了灸法和热熨疗法。灸法所用的材料，最初很可能是可烧灼、烫、熨的各种树枝，后来才发现用艾叶做成的艾绒易于引火缓燃而不起火焰，更适用于灸，遂使艾灸世代相传，沿用至今。

The origin of moxibustion therapy can also be traced back to clan commune period of the primitive Chinese society. It is believed that the use of moxibustion resulted from the discovery of fire by the Chinese people who were nomads and herdsmen living in the northern area. The invention of moxibustion therapy was closely correlated to the cold living conditions. Ancient people found that certain illnesses or pain caused by the cold were alleviated or cured when the body was warmed by fire. Initially, people practiced moxibustion with various kinds of tree branches that were used for burning, warming or burning the body surface. Later on, the moxa leaf (Folium Artemisia Argyi) was found to be more suitable because it was easy to ignite without producing a visible flame; thus the practice of moxibustion therapy was passed down from generation to generation up to this date.

经络的概念来源于医疗实践，与我国针灸、按摩、气功等独特医疗保健方法的应用是分不开的。经络主运行血气。“血气”一词，除《内经》外，在春秋战国时期的不少非医学著作中也有提到，说明那时人们对血气的概念已有较普遍的认识。古文献有关血气的论述常涉及“脉”的概念。脉，本义指血管，《说文解字》解释为“血理分衺（斜）行体者”。脉，原写作“脈”，又作“衇”。从“脉”字的字形构造可看出，古人是将水流现象比拟血流，“𠂢”就是“派”的意思。“经”、“络”名词的出现较“脉”晚，是对“脉”的概念的进一步认识。

The concept of meridians and collaterals derived from medical practice and was closely correlated to the Chinese distinctive therapies such as acupuncture, massage and qigong. The meridians and collaterals are pathways in which blood and qi of the human body are circulated. The term of Xue Qi (blood and qi) was recorded not only in *Nei Jing* (*Internal Classic*) but also in many non-medical literatures during the period of the Spring and Autumn to the Warring States, which shew that the term of blood and qi had been known generally. The description of blood and qi in the ancient literatures was often concerned with the term of Mai. Mai, originally meaned blood vessels as was recorded in *Shuo Wen Jie Zi* (an analytical dictionary of characters) that Mai, meaned vessels distributed around the body in which blood circulated. It is obvious that blood circulation was compared to water stream in ancient time from the font of Chinese character of Mai. The term of Jing (meridians) and Luo (collaterals) appeared after the term of Mai (vessels), as the derivative term from Mai (vessels).

腧穴是人们在长期的医疗保健实践中逐步发现和积累起来的。初期的针灸治疗是没有确定的腧穴的，只是在病痛局部作砭刺、叩击、按摩、针刺或火灸等治疗，这就是《内经》所说的“以痛为输（腧穴）”。人们还在无意识中偶然发现了腧穴，如误伤或按压肢体某一部位而在局部出现疼痛或舒适感觉后，远离部位的脏器病痛得到缓解或随之消失。当再出现这种病痛时，人们就有意识地刺灸这些部位来进行治疗。《内经》中有不少有关这方面的记载，如“疾按之应手如痛，刺之”，“切之坚痛如筋者，灸之”，“以手疾按之，快然乃刺之”等。随着对体表刺激部位及其治疗作用的不断观察，对腧穴认识的逐步加深，人们便开始对腧穴进行定位和命名。通过大量的医疗实践，古医家对腧穴主治进行分析和归类，并结合经络理论，将某些主治作用相似、感传路线一致的腧穴加以归经，现在所谓的经穴，就是指这类腧穴。

Acupoints were discovered and accumulated gradually in the long – term medical care practice. At the initial stage, there were no certain acupoints but local pain points for bian – stone puncturing, percussion, massage or moxibustion manipulating, and acupuncture, just as the record in *Internal Classic* saying "taking the painful locations as acupoints". Acupoints also have been discovered by accident. For example, when some part of limbs accidentally got injured or pressed, then pain or comfort occurred while the ailment of the remote organs got relieved or cured. Then when the same ailment occured again, these parts would be consciously selected as the therapeutic point to manipulate acupuncture and moxibustion. There were many such records in *Internal Classic* as "puncturing where pain appeared by palpation", "manipulating moxibustion where was painful and felt hard like tendon when palpated", "puncturing where comfort feeling appeared when palpated quickly". With the constant observation on such stimulation spots on the surface of human body and their therapeutic effects, acupoints were gradually known and have begun to be located and denominated. Then acupoints indications were analyzed and classified combined with the theory of meridians and collaterals through a great deal of medical practice. Those with similar therapeutic effects and the same propagated sensation route had been classified to pertain to certain meridian, that is so – called acupoints of fourteen meridians nowadays.

二、理论形成
Establishment of the Theory of Meridians, Collaterals and Acupoints

针灸学的发展经历了一个漫长的历史过程。春秋、战国、秦、汉时期，政治、经济、文化的发展，为医药学的发展提供了条件。针刺工具由砭石、骨针发展到金属针具，特别是九针的出现更扩大了针灸实践范围，促进了针灸学发展，针灸理论也不断得以升华。

Acupuncture and moxibustion as academic disciplines have experienced an uninterrupted long course of development. The period from the Spring and Autumn (770 B. C. – 476 B. C.), the Warring States (475 B. C. – 221 B. C.) and the Qin (221 B. C. – 206 B. C.) to Han Dynasties (206 B. C. – 220 A. D.), the rapid progress in politics, economy and culture all provided a conducive milieu for the development of TCM. The instruments for acupuncture were improved from bian –

stone needles to bone needles and then to metal needles. The advent of the nine kinds of metal needles significantly extended the therapeutic indications for acupuncture and greatly advanced the acupuncture theories.

现存的经络文献原以《内经》最早，但近年出土的古代文物表明，在《内经》之前已有各种较为原始的文字记载。1973 年，湖南长沙马王堆汉墓出土的帛书中载有“十一脉”的内容；1984 年，湖北江陵张家山汉墓出土的竹简中也有同样的记载，且名为《脉书》。这是现存最早的经络学文献，反映了针灸学核心理论经络学说的早期面貌。《脉书》这一名称与《史记仓公列传》所说的仓公淳于意受其师阳庆传授“黄帝、扁鹊之《脉书》”之说相符。《脉书》有属于黄帝的，也有属于扁鹊的，可知有不同的本子。长沙马王堆汉墓出土的帛书就有几种文本：一种内容较简，按先“足三阳三阴脉”后“臂二阴三阳脉排列”，因称“足臂本”（《 足臂十一脉灸经》）；另一种内容较详，按先六阳脉后五阴脉次序排列，因称“阴阳本”（《阴阳十一脉灸经》）。“阴阳本”在帛书中又有甲、乙两写本；又有江陵张家山汉墓出土的简书本，可见其传抄较多，影响更广。帛书的记载见于《马王堆汉墓帛书》和《五十二病方》书中。

Internal Classic was thought to be the earliest extant literature of meridians and collaterals. But ancient relics excavated recently shew that there were all kinds of earlier original records. In 1973, silk books unearthed from a Han Dynasty Tomb at Mawangdui in Changsha city of Hunan province recorded eleven meridians. Likewise, in 1984, *Mai Shu* (Meridian Book) with the similar records about meridians and collaterals was found among the unearthed bamboo manuscripts in the Han Dynasty Tomb at Zhangjiashan in Jiangling city of Hubei province. These books are the earliest classics on meridians and collaterals that have been discovered, and represent the early doctrines of meridians and collaterals, the core theory of acupuncture and moxibustion. The book name of Meridian Book was also recorded in the Canggong Commentary Section of the Historical Records that Canggong, Chun Yuyi was taught knowledge of Huangdi's and Bianque's Meridian Books by his master Yangqing. Obviously, Meridian Book had different versions of Huangdi and Bianque. Even silk books unearthed from Han Dynasty Tomb at Mawangdui in Changsha city also have two following versions: one is Zu (Foot) Bi (Arm) Ben version with simple content edited by the sequence of three foot meridians of yang and yin before two yin meridians and three yang meridians of arm, thus called *Zu Bi Shi Yi Mai Jiu Jing* (the Moxibustion Classic of Eleven Foot – Arm Meridians); the other is Yin Yang Ben version with detailed description edited by the sequence of six yang meridians before five yin meridians, thus called *Yin Yang Shi Yi Mai Jiu Jing* (the Moxibustion Classic of Eleven Yin – Yang Meridians). The Yin Yang Ben version of silk book also had A and B editions. Moreover there was bamboo manuscripts version in the Han Dynasty Tomb at Zhangjiashan in Jiangling city. It was obvious that there were many private copies of a manuscript with a larger scaled effect. The records on silk books could be found in the two books of *Ma Wang Dui Han Mu Bo Shu* (Silk Books of a Han Dynasty Tomb at Mawangdui) and *Wu Shi Er Bing Fang* (Case Reports of Fifty – two Patients).

马王堆汉墓出土的医籍中尚有《脉法》一书。此书虽主要论述脉法，但多处提到用灸法和砭法治疗疾病的内容。如“阳上于环二寸而益为一久（灸）”等。所载砭灸部位虽无规范的名称，但已具备了腧穴的某些特点。《五十二病方》虽然没有明确记载腧穴的具体名称和部位，但有几处描述的施灸部位已明显缩小，从书中“灸泰阴”、“久（灸）左胻”、“久（灸）足中指”等有关施灸部位的记载来看，其施灸范围由大到小，由某一条脉到某一个部位，最后接近腧穴点的范围，说明当时已初步形成了腧穴概念。此外，战国初期医家秦越人（扁鹊）曾“刺三阳五会（输）救治虢太子尸厥”；西汉初期医家淳于意（仓公）称针灸的部位为“俞”（“论俞所居”）和“砭灸处”。这些都是有关腧穴早期临床应用的文献记载。

There was another medical silk book named *Mai Fa* (Pulse Feeling Book) unearthed from a Han Dynasty Tomb at Mawangdui. It was mainly recorded pulse feeling methods and also included some records of clinical application of moxibustion and Bian – stone therapy. Though without formal name for the treating points, they had some characteristics of acupoints. In the other book of *Prescriptions for Fifty – two diseases* there were also no specific name and location of acupoints, but term of acupoints initially formed for some descriptions about sites for applying moxibustion had become smaller from a meridian to a certain location, then come near to the site of acupoint. In addition, the physician Qin Yueren who lived in the early period of Warring States had rescued a crown prince from cadaverous coma in Guo country by puncturing the point of Sanyang Wuhui. The other doctor Chun Yuyi who lived in the early period of Western Han Dynasty named the sites for acupuncture and moxibustion as Shu or location for bian – stone and moxibustion. All are the literatures records that reflected an early clinical application of acupoints.

《黄帝内经》，简称《内经》，分《灵枢》和《素问》两部，成书于战国、秦、汉时期。《内经》的面世标志着针灸学理论体系的基本形成。《内经》以阴阳、五行、脏腑、经络、精神、气血等为主要内容，从整体观阐述了人体生理病理、诊断要领和防治原则，重点论述了经络、腧穴、针法、灸法等。《汉书·艺文志》中有“《黄帝内经》十八卷”的记载，据晋代皇甫谧《针灸甲乙经》序文所说，就是指现存的《素问》九卷和《针经》九卷。《针经》写作在先，《素问》在后。《灵枢》较完整地论述了经络腧穴理论、刺灸方法和临床治疗等，对针灸医学做了比较系统的总结，为后世针灸学的发展奠定了基础。关于经络的记载，以《灵枢》为最详，如《经脉》、《经别》、《脉度》、《根结》等篇；《素问》则是在此基础上做进一步的阐发和讨论，故多以“论”或“解”为名，如《脉解》、《皮部论》、《经络论》、《骨空论》、《太阴阳明论》、《阳明脉解》等。但《素问》所引古文献并不完全与现存的《灵枢》相同，如《脉解》所载经脉文字不同于《灵枢·经脉》，却接近于帛书的记载，这当是古《脉书》的另一传本。凡名为“解”者自然是晚于原书的解释性著述。《内经》对人体腧穴的认识，已经到了从医疗实践上升到理论的阶段。书中所载，有的有名称有定位，有的有定位无名称，还提到了“以痛为输”的取穴形式，除穴名和位置外，其内容涉及与经络的关系、主治病症、刺灸方法及其禁忌等。《内经》对部分腧穴已进行了分类，如各经的“脉气所发”，五输穴、原穴、络穴、下合穴、背俞穴、募穴等，并作了简要的论述，反映了腧穴理论的早期面貌。略晚于《内经》的《明堂孔穴针灸治要》一书，为早期有关腧穴理论的总结性著作，可惜早已散佚，其内容保留于《针灸甲乙经》中。

Huang Di Nei Jing (Huangdi's Internal Classic) or *Internal Classic* for short, was written during the Warring States (475 B. C. –221 B. C.) to Qin Dynasty (221 B. C. –206 B. C.) or Han Dynasty (206 B. C. – 220 A. D.), and comprises of two parts, namely *Ling Shu* (*Miraculous Pivot*) and *Su Wen* (*Plain Questions*) . The completion of *Internal Classic* marked the establishment of the theory of acupuncture and moxibustion. The main contents of *Internal Classic* were yin – yang, five elements, zang – fu organs, meridians and collaterals, essence, qi and blood. It explained the physiology and pathology of the human body, provided guiding principles for diagnosis and prevention and treatment of diseases from a holistic perspective. It also focused on the discussion of meridians and collaterals, points, and techniques of acupuncture and moxibustion. It was recorded in *Book of Han Shu Yi Wen Zhi* (*Chronicles of the Han Dynasty · Bibliraphic Treatise*) that there were eighteen volumes of *Huangdi's Internal Classic*, that is extant *Plain Questions* and *Zhen Jing* (*Classic of Acupuncture*) nine volumes respectively according to the preface of *Zhen Jiu Jia Yi Jing* (*The AB Classic of Acupuncture and Moxibustion*) written by Huang Fumi. *Zhen Jing* (*Acupuncture Classic*) was also called *Jiu Juan* (*the Nine Volumes*) before Tang Dynasty while *Miraculous Pivot* afterward. It is obvious that *Miraculous Pivot* was compiled before the *Plain Questions* through comparison. *Miraculous Pivot* comprehensively discussed the theories of meridians collaterals, and points, techniques of acupuncture and moxibustion, and its clinical application for treatment. It gave a systematic summarization of the science of acupuncture and moxibustion, and laid the theoretical foundation for the development of these disciplines in later generations. There were most minute records of meridians and collaterals in *Miraculous Pivot* such as chapter 10, chapter 11, chapter 17, chapter 5 and so on. Further explanation and discussion were made in *Plain Questions* and the corresponding chapters were named with "Lun (discussion)" or "Jie (explanation)" such as chapter 30, chapter 56, chapter 57, chapter 2, chapter 62, chapter 29, chapter 30, etc. But the reference literatures of *Plain Questions* were not the same as those of *Miraculous Pivot*. For example, the description of meridians in the chapter 30 were different from that in the chapter 10 of *Miraculous Pivot*, while similar to that *in the Silk Books*, It could be one circulating edition of Meridian Book for explanation chapter must written on the basis of relative original book. Records on acupoints in *Internal Classic* shew that knowledge of acupoints had been raised from the medical practice up to theory. It recorded some acupoints with definite name and fixed location and others with fixed location but without definite name, set up the point locating method of taking the painful sites as points, and also recorded the relationship between acupoints and meridians, indications and manipulating method of acupuncture and moxibustion and contraindication of acupoints. Some acupoints where meridian – qi transported of each meridian also had been classified in that book into five – shu points, yuan – source points, luo – connecting points, lower he – sea points, back – shu points and front – mu points and brief discussion was further made. These represented the early outlook of acupoints theory. Slightly later than *Internal Classic* there was another concluding literature of early acupoints theory of *Ming Tang Kong Xue Zhen Jiu Zhi Yao* (*Treatment Essentials of Acupuncture and Moxibustion Points*), had long been lost, and its content had been kept in *The AB Classic of Acupuncture and Moxibustion.*

大约成书于汉代的《难经》，原称《黄帝八十一难经》，以阐明《内经》为要旨，是继《内经》以后又一部中医经典著作。书中就《内经》等古经提出 81 个问题，并进行解答。有关经络的问题特别注重寸口脉诊、元气、奇经八脉以及对"是动"、"所生病"的解释。《难经》首先提出"奇经八脉"这一名称，并对奇经八脉内容作了集中的论述，补充《内经》之不足。《难经》对经络理论的补充、阐发主要体现在奇经八脉、经脉病候、十五络脉等方面，对腧穴理论则主要体现在八会穴、原穴及五输穴的五行配属和治疗作用等方面。《难经》还完善了各经五输穴的五行配属关系，并以刚柔相济理论作了解释，同时对其临床应用加以阐发，使之成为后世子午流注法的理论基础，在此基础上又提出了"虚则补其母，实则泻其子"和"泻南补北"理论，对针灸和中医临床各科均具有启示意义。

总之，从战国至西汉及东汉时期，是《内经》和《难经》的著作年代，也是针灸理论的形成和奠基时期。《内经》、《难经》同属于针灸基础理论的早期文献，都属医学经典。

Written during the Han Dynasty (206 B. C. – 220 A. D.), *Classic on Medical Problems*, originally called *Huangdi's Classic of Eighty – One Problem* was a TCM classic after *Intenal Classic.* It intended to explain *Internal Classic*, raising eighty one questions of the ancient classics such as *Internal Classic* and answering. Among the questions of meridians and collaterals, it focused especially on explaining pulse taking method over radial artery on the wrist, original qi, the eight extra meridians and the indications of meridians like "Shi Dong" and "Suo Sheng Bing". It put forward the term of the eight extra meridians for the first time and described them in detail, supplementing the deficiency of *Internal Classic.* It developed the theory of meridians and collaterals by supplementing and explaining the contents of the eight extra meridians, indications of meridians and fifteen collaterals. The development of Classic on Medical Problems in acupoints theory were mainly manifested in therapeutic effect of the eight confluent points, yuan – source points and the property of five elements and indications of five – shu points. It put forward the term of eight confluent points for the first time and further explained the relationship between the eight confluent points and the qi, blood, tendon, vessel, bone, marrow, zang – organ and fu – organ in detail. It explained the primary qi distributed all over the zangfu organs and twelve regular meridians through pathway of Sanjiao, the yuan – source points were where the original qi passes and gathers, and added the yuan – source point of heart meridian on the basis of *Internal Classic*, which thus brought the theory of yuan – source points to a whole. It defined the property of five elements of five – shu points and recorded their clinical application, which laid the theoretical foundation of later "Ziwu Liuzhu" acupuncture. Then based on the mutual generating relationship of the five elements, *Classic on Medical Problems* established a principle of reinforcing the "mother" when the "son" is deficient and reducing the "son" when the "mother" is excessive and principle of reducing the pathogenic fire of heart and reinforcing the kidney yin, all these principles had great significance to acupuncture and moxibustion and other clinical disciplines of TCM.

In summary, the period from the Warring States (475 B. C. –221 B. C.) to the Western Han (206 B. C. –23 A. D.) and Eastern Han Dynasties (25 –220 A. D.) was not only the period when *Internal Classic* and *Classic on Medical Problems* were compiled, but it also was an era when the theory of acupuncture and moxibustion was established. Both *Internal Classic* and *Classic on Medical Problems* are TCM classic as the early literatures of the basic theory of acupuncture and moxibustion.

魏晋时皇甫谧编集的《针灸甲乙经》，全名《黄帝三部针灸甲乙经》，简称《甲乙经》，是现存最早的针灸学专著和经穴专著，是继《内经》之后对针灸学的又一次总结。《甲乙经》是汇集《素问》、《针经》及《明堂孔穴针灸治要》三部书并加以分类整理而成的。《明堂孔穴针灸治要》又称《黄帝明堂》，原有书有图，自皇甫谧把它编入《甲乙经》后，原书渐趋散佚。"明堂"这一名称，原意是指国君议政的场所。《内经》中假设黄帝做名堂之上鱼类宫灯臣子讨论医道，后来便称经穴之学为"明堂"。这方面的书称"明堂经"，图称"明堂图"。《黄帝明堂》是《内经》之后的经穴专著，约成书于东汉时，现只能从《甲乙经》中间接了解其内容。经络所属穴和交会穴均详见于该书。书中所载各经穴名共 349 个，其中有交会关系者 84 穴。各经都有所属专穴，有些穴位几条经所交会则称交会穴。《甲乙经》以"头身分部，四肢分经"的排列形式，对十四经穴进行整理和归类，将基础理论和针灸治疗内容集合成古代针灸学专著。这是皇甫谧对针灸学的重大贡献。《甲乙经》于公元 6 世纪传到日本、朝鲜等国，是针灸走向世界的先导。

东汉末年，张仲景"撰用《素问》、《九卷》、《八十一难》"等书著成《伤寒杂病论》(《伤寒论》)。《伤寒论》一书运用六经辨证，是对《内经》、《难经》理论的继承和发展，也是对经络理论的灵活应用。

The A. B Classic of Acupuncture and Moxibustion, *The Huangdi's ABC Classic of Acupuncture and Moxibustion* as full name of or *Jia Yi Jing* (*AB Classic*) for short, was written by Huangfu Mi during the period of the Wei and Jin Dynasties (265 –420 A. D.). It is the earliest existing monograph on acupuncture and moxibustion, acupoints monograph as well. It provided another summary on acupuncture and moxibustion after *Internal Classic*. It sorted out relevant contents from *Plain Questions*, *Miraculous Pivot* and *Ming Tang Kong Xue Zhen Jiu Zhi Yao* (*Treatment Essentials of Acupuncture and Moxibustion Points*) into appropriate categories. *Treatment Essentials of Acupuncture and Moxibustion Points* was also called *Huang Di Ming Tang* (*Huangdi's Classic*). The original book with charts had lost gradually after beening compiled into the book *AB Classic*. The term of Mingtang, originally meant the place where emperor discussed political affairs. In *Internal Classic*, Emperor Huangdi was assumed to sit in the Mingtang to discuss medicine issues with his courtiers such as Lei Gong. Since then, the theory of acupoints had been called Mingtang, and the relevant books as Mingtang Jing, the acupoints charts called *Mingtangtu*. *Huang Di Ming Tang*, written in the period of Eastern Han Dynasty, as monograph on acupoints after *Internal Classic*, can only be acquired from *AB Classic* indirectly now. It recorded 349 acupoints of meridians in total and 84 crossing points among them. In the book of *AB Classic*, each meridian had its own points, only those distributed at the place where several meridians met were called crossing points, which made the coincide relationship among meridians clear. And all the distribution charts of meridians and collaterals were drawn with their own acupoints and crossing points. Furthermore, the acupoints of fourteen meridians have been sorted and categorized in the following order: acupoints of head and trunk arranged according to physical region and acupoints of four limbs listed according to meridians. As a ancient monograph including basic theory and clinical application of acupuncture and moxibustion, *AB Classic* was the significant contribution to science of acupuncture and moxibustion that Huangfu Mi had made. Later, *AB Classic* was introduced to other countries such as Korea and Japan in the 6th century A. D. making acupuncture and moxibustion known worldwide.

In the last years of the Eastern Han Dynasty, on the basis of *Plain Questions*, *Miraculous Pivot* and *Eighty - One Problem Classic*, Zhang Zhongjing wrote *Shang Han Za Bing Lun* (*Treatise on Exogenous Febrile Disease*), or *Shang Han Lun* (*Treatise on Febrile Disease*) for short. The method of syndrome - differentiation of six meridians was applied in the book and that was flexible application of theory of meridians and collaterals inherited and developed from the theory of *Intenal Classic* and *Classic on Medical Problems*.

三、学术发展
Academic Development of Meridians, Collaterals and Acupoints

魏晋时皇甫谧《针灸甲乙经》对经络腧穴理论的贡献已进行了介绍。

晋代以炼丹闻名的葛洪所著《抱朴子》和《肘后备急方》（《肘后方》）均提到《明堂流注偃侧图》，这是指关于经穴的前、侧、后图形，简称“明堂图”。《肘后方》载录针灸医方109条，其中99条为灸方，从而使灸法得到了进一步的发展。其妻鲍姑，亦擅长用灸，是中国历史上不可多得的女灸疗家。晋代尚有名医秦承祖、陶弘景等，对针法、灸法均有研究。

The contribution of *The AB Classic of Acupuncture and Moxibustion* written by Huangfu Mi during the period of the Wei and Jin Dynasties (265 –420A. D.) was introduced above.

During the Jin Dynasty (265 – 420 A. D.), Ge Hong, a famous alchemist compiled two books of *Bao Pu Zi* and *Zhou Hou Bei Ji Fang* (*the Handbook of Prescriptions for Emergencies*) or *Zhou Hou Fang* (*Prescriptions Handbook*) for short. In these two books , *Ming Tang Liu Zhu Yan Ce Tu*, *Mingtang Charts* for short, was mentioned about acupoints charts of the front, the back and the side of human body. It recorded 109 prescribed treatments using acupuncture and moxibustion, 99 of which were prescriptions for moxibustion. This made a significant contribution for the development of moxibustion therapy. Bao Gu, Ge Hong's wife, was also adept at applying moxibustion, and was one of the few female practitioners of moxibustion in Chinese medical history. Some other famous physicians included Qin Chengzu and Tao Hongjing, who all specialized in acupuncture and moxibustion.

隋、唐时期，随着经济文化的繁荣，针灸医学也有很大的发展。至唐代，针灸已成为一门专科，针灸教育也占有重要地位，促进了针灸学的全面发展。著名医家孙思邈在其所著《备急千金要方》中绘制了五色"明堂三人图"，还首载阿是穴和指寸法。这一时期灸法最为盛行，尤以王焘著《外台秘要》、崔知悌著《骨蒸病灸方》最享盛名。

When it came to the period of the Sui (581 – 618A. D.) and Tang (618 – 907A. D.) Dynasties, acupuncture and moxibustion also experienced a rapid development along with a prosperous economy and culture. In the Tang Dynasty, acupuncture and moxibustion developed into a medical specialty, where teaching and learning of acupuncture and moxibustion became important, thus enabling its all – round development. The famous physician Sun Simiao drew three multicolored charts of acupuncture and moxibustion in his renowned medical book *Bei Ji Qian Jing Yao Fang* (*Invaluable Prescriptions for Emergencies*). He is the first physician to mention the ashi – points and to introduce the method of locating points by finger – length measurement. Moxibustion therapy was most popular at that time, and *Wai Tai Mi Yao* (*Medical Secrets of an Official*) written by Wang Tao as well as *Gu Zheng Bing Jiu Fang* (*Prescriptions of Moxibustion for Tuberculosis*) by Cui Zhibao are among the most famous medical works on moxibustion.

唐代的杨上善除撰注《黄帝内经太素》之外，又将《内经》与《明堂孔穴》的内容汇合编成《黄帝内经明堂类成》十三卷，即十二经脉各一卷，奇经八脉合一卷，现仅存第一卷。从残存的卷一内容看，该书对经脉、腧穴已按气血流注次序排列，并对部分穴名作了释义，开创了循经考穴的先河，对经络腧穴理论体系的完善有重要意义。

In Tang Dynasty, apart from the book of *Huang Di Nei Jing Tai Su* (*Huangdi's internal classic: Tai Su*), Yang Shangshan also compiled the other book of *Huang Di Nei Jing Ming Tang Lei Cheng* (*Acupuncture Points in Internal Classic*) which revised the relevant contents of *Intenal Classic* and *Ming Tang Kong Xue Zhen Jiu Zhi Yao* (*Treatment Essentials of Acupuncture and Moxibustion Points*). The book had thirteen volumes in total including twelve volumes of twelve regular meridians and one volume of extra meridians, but only the first volume exists now. The remained first volume shew that meridians and acupoints had been sorted by the sequence of circulation of blood and qi, and furthermore the meaning of some acupoints had been explained. That book established a precedence of Textual Researches on acupoints along meridians and was important to improve the theoretical system of meridians, collaterals and acupoints.

宋代注重对医书的编纂和校正，早期组织编写的《太平圣惠方》，其第九十九卷称《针经》，第一百卷称《明堂》(《明堂灸经》)，后人又称为"明堂上经"和"明堂下经"，其中列有"十二人形"的经穴图；后期组织编写《圣济总录》，其中按经排列腧穴，为元代各书所继承。《难经》曾对奇经八脉的分布、功能和病候作了集中论述，《圣济总录》则对奇经八脉的有关腧穴和循行路线作了完整的描述。北宋翰林医官王惟一还奉诏编成了《铜人腧穴针灸图经》三卷，共载354经穴，次年铸成"铜人"经穴模型两座，并以图经刻石，对统一经穴定位影响甚广。

In Song Dynasty, the government attached great importance to compilation and revision of medical books. In the early years, *Tai Ping Sheng Hui Fang* (*Taiping Royal Prescriptions*) was compiled, in which the ninety – ninth volume was *Zhen Jing* (*Classic of Acupuncture*) and the one hundredth volume was *Ming Tang* (*Moxibustion Classic of Ming Tang*). They also have been called *Ming Tang Shang Jing* (*the first half of Ming Tang classic*) and *Ming Tang Xia Jing* (*the second half of Ming Tang classic*) respectively. Twelve figure charts of acupoints were included in the book. In the late years, *Sheng Ji Zong Lu* (*General Medical Collection of Royal Benevolence*) was finished in which acupoints were listed according to meridians that had been adopted by other medical books in Yuan Dynasty. Different from *Classic on Medical Problems* that had expounded the distribution, function and indications of eight extra meridians, it described the distribution and their acupoints of the eight extra meridians completely, obeying the Imperial Edict of the Northern Song government, academician medical officer named Wang Weiyi wrote the book *Tong Ren Shu Xue Zhen Jiu Tu Jing* (*Illustrated Manual on the Points for Acupuncture and Moxibustion on a New Bronze Figure*) of three volumes in total and in which 354 acupoints were recorded. The book was engraved on stone tablets in the subsequent year and two bronze figures of acupoints were cast and made. All these promoted the unification of the location of acupoints.

宋、金时期还将古代"候气而刺"、"顺时而刺"的思想发展为具体的子午流注针法。金代何若愚写成《流注指微针赋》一篇，阎明广加以注解，并收集有关资料扩展成为《子午流注针经》一书，这是子午流注法的初期著作。明代徐凤《针灸大全》又改编成《子午流注逐日按时定穴歌》十首，各书加以转载，影响遂广。此法的特点就是按时选用十二经的井、荥、输、经、合穴。其后，又有将八脉交会穴也结合日时选用，称为"飞腾八法"或"灵龟八法"，初见于元代王国瑞的《扁鹊神应针灸玉龙经》。

During the period of Song and Jin Dynasty, the ancient theory such as puncturing when needle sensation occurred and puncturing in conformance with time had been developed as acupuncture therapy of Ziwuliuzhu (the Midnight – noon Ebb – flow acupuncture). Firstly, He Ruoyu of Jin Dynasty wrote an article of "*Liu Zhu Zhi Wei Zhen Fu*". Then Yan Mingguang made explanatory notes on it and collected relevant materials to write *Ziwuliuzhu Zhen Jing* (*Acupuncture Classic of Ziwuliuzhu*), the initial works of "Ziwuliuzhu" therapy. And in *Zhen Jiu Da Quan* (*Complete Collection of acupuncture and moxibustion*) written by Xu Feng of Ming Dynasty, it was developed into ten formulas put into verse of "*Ziwuliuzhu Zhu Ri An Shi Ding Xue Ge*" and reprinted by other books then and thus spread widely. Ziwuliuzhu (the Midnight – noon Ebb – flow acupuncture) meant five – shu points such as jing – well point, ying – spring point, shu – stream point, jing – river point and he –

sea point would be selected to puncture according to Chinese two – hour time on the basis of Heavenly Stems and Earthly Branches. Later on, eight confluent points were also selected to puncture according to date, called "Feitengbafa" or "Lingguibafa", and was first recorded in the book of "*Bian Que Shen Ying Zhen Jiu Yu Long Jing*" written by Wang Guorui in Yuan Dynasty.

金末元初，窦默（字汉卿）著有《针经指南》一书，内载《标幽赋》、《通玄指要赋》及流注八穴、十四手法等内容，并对络脉提出新的观点："络有一十五，有横络三百余，有丝络一万八千，有孙络不知其纪。"明代钱雷《人镜经附录》对络脉也有新的认识："十二经生十五络，十五络生一百八十系络，系络生一百八十缠络，缠络生三万四千孙络。"这一说法为以后的《医门法律·络脉论》等书所引用，对清代医家有重要影响。

During the last years of Jin Dynasty to the first years of Yuan Dynasty, Doumo (Hanqing as courtesy name) wrote a book of *Zhen Jing Zhi Nan* (*Guidelines of Acupuncture Classic*). It recorded the contents of "Biao You Fu", "Tong Xuan Zhi Yao Fu" and "Liu Zhu Ba Xue" and fourteen kinds of acupuncture manipulation and presented new viewpoint on collaterals that there were fifteen collaterals and over three hundred transverse collaterals, eighteen thousand floating collaterals and uncounted mini – collaterals. It also presented a new views on collaterals in the book of *Ren Jing Jing Fu Lu* written by Qian Lei in Ming Dynasty that the twelve regular meridians branched out into fifteen collaterals, from which one hundred and eighty xi – luo branched out, then one hundred and eighty chan – collaterals branched out and at last thirty four thousand mini – collaterals branched out. This viewpoint was cited by the physician Yu Jiayan in his book of *Yi Men Fa Lv Luo Mai Lun* and thus affected the other physicians in Qing Dynasty.

元代滑寿（字伯仁）在元代忽泰必烈《金兰循经取穴图解》的基础上编著成《十四经发挥》，将任、督二脉与十二经并论。该书对循经考穴影响甚广，明、清各家注解经脉者多以此书为主要参考，如明代夏英以滑氏注解配合经脉原文编成《灵枢·经脉翼》，高武《针灸聚英》也依照此书流注次序排列经穴。

In Yuan Dynasty (1279 – 1368A. D.), on the basis of the book of "*Jin Lan Xun Jing Qu Xue Tu Jie*" written by Hutai Bilie, Hua Shou (Boren as courtesy name) compiled *Shi Si Jing Fa Hui* (*Elaboration on the Fourteen Meridians*), in which the conception vessel and governor vessel were regarded as important as the twelve regular meridians. This had a deep influence on the study of acupoints along meridians. In the following Ming and Qing Dynasty the other physicians took this book as Main reference when they made explanatory notes on meridians. For example, on the basis of *Elaboration on the Fourteen Meridians*, Xia Ying of Ming Dynasty compiled *Ling Shu Jing Mai Yi* (Supplement to the chapter 10, Miraculous Pivot) combined with the original records of meridians and the other physician Gaowu wrote *Zhen Jiu Ju Ying* (*Collective Essentials of Acupuncture and Moxibustion*), in which acupoints was listed according to the sequence of meridian – qi circulation that recorded in Elaboration on the Fourteen Meridians.

明代是针灸学术发展的高潮，名医辈出，理论研究深化，其间以杨继洲《针灸大成》影响最大。此书是以杨继洲原编的《卫生针灸玄机秘要》一书为基础，由靳贤选集有关文献扩充而成，内载经络穴位资料非常丰富，共载经穴 359 个，并载录杨氏的著述和医案等，是继《甲乙经》后对针灸学的第三次总结。明代李时珍就奇经八脉文献进行汇集和考证，作《奇经八脉考》，补《十四经发挥》所未备。

The Ming Dynasty (1368 – 1644A. D.) was the peak time for the development of acupuncture and moxibustion. Many famous acupuncturists emerged in succession, and studies of acupuncture and moxibustion theories deepened. Among a myriad of medical works published during this period, the *Zhen Jiu Da Cheng* (*Great Compendium of Acupuncture and Moxibustion*) written by Yang Jizhou had the most pronounced influence. This book was a grand compilation on the basis of Jin Xian's chrestomathy and *Wei Sheng Zhen Jiu Xuan Ji Mi Yao* (*Mysterious Secrets of Acupuncture and Moxibustion*) written by Yang Jizhou. Abundant record of meridians, collaterals and acupoints of 359 in total and works of Yang and case record were included in that book. It is the third summary of acupuncture and moxibustion after the *Jia Yi Jing* (*AB Classic*). During this period, Li Shizhen collected literatures of the eight extra meridians and made textual research on it, then wrote the book of *Qi Jing Ba Mai Kao* (*Textual Research on the Eight Extra Meridians*), which supplemented the deficiency of Elaboration on the Fourteen Meridians.

清代，除了见于注释《内经》和针灸书中的经络内容外，经络专书较少。《医宗金鉴·刺灸心法要诀》中载有经穴歌诀，分绘经脉图和经穴图。李学川《针灸逢源》一书，共载经穴 361 个，这是对经穴的又一次总结，此经穴数被沿用至今。清代在药物归经和运用方面有所发展，严西亭等人的《得配本草》、赵观澜的《医学指归》及姚澜的《本草分经》，都将经络学说与药物结合起来，认为“何经之病，宜用何经之药”，是掌握药物性能的要领。温病学派叶天士等人注重分经辨证用药，于十二经之外更重视奇经，在辨证上创立“初为气结，在经”，“久则血伤，入络”，以及“卫气营血”的分层理论，还有“八脉辨肝肾”和“厥阴之阳”等说，都为经络理论在方药方面的运用作出贡献。

In Qing Dynasty, there was fewer monographs of meridians and collaterals apart from comments on meridians and collaterals of *Internal Classic* and other books of acupuncture and moxibustion. In the book of *Yi Zong Jin Jian Ci Jiu Xin Fa Yao Jue* (*Golden Mirror of Medicine, Essentials of Acupuncture and Moxibustion in Verse*) the formulas put into verse of acupoints was recorded, the charts of meridians and that of acupoints were drawn respectively. *Zhen Jiu Feng Yuan* (*Achieving the Effect of Acupuncture and Moxibustion*) by Li Xuechuan made a record of 361 acupoints, another conclusion of acupoints, which has since become the standard number of regular meridian points until today. The meridian tropism theory of Chinese herbs developed at that time. In the book of *De Pei Ben Cao* written by Yan Xi Ting, *Yi Xue Zhi Gui* written by Zhao Guanlan and *Ben Cao Fen Jing* written by Yao Lan, theory of meridians and collaterals had been combined with Chinese herbs, and put forward the key point to master the properties of Chinese herbs that the disorder of certain meridians should be treated by the herbs with the corresponding meridians tropism. Ye Tianshi, a representative of the School of Epidemic Febrile Disease, emphasized syndrome differentiation in terms of meridians (not just the twelve regular meridians but the extra meridians were included) when applying Chinese herbs. Furthermore he developed stratification theory of syndrome differentiation such as "pathology of qi stagnation in meridians at the initial stage of diseases, and blood hurt in collaterals long after" and syndrome differentiation in terms of wei, qi, ying and blood system and other theory like liver - yang and syndrome differentiation in terms of the eight extra meridians, all these made great contribution for applying theory of meridians and collaterals in TCM prescription.

清初至民国时期，针灸医学由兴盛逐渐走向衰退。清朝医者多重药轻针，清代竟以“针刺火灸，究非奉君之所宜”为由废除太医院的针灸科。民国时期政府曾下令废止中医，但针灸疗法仍受到广大民众喜爱，在民间广为应用而得以流传。以承淡安先生为代表的许多有识之士为保存和发展针灸学术这一中医学的文化瑰宝，成立了针灸学社，编印针灸书刊，开展针灸函授教育等，为振兴针灸学术作出了贡献。

During the early Qing Dynasty to the Republic of China (1912 - 1949), acupuncture and moxibustion suffered a gradual decline. The physicians regarded herbal medication as superior to acupuncture. The authorities of the Qing Dynasty declared an order to abolish the acupuncture - moxibustion department from the Imperial Medical College because acupuncture and moxibustion were not suitable to be applied to the emperor. In the period of the Republic of China, the government announced to abolish TCM. However, acupuncture and moxibustion remained well - accepted by the general public such that it was still practiced extensively and the techniques were successfully passed down by practicing physicians. In order to preserve and develop this national treasure, many personages with an intellectual vision represented by Cheng Dan'an, established an association of acupuncture and moxibustion. They also compiled and published books and periodicals, carried out the correspondence mode of education and made great contributions to revitalize acupuncture and moxibustion practices.

中华人民共和国成立以来，针灸医学得到前所未有的普及和提高。针灸医疗、教学、科研等各方面取得了明显的发展，同时也加速了针灸医学的对外传播。针灸医学源于中国，几千年来不仅对中国人民的健康事业起了重大作用，而且早在公元6世纪就传到朝鲜、日本等国。随着中外文化交流的不断深入，针灸也随之传到东南亚及印度大陆。公元16世纪末，针灸开始传入欧洲，此后国际上的针灸学术交流甚为频繁，学术团体也日渐增多。在20世纪50年代，我国曾帮助前苏联和东欧国家的一些医疗工作者学习针灸。1975年，受联合国世界卫生组织（WHO）委托，在中国北京、上海、南京设立了三大国际针灸培训中心，为许多国家和地区培训了大批针灸人才。1979年，WHO就列出适宜针灸治疗的43种疾病名称。据统计，目前可用针灸治疗的病证已达300多种，包括内、外、妇、儿、五官和皮肤各科，其中对100种左右的病证有较好或很好的疗效。1987年11月，世界针灸学会联合会成立大会暨第一届世界针灸学术大会在北京召开，至今已召开七届世界针灸学会联合会会员大会暨学术大会。世界针灸学会联合会总部设在北京，由世界55个针灸学会联合组成，是覆盖面最广的世界针灸组织。1990年，WHO宣布针灸已成为世界医学的一个重要组成部分。1997年，美国国立卫生院（National Institutes of Health，NIH）的专家听证会也明确指出，起源于中国的针刺疗法对许多疾病有显著疗效，作用确切而副作用极小，可广泛应用。这对针灸学向世界各国的普及和推广具有重要意义。

Since the founding of the People's Republic of China（1949－），the discipline of acupuncture and moxibustion has been popularized and improved in a scale unmatched by previous periods. Great achievements have been made in many aspects，such as clinical application，teaching and scientific research. All these academic activities have accelerated the worldwide dissemination of acupuncture and moxibustion. Originating from China，the disciplines of acupuncture and moxibustion not only have significant roles in the medical care of the Chinese people for thousands of years，but they were also introduced to other countries such as Korea and Japan as early as the 6th century A. D. With more and more cultural exchanges，acupuncture and moxibustion were spread to Southeast Asia and India. International academic exchange has become a frequent event while more academic associations were established，especially after acupuncture and moxibustion were introduced to Europe in the late 16th century A. D. In the 1950s，medical staff from the Pre－Soviet Union and Eastern Europe began to learn acupuncture in China. In 1975，entrusted by World Health Organization（WHO），three international training centers of acupuncture and moxibustion were set up in the cities of Beijing，Shanghai and Nanjing respectively in China，where a great number of acupuncturists from different countries and regions have been trained. In 1979，WHO assured that 43 kinds of diseases are suitable indications for acupuncture and moxibustion therapy. According to available statistics，more than 300 kinds of diseases in the speciality areas of internal medicine，surgery，gynecology，pediatrics，five sense organs and dermatology can be treated by acupuncture and moxibustion. Among them，about 100 of them have moderate to good responses to acupuncture and moxibustion. In November 1987，the World Federation of Acupuncture－Moxibustion Societies was established and the 1st International Conference on Acupuncture and Moxibustion was held in Beijing. Since then，seven such conferences have been held. Composed of 55 associations worldwide with its headquarters located in Beijing，the World Federation of Acupuncture－Moxibustion Societies is the biggest acupuncture organization in the world. In 1997，it was clearly stated in the specialists' hearing of the National Institute of Health（NIH）of the United States of America that acupuncture can be effectively used for a wide range of diseases because of its significant therapeutic effects and few side effects. This recommendation is of great significance for successful propagation of acupuncture and moxibustion all over the world.

总 论
General Introduction

第一章 经络概述
Meridians and Collaterals

经络是运行气血，联系脏腑、体表及全身各部的通道。经，有路径之义，就是直行主线的意思，是经络系统中的主干，深而在里，沟通内外，贯通上下；络，有网络之义，是经脉别出的分支，浅而在表，纵横交错，遍布全身。经络学说阐述人体经脉的循行分支、生理功能、病理变化及其与脏腑的相互关系，是针灸学科的基础，也是中医基础理论的重要组成部分。经络理论贯穿于中医的生理、病理、诊断和治疗等各个方面，对中医各科的临床实践有重要指导意义。

Meridians and collaterals are pathways that transport qi and blood, and connect the internal zang – fu organs with the every parts of the body. "Jing" originally means "longitudinal line" and is translated as "meridian" or "channel" which has the meaning of path or straight line. Meridians are the main components of the meridian system, and travel at a relatively deeper level and connect the entire body from both the interior to the exterior, upward and downward. "luo" means "network," which is translated as "collaterals" and refers to branches which are separated from meridians and run superficially and transversely all over the body. The theory of meridian and collateral studies the pathway distribution, physiological functions, and pathological changes of the meridians and collaterals in the human body, as well as their relationships with internal zang – fu organs. It is the foundation for science of acupuncture and moxibustion and an important component in the basic theories of traditional Chinese medicine (TCM). Moreover, the theory of meridian and collateral runs through all aspects of physiology, pathology, diagnosis and treatment and plays a significant role in clinical practice of all subjects of TCM.

第一节 经络系统的组成
The Constituent of Meridian and Collateral System

经络系统，包括十二经脉、奇经八脉、十二经别、十五络脉、十二经筋和十二皮部（图1-1）。十二经脉是经络系统的主干，“内属于腑脏，外络于支节”（《灵枢·海论》），将人体内外联系成一个有机的整体。十二经别，是十二经脉在胸、腹及头部的内行支脉。十五络脉，是十二经脉在四肢部及躯干前、后、侧三部的外行支脉。奇经八脉，是具有特殊分布和作用的经脉。此外，经络的外部筋肉也受经络支配分为十二经筋；皮部也按经络的分布分为十二皮部。现将经络系统的内容逐一介绍如下。

The system of meridian and collateral comprises twelve regular meridians, eight extra meridians, twelve divergent meridians, fifteen collaterals, twelve muscular regions, and twelve cutaneous regions (Fig 1-1). Among them, the twelve regular meridians are the dominant part in the system of meridian and collateral. As stated in the chapter 33 of *Miraculous Pivot*, the "twelve regular meridians belong to the zang-fu organs internally, and connect to the extremities and joints externally". In this way, they make whole body as an organic one. The twelve divergent meridians are branches that travel internally in the chest, the abdomen and the head. The fifteen collaterals are branches running externally in the limbs and the anterior, posterior and lateral side of the trunk. The eight extra meridians are the meridians with particular distribution and functions. In addition, the external muscles and tendons along the twelve regular meridians which dominated by the meridians and collaterals are called the twelve muscular regions. The skin covering the body is divided into twelve regions corresponding to the regular meridian distribution, so these are named as twelve cutaneous regions. The content of the system will be introduced as follows in detail.

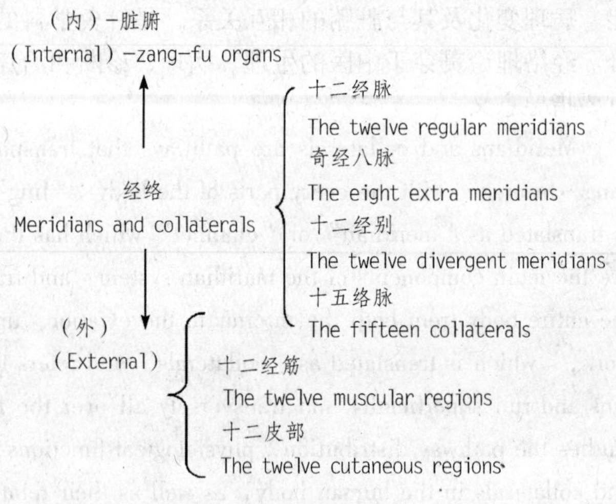

图1-1 经络系统简图

Fig 1-1 Simple list of the meridian system

一、十二经脉
The Twelve Regular Meridians

十二经脉按其流注如环无端，其次序分别为手太阴肺经、手阳明大肠经、足阳明胃经、足太阴脾经、手少阴心经、手太阳小肠经、足太阳膀胱经、足少阴肾经、手厥阴心包经、手少阳三焦经、足少阳胆经和足厥阴肝经。十二经脉是经络系统的主体，故又被称为“正经”。

The qi in the twelve meridians circulates in a cyclical way, and its order of flow starts from the lung meridian of hand – taiyin, traveling to the large intestine meridian of hand – yangming, from there to the stomach meridian of foot – yangming, then onto the spleen meridian of foot – taiyin, then it goes to the heart meridian of hand – shaoyin, from there to the small intestine meridian of hand – taiyang, onto the bladder meridian of foot – taiyang, then travels to the kidney meridian of foot – shaoyin, and then to the pericardium meridian of hand – jueyin, from there to the triple energizer meridian of hand – shaoyang, then it goes to the gallbladder meridian of foot – shaoyang, and finally stops at the liver meridian of foot – jueyin, from which a new cycle of flow restarts. these twelve meridians are the dominant part in the meridian and collateral system, thus named as “regular meridians.”

（一）十二经脉的名称和含义
The Nomenclature and Implication of the Twelve Regular Meridians

十二经脉的名称由手足、阴阳和脏腑三部分组成。手足，表示经脉在上、下肢分布的不同，手经表示其外行路线分布于上肢，足经表示其外行路线分布于下肢。脏腑，表示经脉的脏腑属性，如肺经表示该经脉属肺脏，胃经表示该经脉属胃腑。阴阳表示经脉的阴阳属性及阴阳气的多寡。阴气最盛为太阴，其次为少阴，再次为厥阴；阳气最盛为阳明，其次为太阳，再次为少阳。根据阴阳气的多少，三阴三阳之间组成对应的表里相合关系（图 1 –2）。三阴三阳的名称广泛应用于经络的命名，经别、络脉、经筋也是如此。

The nomenclature of the twelve regular meridians is based on three factors, which are hand or foot, yin or yang, and zang or fu organ. Hand or foot refers to the meridian traveling on the upper or lower limbs respectively along their external pathways. Zang or fu organ indicates the zang or fu to which the meridian belongs. For example, the lung meridian implies that this meridian belongs to the lung, a zang – organ, whereas the stomach meridian belongs to the stomach, a fu – organ. Yin or yang indicates the meridian's yin or yang identity and the amount of yin or yang qi it carries. The yin and yang are then further divided into three yin and three yang categories in order to differentiate the amount of yin or yang qi of the meridians. The meridians that carry the most abundant yin qi are called taiyin. The ones that carry the lesser amount of yin qi are called shaoyin, while the meridians that carry the least yin qi are named jueyin. similarly, the meridians that carry the most abundant yang qi are called yangming, and the ones that carry a lesser amount of yang qi are called taiyang. The meridians that carry the least amount of yang qi are named shaoyang. According to the amount of qi in the meridians, the three yin and three yang meridians are paired with their corresponding yang or yin meridians to become six interior and exterior pairs (Fig 1－2). The names of three yin and three yang are widely used in the nomenclature of the meridian and collateral system, such as regular meridians, divergent meridians, collaterals, and muscular regions.

阴	太阴－阳明 少阴－太阳 厥阴－少阳	阳	Yin	taiyin－yangming shaoyin－taiyang jueyin－shaoyang	Yang

图 1－2 三阴三阳表里相合之对应关系

Fig 1－2 Corresponding relation of interior and exterior pairs between three yang and three yin meridians

(二) 十二经脉的分布
Distribution of the Twelve Regular Meridians

十二经脉是经络系统的主要内容。在内部，十二经脉隶属于脏腑，在外部，分布于四肢、头和躯干。

The twelve meridians are the main content of the meridian and collateral system. Internally, they pertain to the zang or fu organs, externally, they distribute over the extremities, head and trunk.

1. 外行部分
Exterior Pathways

十二经脉对称地分布在四肢、头部和躯干两边（图 1－3）。

The twelve regular meridians are distributed in the four limbs, the head, and the trunk symmetrically (Fig 1－3).

（1）四肢部：手足阴经分布于四肢的内侧，手足阳经分布于四肢的外侧。四肢前缘为太阴经、阳明经，中间为厥阴经、少阳经，后缘为少阴经、太阳经。但下肢内踝上 8 寸以下，前缘为厥阴经，中间为太阴经。下肢内侧面内踝上 8 寸以上恢复为太阴、厥阴、少阴经的分布。

In the four limbs: The three yin meridians of the hand and foot run on the inner surface of the limbs. Conversely, the three yang meridians of the hand and foot occupy the outer surface of the limbs. In terms of the twelve meridians' distribution on the surface of the limbs, the taiyin and yangming meridians lie in the anterior portion. The jueyin and shaoyang meridians run in the middle portion, while the shaoyin and taiyang meridians travel in the posterior portion except in the lower part of the shank and the foot, where the foot – jueyin meridian runs anterior to the foot – taiyin meridian. The foot – jueyin meridian goes back and runs between the foot – taiyin meridian and the foot – shaoyin meridian after the crossing point which is eight cun above the inner malleolus.

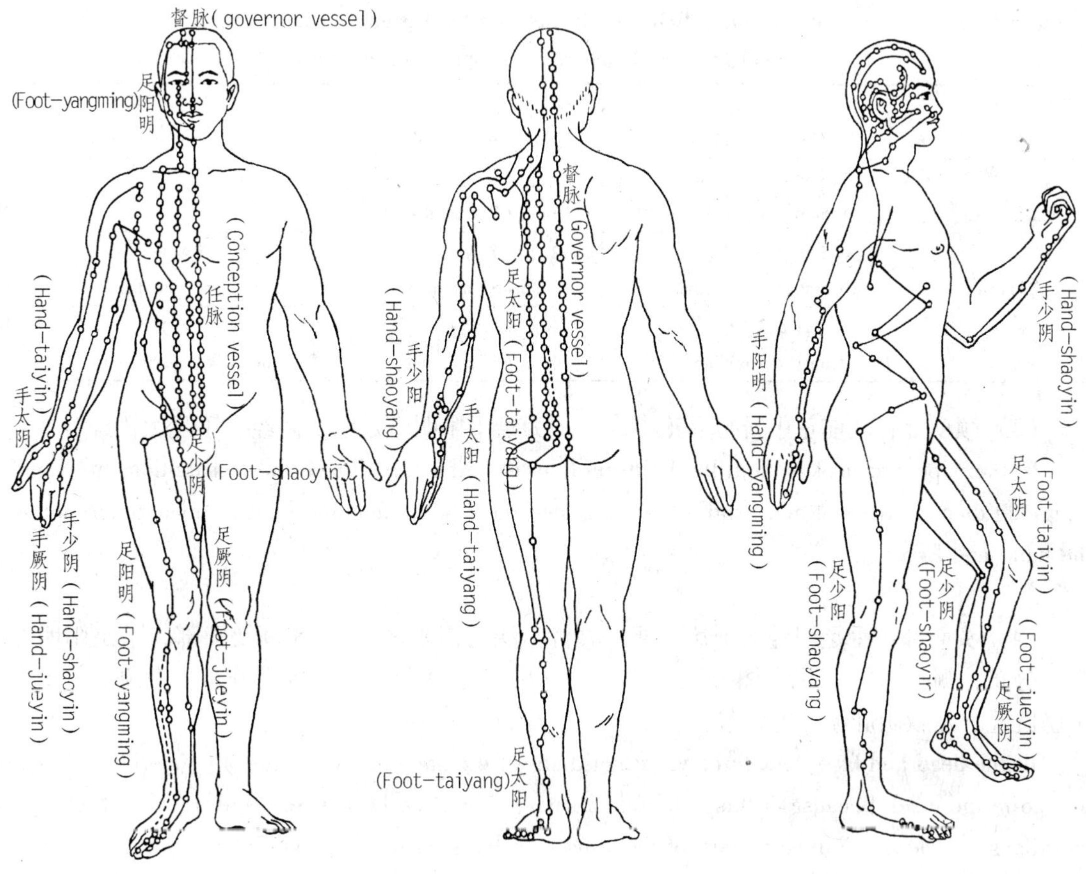

图 1 – 3 十四经分布概括

Fig 1 – 3 Overview for the distribution of the fourteen meridians

（2）躯干部：胸腹部的分布规律是，胸部旁开前正中线 2 寸，腹部旁开前正中线 0.5 寸为足少阴肾经；胸部旁开前正中线 4 寸，经过乳头，腹部旁开前正中线 2 寸为足阳明胃经；胸部旁开前正中线 6 寸，腹部旁开前正中线 4 寸为足太阴脾经。背腰部的分布规律是，旁开后正中线 1.5 寸和 3 寸，分别为足太阳膀胱经第一、第二侧线。侧胸腹部为足少阳胆经和足厥阴肝经分布（表 1 – 1）。

In the body trunk: In the chest and abdomen, it's the kidney meridian which runs lateral to the front midline 2 in the chest and 0.5 cun in the abdomen; the stomach meridian distributes 4 cun lateral to the front midline in the chest, run through the nipple and 2 cun lateral to the front line in the abdomen; the spleen meridian 6 cun laterally in the chest and 4 cun laterally in the abdomen. In the back and waist, there are two lateral branches of the bladder meridian, one is 1.5 lateral to the back midline and the other is 3 cun laterally. In the sides part of the body trunk, the liver meridian and the gallbladder meridian spread (Tab 1 – 1).

表 1 – 1 躯干部侧线的距离及与经脉的对应关系

Tab 1 – 1 The Corresponding Rclationship Between the Distant of the Lateral Line of the Meridians on the Trunk and Meridians

部位 Portion	第一侧线 The first lateral line	第二侧线 The second lateral line	第三侧线 The third lateral line
背腰 Back & waist	1.5 寸（膀胱经） 1.5cun (BL meridian)	3 寸（膀胱经） 3cun (BL meridian)	—
腹部 Abdomen	0.5 寸（肾经） 0.5cun (KI meridian)	2 寸（胃经） 2cun (ST meridian)	4 寸（脾经） 4cun (SP meridian)
胸部 Chest	2 寸（肾经） 2cun (KI meridian)	4 寸（胃经） 4cun (ST meridian)	6 寸（脾经） 6cun (SP meridian)

（3）颈项部：从前正中线至后正中线分别为足手阳明、足手少阳经、手足太阳经分布。

In the nape and neck: From the front midline to the back midline, the distributions are yangming meridians of the foot and hand, shaoyang meridians of the foot and hand, taiyang meridian of the hand and foot.

（4）头面部：手足阳经均到达头部，故言“头为诸阳之会”。前额及面部，手足阳明经为主分布；侧头部位，手足少阳经为主分布；后头部，手足太阳经为主分布；巅顶部，足太阳膀胱经、足厥阴肝经为主分布。

In the head and face: All three yang meridians of the hand and the three yang meridians of the foot go to the head. Because of this, there is a saying that “the head is the convergence of all yang meridians”. The distribution pattern of the yang meridians on the head is that yangming meridians occupy the forehead and face, shaoyang meridians lie on the lateral side of the head, while the taiyang meridians run on the posterior part of the head, and the liver meridian and taiyang meridians distribute the temple part of the head.

2. 内行部分
Interior Pathways

十二经脉“内属于腑脏”，即指其内行部分。脏腑中，脏为阴，腑为阳。手三阴联系于胸部，内属于肺、心包、心；足三阴联系于腹部，其内属于脾、肝、肾，这就是所谓的“阴脉营其脏”。阳经属于腑，足三阳内属于胃、胆、膀胱；手三阳内属于大肠、三焦、小肠，这就是所谓的“阳脉营其腑”。

The twelve regular meridians attach to zang – fu organs interiorly. As zang – organs belong to yin, and fu – organs belong to yang, the three yin meridians of the hand, which enter at the chest, connect to the lung, pericardium, and the heart respectively. The three yin meridians of the foot, which enter at the abdomen, belong to the spleen, liver, and the kidney respectively. The three yang meridians of the foot connect to the stomach, the gallbladder, and the urinary bladder; whereas the three yang meridians of the hand belong to the large intestine, the triple energizer, and the small intestine respectively. That is the saying, "yang meridians manage the fu organs".

(三) 十二经脉的表里属络
The Exterior – Interior Relationship of the Twelve Regular Meridians

脏腑有表里相合关系。十二经脉内属于脏腑，亦有相应的表里相合关系。阴经为里，属于脏，阳经为表，属于腑。互为表里的阴经与阳经在体内有属络关系，阴经属脏络腑，阳经属腑络脏，十二经脉形成了"六合"关系，十二经别和络脉加强了十二经脉的属络关系。(表1-2)。

As stated above, the twelve regular meridians connect to zang – fu organs. The paired yin and yang meridians with an exterior – interior relationship are connected within the body. Among them, yin meridians, which are considered relatively inner, belong to zang – organs and interact with fu – organs. The yang meridians, which run relatively superficially, belong to fu – organs and connect to zang – organs. According to the exterior – interior relationship, the twelve regular meridians can be divided into "six pairs", which can be strengthened by the divergent meridians and collaterals which facilitate the communication between the inner and the outer parts of the body (Tab 1 – 2).

表1-2　　十二经脉的表里属络关系

Tab 1 – 2　　The Relations of Exterior – Interior and Pertaining – Connecting in the Twelve Meridians

阳经（腑） Yang meridian (fu organ)	阴经（脏） Yin meridian (zang organ)
手阳明（大肠）经 Large Intestine meridian of hand – yangming	手太阴（肺）经 lung meridian of hand – taiyin
手少阳（三焦）经 Triple energizer meridian of hand – shaoyang	手厥阴（心包）经 Pericardium meridian of hand – jueyin
手太阳（小肠）经 Small intestine meridian of hand – taiyang	手少阴（心）经 Heart meridian of hand – shaoyin
足阳明（胃）经 Stomach meridian of foot – yangming	足太阴（脾）经 Spleen meridian of foot – taiyin
足少阳（胆）经 Gallbladder meridian of foot – shaoyang	足厥阴（肝）经 Liver meridian of foot – jueyin
足太阳（膀胱）经 Bladder meridian of foot – taiyang	足少阴（肾）经 Kidney meridian of foot – shaoyin

（四）十二经脉的走向和流注
Pathways and the Flow of Qi of the Twelve Regular Meridians

十二经脉的循行有一定的方向，或上行，或下行，形成“脉行之逆顺”，其走向规律是：手三阴经从胸走手，手三阳经从手走头，足三阳经从头走足，足三阴经从足走腹（胸），构成“如环无端”的气血流注关系（图1－4）。

The pathways of the twelve regular meridians follow the rule that run upward or downward to form “frontward and backward of the meridians' pathways”. The principle of the pathways is: the three yin meridians of the hand go from the chest to the hand; the three yang meridians of the hand run from the hand to the head; the three yang meridians of the foot travel from the head to the foot; and the three yin meridians of the foot go from the foot to the abdomen or the chest. The meridians of the hand and foot are connected with each other, forming an “interminable circulation” of qi and blood. The pathways of the twelve regular meridians is shown in Fig 1－4.

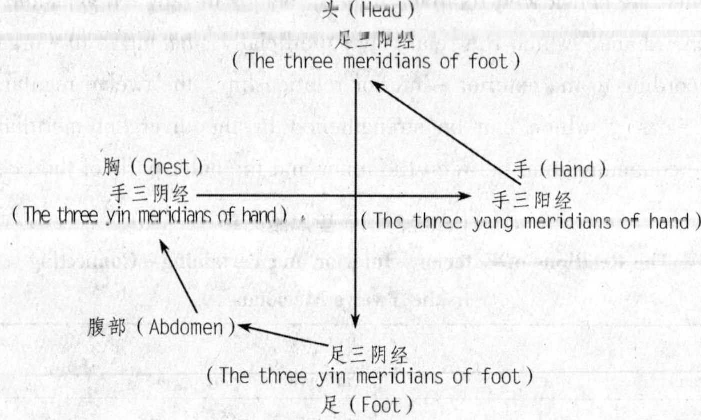

图1－4　十二经脉的走向

Fig 1－4　The pathways of the twelve regular meridians

（五）十二经脉的衔接
The Connection of the Twelve Regular Meridians

十二经脉通过以下三种形式相互衔接（图1－5）。

There are three types of connections through which the twelve regular meridians attach to each other（Fig 1－5）.

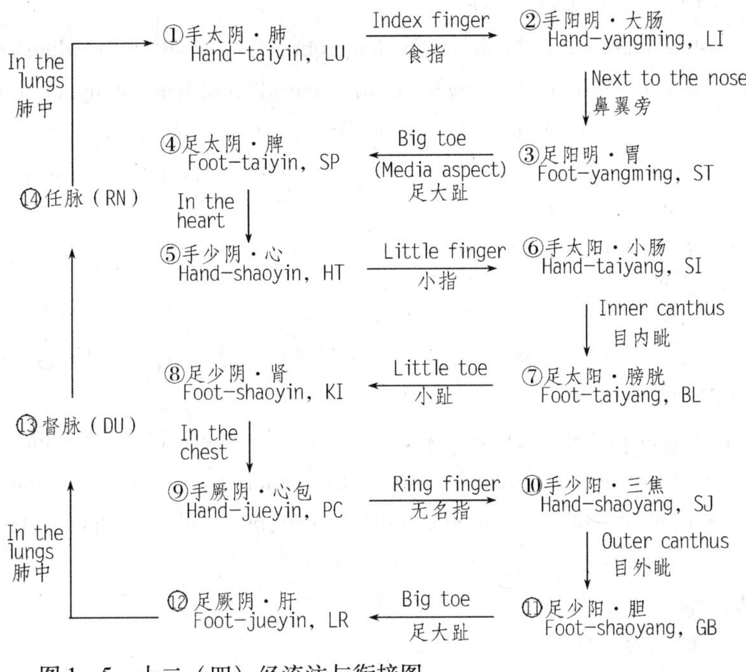

图1-5 十二（四）经流注与衔接图

Fig 1-5 Qi flowing & connection in the twelve (fourteen) meridians

1. 阴经与阳经（表里经）在手足部衔接
Yin Meridians and Yang Meridians (Exterior - Interior Relationship) Connect in the Hand or the Foot

手太阴肺经在食指与手阳明大肠经交接；手少阴心经在小指与手太阳小肠经连接；手厥阴心包经在无名指与手少阳三焦经衔接；足阳明胃经在足大趾（内侧）与足太阴脾经相接；足太阳膀胱经在足小趾与足少阴肾经相连；足少阳胆经在足大趾（外侧）与足厥阴肝经连接。

The lung meridian of hand - taiyin links to the large intestine meridian of hand - yangming at the tip of the index finger. The heart meridian of hand - shaoyin connects to the small Intestine of hand - taiyang at the tip of the little finger. The pericardium meridian of hand - jueyin links to the triple energizer (sanjiao) meridian of hand - shaoyang at the ring finger. The stomach meridian of foot - yangming connects to the spleen meridian of foot - taiyin on the medial side of big toe. The bladder meridian of foot - taiyang links to the kidney meridian of foot - shaoyin at the little toe. The gallbladder meridian of foot - shaoyang connects to the liver meridian of foot - jueyin on the lateral side of the big toe.

2. 阳经与阳经（同名阳经）在头面部衔接
Two Yang Meridians with the Same Name Connect in the Head and Facial Region

手阳明大肠经和足阳明胃经在鼻翼旁连接；手太阳小肠经与足太阳膀胱经在目内眦交

接；手少阳三焦经和足少阳胆经在目外眦衔接。

The large intestine meridian of hand – yangming connects to stomach meridian of the foot – yangming in the region next to the nose. The small intestine meridian of hand – taiyang links to the bladder meridian of foot – taiyang at the inner canthus of the eye. The triple energizer meridian of hand – shaoyang connects to the gallbladder meridian of the foot – shaoyang at the outer canthus of the eye.

3. 阴经与阴经（手足三阴经）在胸部衔接 Hand Yin Meridians and Foot Yin Meridians Connect in the Chest

足太阴脾经与手少阴心经交接于心中；足少阴肾经与手厥阴心包经交接于胸中；足厥阴肝经与手太阴肺经交接于肺中。

The spleen meridian of foot – taiyin connects to the heart meridian of hand – shaoyin in the heart. The kidney meridian of foot – shaoyin links to the pericardium meridian of hand – jueyin in the chest. The liver meridian of foot – jueyin connects to the lung meridian of hand – taiyin in the lung.

二、奇经八脉 Eight Extra Meridians

奇经八脉，包括督脉、任脉、冲脉、带脉、阳跻脉和阴跻脉、阳维脉和阴维脉。它们与十二正经不同，既不直属脏腑，又无表里配合关系，“别道奇行”。这是具有特殊作用的经脉，对其余经络起统率、联络和调节气血盛衰的作用。奇经八脉的分布部位与十二经脉纵横交互。督脉行于后正中线，任脉行于前正中线，任、督脉各有本经所属穴位，故与十二经相提并论。合称为“十四经”。其余的冲、带、跻、维六脉的穴位均交会于十二经和任、督脉中。冲脉行于腹部第一侧线交会足少阴肾经穴。任、督、冲三脉皆起于胞中，同出会阴而异行，称为“一源三歧”。带脉横斜行于腰腹，交会足少阳经穴。阳跻行于下肢外侧及肩、头部，交会足太阳等经穴。阴跻行于下肢内侧及眼，交会足少阴经穴。阳维行于下肢外侧、肩和头项，交会足少阳等经穴及督脉穴。阴维行于下肢内侧、腹第三侧线和颈部，交会足少阴等经穴及任脉穴。

The eight extra meridians encompass governor vessel, conception vessel, thoroughfare vessel, belt vessel, yang heel vessel, yin heel vessel, yang link vessel and yin link vessel. These eight meridians are different from the twelve regular meridians in that they do not belong to any zang – fu organs directly and have no exterior – interior relationship amongst themselves. In addition, they travel in an “extraordinary way” compared to the twelve regular meridians in order to command and communicate with the twelve regular meridians as well as regulate the amount of qi and blood in these regular meridians. The eight extra meridians connect criss – cross with the twelve regular meridians. Governor vessel runs along the middle line on the back while conception vessel travels along the mid – line in the front. Similar to the twelve regular meridians, Governor vessel and the conception vessel have points of their own. Because of this, they are often grouped together with the twelve regular meridians and are collectively known as "the fourteen main meridians". With no pertinent points of their own, the remaining six vessels only connect with the fourteen main meridians by crossing certain points. Thoroughfare vessel runs along the first lateral line on the abdomen and shares crossing points with the kidney meridian of the foot – shaoyin. Conception vessel, governor vessel and thoroughfare vessel all originate from Bao Zhong (literally means within the uterus) in the lower abdomen. After converging at the perineum, the three meridians branch out and run in their own independent ways. The saying "one origin and three branches" is thus devoted to these three vessels. Belt vessel circles around the waist and the abdomen obliquely like a waist belt, and shares crossing points with the gallbladder meridian of foot – shaoyang. Yang heel vessel runs on the lateral side of the lower limbs, shoulders, and the head. It shares crossing points with the bladder meridian of foot – taiyang. Yin heel vessel travels on the inner medial side of the lower limbs, and finally reaches the eyes. It shares crossing points with the kidney meridian of foot – shaoyin. Yang link vessel goes on the lateral side of the lower limbs, shoulders, head, and the nape of the neck. It shares crossing points with the gallbladder meridian of foot – shaoyang and governor vessel. Yin link vessel travels on the inner side of the lower limbs, the third lateral line of the abdomen and the neck. It shares crossing points with the kidney meridian of foot – shaoyin and conception vessel.

三、十二经别
Twelve Divergent Meridians

十二经别，是十二经脉别行深入体腔的支脉，又称“别行之正经”。十二经别有“离、入、出、合”的分布特点。从十二经脉分出称“离”；进入胸腹腔称“入”；在头颈部浅出称“出”；出于头颈部后，阳经经别合于原经脉，阴经经别合于相表里的阳经经脉称“合”，如手阳明经别合于手阳明经脉，手太阴经别也合于手阳明经脉。手足三阴三阳经别，按阴阳表里关系组成六对，称为“六合”。经别通过离、入、出、合的分布，加强了表里两经及经脉与脏腑的联系，突出了心和头的重要性，扩大了经脉的循行联系和经穴的主治范围。

The twelve divergent meridians are branches departing from the twelve regular meridians and traveling deeply into the body cavity. They are also named as "divergent regular meridians". According to the meridian and collateral theory, the twelve divergent meridians have four distribution characteristics, namely "separating", "entering", "resurfacing" and "joining". Separating refers to the branching out of the divergent meridians from the twelve regular meridians. Entering means the entrance of the divergent meridian into the chest or abdominal cavity. Resurfacing refers to the emergence of the divergent meridian out of the body surface, usually at the neck or the face. Joining means that after resurfacing at the head or the neck, the yang divergent meridians then join their own regular meridians again, while the yin divergent meridians join their internally – externally related yang regular meridians. For example, both the divergent meridians of hand – yangming and the hand – taiyin join the large intestine meridian of hand – yangming. According to yin – yang and its internal – external relationship, the three yin and three yang divergent meridians of the hand and foot can be divided into six pairs, which is the so – called "six convergences". By the distribution of separating, entering, resurfacing, and joining, the divergent meridians strengthen the bonds between the interior and exterior – paired regular meridians as well as with their zang – fu organs. The theory of the twelve divergent meridians emphasizes the importance of the heart and the head, and expands the scope of the distribution of the regular meridians and the indication of the acupoints.

四、十五络脉 Fifteen Main Collaterals

十二经脉在四肢部各分出一络，再加躯干前的任脉络、躯干后的督脉络及躯干侧的脾之大络，共十五条，称“十五络脉”。十二络脉在四肢部从相应络穴分出后均走向相应的表里经，躯干部三络则分别分布于身前、身后和身侧。四肢部的十二络，主要起沟通表里两经和补充经脉循行不足的作用；躯干部的三络，起渗灌气血的作用。

The fifteen main collaterals are made up of twelve collaterals which branch out from the twelve regular meridians at the limbs, plus one collateral each for conception vessel on the front and governor vessel on the back, and the major collateral of the spleen on the lateral side of the trunk. The collaterals of the twelve regular meridians spread from the luo – connecting point in the limbs out of their own meridian to connect with their internally – externally paired meridian. The three collaterals on the trunk cover the anterior, posterior and the lateral side of the body. The twelve collaterals on the limbs strengthen the connection between the internally – externally paired meridians and reach areas of the body not supplied or interconnected by the regular meridians. The three collaterals on the trunk adjust the supply of qi and blood on the trunk.

络脉和经别都是经脉的分支，均有加强表里两经的作用。但经别主内，无所属穴位，也无所主病症；络脉则主外，各有一络穴，并有所主病症。络脉按其形状、大小、深浅等的不同又有不同的名称，浮行于浅表的络脉称“浮络”，最细小的络脉称“孙络”，细小的血管称“血络”。

Both the collaterals and the divergent meridians are branches from the regular meridians and have the function of strengthening the connection of the internally – externally paired regular meridians. However, there exist differences between the collaterals and divergent meridians. The divergent meridians dominate the internal part of the body with no points on their pathways, whereas the collaterals dominate the external part of the body and each has its own luo – connecting point with specific purposes. The collaterals have different names according to their shape, size, and depth of their pathways in the body. The collaterals which travel on the superficial surface of the body are called superficial collaterals, the minute collaterals are called tertiary collateral, and the tiny blood vessels are called blood collaterals.

五、十二经筋
Twelve Muscular Regions

十二经筋，是指与十二经脉相应的筋肉部分，其分布范围与十二经脉大体一致。全身筋肉按经络分布部位同样分成手足三阴三阳。经筋均起于四肢末端，结聚于骨骼和关节部，有的进入胸腹腔，但不像经脉那样属络脏腑。手足三阳之筋都到达头面，手三阴之筋到胸膈，足三阴之筋到阴部。经筋的作用是约束骨骼，活动关节，保持人体正常的运动功能，维持人体正常的体位姿势。

The twelve muscular regions refer to the corresponding muscles and tendons around the twelve regular meridians, and their distribution pattern is by and large similar to the twelve regular meridians. Muscles and tendons of the whole body can be divided into three yin and three yang meridians of the hand and foot according to their distribution. In general, the muscular regions originate from the extremities and converge at the bones and joints. Some of them enter the chest or abdominal cavity. However, they do not belong to or relate to zang – fu organs like the regular meridian. The three yang muscular regions of the hand and foot reach the head and the face, while the three yin muscular regions of the hand arrive at the chest and diaphragm. The three yin muscular regions of the foot reach the pudendum. The muscular regions have the function of restraining the bones and mobilizing the joints in order to maintain normal movement and posture of the human body.

六、十二皮部
Twelve Cutaneous Regions

十二皮部，是指与十二经脉相应的皮肤部分，属十二经脉及其络脉的散布部位。体表皮肤也按手足三阴三阳划分。这是十二经脉在体表的功能活动部位，也是络脉之气散布之所在。皮部位于人体最外层，是机体的卫外屏障。《素问·皮部论》指出邪气可经皮→络→经→腑→脏的途径入侵机体而致病；脏腑、经络的病变也可反映到皮部。因此，通过外部的诊察和施治可推断和治疗内部的疾病。皮部具有抗御外邪保卫机体和反映病候、协助诊断的作用。临床上皮肤针、刺络、敷贴等疗法，就是皮部理论的应用（图1－6）。

The twelve cutaneous regions refer to the corresponding skin regions of the twelve regular meridians. These are the spreading parts of the twelve regular meridians and their collaterals which can also be divided into three yin and three yang of the hand and foot. The twelve cutaneous regions are the functional parts of the twelve regular meridians manifested on the skin and the locations where qi in the collaterals is spread. The cutaneous regions constitute the outermost shield of the human body. In chapter 56 of *Plain Question*, it states that the external pathogenic qi penetrates through the skin, spreads to the collaterals, goes to the meridians, then travels to the fu – organ, and finally it reaches the zang – organ in order to cause a disease. Disorders of zang – fu organs and meridians can also manifest on the cutaneous regions. Therefore, disorders of a deep, underlying part of the body can be diagnosed by the symptoms manifested on the skin; and conversely, treatment applied at the level of the skin is able to create a more pronounced therapeutic response. Moreover, the cutaneous regions protect the body from the invasion of external pathogenic qi. Because cutaneous regions can manifest disorders of the body, they are very valuable in disease diagnosis. Certain types of therapies used in clinical practice, such as skin needling, pricking, bloodletting, and topical application therapy, follow the theory of the cutaneous region (Fig 1 – 6).

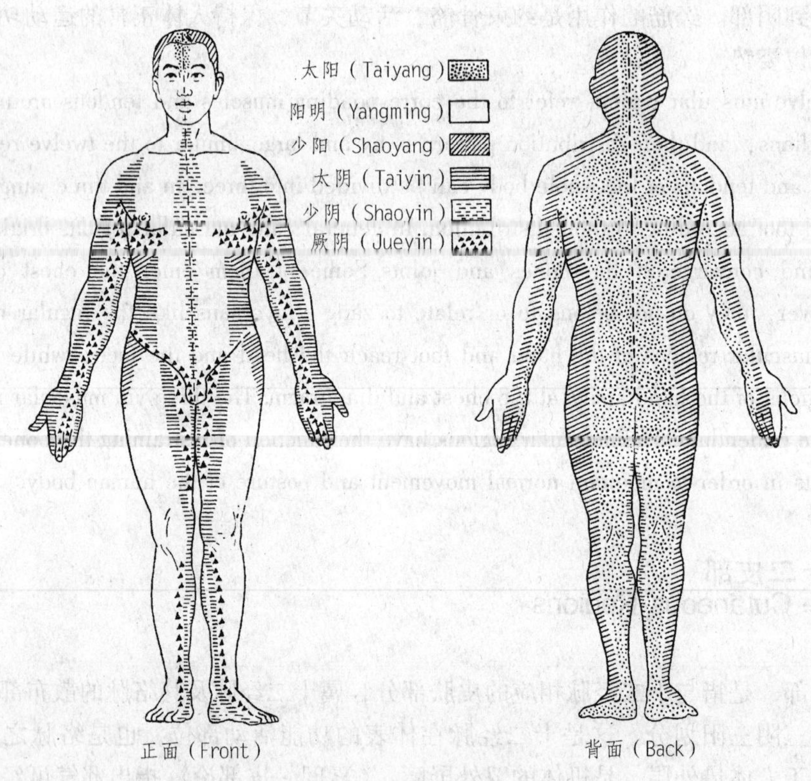

图 1 – 6　六经皮部示意图

Fig 1 – 6　The cutaneous regions of the six meridians

第二节　经络的作用及经络理论的临床应用
Effects and Clinical Applications of Meridian Theory

经络学说不仅在中医基础理论中占有重要地位，经络的作用还体现在中医各科的临床应用中。经络理论与临床实践是相互结合的，经络理论可指导临床实践，而临床实践可不断完善、发展经络理论。

The meridian doctrines occupy an important place in the basic TCM theories. The significance of meridian theory is also embodied in its application in various TCM clinical subjects. The development of meridian theory has been closely linked to TCM clinical practice, they are mutual complementation and interdependent.

一、经络的作用
Meridian Effects

《灵枢·经脉》指出："经脉者，所以能决死生，处百病，调虚实，不可不通。"这概括地说明了经络系统在生理、病理和防治疾病等方面的重要性。其所以能决定人的生和死，是因为其具有联系人体内外和运行气血的作用；处治百病，是因其具有抗御病邪、反映证候的作用；调整虚实，是因其能传导感应而起补虚泻实的作用。

In the chapter 10, *Miraculous Pivot*, it states that "the meridian system can be utilized to tell whether one is healthy or dying, to manage variety of diseases, and to regulate deficiency and excess of the body. It is so important that it must be fully understood". This sentence summarizes the significance of the meridian system with respect to physiology, pathology, and disease prevention. The main functions of meridians are to connect the internal and external parts of the human body and to transport qi and blood, which make it possible to tell whether one is healthy or dying. The effects of fighting pathogenic qi and manifesting symptoms are the reasons why meridians can treat many kinds of diseases. Meridians can regulate deficiency and excess because they have the ability to transmit sensation, tonify the deficiency and reduce the excess.

（一）沟通内外，网络全身
Linking the Whole Body and Communicating the Internal with the External

《灵枢·海论》指出："夫十二经脉者，内属于腑脏，外络于支节。"人体的五脏六腑、四肢百骸、五官九窍、皮肉筋骨等组织器官，虽有各自不同的生理功能，但又互相联系，互相配合，使人体构成一个有机的整体，保持协调统一。这主要是依靠经络系统的联络沟通而实现的。十二经脉及经别着重于人体体表与脏腑，以及脏腑间的联系；十二经脉和十五络脉，着重于体表与体表，以及体表与脏腑间的联系；十二经脉通过奇经八脉，加强了经与经之间的联系；十二经的根结、标本、气街和四海，则加强了人体头面躯干前后腹背的分段联系。

It is said in chapter 33 of *Miraculous Pivot* that "internally, the twelve main meridians connect with the zang-fu organs, and externally with the joints, limbs and other superficial tissues of the body." All tissues and internal organs in the human body, such as the five zang-organs, six fu-organs, limbs, joints, five sense organs, nine orifices, skin, muscles, and tendons have their own physiological functions. They are also intimately interconnected and coordinated in such a way to make the human body into a holistic organism and to maintain coordination. All these effects are carried out by the connection and communication of the meridian system. The twelve regular meridians and the divergent meridians mainly connect the surface of the human body with the internal organs, and maintain the interrelationship of zang – fu organs. The twelve regular meridians and the fifteen main collaterals strengthen the relationship between the skin and the zang – fu organs. With the aid of the eight extra meridians, the relationships amongst the twelve regular meridians are strengthened. The tip – root, branch – foundation, qi thoroughfare, and four seas strengthen the connection between various regions such as the head, face, abdomen and trunk.

（二）运行气血，协调阴阳
Circulating Qi and Blood and Coordinating Yin and Yang

《灵枢·本藏》指出："经脉者，所以行血气而营阴阳，濡筋骨，利关节者也。"气血在全身各部的输布有赖于经络的运行。人体各个脏腑组织器官在气血的濡养后才能发挥其正常的生理作用，而气血必须经过经络输布于周身内外，使"内溉脏腑，外濡腠理"（《灵枢·脉度》）。在经络的联系下，气血盛衰和机能动静保持相对平衡，使人体"阴平阳秘，精神乃治"（《素问·生气通天论》）。

In the chapter 47, *Miraculous Pivot*, it says "the meridians and collaterals transport blood and qi to adjust yin and yang, nourish tendons and bones, and improve joint function". The transportation of qi and blood all over the body is carried out in meridians. All zang – fu organs and tissues conduct their normal physiological functions, relying on the nourishment provided by qi and blood, which are transmitted by meridians. In the chapter 17, *Miraculous Pivot*, it also says that qi and blood "fills into zang – fu organs interiorly, and nourishes interstices exteriorly". Via the linkage of meridians, sufficient amount of qi and blood maintain the dynamic equilibrium so that the body reaches a state where "yin is balanced and yang is firm, and a coordinated spirit is guaranteed" stated in the chapter 3, *Plain Questions.*

（三）抗御病邪，反映证候
Resisting Pathogenic – Qi and Manifesting Symptoms and Signs of Diseases

经络具有抗御病邪、反映证候的作用。经络中的孙络分布广而浅表，是机体的卫外屏障。经络又是外邪入侵的途径，外邪可经孙络、络脉、经脉、脏腑之途径由表及里，逐步深入。《素问·缪刺论》说："夫邪之客于形也，必先舍于皮毛，留而不去，入舍于孙脉，留而不去，入舍于络脉，留而不去，入舍于经脉，内连五脏，散于肠胃"，即是此意。脏腑的病理变化也可经经络途径由内而外地反映到体表，这对临床诊断有重要应用价值。

Meridians have the functional capability of resisting pathogenic – qi and manifesting symptoms and signs of diseases. The tertiary collaterals of meridians distribute widely and superficially and form the external shield of the human body. Meanwhile, meridians can also be the transmitting pathway of exogenous pathogenic – qi. The exogenous pathogenic – qi attack the body through tertiary collaterals, collaterals, meridians, and then into the zang – fu organs gradually. As stated in the chapter 63, *Plain Questions*, "when the body is involved in a pathogenic invasion, the exogenous pathogen first attack the skin. If the pathogen does not go away, it will penetrate the tertiary collaterals. If the pathogen is not expelled, it will attack the collaterals. If the pathogen is not expelled, it will attack the meridians, and go further into the five zang – organs, as well as spread into the stomach and the intestines". On the other hand, the pathological changes of zang – fu organs can be manifested in the skin through the pathway of the meridians. Such manifestation is of practical importance in TCM diagnosis.

（四）传导感应，调整虚实 Transmitting Needling Sensation and Regulating Deficiency and Excess Conditions

针刺时的"得气"、"行气"和"气至病所"现象是经络传导感应的表现。《灵枢·九针十二原》说："刺之要，气至而有效"。针刺感应是针刺取得疗效的关键，而针感是通过经络传导的，针感循经络通路最终到达病变部位而起调整虚实的作用。

During acupuncture, the transmission of needling sensation along meridians is shown in phenomena such as arrival of qi, movement of qi, and spreading of qi to the affected area. Therefore, the first chapter in *Miraculous Pivot* points out, "In acupuncture, the arrival of qi is essential to obtaining therapeutic effects". The sensation induced by needling is the key in achieving therapeutic efficacy in acupuncture. Meanwhile, needling sensation is conducted through meridians to reach the diseased area in order to regulate deficiency and excess.

二、经络理论的临床应用 Clinical Applications of Meridian Theory

经络理论的临床应用可体现在诊断和治疗两个方面。诊断方面包括经络诊法和分经辨证；治疗方面包括循经取穴和药物归经。

The clinical application of meridian theory encompasses both diagnosis and treatment. TCM diagnosis includes meridian diagnosis and pattern identification according to meridians. As with meridian application in disease treatment, it includes selecting points along meridians and meridian entry of herbs on demarcation of meridians.

（一）经络诊法 Meridian Diagnosis

经络诊法对经络部位进行诊察的方法，包括审查、指切、推循、扪摸、按压，以及对局部寒温和气血盛衰现象的观察。

The meridian diagnosis comprises of external meridian reaction detecting, pulse taking according to meridians, regional collaterals detecting and tender point detecting. The commonly used methods for external meridian reaction include observing, nail-pressing, pushing and searching, and pressing, as well as identifying the cold and warm sensations of the local area and the fullness and emptiness of the qi and blood.

经络外诊多用直接的检查。在诊察某些疾病的过程中，常可发现在经络循行路线上有皮肤形态、色泽的变化，或有明显的结节、条索状物等阳性反应物，这些都有助于对疾病的诊断。近代又采用一些客观的检测方法，如皮肤温度、皮肤电阻、红外热像等检测，使探测方法更趋于多样化、客观化和现代化。

By examining the positive manifestations such as changes in skin appearance and color, nodules, or enlarged fibers along the pathways of meridians, one can make a proper diagnosis. More recently, some new meridian detecting methods have been introduced into clinical practice, such as skin temperature measuring, skin electrical resistance detecting, and infrared thermal detecting techniques. All these detecting methods make meridian diagnosis more diverse, objective and quantitative.

分经切脉，原是经络诊法的主要内容。如《灵枢》以寸口脉诊候阴经病症的虚实，人迎脉诊候阳经病症的虚实。因以阳明脉气最盛，其下部可诊候冲阳（趺阳）脉，肾气盛衰则可诊候太溪脉。

Pulse taking according to meridians used to be the main component in meridian diagnosis. For example, the *Miraculous Pivot* records that the pulse in Cunkou on the wrist may be used to differentiate deficiency or excess in yin meridians, and the pulse of Renying（ST 9）on the neck may be used to identify the deficiency or excess in yang meridians. Because of the abundance of qi in the yangming meridian, one can diagnose lower regions conditions of the body by checking on the Fuyang（ST 42）pulse on the foot. Similarly, the condition of the kidney qi can be diagnosed by checking the Taixi（KI 3）pulse on the ankle.

分部诊络，是诊察皮部血络的色泽，以辨痛、痹、寒、热等。近年的皮疹辨证，也属于诊络法。

Regional collateral detecting is another meridian diagnosis method used to observe the color of blood collaterals in the skin regions in order to differentiate pain, blockage, cold, heat, and so on. The pattern identification of rashes on the skin, a technique used recently, also belongs to collateral detecting in meridian diagnosis.

压痛的检查，对临床取穴尤为重要。《灵枢·背腧》说："按其处，应在中而痛解

(懈)”。这种以痛为腧的取穴方法，实际上也是一种经络诊法。

Finding a tender point is especially important in acupuncture and moxibustion. The chapter 51, *Miraculous Pivot*, indicated that “pressing at a tender point at the back can lead to the relief of the internal painful condition”. Such tender point pressing actually is the application of meridian diagnosis.

(二) 分经辨证
Pattern Identification According to Meridians

十二经穴能主治其所发生的病症，这就是经脉的主病。各经脉既有其循行所过部位的外经病（证），又有其有关的脏腑病（证）。此外，络脉、经筋也各有主病；皮部病症实际上是经络病候的综合反映。奇经八脉与各经相交会，其所主病症又有其特殊性。临床上可根据所出现的病症，结合经络循行部位及所联系的脏腑进行辨证归经。分经辨证，主要分十二经（合为六经）和奇经八脉。

The points of the twelve regular meridians can be needled for the treatment of diseases related to the twelve regular meridians. This is to say that a regular meridian point can treat disorders of its meridian, and each meridian has its indications, which may include the external disorders along its meridian pathway and the internal disorders of its related zang－fu organs. Besides, collaterals and muscular regions have their own indications too. Actually, symptoms of the cutaneous region are manifestations of its pertaining meridian's disorder. By intersecting with the twelve regular meridians, the eight extra meridians have their own characteristics in disease detection. In clinical practice, meridian pattern identification is made by observing reaction on the course of the affected meridians, analyzing their indications and the related zang－fu organs. It is generally divided into twelve meridians (or combined as six meridians) for pattern identification and eight extra meridians for pattern identification.

通过分经辨证对经气虚实、经气厥逆，甚或经气终厥等的观察，可明确病位，了解疾病的性质、程度、发展和预后，对疾病的诊断和治疗有重要意义。

Through meridian pattern identification, the condition of the meridian－qi such as excess, deficiency, blockage, adverse flow or even depletion of qi may be detected. Moreover, the nature, severity, development and prognosis of a disease can be clarified. Meridian identification, therefore, plays an important role in the diagnosis and treatment of disease.

(三) 循经取穴
Selecting Points Along Meridians

循经取穴，是以经络理论为指导，通常是在分经辨证的基础上，选用病变相关经脉的远道经穴，是针灸临床上的常用和基本取穴方法。《四总穴歌》所说的“肚腹三里留，腰背委中求，头项寻列缺，面口合谷收”，是典型的循经取穴。

Selecting points along meridians is guidance under the meridian theory and usually based on meridian pattern identification, and remains as a common method and one of the basic point selection methods in acupuncture practice. This point selection method is exemplified by the famous *The Song of Four General Points* (*Si Zong Xue Ge*) which says that "abdominal disorders can be treated with Zusanli (ST 36). One can search that Weizhong (BL 40) can be used for back and lumbar problems; head and neck conditions can be dealt with by selecting Lieque (LU 7); and illness of the face and mouth can be cleared by needling Hegu (LI 4)".

(四) 药物归经
Meridian Entry of Herbs

在中药中，药物按其主治性能归入某经或某几经，简称药物归经。此说是在分经辨证的基础上发展而来，因病症可以分经，主治某些病症的药物也就成为某经或某几经之药。

清代徐灵胎《医学源流论》说：“因其能治何经之病，后人即指为何经之药。”可见，药物归经实际上是指某药能主治某经或某几经所属的病症，是运用经络理论对药物性能进行分析和归类。

In Chinese medicine, each herb has the tendency to enter one or several meridians, and the theory is called the "meridian entry of herbs", which was developed from meridian pattern identification. Since a disease is caused by dysfunction of one or several meridians, a herb which treats the disease usually enters the same meridians as well. Xu Lingtai, a famous physician in the Qing Dynasty (1644 – 1911), recorded in his book *Discussion on the Origin of Medicine* (*Yi Xue Yuan Liu Lun*) that "people categorized the meridian entry of a herb by its indications". So the meridian entry of an herb is actually an analysis and classification for the indications of the herb using meridian theory.

经络不仅在人体生理功能的调控上具有重要作用，而且是临床上说明人体病理变化，指导辨证归经和针灸治疗的重要理论依据。

Meridians and collaterals play important roles not only in regulating the physiological function of the human body, but they are also manifested in pathogenic changes of a disease. Moreover, they constitute the significant theoretical evidence for pattern identification, diagnosis and acupuncture treatment.

第三节 经络的纵横关系
Vertical – Horizontal Relations in the Meridian Theory

根结、标本、气街和四海是关于经络纵横关系的理论，它是从各经的纵向或横向方面阐述若干规律性的认识，以指导临床辨证和用穴。根结和标本，主要分析经络的纵向关系，气街和四海主要从大范围分析经络的横向关系，其间又是相互联系的。

The tip – root, branch – foundation, qi thoroughfare, and four seas theories discuss the vertical or horizontal relationship of meridians in order to interpret the common rules in each meridian and provide guidance in diagnosis and point selection in acupuncture practice. The tip – root and branch – foundation theories analyze the vertical relationship of meridians, while the qi thoroughfare and four seas theories explain from a grand perspective the horizontal relationship of meridians and their intercommunication.

一、根与结
Root - Tip Theory

"根"和"结"，是指十二经脉之气起始和归结的部位。根，有起始的含义，此指四肢末端的井穴；结，是结聚、归结的意思，在头、胸、腹部。

Root and tip, or "Gen Jie" in Chinese, refer to the originating and terminating points of qi in the twelve regular meridians. The word "Gen", means root or originating, and it refers to the jing – well point of the individual meridian in the extremities. The word "Jie" means tip or gathering, and it lies on the head, chest, and abdomen.

根结理论说明了经气活动的上下联系，强调以四肢末端为出发点，着重经气循行的根源与归结，强调四肢腧穴对于头、胸、腹部的重要作用。

The root – tip theory explains the upward and downward movement of the meridian – qi, and emphasizes the importance of extremities as the starting points of the meridian – qi in its circulation. It reiterates that points located in the limbs have important implications in the therapeutic effect on the head, chest and abdomen.

二、标与本
Branch - Foundation Theory

"标"和"本"，是指经脉的上下对应关系。"标"，原意指树梢，此指人体上部的头面胸背部位。"本"，原意指树的下部，此指人体下部的四肢部。

Branch and foundation, or "Biao Ben" in Chinese, refers to the up and down corresponding relationship in the meridians. The original meaning of "Biao" is the branches or the top of a tree. Here it means the upper part of the body including the head, face, chest, and back. "Ben" refers to the lower part or the foundation of a tree. Here it means the lower part of a human body, such as the extremities.

标本与根结两者都是论述四肢与头面躯干之间的相互关系，以四肢为"根"，为"本"，以头面躯干为结，为标。"根"专指井穴，"本"则扩及四肢肘膝以下的一定部位；"结"在头、胸、腹部，"标"扩及背部的背俞。《内经》论根结仅以足六经为代表，论标本则有手足六经，范围更为全面。

Both root - tip and branch - foundation theories discuss the interrelation of the limbs with the trunk, head and face. The limbs are the root or foundation, and the trunk, head, and face are the tip or branch. It is worthy to note that the root only refers to the Jing - Well point. Foundation refers to a certain area beneath the elbow or the knee joints. The tip lies on the head, the chest, or the abdomen. The branch enlarges the area and covers the Back - Shu points on the back. *Huangdi's Internal Classic* uses six foot meridians to represent the root and the tip, while it uses six hand meridians as well as six foot meridians when explaining the branch - foundation theory.

根结和标本理论在意义上大体是一致的，都是强调经气其"源"在四肢，以此为"根"，为"本"；而其"流"在头面躯干，以此为"结"，为"标"。根结、标本理论主要阐明四肢肘膝以下的经穴对头面躯干远隔部位的重要治疗作用，从而指导临床取穴。

Overall, the root - tip and branch - foundation theories share similar meanings. Both theories emphasize that the source of the meridian - qi lies in the limbs, which is the root or the foundation; and the meridian - qi flows into the trunk, head, and face, which are the tips or the branches. The root - tip and branch - foundation theories have important clinical implications in that the meridian points beneath the elbow and the knee joint of the limbs possess important therapeutic effects on the distal areas, such as the trunk, head, and face. As such, these theoretical frameworks help guide point selection in clinical practice.

三、气街
Qi Thoroughfare

气街是经气在头面躯干部横斜扩散的通路。《灵枢·卫气》记载："胸气有街，腹气有街，头气有街，胫气有街。故气在头者，止之于脑；气在胸者，止之膺与背腧；气在腹者，止之背腧与冲脉于脐左右之动脉者；气在胫者，止之于气街与承山踝上以下。"

Qi thoroughfare is the direct pathway where the meridian - qi spreads in the trunk, head, and face transversely and obliquely. As stated in the chapter 52, *Miraculous Pivot*, "the chest qi, abdomen qi, head qi, and shank qi have their own qi thoroughfare respectively. So qi in the head terminates at the brain; qi in the chest ends at the breast and back - shu points; qi in the abdomen terminates in the area between the back - shu points, thoroughfare vessel and around the pulsing arteries of the left and right side of the umbilicus; and qi in the shank ends at the region inferior to Qijie (ST 30, Qichong), and Chengshan (BL 57) which are located above to the ankle".

气街，主要说明头、胸、腹、胫这些部位是经气循行的共同通道，说明了经络的横向联系，是经气横向输注及脏腑之气前后布散的路径，为临床处方配穴提供了理论依据。

Qi thoroughfare theory shows that regions like the head, chest, abdomen, and shank are the common pathways for circulation of the channel - qi, and it provides an explanation for the horizontal relationship of various meridians. These common pathways are for horizontal transportation of the meridian - qi and the anterior and posterior distribution of the zang - fu qi. The qi thoroughfare theory provides theoretical evidence for point selection in clinical practice.

四、四海
Four Seas Theory

四海即髓海、血海、气海、水谷之海的总称。《灵枢·海论》指出："胃者，水谷之海，其输上在气街（气冲），下至三里；冲脉者，为十二经之海，其输上在于大杼，下出于巨虚之上下廉（上、下巨虚）；膻中者，为气之海，其输上在于柱骨之上下（大椎），前在于人迎；脑为髓之海，其输上在于盖（百会），下在风府。"《灵枢·海论》还描述了四海有余、不足的有关病候，对针灸临床有重要指导意义。

The four seas include the sea of marrow, the sea of blood, the sea of qi, and the sea of grain and water. In the chapter 33, *Miraculous Pivot*, it points out that "the stomach is the sea of grain and water, its qi transports superiorly to Qijie (ST 30, Qichong), and inferiorly to Zusanli (ST 36). The Thoroughfare Vessel is the sea of the twelve regular meridians, and its transportation reaches superiorly to Dazhu (BL 11), inferiorly to Shangjuxu (ST 37) and Xiajuxu (ST 39). Danzhong is the sea of qi, and its transportation reaches superiorly around Zhugu (DU 14, Dazhui) and anteriorly to Renying (ST 9). The brain is the sea of marrow, and its transporting region of qi locates superiorly at Baihui (DU 20) and inferiorly at Fengfu (DU 16)". In the same chapter, it also records symptoms of excess and insufficiency of the four seas, and provides an important guidance in acupuncture practice.

四海与"气街"、"结"、"标"有其一致性。经气从"根"、"本"部汇集到"结"、"标"部时，通过气街的弥散形成四海。

There is some consistency amongst the four seas, root - tip, and branch - foundation theories. The meridian - qi originates from the root or foundation, and converges at the tip or branch, and then spreads through the qi thoroughfare to form the four seas.

复习思考题
Review Questions

1. 什么是经络？其临床意义是什么？

What is a meridian? What is its clinical significance?

2. 十二经脉在四肢的分布如何？

What are the distribution rules of the twelve regular meridians in the limbs?

3. 营气在十二经脉中是如何流注的？十二经脉的循行走向如何？

How does the nutritive qi flow in the twelve regular meridians? What is the rule of "the distributing directions of meridians"?

4. 十二经脉的衔接规律是什么？

How do the twelve meridians connect to each other?

5. 十二经别的分布规律是什么？有什么作用？

What is the distribution characteristic of the twelve divergent meridians? What are their effects?

6. 十二经别和十二络脉有什么异同点？

What are the similarities and differences between the twelve divergent meridians and the twelve collaterals?

第二章 腧穴概述
General Introduction to Acupuncture Points

腧穴是脏腑经络气血输注于躯体外部的特殊部位，也是疾病的反应点和针灸等治法的刺激点。腧，又作“俞”，通“输”，有输注、转输的意思；穴，原意为“土室”，引申为孔隙、空窍、凹陷处。腧穴在《内经》中又有“节”、“会”、“气穴”、“气府”、“骨空”等名称。

The places for acupuncture and moxibustion, also known as acupuncture points, acupoints or points, are the specific sites where the qi of zang - fu organs and meridians is transported to the body surface. Points are not only the reflecting places of disorders but also the sites to receive the stimulation by acupuncture and moxibustion. An acupuncture point is “Shu Xue” in Chinese. “Shu” means transporting, while “Xue” means valley or hole. In *Huangdi's Internal Classic*, there exist some other descriptions of acupoints such as a “Joint”, “Meeting Place”, “Qi Valley”, “Qi House” and “Bone Cleft”.

腧穴与脏腑、经络有密切关系。腧穴归于经络，经络属于脏腑，故腧穴与脏腑脉气相通。历代医著记载了腧穴的定位、主治等，形成了系统的腧穴理论。

There is a close relation between points, zang - fu organs and meridians. Since a point is distributed along the course of a meridian, the meridian links with certain zang - fu organs, and there exists a close link between the points and internal zang - fu organs. Medical practitioners of past ages have left plentiful recordings describing the locations and indications of acupuncture points, formulation a systematical theory.

第一节 腧穴的分类和命名
Classification and Nomenclature of Acupoints

一、腧穴的分类
Classification of Acupoints

腧穴的类别，一般将归属于十四经系统的称为“经穴”，未归入十四经的补充穴称为

"经外奇穴"，还有按压痛点取穴则称为"阿是穴"。

Points are classified into three categories，namely meridian points，which all distribute in the fourteen meridians；extra points，which are not attributed to the fourteen meridians；and ashi - points，which selected by pressing the tender spots.

（一）经穴
Meridian Points

凡归属于十二经脉和任脉、督脉的腧穴，亦即归属于十四经的穴位，总称"经穴"。经穴均有具体的穴名和固定的位置，分布在十四经循行路线上，有明确的针灸主治证。《内经》多处提到"三百六十五穴"之数，但实际其载有穴名者约160穴左右；经穴专书《针灸甲乙经》和《千金翼方》载共349穴；宋代《铜人腧穴针灸图经》（《十四经发挥》同）穴数有所增加，穴名数达354；明代《针灸大成》载有359穴；至清代《针灸逢源》，经穴总数才达361，目前经穴总数即以此为准。穴位有单穴和双穴之分，十二经脉腧穴左右对称分布，是一名双穴；任脉、督脉位于正中，是一名一穴，分布在前后正中线上。历代代表性针灸医籍所载经穴数见表2-1。

The points distributed along the course of the fourteen meridians（twelve regular meridians plus governor and conception vessels）are called "points of the fourteen meridians" or "meridian points" for short. A meridian point has its definite name，fixed location and specific indication. In *Huangdi's Internal Classic*，it mentioned "365 points"，but the actual number of points with their names recorded in this classic is around 160；*The AB Classic of Acupuncture and Moxibustion* and Supplement to the Invaluable Prescriptions recorded 349 points；Illustrated Manual of Points on Bronze Figure in the Song Dynasty and Exposition of the Fourteen Meridians recorded 354 points respectively；Great Compendium of Acupuncture and Moxibustion recorded 359 points；Source of Acupuncture and Moxibustion compiled in the late Qing Dynasty recorded 361 points，which is the number of meridian points still used today. Those of the twelve main meridians are distributed symmetrically in pairs on the left and right sides of the body，while those of governor and conception vessels are single ones，aligning on the posterior and anterior midlines respectively（Tab 2-1）.

表2-1　历代医籍记载的十四经穴数

Tab 2-1　The Total Acupoints in the Fourteen Meridians Recorded in All Ages Literatures

年代（公元） Year	作者 Author	书名 Name	穴名数 Number of points		
			正中单穴 Middle single point	两侧双穴 Bilateral dual points	穴名总数 Total
战国（公元前475-公元前221） Warring States period （475B. C. -221B. C.）		《内经》 Internal Classic（Huangdi's Canon of Acupuncture and Plain Questions）	约25 About 25	约135 About 135	约160 About 160

续表

年代（公元）Year	作者 Author	书名 Name	穴名数 Number of points		
			正中单穴 Middle single point	两侧双穴 Bilateral dual points	穴名总数 Total
三国魏晋（256－260 年）Three Kingdoms Period，Wei and Jin Dynasties（256A. D. －260A. D. ）	皇甫谧 Huangfu Mi	《甲乙经》录《明堂》AB Classic of Acupuncture and Moxibustion	49	300	349
唐（680－682 年）Tang Dynasty（680A. D. －682 A. D. ）	孙思邈 Su Simiao	《千金翼方》Supplement to the Invaluable Prescriptions			
宋（1026 年）Song Dynasty（1026 A. D）	王惟一 Wang Weiyi	《铜人》Illustrated Manual of Points on Bronze Figure	51	303	354
元（1341 年）Yuan Dynasty（1341 A. D. ）	滑伯仁 Hua Boren	《发挥》Exposition of the Fourteen Meridians			
明（1601 年）Ming Dynasty（1601 A. D. ）	杨继洲 Yang Jizhou	《大成》Great Compendium of Acupuncture and Moxibustion	51	308	359
清（1742 年）Qing Dynasty（1742 A. D. ）	吴谦 Wu Qian	《金鉴》Golden Mirror of Medicine	52	308	360
清（1817 年）Qing Dynasty（1817 A. D. ）	李学川 Li Xuechuan	《逢源》The Source of Acupuncture and Moxibustion	52	309	361

（二）奇穴
Extra Points

凡未归入十四经穴范围，而有具体的位置和名称的经验效穴，统称“经外奇穴”，简称“奇穴”。奇穴是在“阿是穴颈”的基础上发展起来的，这类腧穴的主治范围比较单一，多数对某些病症有特殊疗效，如颈百劳穴治瘰疬，四缝穴治小儿疳积等。

The points that have definite locations but have not been recognized as points of the fourteen meridians have specific names and effective indications and are named as “extra points outside the meridians” or “extra points” for short. Extra points were originally derived from the “ashi－points”. Points in this category have relatively fixed indications，and most of them are indicated for some specific disorders. For example，Jingbailao（EX－HN 14）is effective for scrofula，and Sifeng（EX－UE 10）is for infantile malnutrition.

奇穴的分布较为分散，有的在十四经循行路线上，如印堂与督脉相关，阑尾与胃经相关。有的虽不在十四经循行路线上，但却与经络系统有着密切联系。有的奇穴并不是指一个穴位，而是多个穴位的组合，如十宣、八邪、八风、华佗夹脊等。

Although scattered over the body, some extra points are distributed along the courses of the fourteen meridians, for example, Yintang (EX - HN 3) is related to governor vessel, Lanwei (EX - LE 7) to the stomach meridian of foot - yangming. While some of them are not located on the fourteen meridians, but they are close related with the meridian system. Some extra points are not one point but a group of points. For instance, there is the group that consists of Shixuan (EX - UE 11), Baxie (EX - UE 9), Bafeng (EX - LE 9), Jiaji (EX - B 2).

(三) 阿是穴 Ashi - Points

阿是穴，又称天应穴、不定穴等，通常是指该处既不是经穴，又不是奇穴，只是按压痛点取穴。这类穴既无具体名称，又无固定位置，而是以压痛或其他反应点作为刺灸的部位。阿是穴多在病变附近，也可在与其距离较远处。

An ashi - point refers to the site which is neither a point of the fourteen meridians nor an extra point, but solely the tender spot instead. This category of points has neither definite names nor fixed locations, and is used for acupuncture and moxibustion by means of the tender spots or other reflecting spots. Most of the ashi - points are localized near the affected areas, but some are located distant to the disease site.

"阿是"之名见于唐代《备急千金要方》。其取穴法，出自《内经》所说"以痛为腧"。这体现了初时腧穴选穴是以所在部位的压痛或特殊反应为取穴根据的。临床上对于压痛取穴多用于治疗痛证。

The name of "ashi" points was first mentioned in the book *Invaluable Prescriptions for Emergencies.* However, the point - locating method was mentioned much earlier in the chapter 13 of *Miraculous Pivot* as "Tender spots can be used as acupuncture points". Ashi - points are considered to represent the earliest stage of acupuncture point evolution. Clinically, they are mostly used for pain syndromes.

二、腧穴的命名 Nomenclature of Acupoints

十四经腧穴各有一定的部位和命名。《素问·阴阳应象大论》说："气穴所发，各有处名。"腧穴的名称都有一定的意义。故孙思邈《千金翼方》说："凡诸孔穴，名不徒设，皆有深意。"有关腧穴命名含义的解释在古代文献中早有记载。古人对腧穴的命名，取义十分广泛，可谓上察天文，下观地理，中通人事，远取诸物，近取诸身，结合腧穴的分布特点、作用、主治等内容赋予一定的名称。现将腧穴命名归纳介绍如下：

Acupuncture points of the fourteen meridians have their definite locations and names. It is stated in chapter 5 of *Plain Questions*, "Acupuncture points are the sites into which qi and blood are infused. Each has its own location and name". The name of a point usually has its specific meaning. Sun Simiao said in his book *Supplement to the Invaluable Prescriptions* that "the nomenclature for points is not at random, but with profound meanings". The explanation to the meaning of points was recorded in ancient literature. The nomenclature of points by ancient scholars was based on a myriad of subjects ranging from astronomy, geography, daily life, natural objects, anatomy, all the way to distribution characteristics, functions and indications of points. The nomenclature of points is summarized below.

(一) 天象地理类
Nomenclature Based on Astronomy and Geography

1. 以日月星辰命名
Points Named After the Sun, Moon or Stars

如日月、上星、璇玑、华盖、太乙、太白、天枢等。

Riyue (CB 24) means the sun and the moon; Shangxing (DU 23) is the upper star; Xuanji (RN 21), Huagai (RN 20), Taiyi (ST 23), and Taibai (SP 3) all are names of stars; Tianshu (ST 25) means the pivot between the heaven and earth.

2. 以山、谷、丘、陵命名
Points Named After Mountains, Hills or Valleys

如承山、合谷、大陵、梁丘、丘墟等。

Chengshan (BL 57) means sustaining mountain; Hegu (LI 4) is the junction of valleys; Daling (PC 7) is a large mound; Liangqiu (ST 34) is a ridge in the hills; and Qiuxu (GB 40) is a large mound.

3. 以海、江河、溪沟命名
Points Named After the Sea, River, Stream, or Pond

如后溪、支沟、四渎、少海、尺泽、曲池、曲泉、经渠、太渊等。

Houxi (SI 3) means back stream; Zhigou (SJ 6) is a small ditch; Sidu (SJ 9) is the four rivers; Shaohai (HT 3) is a young sea; Chize (LU 5) is a marsh; Quchi (LI 11) is a crooked pond; Ququan (LR 8) is a crooked spring; Jingqu (LU 9) is a passing river; and Taiyuan

（LU 9）is a great deep pool.

4. 以路径等交通要冲命名
Points Named After Road，Path，or Pass

如气冲、水道、关冲、内关、风市等。

Qichong（ST 30）is a pathway of qi；Shuidao（ST 28）is a water pathway；Guanchong（SJ 1）is a key pass；Neiguan（PC 6）is an internal pass；and Fengshi（GB 33）is a wind market.

（二）人事物象类
Nomenclature Based on the Activities of Human Being and Objects

1. 以动植物名称命名
Points Named After Animals and Plants

如鱼际、鸠尾、伏兔、犊鼻、攒竹、禾髎等。

Yuji（LU 10）means the fish border；Jiuwei（RN 15）is a turtledove tail；Futu（ST 32）is a lying rabbit；Dubi（ST 35）is a calf nose；Cuanzhu（BL 2）is assembled bamboo；and Heliao（LI 9）is a grain foramen.

2. 以建筑居处命名
Points Named After Architectures

如天井、玉堂、巨阙、曲垣、库房、府舍、天窗、地仓、梁门、紫宫、内庭、气户等。

Tianjing（SJ 10）is a patio；Yutang（RN 18）is a jade palace；Juque（RN 14）is a great palace gate；Quyuan（SI 13）is a curved wall；Kufang（ST 14）is a storehouse；Fushe（SP 13）is a dwelling；Tianchuang（SI 16）is an upper window；Dicang（ST 4）is an earth granary；Liangmen（ST 21）is a beam gate；Zigong（RN 19）is a purple palace；Neiting（ST 44）is an internal courtyard；and Qihu（ST 13）is an air door.

3. 以生活用具命名
Points Named After Living Utensils

如大杼、地机、阳辅、缺盆、天鼎、悬钟等。

Dazhu（BL 11）is a large shuttle；Diji（SP 8）is a trigger of the earth；Yangfu（GB 38）is an auxiliary tool；Quepen（ST 12）is a basin；Tianding（LI 17）is a heavy cooking vessel；and Xuanzhong（GB 39）is a hanging bell.

4. 以人事活动命名
Points Named After Human Affairs

如人迎、百会、归来、足三里等。

Renying (ST 9) is a meeting of people; Baihui (DU 20) is a meeting of hundreds of people; Guilai (ST 29) is returning home; and Zusanli (ST 36) is a distance of three miles.

(三) 形态功能类
Nomenclature Based on Locations and Functions of the Point

1. 以解剖部位命名
Points Named According to the Anatomic Location of the Point

如腕骨、完骨、大椎、曲骨、京骨、巨骨等。

Wangu (SI 4) is the wrist bone; Wangu (GB 12) is the mastoid process; Dazhui (DU 14) is a large vertebra; Qugu (RN 2) is the name of the pubic bone; Jinggu (BL 64) is the name of the tuberosity of the 5th metatarsus; and Jugu (LI 16) is a big bone.

2. 以脏腑功能命名
Points Named According to the Function of Zang - Fu Organs

如神堂、魄户、魂门、意舍、志室等。

Shentang (BL 44) is the palace of the spirit; Pohu (BL 42) is the door of the corporeal soul; Hunmen (BL 47) is the door of the ethereal soul; Yishe (BL 49) is the house of reflection; and Zhishi (BL 52) is the room of the will.

3. 以经络阴阳命名
Points Named According to the Meridians, Collaterals and Yin - Yang

如三阴交、三阳络、阴都(腹)、阳纲(背)、阴陵泉、阳陵泉等。

Sanyinjiao (SP 6) is the interlogtion of the three yin meridians; Sanyangluo (TE 8) connects the three yang meridians; Yindu (KI 19) is a yin gathering place; Yanggang (BL 48) is an outline of yang; Yinlingquan (SP 9) is a spring on the yin aspect of hill; and Yanglingquan (GB 34) is a spring on the yang aspect of hill.

4. 以穴位作用命名
Points Named According to the Functions of the Point

如承浆、承泣、听会、迎香、廉泉、劳宫、气海、血海、光明、水分等。

Chengjiang (RN 24) is for receiving fluids; Chengqi (ST 1) is for receiving tears; Tinghui (GB 2) is for hearing; Yingxiang (LI 20) is for restoring olfactory sensation; and Lian quan (RN 23) is for promoting secretion of saliva. Other points are Laogong (PC 9) which is a labor's palace; Qihai (RN 6) is the sea of qi; Xuehai (SP 10) is the sea of blood; Guangming (GB 37) is for brightening vision; and Shuifen (RN 9) is for separating water to treat edema.

第二节 腧穴的作用及主治规律
Principles for the Effects and Indications of Acupoints

一、腧穴的作用
The Effects of Acupoints

腧穴具有接受刺激和防治疾病的作用。腧穴作为脏腑经络气血转输出入的特殊部位，也是病邪入侵之所，又是针灸防治疾病施术之处。通过针刺、艾灸等对腧穴的刺激以通其经脉，调其气血，使阴阳归于平衡，脏腑趋于和调，从而达到扶正祛邪的目的。腧穴的治疗作用有以下三个方面的特点：

Points have the function of receiving stimulation and preventing and curing diseases. Points are the sites where qi and blood are transported, as well as the place where pathogenic - qi invade. They are also stimulation spots for acupuncture and moxibustion used for prevention and treatment of diseases. The stimulation of points by acupuncture and moxibustion may dredge meridians, regulate the flow of qi and blood, and restore the balance of yin and yang, so that harmony can be achieved between yin - yang and the functions of zang - fu organs as well as strengthen the healthy qi and remove pathogenic qi. The rules of the effects of points can be classified into the following three aspects.

(一) 邻近作用
Local and Adjacent Therapeutic Effects

这是经穴、奇穴和阿是穴所共有的主治作用特点，即腧穴都能治疗其所在部位及邻近部位的病症，如胃部的中脘、建里、梁门等穴；均能治疗胃病；眼区的睛明、承泣、四白各穴，均能治疗眼病；耳区的听宫、听会、翳风诸穴，均能治疗耳病。

This is a characteristic therapeutic property for all points, including meridian points, extra points and ashi - points. All points can treat the disorders of their local and adjacent locations. For examples, Zhongwan (RN 12), Jianli (RN 11) and Liangmen (ST 21) on the upper abdomen can be used to treat gastric disorders; Jingming（BL 1）, Chengqi（ST 1）and Sibai（ST 2）located around the eyes are for ophthalmic diseases; and Tinggong（SI 19）, Tinghui（GB 2）and Yifeng（SJ 17）located around the ears can treat hearing disorders.

（二）远道作用
Remote Therapeutic Effect

这是经穴，尤其是十二经脉在四肢肘、膝关节以下的腧穴的主治作用特点。这些要穴不仅能治疗局部病症，而且能治疗本经循行所到达的远隔部位的病症。这就是常说的“经络所通，主治所及”。如合谷穴，不仅能治疗上肢病症，而且能治疗颈部和头面部病症；足三里穴不但能治疗下肢病症，而且能治疗胃肠以及更高部位的病症等。

The remote therapeutic effect is a property of the meridian points, especially for those of the twelve regular meridians located distally to the elbow and knee joints. They are effective not only for local disorders but also for the disorders of remote locations on the course of their pertaining meridians. This is what the saying “the indications of points extend to where their pertinent meridians reach”. For example, Hegu（LI 4）not only treats diseases of the upper limb, but it also treats diseases of the neck, head and face. Zusanli（ST 36）treats not only disorders of the lower limbs, but also the disorders of gastro – intestinal and the upper part of the body.

（三）整体作用
Special Therapeutic Effects

除以上邻近和远道作用以外，某些腧穴可起双向的、整体性的或特殊的调治作用。多数穴位具有双向调整作用，如泄泻时，针刺天枢能止泻；便秘时，针刺则能通便。心动过速时，针刺内关能减慢心率；心动过缓时，针刺则可加快心率。有些穴位还能调治全身性的病症，这在手足阳明经穴和任督脉经穴中更为多见。如合谷、曲池、大椎可治外感发热；足三里、关元、膏肓俞作为强壮穴，具有增强人体防卫功能的作用。一些穴位具有对疾病相对特异的作用，如至阴穴纠正胎位，阑尾穴治疗阑尾炎等。

Besides the above local and remote therapeutic effects, some points have certain special effects such as bi – directional regulation, general regulation, and other specific actions. Many points have the therapeutic effects of bi – directional regulation. For instance, needling Tianshu（ST 25）can relieve diarrhea or constipation; puncturing Neiguan（PC 6）can decrease heart rate in patients with tachycardia, but it can also increase the heart rate when bradycardia is present. Some points can treat general disorders, especially points of the yangming meridians, conception and governor vessels. For instance, Hegu（LI 4）, Quchi（LI 11）and Dazhui（DU 14）are used to treat fever caused by exopathogenic qi; Zusanli（ST 36）, Guanyuan（RN 4）and Gaohuang（BL 43）have the effects of tonification and health preservation. Some other points have relatively specific effects depending on the diseases. For instance, Zhiyin（BL 67）corrects a breech presentation, while Lanwei（EX－LE 7）is effective in treating appendicitis.

二、腧穴的主治规律
Principles for the Indications of Acupoints

每个腧穴都有较广泛的主治范围，这与其所属经络和所在部位的不同有直接关系。无论腧穴的局部治疗作用，还是远隔部位的治疗作用，都是以经络学说为依据的。如要掌握腧穴的主治规律，一般可以从腧穴的分经、分部两方面来归纳。

Each point has its broad scope of functions, which is directly related to its location and meridian. Both of its local and remote therapeutic effects are based on meridian theory. There exist some rules or similarities for indications amongst points, which can be understood from the perspective of meridian distribution and physical region of the points.

（一）分经主治规律
Rules of Indication in Meridians

十二经脉在四肢部的五输、原、络、郄穴对于头身部及脏腑病症有特殊治疗作用，这是腧穴分经主治的基础，也是古人所总结的“四根三结”主治规律的由来。四肢是经脉的“根”和“本”部，对于头身的“结”和“标”部有远道主治作用。各经有其主要治症（主病），邻近的经又有类似作用，或两经相同，或三经相同，这是“三阴”、“三阳”在治疗作用上的共性。现归纳为手足三阴三阳经穴主治表，并配合四肢经穴图，以便于理解（表2－2～5）。

The meridian points on the four limbs, such as the five－shu points, yuan－source points, luo－connecting points, and xi－cleft points, have special therapeutic effects for the disorders of the head, trunk and zang－fu organs. These are the foundation for point indications according to meridian distribution, and the origin of the therapeutic rules of so－called “Four Roots and Three Tips” summarized by ancient doctors. The four limbs are considered the “roots” of meridians, so points in the limbs have the remote therapeutic effects for disorders of the head and trunk, which are the “tips” of the meridians. Each meridian has its own indications and the adjacent meridians may have similar indications. This is a common therapeutic sign shared by the “three yin” and “three yang”. The rules of indications for the meridians are summarized in the following tables（Tab 2－2 to Tab 2－5）.

表 2-2 手三阴经穴主治规律

Tab 2-2 Indications for Points of the Three Yin Meridians of the Hand

经名 Meridians	本经主病 Indications for the meridian	二经相同 Common indications for the two meridians	三经相同 Common indications for the three meridians
手太阴经 hand-taiyin meridian	肺、喉病 Disorders of lungs and throat	—	胸部病 Disorders in the chest
手厥阴经 Hand-jueyin meridian	心、胃病 Disorders of heart and stomach	神志病 Mental disorders	
手少阴经 Hand-shaoyin meridian	心病 Disorders of heart		

表 2-3 手三阳经穴主治规律

Tab 2-3 Indications for Points of the Three Yang Meridians of the Hand

经名 Meridians	本经主病 Indications for the meridian	二经相同 Common indications for the two meridians	三经相同 Common indications for the three meridians
手阳明经 Hand-yangming meridian	前头、鼻、口齿病 Disorders of forehead, nose, mouth and teeth	—	眼病、咽喉病、热病 Disorders of eyes, throat and fever
手少阳经 Hand-shaoyang meridian	侧头、胁肋病 Disorders of temporal region and costal-hypochondriac region	耳病 Ear diseases	
手太阳经 Hand-taiyang meridian	后头、肩胛、神志病 Disorders of occipital region, scapula and mind		

表 2-4 足三阳经穴主治规律

Tab 2-4 Indications for Points of the Three Yang Meridians of the Foot

经名 Meridians	本经主病 Indications for the meridian	二经相同 Common indications for the two meridians	三经相同 Common indications for the three meridians
足阳明经 Foot-yangming meridian	前头、口、齿、咽喉、胃肠病 Disorders of forehead, mouth, teeth, throat, stomach and intestines	—	神志病、热病 Mental disorders and fever
足少阳经 Foot-shaoyang meridian	侧头、耳病、项、胁肋、胆病 Disorders of temporal region, ear, neck, costal-hypochondriac region and gallbladder	眼病 Eyes diseases	
足太阳经 Foot-taiyang meridian	后头、项、背腰、肛肠病 Disorders of occipital region, neck, back and waist, anal-intestinal disease		

表 2 – 5 足三阴经穴主治规律

Tab 2 – 5 **Indications for Points of the Three Yin Meridians of the Foot**

经名 Meridians	本经主病 Indications for the meridian	二经相同 Common indications for the two meridians	三经相同 Common indications for the three meridians
足太阴经 Foot – taiyin meridian	脾胃病 Disorders of spleen and stomach	—	腹部病 Disorders in the abdomen and gynecological diseases
足厥阴经 Foot – jueyin meridian	肝病 Disorders of liver	前阴病 Disorders of external genitalia	
足少阴经 Foot – shaoyin meridian	肾、肺、咽喉病 Disorders of kidney, lungs and throat		

（二）分部主治规律
Rules of Indication According to the Physical Region

头身部是四海和气街所在部位，是十二经脉的“结”和“标”之部。“脏腑腹背，气相通应”。这是分部主治的规律，体现经脉在纵行分经的基础上又有横行分部的关系。比如，肩胛部腧穴不仅能治疗局部疾患，同时可以治疗咽喉、上肢和发热疾病；胁肋部腧穴相应于肝胆，腹部外侧相应于内侧的脾胃，这些区域的腧穴可以治疗中焦之疾，也可以治疗下肢疾患。各部经穴主治分别见表 2 – 6 ~ 8。

The head and trunk of the body are the locations of the “Four seas” and “Qi Jie”, “Tips” and “Branches” of the twelve meridians. “The qi of zang – fu organs, abdomen and back connect and correspond with each other”. These are the rules for point indications according to the physical region, and they show that there is a transverse relationship between meridians in addition to their own longitudinal pathways.

For example, the neck and scapular regions are located between the head and back, thus the points in this region can not only treat local disorders but also the disorders of the throat, upper limbs, and fever. The lateral costal region corresponds to the liver and gallbladder, and the lateral abdominal region corresponds internally to the spleen and stomach. The points in these regions can therefore treat the disorders in the middle energizer. The region of the waist and hips corresponds to the organs in the lower energizer, and the points located in this region can mainly treat the disorders of the lower limbs. The rules for point indication in different regions are listed below (Tab 2 – 6 to Tab 2 – 8).

表 2－6　　任督二脉经穴主治规律

Tab 2－6　　Indications for Points of Governor and Conception Vessels

经名 Meridians	本经主病 Indications for the meridian	二经相同 Common indications for the two meridians
任脉 Governor vessel	中风脱证、虚寒、下焦病 Flaccid syndrome by wind stroke, deficiency and cold syndromes, disorders in the lower－jiao	神志病、脏腑病 Mental disorders and diseases of zang－fu organs
督脉 Conception vessel	中风昏迷、热病、头部病 Coma by wind stroke, fever, disorders of head	

表 2－7　　头面颈项部经穴主治规律

Tab 2－7　　Indications for Points in the Regions of the Head, Face and Neck

分部 Regions of points	主治 Indications
前头、侧头区 Forehead, temple	眼、鼻病 Disorders of eye and nose
后头区 Occipital region	神志、头部病 Mental disorders and head diseases
项区 Nape	神志、咽喉、眼、头项病 Mental disorders and diseases of the throat, eye, head and nape of neck
眼区 Eye	眼病 Eye diseases
鼻区 Nose	鼻病 Nose disease
颈区 Neck	舌、咽喉、气管、颈部病 Disorders of tongue, throat, trachea, and neck

表 2－8　　胸腹腰背部经穴主治规律

Tab 2－8 Indications for Points in the Regions of the Chest, Abdomen, Back and Waist

前 Front	后 Back	主治 Indications
胸膺部 Chest	上背部 Upper back	肺、心（上焦病） Disorders of lungs, heart (upper－jiao)
胁腹部 Hypochondrium and upper abdomen	下背部 Lower back	肝、胆、脾、胃（中焦病） Disorders of liver, gallbladder, spleen, stomach (middle－jiao)
少腹部 Lower abdomen	腰尻部 Lumbosacral region	前后阴、肾、肠、膀胱（下焦病） Disorders of external genitalia and anus, kidney, intestines and urinary bladder (lower－jiao)

第三节 特定穴
Specific Acupoints

十四经中具有特殊治疗作用，并按特定称号归类的腧穴，称为特定穴。包括在四肢肘、膝以下的五输穴、原穴、络穴、郄穴、八脉交会穴、下合穴；在胸腹、背腰部的背俞穴、募穴；在四肢躯干的八会穴以及全身经脉的交会穴。这些腧穴在十四经中不仅在数量上占有相当的比例，而且在针灸学的基本理论和临床应用方面也有着极其重要的意义。

Specific points refer to those points of the fourteen meridians that have special therapeutic effects and are specifically named under certain categories, include the five – shu points, yuan – source points, luo – connecting points, xi – cleft points, eight – influential points and lower he – sea points which all located beneath the elbow and knee of the limbs; the back – shu points, front – mu points which distributed in the chest, abdomen, back and waist; the eight – confluent points on the trunk and four limbs and crossing points all over the meridians. These specific points not only make up a considerable proportion of the points of the fourteen meridians, but they also play an important role in the basic theory and clinical application of acupuncture and moxibustion.

一、五输穴
Five - Shu Points

十二经脉在肘膝关节以下各有称为井、荥、输、经、合的五个腧穴，合称“五输穴”。有关记载首见于《灵枢·九针十二原》：“所出为井，所溜为荥，所注为输，所行为经，所入为合”（表2－9，表2－10）。

Each of the twelve regular meridians has, below the elbow or knee, five specific points, namely jing – well, ying – spring, shu – stream, jing – river and he – sea, which are termed five shu points in general. They were first stated in the first chapter of *miraculous pivot* that “The points at which qi springs up are called well points; the points where qi flows copiously are called spring points; the points where qi flows like a stream are called stream points; the points where qi flows through are called river points; and the points where qi gathers are called sea points” (Tab 2 – 9, Tab 2 – 10).

表 2 – 9　　六阴经五输穴及与五行配属表

Tab 2 – 9　Five – Shu Points and its Corresponding Five Elements of the Six Yin Meridians

六阴经 Six yin meridians		井（木） Well (Wood)	荥（火） Spring (Fire)	输（土） Stream (Earth)	经（金） River (Metal)	合（水） Sea (Water)
手三阴 Three hand yin meridians	肺（金） Lung (Metal)	少商 LU11	鱼际 LU 10	太渊 LU 9	经渠 LU 8	尺泽 LU 5
	心包（相火） Pericardium (Ministerial fire)	中冲 PC 9	劳宫 PC 8	大陵 PC 7	间使 PC 5	曲泽 PC 3
	心（火） Heart (Fire)	少冲 HT 9	少府 HT 8	神门 HT 7	灵道 HT 4	少海 HT 3
足三阴 Three foot yin meridians	脾（土） Spleen (Earth)	隐白 SP 1	大都 SP 2	太白 SP 3	商丘 SP 5	阴陵泉 SP 9
	肝（木） Liver (Wood)	大敦 LR 1	行间 LR 2	太冲 LR 3	中封 LR 4	曲泉 LR 8
	肾（水） Kidney (Water)	涌泉 KI 1	然谷 KI 2	太溪 KI 3	复溜 KI 7	阴谷 KI 10

表 2 – 10　　六阳经五输穴及与五行配属表

Tab 2 – 10　Five – Shu Points and its Corresponding Five Elements of the Six Yang Meridians

六阳经 Six yang meridians		井（金） Well (Metal)	荥（水） Spring (Water)	输（木） Stream (Wood)	经（火） River (Fire)	合（土） Sea (Earth)
手三阳 Three hand yang meridians	大肠（金） Large intestine (Metal)	商阳 LI 1	二间 LI 2	三间 LI 3	阳溪 LI 5	曲池 LI 11
	三焦（相火） Sanjiao (Ministerial fire)	关冲 SJ 1	液门 SJ 2	中渚 SJ 3	支沟 SJ 6	天井 SJ 10
	小肠（火） Small intestine (Fire)	少泽 SI 1	前谷 SI 2	后溪 SI 3	阳谷 SI 5	小海 SI 8
足三阳 Three foot yang meridians	胃（土） Stomach (Earth)	厉兑 ST 45	内庭 ST 44	陷谷 ST 43	解溪 ST 41	足三里 ST 36
	胆（木） Gallbladder (Wood)	足窍阴 GB 44	侠溪 GB 43	足临泣 GB 41	阳辅 GB 38	阳陵泉 GB 34
	膀胱（水） Bladder (Water)	至阴 BL 67	足通谷 BL 66	束骨 BL 65	昆仑 BL 60	委中 BL 40

古人把经气运行过程用自然界的水流由小到大，由浅入深的变化来形容，把五输穴按井、荥、输、经、合的顺序，从四肢末端向肘、膝方向依次排列。“井”穴多位于手足之端，喻作水的源头，是经气所出的部位，即“所出为井”。“荥”穴多位于掌指或跖趾关节之前，喻作水流尚微，萦迂未成大流，是经气流行的部位，即“所溜为荥”。“输”穴多位于掌指或跖趾关节之后，喻作水流由小而大，由浅注深，是经气渐盛，由此注彼的部位，即“所注为输”。“经”穴多位于腕踝关节以上，喻作水流变大，畅通无阻，是经气正盛运行经

过的部位，即“所行为经”。“合”穴位于肘膝关节附近，喻作江河水流汇入湖海，是经气由此深入，进而会合于脏腑的部位，即“所入为合”。

The ancient doctors described qi and blood flowing in the meridians as water flowing from the well, spring into the sea, or going from the shallow to the deep in the natural world. The qi of meridians flows from the distal extremities to the elbows or knees in the sequence of jing - well, ying - spring, shu - stream, jing - river and he - sea. The jing - well points are mostly situated on the tips of the fingers or toes where the meridian - qi starts to bubble, just like water coming out of a well, hence the name jing - well points. The ying - spring points are situated distal to the metacarpal - phalangeal joints or the metatarsophalangeal joints where the meridian - qi starts to rush, just like a spring, hence the name ying - spring points. The shu - stream points are situated proximal to the metacarpal - phalangeal joints or the metatarsophalangeal joints where the meridian - qi flows, just like a stream, hence the name shu - stream points. The jing - river points are situated proximal to the wrist joints or ankle joints where the meridian - qi is pouring abundantly, just like a river, hence the name jing - river points. Finally, the he - sea points are situated near the elbows and knees, where the meridian - qi goes into the body and gathers in the zang - fu organs, just like the convergence of rivers into the sea, hence the name he - sea points.

《难经·六十八难》则说：“井主心下满，荥主身热，输主体重节痛，经主喘咳寒热，合主逆气而泄。”临床上井穴可用来治疗神志病、脏病；荥穴、输穴、经穴主治外经之病。阴经诸穴主治内脏之病；合穴主治腑病。

The sixty - eight problem in *Classic on Medical Problems* says that “jing - well points are indicated in the fullness of the chest; ying - spring points in the febrile diseases; shu - stream points in the heavy sensation of the body and painful joints; jing - river points in cough and asthma due to pathogenic cold and heat; and he - sea points in diarrhea due to perversive flow of qi”. Generally speaking, jing - well points are indicated in mental illness related to the zang organs; ying - spring; shu - stream and jing - river points are indicated in disorders along the outer course of the affected meridians. Points on the yin meridians are indicated in the disorders of the internal organs. The he - sea points are indicated in problems related to the fu organs.

五输穴又配属五行，即“阴井木，阳井金；阴荥火，阳荥水；阴俞土，阳俞木；阴经金，阳经火；阴合水，阳合土”。均依五行相生的顺序，并根据生克乘侮进行临床应用。根据《难经·六十九难》“虚者补其母，实者泻其子”的理论，按五输穴五行属性以生我者为母，我生者为子的原则进行选穴，虚证选用母穴，实证选用子穴。这就是临床上所称的补母泻子法，如肺属金，虚则取太渊（土），实则取尺泽（水）等。

In addition to the selection of the five - shu points according to their therapeutic properties, the five - shu points can be selected according to the interpromoting, interacting, overacting and counteracting relations of the five elements to which they are respectively attributed. The jing - well, ying – spring, shu – stream, jing – river and he – sea points of the yin meridians are attributed to the five elements in the order of wood, fire, earth, metal and water, but those of the yang meridians in the order of metal, water, wood, fire and earth. Based on the interpromoting relation of the five elements, each meridian has a "mother" point and a "son" point. It's recorded in the sixty – nine problem in *Classic on Medical Problems* that "reinforce the mother for deficiency syndrome and reduce the son for excess syndrome when this principle is applied for treatment". For instance, the lung meridian relates to metal, the "mother" of metal is earth, then the "mother point" of the lung meridian is Taiyuan (LU 9) which attributes to earth, which is used with the reinforcing method for the deficiency syndrome in the lung meridian; the "son" of metal is water, so the "son point" of the lung meridian is Chize (LU 5) which attributes to water, which is used with the reducing method for the excess syndrom in the lung meridian.

二、原穴
Yuan - Source Points

十二经脉在腕、踝关节附近各有一个腧穴，是脏腑原气留止的部位，称为"原穴"，合称"十二原"。"原"即本原、原气之意，是人体生命活动的原动力。

原穴名称，首载于《灵枢·九针十二原》。阴经五脏之原穴，即是五输穴中的输穴，阳经则输穴与原穴分立（表2–11）。

Yuan – source points are a group of regular meridian points located near the wrist or ankle, and these are the places where the original qi of zang – fu organs and meridians passes and gathers, thus they are termed yuan – source points, or collectively called the twelve yuan – source points. "Yuan" means source or original qi, which is the original power of vital activities.

The term of the yuan – source points was first mentioned in the chapter 1, *Miraculous Pivot*. The yuan – source point of a yin meridian actually is identical to its shu – stream point of five – shu points, whereas a Yuan – Source point on a yang meridian is independent of the shu – stream point (Tab 2 – 11).

表2–11 十二经原穴表

Tab 2 – 11 The Yuan – Source Points of the Twelve Regular Meridians

经脉 Meridians	经脉穴位 Meridian yuan – source point	经脉穴位 Meridian yuan – source point	经脉穴位 Meridian yuan – source point
手三阴经 Three yin meridians of hand	肺经 – 太渊 Lung meridian – LU 9	心经 – 神门 Heart meridian – HT 7	心包经 – 大陵 Pericardium meridian – PC 7
手三阳经 Three yang meridians of hand	大肠经 – 合谷 Large intestine meridian – LI 4	小肠经 – 腕骨 Small intestine meridian – SI 4	三焦经 – 阳池 Sanjiao meridian – SJ 4

续表

经脉 Meridians	经脉穴位 Meridian yuan - source point	经脉穴位 Meridian yuan - source point	经脉穴位 Meridian yuan - source point
足三阴经 Three yin meridians of foot	脾经 - 太白 Spleen meridian - SP 3	肾经 - 太溪 Kidney meridian - KI 3	肝经 - 太冲 Liver meridian - LR 3
足三阳经 Three yang meridians of foot	胃经 - 冲阳 Stomach meridian - ST 42	膀胱经 - 京骨 Bladder meridian - BL 64	胆经 - 丘墟 Gallbladder meridian - GB 40

原穴是脏腑原气留止之处，因此脏腑发生病变时，就会相应的反映到原穴上来。正如《灵枢·九针十二原》所说："五脏有疾也，应出十二原，十二原各有所出，明知其原，睹其应而知五脏之害矣。"原穴与三焦、原气有密切关系。原气导源于肾间动气，运行周身，与气机相关，通过三焦运行于脏腑。原穴是脏腑原气留止之处，因此原穴有调整其脏腑经络虚实各证的功能。

The yuan - source points are the points where the primary qi of the zang - fu organs is retained. So disorders of the zang - fu organs are usually relieved by needling the twelve yuan source points. The first chapter of *Miraculous Pivot* says, "when the five zang organs are diseased, the symptoms will manifest themselves in the conditions of the twelve yuan - source points with which they are connected. Each of the five zang organs is connected with its own yuan - source point. For this reason, if we fully grasp the connections between zang organs and their corresponding yuan - source point as well as the latter's external manifestations, there will be no difficulty for us to understand the nature of the diseases of the five zang organs, The twelve yuan - source points are effective for treating the diseases of the five zang and six fu organs" . They are closely related to triple energizer and primary qi. The primary qi originates from the kidneys, distributing over the whole body and concerning the qi activities. It travels over each yang meridian through triple energizer. The place where the primary qi is centred is the location of the yuan - source point. Therefore, they are indicated in deficiency and excess syndromes of their respective related organs.

三、络穴
Luo - Connecting Points

络脉由经脉分出之处各有一穴，称络穴。络穴名称首载于《灵枢·经脉》。十二经在肘膝关节以下各有一络穴，加上躯干前的任脉络穴、躯干后的督脉络穴和躯干侧的脾之大络，合称"十五络穴"（表2-12）。

Luo - connecting points are the sites where the fifteen collaterals branch out from the meridians (including governor vessel and conception vessel) means connecting. The term of luo - connecting points, was first recorded in the chapter 10, *Miraculous Pivot*. There is one luo - connecting point distal to the elbow or knee joint on each of the twelve meridians, in addition to the three luo – connecting points of the conception vessel, governor vessel, and the major collateral of the spleen which are respectively located in the front, back and lateral side of the trunk. Together, they are called "fifteen luo – connecting points" (Tab 2 – 12).

表 2 – 12　　十五络穴表

Tab 2 – 12　　The Luo – Connecting Points of the Fifteen Major Collaterals

经脉 Meridians	经脉穴位 Meridian luo – connecting point	经脉穴位 Meridian luo – connecting point	经脉穴位 Meridian luo – connecting point
手三阴经 Three yin meridians of hand	肺经 – 列缺 Lung meridian – LU 7	心经 – 通里 Heart meridian – HT 5	心包经 – 内关 Pericardium meridian – PC 6
手三阳经 Three yang meridians of hand	大肠经 – 偏历 Large intestine meridian – LI 6	小肠经 – 支正 Small intestine meridian – SI 7	三焦经 – 外关 Sanjiao meridian – SJ 5
足三阴经 Three yin meridians of foot	脾经 – 公孙 Spleen meridian – SP 4	肾经 – 大钟 Kidney meridian – KI 4	肝经 – 蠡沟 Liver meridian – LR 5
足三阳经 Three yang meridians of foot	胃经 – 丰隆 Stomach meridian – ST 40	膀胱经 – 飞扬 Bladder meridian – BL 58	胆经 – 光明 Gallbladder meridian – GB 37
任、督、脾大络 Conception vessel, governor vessel and major spleen collateral	任脉　鸠尾 Conception vessel – RN 15	督脉 – 长强 Governor vessel – DU 1	脾大络 – 大包 The major spleen collateral – SP 21

络穴各主治其络脉的病症。十二络穴能沟通表里两经，故有“一络通两经”之说。因此，络穴不仅能治本经病，也能治其相表里之经的病症，如手太阴经的络穴列缺，既能治肺经的咳嗽、喘息，又能治手阳明大肠经的齿痛、头项强痛等疾患。

Each luo – connecting point can be used to treat the disorders of its collaterals respectively. The luo – connecting points of the twelve meridians can treat not only the diseases in its pertaining meridian, but also its respective exterior – interior related meridians' disorders, because they are located the cross of the exteriorly – interiorly related meridians, so there's a saying "a luo – connecting point related two meridians". For instance, Lieque (LU 7), the luo – connecting point of the hand – taiyin, can used for relieving cough and asthma of the lung meridian, but for treating toothache and stiffness pain of head and neck of the large intestine meridian of hand – yangming.

原穴和络穴在临床上既可单独使用，也可相互配合使用。原络合用称“主客原络配穴”。

The yuan – source point and luo – connecting points may be used independently or in combination. The combination of them is called the "host and guest combination."

四、郄穴
Xi - Cleft Points

郄穴是各经脉在四肢部经气深聚的部位，郄与"隙"通，是空隙、间隙的意思。大多分布于四肢肘膝关节以下。郄穴的名称和位置首载于《针灸甲乙经》。十二经脉、阴阳跻脉和阴阳维脉各有一郄穴，总为十六郄穴（表2-13）。

Xi - cleft points are situated at the sites where the meridian - qi is deeply converged and accumulated in the limbs. "Xi" means hollow or cleft. Most xi - cleft points are situated distal to the elbow or knee joints. The term of xi - cleft point was first mentioned in *The A, B Classic of Acupuncture and Moxibustion.* Each of the twelve regular meridians and four extra meridians, i. e. the yin heel vessel, yang heel vessel, yin link vessel and yang link vessel, has one xi - cleft point. Together, there are sixteen xi - cleft points (Tab 2 - 13).

表 2-13　十八经郄穴表

Tab 2 - 13　The Xi - Cleft Points of the Sixteen Meridians

阴经 Yin meridians	郄穴 Xi - cleft points	阳经 Yang meridians	郄穴 Xi - cleft points
手太阴肺经 Lung meridian of hand - taiyin	孔最 LU 6	手阳明大肠经 Large intestine meridian of hand - yangming	温溜 LI 7
手厥阴心包经 Pericardium meridian of hand - jueyin	郄门 PC 4	手少阳三焦经 Sanjiao meridian of hand - shaoyang	会宗 SJ 7
手少阴心经 Heart meridian of hand - shaoyin	阴郄 HT 6	手太阳小肠经 Small intestine meridian of hand - taiyang	养老 SI 6
足太阴脾经 Spleen meridian of foot - taiyin	地机 SP 8	足阳明胃经 Stomach meridian of foot - yangming	梁丘 ST 34
足厥阴肝经 Liver meridian of foot - jueyin	中都 LR 6	足少阳胆经 Gallbladder meridian of foot - shaoyang	外丘 GB 36
足少阴肾经 Kidney meridian of foot - shaoyin	水泉 KI 5	足太阳膀胱经 Bladder meridian of foot - taiyang	金门 BL 63
阴维脉 Yin link meridian	筑宾 KI 9	阳维脉 Yang link meridian	阳交 GB 35
阴跻脉 Yin heel meridian	交信 KI 8	阳跻脉 Yang heel meridian	跗阳 BL 59

临床上郄穴常用来治疗本经循行部位及所属脏腑的急性病症。阴经郄穴多治血证，如孔最治咳血。阳经郄穴多治急性疼痛，如胃脘痛取梁丘等。此外，当脏腑发生病变时，可按压郄穴进行检查，作协助诊断之用。

The xi – cleft points are used primarily in treatment of the acute diseases appearing in their meridians'distributions and corresponding organs. The xi – cleft points of the yin meridians mostly are used in the treatment of bleeding diseases, for example, Kongzui (LU 6), the xi – cleft Points of the lung meridian of hand – taiyin is effective to hemoptysis; while the xi – cleft point of the yang meridians usually treat acute pain, for instance, Liangqiu (ST 34) of the stomach meridian of foot – yangming works for epigastric pain. In addition, the xi – cleft points also can apply for the supplement diagnosis by pressing the corresponding one as diseases of the respective zang – fu organs happened.

五、背俞穴
Back - Shu Points

背俞穴，是脏腑之气输注于背腰部的腧穴，首见于《灵枢·背腧》。背俞穴位于背腰部足太阳膀胱经的第一侧线上，大体依脏腑位置而上下排列，位于脊柱两旁（表2－14）。

Back – shu points are the corresponding points on the back where the qi of the respective zang – fu organs is infused. The term of the back – shu points was first recorded in the chapter 51, *Miraculous Pivot*. All these back – shu points are situated on the first lateral line of the bladder meridian of the foot – taiyang, and are longitudinally distributed roughly according to the anatomic position of the zang – fu organs. Each of the zang – fu organs has one back – shu point on each side of the spine, therefore there is a total of twelve back – shu points corresponding to the twelve zang – fu organs (Tab 2 – 14).

表 2 – 14 脏腑背俞穴表

Tab 2 – 14 The Back – Shu Points of the Twelve Zang – Fu Organ

上部 Upper part	背俞 Back – shu points	下部 Lower part	背俞 Back – shu points
肺 Lung	肺俞 BL 13	胃 Stomach	胃俞 BL 21
心包 Pericardium	厥阴俞 BL 14	三焦 Triple energizer	三焦俞 BL 22
心 Heart	心俞 BL 15	肾 Kidney	肾俞 BL 23
肝 Liver	肝俞 BL 18	大肠 Large intestine	大肠俞 BL 25
胆 Gallbladder	胆俞 BL 19	小肠 Small intestine	小肠俞 BL 27
脾 Spleen	脾俞 BL 20	膀胱 Bladder	膀胱俞 BL 28

背俞穴不但可以治疗与其相应的脏腑病症，也可以治疗与五脏相关的五官九窍、皮肉筋

骨等病症。如肝俞既能治疗肝病，又能治疗与肝有关的目疾、筋急等病；肾俞既能治疗肾病，也可治疗与肾有关的耳鸣、耳聋、阳痿及骨病等。

The Back – shu points not only are indicated in diseases of the corresponding zang – fu organs, but also can be used for the illness of the five sense organs and the nine orifices, skin, muscles, tendons and bones. For instance, Ganshu (BL 18), the back – shu points of the liver, may be chosen to treat liver disorders, but the eye troubles and muscular contracture; Shenshu (BL 23), the back – shu points of the kidney, can be prescribed to treat kidney diseases, but the ear disorders, such as tinnitus, deafness and impotence and bone disorders.

六、募穴
Front - Mu Points

脏腑之气结聚于胸腹部的腧穴，称募穴。始见于《素问·奇病论》。"募"有汇聚之义。五脏六腑各有一募穴，与其相应脏腑部位对应（表2-15）。

Front – mu points are a group of regular meridian points located on the chest and abdomen where the qi of the respective zang – fu organ infuses and converges. The term for the front – mu Points was first stated in *Plain Questions*. "Mu" means converging and recruiting. Each of the zang – fu organs has one front – mu point. There is a total of twelve front – mu points which are situated close to their corresponding zang or fu – organs (Tab 2 – 15).

表2-15　脏腑募穴表

Tab 2 – 15　The Front – Mu Points of the Twelve Zang – Fu Organ

两侧募穴 Front – mu points on the bilateral sides	正中募穴 Front – mu points on the midline
肺-中府 Lung – LU 1	心包-膻中 Pericardium – RN 17
肝-期门 Liver – LR 14	心-巨阙 Heart – RN 14
胆-日月 Gallbladder – GB 24	胃-中脘 Stomach – RN 12
脾-章门 Spleen – LR 13	三焦-石门 Triple energizer – RN 5
肾-京门 Kidney – GB 25	小肠-关元 Small intestine – RN 4
大肠-天枢 Large intestine – ST 25	膀胱-中极 Bladder – RN 3

俞募穴用于治疗相应的脏腑疾病，俞穴位于背部属于阳，募穴位于胸腹部属于阴。《难经·六十七难》说："阴病行阳，阳病行阴，故令募在阴，俞在阳。"因此，俞穴多用于治疗五脏之病；募穴多用于治疗六腑之疾，如心脏病取心俞，肝病取肝俞；胃病取中脘，大肠

病取天枢。这就是“阳病治阴，阴病治阳”。俞募同用属“前后配穴”。

The back – shu pointss and the front – mu points work for diseases of the zang – fu organs. In addition, they are of different nature of yin and yang. The back – shu points located on the back pertain to yang, while the front – mu points located on the chest and abdomen pertain to yin. It is stated in the sixty – seventh problem of *Classic on Medical Problems*, “diseases of the zang organs (yin) are manifested in the back – shu points, and the diseases of fu organs (yang) are manifested in the front – mu points”. Therefore, the back – shu points are mainly used to treat the problems of five zang organs, and the front – mu points are mainly effective to the problems of six fu organs. For example, Xinshu (BL 15) is helpful to the heart diseases; Ganshu (BL 18) works for the liver diseases; Zhongwan (RN 12) is effective to the stomach diseases and Tianshu (ST 25) is good for the large intestine diseases. This is one of the methods to treat yang disease from yin and vice versa. And it is known as the combination of the anterior – posterior points.

七、八会穴
Eight Influential Points

八会穴是指脏、腑、气、血、筋、脉、骨、髓所会聚的八个腧穴。八会穴首载于《难经·四十五难》（表2－16）。

The Eight Influential Points refer to the eight points which are the gathering places for the zang – organs, fu – organs, qi, blood, tendon, vessel, bone and marrow respectively. The term was first recorded in the forty – five problems of *Classic on Medical Problems* (Tab 2 – 16).

表2－16　　八会穴表

Tab 2 – 16　　The Eight Influential Points

八会 Tissue	脏会 Zang organs	腑会 Fu organs	气会 Qi	血会 Blood	筋会 Tendom	脉会 Pulse, vessels	骨会 Bone	髓会 Marrow
穴位 Influential point	章门 LR 13	中脘 RN 12	膻中 RN 17	膈俞 BL 17	阳陵泉 GB 34	太渊 LU 9	大杼 BL 11	悬钟 GB 39

八会穴分布在躯干和四肢，其中脏、腑、气、血、骨之会穴位于躯干部，而筋、脉、髓之会穴位于四肢部。临床上，凡与此八者有关的病症均可选用相关的八会穴来治疗。比如章门用于治疗脏病，膈俞用于治疗血病。另外，《难经·四十五难》还说：“热病在内者，取其会之气穴也。”说明八会穴还能治某些热病。

The eight influential points are distributed on the trunk and the four limbs, amongst which the influential points of the zang – organs, fu – organs, qi, blood and bone are located on the trunk, while those of the tendon, vessel and marrow are on the four limbs. In clinics, they are used for all kinds of diseases of the eight tissues respectively. For example, Zhangmen (LR 13) may be selected for diseases of the zang organs and Geshu (BL 17) may be used for disorders of blood. In addition, there is record in the forty – five problem of the *Classic on Medical Problems*, “For interior heat syndrome, Danzhong (RN 17), the influential of qi is applied". which means the Influential Points are also used for some heat syndromes.

八、八脉交会穴
Eight Confluent Points

八脉交会穴是指四肢部通向奇经八脉的八个经穴，首见于窦汉卿《针经指南》。八穴均分布于腕踝关节附近（表2－17）。

Eight confluent points refer to the eight points on the four limbs where the twelve regular meridians communicate with the eight extra meridians. The term was first stated in *Zhen Jing Zhi Nan* (*Guideline to Acupuncture Classic*), written by Dou hanqing. eight confluent points are distributed distal to the wrists or the ankles (Tab2－17).

表2－17　　八脉交会穴表

Tab 2－17　　The Eight Confluent Points of the Eight Extra Meridians

经脉 Regular meridian	八穴 Confluent point	通八脉 Extra meridian	会合部位 Confluent portion
足太阴 Foot－taiyin	公孙 SP 4	冲脉 Thoroughfare vessel	胃、心、胸 Stomach, heart, chest
手厥阴 Hand－jueyin	内关 PC 6	阴维脉 Yin link vessel	
手少阳 Hand－shaoyang	外关 SJ 5	阳维脉 Yang link vessel	目外眦、颊、颈、耳后、肩 Outer canthus, cheek, neck, back of ears, shoulder
足少阳 Foot－shaoyang	足临泣 GB 41	带脉 Belt vessel	
手太阳 Hand－taiyang	后溪 SI 3	督脉 Governor vessel	目内眦、项、耳、肩胛 Inner canthus, nape of the neck, ear, scapular
足太阳 Foot－taiyang	申脉 BL 62	阳跻脉 Yang heel vessel	
手太阴 Hand－taiyin	列缺 LU 7	任脉 Conception vessel	胸、肺、膈、喉咙 Chest, lungs, diaphragm, throat
足少阴 Foot－shaoyin	照海 KI 6	阴跻脉 Yin heel vessel	

八穴与八脉的相会（通）关系是：公孙从足太阴脾经入腹，与冲脉相通；内关从手厥阴心包经，于胸中与阴维脉相通；外关从手少阳三焦经上肩，与阳维脉相通；足临泣从足少阳胆经过季胁，与带脉相通；申脉从足太阳膀胱经，与阳跻脉相通；后溪从手太阳小肠经交肩会于大椎，与督脉相通；照海从足少阴肾经，与阴跻脉相通；列缺从手太阴肺经循喉咙，与任脉相通。由于八穴与八脉相会通，所以此八穴既能治本经病，又能治奇经病。如公孙通冲脉，能治足太阴脾经病，又能治冲脉病；内关通阴维脉，能治手厥阴心包经病，又能治阴

维脉病，都属主治范围的扩展。

The relations between the eight confluent points and the eight extra meridians are: Gongsun (SP 4) of the spleen meridian of foot – taiyin connects with thoroughfare vessel from abdomen; and Neiguan (PC 6) of the pericardium meridian of hand – jueyin links with yin link vessel in the chest. These two meridians are confluent in the chest, heart and stomach. Zulinqi (GB 41) of the gallbladder meridian connects with belt vessel from the costal region; and Waiguan (SJ 5) of the triple energizer meridian connects with yang link vessel from the shoulder. Houxi (SI 3) of the small intestine meridian leads to governor vessel from the Dazhui (DU 14) by crossing the shoulders; and Shenmai (BL 62) of the bladder meridian connects with yang heel vessel. These two meridians are confluent at the inner canthus, nape, ear, shoulder and back. Lieque (LU 7) of the lung meridian leads to conception vessel by following the throat; and Zhaohai (KI 6) of the kidney meridian connects with yin heel vessel.

八脉交会穴在临床上应用甚为广泛，可治疗奇经八脉之疾，也可以治疗相应经脉之病。李梴《医学入门》说："周身三百六十穴统于手足六十六穴，六十六穴又统于八穴。"强调了八脉交会穴的重要意义。八脉交会穴临床上可作为远道取穴单独选用，再配上头身部的邻近穴，成为远近配穴，又可上下配合应用，如公孙配内关，治疗胃、心、胸部病症；后溪配申脉，治内眼角、耳、项、肩胛部位病及发热恶寒等表证。

The eight confluent points are indicated in wide range, in diseases of the eight extra meridians and their related regular meridians and their related regular meridians according to their connexions. *Yi Xue Ru Men* (*Introduction to Medicine*) wrote by Li ting says that "among the 360 points on the whole body, 66 points located at the four extremities are important, and among these 66 points, the eight confluent points are considered the most important." In practice, the eight confluent points may be used independently. For instance, problems of governor vessel are treated by Houxi (SI 3), disorders of thoroughfare vessel are treated by Gongsun (SP 4) or the confluent point on the upper limb can be combined with the confluent point on the lower limb. For example, Neiguan (PC 6) is combined with Gongsun (SP 4) to treat diseases of the heart, chest and stomach. Houxi (SI 3) is combined with Shenmai (BL 62) for diseases of the inner canthus, ears, neck, scapular regions, and the external illness, such as fever, aversion to cold, etc.

九、下合穴
Lower He - Sea Points

下合穴，即六腑下合穴，是六腑之气下合于足三阳经的六个腧穴。首载于《灵枢·本输》中。胃、胆、膀胱三腑的下合穴，即本经五输穴中的合穴，而大肠、小肠、三焦三腑在下肢则另有合穴。

Lower he – sea points, also called lower he – sea points of the six fu – organs, refer to the six points where the qi of the six fu – organs pours downward toward the three yang meridians of the foot. lower he – sea points were first recorded in the chapter 2, *Miraculous Pivot*. There are six lower he – sea points in total. Among them, the lower he – sea points of the stomach, gallbladder and bladder are identical to their he – sea points, while the large intestine, small intestine and triple energizer have other lower he – sea points in the lower limbs.

"胃合于三里，大肠合于巨虚上廉，小肠合入于巨虚下廉"，大肠、小肠皆属于胃，下合于胃经，其意义在于调和上下生理作用。"三焦合入于委阳，膀胱合入于委中央"，三焦联络膀胱主水液代谢，下合于足太阳膀胱经。"胆合入于阳陵泉"，属足少阳胆经。《灵枢·邪气脏腑病形》又提出了"合治内府"的理论，如足三里治胃脘痛、呕吐酸水；上巨虚治肠痈、痢疾；阳陵泉治胆痛、呕吐等（表2-18）。

"The stomach communicates with Zusanli (ST 36); the large intestine with Shangjuxu (ST 37); the small intestine with Xiajuxu (ST 39)", all pertaining to the stomach meridian of foot – yangming. The large intestine and the small intestine pertain to the stomach. It means that their physiological aotivitioc work upward and downward. "The bladder and triple energizer communicating with Weizhong (BL 40) and Weiyang (BL 31) respectively" pertain to the bladder meridian of foot – taiyang, owing to the water passage of triple energizer connected with the bladder. The gallbladder communicates with Yanglingquan (GB 34), a point of the gallbladder meridian of foot – shaoyang. As it is mentioned in the fourth chapter of *Miraculous Pivot*, "The disorders of the six fu organs can be treated by the he – sea points." For example, gastric pain and sour regurgitation are treated by Zusanli (ST 36); dysentery or appendicitis is treated by Shangjuxu (ST 37); biliary pain and vomiting are treated by Yanglingquan (GB 34) (Tab 2 – 18).

表 2 – 18 下合穴表

Tab 2 – 18 The Lower He – Sea Points

六腑 Six fu organs	胃 Stomach	大肠 Large intestine	小肠 Small intestine	三焦 Triple energier	膀胱 Bladder	胆 Gallbladder
下合穴 Lower He – Sea points	足三里 ST 36	上巨虚 ST 37	下巨虚 ST 39	委阳 BL 39	委中 BL 40	阳陵泉 GB 34

十、交会穴
Crossing Points

交会穴是指两经或数经相交会合的腧穴。交会穴的记载始见于《针灸甲乙经》。交会穴多分布于头面、躯干部。交会穴不但能治本经病，还能兼治所交经脉的病症，如关元、中极是任脉经穴，又与足三阴经相交会，故既可治任脉病症，又可治足三阴经的病症；三阴交是足太阴脾经穴，又与足少阴肾经和足厥阴肝经相交会，故不但能治脾经病，又能治肝、肾两经的疾病。

Crossing points are those points at which two or more meridians intersect. They were first recorded in *The A, B Classic of Acupuncture and Moxibustion*. Most of them are distributed on the head, face and trunk. They can be used to treat disorders of the pertaining meridians and the intersected meridians. Generally, they are often used to treat the diseases appearing simultaneously in meridians intersecting each other. For example, Guanyuan (RN 4) and Zhongji (RN 3) located at the intersection of three yin meridians and the conception vessel may be used to treat diseases of the three foot yin meridians. Sanyinjiao (SP 6), a crossing point in the three foot yin meridians is used for diseases of the liver, spleen and kidney meridians.

第四节 腧穴定位法
Methods for Locating Points

腧穴定位法，又称取穴法，是指确定腧穴位置的基本方法。确定腧穴位置，要以体表标志为主要依据，在距离标志较远的部位，则于两标志之间折合一定的比例寸，称"骨度分寸"，用此"寸"表示上下左右的距离；取穴时，用手指比量这种距离，则有手指"同身寸"的应用。以下就分体表标志、骨度分寸和手指同身寸、简便定位法进行介绍。

The methods for locating points, also called selecting points, refer to the basic methods of determining the locations of a point. To locate points accurately, the anatomic landmarks on the body surface must be used. For the points away from these landmarks, the distance between any two landmarks may be converted into certain proportional units (bone – length proportional cun). In addition to the above two methods, measurement of cun using the fingers is acceptable for locating points. In general, the commonly used methods for locating points include measurement utilizing anatomic landmarks, measurement with bone – length proportional units, measurement with fingers, and simple measurement.

一、骨度分寸法
Bone - Length Proportional Measurement

骨度分寸法，古称"骨度法"，即以骨节为主要标志测量周身各部的大小、长短，并依其尺寸按比例折算作为定穴的标准。此法的记载，最早见于《灵枢·骨度》，将设定的骨节两端之间的长度折成为一定的等分，每一等分为一寸。不论男女老幼，肥瘦高矮，一概以此标准折量作为量取腧穴的依据。现将全身各部骨度折量寸列表、图示如下（表 2 – 19，图 2 – 1）。

Bone – length proportional measurement is a point locating method by taking the bones and joints of the body as major markers used to measure the length and size of certain body parts and converting their length or size into proportional units based on the measuring criteria for locating points. This measurement was first recorded in the chapter 14, *Miraculous Pivot*. Proportional measurement is based on the patient's body figure. The length of a given bone or between two joints is divided into absolute numbers of equal units, and each unit is considered as one cun. This measurement is applicable for locating points on patients of different sexes, ages and body types. The proportional measurements of the different parts of the body are introduced in Tab 2 – 19, Fig 2 – 1.

表 2 – 19　　常用骨度表

Tab 2 – 19　　Standards for Bone – Length Proportional Measurement

部位 Body portion	起止点 Distance	折量寸 Proportional measurement	度量法 Method	说明 Explanation
头部 Head	前发际至后发际 From the anterior hairline to the posterior hairline	12 寸 12 cun	直 Longitudinal measurement	如前发际不明，从眉心至大椎穴作 18 寸，眉心至前发际 3 寸，大椎穴至后发际 3 寸 If the anterior and posterior hairline are indistinguishable, the distance from the glabella to DU 14 is taken as 18 cun. The distance from the glabella to the anterior hairline is taken as 3 cun. The distance from DU 14 to the posterior hairline is taken as 3 cun
	前额两发角之间 Between the two frontal angle along hairline	9 寸 9 cun	横 Transverse measurement	用于量头部得横寸 The transverse measurement is also used to localize other points on the head
	耳后两完骨（乳突）之间 Between the two mastoid processes	9 寸 9 cun		
胸腹部 Chest and abdomen	天突至歧骨（胸剑联合） From the RN 22 to the xiphosternal symphysis	9 寸 9 cun	直 Longitudinal measurement	胸部与胁肋部取穴直寸，一般根据肋骨计算，每一肋骨折作 1.6 寸（天突穴至璇玑穴可作 1 寸，璇玑穴至中庭穴，各穴间可作 1.6 寸计算） The longitudinal measurement of the chest and the hypochondriac region is generally based on the intercostal space. Each intercostal space is taken as 1.6 cun (the distance between RN 22 and RN 21 as 1 cun is an exception)
	歧骨至脐中 From the xiphosternal symphysis to the centre of the umbilicus	8 寸 8 cun		
	脐中至横骨上廉（耻骨联合上缘） Between the centre of the umbilicus and the upper border of symphysis pubis	5 寸 5 cun		
	两乳头之间 Between the two nipples	8 寸 8 cun	横 Transverse measurement	胸腹部取穴横寸，可根据两乳头间的距离折量，女性可用锁骨中线代替 For females, the distance between two mid – clavicular lines can be taken as the substitute of the transverse measurement of the two nipple

续表

部位 Body portion	起止点 Distance	折量寸 Proportional measurement	度量法 Method	说明 Explanation
背腰部 Back	大椎以下至尾骶 From DU 14 to the sacrum	21 椎 21 vertebra	直 Longitudinal measurement	背腰部腧穴以脊椎棘突作为标志作定位依据。一般两肩胛骨下角连线平第 7 胸椎棘突；两髂嵴相当于第 4 腰椎棘突 The longitudinal measurement f the back is based on the spinous processes of the vertebral column. Usually, the lower angle of the scapula is about at the same level of the 7th thoracic spinous process, and the iliac spine is about at the same level as the 4th lumbar spinous process
	两肩胛骨内侧缘 Between the two medial borders of the scapula	6 寸 6cun	横 Transverse measurement	
身侧部 Lateral side of the trunk	腋以下至季胁 From the tip of the axillary fossa on the lateral side of the chest to the tip of the 11th rib	12 寸 12 cun	直 Longitudinal measurement	季胁此指第 11 肋端下方 Ji xie indicates the underneath of the 11th rib
身侧部 Lateral side of the trunk	季胁以下至髀枢 From the tip of the 11th rib to the prominence of the greater trochanter of femur	9 寸 9 cun	直 Longitudinal measurement	髀枢指股骨大转子高点 Bi shu means The prominence of the greater trochanter of femur
上肢部 Upper limbs	腋前纹头（腋前皱襞）至肘横纹 From the end of the axillary anterior fold to the transverse cubital crease	9 寸 9 cun	直 Longitudinal measurement	用于手三阴、手三阳经骨度分寸 For locating points of three yin and three yang meridians of the hand
	肘横纹至腕横纹 From the transverse cubital crease to the transverse wrist crease	12 寸 12 cun		
下肢部 Lower limbs	横骨上廉至内辅骨上廉 From the upper border of symphysis pubis to the medial condyle of femur	18 寸 18 cun	直 Longitudinal measurement	—
	内辅骨下廉至内踝尖 From the lower border of medial condyle of the tibia to the tip of medial malleolus	13 寸 13 cun		
	髀枢至膝中 From the prominence of the greater trochanter of the femur to the popliteal transverse crease	19 寸 19 cun		臀横纹至膝中，可作 14 寸折量 The distance between the transverse crease of the hip to the middle of the patella is measured as 14 cun

续表

部位 Body portion	起止点 Distance	折量寸 Proportional measurement	度量法 Method	说明 Explanation
下肢部 Lower limbs	膝中至外踝尖 From the popliteal transverse crease to the tip of lateral malleolus	16寸 16 cun		
	外踝尖至足底 From the tip of lateral malleolus to the sole	3寸 3 cun		

骨度分寸法借助体表标准定位法来对身体绝大多数部位进行定位。实际上，这个方法是体表标志定位法的扩展，并补充了后者的不足。是临床最常用、最精确也最广泛使用的定位方法。

Bone-length proportional measurement is to measure the length and width of all parts of the body by means of anatomic landmarks on the body surface. Actually, this method is the extension of the anatomic landmarks measurement, and supplements the limitation of the latter measurement. It is considered to be an accurate points-locating method, thus bone-length proportional measurement is most often used clinically and is widely applicable for most points.

二、体表标志定位法 Measurement with Anatomic Landmarks

体表标志，主要指分布于全身体表的骨性标志和肌性标志，可分为固定标志和活动标志两类。

Measurement with anatomic landmarks is a method for locating points by referring to the anatomic landmarks on the body surface. The anatomic landmarks include bone and muscle landmarks. Anatomic landmarks may be classified into fixed and moving landmarks.

（一）固定标志 Fixed Anatomic Landmarks

固定标志定位，是指利用五官、毛发、爪甲、乳头、脐窝和骨节凸起、凹陷及肌肉隆起等固定标志来取穴的方法。比较明显的标志，如鼻尖取素髎；两眉中间取印堂；两乳中间取膻中；脐旁2寸取天枢；腓骨小头前下缘取阳陵泉；俯首显示最高的第7颈椎棘突下取大椎等。在两骨分歧处，如锁骨肩峰端与肩胛冈分歧处取巨骨；胸骨下端与肋软骨分歧处取中庭等。此外，肩胛冈平第3胸椎棘突，肩胛骨下角平第7胸椎棘突，髂嵴平第4腰椎棘突，这些可作为背腰部穴位的取穴标志。

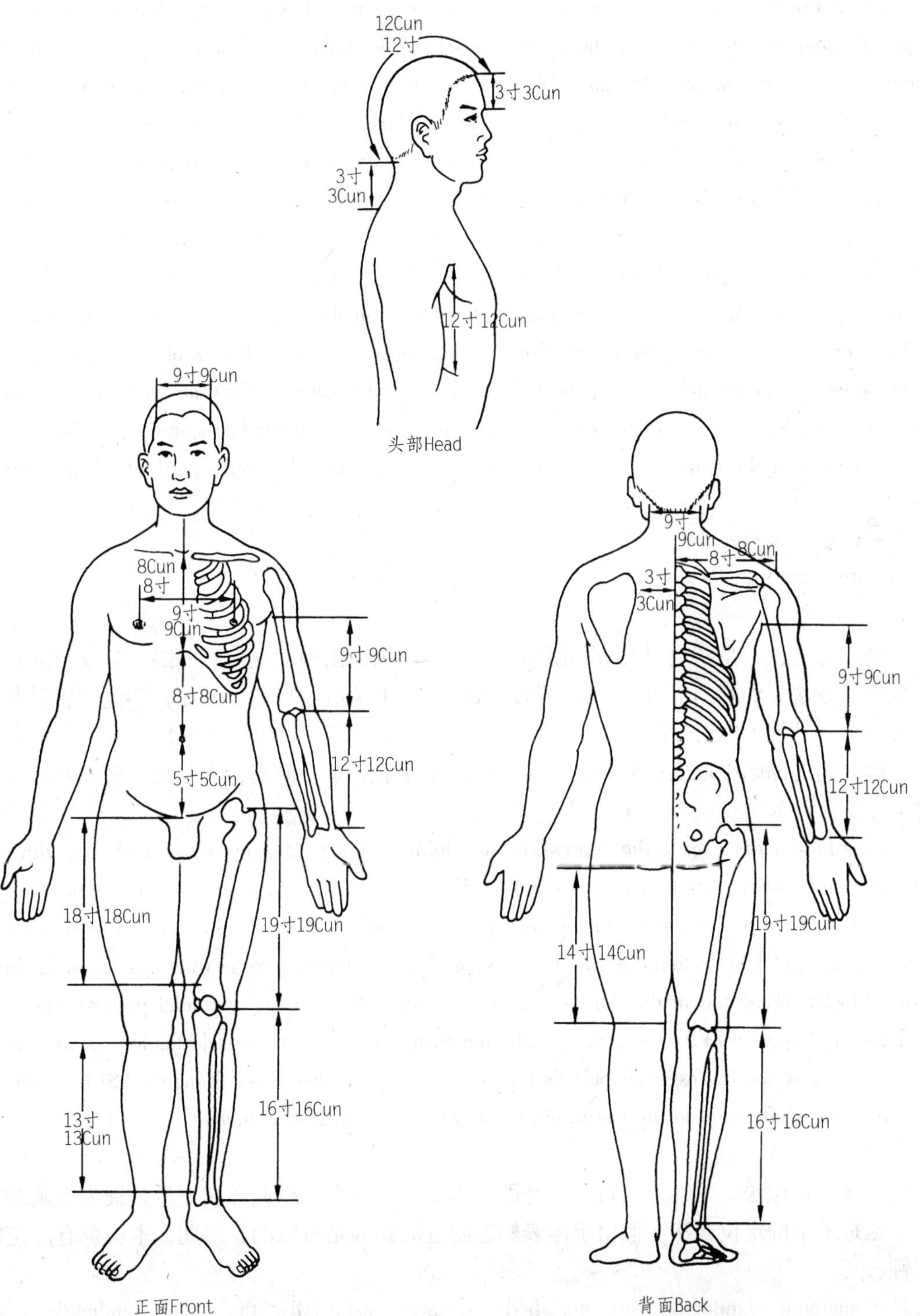

图 2－1 常用骨度分寸示意图

Fig 2－1 Bone－length proportional measurement

Fixed anatomic landmarks include the five sensory organs, hair, nails, nipples, umbilicus, and prominences and depressions of bones and muscles. The obvious landmarks can be used directly to locate points. For example, Suliao (DU 25) is situated on the tip of nose; Yintang (EX – HN3) is the point in the center of the two eyebrows; Danzhong (RN 17) is the point directly in the center between the two nipples; Tianshu (ST 25) is the point 2 cun lateral to the umbilicus; Yanglingquan (GB 34) is the point anterior – inferior to the capitulum fibulae; and Dazhui (DU 14) is under the 7th cervical spinous process. Some points are situated at the bifurcation of two bones. For example, Jugu (LI 16) is located on the bifurcation of the scapular extremity of the clavicle and scapular spine; and Zhongting (RN 16) is on the bifurcation of the costal cartilage and the lower border of the xiphoid bone. The scapular spine is on the same level as the 3rd thoracic spinous process, but the inferior angle of the scapula is on the same level as the 7th thoracic spinous process. Meanwhile, the iliac crest is on the same level as the 4th lumbar spinous process. The above landmarks may be employed as reference markers for locating the points on the back and waist.

(二) 活动标志
Moving Landmarks

活动标志定位，是指利用关节、肌肉、皮肤随活动而出现的孔隙、凹陷、皱纹等活动标志来取穴的方法。如耳门、听宫、听会等应张口取；下关应闭口取。又如，曲池宜屈肘于横纹头处取之；外展上臂时肩峰前下方的凹陷中取肩髃；取阳溪穴时应将拇指跷起，当拇长、短伸肌腱之间的凹陷中取之；取养老穴时，应正坐屈肘，掌心向胸，当尺骨小头桡侧骨缝中取之。

Moving landmarks refer to the depressions and folds on the joints, muscles, and skin with reference to specific body movements. For example, Ermen (SJ 21), Tinggong (SI 19) and Tinghui (GB 2) are located where the mouth opens, while Xiaguan (ST 7) is located where the mouth closes; Quchi (LI 11) is found on the lateral side of the transverse crease when the elbow is bent; Jianyu (LI 15) is located in the depression anterior and inferior to the acromial process when the arm abducts; Yangxi (LI 5) is located in the depression between the muscle tendons of the extensor pollicis longus and the extensor pollicis brevis when the thumb erects; Yanglao (SI 6) is located in the bone cleft radial to the capitulum ulnae when the forearm adducts.

体表标志定位法，尤其是固定标志是固定不变的，因而，以此方法定位是最为准确的定位法，也是最早的定位方法。但由于体表标志附近的腧穴是有限的，因此，本法也有一定的局限性。

The anatomic landmarks on the body surface, especially the fixed landmarks, are invariable. Therefore, locating a point with these landmarks is the most accurate method, and it remains as the primary way of locating points. However, because the number of points situated near these landmarks on the body surface is limited, the measurement of them using anatomic landmarks has certain limitations.

三、手指同身寸定位法
Finger Measurement

手指比量，原是指以患者本人的手指为标准度量取穴，称为“同身寸”。最常用的有中指同身寸、拇指同身寸和四指同身寸。

Finger measurement is a point – locating method using the length and width of the patient's fingers as a standard to locate points. The commonly used finger measurement methods use the middle finger, thumb and four – finger for making measurements.

（一）中指同身寸
Middle Finger Measurement

中指同身寸法，即以患者中指屈曲时中节内侧两端纹头之间的距离为 1 寸（图 2 –2）。这种“同身寸”法与骨度分寸相比偏长，只可用于小腿部和下腹部的直量，不适合普遍使用。

When the patient's middle finger is bent, the distance between the two medial ends of the creases of two interphalangeal joints is taken as one cun（Fig 2 –2）. Compared with bone – length proportional measurement, the middle finger measurement may be a little longer, and this should be kept in mind when using it for points locations on the lower leg and abdomen. It's not available in common use.

（二）拇指同身寸
Thumb Measurement

拇指同身寸法，即以患者拇指指间关节的宽度为 1 寸（图 2 –3）。与中指同身寸相比较，本法具有更清晰、简易的优点，是常用的定位方法。

The width of the interphalangeal joint of the patient's thumb is taken as one cun（Fig 2 –3）. Compared to the middle finger measurement, this method has the advantage of being clearer and simpler, and remains as a commonly used point location method.

（三）四指同身寸
Four – Finger Measurement

四指同身寸法，即以患者的四指（食指、中指、无名指和小指）并拢时，以中指近侧指间关节横纹水平的四指宽度为3寸。此法也是手指同身寸法中最常用的方法，称“一夫法”（图2-4）。

When the patient's four fingers (the index, middle, ring and little fingers) extend and touch closely together, the width of the four fingers at the level of the crease of the proximal interphalangeal joint of the middle finger is measured to be three cun (Fig 2-4). This method is also commonly used amongst the finger measurements, so called "one method of finger breadth measurement".

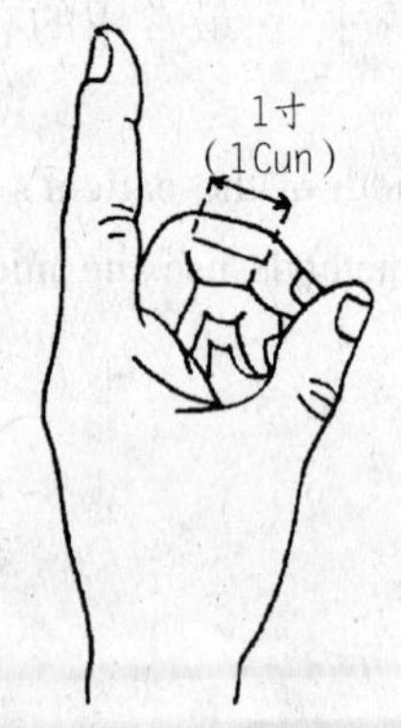

图2-2 中指同身寸
Fig 2-2 Middle finger measurement

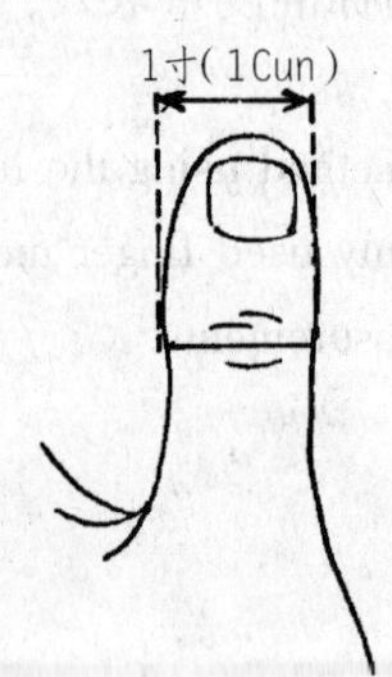

图2-3 拇指同身寸
Fig 2-3 Thumb measurement

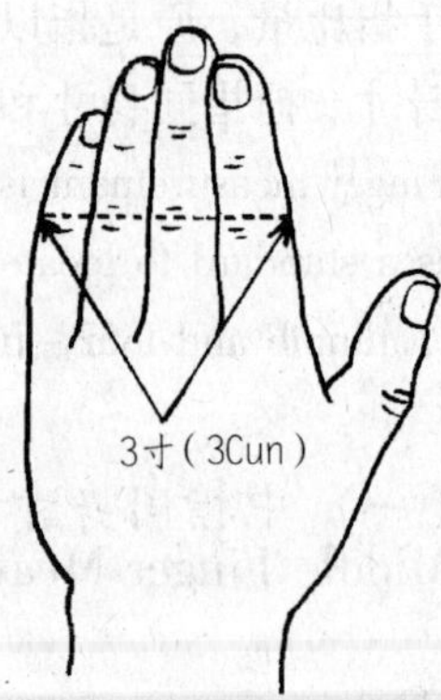

图2-4 四指同身寸
Fig 2-4 Four-finger measurement

四、简便定位法 Simplified Measurement

简便定位法，是用简便方法来定穴位的一种方法。比如：两手伸开，于虎口交叉，当食指端处取列缺；半握拳，当中指端所指处取劳宫；两手自然下垂，于中指端处取风市；垂肩屈肘于平肘尖处取章门；两耳角直上连线中点取百会等。这些取穴方法只是作为其他定位取穴法的参考。

Simplified measurement is a simple method used to locate points. For instance, when the index fingers and thumbs of both hands are crossed with the index finger of one hand in an outstretched position, Lieque (LU 7) is under the tip of the index finger; when making a fist loosely, Laogong (PC 8) is just under the tip of the middle finger; when the patient stands erect with the hands close to the legs, Fengshi (GB 31) is where the tip of the middle finger touches the leg; when the shoulder drops and the elbow is bent, Zhangmen (LR 13) is located at the level of the tip of elbow joint. Baihui (DU 20) is situated in the center of the line directly above the two ear apexes. A simplified measurement is usually employed as an auxiliary to the other point-locating methods.

复习思考题
Review Questions

1. 腧穴的含义和治疗作用是什么?

What are the definition and therapeutic properties of points?

2. 古人如何以自然水流来描述五输穴的?

How did the ancient doctors figuratively describe the distribution of the five - shu points with the phenomenon of water flowing in the natural world?

3. 阿是穴的定义和特点是什么?

What are the definition and characteristics of ashi - points?

4. 下合穴的定义和分布特点是什么?

What are the definition and the distribution characteristics of Lower he - sea points?

5. 何谓骨度分寸定位法? 骨度分寸定位法和体表标志定位法有何区别?

What is the definition of bone - length proportional measurement? What are the differences between the bone - length proportional measurement with the anatomic landmarks measurement?

经络腧穴各论
Meridians and Collaterals，Acupoints

第三章　手太阴经络与腧穴
Meridian and Collateral and Its Acupoints of Hand – Taiyin

第一节　手太阴经络
Meridian and Collateral of Hand – Taiyin

一、手太阴经脉
Meridian of Hand - Taiyin

（一）经脉循行
The Course of Meridian

手太阴肺经，起始于中焦，向下联络大肠，回过来沿着胃上口，穿过膈肌，属于肺脏。从肺系（气管、喉咙部）横出腋下（中府、云门），下循上臂内侧，行于手少阴、手厥阴经之前（天府、侠白），下过肘中（尺泽），沿前臂内侧桡骨边缘（孔最），进入寸口（桡动脉搏动处，经渠、太渊），上行至大鱼际部，沿其边际，出大指的末端（少商）。其支脉，从腕后（列缺）走向食指内（桡）侧，出其末端，接手阳明大肠经（图3－1）。

《灵枢·经脉》原文："肺手太阴之脉，起于中焦，下络大肠，还循胃口，上膈属肺。从肺系，横出腋下，下循臑内，行少阴、心主之前，下肘中，循臂内上骨下廉，入寸口，上鱼，循鱼际，出大指之端。其支者，从腕后，直出次指内廉，出其端。"

The chapter "Discussion on the Meridians" *in Miraculous Pivot*：the lung meridian originates from the middle energizer, running downward to connect with large intestine. Winding back, it goes along the upper orifice of the stomach, passes upward through the diaphragm, and enters the lung, its pertaining organ. From the lung, it comes out transversely from the axilla, running downward along the medial aspect of the upper arm, it reaches the cubital fossa, then it goes continuously downward along the anterior border of the radial side in the medial aspect of the forearm and enters cunkou. Passing the thenar eminence, and going along its radial border, it ends at the medial side of the tip of the thumb.

The branch emerges from the posterior wrist and runs along the dorsum of the hand onto the radial side of the tip of the index finger (Fig 3－1).

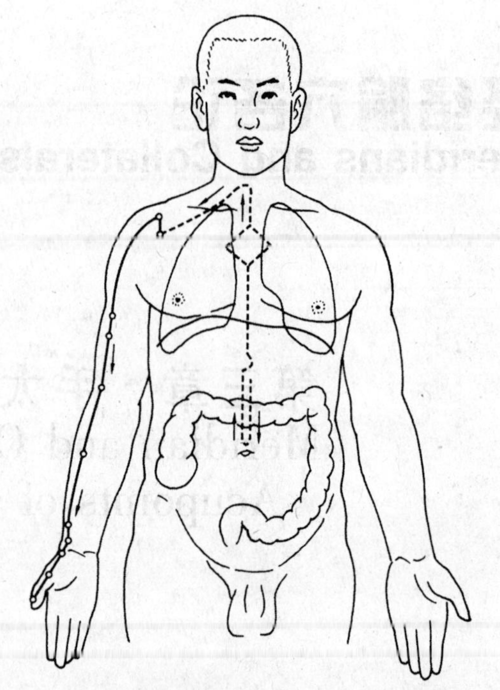

图例——本经有穴通路　　……本经无穴通路

Note ——Pathway with points

……Pathway without points

图 3－1　手太阴经脉、络脉循行示意图

Fig 3－1　The course of the meridianand and collateral of hand－taiyin

(二) 经脉病候
The Syndromes of Meridian

本经异常就出现下列病症：肺部胀闷，膨膨而咳喘，咽喉肿痛，严重时交捧双手，心胸闷乱，视物模糊，还可发生前臂部的气血阻逆，如厥冷、麻木、疼痛等。

本经穴主治有关“肺”方面所发生的病症：咳嗽，气急，喘息，心烦，胸闷，上臂、前臂的内侧前缘酸痛或厥冷，或掌心发热。

当气盛有余时，可见肩背酸痛，感受风寒而汗出，伤风，小便频数，张口嘘气；而气虚不足时，则见肩背冷痛，气短，小便颜色异常。

Diseases of throat, chest, lung and diseases of the regions along the course of this meridian.

二、手太阴络脉
Collateral of Hand - Taiyin

手太阴络脉，名列缺，起于腕横纹约上 1.5 寸处的分肉之间，走向手阳明经脉；与手太阴经并行，直走入手掌中，散布在大鱼际部。

其病：实证，手腕和手掌部灼热；虚证，张口出气、尿频、遗尿。可取手太阴络穴治疗。

The collateral of the lung meridian of hand－taiyin. It arises from Lieque (LU7) and runs to the large intestine meridian of hand – yangming. Another branch follows the lung meridian of hand – tanyin into the palm of the hand and spreads through thenar eminence.

三、手太阴经别
Divergent Meridian of Hand - Taiyin

手太阴经别，从手太阴经脉分出，进入腋下，行于手少阴经别之前，入体腔后走向肺脏，散到大肠，上方通过缺盆部，沿喉咙，在约当扶突穴处又合于手阳明经脉（图 3 –2）。

Divergent meridian of the lung meridian of hand – taiyin after deriving from the lung meridian at the axilla. It runs anterior to the pericardium meridian of hand – shaoyin into the chest, and there it connects with the lung and then disperses in the large intestine. A branch extends upward from the lung and emerges at the clavicle, it ascends across the throat and converges with the large Intestine meridian（Fig 3 –2）.

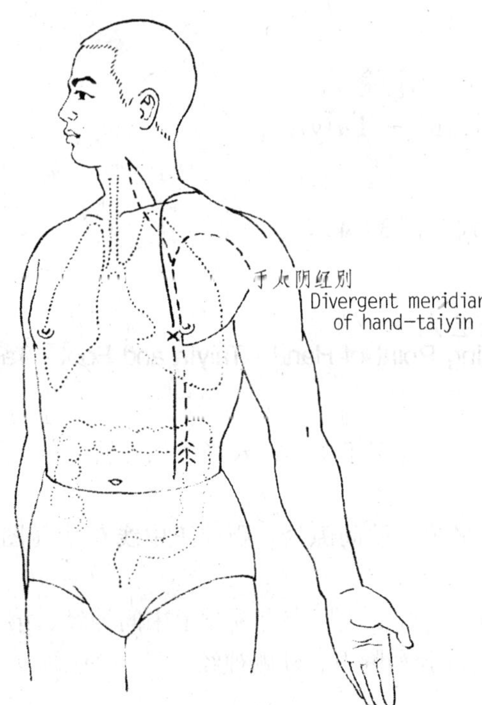

图 3 –2　手太阴经别循行示意图

Fig 3 –2　The course of the divergent meridian of hand – taiyin

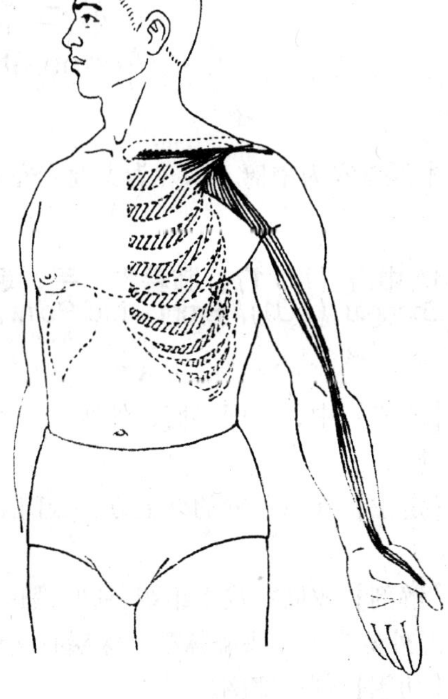

图 3 –3　手太阴经筋分布示意图

Fig 3 –3　The course of the muscular region of hand – taiyin

四、手太阴经筋
Muscular Region of Hand - Taiyin

手太阴经筋，起于大指之上，沿大指上行，结于鱼际之后；行寸口动脉外侧，上行沿前臂，结于肘中；向上经过臂内侧，进入腋下，出缺盆部，结于肩峰前方；其上行结于缺盆，向下内行结于胸里；分散通过膈部，会合于膈下，到达季胁（图3-3）。

The muscular region of the lung of hand - taiyin arises from the tip of the thumb and knots at the lower thenar eminence. Proceeding up laterally to the pulse and along the forearm, it knots at the elbow, then ascends along the medial aspect of the arm and enters the chest below the axilla. Emerging from Quepen（ST 12）, it knots anteriorly to Jianyu（LI15）. Above, it knots with the clavicle, and below it knots in the chest, dispersing over the diaphragm and converging again at the lowest rib（Fig 3-3）.

第二节 手太阴腧穴
Acupoints of Hand - Taiyin

本经首穴为中府，末穴为少商，左右各11穴（图3-4）。

1. 中府（LU 1），肺募穴，手、足太阴交会穴
Zhongfu（LU1），Front - Mu Point，Crossing Point of Hand - Taiyin and Foot - Taiyin

【释义】中，中间；府，处所。中，指中焦，肺经起于中焦，穴当中焦脾胃之气汇聚肺经之处。

【定位】在胸前壁的外上方，云门下1寸，平第一肋间隙处，距前正中线6寸（图3-5）。

【解剖】皮肤→皮下组织→胸大肌→胸小肌→胸腔。浅层布有锁骨上中间神经、第一肋间神经外侧皮支、头静脉等。深层有胸肩峰动、静脉和胸内、外侧神经。

【功用】理气宽胸。

【主治】咳嗽，气喘，胸痛，肩背痛。

【操作】向外斜刺或平刺0.5~0.8寸，不可向内深刺，以免伤及肺脏。

【Meaning】zhong，middle；fu，place. Zhong refers to the middle energizer. The lung meridian starts from the middle energizer. The point is in the place where qi of spleen and stomach in the middle energizer is gathered into the lung meridian.

【Location】In the superior lateral aspect of the anterior thoracic wall，1 cun below Yunmen（LU 2），on the level of the 1st intercostal space，6 cun lateral to the anterior midline（Fig 3-5）.

【Regional anatomy】skin→subcutaneous tissue→pectoralis major→pectoralis minor→thoracic cavity. The superficial layer have intermediate supraclavicular nerves, lateral cutaneous branch of the first intercostal nerve, cephalic vein. etc. the deep layer have thoracoacromial artery and vein, medial and lateral pectoral nerve.

【Properties】Regulate vital energy and relax the chest.

【Indications】Cough, asthma, chest pain and pain in the shoulder and back.

【Needling method】Puncture outward obliquely or transversely 0.5～0.8 cun; moxibustion is applicable.

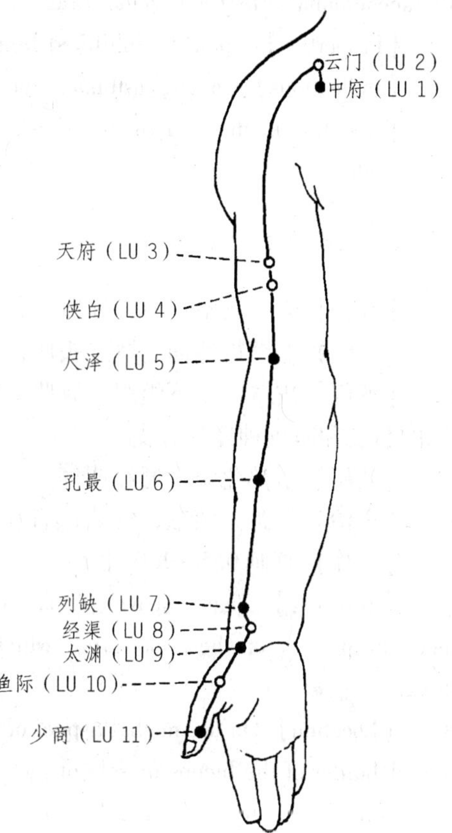

图例 ● 常用腧穴 ○ 一般腧穴
Note ● Main point ○ Common point
图 3－4 手太阴肺经腧穴总图
Fig 3－4 Points of the lung meridian of hand－taiyin

2. 云门 Yunmen（LU 2）

【释义】云，云雾的云；门，门户。云，指肺气。穴在胸上部，如肺气出入的门户。

【定位】在胸前壁的外上方，肩胛骨喙突上方，锁骨下窝凹陷中，距前正中线6寸（图3－5）。

【解剖】皮肤→皮下组织→三角肌→锁胸筋膜→喙锁韧带。浅层布有锁骨上中间神经、头静脉。深层有胸肩峰动、静脉支和胸内、外侧神经的分支。

【功用】宣肺理气。

【主治】咳嗽，气喘，胸痛，肩痛。

【操作】向外斜刺或平刺0.5～0.8寸，不可向内深刺，以免伤及肺脏。

【Meaning】Yun, cloud; men, door. Yun refers to the qi of lung. The point is on the upper part of the chest, serving as a door for the qi of lung.

【Location】In the superior lateral aspect of the anterior thoracic wall, superior to the coracoid process of scapula, in the depression of the infraclavicular fossa, 6 cun lateral to the anterior midline（Fig 3－5）.

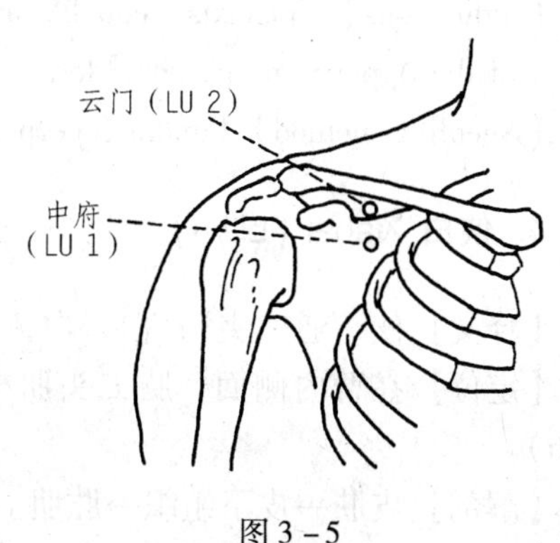

图 3－5
Fig 3－5

【Regional anatomy】skin→subcutaneous tissue→deltoid→clavipectoral fascia→coracoclavicular ligament. The superficial layer have intermediate supraclavicular nerves, and cephalic vein. etc. the deep layer have thoracoacromial artery and vein, branches of medial and lateral pectoral nerve.

【Properties】Open the inhibited lung – energy and regulate the flow of lung qi.

【Indications】Cough, asthma, chest pain, and pain in the back and shoulder.

【Needling method】Puncture outward obliquely or transversely 0.5 ~0.8 cun; moxibustion is applicable.

3. 天府 Tianfu (LU 3)

【释义】天，天空；府，处所。天，指上而言。穴在臂部，是肺气聚焦之处。

【定位】在臂内侧面，肱二头肌桡侧缘，腋前纹头下3寸处（图3–6）。

【解剖】皮肤→皮下组织→肱肌。浅层布有臂外侧皮神经、头静脉等；深层有肱、动静脉的肌支和肌皮神经的分支。

【功用】清热化痰，通经调气。

【主治】鼻衄，咳嗽，气喘，肩及上肢内侧疼痛。

【操作】直刺0.5~1.0寸。

【Meaning】Tian, heaven; fu, place. Tian refers to upper. The point is on the upper arm, which in a confluence of qi of lung.

【Location】On the medial aspect of the upper arm and on the radial border of the biceps muscle of the arm, 3 cun below the anterior end of axillary fold (Fig 3 – 6).

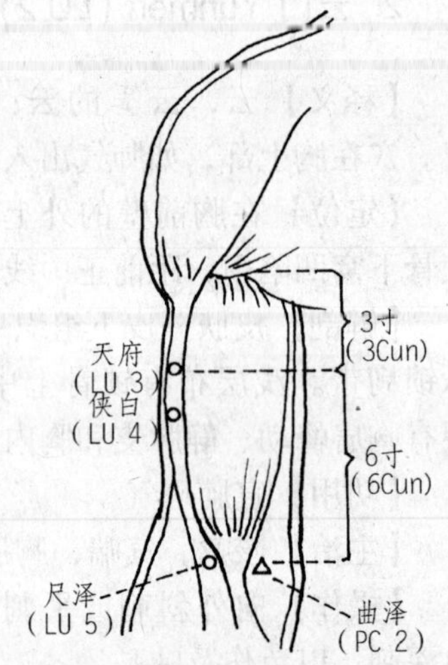

图3–6
Fig 3–6

【Regional anatomy】skin → subcutaneous tissue → brachialis. The superficial layer have nervus cutaneus brachii lateralis and cephalic vein. etc. the deep layer have muscular banches of brachial artery and vein and the branch of musculo cutaneous nerve.

【Properties】Clearing heat and expectoration, dredge the meridians and collaterals, and regulate the flow of lung qi.

【Indications】Epistaxis, cough, asthma, pain in the medial aspect of the upper arm and shoulder.

【Needling method】Puncture perpendicularly 0.5 ~1.0cun.

4. 侠白 Xiabai (LU 4)

【释义】侠，通“夹”；白，白色。白色属肺。两臂下垂，本穴夹于肺的两旁。

【定位】在臂内侧面，肱二头肌桡侧缘，腋前纹头下4寸处，或肘横纹上5寸处（图3–6）。

【解剖】皮肤→皮下组织→肱肌。浅层布有臂外侧皮神经、头静脉等；深层有肱动、静脉的肌支和肌皮神经的分支。

【功用】调肺气，理心血。

【主治】咳嗽，气喘，上臂内侧痛。

【操作】直刺0.5~1.0寸。

【Meaning】Xia, to press from both sides; bai, white. White color pertain to the lung. With both arms hanging freely, this point is precisely on both sides of the lung.

【Location】On the medial aspect of the upper arm and on the radial border of the biceps muscle of the arm, 4 cun below the anterior end of axillary fold, or 5 cun above the cubital crease (Fig 3-6).

【Regional anatomy】skin→subcutaneous tissue→brachialis. The superficial layer have nervus cutaneus brachii lateralis and cephalic vein. etc. the deep layer have muscular banches of brachial artery and vein and the branch of musculo cutaneous nerve.

【Properties】Regulate the flow of lung qi, control the circulation of blood and vessel of heart.

【Indications】Cough, asthma, and pain in the medial aspect of the upper arm.

【Needling method】Puncture perpendicularly 0.5~1.0cun.

5. 尺泽（LU 5），合穴
Chize（LU 5），He - Sea Point

【释义】尺，长度单位，十寸为尺；泽，沼泽。尺，指尺部（腕至肘之前臂）。穴在尺部肘窝陷中，脉气流注于此，如水注沼泽。

【定位】在肘横纹中，肱二头肌腱桡侧凹陷处（图3-7）。

【解剖】皮肤→皮下组织→肱桡肌→桡神经→肱肌。浅层布有臂外侧皮神经、头静脉等。深层有桡神经，桡侧副动、静脉前支，桡侧返动、静脉等。

【功用】养阴清肺。

【主治】咳嗽，气喘，咳血，潮热，胸部胀满，咽喉肿痛，急性腹痛吐泻，肘臂挛痛。

【操作】直刺0.8~1.2寸；或点刺出血。

【Meaning】Chi, ruler or ulnar; ze, marsh. Chi refers to the ulnar aspects (from the wrist to the elbow). The point is in the depression of the elbow fossa at the ulnar aspect. The qi of the meridian is infused here, like water flowing into a marsh.

【Location】In the cubital crease, in the depression of the radial aspect of the tendon of the biceps muscle of the arm (Fig 3-7).

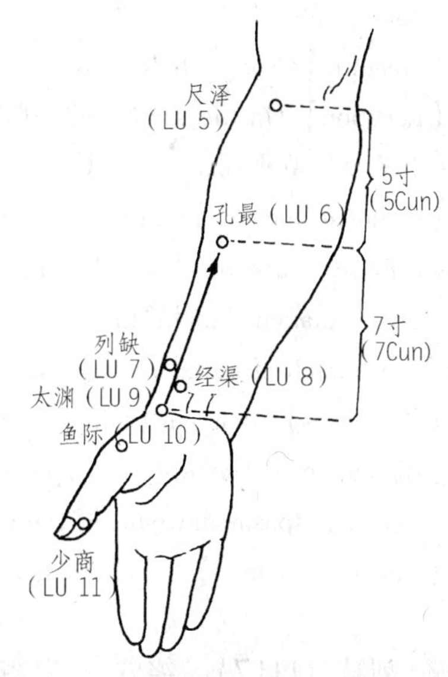

图3-7

Fig 3-7

【Regional anatomy】 skin → subcutaneous tissue → brachioradialis → radial nerve → brachialis. The superficial layer have nervus cutaneus brachii lateralis and cephalic vein, etc. the deep layer have radial nerve, anterior branch of radial collateral artery and vein, and radial recurrent artery and vein, etc.

【Properties】 Clear away lung heart and nourish yin of lung.

【Indications】 Cough, asthma, hemoptysis, hot flush, distension and fullness in the chest, swelling and pain in the throat, acute vomiting and diarrhea, infantile convulsion, and spasmodic pain of the elbow and arm.

【Needling method】 Puncture perpendicularly 0. 8 ~ 1. 2 cun, or prick the acupoint to cause bleeding.

6. 孔最（LU 6），郄穴
Kongzui（LU 6），Xi - Cleft Point

【释义】孔，孔隙；最，副词。

【定位】在前臂掌面桡侧，当尺泽与太渊连线上，腕横纹上 7 寸处（图 3 – 7）。

【解剖】皮肤→皮下组织→肱桡肌→桡侧腕屈肌→指浅层肌与旋前圆肌之间→拇长屈肌。浅层布有前臂外侧皮神经、头静脉等。深层有桡动、静脉，桡神经浅支等结构。

【功用】润肺止血，解表清热。

【主治】咳血，鼻衄，咳嗽，气喘，咽喉肿痛，热病无汗，肘臂挛痛，痔血。

【操作】直刺 0. 5 ~ 1. 0 寸。

【Meaning】 Kong, hole; zui, the most.

【Location】 On the radial side of the palmar surface of the forearm, and on the line connecting Chize（LU 5）and Taiyuan（LU 9）, 7 cun above the cubital crease（Fig 3 – 7）.

【Regional anatomy】 skin→subcutaneous tissue→brachioradialis→flexor carpi radialis muscle→between muscle superficialis and pronator teres→flexor pollicis longus muscle. The superficial layer have nervus cutaneus brachii lateralis, cephalic vein, etc. the deep layer have radial artery and vein, superficial branch of radial nerve, etc.

【Properties】 Moisten the lung, stop bleeding, relieve exterior syndrome and clear away heat.

【Indications】 Hemoptysis, epistaxis, cough, swelling and pain in the throat, febrile disease without sweat, spasmodic pain of the elbow and arm, hemorrhoids and bloody stool.

【Needling method】 Puncture perpendicularly 0. 5 ~ 1. 0cun.

7. 列缺（LU 7），络穴，八脉交会穴（通任脉）
Lieque（LU 7），Luo - Connecting Point，One of th Eight Confluent Points（Connecting with Conception Vessel）

【释义】列，排列；缺，凹陷。古代称闪电和天际裂缝为列缺。手太阴脉从这里别走手阳明脉，本穴位列于桡骨茎突上方凹陷处。

【定位】在前臂桡侧缘，桡骨茎突上方，腕横纹上 1.5 寸，当肱桡肌与拇长展肌腱之间（图 3－7）。

简便定位：两手虎口自然平直交叉，一手食指按在另一手桡骨茎突上，指尖下凹陷中是穴。

【解剖】皮肤→皮下组织→拇长展肌腱→肱桡肌腱→旋前方肌。浅层布有头静脉，前臂外侧皮神经和桡神经浅支；深层有桡动、静脉的分支。

【功用】宣肺止痛，通调任脉。

【主治】外感头痛，项强，咳嗽，气喘，咽喉肿痛，口㖞，齿痛。

【操作】向上斜刺 0.3～0.5 寸。

【Meaning】Lie, arrangement; que, depression. The lighting and the rift in the sky were called Lieque in ancient times. The meridian of hand－taiyin diverges from this point to the meridian of hand－yangming. The point is in the depression superior to the styloid process of the radius.

【Location】On the radial side of the forearm, proximal to the styloid process of radius, 1.5 cun above the crease of the wrist, between branchioradial muscle and the tendon of long abductor muscle of the thumb（Fig 3－7）.

Simplified Measurement: under the tip of the index, when the left and right hukou of both hands are intercrossed and the index finger are pressed on another styloid process behind the wrist of the radius.

【Regional anatomy】skin→subcutaneous tissue→tendon of abductor pollicis longus→tendon of brachioradialis→pronator quadratus. The superficial layer have cephalic vein, nervus cutaneus brachii lateralis and superficial branch of radial nerve, the deep layer have branches of radial artery and vein.

【Properties】Open the inhibited lung－energy and alleviate pain, dredge conception vessel.

【Indications】headache caused by external factors, neck rigidity, cough, asthma, swelling and pain in the throat, deviated mouth and toothache.

【Needling method】Puncture obliquely upward the elbow 0.3～0.5 cun.

8. 经渠（LU 8），经穴
Jingqu（LU 8), Jing－River Point

【释义】经，经过；渠，渠道。经脉通过的渠道。

【定位】在前臂掌面桡侧，桡骨茎突与桡动脉之间凹陷处，腕横纹上 1 寸（图 3－7）。

【解剖】皮肤→皮下组织→肱桡肌腱尺侧缘→旋前方肌。浅层布有前臂外侧皮神经和桡神经浅支；深层有桡动、静脉。

【功用】疏调肺气。

【主治】咳嗽，气喘，咽喉肿痛，手腕痛。

【操作】避开桡动脉，直刺 0.3～0.5 寸。

【Meaning】Jing, to pass; qu, ditch. A ditch where the meridian passes.

【Location】On the radial side of the palmar surface of the forearm, 1 cun above the cubital crease, in the depression between the styloid process of the radius and the radial artery (Fig 3 –7).

【Regional anatomy】skin→subcutaneous tissue→the ulnar aspect of tendon of brachioradialis→pronator quadratus. The superficial layer have nervus cutaneus brachii lateralis and superficial branch of radial nerve, the deep layer have radial artery and vein.

【Properties】Regulate the flow of lung qi.

【Indications】Cough, asthma, swelling and pain in the throat, pain in the wrist.

【Needling method】Keep off radial artery, puncture perpendicularly 0. 3 ~0. 5 cun.

9. 太渊（LU 9），输穴，原穴，八会穴（脉会）
Taiyuan (LU 9), Shu - Stream Point, Yuan - Source Point, One of the Eight Influential Points (Influential Point of Vessel)

【释义】太，甚大；渊，深渊。太，有旺盛的意思。穴位局部脉气旺盛如深渊。

【定位】在腕掌侧横纹桡侧，桡动脉搏动处（图 3 –7）。

【解剖】皮肤→皮下组织→桡侧腕屈肌腱与拇长展肌腱之间。浅层布有前臂外侧皮神经、桡神经浅支和桡动脉掌浅支；深层有桡动、静脉等。

【功用】理气止咳。

【主治】外感，咳嗽，气喘，咳血，胸痛，咽喉肿痛，腕臂痛，无脉症。

【操作】避开桡动脉，直刺 0. 3 ~0. 5 寸。

【Meaning】Tai, great; yuan, deep pool. Tai means abundance. The qi of meridian in the local part of this point is abundant as in a deep pool.

【Location】At the radial end of the crease of the wrist, where the pulsation of radial artery is palpable (Fig 3 –7).

【Regional anatomy】skin→subcutaneous tissue→between tendon of flexor carpi radialis and tendon of abductor pollicis longus. The superficial layer have nervus cutaneus antebrachii lateralis, superficial branch of radial nerve, and superficial palmar branch of radial artery, the deep layer have radial artery and vein.

【Properties】Regulate vital energy and alleviate cough.

【Indications】External contraction, cough, asthma, hemoptysis, pain in the chest, swelling and pain in the throat, the diseases of the radius and wrist , acrotism.

【Needling method】Keep off radial artery, puncture perpendicularly 0. 3 ~0. 5 cun.

10. 鱼际（LU 10），荥穴
Yuji (LU 10), Ying - Spring Point

【释义】鱼，鱼腹；际，边际；拇短展肌隆起似鱼腹，穴位位于它的边际。鱼际现已用

作现代解剖学名词。

【定位】在手拇指本节（第 1 掌指关节）后凹陷处，约当第 1 掌骨中点桡侧，赤白肉际处（图 3－7）。

【解剖】皮肤→皮下组织→拇短展肌→拇对掌肌→拇短屈肌。浅层有正中神经掌皮支及桡神经浅支；深层有正中神经肌支和尺神经肌支等结构。

【功用】通调肺气，清热利咽。

【主治】咳嗽，哮喘，咳血，咽喉肿痛，发热。

【操作】直刺 0.5～0.8 寸。

【Meaning】Yu, fish; ji, border. Abductor pollicis brevis in the palm is prominent as fish, the point is located just at its border. Yuji (thenar) is used as an anatomical word at present.

【Location】In the depression proximal to the 1st metacarpophalangeal joint, on the side of the midpoint of the 1st metacarpal bone, and on the junction of the red and white skin (Fig 3－7).

【Regional anatomy】skin→subcutaneous tissue→abductor pollicis brevis→opponens pollicis→flexor pollicis brevis. The superficial layer have ramus cutaneus volaris of median nerve and superficial branch of radial nerve, the deep layer have median nerve muscular branches, ulnar nerve muscular branches. etc.

【Properties】Regulate the flow of lung qi, clear hot detoxify and benefit pharynx.

【Indications】cough, asthma, hemoptysis, swelling and pain in the throat, and febrile disaese.

【Needling method】Puncture perpendicularly 0.5～0.8 cun.

11. 少商（LU 11），井穴
Shaoshang (LU 11), Jing - Well Point

【释义】少，幼小；商，五音之一，属金。少有少量的意思，肺属金，在五音为商，此为肺经末穴，其气小而不充。

【定位】在手拇指末节桡侧，距指甲角 0.1 寸（图 3－7）。

【解剖】皮肤→皮下组织→指甲根。有正中神经的指掌侧固有神经之指背支和拇主要动、静脉与第 1 掌背动、静脉分支所形成的动、静网。

【功用】清肺利咽，泄热醒神。

【主治】咽喉肿痛，发热，咳嗽，失音，鼻衄，昏迷，癫狂，指肿，麻木。

【操作】浅刺 0.1～0.2 寸，或点刺出血。

【Meaning】Shao, immaturity; shang, one of the Five Sounds, pertaining to metal.

【Location】On the radial aspect of the end of the thumb, 0.1 cun posterior to the corner of the nail (Fig 3－7).

【Regional anatomy】skin→subcutaneous tissue→the corner of the nail. There are dorsal branch of nervi digitales palmares proprii of the median nerve, the arterial and venous network formed by the palmar digital arteries and veins, and the branches of the first volardorsal artery and vein.

【Properties】 Clear away heat from the lung, benefit the throat, purge heat and restore consciousness.

【Indications】 Swelling and pain in the throat, febrile disease, cough, obmutescence, epistaxis, unconsciousness, manic and depressive psychosis, swollen and numbness fingers.

【Needling method】 Puncture superficially 0.1 ~0.2 cun, or prick to cause bleeding.

复习思考题
Review Questions

1. 手太阴肺经与哪些脏腑、组织器官有联系？

What are the organs and tissues connected with the lung meridian of hand – tanyin?

2. 为什么列缺穴可治头面五官疾病？

Why is Lieque（LU 7）indicated for diseases of the head and the five sense organs?

3. 肺经的五输穴是哪几个？

What are the five – shu points of the lung meridian?

4. 尺泽、孔最、太渊穴属哪种特定穴？如何定位？可治何病？

Which specific point is of Chize（LU 5）, Kongzui（LU 6）and Taiyuan（LU 9）respectively? How do you locate them and what are their indications?

5. 中府、云门穴针刺时应注意什么？为什么？

What are the needling precautions of Zhongfu（LU 1）and Yunmen（LU 2）? Why?

第四章　手阳明经络与腧穴
Meridian and Collateral and Its Acupoints of Hand - Yangming

第一节　手阳明经络
Meridian and Collateral of Hand - Yangming

一、手阳明经脉
Meridian of Hand - Yangming

（一）经脉循行
The Course of Meridian

手阳明大肠经，起始于食指末端，沿食指桡侧缘，经第1、2掌骨间，进入两筋（拇长伸肌腱和拇短伸肌腱）之间，沿前臂外侧前缘，上肘外侧，经上臂外侧前缘，上肩，出肩峰部前边，上行颈部交会督脉，从缺盆部进入胸腔，联络于肺脏，通过横膈，属于大肠。颈部支脉，从缺盆部上行颈旁，上面颊，进入下齿，出来夹口旁，交会于人中部，左脉向右，右脉向左，上夹鼻翼两旁，连接足阳明胃经（图4-1）。

《灵枢·经脉》原文："大肠手阳明之脉，起于大指次指之端，循指上廉，出合谷两骨之间，上入两筋之中，循臂上廉，入肘外廉，上臑外前廉，上肩，出髃骨之前廉，上出于柱骨之会上，下入缺盆，络肺，下膈，属大肠。其支者，从缺盆上颈，贯颊，入下齿中；还出夹口，交人中，左之右，右之左，上夹鼻孔"（图4-1）。

The large intestine meridian of hand - yangming starts from the tip of the index finger, proceeding upward along the radial side of the index finger, through the interspace of the first and second metacarpal bones and entering the depression between the two tendons (extensor pollicis longus and brevis). It then goes upwards along the lateral anterior aspect of the forearm and enters the lateral side of the elbow. From the elbow it proceeds upwards along the lateral anterior aspect of the upper arm and reaches the highest point of the shoulder joint. From there, it crosses the anterior border of the acromion upwards and reaches the Governor Vessel. It then enters the supraclavicular fossa and descends to connect with the Lung Meridian. It continues to travel through the diaphragm further, where it enters the large intestine, its pertaining organ. Its branch splits from the supraclavicular fossa and runs upwards along the neck, passes through the cheek and enters the gums of the lower teeth. It then curves around the corner of the mouth and intersects at the philtrum with the opposite side of the same channel, with this intersection the channel on the right hand proceeds to the left while the left to right. It finally terminates on the lateral side of the nose (Fig 4 –1).

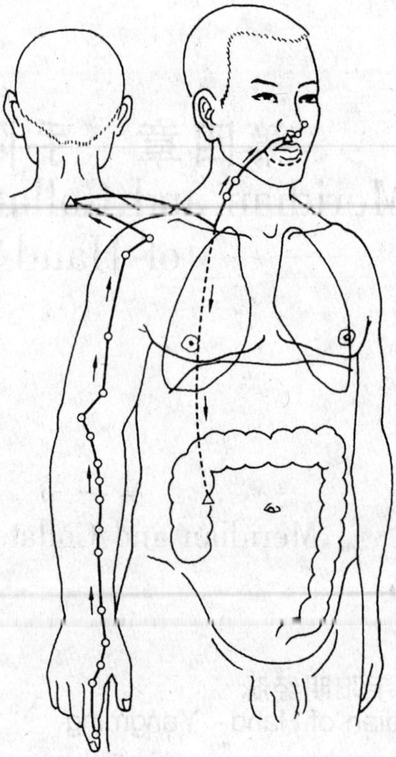

图例 ——本经有穴通路 ……本经无穴通路

Note ——Pathway with points ……Pathway without points

图 4 –1 手阳明大肠经循行示意图

Fig 4 –1 The course of the large intestine meridian of hand – yangming

(二) 经脉病候
The Syndromes of Meridian

本经异常就出现下列病症：齿痛，面颊部肿胀。

本经穴主治有关"津"方面所发生的病症：眼睛昏黄，口干，鼻流清涕或出血，喉咙痛，肩前、上臂部痛，食指疼痛、活动不利。

当气盛有余时，经脉所过部位发热、肿胀；而气虚不足时，则发冷、战栗，难以复温。

Disorder of the meridian causes: toothache and swelling of the cheeks.

Diseases of the large intestine and disorder of body fluid metabolism: icteric sclera, dry mouth, cold sensation of nose, nasal discharge or epistaxis, pharyngitis, pain along the anterior border of the shoulder and the upper arm, and limitation of the index finger due to pain.

Those whose qi of the meridian is excessive, probably suffer from heat and swelling of the regions where meridian passes; while those whose qi of the meridian deficient, often suffer from chilly sensation or severe shivering.

二、手阳明络脉
Collateral of Hand - Taiyin

手阳明络脉，名偏历。在腕关节后 3 寸处分出，走向手太阴经脉；其支脉向上沿着臂膊，经过肩髃部位，上行到下颌角处，遍布于牙齿根部；其支脉进入耳中，与耳目所聚集的许多经脉（宗脉）会合（图 4－2）。

其病症：实证，见龋齿痛、耳聋；虚证，见齿冷、胸膈痹阻不畅通，可取手阳明络穴治疗。

It starts from Pianli（LI 6）and joins the lung meridian of hand－taiyin three cun above the wrist. Another branch runs along the arm to Jianyu（LI 15）, crosses the jaw and extends to the teeth. Still another branch derives at the jaw and enters the ear to join the zong meridian（Fig 4－2）

Its repletion disorders are dental caries and deafness. Its vacuity disorders are cold teeth and numb and blockaded gums. Use this point.

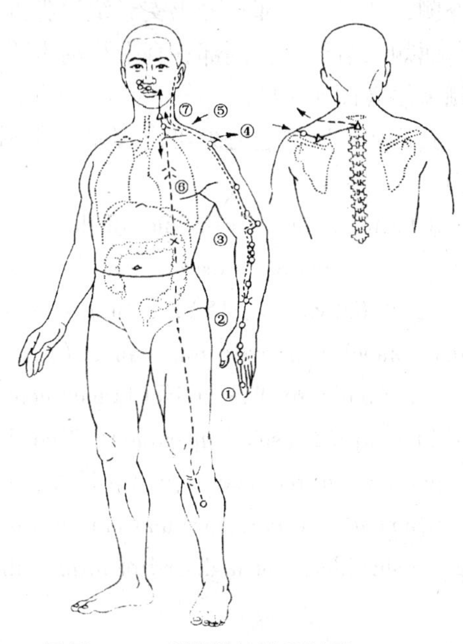

图例 ——手阳明经脉循行线
……手阳明络脉循行线

Note ——The course of the meridian of hand－yangming
……The course of the collateral of hand－yangming

图 4－2 手阳明经脉、络脉循行示意图

Fig 4－2 The course of the meridian and collateral of hand－yangming

三、手阳明经别
Divergent Meridian of Hand - Yangming

手阳明经别，在肩上部肩髃穴处分出，从第 7 颈椎处进入体腔，下行到达大肠，归属于肺脏，向上沿喉咙，浅出于缺盆部，脉气仍旧流入手阳明本经（图 4－3）。

After deriving from the large intestine meridian on the hand, it continues upward, crossing the arm and shoulder to reach the breast. A branch separates at the top of the shoulder and enters the spine at the nape. It runs downward to connect with the large intestine and lung. Another branch runs upward from the shoulder along the throat and emerges at the supraclavicular fossa; there it rejoins the large intestine meridian（Fig 4－3）.

四、手阳明经筋
Muscular Region of Hand - Yangming

手阳明经筋，起始于第 2 手指桡侧端，结于腕背部，向上沿前臂，结于肘外侧，上经上臂外侧，结于肩髃部；分出支经绕肩胛处，夹脊柱两旁；直行的经筋从肩髃部上走颈；分支走向面颊，结于鼻旁颧部；直上行的走手太阳经筋前方，上左侧额角者，结络于头部向下至右侧下颔（图4－4）。

其病症：所经过之处可出现牵扯不适、酸痛及痉挛，肩关节不能高举，颈不能向两侧转动。

It begins from the extremity of the index finger and knots at the dorsum of the wrist, then it goes upward along the forearm, and knots at the lateral aspect of the elbow. Continuing up the arm, it knots at Jianyu（LI 15）, a branch moves around the scapula and attaches to the spine. The straight branch continues from Jianyu（LI 15）to the neck, where a branch separates and knots at the side of the nose. The straight branch continues upward and emerges in front of muscular meridian of hand－taiyang（small intestine）. Then it crosses over the head, connecting at the mandible on the opposite side the face（Fig 4－4）.

Symptoms: Contracture and pain in the region of the path of this muscle region, failure of raising the shoulder joint high and of turning the neck round.

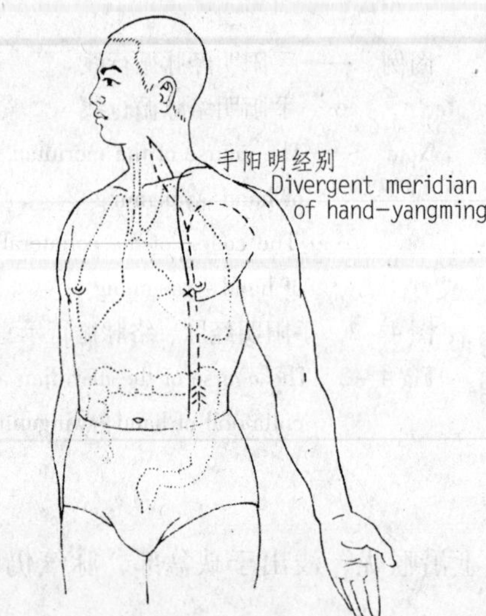

图4－3 手阳明经别循行示意图
Fig 4－3 The course of the divergent meridian of hand－yangming

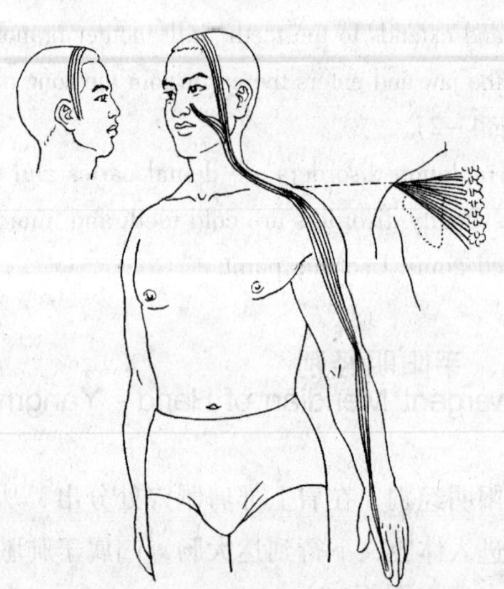

图4－4 手阳明经筋分布示意图
Fig 4－4 The course of the muscular region of hand－yangming

第二节 手阳明腧穴
Acupoints of Hand－Yangming

本经左右各20个穴位，首穴为商阳，末穴为迎香（图4－5）。

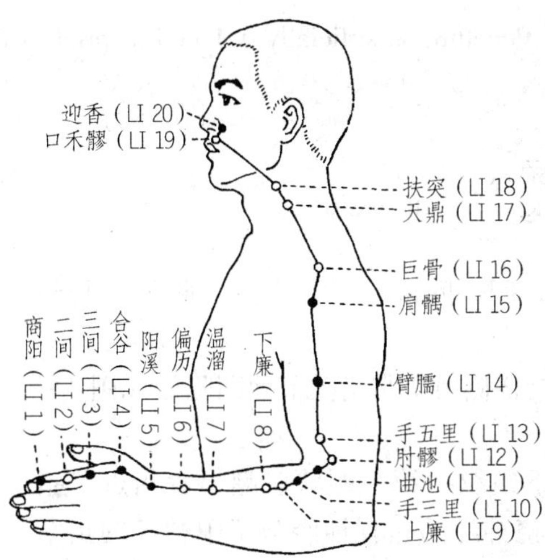

图例 ● 常用腧穴 ○ 一般腧穴

Note ● Main point ○ Common point

图 4－5 手阳明大肠经腧穴总图

Fig 4－5 Points of the large intestine meridian of hand－yangming

1. 商阳（LI 1），井穴
Shangyang（LI 1），Jing－Well Point

【释义】商，五音之一，属金；阳，阴阳之阳。大肠属金，在音为商；阳，指阳经。

【定位】食指末节桡侧，距指甲角 0.1 寸（图 4－6）。

【解剖】皮肤→皮下组织→指甲根。有正中神经的指掌侧固有神经之指背支和食指桡侧动脉与第一掌背动脉分支所形成的动、静脉网。

【功用】泄热，利咽，开窍。

【主治】咽喉肿痛，齿痛，昏迷，中暑，热病。

【操作】浅刺 0.1 寸，或点刺放血。

【Meaning】Shang, one of the Five Sounds, pertaining to metal; yang, yang of yin－yang. The large intestine pertains to metal and is ascribed to shang sound. yang implies the yang meridian.

【Location】0.1 cun lateral to the radial nail corner of the index finger（Fig 4－6）.

【Regional anatomy】: Skin→subcutaneous tissue→the root of the nail. There are the dorsal digital branches of the proper palmar digital nerve of the median nerve, the arteriovenous network formed by the arteries and veins in the radial side of the index finger and the branches of the first dorsal metacarpal artery and vein in this area.

【Properties】Discharge heat, soothe the throat and open the orifices.

【Indications】Swollen and sore throat, toothache, loss of consciousness, sunstroke, febrile disease.

【Needling method】Puncture superficially 0.1 cun or prick with a three - edged needle to induce bleeding.

2. 二间（LI 2），荥穴
Erjian（LI 2），Ying - Spring Point

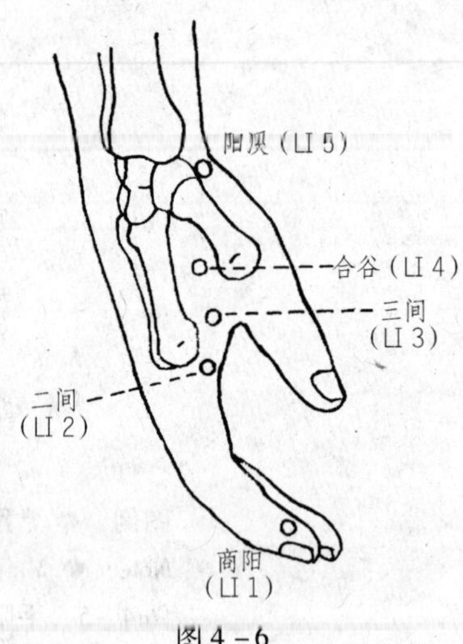

图 4 – 6
Fig 4 – 6

【释义】二，第二；间，间隙。间，指穴。此为大肠经第二穴。

【定位】微握拳食指桡侧第 2 掌指关节前凹陷处（图 4 – 6）。

【解剖】皮肤→皮下组织→第一蚓状肌腱→食指近节指骨基底部。浅层神经由桡神经的指背神经与正中神经的指掌侧固有神经双重分布。血管有第一掌背和食指桡侧动、静脉的分支。

【功用】清热，利咽，明目。

【主治】鼻衄，齿痛，目赤痛，咽喉肿痛，口眼㖞斜，热病。

【操作】直刺 0.2 ~ 0.3 寸。

【Meaning】Er, two, second; jian, clearance. Jian, indicates the point. This is the second point of the Large Intestine Meridian.

【Location】When a loose fist is formed, it is on the radial side of the index finger, in the depression distal to the 2nd metacarpophalangeal joint（Fig 4 – 6）.

【Regional anatomy】Skin→subcutaneous tissue→the 1st lumbrical muscle tendon→the base of the proximal phalanx of the index finger. In the superficial layer, there is the dorsal digital nerve of the radial nerve, the proper palmar digital nerve of the median nerve, the branches of the 1st dorsal metacarpal artery and vein and the branches of the radial artery and vein of the index finger.

【Properties】Clear heat, soothe the throat and improve eyesight.

【Indications】Nosebleed, toothache, conjunctival congestion, sore throat, deviated mouth and eye, febrile disease.

【Needling method】Puncture perpendicularly 0.2 ~ 0.3 cun.

3. 三间（LI 3），输穴
Sanjian（LI 3），Shu - Stream Point

【释义】三，第三；间，间隙。间，指穴。此为大肠经第三穴。

【定位】微握拳，食指桡侧，第 2 掌指关节后凹陷处（图 4 – 6）。

【解剖】皮肤→皮下组织→第一骨间背侧肌→第一蚓状肌与第二掌骨之间→食指的指浅、深屈肌腱与第一骨间掌侧肌之间。浅层神经由桡神经的指背神经与正中神经的指掌侧固有神经双重分布。血管有手背静脉网，第一掌背动、静脉和食指桡侧动、静脉的分支。深层有尺神经深支和正中神经的肌支。

【功用】清热，利咽，止痛。

【主治】齿痛，咽喉肿痛，身热。

【操作】直刺0.3~0.5寸。

【Meaning】San, three, 3rd; jian, clearance. Jian, indicates the point. This is the 3rd point of the Large Intestine Meridian.

【Location】With a loose fist, on the radial side of the index finger, in the depression proximal to the 2nd metacarpophalangeal joint (Fig 4-6).

【Regional anatomy】Skin→subcutaneous tissue→the 1st dorsal interosseous muscle→between the 1st lumbrical muscle and 2nd metacarpal bone→between the tendons of the superficial and deep flexor muscles of the index finger and the 1st palmar interosseus muscle. In the superficial layer, there is the dorsal digital nerve of the radial nerve and the proper palmar digital nerve of the median nerve, the dorsal venous network of the hand, the branches of the 1st dorsal metacarpal artery and vein and the branches of the radial artery and vein of the index finger. In the deep layer, there are the deep branches of the ulnar nerve and the muscular branches of the median nerve.

【Properties】Clear heat, soothe the throat and relieve pain.

【Indications】Toothache, swollen and sore throat, fever.

【Needling method】Puncture perpendicularly 0.3~0.5 cun.

4. 合谷（LI 4），原穴
Hegu (LI 4), Yuan-Source Point

【释义】合，结合；谷，山谷。穴在第1、2掌骨之间，局部呈山谷样凹陷。

【定位】手背，第1、2掌骨间，当第2掌骨桡侧中点处（图4-6）。

【解剖】皮肤→皮下组织→第一骨间背侧肌→拇收肌。浅层布有桡神经浅支、有手背静脉网桡侧部和第一掌背动、静脉的分支或属支。深层分布有尺神经深支的分支等。

【功用】疏散风邪，清热解表，开窍止痛，通调胃肠，调经引产，通经活络。

【主治】①头痛，口眼㖞斜，齿痛，目赤肿痛，鼻衄，耳聋。②发热恶寒，多汗，无汗。③经闭，滞产。④上肢痿痹、不遂，手指挛痛。

【操作】直刺0.5~1.0寸；孕妇禁针。

【Meaning】He, junction; gu, valley. This point is between the 1st and the 2nd metacarpal bones, location of the point is depressed as a valley.

【Location】On the dorsum of the hand, between the 1st and 2nd metacarpal bones, approximately in the middle of the 2nd metacarpal bone on the radial side (Fig 4-6).

【Regional anatomy】Skin→subcutaneous tissue→the 1st dorsal interosseous muscle→the abductor muscle of the thumb. In the superficial layer, there are the superficial branches of the radial nerve, the radial part of the dorsal venous network of the hand and the branches or tributaries of the

1st dorsal metacarpal artery and vein. In the deep layer, there are the deep branches of the ulnar nerve.

【Properties】Disperse wind, clear heat and resolve superficies, open the orifices and relieve pain, harmonize intestines and stomach, regulate menstruation and induce labor, unblock the meridian and activate collaterals.

【Indications】①Headache, deviated mouth and eye, toothache, conjunctival congestion, nosebleed, deafness. ②Fever and aversion to cold with or without sweating. ③Amenorrhea, delayed labour. ④Paralysis of the forearm, unable to move voluntarily, painful wrist and forearm.

【Needling method】Puncture perpendicularly 0.5 ~ 1.0 cun. Do not use this point in pregnant women.

5. 阳溪（LI 5），经穴
Yangxi（LI 5），Jing - River Point

【释义】阳，阴阳之阳；溪，沟溪。阳，指阳经。局部呈凹陷，好像山间沟溪。

【定位】腕背横纹桡侧，拇短伸肌腱与拇长伸肌腱之间的凹陷中（图 4 - 6）。

【解剖】皮肤→皮下组织→拇长伸肌腱与拇短伸肌腱之间→桡侧腕长伸肌腱的前方。浅层布有头静脉和桡神经浅支。深层分布桡动、静脉的分支或属支。

【功用】清热祛风，通利关节。

【主治】手腕痛，头痛，齿痛，咽喉肿痛。

【操作】直刺 0.3 ~ 0.5 寸。

【Meaning】Yang, yang of yin - yang; xi, brook. Yang, refers to the yang meridian. The local depression is like a brook in the mountains.

【Location】On the transverse crease of the radial side of the wrist, between the hollow of the tendons of the extensor pollicis longus and brevis（Fig 4 - 6）

【Regional anatomy】Skin→subcutaneous tissue→between the short extensor muscle tendon of the thumb and the long extensor muscle tendon of the thumb→the front part of the long radial extensor muscle of the wrist. In the superficial layer, there are the branches of the cephalic vein and the superficial branches of the radial nerve. In the deep layer, there are the branches or tributaries of the radial artery and vein.

【Properties】Clear heat, dispel wind and disinhibit joints.

【Indications】Pain in the wrist, headache, toothache, swollen and sore throat.

【Needling method】Puncture perpendicularly 0.3 ~ 0.5 cun.

6. 偏历（LI 6），络穴
Pianli（LI 6），Luo - Connecting Point

【释义】偏，偏离；历，行径。大肠经从这里分出络脉，偏行肺经。

【定位】屈肘，在阳溪与曲池连线上，腕横纹上3寸（图4-7）。

【解剖】皮肤→皮下组织→拇短伸肌→桡侧腕长伸肌腱→拇长展肌腱。浅层布有头静脉的属支，前臂外侧皮神经和桡神经浅支。深层有桡神经的骨间后神经分支。

【功用】疏风解表，调水道，通脉络。

【主治】鼻衄，耳鸣，耳聋，手臂酸痛，水肿。

【操作】直刺或斜刺0.3~0.5寸。

【Meaning】Pian, divergence; li, pathway. The large intestine meridian separates a collateral from here and diverges to the lung.

【Location】With the elbow flexed, on the line linking the Yangxi (LI 5) and Quchi (LI 11) points, 3 cun above the wrist crease (Fig 4-7).

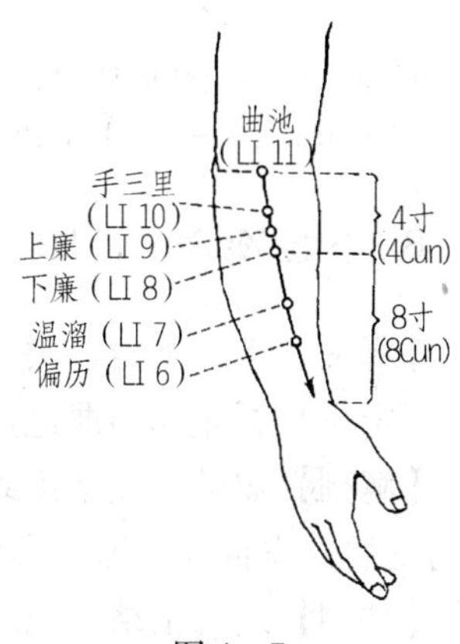

图4-7
Fig 4-7

【Regional anatomy】Skin→subcutaneous tissue→the short extensor muscle of the thumb→the long radial extensor muscle tendon of the wrist→the long abductor muscle tendon of the thumb. In the superficial layer, there are the tributaries of the cephalic vein, the lateral cutaneous nerve of the forearm and the superficial branches of the radial nerve. In the deep layer, there are the branches of the posterior interosseous nerve of the radial nerve.

【Properties】Disperse wind and resolve superficies, regulate waterways and free the collateral vessels.

【Indications】Nosebleed, tinnitus, deafness, pain in the forearm, edema.

【Needling method】Puncture perpendicularly or obliquely 0.3 ~ 0.5 cun.

7. 温溜（LI 7），郄穴
Wenliu (LI 7), Xi - Cleft Point

【释义】温，温暖；溜，流通；本穴有温通经脉之功，善治肘臂寒痛。

【定位】屈肘，在阳溪与曲池连线上，腕横纹上5寸（图4-7）。

【解剖】皮肤→皮下组织→桡侧腕长伸肌腱→桡侧腕短伸肌腱。浅层布有头静脉，前臂外侧皮神经和前臂后皮神经。深层在桡侧腕长伸肌和桡侧腕短伸肌腱之前有桡神经浅支。

【功用】清邪热，理肠胃。

【主治】头痛，面肿，咽喉肿痛，肩背酸痛，肠鸣腹痛。

【操作】直刺0.5~1.0寸。

【Meaning】Wen, to warm; liu, circulation. This point is able to warm the meridian and promote its circulation, and is good for treating cold - pain of the elbow and arm.

【Location】With the elbow flexed, on the line linking the Yangxi (LI 5) and Quchi (LI 11) points, 5 cun above the wrist crease (Fig 4-7).

【Regional anatomy】Skin→subcutaneous tissue→the long radial extensor muscle tendon of the wrist→the short radial extensor muscle of the wrist. In the superficial layer, there are the cephalic vein, the lateral cutaneous nerve of the forearm and the posterior cutaneous nerve of the forearm. In the deep layer, there are the superficial branches of the radial nerve before the tendons of the long and short radial extensor muscle of the wrist.

【Properties】Clear evil heat, harmonize intestines and stomach.

【Indications】Headache, swelling of the face, sore throat, aching of shoulders and back; abdominal pain, borborygmus.

【Needling method】Puncture perpendicularly 0.5 ~ 1.0 cun.

8. 下廉 Xialian (LI 8)

【释义】下，下方；廉，边缘。穴在前臂背面近桡侧缘，上廉穴之下。

【定位】在阳溪与曲池连线上，肘横纹下4寸（图4-7）。

【解剖】皮肤→皮下组织→肱桡肌→桡侧腕短伸肌→旋后肌。浅层布有前臂外侧皮神经和前臂后侧皮神经。深层有桡神经深支的分支。

【功用】通经活络，调理肠胃。

【主治】肘臂痛麻，上肢不遂，腹痛，腹胀。

【操作】直刺0.5~0.8寸。

【Meaning】Xia, inferior; lian, edge. The point is inferior to Shanglian at the dorsal side of the forearm, close to the radial aspect.

【Location】On the line linking the Yangxi (LI 5) and Quchi (LI 11) points, 5 cun below the cubital crease (Fig 4-7).

【Regional anatomy】Skin→subcutaneous tissue→branchioradial muscle→the short radial extensor muscle of the wrist→supinator muscle. In the superficial layer, there are the lateral and posterior cutaneous nerves of the forearm. In the deep layer, there are the deep branches of the radial nerve.

【Properties】Unblock the meridian and activate collaterals, harmonize intestines and stomach.

【Indications】Pain in the elbow and arm, paralysis of the forearm, abdominal distention, abdominal pain.

【Needling method】Puncture perpendicularly 0.5 ~ 0.8 cun.

9. 上廉 Shanglian (LI 9)

【释义】上，上方；廉，边缘。穴在前臂背面近桡侧缘，下廉穴之上。

【定位】在阳溪与曲池连线上，肘横纹下3寸（图4-7）。

【解剖】皮肤→皮下组织→桡侧腕长伸肌腱后方→桡侧腕短伸肌→旋后肌→拇长展肌。浅层布有前臂外侧皮神经、前臂后皮神经和浅静脉。深层有桡神经深支穿旋后肌。

【功用】舒筋通络，散寒祛湿。

【主治】肘臂痛麻，上肢不遂，腹痛，肠鸣。

【操作】直刺0.5~1.0寸。

【Meaning】Shang, superior; lian, edge. The point is superior to Xialian (LI 8) at the dorsal side of the forearm, close to the radial aspect.

【Location】On the line linking the Yangxi (LI 5) and Quchi (LI 11) points, 3 cun below the cubital crease (Fig 4-7).

【Regional anatomy】Skin→subcutaneous tissue→the long radial extensor muscle tendon of the wrist→the short radial extensor muscle of the wrist→supinator muscle→abductor pollicis longus. In the superficial layer, there are the lateral and posterior cutaneous nerves of the forearm and superficial vein. In the deep layer, there are the deep branches of the radial nerve.

【Properties】Relax sinews and activate collaterals, diffuse the cold and dispel dampness.

【Indications】Pain and numbness in the elbow and arm, paralysis of the forearm, abdominal pain, borborygmus.

【Needling method】Puncture perpendicularly 0.5~1.0cun.

10. 手三里 Shousanli (LI 10)

【释义】手，上肢；三，数词；里，古代有以里为寸之说。穴在上肢，若直臂取穴，当曲池穴下3寸。

【定位】在阳溪与曲池连线上，肘横纹下2寸（图4-7）。

【解剖】皮肤→皮下组织→桡侧腕长伸肌→桡侧腕短伸肌→指伸肌的前方→旋后肌。浅层布有前臂外侧皮神经、前臂后皮神经。深层有桡侧返动、静脉的分支或属支及桡神经深支。

【功用】通经活络，调理肠胃。

【主治】上肢不遂，肘臂痛，齿痛，颊肿，腹痛，腹泻。

【操作】直刺0.5~0.8寸。

【Meaning】Shou, arm; san, three; li, taken as cun in ancient times. The point is on the forearm. With the arm outstretched, the point is 3cun below Quchi.

【Location】On the line linking the Yangxi (LI 5) and Quchi (LI 11) points, 2 cun below the cubital crease (Fig 4-7).

【Regional anatomy】Skin→subcutaneous tissue→the long radial extensor muscle of the wrist→the short radial extensor muscle of the wrist→the front part of the extensor muscle of the fingers→the supinator muscle. In the superficial layer, there are the lateral and posterior cutaneous nerves of the forearm. In the deep layer, there are branches tributaries of the radial recurrent artery and vein, at the deep branches of the radial nerve.

【Properties】Unblock the meridian and activate collaterals, harmonize intestines and stomach.

【Indications】Paralysis of the forearm, pain and numbness in the elbow and arm, toothache, swollen cheek, abdominal pain, diarrhea.

【Needling method】Puncture perpendicularly 0. 5 ~0. 8 cun.

11. 曲池（LI 11），合穴 Quchi（LI 11），He - Sea Point

【释义】曲，弯曲；池，池塘。屈肘，肘桡侧纹头凹陷如池，穴在其中。

【定位】屈肘，肘横纹外侧端，当尺泽与肱骨外上髁连线中点（图 4 –7）。

【解剖】皮肤→皮下组织→桡侧腕长伸肌和桡侧腕短伸肌→肱桡肌。浅层布有头静脉的属支和前臂后皮神经。深层有桡神经，桡侧返动、静脉和桡侧副动、静脉间的吻合支。

【功用】疏风清热，调理肠胃，通经活络，运行气血。

【主治】①咽喉肿痛，齿痛，目赤痛。②热病。③风疹，湿疹。④高血压。⑤上肢不遂，肘臂疼痛无力。⑥癫狂。⑦腹痛腹泻。

【操作】直刺0. 8 ~1. 5 寸。

【Meaning】Qu, crooked; chi, pond. When the arm is flexed, a depression at the elbow is like a pool and the point is inside it.

【Location】With the elbow flexed, at the lateral end of the transverse cubital crease, midway between Chize（LU 5）and the lateral epicondyle of the humerus（Fig 4 –7）.

【Regional anatomy】Skin→subcutaneous tissue→the long radial extensor muscle of the wrist and short radial extensor muscle of the wrist→the branchioradial muscle. In the superficial layer, there are the tributaries of the cephalic vein and the posterior cutaneous nerve of the forearm. In the deep layer, there are the radial nerve and the anastomotic branches of the radial recurrent artery and vein, the radial collateral artery and vein.

【Properties】Disperse wind and clear heat, harmonize intestines and stomach, unblock the meridian and activate collaterals, circulate qi and blood.

【Indications】①Swollen and sore throat, toothache, redness and pain in the eyes. ②Febrile disease. ③Rubella, eczema. ④Hypertension. ⑤Paralysis of the arm, pain and weakness in the elbow. ⑥Psychosis. ⑦Abdominal pain, diarrhea.

【Needling method】Puncture perpendicularly 0. 8 ~1. 5 cun.

12. 肘髎 Zhouliao（LI 12）

【释义】肘，肘部；髎，骨隙；穴在肘部，靠近骨隙处。

【定位】屈肘，曲池上方 1 寸，当肱骨边缘处（图 4 –8）。

【解剖】皮肤→皮下组织→肱桡肌→肱肌。浅层布有前臂后皮神经等结构，深层有桡侧副动、静脉的分支或属支。

【功用】疏利肢节。

【主治】肘臂疼痛，挛急，麻木。

【操作】直刺0.5～1.0寸。

【Meaning】Zhou, elbow; liao, foremen. The point is at the elbow and close to foramen.

【Location】With the elbow flexed, 1 cun above the Quchi (LI 11) point, on the border of the humerus (Fig 4－8)

【Regional anatomy】Skin→subcutaneous tissue→the branchioradial muscle→brachial muscle. In the superficial layer, there is the posterior cutaneous nerve of the forearm. In the deep layer, there are the branches or tributaries of the radial collateral artery and vein.

【Properties】Disinhibit the elbow joint.

【Indications】Aching, numbness and spasm of the elbow and arm.

【Needling method】Puncture perpendicularly 0.5～1.0 cun.

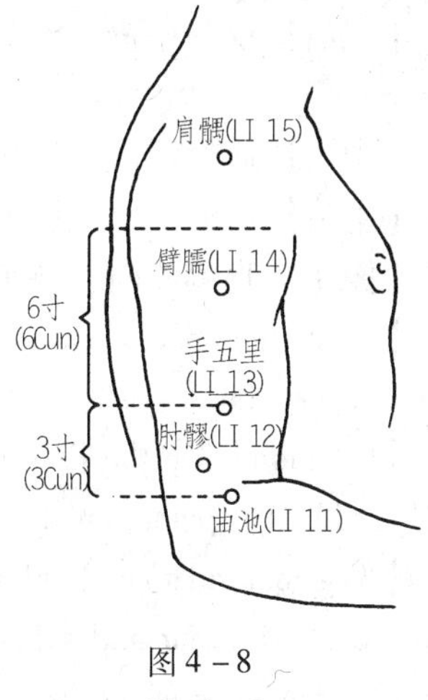

图4－8

Fig 4－8

13. 手五里 Shouwuli (LI 13)

【释义】手，上肢；五，数词；里，古代有以里为寸之说。穴在上肢，当天府穴下5寸。

【定位】在曲池与肩髃连线上，曲池穴上3寸（图4－8）。

【解剖】皮肤→皮下组织→肱肌。浅层布有臂外侧下皮神经和前臂后皮神经。深层有桡侧副动、静脉和桡神经。

【功用】通经活络，理气散结。

【主治】肘臂挛痛；瘰疬。

【操作】直刺0.5～1.0寸。

【Meaning】Shou, arm; wu, five; li, taken as cun in ancient times. The point is on the upper arm, 5 cun below Tianfu.

【Location】On the line linking Jianyu (LI 15) and Quchi (LI 11) points, 3 cun above the Quchi (LI 11) point (Fig 4－8).

【Regional anatomy】Skin→subcutaneous tissue－brachial muscle. In the superficial layer, there are the lateral inferior cutaneous nerve of the arm and the posterior cutaneous nerve of the forearm. In the deep layer, there are the radial collateral artery and vein and the radial nerve.

【Properties】Unblock the meridian and activate collaterals, regulate qi and dissipate binds.

【Indications】Spasm and pain of the elbow and arm; scrofula (use another term).

【Needling method】Puncture perpendicularly 0.5～1.0 cun.

14. 臂臑 Binao (LI 14)

【释义】臂，多指上臂；臑，臂部肌肉隆起点。穴在上臂肌肉隆起点。

【定位】在曲池与肩髃连线上，曲池上7寸，三角肌止点处（图4-8）。

【解剖】皮肤→皮下组织→三角肌。浅层布有臂外侧上、下皮神经。深层有肱动脉的肌支。

【功用】通经活络，清热明目。

【主治】肩臂痛，上肢不遂；目疾；瘰疬。

【操作】直刺或向上斜刺0.8~1.5寸。

【Meaning】Bi, arm; nao, muscle prominence of the arm. The point is on the muscle prominence of the arm.

【Location】On the line linking Jianyu (LI 15) and Quchi (LI 11) points, 7 cun above the Quchi (LI 11) point, at the distal end of the deltoid muscle (Fig 4-8).

【Regional anatomy】Skin→subcutaneous tissue→deltoid muscle. In the superficial layer, there are the inferior and superior lateral cutaneous nerves of the arm. In the deep layer, there are muscular branches of the branchial artery.

【Properties】Unblock the meridian and activate collaterals, clear heat and improve eyesight.

【Indications】Painful upper arm and shoulder, impaired arm movement; eye diseases; scrofula.

【Needling method】Puncture perpendicularly or obliquely upwards 0.8 ~ 1.5 cun.

15. 肩髃（LI 15），手阳明经、阳跻脉交会穴
Jianyu (LI 15), Crossing Point of Hand - Yangming Meridian and Yang Heel Vessel

【释义】肩，肩部；髃，隅角。穴在肩角部。

【定位】在肩部三角肌下，臂外展或向前平伸时肩峰前下方凹陷中（图4-8）。

【解剖】皮肤→皮下组织→三角肌→三角肌下囊→冈上肌腱。浅层布有锁骨上外侧神经、臂外侧上皮神经。深层有旋肱后动、静脉和腋神经的分支。

【功用】通经活络，通利关节，祛风除湿。

【主治】肩痛不举，上肢不遂；瘰疬。

【操作】直刺或向下斜刺0.5~0.8寸。

【Meaning】Jian, shoulder; yu, corner. The point is at the corner of the shoulder.

【Location】With the arm abducted and parallel to the ground, at the upper border of the deltoid muscle, in the inferior anterior depression of the shoulder (Fig 4-8).

【Regional anatomy】Skin→subcutaneous tissue→deltoid muscle→subdeltoid bursa→supraspinous muscle tendon. In the superficial layer, there is the lateral supraclavicular nerve and the superior lateral cutaneous nerve of the arm. In the deep layer, there is the posterior humoral circumflex artery and vein and the branches of the axillary nerve.

【Properties】Unblock the meridian and activate collaterals, disinhibit the shoulder joint, dispel wind and dampness.

【Indications】Pain and numbness in the upper arm and shoulder, impaired movement of arm;

scrofula.

【Needling method】 Puncture perpendicularly or obliquely downwards 0.5 ~ 0.8cun.

16. 巨骨（LI 16），手阳明经、阳跻脉交会穴
Jugu（LI 16), Crossing Point of Hand - Yangming Meridian and Yang Heel Vessel

【释义】巨，大；骨，骨骼。古称锁骨为巨骨，穴近锁骨峰端。

【定位】在肩上部，锁骨肩峰端与肩胛冈之间凹陷处（图4－9）。

【解剖】皮肤→皮下组织→肩锁韧带→冈上肌。浅层布有锁骨上外侧神经。深层布有肩胛上神经的分支和肩胛上动、静脉的分支或属支。

【功用】消肿散结。

【主治】肩背疼痛；瘰疬，瘿气。

【操作】直刺0.5～0.8寸。深部有肺脏，不可向下深刺，以免造成气胸。

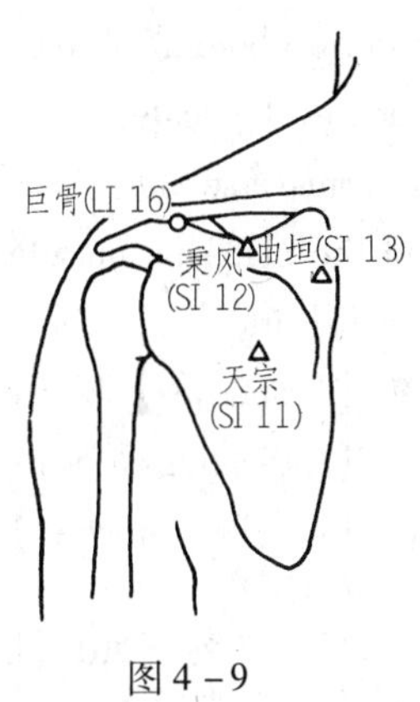

图4－9

Fig 4－9

【Meaning】 Ju, huge; gu, bone. The clavicle was called Jugu in ancient times. The point is close to the acromial end of the clavicle.

【Location】 In the upper portion of the shoulder, in the depression between the acromial extremity of the clavicle and the scapular spine（Fig 4－9）.

【Regional anatomy】 Skin→subcutaneous tissue→acromioclavicular ligament→the supraspinous muscle. In the superficial layer, there are the lateral supraclavicular nerve. In the deep layer, there are the branches of the suprascapular nerve and the branches or tributaries of the suprascapular artery and vein

【Properties】 Disperse swelling and dissipate binds.

【Indications】 Pain of the shoulder and upper back; scrofula, goiter.

【Needling method】 Puncture perpendicularly 0.5～0.8 cun. Deep perpendicular insertion is prohibited in order to avoid puncturing the lungs and causing pneumothorax.

17. 天鼎 Tianding（LI 17)

【释义】天，天空；鼎，古器物名。天，指上而言。头形似鼎，穴在其耳下颈部。

【定位】在颈外侧，胸锁乳突肌后缘，扶突与缺盆连线中点（图4－10）。

【解剖】皮肤→皮下组织→胸锁乳突肌后缘→斜角肌间隙。浅层内有颈横神经、颈外静脉和颈阔肌。深层布有颈升动、静脉分支或属支，在斜角肌间隙内分布着臂丛神经等结构。

【功用】利咽散结。

【主治】咽喉肿痛，暴喑；瘿气，瘰疬。

【操作】直刺0.3～0.5寸。

【Meaning】Tian, heaven; ding, an ancient cooking vessel with two loop handles. Tian implies upper. The head looks like a ding. The point is below the ear at the neck.

【Location】On the lateral side of the neck, on the posterior border of sternocleidomastoid muscle, at the midpoint of the line linking the Futu (LI 18) and Quepen (ST 12) points (Fig 4 – 10)

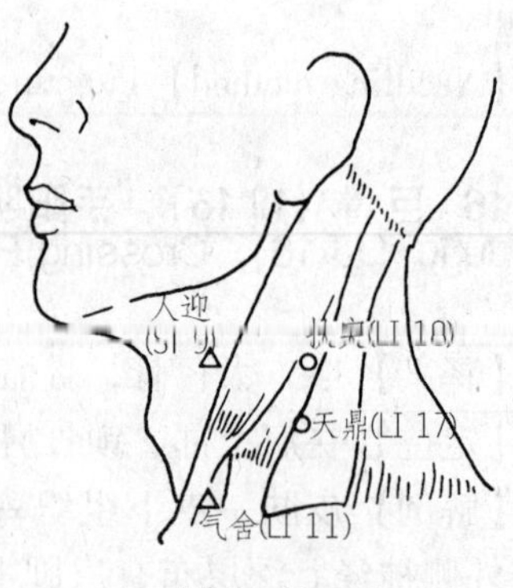

图 4 – 10

Fig 4 – 10

【Regional anatomy】Skin→subcutaneous tissue→the posterior border of the sternocleidomastoid muscle→interspace of the scalene muscle. In the superficial layer, there is the transverse nerve of the neck, the external jugular vein and the platysma muscle. In the deep layer, there are the branches or tributaries of the ascending cervical artery and vein and the branchial plexus in the interspace of the scalene muscle.

【Properties】Soothe the throat and dissipate binds.

【Indications】Sore throat, sudden loss of voice; scrofula, goiter.

【Needling method】Puncture perpendicularly 0. 3 ~ 0. 5 cun.

18. 扶突 Futu (LI 18)

【释义】扶，旁边；突，隆起。突，指喉结，穴在喉结旁。

【定位】结喉旁3寸，当胸锁乳突肌的胸骨头和锁骨头之间（图4－10）。

【解剖】皮肤→皮下组织→胸锁乳突肌的胸骨头与锁骨头之间→颈血管鞘的后缘。浅层内有颈横神经、颈阔肌。深层有颈血管鞘。

【功用】消肿散结，清咽开音。

【主治】咽喉肿痛，暴喑；瘿气，瘰疬；咳喘。

【操作】直刺0.5～0.8寸。

【Meaning】Fu, side; tu, prominence. Tu refers to prominentia laryngea. The point is beside the Adam's apple.

【Location】3 cun lateral to the tip of the Adam's apple, between the sternal head and clavicular head of sternocleidomastoid muscle (Fig 4 – 10).

【Regional anatomy】Skin→subcutaneous tissue→between the sternal head and the clavicular head of the sternocleidomastoid muscle→the posterior border of the carotid sheath. In the superficial layer, there is the transverse nerve of the neck and the platysma muscle. In the deep layer, there is the carotid sheath.

【Properties】Disperse swelling and dissipate binds, soothe the throat and ease – up the voice.

【Indications】Sore throat, sudden loss of voice; scrofula, goiter; cough and asthma.

【Needling method】Puncture perpendicularly 0. 5 ~ 0. 8 cun.

19. 口禾髎 Kouheliao (LI 19)

【释义】口，口部；禾，谷物；髎，骨隙。谷物从口入胃，穴在口旁骨隙中。

【定位】鼻孔外缘直下，平水沟穴（图4－11）。

【解剖】皮肤→皮下组织→口轮匝肌。浅层有上颌神经的眶下神经分支等结构。深层有上唇动、静脉和面神经颊支等分布。

【功用】祛风清热，开窍。

【主治】鼽衄，鼻塞，口㖞，口噤。

【操作】直刺或斜刺0.3～0.5寸。

【Meaning】Kou, mouth; he, grain; liao, foramen. The grain enters the stomach through the mouth. The point is in the foramen beside the mouth.

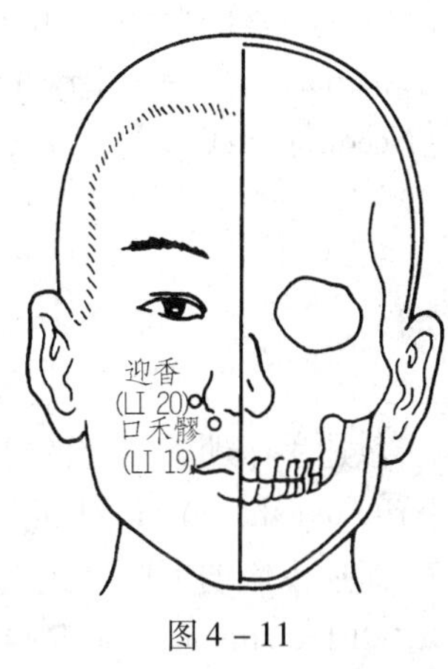

图4－11

Fig 4－11

【Location】Below the lateral margin of the nostril, level with the Shuigou (DU 26) point (Fig 4－11).

【Regional anatomy】Skin→subcutaneous tissue→the orbicular muscle of the mouth. In the superficial layer, there are the branches of the infraorbital nerve of the maxillary nerves, etc. In the deep layer, there are artery and vein of the upper lip and the buccal branches of the facial nerve.

【Properties】Dispel wind and clear heat, open the orifices.

【Indications】Nosebleed, nasal obstruction, deviated face, trismus.

【Needling method】Puncture perpendicularly or obliquely 0.3～0.5 cun.

20. 迎香 Yingxiang (LI 20)，手、足阳明经交会穴 Yingxiang (LI 20), Crossing Point of the Meridians of Hand－Yangming and Foot－Yangming

【释义】迎，迎接；香，香气。本穴在鼻旁，治鼻病，改善嗅觉，能迎来香气。

【定位】鼻翼外缘中点旁，当鼻唇沟中（图4－11）。

【解剖】皮肤→皮下组织→提上唇肌。浅层有上颌神经的眶下神经分支。深层有面动、静脉的分支或属支，面神经颊支。

【功用】通鼻窍，散风邪，清气火。

【主治】鼻塞，鼻衄，鼻渊；口㖞，面痒；胆道蛔虫症。

【操作】斜刺或平刺0.3～0.5寸。

【Meaning】Ying, to meet; xiang, fragrance. This point is at either side of the nose. It is used to treat disorders of the nose to improve the sense of smell, to enable the nose to "sense fragrance".

【Location】In the naso－labial groove, at the center of the lateral border of the ala nasi (Fig

4－11)

【Regional anatomy】Skin→subcutaneous tissue→the levator muscle of the upper lip. In the superficial layer, there are the branches of the infraorbital nerve from the maxillary nerve. In the deep layer, there are buccal branches of the facial nerve and the branches or tributaries of the facial artery and vein.

【Properties】Relieve the stuffy nose, disperse wind and clear heat.

【Indications】Nasal obstruction, nosebleed, sinusitis; facial paralysis of spasm, facial itchiness; ascariasis of the biliary tract.

【Needling method】Puncture obliquely or transversely 0.3～0.5 cun.

复习思考题
Review Questions

1. 叙述手阳明大肠经的经脉循行。

Write out the course of the large intestine meridian of hand－yangming.

2. 简述手阳明大肠经经穴主治概要。

Retell the summary of the indications of the large intestine meridian of hand－yangming.

3. 简述合谷、曲池、迎香等穴的定位、主治与操作。

Retell the location, indications and needling method of Hegu (LI 4), Quchi (LI 11) and Yingxiang (LI 20).

第五章 足阳明经络与腧穴 Meridian and Collateral and Its Acupoints of Foot – Yangming

第一节 足阳明经络 Meridian and Collateral of Foot – Yangming

一、足阳明经脉 Meridian of Foot - Yangming

(一) 经脉循行 The Course of Meridian

足阳明胃经，从鼻旁开始，上行鼻根处，与足太阳经交会，向下沿鼻外侧，入上齿，出来夹口旁，环绕口唇，向下交会于颏唇沟的承浆；内后沿下颌面动脉部，经下颌角，上耳前，经颧弓上部，沿额角发际，至额前中部。颈部支脉，从大迎前向下，经颈动脉，沿喉咙，进入锁骨上窝，通过膈肌，属于胃，络于脾。胸腹部主脉，从锁骨上窝向下，经乳中（在胸部旁开前正中线 4 寸），向下夹脐两旁（在腹部旁开前正中线 2 寸），进入腹股沟。腹内支脉，从胃口向下，沿腹里，至腹股沟与前外行脉会合。由此下行经髋关节前，到股四头肌隆起处，下入膝关节中，沿胫骨外侧，下行足背，进入足中趾内侧趾缝至足第二趾外侧端。小腿部支脉从膝下 3 寸处分出，向下进入中趾外侧趾缝，出中趾末端。足部支脉，从足背部分出，进入大趾内侧，出大趾末端，连接足太阴脾经（图 5 – 1）。

《灵枢·经脉》原文：胃足阳明之脉，起于鼻，交頞中，旁约太阳之脉，下循鼻外，入上齿中，还出夹口，环唇，下交承浆，却循颐后下廉，出大迎，循颊车，上耳前，过客主人，循发际，至额颅（图 5 – 1）。

其支者，从大迎前，下人迎，循喉咙，入缺盆，下膈，属胃，络脾。

其直者，从缺盆下乳内廉，下夹脐，入气街中。

其支者，起于胃下口，循腹里，下至气街中而合。以下髀关，抵伏兔，下膝膑中，下循胫外廉，下足跗，入中指内间。

其支者，下膝三寸而别，下入中指外间。

其支者，别跗上，入大指间，出其端。

The stomach meridian of foot – yangming starts from the lateral side of the nose. It travels upward to the root of the nose where it meets the meridian of foot – taiyang. Turning downward along the lateral side of the nose, it enters the upper gum. Curving around the lips, it meets Chengjiang (RN 24) in the mentolabial groove. It then travels to the posterior aspect of the mandible passing through the facial artery, ascending in front of the ear and following the anterior hairline, it reaches the forehead. Its cheek branch splits from the front of the Daying (ST 5) point and passes through the carotid artery. Passing along the throat, it enters the supraclavicular fossa. It further descends and passes through the diaphragm, and then enters its pertaining organ, the stomach, and connects to the spleen, the related organ. The straight branch of the meridian in the chest and abdomen arises from the supraclavicular fossa, which descends and passes through the nipple (4 cun lateral to the midline of the chest). It then reaches the lateral side of the umbilicus (2 cun lateral to the anterior midline of the abdomen) and enters the inguinal groove. The branch of the abdomen starts from the lower orifice of the stomach, and descends inside the abdomen, reaching the inguinal groove, where it merges with the previous branch of the channel. From there, it further descends to the front of the coxa joint, reaches the quadriceps muscle and enters the knee. From the knee, it continues further down along the anterior border of the lateral aspect of the tibia to the dorsum of the foot and reaches the lateral side of the tip of the second toe. The tibial branch of the chanel splits from the place 3 cun below the knee and runs downward and ends at the lateral side of the middle toe. Another branch on the foot emerges from the dorsum of the foot to enter the medial side of the tip of the big toe, where it links with the spleen meridian (Fig 5 – 1).

（二）经脉病候
The Syndromes of Meridian

本经有了异常就表现为下列病症：颤抖发冷，喜欢伸腰，屡屡呵欠，面黑。病发时，厌恶别人和火光，听到木器声音就惕惕惊慌，心要跳动，独自关闭户门、遮塞窗户而睡。严重的则可能登高而歌，不穿衣服就走。胸膈部响，腹部胀满。还可发为小腿部的气血阻逆，如厥冷、麻木、酸痛等。

本经穴能主治有关“血”方面所发生的病症：躁狂，疟疾，温热病，自汗出，鼻塞流涕或出血，口㖞，唇生疮疹，颈部肿，喉咙痛，大腹水肿，膝关节肿痛；沿着胸前、乳部、气街（气冲穴部）、腹股沟部、大腿前、小腿外侧、足背上均痛，足中趾不能运用。

凡属于气盛有余的症状，则身体前面都发热，有余的症状表现在胃部，则消化强而容易饥饿，小便颜色黄。属于气虚不足的症状，则身体前面都发冷、寒战，胃部寒冷则感到胀满。

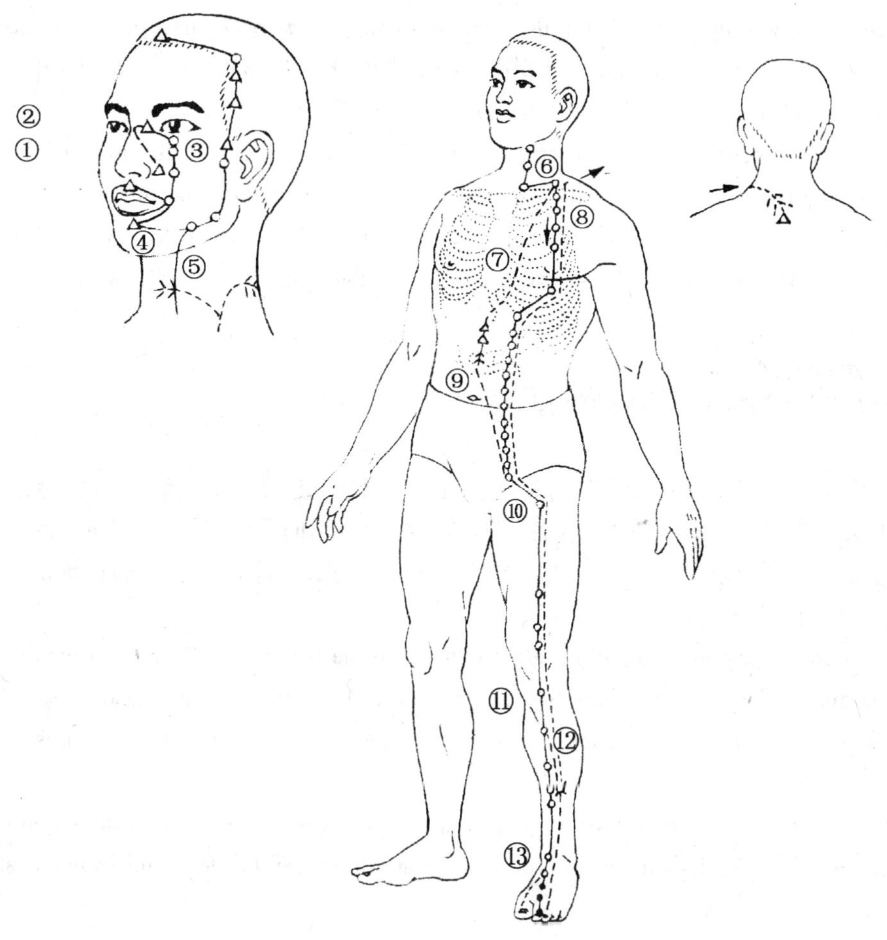

图例 ——足阳明经脉循行线 ……足阳明络脉循行线

Note ——The course of the meridian of foot – yangming

……The course of the collateral of foot – yangming

图 5 – 1 足阳明经脉、络脉循行示意图

Fig 5 – 1 The course of the meridian and collateral of foot – yangming

The manifestations of this meridian with abnormal functions includes: shivering with chills sprinkling over the body, groaning and yawning, dark facial complexion. In fulminate stage, he fears fire and people, frightened by sound of wooden utensils and preference for staying alone. Serious case shows singing aloud and standing high or running round naked, borborygmus and abdominal distention. There may be the stagnation of qi and blood in the shank, presenting with coldness, numbness, aching pain, etc.

The meridian and its acupoints can cure the diseases caused by the disorder of blood, mania, malaria, febrile disease, spontaneous sweating, stuffy nose, running nose with turgid discharge, or nasal bleeding, deviated mouth, sore and rash in the lip, swelling in the neck, pain in the throat, ascites, swelling and pain of the patella; pain along the course of the meridian in the chest, breast, location of Qichong (ST 30), groin, thigh, the anterior – lateral side of the tibia and the dorsum of the foot, and the limitation of the middle toe.

The symptoms caused by the excessive qi include a hot sensation in the front of the body. The symptoms in the stomach caused by the excessive qi include hyperfunction of digestion, easy to be hungry and yellowish urine. The symptoms caused by the deficient qi induce coldness in the front part of body, shivering, and fullness and distention in the epigastrium with coldness.

二、足阳明络脉 Collateral of Foot - Yangming

足阳明络脉，名丰隆，在距离外踝上 8 寸处分出，走向足太阴经；其支脉沿着胫骨外缘，向上联络头项部（会大椎），与各经的脉气相会合，向下联络喉咙和咽峡部。

其病症：气厥逆就会患喉部肿痛，突然音哑。实证，发生癫病，狂病；虚证，见下肢弛缓无力，肌肉萎缩。可取足阳明络穴治疗。

It starts from Fenglong (ST 40), eight cun above the external malleolus, it connects with the spleen meridian. A branch runs along the lateral aspect of the tibia upward to the top of the head, and converges with the other yang meridians on the head and neck. From there it runs downward to connect with the throat.

If the qi is reverse, numb throat and sudden inability to speak will occur. Its repletion disorders are mania and madness. Its vacuity disorders are inability to flex the legs and withered shanks. Use this point.

三、足阳明经别 Divergent Meridian of Foot - Yangming

足阳明经别，在大腿前面从足阳明经分出，进入腹腔之内，属于胃腑，散布到脾脏，向上通连心脏，沿着食道浅出于口腔，上达于鼻根和眼眶下部，回过来联系到眼后与脑相连的组织（目系），脉气仍会合于足阳明经（图 5 – 2）。

After deriving from the stomach meridian on the thigh, it enters the abdomen, connects with the stomach and disperses in the spleen. It then ascends through the heart and alongside the esophagus to reach the mouth. It then runs upward beside the nose and connects with the eye before finally joining the stomach meridian of foot – yangming (Fig 5 – 2).

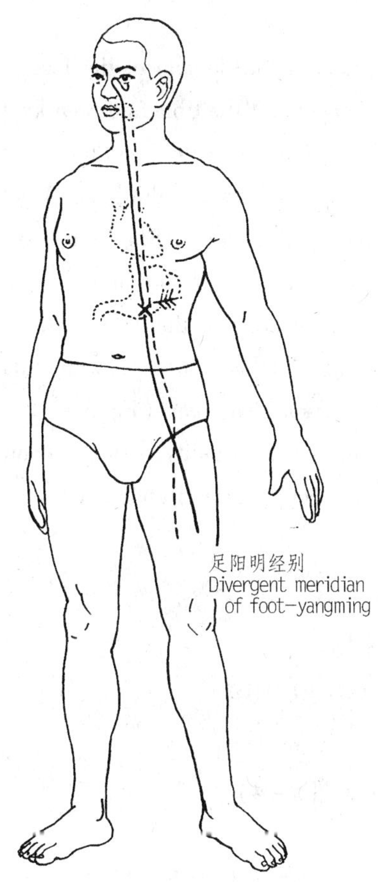

图 5－2　足阳明经别循行示意图

Fig 5－2　The course of the divergent meridian of foot－yangming

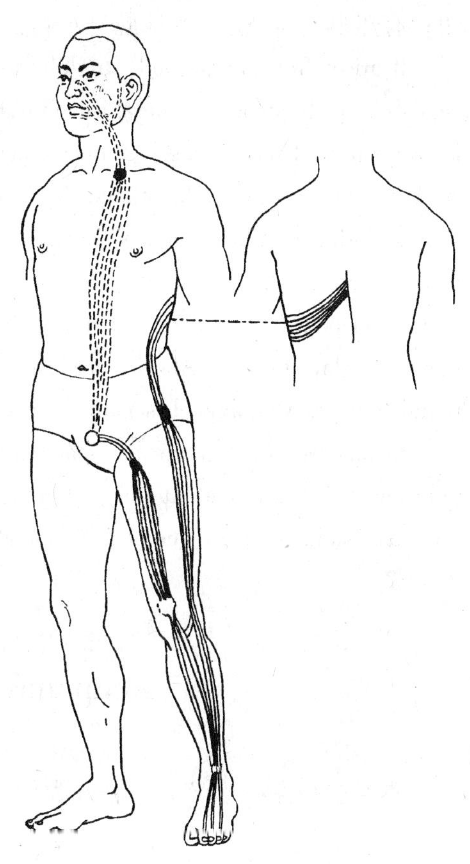

图 5－3　足阳明经筋分布示意图

Fig 5－3　The muscular region of foot－yangming

四、足阳明经筋 Muscular Region of Foot - Yangming

足阳明经筋，起始于足次趾、中趾及无名趾，结于足背，斜向外行加附于腓骨，上结于胫外侧，直上结于髀枢，又向上沿胁部属于脊；其直行的上沿胫骨，结于膝部，分支之筋结于外辅骨部，合并足少阳经筋；直行的沿伏兔上行，结于大腿部而聚会于阴器。再向上分布到腹部，至缺盆处结集；再向上至颈，夹口旁，合于鼻旁颧部，相继下结于鼻，从鼻旁合于足太阳经筋。太阳经筋为“目上纲”（上睑），阳明经筋为“目下纲”（下睑）。另一分支之筋，从面颊结于耳前部（图 5－3）。

其病症：可出现足中趾掣强，胫部筋肉痉挛，下肢跳动、僵硬不舒，股前筋肉拘紧，股前部肿，疝气，腹部筋肉拘紧，向上牵掣到缺盆和颊部。突然发生口角歪斜，如有寒邪则掣引眼睑不能闭合；有热则筋松弛使眼睑不能睁开。颊筋有寒，则使筋肉紧急，牵引面颊和口角；有热则筋肉松弛，不能胜过对侧收缩，所以口歪。

It arises from the second, middle and fourth toes, knots at the dorsum of the foot, and ascends obliquely along the lateral aspect of the leg where it disperses at the tibia and then knots at the lateral aspect of the knee. Ascending directly to knot at the hip joint, it extends to the lower ribs to connect with the spine. The straight branch runs along the tibia and knots at the knee. A subbranch connects with the fibula, and joins with the foot – shaoyang (gallbladder). From the knee, it ascends across the thigh and knots in the pelvic region. Dispersing upward on the abdomen and knotting at Quepen (ST 12), it extends to the neck and mouth, meeting at the side of the nose and knotting below the nose. Above, it joins with the foot – taiyang (bladder) to form a muscular net around the eye. A subbranch separates at the jaw and knots in front of the ear (Fig 5 – 3).

Symptoms: Contracture and pain of the middle toe and tibia, rigidity of foot, contracture, pain and swelling in the anterior portion of the thigh, hernia, contracture of abdominal muscles and tendons, sudden occurrence of facial paralysis.

第二节 足阳明腧穴
Acupoints of Foot – Yangming

本经左右各45个穴位，首穴为承泣，末穴为厉兑（图5－4）。

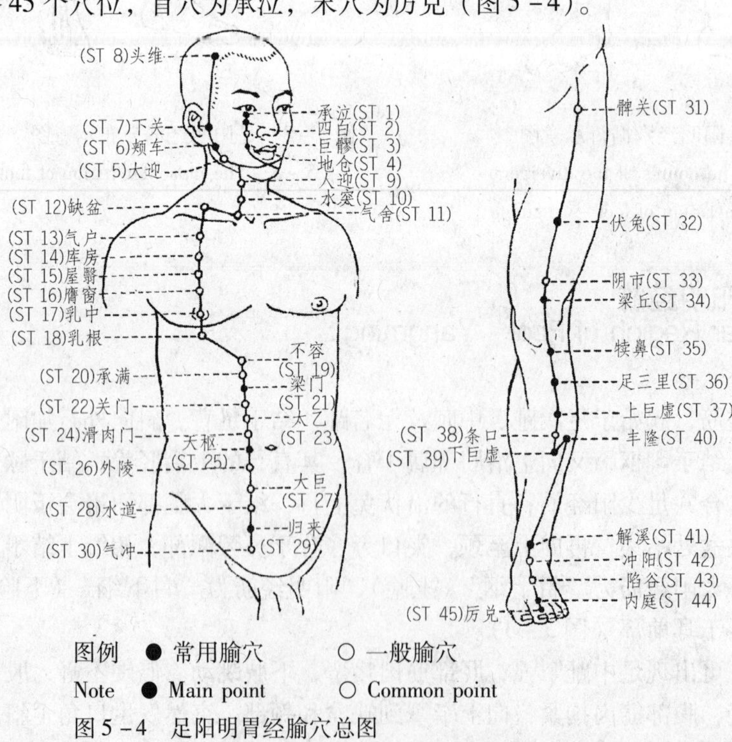

图5－4 足阳明胃经腧穴总图

Fig 5 – 4 Points of the stomach meridian of foot – yangming

1. 承泣（ST 1），阳跻脉、任脉、足阳明经交会穴
Chengqi (ST 1), Crossing Point of Foot - Yangming Meridian, Yang Heel Vessel and Conception Vessel

【释义】承，承受；泣，泪水。穴在目下，犹如承受泪水的部位。

【定位】目正视，瞳孔直下，眼球与眶下缘之间（图5-5）。

【解剖】皮肤→皮下组织→眼轮匝肌→眶脂体→下斜肌。浅层布有眶下神经的分支，面神经的颧支。深层有动眼神经的分支，眼动、静脉的分支或属支。

【功用】祛风清热，明目。

【主治】目赤肿痛，迎风流泪，夜盲，视物不明；眼睑瞤动，口眼㖞斜。

【操作】让患者闭目，医者以左手拇指向上轻推眼球，紧靠眶下缘缓慢直刺0.5~1.0寸，不宜提插，出针时按压针孔，以防出血。禁灸。

【Meaning】Cheng, to receive; qi, tears. The point is below the eye, a place for receiving tears.

【Location】With the eyes looking straight forward, the point is vertically below the pupil, between the eyeball and the infraorbital border (Fig 5-5).

【Regional anatomy】Skin→subcutaneous tissue→the orbicular muscle of the eye→adipose body of the orbit→the inferior oblique muscle. In the superficial layer, there are the branches of the infraorbital nerve and the zygomatic branches of the facial nerve. In the deep layer, there are the branches of the oculomotor nerve and the branches or tributaries of the ophthalmic artery and vein.

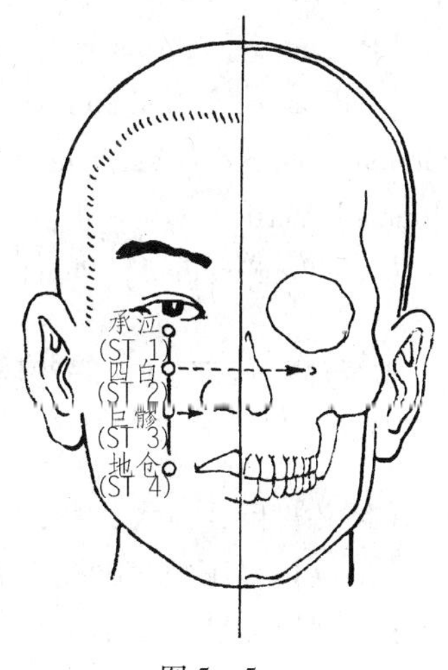

图5-5
Fig 5-5

【Properties】Dispel wind, clear heat and improve eyesight.

【Indications】Red and painful eyes, lacrimation upon exposure to wind, night blindness, blurred vision; twitching of the eyelids, deviated mouth and eye.

【Needling method】With the eyes closed, push the eyeball upward slightly with the left thumb and puncture slowly and perpendicularly 0.5~1.0cun closely along the infraorbital ridge, without lifting and thrusting manipulation. Moxibustion is prohibited.

2. 四白 Sibai (ST 2)

【释义】四，四方；白，光明。穴在目下，治眼病，能改善视觉，明见四方。

【定位】目正视，瞳孔直下，当眶下孔凹陷中（图5-5）。

【解剖】皮肤→皮下组织→眼轮匝肌、提上唇肌→眶下孔或上颌骨。浅层布有眶下神经

的分支，面神经的颧支。深层在眶下孔内有眶下动、静脉和神经穿出。

【功用】祛风明目。

【主治】目赤肿痛，迎风流泪，目翳，视物不明；口眼㖞斜，眼睑瞤动，面痛、面痒；眩晕。

【操作】直刺或斜刺0.2～0.3寸。

【Meaning】Si, four directions; bai, brightness. This point is below the eye and is indicate in eye diseases. It is said to improve the vision and give one sharp eyes in all four directions.

【Location】With the eyes looking straight forward, the point is vertically below the pupil, in the depression at the infraorbital foramen (Fig 5－5).

【Regional anatomy】Skin→subcutaneous tissue→the orbicular muscle of the eye, the levator muscle of the upper lip→the infraorbital foramen or the maxilla. In the superficial layer, there are the branches of the infraorbital nerve and the zygomatic branches of the facial nerve. In the deep layer, there are the infraorbital artery, vein and nerve which pass through the infraorbital foramen.

【Properties】Dispel wind and improve eyesight.

【Indications】Red and painful eyes, lacrimation upon exposure to wind, superficial visual obstruction, blurred vision; deviation of the mouth and eye, twitching of the eyelids, facial pain and itchiness; Vertigo.

【Needling method】Puncture perpendicularly or obliquely upward 0.2～0.3 cun.

3. 巨髎（ST 3），阳跻脉、足阳明经交会穴
Juliao (ST 3), Crossing Point of Foot - Yangming Meridian and Yang Heel Vessel

【释义】巨，巨大；髎，骨隙。穴在上颌骨与颧骨交接处的大骨隙中。

【定位】目正视，瞳孔直下，平鼻翼下缘处，鼻唇沟外侧（图5－5）。

【解剖】皮肤→皮下组织→提上唇肌→提口角肌。布有上颌神经的眶下神经，面神经的颊支，面动、静脉和眶下动、静脉分支或属支的吻合支。

【功用】祛风通窍。

【主治】口眼㖞斜，口角瞤动，鼻衄，齿痛。

【操作】直刺0.3～0.5寸。

【Meaning】Ju, huge; liao, foramen. The point is in the big foramen at the junction of the superior maxillary and zygomatic bones.

【Location】With the eyes looking straight forward, the point is vertically below the pupil, at the level of the lower border of the ala nasi, on the lateral side of the nasolabial groove (Fig 5－5).

【Regional anatomy】Skin→subcutaneous tissue→the levator muscle of the upper lip→the levator muscle the angle of the mouth. There are the infraorbital nerve of the maxillary nerve, the buccal branches of the facial nerve, the anastomotic branches formed by the branches or tributaries of the facial artery and vein and the infraorbital artery and vein in this area.

【Properties】Dispel wind and relieve the stuffy nose.

【Indications】Deviation of the mouth and eye, twitching at the angle of the mouth, nosebleed, toothache.

【Needling method】Puncture perpendicularly 0.3 ~0.5 cun.

4. 地仓（ST4），阳跻脉、手足阳明经交会穴
Di cang（ST4），Crossing Point of the Meridians of Hand - Yangming and Foot - Yangming，Yang Heel Vessel

【释义】地，土地；仓，粮仓。土生五谷，谷从口入，如进粮仓。穴在口角旁。

【定位】目正视，瞳孔直下，平口角处（图5-5）。

【解剖】皮肤→皮下组织→口轮匝肌→降口角肌。布有三叉神经的颊支和眶下支，面动、静脉的分支或属支。

【功用】祛风行滞，利口齿。

【主治】口眼㖞斜，流涎，齿痛，面痛，面肌瞤动。

【操作】斜刺或平刺0.5~0.8寸，或向迎香、颊车方向透刺1.0~2.0寸。

【Meaning】Di, earth; cang, granary. The five grains grow on the earth. The grain enters the stomach via the mouth, as entering a granary. The point is at the corners of the mouth.

【Location】With the eyes looking straight forward, the point is vertically below the pupil, at the level of the angle of the mouth（Fig 5-5）.

【Regional anatomy】Skin→subcutaneous tissue→the orbicular muscle of the mouth→the depressor muscle of the angle. There are the buccal and infraobital branches of the trigeminal nerve and the branches or tributaries of the facial artery and vein in this area.

【Properties】Dispel wind, move stagnation and disinhibit buccal teeth.

【Indications】Deviation of the mouth and eye, excessive salivation, toothache, facial pain and twitching of the facial muscles.

【Needling method】Puncture obliquely or transversely 0.5 ~0.8cun or 1.0 ~2.0 cun in the direction of Yingxiang or Jiache.

5. 大迎 Daying（ST5）

【释义】大，大小之大；迎，迎接。穴在大迎脉（颌外动脉）旁。

【定位】在下颌角前方咬肌附着部的前缘，当面动脉搏动处（图5-6）。

【解剖】皮肤→皮下组织→降口角肌与颈阔肌→咬肌前缘。浅层布有三叉神经第三支下颌神经的颊神经，面神经的下颌缘支。深层有面动、静脉。

【功用】祛风通络，利口齿。

【主治】齿痛，口眼㖞斜，颊肿，面痛，面肌瞤动。

【操作】直刺0.2~0.3寸。

【Meaning】Da, large; ying, to receive. The point lies beside the Daying artery（the extramaxillary artery).

【Location】 Anterior to the angle of the mandible, on the anterior border of the attached portion of masseter muscle, where the facial artery pulsates (Fig 5 –6).

【Regional anatomy】 Skin→subcutaneous tissue→the depressor muscle of the mouth and platysma muscle→the anterior border of the masseter muscle. In the superficial layer, there are the buccal nerve of the mandibular branch of the trigeminal nerve and the marginal mandibular branch of the facial nerve. In the deep layer, there are the facial artery and vein.

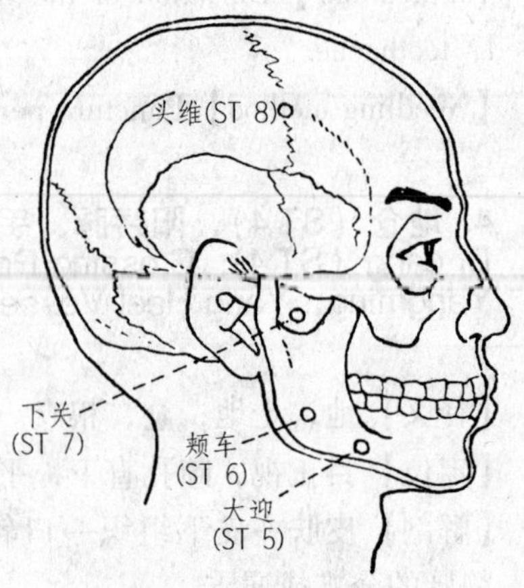

图 5 –6

Fig 5 –6

【Properties】 Dispel wind to free the collateral vessels and disinhibit buccal teeth.

【Indications】 Toothache, deviation of the mouth and eye, swelling of the cheek, facial pain, twitching of the facial muscles.

【Needling method】 Puncture perpendicularly 0. 2 ~ 0. 3 cun.

6. 颊车 Jiache (ST 6)

【释义】颊，颊部；车，车辆。车，指牙车（下颌骨）。穴在颊部，近下颌骨角。

【定位】下颌角前上方约一横指，当咀嚼时咬肌隆起高点处（图 5 –6）。

【解剖】皮肤→皮下组织→咬肌。布有耳大神经的分支，面神经下颌缘支的分支。

【功用】祛风通络，利口齿。

【主治】口眼㖞斜，齿痛，面痛，面肌瞤动，颊肿。

【操作】直刺 0. 3 ~0. 5 寸，平刺 0. 5 ~0. 8 寸。

【Meaning】 Jia, cheek; che, vehicle. Che refers to the mandible. The point is on the cheek, close to the angle of the mandible.

【Location】 One finger width anterior and superior to the lower angle of the mandible, at the prominence of the masseter muscle when teeth are clenched (Fig 5 –6).

【Regional anatomy】 Skin→subcutaneous tissue→masseter muscle. There are the branches of the great auricular nerve and the marginal mandibular branches of the facial nerve in this area.

【Properties】 Dispel wind to free the collateral vessels and disinhibit buccal teeth.

【Indications】 Deviation of the mouth and eye, toothache, facial pain, twitching of the facial muscles, swelling of cheeks.

【Needling method】 Puncture perpendicularly 0. 3 ~ 0. 5 cun, or transversely 0. 5 ~ 0. 8 cun.

7. 下关（ST 7），足少阳、阳明经交会穴
Xiaguan（ST 7），Crossing Point of the Meridians of Foot - Yangming and Foot - Shaoyang

【释义】下，下方；关，关界。关，指颧骨弓，穴在其下缘。

【定位】在面部耳前方，颧弓与下颌切迹所形成的凹陷中（图 5－6）。

【解剖】皮肤→皮下组织→腮腺→咬肌与颞骨颧突之间→翼外肌。浅层布有耳颞神经的分支，面神经的颧支，面横动、静脉等。深层有上颌动、静脉，舌神经，下牙槽神经，脑膜中动脉和翼丛等。

【功用】祛风，聪耳，利牙关。

【主治】下颌疼痛，口噤，口眼㖞斜，齿痛，颊肿，面痛；耳聋，耳鸣，聤耳。

【操作】直刺 0.3～0.5 寸。

【Meaning】 Xia, lower; guan, pass. Guan indicates the zygomatic arch; the point is below it.

【Location】 At the depression between the zygomatic arch and mandibular notch（Fig 5－6）.

【Regional anatomy】 Skin→subcutaneous tissue→the parotid gland→between the masseter muscle and the zygomatic process of the temporal bone→the lateral pterygoid muscle. In the superficial layer, there are the branches of the auriculotemporal nerve, the zygomatic branches of the facial nerve and the transverse facial artery and vein. In the deep layer, there are extramaxillary artery and vein, the lingual nerve, the inferior alveolar nerve, the middle meningeal artery and the pterygoid plexus.

【Properties】 Dispel wind, improve hearing and disinhibit maxillary joint.

【Indications】 Lower mandible pain, locked jaw, deviated mouth and eyes, toothache, swelling of cheek, facial pain; deafness, tinnitus, ear infection.

【Needling method】 Puncture perpendicularly 0. 3 ～ 0. 5 cun.

8. 头维（ST 8），足阳明、足少阳、阳维脉交会穴
Touwei（ST 8），Crossing Point of the Meridians of Foot - Yangming，Foot - Shaoyang and Yang Link Vessel

【释义】头，头部；维，隅角。穴在头之额角部位。

【定位】额角发际上 0.5 寸，头正中线旁开 4.5 寸（图 5－6）。

【解剖】皮肤→皮下组织→颞肌上缘的帽状腱膜→腱膜下疏松结缔组织→颅骨外膜。布有耳颞神经的分支，面神经的颞支，颞浅动、静脉的额支等。

【功用】祛风泻火，止痛明目。

【主治】头痛，眩晕；目痛，迎风流泪；眼睑瞤动。

【操作】平刺 0.5～0.8 寸。

【Meaning】Tou, head; wei, corner or angle. The point is at the angle between two hairlines at the front.

【Location】0. 5 cun straight above the corner of the anterior hairline, 4. 5 cun lateral to the anterior midline of the forehead (Fig 5 -6).

【Regional anatomy】Skin→subcutaneous tissue→epicranial aponeurosis→subaponeurotic loose connective tissue→pericranium. There are the branches of the auriculotemporal nerve, the temporal branches of the facial nerve and the frontal branches of the superficial temporal artery and vein in this area.

【Properties】Dispel wind and discharge fire, relieve pain and improve eyesight.

【Indications】Headache, vertigo; painful eyes, lacrimation upon exposure to wind; twitching of the eyelids.

【Needling method】Puncture transversely 0. 5 ~ 0. 8 cun.

9. 人迎（ST 9），足阳明、少阳经交会穴
Renying (ST 9), Crossing Point of the Meridians of Foot - Yangming and Foot - Shaoyang

【释义】人，人类；迎，迎接。穴在人迎脉（颈总动脉）旁，故名。

【定位】在颈部结喉旁，当胸锁乳突肌前缘，颈总动脉搏动处（图5 -7）。

【解剖】皮肤→皮下组织和颈阔肌→颈固有筋膜浅层及胸锁乳突肌前缘→颈固有筋膜深层和肩胛舌骨肌后缘→咽缩肌。浅层布有颈横神经，面神经颈支。深层有甲状腺上动、静脉的分支或属支，舌下神经袢的分支等。

【功用】理气降逆。

【主治】咽喉肿痛；瘰疬，瘿气；高血压；气喘。

【操作】避开动脉直刺0. 3 ~0. 5 寸。

【Meaning】Ren, mankind; ying, to meet. The point lies beside the Renying artery (common carotid artery).

【Location】Lateral to the Adam's apple, on the anterior border of sternocleidomastoid muscle, where the common carotid artery pulsates (Fig 5 -7).

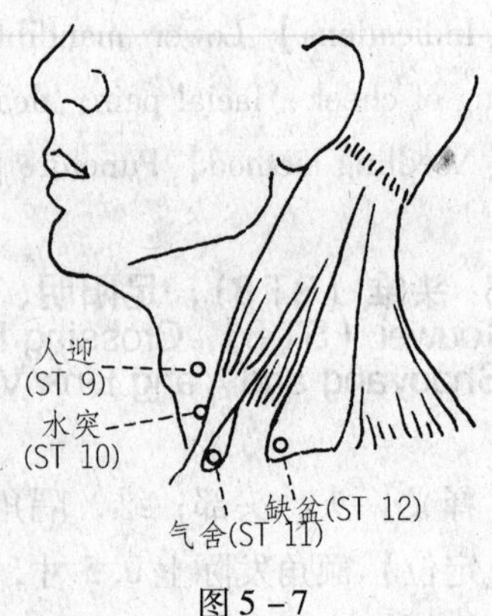

图5 -7
Fig 5 -7

【Regional anatomy】Skin→subcutaneous tissue and the platysma muscle→the superficial layer of the cervical proper fascia and the anterior border of the sternocleidomastoid muscle→the deep layer of the cervical proper facia and the posterior border of the omohyoid muscle→the constrictor muscle of the pharynx. In the superficial layer, there are the transverse nerve of the neck and the cervical branches of the facial nerve. In the deep layer, there are the branches or tributaries of the superior thyroid artery and vein and the branches of the loop of the hypoglossal nerve.

【Properties】 Regulate qi and downbear counterflow.

【Indications】 Swollen and sore throat; scrofula, goiter; hypertension; asthma.

【Needling method】 Puncture perpendicularly 0. 3 ~0. 5 cun, avoid needling the artery.

10. 水突 Shuitu (ST 10)

【释义】水，水谷；突，穿过。穴在颈部，临近通过食物的食管。

【定位】在颈部，胸锁乳突肌的前缘，当人迎与气舍连线的中点（图5－7）。

【解剖】皮肤→皮下组织和颈阔肌→颈固有筋膜浅层及胸锁乳突肌→颈固有筋膜深层及肩胛舌骨肌，胸骨甲状肌。浅层布有颈横神经。深层有甲状腺。

【功用】降逆，利咽。

【主治】咽喉肿痛；咳嗽，喘息；瘰疬，瘿气。

【操作】直刺0. 3 ~0. 5 寸。

【Meaning】 Shui, water and food; tu, passing through. The point is at the neck close to the esophagus, where water and food pass.

【Location】 On the neck, on the anterior border of sternocleidomastoid muscle, at the midpoint of the line linking the Renying and Qishe (Fig 5 –7).

【Regional anatomy】 Skin→subcutaneous tissue and the platysma muscle→the superficial layer of the cervical proper fascia and the sternocleidomastoid muscle→the deep layer of the cervical proper fascia, the omohyoid muscle and the sternothyroid muscle. In the superficial layer, there is the transverse nerve of the neck. In the deep layer, there is the thyroid gland.

【Properties】 Downbear counterflow and soothe the throat.

【Indications】 Sore throat; cough, gasp; scrofula, goiter.

【Needling method】 Puncture perpendicularly 0. 3 ~0. 5 cun.

11. 气舍 Qishe (ST 11)

【释义】气，空气；舍，宅舍。气，指肺胃之气。穴在气管旁，犹如气之宅舍。

【定位】在颈部，锁骨内侧端上缘，胸锁乳突肌的胸骨头与锁骨头之间（图5－7）。

【解剖】皮肤→皮下组织和颈阔肌→胸锁乳突肌的胸骨头与锁骨头之间。浅层布有锁骨上内侧神经，颈横神经的分支和面神经颈支。深层有联络两侧颈前静脉的颈前静脉弓和头臂静脉。

【功用】利咽，消瘿。

【主治】咽喉肿痛，喘息，呃逆，瘿气，瘰疬，颈项强痛。

【操作】直刺0. 3 ~0. 5 寸。穴位深部有大动脉，不可深刺。

【Meaning】 Qi, vital energy; she, residence. Qi refers to the vital energy of the lung and stomach. The point is beside the trachea and like a dwelling for qi.

【Location】 On the neck, on the superior border of the sternal extremity of the clavicle, between the sternal head and clavicular head of sternocleidomastoid muscle (Fig 5 –7).

【Regional anatomy】Skin→subcutaneous tissue and the platysma muscle→between the sternal head and the clavicular head of the sternocleidomastoid muscle. In the superficial layer, there are the branches of the medial supraclavicular nerve, the transverse nerve of the neck and the cervical branches of the facial nerve. In the deep layer, there are the each connecting the bilateral anterior jugular veins and the brachiocephalic vein.

【Properties】Soothe the throat and disperse the goiter.

【Indications】Swollen and sore throat, gasp, hiccup, goiter, scrofula, pain and rigidity of the neck.

【Needling method】Puncture perpendicularly 0. 3 ~ 0. 5 cun. Avoid a deep insertion to prevent puncturing the main, deep artery.

12. 缺盆 Quepen (ST 12)

【释义】缺，凹陷；盆，器物名。缺盆，指锁骨上窝，穴在其中。

【定位】在锁骨上窝中央，前正中线旁开4寸（图5 –7）。

【解剖】皮肤→皮下组织和颈阔肌→锁骨与斜方肌之间→肩胛舌骨肌（下腹）与锁骨下肌之间→臂丛。浅层布有锁骨上中间神经，深层有颈横动、静脉，臂丛的锁骨上部等重要结构。

【功用】利肩臂，泄胸中之热。

【主治】咳嗽，气喘，咽喉肿痛，缺盆痛，瘰疬。

【操作】直刺0. 3 ~0. 5 寸。穴位深部有肺脏，不可深刺。

【Meaning】Que, depression; pen, basin. Quepen refers to the supraclavicular fossa, where the point is located.

【Location】In the midpoint of the supraclavicular fossa, 4 cun lateral to the anterior midline of the chest (Fig 5 –7).

【Regional anatomy】Skin→subcutaneous tissue and the platysma muscle→between the clavicle and the trapezius muscle→between inferior belly of the omohyoid muscle and the subclavicular muscle→brachial plexus. In the superficial layer, there is the intermediate supraclavicular nerve. In the deep layer, there are the transverse cervical artery and vein and the supraclavicular portion of the brachial plexus.

【Properties】Disinhibit shoulder and arm, purge fire of thorax cavity.

【Indications】Cough, asthma, swollen and sore throat, pain in the supraclavicular fossa, scrofula.

【Needling method】Puncture perpendicularly 0. 3 ~0. 5 cun. Avoid a deep insertion to prevent puncturing the lung.

13. 气户 Qihu (ST 13)

【释义】气，空气；户，门户。气，指肺胃之气。穴在胸上部，故喻为气的门户。

【定位】在锁骨中点下缘，前正中线旁开4寸（图5-8）。

【解剖】皮肤→皮下组织→胸大肌。浅层布有锁骨上中间神经。深层有腋动脉和它的分支胸肩峰动脉。

【功用】宣肺理气。

【主治】咳喘，呃逆，胸痛。

【操作】斜刺或平刺0.2~0.4寸。穴位深部有肺脏，不可深刺。

【Meaning】Qi, vital energy; hu, door. The point is on upper chest and is like a door for qi, the vital energy of the lung and stomach.

【Location】At the lower border in the center of the clavicle, 4 cun lateral to the anterior midline of the chest (Fig 5-8).

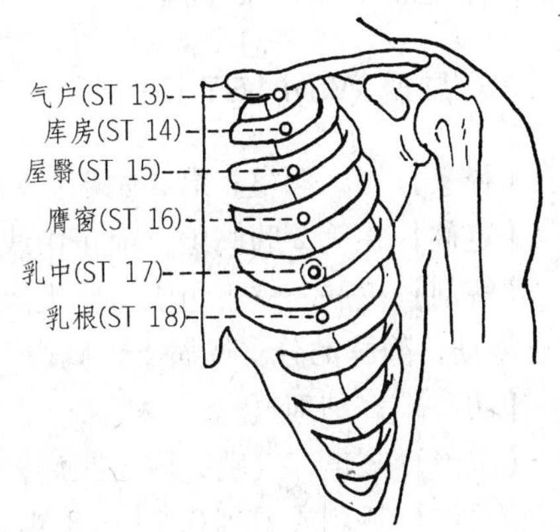

图5-8

Fig 5-8

【Regional anatomy】Skin→subcutaneous tissue→the pectoral muscle. In the superficial layer, there is the intermediate supraclavicular nerve. In the deep layer, there are the axillary artery and the thoracoacromial artery.

【Properties】Diffuse the lung and regulate qi.

【Indications】Cough, asthma, hiccups, chest pain.

【Needling method】Puncture obliquely or transversely 0.2~0.4 cun. Avoid a deep insertion to prevent puncturing the lung.

14. 库房 Kufang (ST 14)

【释义】库，府库；房，旁室。呼吸之气存于肺如储府库；从上至下，犹如从门户进入旁室。

【定位】在第1肋间隙前正中线旁开4寸（图5-8）。

【解剖】皮肤→皮下组织→胸大肌→胸小肌。浅层布有锁骨上神经，肋间神经的皮支。深层有胸肩峰动、静脉的分支和属支，胸内、外侧神经的分支。

【功用】宣肺理气。

【主治】咳嗽，气喘；胸胁胀痛。

【操作】斜刺或平刺0.5~0.8寸。穴位深部有肺脏，不可深刺。

【Meaning】Ku, storehouse; fang, side room. Inhaled air is stored in the lungs as if in a storehouse and descends as if through a door into a side room.

【Location】In the 1st intercostal space, 4 cun lateral to the anterior midline of the chest (Fig 5 – 8).

【Regional anatomy】Skin → subcutaneous tissue → the greater pectoral muscle → the smaller pectoral muscle. In the superficial layer, there are the supraclavicular nerve and the cutaneous branches of the intercostal nerve. In the deep layer, there are the branches or tributaries of the thoracoacromial artery and vein and the branches of the medial pectoral and lateral pectoral nerve.

【Properties】Diffuse the lung and regulate qi.

【Indications】Cough, asthma; distension and pain in the chest.

【Needling method】Puncture obliquely or transversely 0.5 ~ 0.8 cun. Avoid a deep insertion to prevent puncturing the lung.

15. 屋翳 Wuyi (ST 15)

【释义】屋，深室；翳，隐蔽。穴在胸中部，呼吸之气至此如达深室隐蔽。

【定位】在第2肋间隙，前正中线旁开4寸（图5－8）。

【解剖】皮肤→皮下组织→胸大肌→胸小肌。浅层布有第2肋间神经外侧皮支。深层有胸肩峰动、静脉的分支或属支，胸内、外侧神经的分支。

【功用】宣肺理气。

【主治】咳嗽，气喘，胸胁胀痛，乳痈。

【操作】斜刺或平刺0.5～0.8寸。穴位深部有肺脏，不可深刺。

【Meaning】Wu, room; yi, concealment. The point is at the mid – chest. When the inhaled air reaches this point, it "conceals" itself in the underlying room.

【Location】In the 2nd intercostal space, 4 cun lateral to the anterior midline of the chest (Fig 5 – 8).

【Regional anatomy】Skin → subcutaneous tissue → the greater pectoral muscle → the smaller pectoral muscle. In the superficial layer, there are the lateral cutaneous branches of the second intercostal nerve. In the deep layer, there are the branches or tributaries of the thoracoacromial artery and vein and the branches of the medial pectoral and lateral pectoral nerves.

【Properties】Diffuse the lung and regulate qi.

【Indications】Cough, asthma, distension and pain in the chest, mammary abscess.

【Needling method】Puncture obliquely or transversely 0.5 ~ 0.8 cun. Avoid a deep insertion to prevent puncturing the lung.

16. 膺窗 Yingchuang (ST 16)

【释义】膺，胸膺；窗，窗户。穴在胸膺部，犹如胸室之窗。

【定位】在第3肋间隙，前正中线旁开4寸（图5－8）。

【解剖】皮肤→浅筋膜→胸大肌→肋间肌。浅层布有肋间神经的外侧皮支，胸腹壁静脉的属支。深层有胸内、外侧神经，胸肩峰动、静脉的分支或属支，第 3 肋间神经和第 3 肋间后动、静脉。

【功用】理气通乳。

【主治】咳嗽，气喘；胸胁胀痛；乳痈。

【操作】斜刺或平刺 0. 5 ~0. 8 寸。穴位深部有肺脏，不可深刺。

【Meaning】Ying, chest; chuang, window. The point is like a window in the chest.

【Location】Location In the 3rd intercostal space, 4 cun lateral to the anterior midline of the chest (Fig 5 –8).

【Regional anatomy】Skin – subcutaneous tissue→the greater pectoral muscle→the intercostal muscle. In the superficial layer, there are the lateral cutaneous branches of the intercostal nerve and the tributaries of the thoracoepigastric vein. In the deep layer, there are the medial and the lateral pectoral nerves, the branches or tributaries of the thoracoacromial artery and vein, the third intercostal nerve and the third posterior intercostal artery and vein.

【Properties】Regulate qi and promote lactation.

【Indications】Cough, asthma; distension and pain in the chest; mammary abscess.

【Needling method】Puncture obliquely or transversely 0. 5 ~0. 8 cun. Avoid a deep insertion to prevent puncturing the lung.

17. 乳中 Ruzhong (ST 17)

【释义】乳，乳头；中，正中。穴在乳头正中。

【定位】在第 4 肋间隙，前正中线旁开 4 寸，乳头中央（图 5 –8）。

【解剖】乳头皮肤→皮下组织→胸大肌。浅层有第 4 肋间神经外侧皮支，皮下组织内男性主要由结缔组织构成，只有腺组织的迹象，而无腺组织的实质。深层有胸内、外侧神经的分支，胸外侧动、静脉的分支或属支。

【功用】本穴不针不灸。只作胸腹部腧穴定位标志。

【Meaning】Ru, breast; zhong, center. The point is at the center of the nipple.

【Location】In the 4th intercostal space, 4 cun lateral to the anterior midline of the chest, at the center of the nipple (Fig 5 –8).

【Regional anatomy】Skin of the mammary nipple→subcutaneous tissue→the greater pectoral muscle. In the superficial layer, there are the lateral cutaneous branches of the fourth intercostal nerve. In males, the subcutaneous tissue is mainly composed of the connective tissue and the trace, but not parenchyma, of the mammary gland. In the deep layer, there are the branches of the medial and lateral pectoral nerves and the branches or tributaries of the lateral pectoral artery and vein.

【Properties】Acupuncture and moxibustion are prohibited. Only used as the landmark for localization of the acupoints on the chest.

18. 乳根 Rugen（ST 18）

【释义】乳，乳房；根，根部。穴在乳房根部。

【定位】在乳头直下，第5肋间隙，前正中线旁开4寸（图5－8）。

【解剖】皮肤→皮下组织→胸大肌。浅层有第5肋间神经外侧皮支，胸腹壁静脉的属支。深层有胸外侧动、静脉的分支或属支，胸内、外侧神经的分支，第5肋间神经，第5肋间后动、静脉。

【功用】理气通乳。

【主治】乳痈，乳汁少；咳嗽，气喘，呃逆；胸痛。

【操作】斜刺0.5～0.8寸。穴位深部有肺脏，不可深刺。

【Meaning】Ru，breast；gen，root or base. The point is at the base of the breast.

【Location】In the 5th intercostal space，vertically below the nipple，4 cun lateral to the anterior midline of the chest（Fig 5－8）.

【Regional anatomy】Skin→subcutaneous tissue→the greater pectoral muscle. In the superficial layer，there are the lateral cutaneous branches of the 5th intercostal nerve and the tributaries of the thoracoepigastric vein. In the deep layer，there are the branches or tributaries of the lateral pectoral artery and vein，the branches of the medial and lateral pectoral nerves，the 5th intercostal nerve and the 5th posterior intercostal artery and vein.

【Properties】Regulate qi and promote lactation.

【Indications】Mastitis，insufficient lactation；cough，asthma，hiccups；chest pain.

【Needling method】Puncture obliquely 0.5～0.8 cun. Avoid a deep insertion to prevent puncturing the lung.

19. 不容 Burong（ST 19）

【释义】不，不可；容，容纳。穴之上腹部，意指胃纳水谷达此高度，不可再纳。

【定位】脐中上6寸，前正中线旁开2寸（图5－9）。

【解剖】皮肤→皮下组织→腹直肌鞘前壁→腹直肌。浅层布有第6、7、8胸神经前支的外侧皮支和前皮支及腹壁浅静脉。深层有腹壁上动、静脉的分支或属支，第6、7胸神经前支的肌支。

【功用】和胃止呕。

【主治】呕吐，胃痛，腹胀，食欲不振。

【操作】直刺0.5～0.8寸。过饱或肝肿大者不宜针。

【Meaning】Bu，not；rong，contain. The point is on the upper abdomen and marks the upper limitation level for the stomach to receive water and food.

【Location】On the upper abdomen，6 cun above the center of the umbilicus，2 cun lateral to the anterior midline of the abdomen（Fig 5－9）.

【Regional anatomy】 Skin→subcutaneous tissue→the anterior sheath of rectus muscle of the abdomen→the rectus muscle of the abdomen. In the superficial layer, there are the lateral and anterior cutaneous branches of the anterior branches of the 6th to the 8th thoracic nerves and the superficial epigastric vein. In the deep layer, there are the branches or tributaries of the superior epigastric artery and vein and the muscular branches of the anterior branches of the 6th and the 7th thoracic nerves.

【Properties】 Harmonize the stomach and arresting vomiting.

【Indications】 Vomiting, stomachache, abdominal distension, and poor appetite.

【Needling method】 Puncture perpendicularly 0.5 ~0.8 cun. Needling is not advisable for people who have recently eaten a large meal or with hepatomegaly.

20. 承满 Chengman (ST 20)

【释义】承，承受；满，充满。穴在上腹部，意指胃承受水谷至此充满。

【定位】脐中上5寸，前正中线旁开2寸（图5-9）。

【解剖】皮肤→皮下组织→腹直肌鞘前壁→腹直肌。浅层布有第6、7、8胸神经前支的外侧皮支和前皮支及腹壁浅静脉。深层有腹壁上动、静脉的分支或属支，第6、7、8胸神经前支的肌支。

【功用】和胃消胀。

【主治】胃痛，呕吐，腹胀肠鸣，食欲不振。

【操作】直刺0.5~0.8寸。过饱或肝肿大者不宜针。

【Meaning】 Cheng, receive; man, full. The point is on the upper abdomen. The stomach is full when water and food reach this level.

【Location】 On the upper abdomen, 5 cun above the center of the umbilicus, 2 cun lateral to the anterior midline of the abdomen (Fig 5-9).

【Regional anatomy】 Skin → subcutaneous tissue→the anterior sheath of rectus muscle of the abdomen→the rectus muscle of the abdomen. In the superficial layer, there are the lateral and anterior cutaneous branches of the anterior branches of the 6th to the 8th thoracic nerves and the superficial epigastric vein. In the deep layer, there are the branches or tributaries of the superior epigastric artery and vein and the muscular branches of the anterior branches of the 6th and the 8th tho-

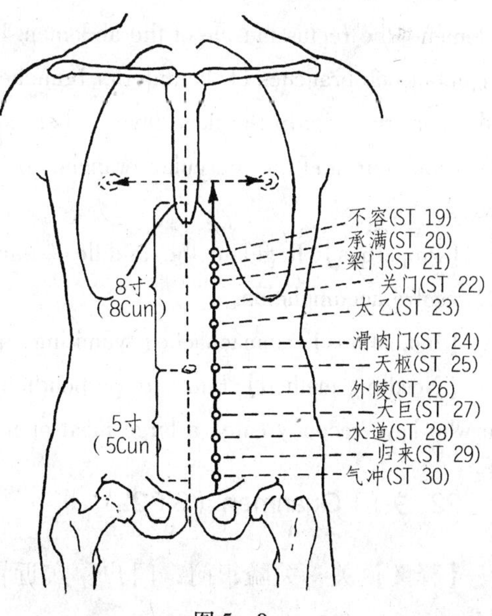

图5-9

Fig 5-9

racic nerves.

【Properties】Harmonize the stomach and relieving flatulence.

【Indications】Stomachache, vomiting, abdominal distension, borborygmus, poor appetite.

【Needling method】Puncture perpendicularly 0.5 ~0.8 cun. Needling is not advisable for people who have recently eaten a large meal or with hepatomegaly.

21. 梁门 Liangmen（ST 21）

【释义】梁，指谷粮；门，门户。穴在上腹部，寓意饮食入胃之门户。

【定位】脐中上4 寸，前正中线旁开2 寸（图5 –9）。

【解剖】皮肤→皮下组织→腹直肌鞘前壁→腹直肌。浅层布有第7、8、9 胸神经前支的外侧皮支和前皮支及腹壁浅静脉。深层有腹壁上动、静脉的分支或属支，第7、8、9 胸神经前支的肌支。

【功用】调中气，和肠胃，化积滞。

【主治】胃痛，呕吐，食欲不振，腹胀。

【操作】直刺0.5 ~0.8 寸。过饱或肝肿大者不宜针。

【Meaning】Liang, grain or food; men, door. The point, on the upper epigastric region, is the door for passage of food to stomach.

【Location】On the upper abdomen, 4 cun above the center of the umbilicus, 2 cun lateral to the anterior midline of the abdomen（Fig 5 –9）.

【Regional anatomy】Skin→subcutaneous tissue→the anterior sheath of rectus muscle of the abdomen→the rectus muscle of the abdomen. In the superficial layer, there are the lateral and anterior cutaneous branches of the anterior branches of the 7th to the 9th thoracic nerves and the superficial epigastric vein. In the deep layer, there are the branches or tributaries of the superior epigastric artery and vein and the muscular branches of the anterior branches of the 7th and the 9th thoracic nerves.

【Properties】Regulate the middle – warmer energy, harmonize the intestines and stomach, and resolve accumulation.

【Indications】Stomachache, vomiting, poor appetite, abdominal distension.

【Needling method】Puncture perpendicularly 0.5 ~0.8 cun. Needling is not advisable for people who have recently eaten a large meal or with hepatomegaly.

22. 关门 Guanmen（ST 22）

【释义】关，关隘；门，门户。穴近胃脘下部，约当胃肠交界之关，有开有关，如同门户。

【定位】脐中上3 寸，前正中线旁开2 寸（图5 –9）。

【解剖】皮肤→皮下组织→腹直肌鞘前壁→腹直肌。浅层布有第7、8、9 胸神经前支的外侧皮支和前皮支及腹壁浅静脉。深层有腹壁上动、静脉的分支或属支，第7、8、9胸神经前支的肌支。

【功用】调胃肠，消胀满，化积滞。

【主治】腹痛，腹胀，肠鸣泄泻，食欲不振。

【操作】直刺0.8～1.2寸。

【Meaning】Guan, pass; men, door. The point is close to lower stomach and corresponds to the junction between the stomach and the intestines, opening and closing like a door.

【Location】On the upper abdomen, 3 cun above the center of the umbilicus, 2 cun lateral to the anterior midline of the abdomen (Fig 5－9).

【Regional anatomy】Skin→subcutaneous tissue→the anterior sheath of rectus muscle of the abdomen→the rectus muscle of the abdomen. In the superficial layer, there are the lateral and anterior cutaneous branches of the anterior branches of the 7th to the 9th thoracic nerves and the superficial epigastric vein. In the deep layer, there are the branches or tributaries of the superior ecpigastric artery and vein and the muscular branches of the anterior branches of the 7th and the 9th thoracic nerves.

【Properties】Harmonize the intestines and stomach, relieve flatulence and resolve accumulation.

【Indications】Abdominal pain and distension, borborygmus, diarrhea, and poor appetite.

【Needling method】Puncture perpendicularly 0.8～1.2 cun.

23. 太乙 Taiyi (ST 23)

【释义】太，甚大；乙，十天干之一。古以中央为太乙，即中宫；脾土居中，喻腹中央为太乙。穴在胃脘下部，约当腹中央。

【定位】脐中上2寸，前正中线旁开2寸（图5－9）。

【解剖】皮肤→皮下组织→腹直肌鞘前壁→腹直肌。浅层布有第8、9、10胸神经前支的外侧皮支和前皮支及腹壁浅静脉。深层有腹壁上动、静脉的分支或属支，第8、9、10胸神经前支的肌支。

【功用】散热除湿。

【主治】腹痛，腹胀；心烦，癫狂。

【操作】直刺0.8～1.2寸。

【Meaning】Tai, great; yi, one of the ten Heavenly Stems. The center was considered as Taiyi in ancient times, Taiyi being the Central Palace of Hetu (the Eight Diagrams). The Spleen is at the center, and the center of the abdomen is identified with Taiyi. The point is on the lower stomach, corresponding to the center of the abdomen.

【Location】On the upper abdomen, 2 cun above the center of the umbilicus, 2 cun lateral to the anterior midline of the abdomen (Fig 5－9).

【Regional anatomy】Skin→subcutaneous tissue→the anterior sheath of rectus muscle of the abdomen→the rectus muscle of the abdomen. In the superficial layer, there are the lateral and anterior cutaneous branches of the anterior branches of the 8th to the 10th thoracic nerves and the superficial epigastric vein. In the deep layer, there are the branches or tributaries of the superior epigastric artery and vein and the muscular branches of the anterior branches of the 8th and the 10th thoracic nerves.

【Properties】 Disperse heat and eliminate dampness.

【Indications】 Abdominal pain and distension; vexation, psychosis.

【Needling method】 Puncture perpendicularly 0.8 ~ 1.2 cun.

24. 滑肉门 Huaroumen (ST 24)

【释义】滑，美好；肉，肌肉；门，门户。滑肉，为初步消化后的精细食物。穴平脐上1寸，食物至此已分清别浊，犹如精细食物通过之门户。

【定位】脐中上1寸，前正中线旁开2寸（图5－9）。

【解剖】皮肤→皮下组织→腹直肌鞘前壁→腹直肌。浅层布有第8、9、10胸神经前支的外侧皮支和前皮支及脐周静脉网。深层有腹壁上动、静脉的分支或属支，第8、9、10胸神经前支的肌支。

【功用】运脾化湿。

【主治】腹痛，呕吐；癫狂。

【操作】直刺0.8～1.2寸。

【Meaning】 Hua, good; rou, muscle; men, door. Huarou refers to the partially digested fine food. The point is at a level 1 cun above the navel where the food is separated into clear and turbid. It is also like a door where the fine food passes through.

【Location】 On the upper abdomen, 1 cun above the center of the umbilicus, 2 cun lateral to the anterior midline of the abdomen (Fig 5－9).

【Regional anatomy】 Skin→subcutaneous tissue→the anterior sheath of rectus muscle of the abdomen→the rectus muscle of the abdomen. In the superficial layer, there are the lateral and anterior cutaneous branches of the anterior branches of the 8th to the 10th thoracic nerves and the periumbilical venous network. In the deep layer, there are the branches or tributaries of the superior epigastric artery and vein and the muscular branches of the anterior branches of the 8th and the 10th thoracic nerves.

【Properties】 Fortify the spleen and resolve dampness.

【Indications】 Abdominal pain, vomiting; psychosis.

【Needling method】 Puncture perpendicularly 0.8 ~ 1.2 cun.

25. 天枢（ST 25），大肠募穴 Tianshu (ST 25), Front - Mu Point of the Large Intestine

【释义】天，天空；枢，枢纽。脐上为天属阳，脐下为地属阴。穴位平脐，如天地间枢纽。

【定位】脐中旁开2寸（图5-9）。

【解剖】皮肤→皮下组织→腹直肌鞘前壁→腹直肌。浅层布有第9、10、11胸神经前支的外侧皮支和前皮支及脐周静脉网。深层有腹壁上、下动、静脉的吻合支，第9、10、11胸神经前支的肌支。

【功用】调理脾胃，疏调大肠，理气消滞，和营调经。

【主治】①腹痛，腹胀，肠鸣，泄泻，痢疾，便秘，肠痈。②月经不调，痛经。③水肿。

【操作】直刺0.8~1.2寸。

【Meaning】Tian, heaven; shu, pivot. The region above the navel is considered as heaven, pertaining to yang, while the region below the navel is earth, pertaining to yin. The point is on a level with the navel, like the pivot between heaven and earth.

【Location】2 cun lateral to the umbilicus (Fig 5-9).

【Regional anatomy】Skin→subcutaneous tissue→the anterior sheath of rectus muscle of the abdomen→the rectus muscle of the abdomen. In the superficial layer, there are the lateral and anterior cutaneous branches of the anterior branches of the 9th to the 11th thoracic nerves and the periumbilical venous network. In the deep layer, there are the branches or tributaries of the superior epigastric arteries and veins and the muscular branches of the anterior branches of the 9th and the 11th thoracic nerves.

【Properties】Harmonize the spleen and stomach, relax the bowels and regulate qi to move stagnation, harmonize the nutrient and regulate menstruation.

【Indications】①Abdominal pain, abdominal distension, borborygmus, diarrhea, dysentery, constipation, intestinal abscess. ②Irregular menstruation, dysmenorrhea. ③Edema.

【Needling method】Puncture perpendicularly 0.8 ~ 1.2 cun.

26. 外陵 Wailing (ST 26)

【释义】外，内外之外；陵，山陵。穴位局部隆起如山陵。

【定位】脐中下1寸，前正中线旁开2寸（图5-9）。

【解剖】皮肤→皮下组织→腹直肌鞘前壁→腹直肌。浅层布有第10、11、12胸神经前支的外侧皮支和前皮支及腹壁浅静脉。深层有腹壁下动、静脉的分支或属支。第10、11、12胸神经前支的肌支。

【功用】行气调肠。

【主治】腹痛，疝气；痛经。

【操作】直刺1.0~1.5寸。

【Meaning】Wai, exterior; ling, hill. The local prominence of the point is like a hill.

【Location】On the lower abdomen, 1 cun below the center of the umbilicus, 2 cun lateral to the anterior midline of the abdomen (Fig 5-9).

【Regional anatomy】Skin→subcutaneous tissue→the anterior sheath of rectus muscle of the abdomen→the rectus muscle of the abdomen. In the superficial layer, there are the lateral and anterior cutaneous branches of the anterior branches of the 10th to the 12th thoracic nerves and the superficial epigastric vein. In the deep layer, there are the branches or tributaries of the inferior epigastric artery and vein and the muscular branches of the anterior branches of the 10th and the 12th thoracic nerves.

【Properties】Move qi and relax the bowels.

【Indications】Abdominal pain, hernia; dysmenorrhea.

【Needling method】Puncture perpendicularly 1. 0 ~1. 5 cun.

27. 大巨 Daju（ST 27）

【释义】大，大小之大；巨，巨大。穴在腹壁最大隆起的部位。

【定位】脐中下2寸，前正中线旁开2寸（图5－9）。

【解剖】皮肤→皮下组织→腹直肌鞘前壁→腹直肌。浅层布有第10、11、12胸神经前支的外侧皮支和前皮支，腹壁浅动脉及腹壁浅静脉。深层有腹壁下动、静脉的分支或属支，第10、11、12胸神经前支的肌支。

【功用】行气利水消胀。

【主治】小腹胀满，小便不利；遗精，早泄；疝气。

【操作】直刺0. 8 ~1. 2寸。

【Meaning】Da, large; ju, huge. The point is on the greatest prominence of the abdominal wall.

【Location】On the lower abdomen, 2 cun below the center of the umbilicus, 2 cun lateral to the anterior midline of the abdomen（Fig 5－9）.

【Regional anatomy】Skin→subcutaneous tissue→the anterior sheath of rectus muscle of the abdomen→the rectus muscle of the abdomen. In the superficial layer, there are the lateral and anterior cutaneous branches of the anterior branches of the 10th to the 12th thoracic nerves and the superficial epigastric artery and vein. In the deep layer, there are the branches or tributaries of the inferior epigastric artery and vein and the muscular branches of the anterior branches of the 10th and the 12th thoracic nerves.

【Properties】Move qi and induce diuresis to alleviate edema.

【Indications】Lower abdominal distension, difficulty in micturition; spermatorrhea, premature ejaculation; hernia.

【Needling method】Puncture perpendicularly 0. 8 ~1. 2 cun.

28. 水道 Shuidao（ST 28）

【释义】水，水液；道，道路。穴位深部相当于小肠并靠近膀胱，属下焦，为水道之所出。

【定位】脐中下3寸，前正中线旁开2寸（图5－9）。

【解剖】皮肤→皮下组织→腹直肌鞘前壁外侧缘→腹直肌外侧缘。浅层布有第11、12胸神经前支和第1腰神经前支的前皮支及外侧皮支，腹壁浅动、静脉。深层有第11、12胸神经前支的肌支。

【功用】利水消胀，调经。

【主治】小腹胀痛，小便不利；痛经；疝气。

【操作】直刺1.0～1.5寸。

【Meaning】Shui，water；dao，pathway. The deep region of the point corresponds to the small intestine and is close to the urinary bladder. It pertains to the lower Jiao，where the waterway passes.

【Location】On the lower abdomen，3 cun below the center of the umbilicus，2 cun lateral to the anterior midline of the abdomen（Fig 5－9）.

【Regional anatomy】Skin→subcutaneous tissue→the lateral border of the anterior sheath of rectus muscle of abdomen→the lateral border of the rectus muscle of the abdomen. In the superficial layer，there are the anterior and lateral cutaneous branches of the anterior branches of the 11th and 12th thoracic nerves and the 1st lumbar nerve，and the superficial epigastric artery and vein. In the deep layer，there are the muscular branches of the anterior branches of the 11th and 12th thoracic nerves.

【Properties】Induce diuresis to alleviate edema and regulate menstruation.

【Indications】Lower abdominal distension，difficulty in micturition；dysmenorrhea；hernia.

【Needling method】Puncture perpendicularly 1.0 ～ 1.5 cun.

29 归来 Guilai（ST 29）

【释义】归，归回；来，到来。本穴能治宫脱、疝气等病，有归复还纳之功。

【定位】脐中下4寸，前正中线旁开2寸（图5－9）。

【解剖】皮肤→皮下组织→腹直肌鞘前壁外侧缘→腹直肌外侧缘。浅层布有第11、12胸神经前支和第1腰神经前支的外侧皮支及前皮支，腹壁浅动、静脉的分支或属支。深层有腹壁下动、静脉的分支或属支和第11、12胸神经前支的肌支。

【功用】理气，治疝，调经。

【主治】经闭，阴挺，痛经，带下，月经不调；小腹痛，疝气。

【操作】直刺1.0～1.5寸。

【Meaning】Gui，return；lai，arrival. This point is indicated in prolapse of uterus and hernia，returning the organs to their original place.

【Location】4 cun below the umbilicus，2 cun lateral to the anterior midline of the abdomen（Fig 5－9）.

【Regional anatomy】Skin→subcutaneous tissue→the lateral border of the anterior sheath of the rectus muscle of the abdomen→the lateral border of rectus muscle of the abdomen. In the superficial layer, there are the superficial epigastric artery and vein, the lateral and the anterior branches of the 11th and 12th thoracic nerves and the 1st lumber nerve, and the branches or tributaries of the superficial epigastric artery and vein. In the deep layer, there are the branches or tributaries of the inferior epigastric artery and vein, and the muscular branches of the anterior branches of the 11th and 12th thoracic nerves.

【Properties】Regulate qi, treat hernia and regulate menstruation.

【Indications】Amenia, prolapse of the uterus, dysmenorrhea, leukorrhea, irregular menstruation; lower abdominal pain, hernia.

【Needling method】Puncture perpendicularly 1.0 ~ 1.5 cun.

30. 气冲 Qichong（ST 30）

【释义】气，指经气；冲，冲要。穴在气街部位，为经气流注之冲要。

【定位】脐中下 5 寸，前正中线旁开 2 寸（图 5－9）。

【解剖】皮肤→皮下组织→腹外斜肌腱膜→腹内斜肌→腹横肌。浅层布有腹壁浅动、静脉，第 12 胸神经前支和第 1 腰神经前支的外侧皮支及前皮支。深层：下外侧在腹股沟管内有精索（或子宫圆韧带）、髂腹股沟神经和生殖股神经生殖支。

【功用】疏调膀胱，和营调经。

【主治】腹痛，疝气；月经不调，不孕，阳痿，阴肿痛。

【操作】直刺 0.8 ~1.2 寸。

【Meaning】Qi, qi of meridian; chong, gushing. The point is locate on Qijie and is a passage for qi of the meridian to circulate.

【Location】On the lower abdomen, 5 cun below the center of the umbilicus, 2 cun lateral to the anterior midline of the abdomen（Fig 5－9）.

【Regional anatomy】Skin→subcutaneous tissue→the aponeurosis of the external oblique muscle of the abdomen→the interal oblique muscle of the abdomen→the transverse muscle of the abdomen. In the superficial layer, there are the superficial epigastric artery and vein, the lateral and anterior cutaneous branches of the anterior branches of the 12th thoracic nerve and the 1st lumbar nerve. In the deep layer, there are the spermatic cord（or the round ligament of the uterus）, the ilioinguinal nerve, and the genital branch of the genitofemoral nerve in the inguinal canal at the inferior lateral side of this area.

【Properties】Regulate the bladder, harmonize the nutrient and regulate menstruation.

【Indications】Abdominal pain, hernia; irregular menstruation, infertility, impotence, swelling of the vulva.

【Needling method】Puncture perpendicularly 0.8 ~ 1.2 cun.

31. 髀关 Biguan（ST 31）

【释义】髀，股；关，关节。穴在股关节部位。

【定位】在髂前上棘与髌骨底外侧端的连线上，屈股时平会阴，缝匠肌外侧凹陷处（图5－10）。

【解剖】皮肤→皮下组织→阔筋膜张肌与缝匠肌之间→股直肌→股外侧肌。浅层布有股外侧皮神经。深层有旋股外侧动、静脉的升支，股神经的肌支。

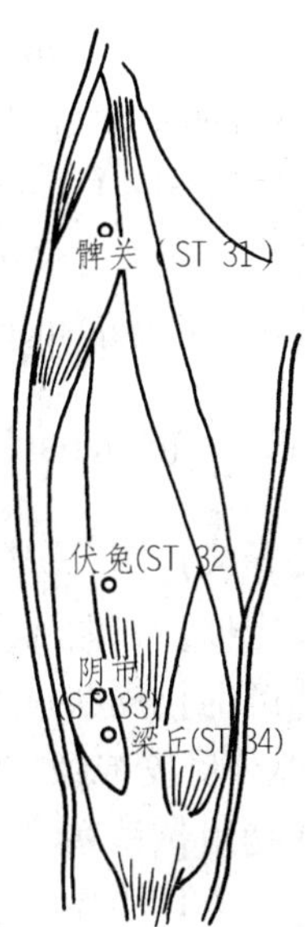

图5－10

Fig 5－10

【功用】祛风通络，利腰膝。

【主治】下肢痿痹、不遂，腰腿疼痛。

【操作】直刺0.6～1.2寸。

【Meaning】Bi, thigh; guan, joint. The point is at the femora junction.

【Location】On the line linking the anterior superior iliac spine and the lateral border of the patella, level with the gluteal groove in the depression lateral to the sartorius muscle（Fig 5－10）.

【Regional anatomy】Skin→subcutaneous tissue→between the tensor muscle of the fascia lata and the sartorius muscle→the rectus muscle of the thigh→the lateral vastus muscle of the thigh. In the superficial layer, there is the lateral cutaneous nerve of the thigh. In the deep layer, there are the ascending branches of the lateral circumflex femoral artery and vein and the muscular branches of the femoral nerve.

【Properties】Dispel wind to free the collateral vessels and disinhibit the waist and knee.

【Indications】Weakness, numbness and pain of the lower limbs, pain of the lower back and leg.

【Needling method】Puncture perpendicularly 0.6 ～1.2 cun.

32. 伏兔 Futu（ST 32）

【释义】伏，俯伏；兔，兔子。穴位局部肌肉隆起，形如俯伏之兔。

【定位】在髂前上棘与髌骨底外侧端的连线上，髌骨底上6寸（图5－10）。

【解剖】皮肤→皮下组织→股直肌→股中间肌。浅层布有股外侧静脉，股神经前皮支及股外侧皮神经。深层有旋股外侧动、静脉的降支，股神经的肌支。

【功用】祛寒湿，利腰膝。

【主治】下肢痿痹、不遂，腰膝冷痛。

【操作】直刺0.6～1.2寸。

【Meaning】Fu, lying prostrate; tu, rabbit. The prominence of the local muscle of the point looks like a rabbit in prostration.

【Location】 On the line linking the anterior superior iliac spine and the lateral border of the patella, 6 cun above the patella (Fig 5 – 10).

【Regional anatomy】 Skin→subcutaneous tissue→the rectus muscle of the thigh→the intermediate vastus muscle of the thigh. In the superficial layer, there are the lateral femoral vein, the anterior cutaneous branches of the femoral nerve and the lateral cutaneous nerve of the thigh. In the deep layer, there are the descending branches of the lateral circumflex artery and vein and the muscular branches of the femoral nerve.

【Properties】 Dispel cold – dampness, disinhibit the waist and knee.

【Indications】 Atrophy and paralysis of the legs, coldness, pain of the lower back and knees.

【Needling method】 Puncture perpendicularly 0. 6 ~ 1. 2 cun.

33. 阴市 Yinshi (ST 33)

【释义】阴，阴阳之阴；市，集市。阴，指寒邪；市，聚散之意。穴能疏散膝部寒邪。

【定位】在髂前上棘与髌骨底外侧端的连线上，髌骨底上 3 寸（图 5 – 10)。

【解剖】皮肤→皮下组织→股直肌腱与股外侧肌之间→股中间肌。浅层布有股神经前皮支和股外侧皮神经。深层有旋股外侧动、静脉的降支和股神经肌支。

【功用】祛寒湿，利膝关。

【主治】膝痛，下肢痿痹、不遂。

【操作】直刺 0. 5 ~ 1. 0 寸。

【Meaning】 Yin, yin of yin – yang; shi, market. Yin refers to pathogenic cold, while shi means dispersion. The point is used to disperse pathogenic cold from the knee.

【Location】 On the line linking the anterior superior iliac spine and the lower lateral border of the patella, 3 cun above the upper lateral border of the kneecap (Fig 5 – 10).

【Regional anatomy】 Skin→subcutaneous tissue→between the tendons of the rectus muscle and the lateral vastus muscle of the thigh→the intermediate vastus muscle of the thigh. In the superficial layer, there are the anterior cutaneous branches of the femoral nerve and the lateral cutaneous nerve of the thigh. In the deep layer, there are the descending branches of the lateral circumflex femoral artery and vein and the muscular branches of the femoral nerve.

【Properties】 Dispel cold – dampness and disinhibit the knee joint.

【Indications】 Knee pain, atrophy and paralysis of the legs.

【Needling method】 Puncture perpendicularly 0. 5 ~ 1. 0 cun.

34. 梁丘 (ST 34)，郄穴
Liangqiu (ST 34), Xi - Cleft Point

【释义】梁，山梁；丘，丘陵。形如山梁丘陵，穴当其处。

【定位】在髂前上棘与髌骨底外侧端的连线上，髌骨底上2寸（图5－10）。

【解剖】皮肤→皮下组织→股直肌腱与股外侧肌之间→股中间肌腱的外侧。浅层布有股神经的前皮支和股外侧皮神经。深层有旋股外侧动、静脉的降支和股神经的肌支。

【功用】通调胃气，祛风化湿，利膝关。

【主治】胃痛；膝痛，下肢痿痹、不遂；乳痈。

【操作】直刺0.5～0.8寸。

【Meaning】Liang, ridge; qiu, hills. The prominent muscle above the knee looks like a ridge in hills, and there the point is located.

【Location】On the line connecting the anterior superior iliac spine and the lower lateral border of the patella, 2 cun above the upper lateral border of the patella (Fig 5－10).

【Regional anatomy】Skin→subcutaneous tissue→between the tendons of the rectus muscle of the thigh and the lateral vastus muscle of the thigh→the lateral side of the tendon of the intermediate vastus muscle of the thigh. In the superficial layer, there are the anterior cutaneous branches of the femoral nerve and the lateral cutaneous nerve of the thigh. In the deep layer, there are the descending branches of the lateral circumflex femoral artery and vein and the muscular branches of the femoral nerve.

【Properties】Harmonize the gastric qi, dispel wind to resolve dampness and disinhibit the knee joint.

【Indications】Stomach pain; knee pain, atrophy and paralysis of the legs; mastitis.

【Needling method】Puncture perpendicularly 0.5～0.8 cun.

35. 犊鼻 Dubi (ST 35)

【释义】犊，小牛；鼻，鼻子。髌骨下两侧凹陷，形如牛犊鼻孔，穴在外孔中。

【定位】屈膝，在膝部髌骨与髌韧带外侧凹陷中（图5－11）。

【解剖】皮肤→皮下组织→髌韧带与髌外侧支持带之间→膝关节囊、翼状皱襞。浅层布有腓肠外侧皮神经，股神经前皮支，隐神经的髌下支和膝关节动、静脉网。深层有膝关节腔。

【功用】祛风湿，利膝关。

【主治】膝肿痛，屈伸不利，脚气。

【操作】向后内斜刺0.8～1.5寸。

【Meaning】Du, calf; bi, nose. The depression on both sides below the kneecap are likened to the nostrils of a calf. The point is at the external foramen.

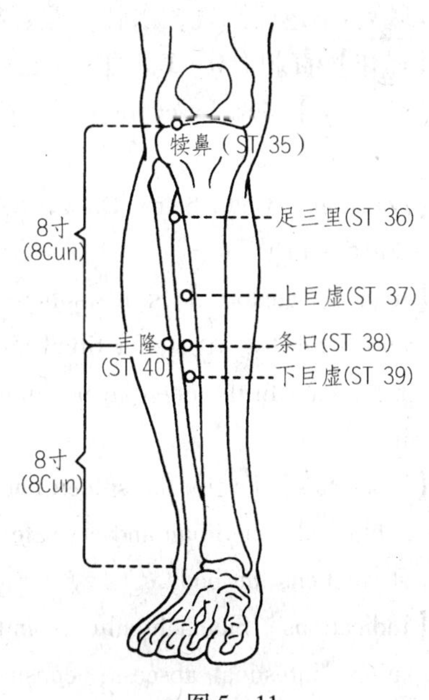

图5－11
Fig 5－11

【Location】When the knee is flexed, at the lower border of the patella, in the depression lateral to the patella ligament (Fig 5 – 11).

【Regional anatomy】Skin→subcutaneous tissue→between the ligament of the patella and the lateral patellar retinaculum→the capsule of the knee joint and the alar folds. In the superficial layer, there are the lateral cutaneous nerve of the calf, the anterior cutaneous branches of the femoral nerve, the infrapatellar branches of the saphenous nerve and the arteriovenous network of the knee joint. In the deep layer, there is the cavity of the knee joint.

【Properties】Dispel wind – dampness and disinhibit the knee joint.

【Indications】Swelling and pain in the knees, difficulty in flexing and extending the knees, and beriberi.

【Needling method】Puncture obliquely from the posterior to interior direction 0.8 ~1.5 cun.

36. 足三里（ST 36），合穴；胃下合穴
Zu san li (ST 36), He - Sea Point; Lower He - Sea Point of the Stomach

【释义】足，下肢；三，数词；里，古代有以里为寸之说。穴在下肢，位于膝下3寸。

【定位】犊鼻穴下3寸，胫骨前缘外一横指（中指）（图5–11）。

【解剖】皮肤→皮下组织→胫骨前肌→小腿骨间膜→胫骨后肌。浅层布有腓肠外侧皮神经。深层有胫前动、静脉的分支或属支。

【功用】健脾和胃，通肠消滞，通经活络，补益气血，为全身强壮要穴。

【主治】胃痛，呕吐，腹痛，腹胀，泄泻，痢疾，便秘，肠痈；虚劳羸瘦，心悸气短；下肢痿痹、不遂，脚气，水肿；癫、狂、痫。

【操作】直刺1.0~1.5寸。

【Meaning】Zu, lower limbs; san, three; li, taken as cun in ancient times. The point is 3 cun below the knee.

【Location】3 cun below Dubi (ST 35), one finger width lateral to the anterior crest of the tibia (Fig 5 – 11).

【Regional anatomy】Skin→subcutaneous tissue→the anterior tibial muscle→the interosseous membrane of the leg→posterior tibial muscle. In the superficial layer, there is the lateral cutaneous nerve of the calf. In the deep layer, there are the branches or tributaries of the anterior tibial artery and vein.

【Properties】Fortify the spleen and harmonize the stomach, relax the bowel and move stagnation, unblock the meridian and activate collaterals, tonify qi and replenish blood. It is the key point which strengthens the body.

【Indications】Stomach pain, vomiting, abdominal pain and distension, diarrhea, dysentery, constipation, intestinal abscess; consumptive disease, palpitation, shortness of breath; atrophy and paralysis of the legs, beriberi, edema; psychosis and epilepsy.

【Needling method】Puncture perpendicularly 1.0 ~1.5 cun.

37. 上巨虚 Shangjuxu（ST 37），大肠下合穴 Shangjuxu（ST 37），Lower He - Sea Point of the Large Intestine

【释义】上，上方；巨，巨大；虚，中空。胫、腓骨髓间形成较大间隙，即中空。穴在此空隙之上方。

【定位】犊鼻穴下6寸，胫骨前缘外一横指（中指）（图5-11）。

【解剖】皮肤→皮下组织→胫骨前肌→小腿骨间膜→胫骨后肌。浅层布有腓肠外侧皮神经。深层有胫前动、静脉和腓深神经。如深刺可能刺中胫后动、静脉和胫神经。

【功用】调理脾胃，通肠消滞，通经活络。

【主治】腹痛，泄泻，痢疾，便秘，肠痈；下肢痿痹、不遂，脚气。

【操作】直刺1.0~1.5寸。

【Meaning】Shang, upper; ju, great; xu, void. A large void is formed between the tibia and fibula. The point is in the upper part of the void.

【Location】6 cun below Dubi（ST 35）, one finger width lateral to the anterior crest of the tibia（Fig 5-11）.

【Regional anatomy】Skin→subcutaneous tissue→the anterior tibial muscle→interosseous membrane of the leg→the posterior tibial muscle. In the superficial layer, there is the lateral cutaneous nerve of the calf. In the deep layer, there are the anterior tibia artery and vein and the deep peroneal nerve. If the needle is inserted too deep, it may injure the posterior tibia artery and vein and the tibia nerve.

【Properties】Harmonize the spleen and stomach, relax the bowels and move stagnation, unblock the meridian and activate collaterals.

【Indications】Abdominal pain, diarrhea, dysentery, constipation, intestinal abscess; atrophy and paralysis of the legs, beriberi.

【Needling method】Puncture perpendicularly 1.0 ~1.5 cun.

38. 条口 Tiaokou（ST 38）

【释义】条，长条；口，空隙。穴在腓、胫骨之间的长条空隙之中。

【定位】犊鼻穴下8寸，距胫骨前缘一横指（中指）（图5-11）。

【解剖】皮肤→皮下组织→胫骨前肌→小腿骨间膜→胫骨后肌。浅层布有腓肠外侧皮神经。深层有胫前动、静脉和腓深神经。如深刺可能刺中腓动、静脉。

【功用】调理肠胃，行气通络。

【主治】下肢痿痹；脘腹疼痛；肩臂痛。

【操作】直刺1.0~1.5寸。

【Meaning】Tiao, strip; kou, space. The point is in the strip space between the fibula and tibia.

【Location】8 cun below Dubi (ST 35), one finger width Lateral to the anterior crest of the tibia (Fig 5 – 11).

【Regional anatomy】Skin → subcutaneous tissue → the anterior tibial muscle → interosseous membrane of the leg→the posterior tibial muscle. In the superficial layer, there is the lateral cutaneous nerve of the calf. In the deep layer, there are the anterior tibial artery and vein and the deep peroneal nerve. If the needle is inserted too deep, it may injure the posterior tibial artery and vein.

【Properties】Harmonize the intestines and stomach, move qi to free the collateral vessels.

【Indications】Atrophy and paralysis of the legs; pain in the abdomen and stomach; pain in the shoulders and arms.

【Needling method】Puncture perpendicularly 1. 0 ~ 1. 5 cun.

39. 下巨虚 (ST 39), 小肠下合穴
Xiajuxu (ST 39), Lower He - Sea Point of the Small Intestine

【释义】下，下方；巨，巨大；虚，中空。胫、腓骨髓间形成较大间隙，即中空。穴在此空隙之下方。

【定位】犊鼻穴下9寸，胫骨前缘外一横指（中指）（图5－11)。

【解剖】皮肤→皮下组织→胫骨前肌→小腿骨间膜→胫骨后肌。浅层布有腓肠外侧皮神经。深层有胫前动、静脉和腓深神经。

【功用】调理肠胃，行气止痛。

【主治】小腹痛，肠鸣，泄泻；下肢痿痹、不遂。

【操作】直刺1.0~1.5寸。

【Meaning】Xia, lower; ju, great; xu, void. A large void is formed between the tibia and fibula. The point is in the lower part of the void.

【Location】9 cun below Dubi (ST 35), one finger width lateral to the anterior crest of the tibia (Fig 5 – 11).

【Regional anatomy】Skin → subcutaneous tissue → the anterior tibial muscle → interosseous membrane of the leg→the posterior tibial muscle. In the superficial layer, there is the lateral cutaneous nerve of the calf. In the deep layer, there are the anterior tibial artery and vein and the deep peroneal nerve.

【Properties】Harmonize the intestines and stomach, move qi to relieve pain.

【Indications】Lower abdominal pain, borborygmus, diarrhea; atrophy and paralysis of the legs.

【Needling method】Puncture perpendicularly 1. 0 ~ 1. 5 cun.

40. 丰隆 (ST 40), 络穴
Fenglong (ST 40), Luo - Connecting Point

【释义】丰，丰满；隆，隆盛。胃经谷气隆盛，至此处丰满溢出于大络。

【定位】外踝尖上8寸，距胫骨前缘外二横指（中指）（图5-11）。

【解剖】皮肤→皮下组织→趾长伸肌→长伸肌→小腿骨间膜→胫骨后肌。浅层布有腓肠外侧皮神经。深层有胫前动、静脉的分支或属支和腓深神经的分支。

【功用】和胃，化痰。

【主治】咳嗽痰多，头痛，眩晕，癫狂痫，下肢痿痹。

【操作】直刺1.0~1.5寸。

【Meaning】Feng, plentiful; long, abundance. The plentiful grain qi of the stomach meridian overflows into its collateral at this point.

【Location】8 cun above the external malleolus, two finger widths lateral to the anterior crest of the tibia (Fig 5-11).

【Regional anatomy】Skin→subcutaneous tissue→the long extensor muscle of toes→the long extensor muscle of the great toe→the interosseous membrane of the leg→the posterior tibial muscle. In the superficial layer, there is the lateral cutaneous nerve of the calf. In the deep layer, there are the branches of tributaries of the anterior tibial artery and vein and the branches of the deep peroneal nerve.

【Properties】Harmonize the stomach and resolve phlegm.

【Indications】Cough with phlegm, headache, vertigo, psychosis, epilepsy, atrophy and paralysis of the legs.

【Needling method】Puncture perpendicularly 1.0~1.5 cun.

41. 解溪（ST 41），经穴
Jiexi (ST 41), Jing - River Point

【释义】解，分解；溪，沟溪。溪，指体表较小凹陷。穴在踝关节前骨节分解凹陷中。

【定位】足背踝关节横纹的中央，拇长伸肌腱与趾长伸肌腱之间（图5-12）。

【解剖】皮肤→皮下组织→拇长伸肌腱与趾长伸肌腱之间→距骨。浅层布有足背内侧皮神经及足背皮下静脉。深层有腓深神经和胫前动、静脉。

【功用】健脾化湿。

【主治】下肢痿痹，足踝肿痛；腹胀，便秘；头痛，眩晕，癫狂痫。

【操作】直刺0.5~1.0寸。

【Meaning】Jie, separation; xi, stream. Xi refers to a minor depression on the body surface. The point is in the anterior articular depression of the ankle joint.

【Location】At the midpoint of the transverse crease of the

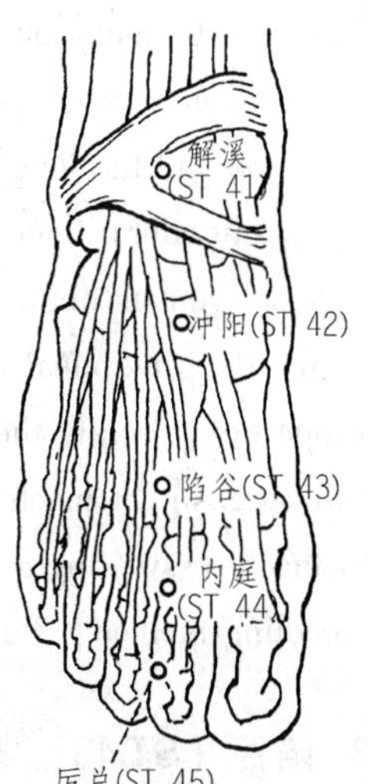

图5-12

Fig 5-12

ankle joint, between the tendons of the digitorum longus and hallucis longus (Fig 5 – 12).

【Regional anatomy】Skin→subcutaneous tissue – between tendons of the long extensor muscle of the great toe and the long extensor muscle of the toes→talus. In the superficial layer, there are the medial dorsal cutaneous nerves and the subcutaneous veins. In the deep layer, there are the deep peroneal nerve and the anterior tibial artery and vein.

【Properties】Fortify the spleen and resolve dampness.

【Indications】Atrophy and paralysis of the legs, pain in the ankle and wrist; abdominal distension, constipation; headache, vertigo, psychosis, epilepsy.

【Needling method】Puncture perpendicularly 0.5 ~ 1.0 cun.

42. 冲阳 (ST 42), 原穴
Chongyang (ST 42), Yuan - Source Point

【释义】冲，冲要；阳，阴阳之阳。穴在冲阳脉（足背动脉）所在之处。

【定位】足背最高处，拇长伸肌腱与趾长伸肌腱之间，足背动脉搏动处（图 5 – 12）。

【解剖】皮肤→皮下组织→拇长伸肌腱与趾长伸肌腱之间→短伸肌→中间楔骨。浅层布有足背内侧皮神经，足背静脉网。深层有足背动、静脉和腓深神经。

【功用】扶土化湿，和胃宁神。

【主治】胃痛，腹胀；口㖞，面肿，齿痛；足背肿痛，足痿无力。

【操作】避开动脉，直刺 0.3 ~0.5 寸。

【Meaning】Chong, important place; yang, yang of yin – yang. The point is where the chongyang pulse is located (arteria dorsalis pedis).

【Location】At the highest point of the dorsum of the foot, between the tendons of the digitorum longus and hallucis longus, where the dorsal artery of the foot pulsates (Fig 5 – 12).

【Regional anatomy】Skin→subcutaneous tissue→between tendons of the long extensor muscle of the great toe and the long extensor muscle of toes→the short extensor muscle of the great toe→the intermediate cuneiform bone. In the superficial layer, there are the medial dorsal cutaneous nerve and the dorsal venous network of the foot. In the deep layer, there are the dorsal pedal artery and vein and the deep peroneal nerve.

【Properties】Tonify the spleen and resolve dampness, harmonize the stomach and tranquilize.

【Indications】Stomach pain, abdominal distension; deviation of the mouth, swelling of the face, toothache; swelling and pain in the dorsa of the foot, weakness and numbness of the the foot.

【Needling method】Puncture perpendicularly 0.3 ~ 0.5 cun; avoid needling the artery.

43. 陷谷 (ST 43), 输穴
Xiangu (ST 43), Shu - Stream Point

【释义】陷，凹陷；谷，山谷。谷，指体表凹陷。穴在第 2 跖骨间隙凹陷中。

【定位】足背，第2、3跖骨结合部前方凹陷处（图5－12）。

【解剖】皮肤→皮下组织→趾长伸肌腱→趾短伸肌腱内侧→第2骨间背侧肌→拇收肌斜头。浅层布有足背内侧皮神经和足背静脉网。深层有第2跖背动、静脉。

【功用】行气利水。

【主治】面目浮肿，水肿；肠鸣腹泻；足背肿痛。

【操作】直刺0.3~0.5寸。

【Meaning】Xian, depression; gu, valley. Gu implies a depression on the body surface. The point is in the depression between the second and third metatarsal bones.

【Location】On the dorsum the foot, in the depression distal to the junction of the 2nd and 3rd metatarsal bones (Fig 5－12).

【Regional anatomy】Skin→subcutaneous tissue→tendons of the long extensor muscle of the toes→the medial side of the tendon of the short extensor muscle of the toes→the 2nd dorsal interosseous muscle→the oblique head of the abductor of the great toe. In the superficial layer, there are the medial dorsal cutaneous nerve and the dorsal venous network of the foot. In the deep layer, there are the 2nd dorsal metatarsal artery and vein.

【Properties】Move qi and induce diuresis.

【Indications】Facial and general edema; borborygmus, diarrhea; swelling and pain of the dorsum of the foot.

【Needling method】Puncture perpendicularly 0.3~0.5 cun.

44. 内庭（ST 44），荥穴
Neiting (ST 44), Ying - Spring Point

【释义】内，里边；庭，庭院。本穴在厉兑之里，犹如门内的庭院。

【定位】足背第2、3趾间，趾蹼缘后方赤白肉际处（图5－12）。

【解剖】皮肤→皮下组织→在第2与第3趾的趾长、短伸肌腱之间→第2、第3跖骨头之间。浅层布有足背内侧皮神经的趾背神经和足背静脉网。深层有趾背动、静脉。

【功用】清胃热，化积滞。

【主治】齿痛，咽喉肿痛，鼻衄，口㖞；热病；胃痛，吐酸，泄泻，痢疾，便秘；足背肿痛。

【操作】直刺或斜刺0.3~0.5寸。

【Meaning】Nei, interior; ting, courtyard. This point is proximal to Lidui (ST 45), likened to its courtyard.

【Location】Proximal to the web margin between the 2nd and 3rd toes, at the junction posterior to the toe web of the red and the white skin (Fig 5－12).

【Regional anatomy】Skin→subcutaneous tissue→between the tendons of the long and the short extensor muscle of the 2nd and 3rd toes→between the heads of the 2nd and 3rd metatarsal bones. In the superficial layer, there are the dorsal digital nerve of the medial dorsal pedal cutaneous nerve and the dorsal arteriovenous network of the foot. In the deep layer, there are the dorsal artery and vein.

【Properties】 Clear stomach fire and move stagnation.

【Indications】 Toothache, swollen and sore throat, nosebleed, deviated mouth; febrile diseases; stomach pain with sour regurgitation, diarrhea, dysentery, constipation; swelling and pain in the dorsum of the foot.

【Needling method】 Puncture perpendicularly or obliquely 0.3 ~0.5 cun.

45. 厉兑（ST 45），井穴
Lidui (ST 45), Jing - Well Point

【释义】厉，指胃；兑，代表门。本穴在趾端，犹如胃经之门户。

【定位】足第2趾外侧，距趾甲角0.1寸（图5－12）。

【解剖】皮肤→皮下组织→甲根。布有足背内侧皮神经的趾背神经和趾背动、静脉网。

【功用】苏厥醒神，清胃热。

【主治】齿痛，鼻衄，咽喉肿痛；热病；多梦，梦魇，癫狂。

【操作】浅刺0.1寸。

【Meaning】 Li, stomach; dui, door. This point is at the end of the second toe, like a door of the Stomach Meridian.

【Location】 On the lateral side at the end of the 2nd toe, 0.1 cun lateral to the corner of the nail (Fig 5 – 12).

【Regional anatomy】 Skin→subcutaneous tissue→root of the nail. There are the dorsal digital nerve of the medial dorsal pedal cutaneous nerve and the dorsal digital arteriovenous network in this area.

【Properties】 Induce resuscitation and clear stomach fire.

【Indications】 Toothache, nosebleed, swollen and sore throat; febrile diseases; profuse dreaming, nightmares, psychosis.

【Needling method】 Puncture superficially 0.1 cun.

复习思考题
Review Questions

1. 以《灵枢·经脉》原文叙述足阳明胃经的循行。

Write out the course of the stomach meridian of foot – yangming according the chapter "Discussion on the Meridians" in *Miraculous Pivot*.

2. 简述足阳明胃经经穴主治概要。

Retell the major indications of the points of the stomach meridian of foot – yangming.

3. 简述承泣穴的定位与针刺操作。

Retell the location and needling method of Chengqi (ST 1).

4. 简述下关、天枢、梁丘和内庭的定位、主治与操作。

Retell the location, indications and needling method of Xia guan (ST 7), Tian shu (ST 25), Liangqiu (ST 34) and Nèitíng (ST 44).

5. 试述足三里、上巨虚、下巨虚的定位与主治异同。

Try to retell the differences of location and indications among Zusanli (ST 36), Shangjuxu (ST 37) and Xiajuxu (ST 39).

6. 简述条口、丰隆的定位、主治和操作。

Retell the location, indications and needling method of Tiaokou (ST 38) and Fenglong (ST 40).

第六章 足太阴经络与腧穴
Meridian and Collateral and Its Acupoints of Foot – Taiyin

第一节 足太阴经络
Meridian and Collateral of Foot – Taiyin

一、足太阴经脉
Meridian of Foot - Taiyin

（一）经脉循行
The Course of Meridian

足太阴脾经，从大趾末端开始，沿大趾内侧赤白肉际，经第一跖骨基底粗隆部后，上向内踝前边，再上小腿内侧，沿胫骨后，交出足厥阴肝经之前，上膝股内侧前边，进入腹部，属于脾，络于胃；通过膈肌，夹食管旁，连舌根，散布舌下。

其支脉，从胃部分出，向上通过膈肌，流注心中，接手少阴心经。

脾之大络，穴名大包，位在渊腋穴下三寸，分布于胸胁（图6-1）。

《灵枢·经脉》原文：脾足太阴之脉，起于大指之端，循指内侧白肉际，过核骨后，上内踝前廉，上腨内，循胫骨后，交出厥阴之前，上膝股内前廉，入腹，属脾，络胃，上膈，夹咽，连舌本，散舌下。

其支者，复从胃别，上膈，注心中。

脾之大络，名曰大包，出渊腋下三寸，布胸胁（图6-1）。

The spleen meridian starts from the tip of the big toe. It runs along the medial aspect of the big toe between the red and white skin and ascends to the front of the medial malleolus and further up to the medial aspect of the leg. It follows the posterior aspect of the tibia and passes through the front of the liver meridian 8cun above the medial malleolus. Going on along the anterior medial aspect of the knee and then the thigh, it enters the abdomen, reaches the spleen, its pertaining organ, and connects with the stomach. From there it ascends, passing through the diaphragm and running alongside the esophagus. When it reaches the root of the tongue, it spreads over under the tongue.

The abdominal branch of the meridian goes from the stomach through the diaphragm, then flows into the heart to link with the heart meridian of hand – shaoyin.

The major collateral of the spleen meridian distributes in the 3rd sidetrack of the thoracic – abdominal aspect, passing beneath the clavicle and terminates at the acupoint——Dabao (SP 21) below the axilla (Fig 6 – 1).

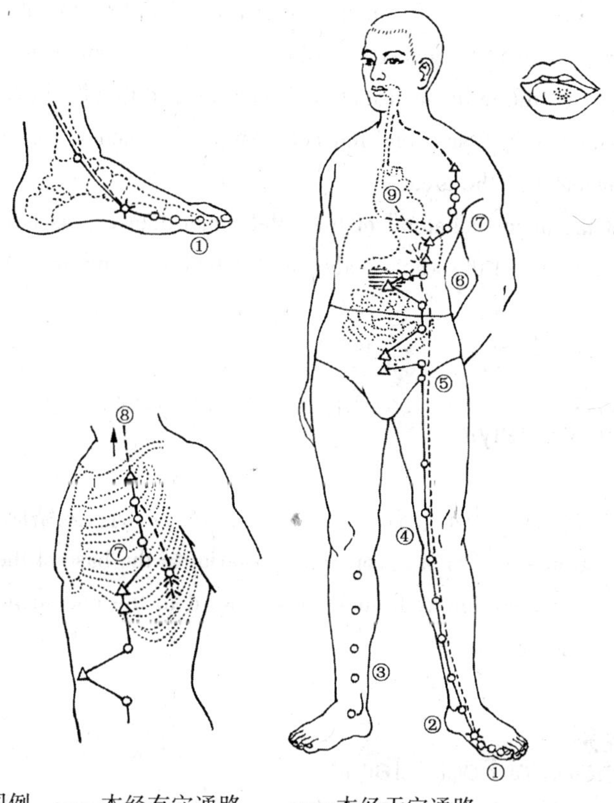

图例 ——本经有穴通路 ……本经无穴通路

Note ——Pathway with points ……Pathway without points

图 6 – 1 足太阴经脉、络脉循行示意图

Fig 6 – 1 The course of the meridian and collateral of foot – taiyin

(二) 经脉病候
The Syndromes of Meridian

本经异常表现为下列病症：舌根部发强，食后就要呕，胃脘痛，腹胀，好嗳气，大便或矢气后就感到轻松，全身感到沉重无力。

本经穴主治"脾"方面所发生的病症：舌根部痛，身体不能活动，吃不下，心胸烦闷，心窝下急痛，大便溏，腹有痞块，泄泻，或小便不通，黄疸，不能安睡，想打呵欠而气不畅，大腿和小腿内侧肿、厥冷，足大趾不能运用。

脾大络病症：实证，浑身酸痛；虚证，百节松弛软弱。

The manifestations of this meridian with abnormal functions includes: stiffness of the tongue root, bitter vomitus just after a meal, stomach pain, abdominal distention, frequent belching, feeling relaxed after a defecation or fart, feeling heaviness and weakness of the whole body.

Acupoints on the meridian are used for the syndromes caused by the disorders of the spleen - organ. They are as follows: pain of the tongue root, limited movement of the body, aversion to food, restlessness, oppression in the chest, cardiac pain, loose stools with undigested food, mass in the abdomen, diarrhea, difficulty in urination, jaundice, difficulty in falling asleep, yawning but leading to a stagnation of qi, swelling and coldness in the medial aspect of the thigh and the lower leg, limited movement of the great toe.

The syndromes of the major collateral of the spleen meridian are as follows: excess syndrome manifests as soreness and pain of the whole body, and deficiency syndrome manifests as weakness of the limbs.

二、足太阴络脉
Collateral of Foot - Taiyin

足太阴之别，名曰公孙。去本节后一寸，别走阳明；其别者入络肠胃（图6-1）。

It branches out at Gongsun (SP 4), one cun posterior to the base of the first metatarsal bone, and then joins the stomach meridian. A branch runs upward to the abdomen and connects with the stomach and intestines (Fig 6-1).

三、足太阴经别
Divergent Meridian of Foot - Taiyin

足太阴之正，上至髀，合于阳明。与别俱行，上结于咽，贯舌本（图6-2）。

After deriving from the spleen meridian on the thigh, It converges with the divergent meridian of the stomach meridian of foot - yangming and runs upward to the throat, and finally enters the tongue (Fig 6-2).

四、足太阴经筋
Muscular Region of Foot - Taiyin

足太阴之筋，起于大指之端内侧，上结于内踝。其直者，结于膝内辅骨；上循阴股，结于髀，聚于阴器。上腹，结于脐；循腹里，结于肋，散于胸中；其内者着于脊（图6-3）。

It starts from the medial side of the big toe and knots at the internal malleolus. Continuing upward and knotting at the medial side of the knee, it traverses the medial aspect of the thigh, and knots at the hip. Then it joins with the external genitalia and extends to the abdomen, knotting with the umbilicus. From there, it enters the abdominal cavity, knots with the ribs, and disperses through the chest. An internal branch adheres to the spine（Fig 6-3）.

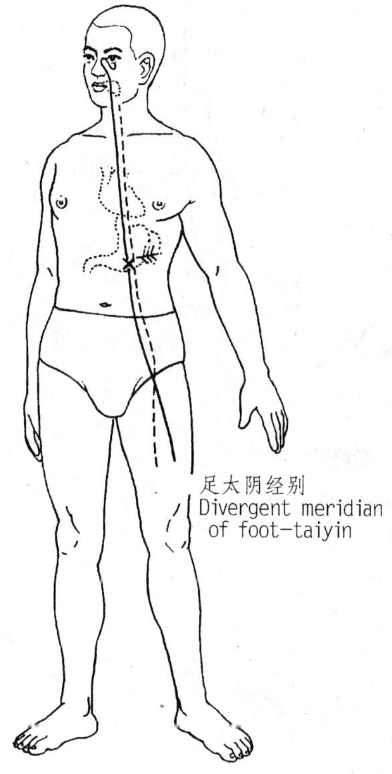

图6-2 足太阴经别循行示意图
Fig 6-2 The courses of the divergence meridian of foot - taiyin

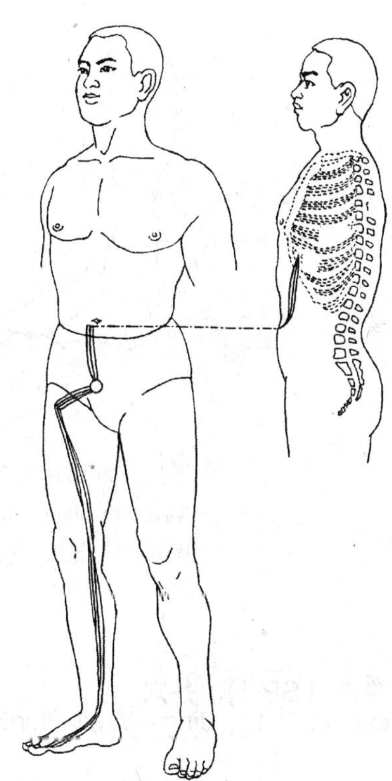

图6-3 足太阴经筋分布示意图
Fig 6-3 The muscular region of foot - taiyin

第二节 足太阴腧穴
Acupoints of Foot - Taiyin

本经左右各21个穴位，首穴为隐白，末穴为大包（图6-4）。

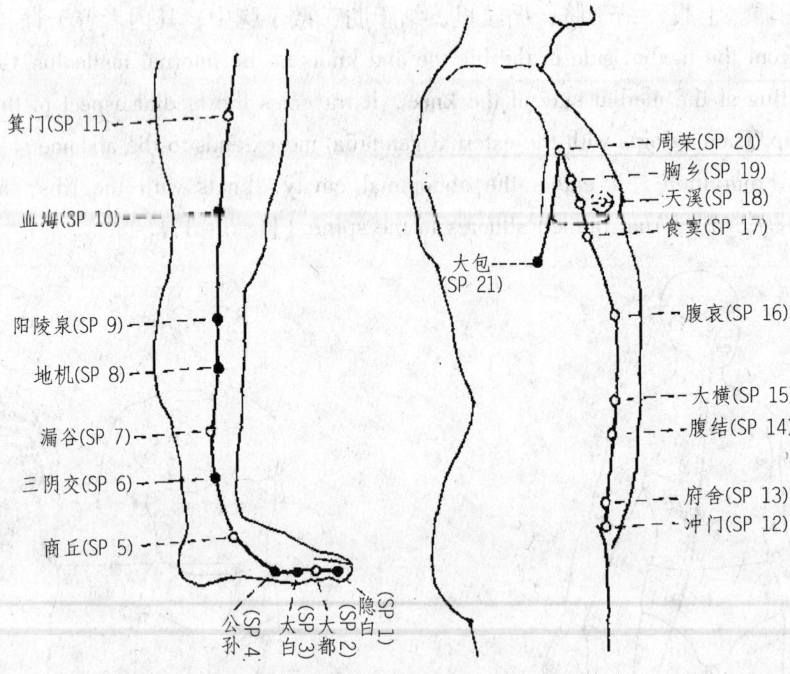

图 6-4 足太阴脾经腧穴总图

Fig 6-4 Points of the spleen meridian of foot-taiyin

1. 隐白（SP 1），井穴
Yinbai（SP 1），Jing-Well Point

【释义】隐，隐蔽；白，白色。穴居隐蔽之处，其处色白。

【定位】在足趾，大趾末节内侧，趾甲根角侧后方 0.1 寸（指寸），沿趾甲内侧画一直线与趾甲基底缘水平线交点处（图 6-5）。

【解剖】皮肤→皮下组织→甲根。有趾背动脉；有腓浅神经的趾背神经与趾底固有神经的吻合处。

【功用】健脾消食，统血止血。

【主治】崩漏，月经过多，便血，尿血；腹胀；癫狂，多梦，惊风。

【操作】浅刺 0.1 寸；或灸。

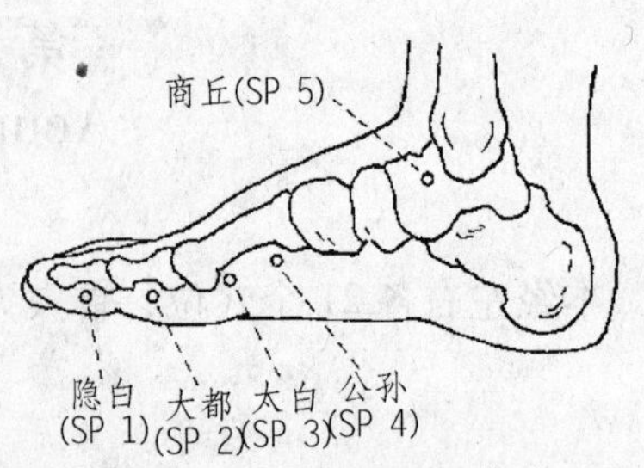

图 6-5

Fig 6-5

【Meaning】Yin, hidden; bai, white. The acupoint is in a hidden region, where the color is white.

【Location】On the great toe, medial to the distal phalanx, 0.1 cun proximal to the medial corner of the toenail, at the intersection of the vertical line of the medial border and horizontal line of the base of the toenail (Fig 6 – 5).

【Regional anatomy】Skin→subcutaneous tissue→nail root. Vasculature: The dorsal digital artery. Innervation: On the anastomosis of the dorsal digital nerve derived from the superficial peroneal nerve and the plantar digital proprii nerve.

【Properties】Strengthening the spleen and eliminating nutrition congestion, controlling the blood within vessels to prevent extravasating, stopping bleeding.

【Indications】Uterine bleeding, menorrhea, blood in the stool, blood in the urine; abdominal distention; psychosis, profuse dreaming, convulsions.

【Needling method】Puncture superficially 0.1 cun, or use moxibustion.

2. 大都 (SP 2), 荥穴
Dadu (SP 2), Ying - Spring Point

【释义】大，大小之大；都，聚会。穴在大趾，为经气所留聚之处。

【定位】在足趾，第1跖趾关节远端赤白肉际凹陷中（图6－5）。

【解剖】皮肤→皮下组织→第1趾骨基底部。有足底内侧动、静脉的分支。分布着足底内侧神经的趾底固有神经。

【功用】健脾和胃。

【主治】腹胀，胃痛，泄泻，便秘；热病无汗。

【操作】直刺0.3～0.5寸。

【Meaning】Da, big; du, assembling. The acupoint is at the big toe, where the qi of meridian gathers.

【Location】On the great toe, in the depression distal to the first metatarsophalangeal joint, at the border between the red and white flesh (Fig 6 – 5).

【Regional anatomy】Skin → subcutaneous tissue → the base of the great phalanges of toes. Vasculature: The branches of the medial plantar artery and vein. Innervation: The plantar digital proprii nerve derived from the medial plantar nerve.

【Properties】Strengthening the spleen and harmonizing the stomach.

【Indications】Abdominal distention, stomach pain, diarrhea, constipation; febrile disease with absence of sweating.

【Needling method】Puncture perpendicularly 0.3～0.5 cun.

3. 太白 (SP 3), 输穴, 原穴
Taibai (SP 3), Shu - Stream and Yuan - Source Points

【释义】太，甚大；白，白色。穴在大趾赤白肉际上；此处之白肉更为宽阔。

【定位】在足内侧，第1跖趾关节近端赤白肉际凹陷中（图6－5）。

【解剖】皮肤→皮下组织→展肌→短屈肌。有足背静脉网，足底内侧动脉及跗内侧动脉的分支。分布着隐神经与腓浅神经分支。

【功用】健脾化湿，理气和胃。

【主治】胃痛，腹胀，腹痛，泄泻，痢疾，纳呆；体重节痛。

【操作】直刺0.5～0.8寸。

【Meaning】Tai, great; bai, white. The acupoint is at the white skin of the big toe, where the white skin is widest.

【Location】On the medial aspect of the foot, in the depression proximal to the first metatarsophalangeal joint, at the border between the red and white flesh (Fig 6－5).

【Regional anatomy】Skin→subcutaneous tissue→extensor hallucis longus→flexor hallucis brevis. Vasculature: The dorsal venous network of the foot, the medial plantar artery and the branches of the medial tarsal artery. Innervation: The branches of the saphenous nerve and superficial peroneal nerve.

【Properties】Strengthening the spleen, eliminating dampness, regulating qi, and harmonizing the stomach.

【Indications】Stomach pain, abdominal distention, abdominal pain, diarrhea, dysentery, anorexia; heaviness of the body, pain in joints.

【Needling method】Puncture perpendicularly 0.5～0.8 cun.

4. 公孙（SP 4），络穴，八脉交会穴（通冲脉）
Gongsun (SP 4), Luo - Connection Point and One of the Eight Confluent Points (Associating with Thoroughfare Vessel)

【释义】公，有通的意思；孙，孙络。孙，在此特指络脉，脾经之络脉是从此通向胃经的。

【定位】在足内侧，第1跖骨底的前下缘赤白肉际处（图6－5）。

【解剖】皮肤→皮下组织→展肌→短屈肌→长屈肌腱。有跗内侧动脉及足背静脉网。分布着隐神经及腓浅神经分支。

【功用】健脾化湿和胃，调冲脉。

【主治】胃痛，呕吐，腹胀，腹痛，泄泻，痢疾；心痛，胸闷。

【操作】直刺0.5～1.0寸。

【Meaning】Gong, connection; sun, minute collateral. Sun here indicates collateral. From this acupoint the collateral of the spleen meridian connects with the stomach meridian.

【Location】On the medial aspect of the foot, anteroinferior to the base of the first metatarsal bone, at the border between the red and white flesh (Fig 6－5).

【Regional anatomy】Skin→subcutaneous tissue→extensor hallucis longus→flexor hallucis brevis→the tendon of flexor hallucis longus. Vasculature: The medial tarsal artery and the dorsal venous network of the foot. Innervation: The saphenous nerve and the branch of the superficial peroneal nerve.

【Properties】Invigorating the spleen, eliminating dampness, harmonizing the stomach, and regulating the Thoroughfare Vessel.

【Indications】Stomach pain, vomiting, abdominal distention, abdominal pain, diarrhea, dysentery; epigastric pain, oppression in the chest.

【Needling method】Puncture perpendicularly 0.5 ~1.0 cun.

5. 商丘（SP 5），经穴
Shangqiu（SP 5），Jing - River Point

【释义】商，五音之一，属金；丘，丘陵。此系脾经经穴，属金，在丘陵样内踝的下方。

【定位】在足内侧，内踝前下方，足舟骨粗隆与内踝尖连线中点凹陷中（图6－5）。

【解剖】皮肤→皮下组织→三角韧带→内踝。有跗内侧动脉，大隐静脉。分布着小腿内侧皮神经及腓浅神经分支。

【功用】健脾止泻。

【主治】腹胀，肠鸣，泄泻，便秘，痔疾；足踝痛。

【操作】直刺0.5 ~0.8寸。

【Meaning】Shang, one of the Five Sounds, pertaining to metal; qiu, hills. This is the jing – xue river acupoint of the spleen meridian and pertains to metal. The acupoint is below the medial malleolus, which resembles a hill.

【Location】On the medial aspect of the foot, anteroinferior to the medial malleolus, in the depression midway between the tuberosity of the navicular bone and the prominence of the medial malleolus（Fig 6 –5）.

【Regional anatomy】Skin → subcutaneous tissue → triangular ligament → medial malleolus. Vasculature: The medial tarsal artery and the great saphenous vein. Innervation: The medial crural cutaneous nerve and the branch of the superficial peroneal nerve.

【Properties】Strengthening the spleen, and calming diarrhoea.

【Indications】Abdominal distention, borborygmus, diarrhea, constipation, hemorrhoids; pain in the foot and ankle.

【Needling method】Puncture perpendicularly 0.5 ~0.8 cun.

6. 三阴交（SP 6），足太阴、厥阴、少阴经交会穴
Sanyinjiao（SP 6），Crossing Point of the Meridians of Foot - Taiyin，Foot - Jueyin and Foot - Shaoyin

【释义】三阴，指三条阴经；交，交会。此系脾、肝、肾三阴经之交会穴。

【定位】在小腿内侧，内踝尖上3寸，胫骨内侧缘后际（图6－6）。

【解剖】皮肤→皮下组织→趾长屈肌→胫骨后肌→长屈肌。有大隐静脉，胫后动、静脉。分布着小腿内侧皮神经，深层后方有胫神经。

【功用】健脾利湿，补肾养阴，镇静安神。

【主治】①腹痛，腹胀，肠鸣，泄泻。②月经不调，痛经，经闭，带下，阴挺，滞产，不孕，不育，阳痿，遗精。③小便不利，遗尿，水肿。④失眠，眩晕。⑤下肢痿痹，脚气。

【操作】直刺1.0～1.5寸；孕妇禁针。

【Meaning】Sanyin, three yin meridian; jiao, crossing. This is an intersecting acupoint of the spleen, liver and kidney meridians.

【Location】On the tibial aspect of the leg, posterior to the medial border of the tibia, 3 cun superior to the prominence of the medial malleolus (Fig 6－6).

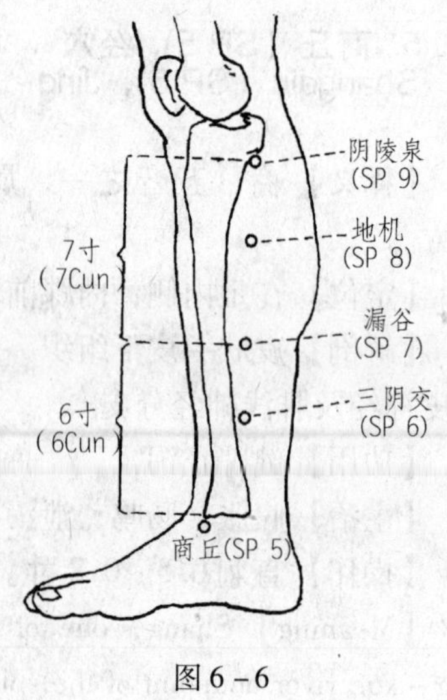

图6－6

Fig 6－6

【Regional anatomy】Skin→subcutaneous tissue→flexor digitorum longus → tibialis posterior → flexor hallucis longus. Vasculature: The great saphenous vein, the posterior tibial artery and vein. Innervation: Superficially, the medial crural cutaneous nerve; deeply, in the posterior aspect, the tibial nerve.

【Properties】Strengthening the spleen, resolving and expelling dampness; invigorating the kidney and nourishing yin, tranquilizing the mind.

【Indications】①Abdominal pain, abdominal distention, borborygmus, diarrhea. ②Irregular menstruation, dysmenorrhea, menostasis, leukorrhea, prolapse of the uterus, prolonged labor, infertility, impotence, spermatorrhea. ③Difficulty in micturition, enuresis, edema. ④Insomnia, dizziness. ⑤Atrophy and paralysis of the legs, beriberi.

【Needling method】Puncture perpendicularly 1.0～1.5 cun. Contraindicated for pregnant women.

7. 漏谷 Lougu (SP 7)

【释义】漏，穴窍；谷，山谷。穴居胫骨内侧缘后方山谷样凹陷中。

【定位】在小腿内侧，内踝尖上6寸，胫骨内侧缘后际（图6－6）。

【解剖】皮肤→皮下组织→小腿三头肌→趾长屈肌→胫骨后肌。血管、神经分布同三阴交（SP 6）。

【功用】健脾除湿。

【主治】腹胀，肠鸣；小便不利；遗精；下肢痿痹。

【操作】直刺1.0～1.5寸。

【Meaning】Lou, aperture; gu, valley. The acupoint is located in the depression posterior to the tibia, like in a valley.

【Location】On the tibial aspect of the leg, posterior to the medial border of the tibia, 6 cun superior to the prominence of the medial malleolus (Fig 6 – 6).

【Regional anatomy】Skin→subcutaneous tissue→triceps surae muscle→flexor digitorum longus→tibialis posterior. See Sanyinjiao (SP 6).

【Properties】Strengthening the spleen and expelling dampness.

【Indications】Abdominal distention, borborygmus; difficulty in micturition; spermatorrhea; atrophy and paralysis of the legs.

【Needling method】Puncture perpendicularly 1.0 ~ 1.5 cun.

8. 地机（SP 8），郄穴 Diji (SP 8), Xi - Cleft Point

【释义】地，土地；机，机要。地，指下肢。穴在下肢，局部肌肉最为丰富，是小腿运动的机要部位。

【定位】在小腿内侧，阴陵泉（SP 9）下3寸，胫骨内侧缘后际（图6 –6）。

【解剖】皮肤→皮下组织→腓肠肌→比目鱼肌。前方有大隐静脉及膝最上动脉的分支，深层有胫后动、静脉。神经分布同三阴交（SP 6）。

【功用】健脾除湿，调经止痛。

【主治】①腹胀，腹痛，泄泻。②月经不调，痛经，崩漏。③小便不利，水肿。④下肢痿痹。

【操作】直刺0.5 ~0.8 寸。

【Meaning】Di, earth; ji, importance. Di refers to the lower limbs where the acupoint is located. The local muscle is very thick and is an important region of the leg movement.

【Location】On the tibial aspect of the leg, posterior to the medial border of the tibia, 3 cun inferior to SP 9 (Fig 6 – 6).

【Regional anatomy】Skin → subcutaneous tissue → gastrocnemius muscle → soleus muscle. Vasculature: Anteriorly, the great saphenous vein and the branch of the genu suprema artery; deeply, the posterior tibial artery and vein. Innervation: See Sanyinjiao (SP 6).

【Properties】Strengthening the spleen and expelling dampness, regulating menstruation and alleviating the pain.

【Indications】①Abdominal distention, abdominal pain, diarrhea. ②Irregular menstruation, dysmenorrhea, uterine bleeding. ③Difficulty in micturition, edema. ④Atrophy and paralysis of the legs.

【Needling method】Puncture perpendicularly 0.5 ~ 0.8 cun.

9. 阴陵泉（SP 9），合穴
Yinlingquan（SP 9），He - Sea Point

【释义】阴，阴阳之阴；陵，山陵；泉，水泉。内为阴，穴在胫骨内上髁下缘陷中，如山陵下之水泉。

【定位】在小腿内侧，胫骨内侧髁下缘与胫骨内侧缘之间的凹陷中（图6-6）。

【解剖】皮肤→皮下组织→半腱肌腱→腓肠肌内侧头。前方有大隐静脉，膝最上动脉，深层有胫后动、静脉。分布着小腿内侧皮神经，深层有胫神经。

【功用】健脾除湿，通调水道。

【主治】①腹胀，泄泻，黄疸。②小便不利，水肿。③遗精，阴痛。④膝痛。

【操作】直刺1.0~2.0寸。

【Meaning】Yin，yin of yin - yang；ling，hill；quan，spring. The interior is yin. The acupoint is in the depression at the inferior border of the medial epicondyle of the tibia，like a spring at the foot of a hill.

【Location】On the tibial aspect of the leg，in the depression between the inferior border of the medial condyle of the tibia and the medial border of the tibia（Fig 6-6）.

【Regional anatomy】Skin→subcutaneous tissue→the tendon of semitendinosus→the medial head of the gastrocnemius. Vasculature：Anteriorly，the great saphenous vein，the genu suprema artery；deeply，the posterior tibial artery and vein. Innervation：Superficially，the medial crural cutaneous nerve；deeply，the tibial nerve.

【Properties】Strengthening the spleen and expelling dampness，dredging the water passage.

【Indications】①Abdominal distention，diarrhea，jaundice. ②Difficulty in micturition，edema. ③Spermatorrhea，pudendal pain. ④Pains in the knees.

【Needling method】Puncture perpendicularly 1.0 ~2.0 cun.

10. 血海 Xuehai (SP 10)

【释义】血，气血的血；海，海洋。本穴善治各种血证，犹如聚溢血重归于海。

【定位】在股前内侧，髌底内侧端上2寸，股内侧肌隆起处（图6-7）。

【解剖】皮肤→皮下组织→股内侧肌。有股动、静脉肌支。分布着股前皮神经及股神经肌支。

【功用】健脾除湿，调经理血。

【主治】月经不调，崩漏，经闭；瘾疹，湿疹，丹毒；膝肿痛。

【操作】直刺1.0~1.5寸。

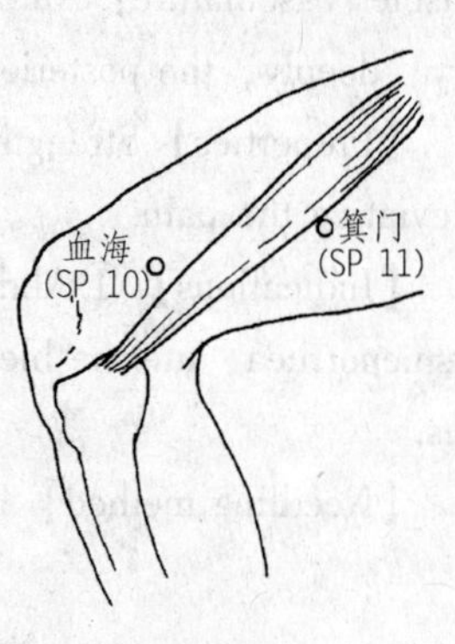

图6-7
Fig 6-7

【Meaning】Xue, blood; hai, sea. This acupoint is indicated in hematological diseases, in the sense of returning overflowed blood into the sea.

【Location】On the anteromedial aspect of the thigh, on the bulge of the vastus medialis muscle, 2 cun superior to the medial end of the base of the patella (Fig 6 – 7).

【Regional anatomy】Skin→subcutaneous tissue→vastus medialis. Vasculature: The muscular branches of the femoral artery and vein. Innervation: The anterior femoral cutaneous nerve and the muscular branch of the femoral nerve.

【Properties】Strengthening the spleen and expelling dampness, regulating menstruation and nourishing the blood.

【Indications】Irregular menstruation, heavy uterine bleeding, amenorrhea; urticaria, eczema, erysipelas; pain and swelling in the knees.

【Needling method】Puncture perpendicularly 1.0 ~ 1.5 cun.

11. 箕门 Jimen (SP 11)

【释义】箕，簸箕；门，门户。两腿张开席地而坐，其形如箕。穴在大腿内侧，左右对称，恰似箕之门户。

【定位】在股内侧，髌底内侧端与冲门（SP 12）的连线上1/3与下2/3交点，长收肌和缝匠肌交角的股动脉搏动处（图6 – 7）。

【解剖】皮肤→皮下组织→股内侧肌。有大隐静脉，深层之外方有股动、静脉。分布着股前皮神经，深部有隐神经。

【功用】清热利尿通淋。

【主治】小便不通，遗尿；腹股沟肿痛。

【操作】直刺0.3 ~0.5寸。针刺时必须避开动脉。

【Meaning】Ji, dustpan; men, door. With the subject sitting with the legs stretched out in the shape of a dustpan, the acupoint is at the medial aspect of either, just like the open side of the dustpan.

【Location】On the medial aspect of the thigh, at the junction of the upper one third and lower two thirds of the line connecting the medial end of the base of the patella with SP 12, between the sartorius muscle and the adductor longus muscle, over the femoral artery (Fig 6 – 7).

【Regional anatomy】Skin→subcutaneous tissue→vastus medialis. Vasculature: Superficially, the great saphenous vein, deeply on the lateral side, the femoral artery and vein. Innervation: The anterior femoral cutaneous nerve; deeply, the saphenous nerve.

【Properties】Clearing away the heat, mobilising the urinary tract, and promoting urination.

【Indications】Dysuria, enuresis; swelling and pain of the groin.

【Needling method】Puncture perpendicularly 0.3 ~0.5 cun. Avoid needling the artery.

12. 冲门（SP 12），足太阴、厥阴经交会穴
Chongmen（SP 12), Crossing Point of the Meridians of Foot - Taiyin and Foot - Jueyin

【释义】冲，冲要；门，门户。穴在气街部，为经气通过的重要门户。

【定位】在腹股沟，腹股沟斜纹中，股动脉搏动处的外侧（图6－8）。

【解剖】皮肤→皮下组织→腹外斜肌腱膜→腹内斜肌→腹横肌→髂腰肌。内侧为股动脉。当股神经经过处。

【功用】理气除湿。

【主治】腹痛，疝气；崩漏，带下。

【操作】直刺0.5～1.0寸。

【Meaning】Chong，pass；men，door. The acupoint，in Qijie，is an important door for the passage of the qi of the meridian.

【Location】In the groin region，at the inguinal crease，lateral to the femoral artery（Fig 6－8）.

【Regional anatomy】Skin→subcutaneous tissue→Aponeurosis mi. oblique external abdominis→oblique internal abdominis muscle→transversus abdominis muscle→iliopsoas muscle. Vasculature：On the medial side，the femoral artery. Innervation：Just where the femoral nerve traverses.

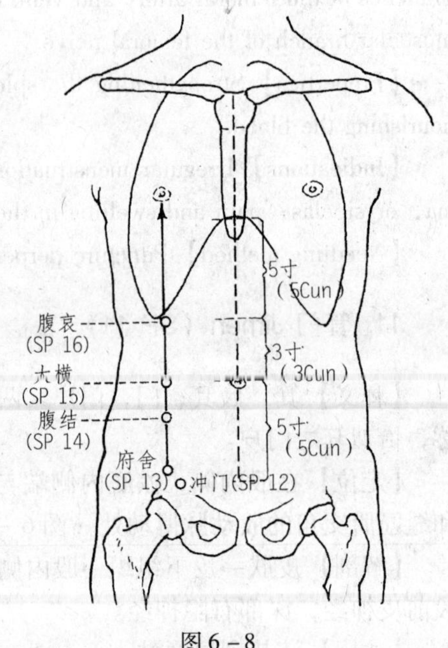

图6－8
Fig 6－8

【Properties】Regulating qi，resolving and expelling dampness.

【Indications】Abdominal pain，hernia；uterine bleeding，leukorrhea.

【Needling method】Puncture perpendicularly 0.5～1.0 cun.

13. 府舍（SP 13），足太阴、厥阴经、阴维脉交会穴
Fushe（SP 13)，Crossing Point of the Meridians of Foot - Taiyin，Foot - Jueyin and Yin Link Vessel

【释义】府，指脏腑；舍，宅舍。穴位深处是腹腔，为脏腑的宅舍。

【定位】在下腹部，脐中下4寸，冲门上方0.7寸，前正中线旁开4寸（图6－8）。

【解剖】皮肤→皮下组织→腹外斜肌腱膜→腹内斜肌→腹横肌。分布着髂腹股沟神经。

【功用】调理肠胃。

【主治】腹痛，疝气，结聚。

【操作】直刺0.8～1.2寸。

【Meaning】Fu, zang - fu organs; she, dwelling. The deep region of the acupoint is the abdominal cavity, which is the dwelling place of the zang - fu organs.

【Location】On the lower abdomen, 4 cun inferior to the centre of the umbilicus, 0.7 cun above chongmen, 4 cun lateral to the anterior median line (Fig 6 - 8).

【Regional anatomy】Skin → subcutaneous tissue → Aponeurosis mi. oblique external abdominis→oblique internal abdominis muscle→transversus abdominis muscle. Innervation: The ilioinguinal nerve.

【Properties】Regulating and harmonizing intestine and stomach.

【Indications】Abdominal pain, hernia, distention, masses in the abdomen.

【Needling method】Puncture perpendicularly 0.8 ~ 1.2 cun.

14. 腹结 Fujie (SP 14)

【释义】腹，腹部；结，结聚。本穴善治腹部结聚不通之证。

【定位】在下腹部，脐中下1.3寸，前正中线旁开4寸（图6-8）。

【解剖】皮肤→皮下组织→腹外斜肌→腹内斜肌→腹横肌。有第11肋间动、静脉及第11肋间神经。

【功用】温脾止泻。

【主治】腹痛，腹泻，便秘。

【操作】直刺1.0~1.5寸。

【Meaning】Fu, abdomen; jie, stagnation. This acupoint is indicated in abdominal stagnation.

【Location】On the lower abdomen, 1.3 cun inferior to the centre of the umbilicus, 4 cun lateral to the anterior median line (Fig 6 - 8).

【Regional anatomy】Skin→subcutaneous tissue→oblique external abdominis muscle→oblique internal abdominis muscle→transversus abdominis muscle. Vasculature: The eleventh intercostal artery and vein. Innervation: The eleventh intercostal nerve.

【Properties】Warming spleen and alleviating diarrhoea.

【Indications】Abdominal pain, diarrhea, constipation.

【Needling method】Puncture perpendicularly 1.0 ~ 1.5 cun.

15. 大横 (SP 15)，足太阴经、阴维脉交会穴
Daheng (SP 15), Crossing Point of the Meridians of Foot - Taiyin and Yin Link Vessel

【释义】大，大小之大；横，横竖之横。穴位内应横行之大肠。

【定位】在上腹部，脐中旁开4寸（图6-8）。

【解剖】皮肤→皮下组织→腹外斜肌→腹内斜肌→腹横肌。有第10肋间动、静脉及第10肋间神经。

【功用】理气止痛，通调腑气。

【主治】绕脐腹痛，泄泻，便秘。

【操作】直刺 1.0 ~ 1.5 寸。

【Meaning】Da, large; heng, horizontal. This acupoint is on the large part of the abdomen, horizontal to the navel.

【Location】On the upper abdomen, 4 cun lateral to the centre of the umbilicus (Fig 6 – 8).

【Regional anatomy】Skin→subcutaneous tissue→oblique external abdominis muscle→oblique internal abdominis muscle→transversus abdominis muscle. Vasculature: The tenth intercostal artery and vein. Innervation: The tenth intercostal nerve.

【Properties】Regulating qi and alleviating pain, harmonizing the fu – qi.

【Indications】Abdominal pain, diarrhea, constipation.

【Needling method】Puncture perpendicularly 1.0 ~ 1.5 cun.

16. 腹哀 Fuai (SP 16)，足太阴经、阴维脉交会穴 Fu'ai (SP 16), Crossing Point of the Meridians of Foot - Taiyin and Yin Link Vessel

【释义】腹，腹部；哀，伤痛。本穴善治腹部各种伤痛。

【定位】在上腹部，脐中上 3 寸，前正中线旁开 4 寸（图 6 – 8）。

【解剖】皮肤→皮下组织→腹外斜肌→腹内斜肌→腹横肌。有第 8 肋间动、静脉及第 8 肋间神经。

【功用】健脾消食，通降腑气。

【主治】腹痛，泄泻，痢疾，便秘，消化不良。

【操作】直刺 1.0 ~ 1.5 寸。

【Meaning】Fu, abdomen; ai, pain. This acupoint is useful in treating abdominal pain.

【Location】On the upper abdomen, 3 cun superior to the centre of the umbilicus, 4 cun lateral to the anterior median line (Fig 6 – 8).

【Regional anatomy】Skin→subcutaneous tissue→oblique external abdominis muscle→oblique internal abdominis muscle→transversus abdominis muscle. Vasculature: The eighth intercostal artery and vein. Innervation: The eighth intercostal nerve.

【Properties】Strengthening the spleen and promoting the congestion, activating and descending the fu – qi.

【Indications】Abdominal pain, diarrhea, dysentery, constipation, dyspepsia.

【Needling method】Puncture perpendicularly 1.0 ~ 1.5 cun.

17. 食窦 Shidou (SP 17)

【释义】食，食物；窦，孔窦。穴在乳头外下方，深部有储藏乳汁的孔窦。本穴能促进食物营养的吸收，为补益之孔穴。

【定位】在前胸部，第5肋间隙，前正中线旁开6寸（图6－9）。

【解剖】皮肤→皮下组织→前锯肌→肋间外肌。有胸腹壁静脉。分布着第5肋间神经外侧皮支。

【功用】理气止痛，和胃降逆。

【主治】嗳气，腹胀；水肿；胸胁胀痛。

【操作】斜刺或平刺0.5～0.8寸，穴位深部有肺脏，不宜深刺。

【Meaning】Shi，food；dou，sinus. This acupoint，infero－lateral to the nipple，has a sinus for storing milk in its deep region. The acupoint is useful in promoting absorption of food nutrients and for tonification.

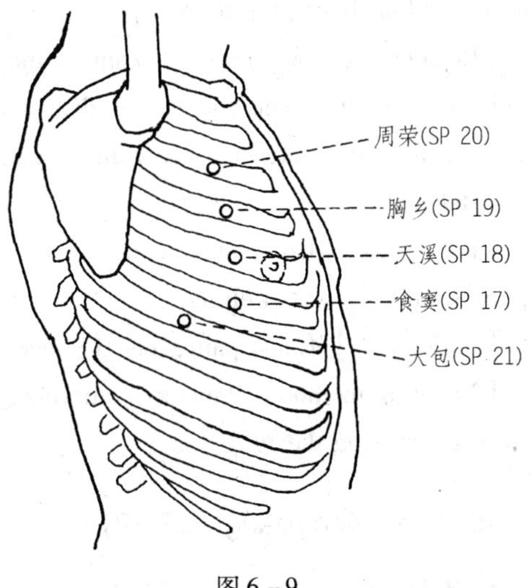

图6－9
Fig 6－9

【Location】In the anterior thoracic region，in the 5th intercostal space，6 cun lateral to the anterior median line（Fig 6－9）.

【Regional anatomy】Skin→subcutaneous tissue→serratus anterior muscle→intercostales external muscles. Vasculature：The thoracoepigastric vein. Innervation：The lateral cutaneous branch of the 5th intercostal nerve.

【Properties】Regulating qi and alleviating pain，harmonizing the stomach and descending inverted qi.

【Indications】Belching，abdominal distention；edema；distention and pain in the chest and hypochondrium.

【Needling method】Puncture transversely or obliquely 0.5～0.8 cun. Avoid a deep insertion to prevent puncturing the lung.

18. 天溪 Tianxi（SP 18）

【释义】天，天空；溪，沟溪。天，指上而言。穴当肋间如沟溪处。

【定位】在前胸部，第4肋间隙，前正中线旁开6寸（图6－9）。

【解剖】皮肤→皮下组织→胸大肌→胸小肌。有胸外侧动、静脉分支，胸腹壁动、静脉，第4肋间动、静脉。分布着第4肋间神经外侧皮支。

【功用】宽胸通乳，止咳消肿。

【主治】胸痛，咳嗽；乳痈，乳汁少。

【操作】斜刺或平刺0.5～0.8寸。穴位深部有肺脏，不宜深刺。

【Meaning】Tian，heaven；xi，valley. Tian refers to upper. The acupoint is in the stream－like intercostal space.

【Location】In the anterior thoracic region, in the 4th intercostal space, 6 cun lateral to the anterior median line (Fig 6 –9).

【Regional anatomy】Skin → subcutaneous tissue → pectoral major muscle → pectoral minor muscle. Vasculature: The branches of the lateral thoracic artery and vein, the thoracoepigastric artery and vein, the 4th intercostal artery and vein. Innervation: The lateral cutaneous branch of the fourth intercostal nerve.

【Properties】Dispersing the depressed chest – qi and stimulating lactation, alleviating coughing and reducing the swelling.

【Indications】Chest pain, cough; acute mastitis, insufficient lactation.

【Needling method】Puncture transversely or obliquely 0.5 ~0.8 cun. Avoid a deep insertion to prevent puncturing the lung.

19. 胸乡 Xiongxiang (SP 19)

【释义】胸，胸部；乡，指部位。穴在胸部，能治胸部疾患。

【定位】在前胸部，第3肋间隙，前正中线旁开6寸（图6–9）。

【解剖】皮肤→皮下组织→胸大肌→胸小肌。有胸外侧动、静脉，第3肋间动、静脉。分布着第3肋间神经外侧皮支。

【功用】宽胸止痛。

【主治】胸胁胀痛。

【操作】斜刺或平刺0.5~0.8寸。穴位深部有肺脏，不宜深刺。

【Meaning】Xiong, chest; xiang, vast place. This acupoint is located on the vast part of the upper chest.

【Location】In the anterior thoracic region, in thc 3rd intercostal space, 6 cun lateral to the anterior median line (Fig 6 –9).

【Regional anatomy】Skin→subcutaneous tissue→pectoral major muscle→pectoral minor muscle. Vasculature: The lateral thoracic artery and vein, the 3rd intercostal artery and vein. Innervation: The lateral cutaneous branch of the third intercostal nerve.

【Properties】Dispersing the depressed chest – qi and alleviating pain.

【Indications】Distention and pain in the chest and hypochondrium.

【Needling method】Puncture transversely or obliquely 0.5 ~0.8 cun. Avoid a deep insertion to prevent Puncturing the lung.

20. 周荣 Zhourong (SP 20)

【释义】周，周身；荣，荣养。本穴可调和营气，荣养周身。

【定位】在前胸部，第2肋间隙，前正中线旁开6寸（图6–9）。

【解剖】皮肤→皮下组织→胸大肌→胸小肌。有胸外侧动、静脉，第2肋间动、静脉。

分布着胸前神经肌支，第2肋间神经外侧皮支。

【功用】宽胸理气，降逆止咳。

【主治】胸胁胀满，咳嗽，气喘。

【操作】斜刺或平刺0.5~0.8寸。穴位深部有肺脏，不宜深刺。

【Meaning】Zhou，general；rong，nourishment. This acupoint functions to harmonize nutrient qi and to nourish the whole body.

【Location】In the anterior thoracic region，in the 2nd intercostal space，6 cun lateral to the anterior median line（Fig 6－9）.

【Regional anatomy】Skin→subcutaneous tissue→pectoral major muscle→pectoral minor muscle. Vasculature：The lateral thoracic artery and vein，the second intercostal artery and vein. Innervation：The muscular branch of the anterior thoracic nerve，the lateral cutaneous branch of the 2nd intercostal nerve.

【Properties】Dispersing the depressed chest－qi，regulating qi，alleviating coughing，and descending the adverse qi.

【Indications】Distention in the chest and hypochondriac regions，cough，asthma.

【Needling method】Puncture transversely or obliquely 0.5~0.8 cun. Avoid a deep insertion to prevent puncturing the lung.

21. 大包 (SP 21)，脾之大络
Dabao（SP 21），the Major Collateral of the Spleen

【释义】大，大小之大；包，包容。穴属脾之大络。脾土居中，与各脏腑有着最广泛的联系。

【定位】在侧胸部，第6肋间隙，当在腋中线（图6－9）。

【解剖】皮肤→皮下组织→前锯肌。有胸背动、静脉及第7肋间动、静脉。分布着第7肋间神经及胸长神经末支。

【功用】宽胸止痛，统血养经。

【主治】咳喘；胸胁痛；全身疼痛，四肢无力。

【操作】斜刺或平刺0.5~0.8寸。穴位深部有肺脏，不宜深刺。

【Meaning】Da，large；bao，containing. The acupoint pertains to the major collateral of the spleen meridian. The spleen（earth）is in the centre and is generally related to the zang－fu organs.

【Location】In the lateral thoracic region，in the 6th intercostal space，on the midaxillary line（Fig 6－9）.

【Regional anatomy】Skin→subcutaneous tissue→serratus anterior muscle. Vasculature：The thoracoepigastric artery and vein，the 7th intercostal artery and vein. Innervation：The 7th intercostal nerve and the terminal branch of the long thoracic nerve.

【Properties】Dispersing the depressed chest－qi and alleviating pain，controlling blood within the vessels to prevent extravasating, nourishing the meridians.

【Indications】Cough, dyspnea; chest and hypochondriac regions; pain of the whole body, weariness of the four limbs.

【Needling method】Puncture transversely or obliquely 0. 5 ~ 0. 8 cun. Avoid a deep insertion to prevent puncturing the lung.

复习思考题
Review Questions

1. 请写出《灵枢·经脉》中足太阴脾经的经脉循行。

Retell the course of the spleen meridian of foot – taiyin according the chapter "Discussion on the Meridians" in *Miraculous Pivot*.

2. 试述隐白、公孙、三阴交、地机、阴陵泉、血海、大横、大包的定位、主治和操作。

Retell the locations, indications, and needling methods of Yinbai (SP 1), Gongsun (SP 4), Sanyinjiao (SP 6), Diji (SP 8), Yinlingquan (SP 9), Xuehai (SP 10), Daheng (SP 15), Dabao (SP 21).

3. 试述三阴交、阴陵泉、血海的临床应用。

Retell the clinical application of Sanyinjiao (SP 6), Yinlingquan (SP 9), Xuehai (SP 10).

第七章 手少阴经络与腧穴
Meridian and Collateral and Its Acupoints of Hand – Shaoyin

第一节 手少阴经络
Meridian and Collateral of Hand – Shaoyin

一、手少阴经脉
Meridian of Hand - Shaoyin

（一）经脉循行
The Course of Meridian

手少阴心经，起于心中，出来属于心系，向下通过横膈，联络小肠。其支脉，从心系向上，沿食管至目系。其直行主脉，从心系上行至肺，再向下浅出腋下，沿上臂内侧后缘到肘，沿前臂内侧后缘至掌后豌豆骨部，进入掌内，沿小指桡侧至末端，与手太阳小肠经相接（图7-1）。

《灵枢·经脉》原文：心手少阴之脉，起于心中，出属心系，下膈，络小肠。

其支者，从心系，上夹咽，系目系。

其直者，复从心系，却上肺，下出腋下，下循臑内后廉，行太阴、心主之后，下肘内，循臂内后廉，抵掌后锐骨之端，入掌内后廉，循小指之内，出其端。

The heart meridian originates from the heart and pertains to the heart system. It goes down through the diaphragm to connect with the small intestine. The ascending branch of the meridian from the heart system runs alongside the esophagus to connect with the eye system. The straight portion of the meridian from the heart system goes upward to the lung, then it runs out from the axilla, it goes along the posterior border of the medial aspect of the upper arm behind the lung meridian and pericardium meridian, it runs downward the medial aspect ot the elbow and descends along the posterior border of the medial aspect of the forearm to the pisiform bone of the wrist and then it enters the palm, follows the radial side of the little finger to terminate at its tip, where it links with the small intestine meridian of hand - taiyang (Fig 7 - 1).

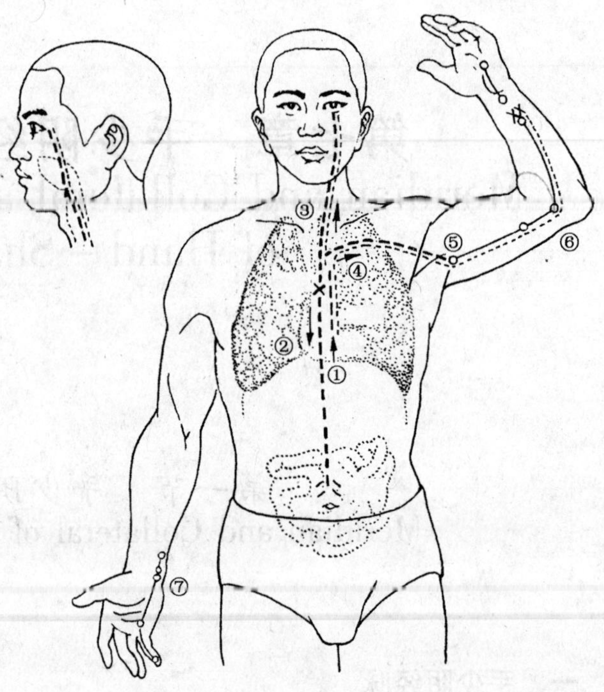

图例 ——本经有穴通路 ……本经无穴通路

Note Pathway with points ……Pathway without points

图 7 - 1 手少阴经脉、络脉循行示意图

Fig 7 - 1 The course of the meridian and collateral of hand - shaoyin

(二) 经脉病候
The Syndromes of Meridian

是动则病，嗌干，心痛，渴而欲饮，是为臂厥。

是主心所生病者，目黄，胁痛，臑臂内后廉痛、厥，掌中热。

The manifestations of this meridian with abnormal functions includes: dryness of the throat, epigastric pain, thirst with a preference to drink, coldness and numbness and pain in the forearm.

Acupoints on the meridian are used for the syndromes caused by the disorders of the heart - organ. They are as follows: yellowing on the eyes, pain in the hypochondriac region, pain and coldness in the posterior border of the medial aspect of the upper arm and forearm, feverish in the palm.

二、手少阴络脉
Collateral of Hand - Shaoyin

手少阴之别，名曰通里，去腕一寸；别而上行，循经入于心中，系舌本，属目系。取之去腕后一寸。别走太阳也（图 7 - 1）。

It branches out at Tongli (HT 5), one cun above the transverse crease of the wrist, it connects with the small intestine meridian of hand - taiyang. About one and a half cun above the wrist, it again follows the meridian and enters the heart; it then runs to the root of the tongue and connects with the eyes (Fig 7 - 1).

三、手少阴经别
Divergent Meridian of Hand - Shaoyin

手少阴之正，别入于渊腋两筋之间，属于心，上走喉咙，出于面，合于内眦（图7-2）。

After deriving from the heart meridian in the axillary fossa, it enters the chest and connects with the heart. Then it runs upward across the throat and emerges on the face, and joins the small intestine meridian at the inner canthus（Fig 7-2）.

四、手少阴经筋
Muscular Region of Hand - Shaoyin

手少阴之筋，起于小指之内侧，结于锐骨；上结于肘后廉；上入腋，交太阴，伏乳里，结于胸中；循贲，下系于脐（图7-3）。

It begins from the medial side of the small finger, knots first at the pisiform bone of the hand, and afterward at the medial aspect of the elbow. Continuing upward and entering the chest below the axilla, it crosses the muscle region of hand-taiyin（lung）in the breast region and knots in the chest. Then it descends across the thoracic diaphragm to connect with the umbilicus（Fig 7-3）.

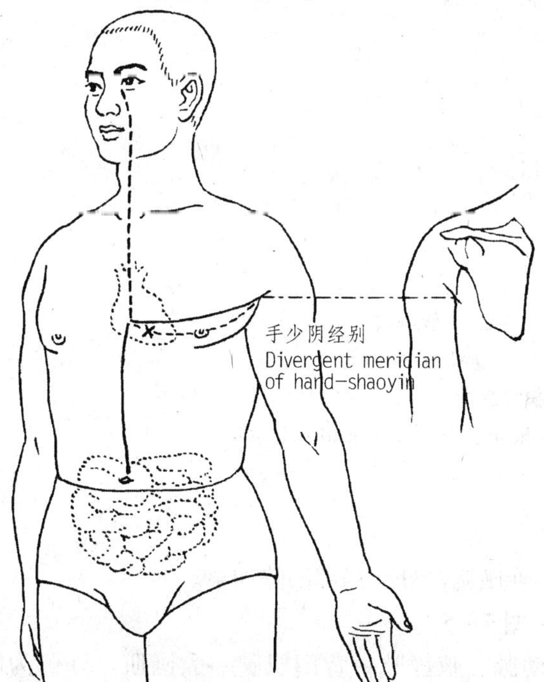

图7-2 手少阴经别循行示意图

Fig 7-2 The courses of divergent meridian of hand-shaoyin

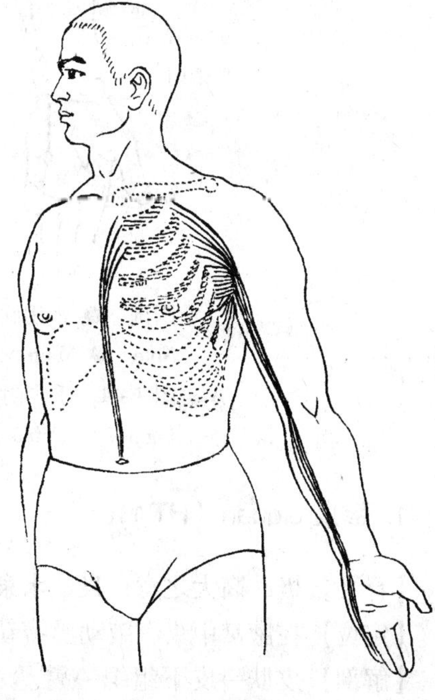

图7-3 手少阴经筋分布示意图

Fig 7-3 The course of the muscular region of hand-shaoyin

第二节　手少阴腧穴
Acupoints of Hand – Shaoyin

本经左右各 9 个穴位，首穴极泉，末穴少冲（图 7 – 4）。

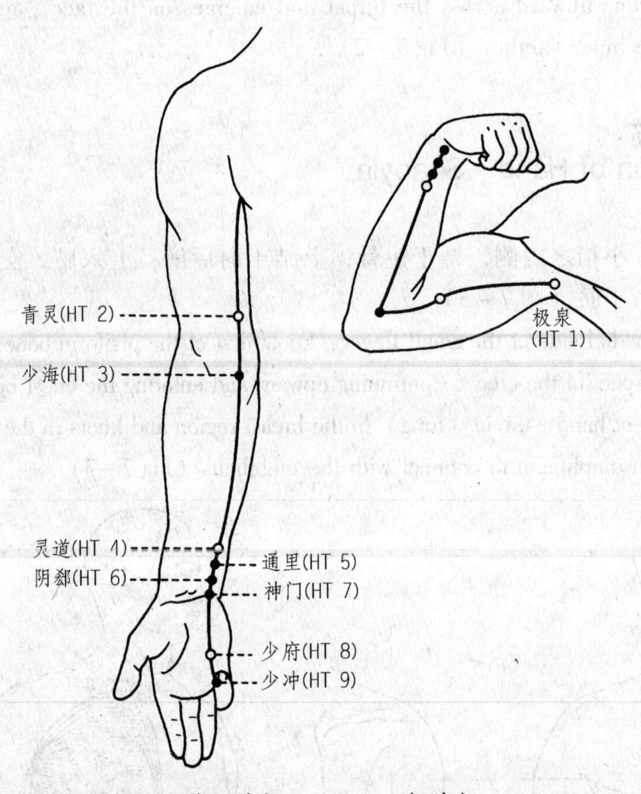

图例 ● 常用腧穴　○ 一般腧穴
Note ● Main point　○ Common point
图 7 – 4　手少阴心经腧穴总图
Fig 3 – 4　Points of the heart meridian of hand – shaoyin

1. 极泉 Jiquan（HT 1）

【释义】极，高大之意；泉，水泉。穴在腋窝高处，局部凹陷如泉。

【定位】在腋窝中央，腋动脉搏动处（图 7 – 5）。

【解剖】皮肤→皮下组织→臂丛、腋动脉、腋静脉→背阔肌腱→大圆肌。外侧为腋动脉。分布着尺神经、正中神经及臂内侧皮神经。

【功用】宽胸理气，舒筋活血。

【主治】①心痛，心悸。②胁肋疼痛。③肩臂疼痛，上肢不遂。④瘰疬。

【操作】避开腋动脉，直刺 0.2 ~ 0.3 寸。

【Meaning】Ji, summit; quan, spring. The acupoint is in the centre of the armpit; the local depression is like a spring.

【Location】In the axilla, in the centre of the axillary fossa, over the axillary artery（Fig 7 – 5）.

【Regional anatomy】Skin→subcutaneous tissue→brachial plexus axillary artery and vein→the tendon of latissimus dorsi→teres major. Vasculature: Laterally, the axillary artery. Innervation: The ulnar nerve, medial nerve and medial brachial cutaneous nerve.

【Properties】Dispersing the depressed chest – qi and regulating qi, relaxing muscles and tendons, promoting blood circulation.

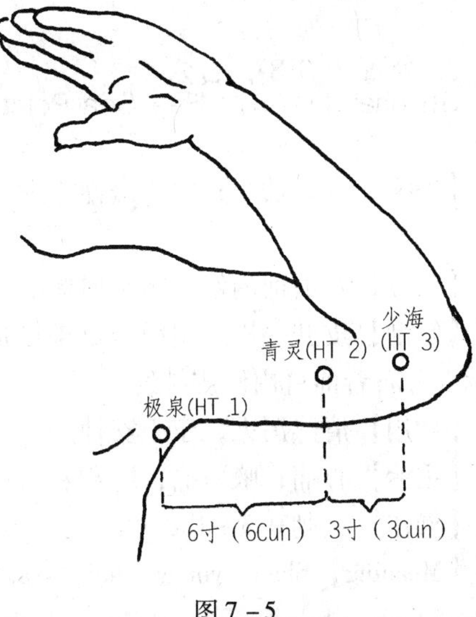

图 7 – 5

Fig 7 – 5

【Indications】①Cardiac pain, palpitations. ②Hypochondriac and costal pain. ③Pain in the shoulder and arm, loss of the use of the upper limb. ④Scrofula.

【Needling method】Puncture perpendicularly 0.2 ~ 0.3 cun; avoid needling the axillary artery.

2. 青灵 Qingling（HT 2）

【释义】青，生发之象；灵，神灵。心为君主之官，通窍藏灵。具有脉气生发之象。

【定位】在臂内侧，肘横纹上 3 寸，肱二头肌的内侧沟中（图 7 – 5）。

【解剖】皮肤→皮下组织→臂内侧肌间隔与肱肌。有贵要静脉，尺侧上副动脉。分布着前臂内侧皮神经及尺神经。

【功用】疏经通络，理气止痛。

【主治】头痛；胁痛；肩臂疼痛。

【操作】直刺 0.5 ~ 1.0 寸。

【Meaning】Qing, origin; ling, mind. The heart is the officer of the monarch with the function of resuscitating and housing the mind. It is the source of the qi of meridian.

【Location】On the medial aspect of the arm, just medial to the biceps brachii muscle, 3 cun superior to the cubital crease（Fig 7 – 5）.

【Regional anatomy】Skin→subcutaneous tissue→medial brachial intermuscular septum and brachialis muscle. Vasculature: The basilic vein, the superior ulnar collateral artery. Innervation: The medial antebrachial cutaneous nerve and the ulnar nerve.

【Properties】Activating the meridian, promoting flow of qi to alleviate pain.

【Indications】Headache; hypochondriac pain; pain in the shoulder and arm.

【Needling method】Puncture perpendicularly 0. 5 ~1. 0 cun.

3. 少海 (HT 3)，合穴
Shaohai（HT 3），He - Sea Point

【释义】少，幼小；海，海洋。少，指手少阴经。此为本经合穴，脉气至此，犹如水流入海。

【定位】在肘前内侧，横平肘横纹，肱骨内上髁前缘（图 7 -5）。

【解剖】皮肤→皮下组织→旋前圆肌→肱肌。有贵要静脉，尺侧下副动脉，尺侧返动、静脉。分布着前臂内侧皮神经。

【功用】清热泻火，宁心安神。

【主治】心痛；腋胁痛；肘臂麻痛；瘰疬。

【操作】直刺 0. 5 ~1. 0 寸。

【Meaning】Shao，young；hai，sea. Shao refers to hand - shaoyin meridian. This is the he - sea point of the heart meridian. The qi of the meridian circulates to this point，like water flowing into the sea.

【Location】On the anteromedial aspect of the elbow，just anterior to the medial epicondyle of the humerus，at the same level as the cubital crease（Fig 7 -5）.

【Regional anatomy】Skin→subcutaneous tissue→pronator teres→brachialis muscle. Vasculature：The basilic vein，the inferior ulnar collateral artery，the ulnar recurrent artery and vein. Innervation：The medial antebrachial cutaneous nerve.

【Properties】Clearing away heat and purging fire，calming the mind.

【Indications】Cardiac pain；axillary and hypochondriac pain；pain of the arm and elbow，paralysis of the upper limbs；scrofula.

【Needling method】Puncture perpendicularly 0. 5 ~1. 0 cun.

4. 灵道（HT 4），经穴
Lingdao（HT 4），Jing - River Point

【释义】灵，神灵；道，通道。心主神灵。穴在尺侧腕屈肌腱桡侧沟，犹如通向神灵之道。

【定位】在前臂前内侧，腕掌侧横纹上 1. 5 寸，尺侧腕屈肌腱的桡侧缘（图 7 -6）。

【解剖】皮肤→皮下组织→尺侧腕屈肌与指浅屈肌之间→指深屈肌→旋前方肌。有尺动脉通过。分布着前臂内侧皮神经，尺侧为尺神经。

【功用】舒筋活络，宁心安神。

【主治】心痛，心悸；暴喑；肘臂挛痛，手指麻木。

【操作】直刺 0. 3 ~0. 5 寸。

【Meaning】Ling，mind；dao，pathway. The heart dominates the mind. The point is in the depression on the radial side of the tendon of m. Flexor carpal ulnaris; it is like a pathway leading toward the mind.

【Location】 On the anteromedial aspect of the forearm, just radial to the flexor carpi ulnaris tendon, 1.5 cun proximal to the palmar wrist crease (Fig 7-6).

【Regional anatomy】 Skin → subcutaneous tissue → between flexor carpi ulnaris and flexor digitorum superficialis→flexor digitorum profundus → pronator quadratus. Vasculature: The ulnar artery. Innervation: The medial antebrachial cutaneous nerve; on the ulnar side, the ulnar nerve.

【Properties】 Relaxing muscles and tendons, promoting flow of blood in the collaterals, tranquilizing the mind.

【Indications】 Cardiac pain, palpitations; sudden loss of voice; pain and spasm in the elbow and arm, numbness of the fingers.

【Needling method】 Puncture perpendicularly 0.3 ~ 0.5 cun.

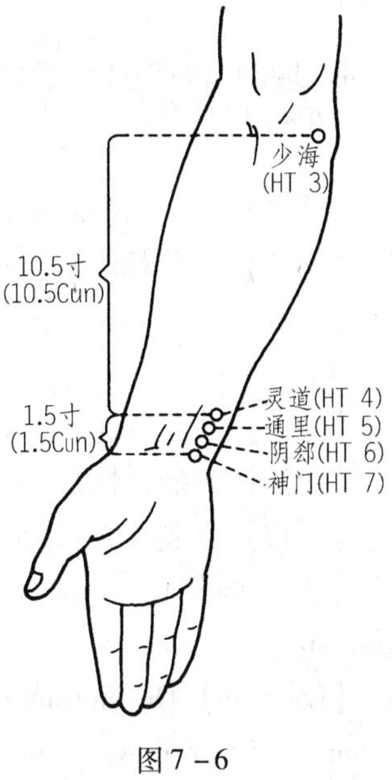

图 7-6
Fig 7-6

5. 通里 (HT 5), 络穴
Tongli (HT 5), Luo - Connecting Point

【释义】通，通往；里，内里。本经络脉由此穴别出，与小肠经互为表里而相通。

【定位】在前臂前内侧，腕掌侧横纹上 1 寸，尺侧腕屈肌腱的桡侧缘（图 7-6）。

【解剖】皮肤→皮下组织→尺侧腕屈肌与指浅屈肌之间→指深屈肌→旋前方肌。血管、神经分布同灵道（HT 4）。

【功用】宁心安神，利咽开音。

【主治】暴喑，舌强不语；心悸；腕臂痛。

【操作】直刺 0.3 ~ 0.5 寸。

【Meaning】 Tong, leading to; li, interior. From this point the collateral of the meridian diverges and relates to the small intestine meridian.

【Location】 On the anteromedial aspect of the forearm, just radial to the flexor carpi ulnaris tendon, 1 cun proximal to the palmar wrist crease (Fig 7-6).

【Regional anatomy】 Skin→subcutaneous tissue→between flexor carpi ulnaris and flexor digitorum superficialis→flexor digitorum profundus→pronator quadratus. See Lingdao (HT 4).

【Properties】 Calm the mind, open the orifices and benefit the functions of tongue.

【Indications】 Sudden loss of voice, stiffness of the tongue, inability to speak; palpitations; pain in the wrist and arm.

【Needling method】Puncture perpendicularly 0. 3 ~0.5 cun.

6. 阴郄（HT 6），郄穴
Yinxi（HT 6），Xi - Cleft Point

【释义】阴，阴阳之阴；郄，孔隙。此为手少阴经之郄穴。

【定位】在前臂前内侧，腕掌侧横纹上0.5寸，尺侧腕屈肌腱的桡侧缘（图7-6）。

【解剖】皮肤→皮下组织→尺侧腕屈肌腱桡侧缘→尺神经。血管、神经分布同灵道（HT 4）。

【功用】滋阴养血，宁心安神。

【主治】心痛，惊悸；吐血，衄血；骨蒸盗汗；暴喑。

【操作】直刺0.3~0.5寸。

【Meaning】Yin，yin of yin - yang；xi，cleft. This is the xi - cleft point of the hand - shaoyin meridian.

【Location】On the anteromedial aspect of the forearm，just radial to the flexor carpi ulnaris tendon，0. 5 cun proximal to the palmar wrist crease（Fig 7 -6）.

【Regional anatomy】Skin→subcutaneous tissue→the radial margin of flexor carpi ulnaris→the ulnar nerve. See Lingdao（HT 4）.

【Properties】Nourishing blood，tranquilizing the mind.

【Indications】Cardiac pain，fright palpitations；hematemesis，epistaxis；bone - steaming heat，night sweats；sudden loss of voice.

【Needling method】Puncture perpendicularly 0. 3 ~0. 5 cun.

7. 神门（HT 7），输穴，原穴
Shenmen（HT 7），Shu - Stream and Yuan - Source Points

【释义】神，心神；门，门户。心藏神。此穴为心神之门户。

【定位】在腕前内侧，腕掌侧横纹上，尺侧腕屈肌腱的桡侧缘（图7-6）。

【解剖】皮肤→皮下组织→尺侧腕屈肌腱桡侧缘。血管、神经分布同灵道（HT 4）。

【功用】镇静安神，宁心通络。

【主治】①失眠，健忘，呆痴，癫狂痫。②心痛，心悸。

【操作】直刺0.3~0.5寸。

【Meaning】Shen，mind；men，door. The heart houses the mind. This point is a door for the mind.

【Location】On the anteromedial aspect of the wrist，radial to the flexor carpi ulnaris tendon，on the palmar wrist crease（Fig 7 -6）.

【Regional anatomy】Skin→subcutaneous tissue→the radial margin of flexor carpi ulnaris. See Lingdao（HT 4）.

【Properties】Tranquilizing the mind, promoting qi and blood circulation in the meridians.

【Indications】①Insomnia, forgetfulness, dementia, psychosis, epilepsy. ②Cardiac pain, palpitations.

【Needling method】Puncture perpendicularly 0. 3 ~0. 5 cun.

8. 少府（HT 8），荥穴 Shaofu（HT 8），Ying - Spring Point

【释义】少，幼小；府，处所。穴属手少阴经，为脉气所溜之处。

【定位】在手掌，第5掌指关节近端，第4、5掌骨之间（图7-7）。

【解剖】皮肤→皮下组织→掌腱膜→环指的浅、深屈肌腱与小指的浅、深屈肌腱之间→第四蚓状肌→第四骨间背侧肌。有指掌侧总动、静脉。分布着来自尺神经的第4指掌侧总神经。

【功用】清心调神。

【主治】①心悸，胸痛。②阴痒痛。③手小指挛痛，掌中热。

【操作】直刺0. 3 ~0. 5寸。

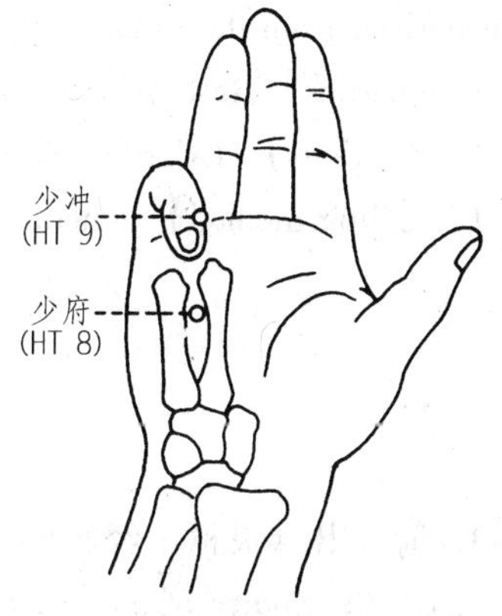

图7-7
Fig 7-7

【Meaning】Shao, young; fu, place. The point pertains to the hand - shaoyin meridian, where the qi of meridian is infused.

【Location】On thc palm of thc hand, in the depression between the 4th and 5th metacarpal bones, proximal to the 5th metacarpophalangeal joint（Fig 7-7）.

【Regional anatomy】Skin→subcutaneous tissue→palmar aponeurosis→between the tendons of flexor digitorum superficialis and profundus of the ring and little fingers→the 4th lumbrical muscle→the 4th dorsal interossei muscle. Vasculature: The common palmar digital artery and vein. Innervation: The 4th common palmar digital nerve derived from the ulnar nerve.

【Properties】Clearing away heat from the heart and regulating the mentality.

【Indications】①Palpitations, chest pain. ②Itching and pain of the genitals. ③Spasmodic pain of the little finger, heat sensations in the palm.

【Needling method】Puncture perpendicularly 0. 3 ~0. 5 cun.

9. 少冲（HT 9），井穴 Shaochong（HT 9），Jing - Well Point

【释义】少，幼小；冲，冲动。本穴是手少阴经井穴，脉气由此涌出沿经脉上行。

【定位】在手指，小指末节桡侧，指甲根角侧上方0. 1寸（指寸），沿指甲桡侧画一直线与指甲基底缘水平线交点处（图 7－7）。

【解剖】皮肤→皮下组织→指甲根。有指掌侧固有动、静脉所形成的动、静脉网。分布着来自尺神经的指掌侧固有神经。

【功用】开窍泄热，宣通气血。

【主治】①心痛，心悸。②癫狂，昏迷。③热病。

【操作】浅刺 0.1～0.2 寸，或点刺出血。

【Meaning】Shao, young; chong, gushing. The point is at the small finger on the hand－shaoyin meridian, where the qi of meridian originates and gushes upwards along the meridian.

【Location】On the little finger, radial to the distal phalanx, 0.1 cun proximal－lateral to the radial corner of the little fingernail, at the intersection of the vertical line of the radial border of the nail and horizontal line of the base of the little fingernail（Fig 7－7）

【Regional anatomy】Skin→subcutaneous tissue→nail root. Vasculature: The arterial and venous network formed by the palmar digital propriae artery and vein. Innervation: The palmar digital nerve derived from the ulnar nerve.

【Properties】Restore resuscitation, purge heat, and promote the flow of qi and blood.

【Indications】①Cardiac pain, palpitations. ②Psychosis, coma. ③Febrile diseases.

【Needling method】puncture superficially 0.1～0.2 cun, or prick to induce bleeding.

复习思考题
Review Questions

1. 请写出《灵枢·经脉》中手少阴心经的经脉循行。

Retell the course of the heart meridian of hand－shaoyin according the chapter "Discussion on the Meridians" in *Miraculous Pivot.*

2. 试述少海、通里、阴郄、神门的定位、主治和操作。

Retell the location, indication, and needling method of Shaohai（HT 3）, Tongli（HT 5）, Yinxi（HT 6）, Shenmen（HT 7）.

3. 试述通里、阴郄、神门的临床应用。

Retell the clinical application of Tongli（HT 5）, Yinxi（HT 6）, Shenmen（HT 7）.

第八章 手太阳经络与腧穴
Meridian and Collateral and Its Acupoints of Hand – Taiyang

第一节 手太阳经络
Meridian and Collateral of Hand – Taiyang

一、手太阳经脉
Meridian of Hand - Taiyang

(一) 经脉循行
The Course of Meridian

手太阳小肠经，起于手小指外侧端，沿着手背尺侧至腕部，出于尺骨小头，直上沿着前臂外侧后缘，经尺骨鹰嘴与肱骨内上髁之间，沿上臂外侧后缘，出于肩关节，绕行肩胛部，交会于肩上，向下进入缺盆（锁骨上窝），联络心脏，沿着食管，通过横膈，到达胃部，属于小肠。颈部支脉，从缺盆上行，沿着颈部，上经面颊至目外眦，弯曲向后进入耳中。面颊部支脉，从面颊部分出，上行颧骨抵于鼻旁，至目内眦，与足太阳膀胱经相接（图8-1）。

《灵枢·经脉》原文：小肠手太阳之脉，起于小指之端，循手外侧上腕，出踝中，直上循臂骨下廉，出肘内侧两骨之间，上循臑外后廉，出肩解，绕肩胛，交肩上，入缺盆，络心，循咽，下膈，抵胃，属小肠。其支者，从缺盆循颈，上颊，至目锐眦，却入耳中。其支者，别颊上䪼，抵鼻，至目内眦（斜络于颧）。

The small intestine meridian of hand – taiyang originates from the ulnar side of the tip of the little finger. It goes along the ulnar side of the dorsum of the hand to the wrist, and emerges at the styloid process of the ulna. It then runs upwards along the posterior border of the lateral aspect of the forearm, and passes between the olecranon of the ulna and the medial epicondyle of the humerus. Ascending along the posterior border of the lateral aspect of the upper arm, it then reaches and emerges at the shoulder joint and proceeds in a zigzag course along the scapular region, arriving at the top of the shoulder. From there, it descends through the supraclavicular fossa and connects with the heart, going downwards along the esophagus, passing through the diaphragm to the stomach, and finally ending at the small intestine. A branch from the supraclavicular fossa ascends to cross the neck and cheek to the outer canthus of the eye, and finally turns and enters the ear. Another branch separates from the previous branch on the cheek and ascends to the zygomatic bone, reaching the side of the nose. It finally terminates at the inner canthus to link with the bladder meridian of foot – taiyang (Fig 8 –1).

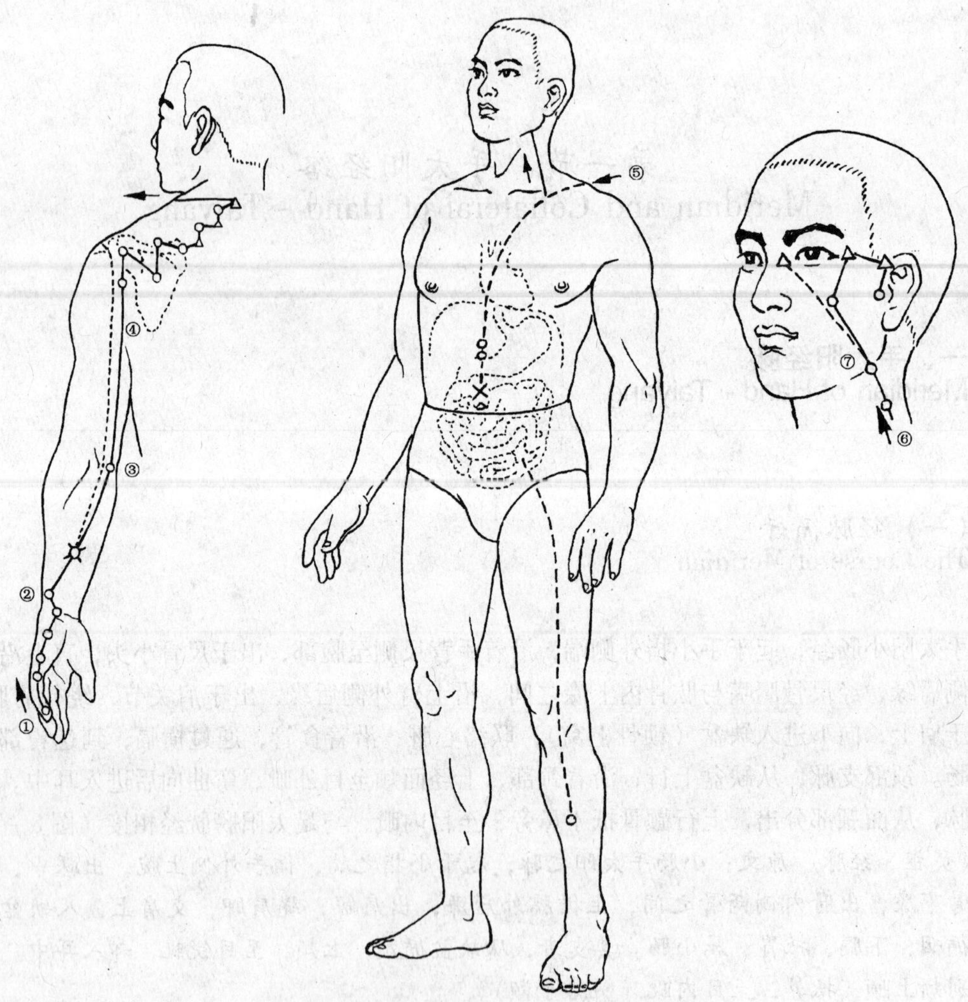

图例 ——本经有穴通路 ……本经无穴通路

Note ——Pathway with points ……Pathway without points

图 8 –1 手太阳经脉、络脉循行示意图

Fig 8 –1 The course of the meridian and collateral of hand – taiyang

（二）经脉病候
The Syndromes of Meridian

本经异常就表现为下列病症：咽喉痛，颏下肿不能回顾，肩部牵拉样疼痛，上臂痛如折断。

本经穴主治“液”方面所发生的病症：耳聋，眼睛发黄，面颊肿，颈部、颌下、肩胛、上臂、前臂的外侧后边疼痛。

The main symptoms of the meridian disorder are: pain in the throat, swelling in the chin, stiff neck, unbearable pain in the shoulder as if extracted, severe pain in the upper arm as if it were fractured.

The main symptoms due to fluid trouble are: deafness, icteric sclera, swelling in the cheek, and the conditions along the pathway of the meridian.

二、手太阳络脉
Collateral of Hand - Taiyang

手太阳络脉，名支正，在腕关节后5寸处，向内侧注入手少阴心经；其支脉上行经肘部，上络于肩髃部。实证，关节弛缓，肘部痿废不用；虚证，皮肤赘生小疣。可取手太阳络穴治疗（图8－1）。

It originates from Zhizheng (SI 7), 5 cun above the wrist, it connects with the heart meridian. Another branch runs upward, crosses the elbow and connects with Jianyu (LI 15). Excess zheng situation joints are chalasia, elbow area couldn't be used; in deficiency zheng situation, there will be little nodules on skin. The luo point could be used to treat (Fig 8－1).

三、手太阳经别
Divergent Meridian of Hand - Taiyang

手太阳经别，在肩关节部从手太阳经分出，进入腋窝部，走向心脏，联系小肠（图8－2）。

After deriving from the small intestine meridian at the shoulder joint, it enters the axilla crosses the heart and runs downward to the abdomen to link up with the small intestine meridian (Fig 8－2).

四、手太阳经筋
Muscular Region of Hand - Taiyang

手太阳经筋，起于手小指之上，结于腕背；上沿前臂内侧，结于肱骨内上髁后，以手弹该骨处，有感传及于手小指之上；上行结于腋下。其分支走腋后侧，向上绕肩胛部，沿着颈旁出走足太阳经筋的前方，结于耳后乳突部；分支进入耳中；直行的出于耳上，向下结于下颌处，上行的连属于目外眦。还有一条支筋从下颌部分出，上行沿耳前，属目外眦，上额，结于额角。

其病症：见小指僵滞不适，肘内锐骨后缘疼痛；沿臂的内侧，上至腋下及腋下后侧等处酸痛；绕肩胛牵引颈部作痛，并感到耳中鸣响，疼痛牵引下颌部，眼睛闭合一会儿才能看清景物；颈筋拘急，可发生筋瘘、颈肿等症（图 8－3）。

It starts from the tip of the small finger, knots at the dorsum of the wrist, and proceeds up along the forearm to knot at the medial condyle of the humerus in the elbow. Then it continues up along the arm and knots below the axilla. A branch runs behind the axilla, curves around the scapula and emerges in front of the foot－taiyang (bladder) on the neck, knotting behind the ear. A branch separates behind the auricle and enters the ear. Emerging above the auricle, the straight branch descends across the face and knots beneath the mandible, then continues upwards to link the outer canthus. Another branch starts at the mandible, ascends in front of the ear, connects the outer canthus and knots at the angle of the forehead.

The main symptoms of this muscular region are: stiffness of the little finger, pain of the posterior border of the ulnar bone, pain along the medial aspect of the arm and upwards to the armpit and its lower posterior side, ache around the scapula radiating to the nape and neck, tinnitus, ear pain radiating to the chin, dim eyesight remedied only by closing the eyes for a while, tensions in the muscles of the neck, carbuncle on the neck (Fig 8－3).

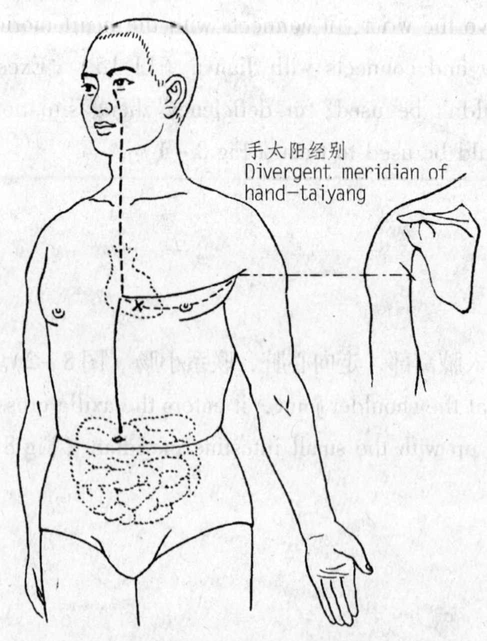

图 8－2　手太阳经别循行示意图

Fig 8－2　The course of the divergent meridian of hand－taiyang

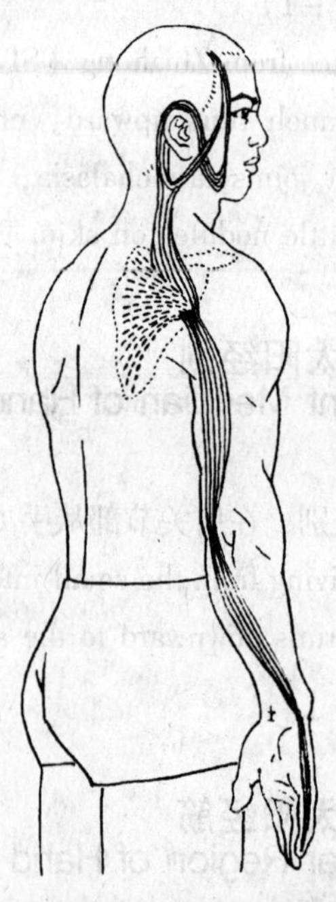

图 8－3　手太阳经筋分布示意图

Fig 8－3　The course of the muscular region of hand－taiyang

第二节 手太阳腧穴
Acupoints of Hand – Taiyang

本经左右各19个穴位，首穴为少泽，末穴为听宫（图8－4）。

1. 少泽（SI 1），井穴
Shaoze（SI 1），Jing - Well Point

【释义】少，幼小；泽，沼泽。穴在小指上，脉气初生之处，始于小泽。

【定位】在手小指末节尺侧，距指甲角0.1寸（图8－5）。

【解剖】皮肤→皮下组织→指甲根。分布有尺神经指掌侧固有神经的指背支和小指尺掌侧动、静脉指背支形成的动、静脉网。

【功用】清热利咽，通乳开窍。

【主治】①头痛，目翳，咽喉肿痛。②乳痈，乳汁少。③昏迷。④热病。

【操作】浅刺0.1～0.2寸，或点刺出血。

【Meaning】shao, young of small; ze, marsh. The point is located on the small finger where the qi of meridian has just originated, like a small marsh.

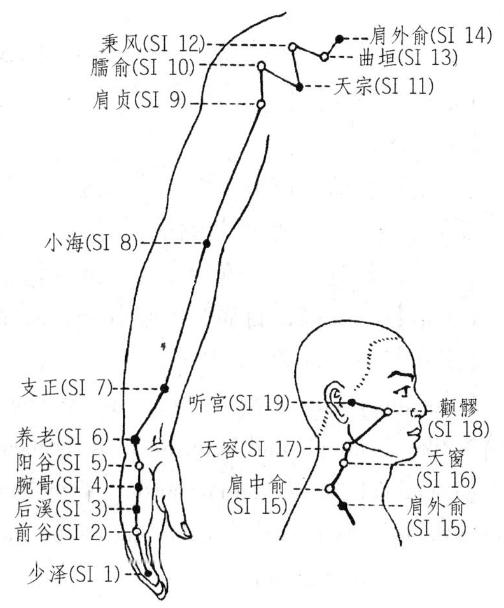

图例 ● 常用腧穴 ○ 一般腧穴

Note ● Main point ○ Common point

图8－4 手太阳小肠经腧穴总图

Fig 8－4 Points of the small intestine meridian of hand – taiyang

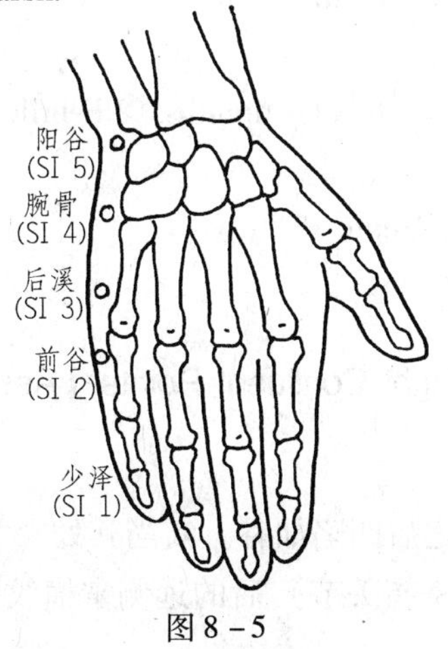

图8－5

Fig 8－5

【Location】On the ulnar side of the little Finger, approximately 0.1 cun from the corner of the nail（Fig 8－5）.

【Regional anatomy】Skin → subcutaneous tissue→the base of nail. The distribution of the palmar digital propriae nerve derived from the ulnar nerve, and the arterial and venous network formed by the little finger palmar digital propriae artery and vein.

【Properties】Clear the heat and soothe the

throat, promote lactation and open the Orifices.

【Indications】①Headache, superficial visual obstruction, sore and swollen throat. ②Mastitis, insufficient lactation. ③Coma. ④Febrile disease.

【Needling method】Puncture superficially 0.1 ~0.2 cun, or prick to induce bleeding.

2. 前谷 (SI 2), 荥穴
Qiangu (SI 2), Ying - Spring Point

【释义】前，前后之前；谷，山谷。第5掌指关节前凹陷如谷。穴当其处。

【定位】在手尺侧，微握拳，当小指本节（第5掌指关节）前的掌指横纹头赤白肉际（图8-5)。

【解剖】皮肤→皮下组织→小指近节指骨基底部。分布有尺神经的指背神经，尺神经的指掌侧固有神经和小指尺掌侧动、静脉。

【功用】清利头目，安神定志，通经活络。

【主治】①头痛，目痛，咽喉肿痛，耳鸣。②热病。③乳少。

【操作】直刺0.2~0.3寸。

【Meaning】Qian, front; gu, valley. The depression in front of the 5th metacarpophalangeal joint is like a valley, and here the point is located.

【Location】On the ulnar border of the hand, when a loose fist is made, distal to the 5th metacarpophalangeal joint, at the end of the transverse crease of the metacarpophalangeal joint, at the junction of the red and white skin (Fig 8-5).

【Regional anatomy】Skin→subcutaneous tissue→the base of the proximal phalanx of the little finger. There are the dorsal digital nerve and the proper palmar digital nerve of the ulnar nerve and little finger ulnar artery and vein.

【Properties】Refresh the mind and improve vision, tranquilize and allay the excitement, dredge the meridian.

【Indications】①Headache, eye pain, sore and swollen throat, tinnitus. ②Febrile diseases. ③Insufficient lactation.

【Needling method】Puncture perpendicularly 0.2 ~ 0.3 cun.

3. 后溪 (SI 3), 输穴；八脉交会穴（通督脉）
Houxi (SI 3), Shu - Stream Point; One of the Eight Confluent Points (Associating with the Governor Vessel)

【释义】后，前后之后；溪，沟溪。第5掌指关节之后凹陷如谷。穴当其处。

【定位】在手掌尺侧，微握拳，当小指本节（第5掌指关节）后的远侧掌横纹头赤白肉际（图8-5)。

【解剖】皮肤→皮下组织→小指展肌→小指短屈肌。浅层分布有神经手背支，尺神经掌

支和皮下浅静脉等。深层有小指尺掌侧固有动、静脉和指掌侧固有神经。

【功用】宁神开窍，通督脉。

【主治】①头项强痛，腰背痛。②目赤，耳聋，咽喉肿痛。③盗汗，疟疾。④癫狂痫。⑤手指及肘臂挛急。

【操作】直刺0.5～0.8寸，或向合谷方向透刺。

【Meaning】Hou, back; xi, brook. The depression at the back of the 5th metacarpophalangeal joint is like a brook, and here the point is located.

【Location】On the ulnar side of the hand, when a loose fist is made, proximal to the 5th metacarpophalangeal joint, at the top of the transverse crease and the border of the red and white skin (Fig 8－5).

【Regional anatomy】Skin→subcutaneous tissue→abductor digiti minimi→flexor digiti minimi brevis. Superficial layer, the dorsal branch and the palmar branch of the ulnar nerve. deep layer, the little finger palmar digital propriae artery, vein and nerve.

【Properties】Calm the heart for resuscitation; promote the function of the Governor Vessel.

【Indications】①Headache and painful stiff nape of the neck, pain of the lumbar and back region. ②Red eye, deafness, sore and swollen throat. ③Night sweats, malaria. ④Psychosis, epilepsy. ⑤Spasm in the fingers, elbows or arms.

【Needling method】Puncture perpendicularly 0.5～0.8 cun, or transversely towards Hegu (LI 4).

4. 腕骨（SI 4），原穴 Wangu (SI 4), Yuan - Source Point

【释义】腕，腕部；骨，骨头。穴在腕部骨间。

【定位】在手掌尺侧，当第5掌骨基底与钩骨之间的凹陷处，赤白肉际（图8－5）。

【解剖】皮肤→皮下组织→小指展肌→豆掌韧带。浅层布有前臂内侧皮神经，尺神经掌支，尺神经手背支和浅静脉等。深层有尺动、静脉的分支或属支。

【功用】舒筋活络，泌别清浊。

【主治】①头项强痛，耳鸣，目翳。②黄疸。③消渴，热病，疟疾。④指挛腕痛。

【操作】直刺0.3～0.5寸。

【Meaning】Wan, wrist; gu, bone. The point is between the bones of the wrist.

【Location】On the ulnar side of the palm, in the depression between the 5th metacarpal bone and the hamate bone, at the junction of the red and white skin (Fig 8－5).

【Regional anatomy】Skin→subcutaneous tissue→the abductor muscle of the little finger→pisometacarpal ligament. In the superficial layer, there are the medial cutaneous nerve of the forearm, the palmar branches of the ulnar nerve, the dorsal branches of the ulnar nerve and the superficial vein. In the deep layer, there are the branches or tributaries of the ulnar artery and vein.

【Properties】Relieve the rigidity of muscles and activating collaterals; separate fluids.

【Indications】①Headache and painful stiff nape of the neck, tinnitus, superficial visual obstruction. ②Jaundice. ③Diabetes, febrile diseases, malaria. ④Pain and spasm in the fingers and wrists.

【Needling method】Puncture perpendicularly 0.3 ~0.5 cun.

5. 阳谷（SI 5），经穴
Yang gu（SI 5），Jing - River Point

【释义】阳，阴阳之阳；谷，山谷。外为阳。腕外骨隙形如山谷，穴当其处。

【定位】在手腕尺侧，当尺骨茎突与三角骨之间的凹陷处（图 8 -5）。

【解剖】皮肤→皮下组织→尺侧腕伸肌腱的前方。浅层有尺神经手背支、贵要静脉等分布。深层有尺动脉的腕背支。

【功用】明目安神，通经活络。

【主治】①头痛，目眩，耳鸣，耳聋。②热病。③癫狂痫。④手腕痛。

【操作】直刺 0.3 ~0.5 寸。

【Meaning】Yang, yang of yin - yang; gu, valley. The exterior is yang. The seam on the exterior aspect of the wrist is like a valley, and here the point is located.

【Location】On the ulnar side of the wrist, in the depression between the styloid process of the ulna and the triquetral bone（Fig 8 -5）.

【Regional anatomy】Skin→subcutaneous tissue→the anterior border of the tendon of the ulnar extensor muscle of the wrist. In the superficial layer, there are the dorsal branches of the ulnar nerve, basilic vein, etc. In the deep layer, there are the dorsal branches of the ulnar artery.

【Properties】Improve the vision and tranquillize; dredge the meridian.

【Indications】①Headache, dizziness, tinnitus, deafness. ②Febrile diseases. ③Psychosis, epilepsy. ④Pain in the wrist.

【Needling method】Puncture perpendicularly 0.3 ~0.5 cun.

6. 养老（SI 6），郄穴
Yanglao（SI 6），Xi - Cleft Point

【释义】养，赡养；老，老人。此穴善治目花、耳聋、腰酸和肩痛等老年人常见病症。

【定位】在前臂背面尺侧，当尺骨小头近端桡侧凹陷中（图 8 -6）。

【解剖】皮肤→皮下组织→尺侧腕伸肌腱。浅层布有前臂内侧皮神经，前臂后皮神经，尺神经手背支和贵要静脉属支。深层有腕背动、静脉网。

【功用】清利头目，舒筋活络。

【主治】①目视不明。②肩背肘臂痛麻，项强，急性腰痛。

【操作】掌心向胸姿势，向肘方向斜刺 0.5 ~0.8 寸。

【Meaning】Yang, to support; lao, the aged. This point is useful in treating such geriatric diseases as blurring of vision, deafness, lumbago and shoulder pain.

【Location】On the dorsal ulnar aspect of the forearm, in the depression on the radial side of the proximal end of the capitulum of the ulna (Fig 8 –6).

【Regional anatomy】Skin→subcutaneous tissue→extensor carpi ulnaris tendon. Superficial layer, the medial branchial cutaneous nerve, the posterior antebrachial cutaneous nerve, the dorsal branch of the ulnar nerve, and the subordinate branches of the basilic vein; deep layer, the dorsal arterial and venous network of the wrist.

【Properties】Clear the head and improve vision, relieve the rigidity of muscles and activate collaterals.

【Indications】①Blurred vision. ②Numbness and pain in the shoulder, back, elbow and arm, stiff neck, acute lumbar pain.

【Needling method】When the palm of the hand is placed on the chest, insert obliquely towards the elbow 0.5 ~0.8 cun.

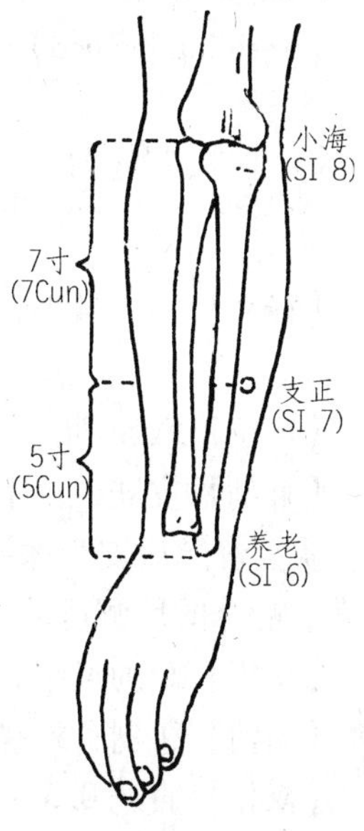

图 8 –6

Fig 8 –6

7. 支正（SI 7），络穴 Zhizheng (SI 7), Luo - Connecting Point

【释义】支，支别；正，正经。小肠经之络脉由此别离正经，走向心经。

【定位】在前臂背面尺侧，当阳谷与小海的连线上，腕背横纹上5寸（图8 –6）。

【解剖】皮肤→皮下组织→尺侧腕屈肌→指深屈肌→前臂骨间膜。浅层布有前臂内侧皮神经，贵要静脉属支。深层有尺动、静脉和尺神经。

【功用】醒神开窍，清热解表。

【主治】①头痛，项强。②热病。③癫狂。④肘臂酸痛。

【操作】直刺或斜刺0.5 ~0.8 寸。

【Meaning】Zhi, divergence; zheng, regular meridian. The collateral of the small intestine meridian diverges from this point to the heart meridian.

【Location】On the dorsal ulnar aspect of the forearm, on the line connecting Yanggu (SI 5) and Xiaohai (SI 8), 5 cun above the dorsal transverse crease of the wrist (Fig 8 –6).

【Regional anatomy】Skin→subcutaneous tissue→the ulnar flexor muscle of the wrist→the deep flexor muscle of the fingers→interosseous membrane of the forearm. In the superficial layer, there is the medial cutaneous nerve of the forearm and the tributaries of the basilic vein. In the deep layer, there is the ulnar artery and vein and the ulnar nerve.

【Properties】Calm the heart for inducing resuscitation, clear the heat for releasing the exterior.

【Indications】①Headache, stiff neck. ②Febrile disease. ③Psychosis. ④Aching pain in the elbow and arm.

【Needling method】Puncture perpendicularly or obliquely 0.5 ~0.8 cun.

8. 小海（SI 8），合穴
Xiaohai（SI 8), He - Sea Point

【释义】小，微小；海，海洋。小，指小肠经。此系小肠经合穴，气血至此，犹如水流入海。

【定位】微屈肘，在尺骨鹰嘴与肱骨内上髁之间凹陷处（图8－6)。

【解剖】皮肤→皮下组织→尺神经沟内。浅层布有前臂内侧皮神经尺侧支，臂内侧皮神经，贵要静脉属支。深层，在尺神经沟内有尺神经，尺神经的后外侧有尺侧上副动、静脉与尺动、静脉的尺侧返动、静脉后支吻合成的动、静脉网。

【功用】疏通经络，清热醒神。

【主治】①肘臂疼痛。②癫痫。

【操作】直刺0.3~0.5寸。

【Meaning】Xiao, small; hai, sea. Xiao refers to the small intestine meridian, and this is its he - sea point. The arrival of qi and blood at this point is like water flowing into the sea.

【Location】With the elbow flexed, in the depression between the olecranon of the ulna and the medial epicondyle of the humerus（Fig 8 -6）.

【Regional anatomy】Skin→subcutaneous tissue→the groove of the ulnar nerve. Superficial layer. the medial branchial cutaneous nerve, the medial antebrachial cutaneous nerve, the subordinate branches of the basilic vein; deep layer, the ulnar nerve in the groove of it. the arterial and venous network formed by the superior ulnar collateral arteries and veins, and the ulnar recurrent arteries and veins.

【Properties】Activate collaterals and clear away heat for resuscitation.

【Indications】①Pain in the elbow and arm. ②Epilepsy.

【Needling method】Puncture perpendicularly 0.3 ~0.5 cun.

9. 肩贞 Jianzhen（SI 9）

【释义】肩，肩部；贞，第一。此为本经入肩部的第一穴。

【定位】在肩关节后下方，臂内收时，腋后纹头上1寸（图8－7)。

【解剖】皮肤→皮下组织→三角肌后分→肱三头肌长头→大圆肌→背阔肌腱。浅层布有第2肋间神经的外侧皮支和臂外侧上皮神经。深层有桡神经等结构。

【功用】活血止痛。

【主治】①肩臂麻痛。②瘰疬。③耳鸣，耳聋。

【操作】直刺1.0~1.5寸。

【Meaning】Jian, shoulder; zhen, first. This is the first point where the small intestine meridian joins the shoulder.

【Location】Posterior and inferior to the shoulder joint, when the arm is adducted, 1 cun above the posterior end of the axillary fold (Fig 8 –7).

【Regional anatomy】Skin→subcutaneous tissue→the back share of deltoid→triceps brachii→teres major→latissimus dorsi tendon. Superficial layer, the lateral cutaneous branches of the second intercostal nerve, and the posterior antebrachial cutaneous nerve; deep layer, the radial nerve.

【Properties】Activate blood to relieve pain.

【Indications】①Numbness and pain in the shoulder and arm. ②Scrofula. ③Tin – nitus, deafness.

【Needling method】Puncture perpendicularly 1.0 ~ 1.5 cun.

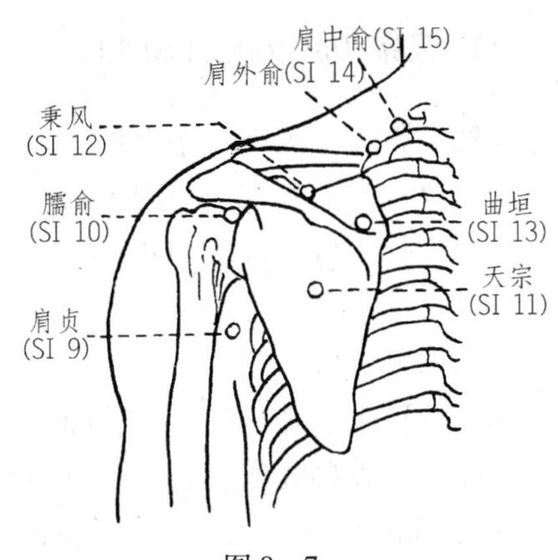

图 8 –7

Fig 8 –7

10. 臑俞（SI 10），手、足太阳经，阳维脉、阳跻脉交会穴 Naoshu (SI 10), Crossing Point of the Meridians of the Hand - Taiyang, Foot - Taiyang, Yang Link Vessel and Yang Heel Vessel

【释义】臑，上臂肌肉隆起处；俞，穴。穴在臑部，为经气输注之处。

【定位】在肩部，当腋后纹头直上，肩胛冈下缘凹陷中（图 8 7）。

【解剖】皮肤→皮下组织→三角肌→冈下肌。浅层布有锁骨上外侧神经。深层有肩胛上动、静脉的分支或属支；旋肱后动、静脉的分支或属支等。

【功用】舒筋活络，化痰消肿。

【主治】①肩臂疼痛。②瘰疬。

【操作】直刺或斜刺 0.5 ~ 1.2 寸。

【Meaning】Nao, muscle prominence of the upper arm; shu, point. The point is on the upper arm, where the qi of meridian is infused.

【Location】On the shoulder, directly above the posterior end of the axillary fold, in the depression inferior to the scapular spine (Fig 8 –7).

【Regional anatomy】Skin → subcutaneous tissue → deltoid muscle → infraspinous muscle. Superficial layer, the lateral supraclavicular nerves. Deep layer, there are the branches or tributaries of the supraclavicular artery and vein, and the branches or tributaries of the posterior humeral circumflex artery and vein.

【Properties】Relieve the rigidity of muscles and activate collaterals, eliminate phlegm for detumescence.

【Indications】①Pain in the shoulder and arm. ②Scrofula.

【Needling method】Puncture perpendicularly or obliquely 0.5 ~ 1.2 cun.

11. 天宗 Tianzong（SI 11）

【释义】天，天空，指上部；宗，尊奉。意为人体上部的重要俞穴。

【定位】在肩胛部，当冈下窝中央凹陷处，与第4胸椎相平（图8－7）。

【解剖】皮肤→皮下组织→斜方肌→冈下肌。浅层有第4胸神经后支的皮支和伴行的动、静脉。深层布有肩胛上神经的分支和旋肩胛动、静脉的分支或属支。

【功用】理气止痛。

【主治】①肩胛疼痛。②乳痈。③气喘。

【操作】直刺或斜刺0.5～1.0寸。

【Meaning】Tian, the upper part; zong, respect. Tianzong means an important point on the upper part of the body.

【Location】In the region of the scapula, in the depression of the center of the subscapular fossa, level with the 4th thoracic vertebra（Fig 8－7）.

【Regional anatomy】Skin→subcutaneous tissue→the trapezius muscle→infraspinous muscle. In the superficial layer, there are the cutaneous branches of the posterior branches of the 4th thoracic nerve and the accompanying arteries and veins. In the deep layer, there are the branches of the suprascapular nerve and the branches or tributaries of the circumflex scapular artery and vein.

【Properties】Regulate qi－flowing for relieving pain.

【Indications】①Scapular pain. ②Mastitis. ③Asthma.

【Needling method】Puncture perpendicularly or obliquely 0.5～1.0 cun.

12. 秉风（SI 12），手三阳经与足少阳经交会穴 Bingfeng（SI 12），Crossing Point of Hand-Taiyang Meridian，Shaoyang Meridians of Hand and Foot

【释义】秉，秉受；风，风邪。穴在易受风邪之处。

【定位】在肩胛部，冈上窝中央，天宗直上，举臂有凹陷处（图8－7）。

【解剖】皮肤→皮下组织→斜方肌→冈上肌。浅层布有第2胸神经后支的皮支和伴行的动、静脉。深层有肩胛上神经的分支和肩胛上动、静脉的分支或属支分布。

【功用】散风活络。

【主治】肩胛疼痛，上肢酸麻。

【操作】直刺或斜刺0.3寸。

【Meaning】Bing, to receive; feng, pathogenic wind. The point is located at a place where it is easily invaded by pathogenic wind.

【Location】In the region of the scapula, in the center of the suprascapular fossa, directly above Tianzong（SI 11）, in the depression when the arm is lifted（Fig 8－6）.

【Regional anatomy】Skin→subcutaneous tissue→trapezius→supraspinatus. Superficial layer, the cutaneous branches of the posterior branches of the second thoracic nerves and the arteries and veins along with them. Deep layer, the branches of the suprascapular nerve, and the branches or the subordinate ramus of the suprascapular artery and vein.

【Properties】Dispelling wind to activate collaterals.

【Indications】Scapular pain and aching numbness of the upper arm.

【Needling method】Puncture perpendicularly or obliquely 0.3 cun.

13. 曲垣 Quyuan (SI 13)

【释义】曲，弯曲；垣，矮墙。肩胛冈弯曲如墙，穴当其处。

【定位】在肩胛部，冈上窝内侧端，当臑俞与第2胸椎棘突连线的中点处（图8-7）。

【解剖】皮肤→皮下组织→斜方肌→冈上肌。浅层有第2、3胸神经后支的皮支和伴行的动、静脉。深层布有肩胛上神经的肌支和肩胛上动、静脉，肩胛背动、静脉的分支或属支。

【功用】舒筋活络，疏风止痛。

【主治】肩胛背项疼痛。

【操作】直刺或向外斜刺0.5~0.8寸。

【Meaning】Qu, curved; yuan, wall. The spine of the scapula is like a curved wall. The point is located on it.

【Location】In the region of the scapula, on the medial end of the suprascapular fossa, midpoint of the line between Naoshu (SI 10) and the spinous process of the 2nd thoracic vertebra (Fig 8-7).

【Regional anatomy】Skin→subcutaneous tissue→the trapezius muscle→supraspinous muscle. In the superficial layer, there are the cutaneous branches of the posterior branches of the 2nd and 3rd thoracic nerves and the accompanying arteries and veins. In the deep layer, there are the muscular branches of the suprascapular nerve, the branches or tributaries of the suprascapular artery and vein and the dorsal scapular artery and vein.

【Properties】Relieving the rigidity of muscles and activating collaterals; dispelling wind for relieving pain.

【Indications】Pain in the scapula, back and neck.

【Needling method】Puncture perpendicularly or obliquely outward 0.5~0.8 cun.

14. 肩外俞 Jianwaishu (SI 14)

【释义】肩，肩部；外，外侧；俞，穴位。穴在肩部，约当肩胛内侧缘之稍外方。

【定位】在背部，当第1胸椎棘突下，旁开3寸（图8-7）。

【解剖】皮肤→皮下组织→斜方肌→菱形肌。浅层有第1、2胸神经后支的皮支和伴行的动、静脉。深层分布有颈横动、静脉的分支或属支和肩胛背神经的肌支。

【功用】舒筋活络，祛风止痛。

【主治】肩背疼痛，颈项强急。

【操作】斜刺0.5~0.8寸。

【Meaning】Jian, shoulder; wai, lateral side, shu, point. The point is on the shoulder, slightly lateral to the vertebral border of the scapula.

【Location】On the back, 3 cun lateral to the lower border of the spinous process of the 1st thoracic vertebra (Fig 8-7).

【Regional anatomy】Skin→subcutaneous tissue→the trapezius muscle→the rhomboid muscle. In the superficial layer, there are the cutaneous branches of the posterior branches of the 1st and 2nd thoracic nerves and accompanying arteries and veins. In the deep layer, there are the branches of tributaries of the transverse cervical artery and vein and muscular branches of the dorsal scapular nerve.

【Properties】Relieve the rigidity of muscles and activate collaterals, dispelling wind for relieving pain.

【Indications】Pain in the shoulder and upper back, spasm and stiff nape of the neck.

【Needling method】Puncture obliquely 0.5~0.8 cun.

15. 肩中俞 Jianzhongshu (SI 15)

【释义】肩，肩部；中，中间；俞，穴位。穴在肩部，约当肩胛骨内侧缘之内侧。

【定位】在背部，当第7颈椎棘突下，旁开2寸（图8-7）。

【解剖】皮肤→皮下组织→斜方肌→菱形肌。浅层有第8颈神经后支，第1胸神经后支的皮支分布。深层有副神经、肩胛背神经的分布和颈横动、静脉。

【功用】舒筋活络，解表宣肺。

【主治】①咳嗽，气喘。②肩背疼痛。

【操作】斜刺0.5~0.8寸。

【Meaning】Jian, shoulder; zhong, central; shu, point. The point is on the shoulder and is central to the vertebral border of the scapula.

【Location】On the back, 2 cun lateral to the lower border of the spinous process of the 7th cervical vertebra (Fig 8-7).

【Regional anatomy】Skin→subcutaneous tissue→the trapezius muscle→the rhomboid muscle. In the superficial layer, there are the posterior branches of the 8th cervical nerve and the cutaneous branches of the posterior branches of the 1st thoracic nerve. In the deep layer, there are the accessory nerve, the branches of the dorsal scapular nerve and the transverse cervical artery and vein.

【Properties】Relieving the rigidity of muscles and activating collaterals, dispersing lung qi for relieving exterior syndrome.

【Indications】①Cough, asthma. ②Pain in the shoulder and upper back.

【Needling method】Puncture obliquely 0.5~0.8 cun.

16. 天窗 Tianchuang (SI 16)

【释义】天，天空，指上部；窗，窗户。穴在颈部，位于上，主治耳病，通耳窍，如开“天窗”。

【定位】在颈外侧部，胸锁乳突肌的后缘，扶突后，与喉结平（图 8-8）。

【解剖】皮肤→皮下组织→胸锁乳突肌后缘→肩胛提肌→头、颈夹肌。浅层有耳大神经、枕小神经和颈外静脉。深层布有颈升动、静脉的分支或属支。

【功用】息风宁神，利咽聪耳。

【主治】①咽喉肿痛，暴喑，耳鸣，耳聋。②颈项强痛。

【操作】直刺 0.5～0.8 寸。

【Meaning】 Tian, upper part; chuang, window. The point is on the neck and indicated in ear disease. Its function is to restore hearing loss, like opening a window.

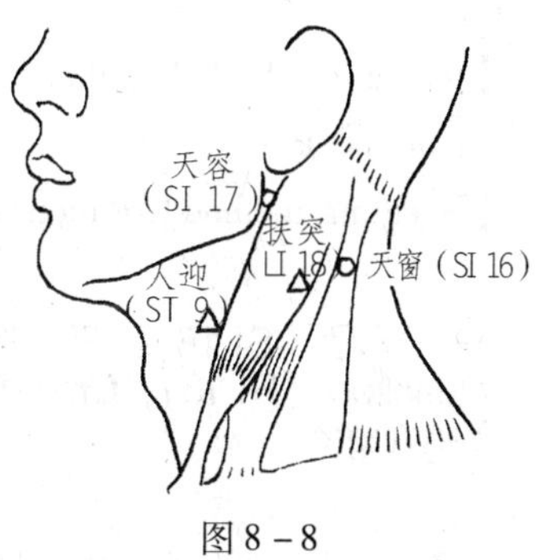

图 8-8
Fig 8-8

【Location】 On the lateral aspect of the neck, on the posterior border of the steraocleidomastoideus, posterior to Futu (LI 18), and level with the Adam's Apple (Fig 8-8).

【Regional anatomy】 Skin→subcutaneous tissue→the posterior border of the sternocleidomastoid muscle→levator muscle of the scapula→splenius muscle of the neck and the head. In the superficial layer, there are the greater auricular nerve, the lesser occipital nerve and the external jugular vein. In the deep layer, there are the branches or tributaries of the ascending cervical artery and vein.

【Properties】 Dispersing liver wind to calm the heart, relieving sore throat and improving hearing.

【Indications】 ①Sore and swollen throat, sudden loss of voice, tinnitus, deafness. ②Pain and stiffness in the nape of the neck.

【Needling method】 Puncture perpendicularly 0.5～0.8 cun.

17. 天容 Tianrong (SI 17)

【释义】天，天空，指上部；容，隆盛。穴在头部，位于上，为经气隆盛之处。

【定位】在颈外侧部，当下颌骨的后方，胸锁乳突肌的前缘凹陷中（图 8-8）。

【解剖】皮肤→皮下组织→面动脉后方→二腹肌腱及茎突舌骨肌。浅层有耳大神经和颈外静脉等结构。深层有面动、静脉，颈内静脉，副神经，迷走神经，舌下神经，颈上神经节等重要结构。

【功用】清热利咽，消肿降逆。

【主治】①耳鸣，耳聋，咽喉肿痛。②颈项肿痛。

【操作】直刺 0.5～0.8 寸。

【Meaning】Tian, upper part; rong, abundance. The point is on the head, where the qi of meridian is abundant.

【Location】On the lateral aspect of the neck, posterior to the angle of the mandible, in the depression of the anterior border of the sternocleidomastoideus (Fig 8－8).

【Regional anatomy】Skin→subcutaneous tissue→the posterior border of the facial artery→tendons of the digastric muscle and the stylohyoid muscle. In the superficial layer, there are the greater auricular nerve and the external jugular vein. In the deep layer, there are the facial artery and vein, the internal jugular vein, the accessory nerve, the vagus nerve, the hypoglossal nerve and the superior cervical ganglion.

【Properties】Clearing heat from throat, eliminating phlegm for detumescence and lowering adverse qi.

【Indications】①Tinnitus, deafness, sore and swollen throat. ②Pain and distension in the nape of the neck.

【Needling method】Puncture perpendicularly 0.5～0.8 cun.

18. 颧髎（SI 18），手少阳、太阳经交会穴
Quanliao (SI 18), Crossing Point of the Meridians of Hand - Shaoyang and Hand - Taiyang

【释义】颧，颧部；髎，骨隙。穴在颧部骨隙中。

【定位】在面部当目外眦直下，颧骨下缘凹陷处（图 8－9）。

【解剖】皮肤→皮下组织→颧肌→咬肌→颞肌。浅层布有上颌神经的眶下神经分支，面神经的颧支、颊支，面横动、静脉的分支或属支。深层有三叉神经的下颌神经分支。

【功用】祛风镇痉。

【主治】口眼㖞斜，眼睑瞤动，面痛，齿痛，颊肿。

【操作】直刺 0.3～0.5 寸，或斜刺 0.5～1.0 寸。

【Meaning】Quan, zygoma; liao, foramen. The point is in the seam of the zygomatic bone.

【Location】On the face, directly below the outer canthus, in the depression on the lower border of the zygomatic bone (Fig 8－9).

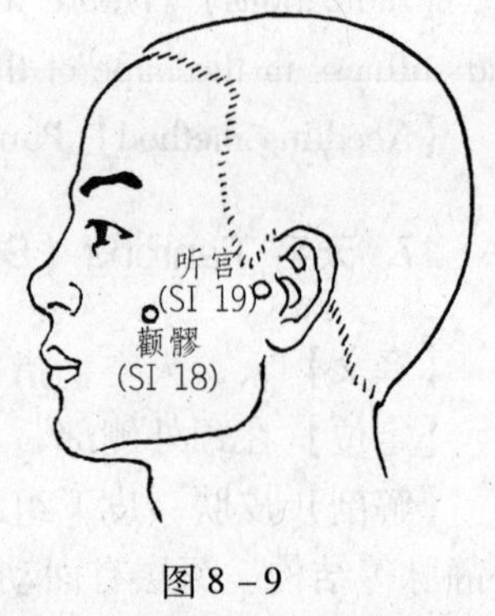

图 8－9
Fig 8－9

【Regional anatomy】Skin→subcutaneous tissue→zygomatic muscle→masseter→temporalis. Superficial layer, the branch of infraorbital nerves of maxillary nerve, the zygomatic branch and the temporal branch of the facial nerve, the branches or the subordinate ramus of the transverse facial artery and vein. deep layer, the maxillary nerve derived from trigeminal nerve.

【Properties】Dispelling pathogenic wind for resolving convulsion.

【Indications】Deviation of the mouth and eye, twitching of the eyelids, facial pain, toothache, and swelling in the cheeks.

【Needling method】Puncture perpendicularly 0.3～0.5 cun, or puncture obliquely 0.5～1.0 cun.

19. 听宫（SI 19），手足少阳、手太阳经交会穴 Tinggong (SI 19), Crossing Point of the Meridians of the Hand - Shaoyang, Hand - Taiyang and Foot - Shaoyang

【释义】听，听闻；宫，宫殿。听宫，指耳窍。穴在耳部，治耳病，有通耳窍之功。

【定位】在面部，耳屏前，下颌骨髁状突的后方，张口时呈凹陷处（图8－9）。

【解剖】皮肤→皮下组织→外耳道软骨。布有耳颞神经，颞浅动、静脉耳前支的分支或属支等结构。

【功用】聪耳开窍。

【主治】①耳鸣，耳聋，齿痛。②癫痫。

【操作】微张口，直刺0.5～1.0寸。

【Meaning】Ting, hearing; gong, palace. Tinggong refers to the ear. The point is located in front of the ear and is indicated in ear disease.

【Location】On the face, anterior to the tragus and posterior to the condyle of the mandible, in the depression formed when the mouth is open (Fig 8－9).

【Regional anatomy】Skin→subcutaneous tissue→the cartilage of the external acoustic meatus. The distribution of the auriculotemporal nerve, and the branches or the subordinate ramus of the auricular branches of the superficial temporal artery and vein.

【Properties】Improving hearing with resuscitation.

【Indications】①Tinnitus, deafness, toothache. ②Epilepsy.

【Needling method】Puncture perpendicularly 0.5～1.0 cun with the mouth open.

复习思考题 Review Questions

1. 请根据《灵枢·经脉》写出手太阳小肠经的循行线路。

Retell the course of the heart meridian of hand－taiyang according the chapter "Discussion on the Meridians" in *Miraculous Pivot*.

2. 试述少泽穴、后溪穴、养老穴和小海穴的定位、主治和操作方法。

Retell the location, indications, and needling method of Shaoze (SI 1), Houxi (SI 3), Yanglao (SI 6), Xiaohai (SI 8).

3. 试述手太阳小肠经穴位的主治内容。

Retell the summary of indications of this meridian.

第九章 足太阳经络与腧穴
Meridian and Collateral and Its Acupoints of Foot – Taiyang

第一节 足太阳经络
Meridian and Collateral of Foot – Taiyang

一、足太阳经脉
Meridian of Foot - Taiyang

（一）经脉循行
The Course of Meridian

足太阳膀胱经，起于目内眦，上额交会于巅顶；头顶部的支脉，从头顶分出到耳上方。巅顶部直行的主脉，从头顶入里联络于脑，返回出项部而分开下行。一支沿着肩胛部内侧，夹着脊柱，到达腰部，从脊柱旁肌肉进入体腔，联络肾脏，属于膀胱；腰部的支脉，向下通过臀部，进入腘窝中。后项的另一支脉，通过肩胛骨内缘直下，经过髋关节下行，沿着大腿后外侧，与腰部下来的支脉会合于腘窝，由此向下通过腓肠肌，出于外踝的后面，沿着第5跖骨粗隆，至小趾外侧端，与足少阴肾经相接（图9–1）。

《灵枢·经脉》原文：膀胱足太阳之脉，起于目内眦，上额，交巅。其支者，从巅至耳上角。其直者，从巅入络脑，还出别下项，循肩髆内，夹脊抵腰中，入循膂，络肾，属膀胱。其支者，从腰中，下夹脊，贯臀，入腘中。其支者，从髆内左右，别下贯胛，夹脊内，过髀枢，循髀外后廉下合腘中，以下贯腨内，出外踝之后，循京骨，至小指外侧。

The bladder meridian of foot – taiyang originates from the inner canthus of the eye. It then goes upwards toward the forehead, and connects at the vertex. Its branch from the vertex descends to the upper corner of the ear. The straight branch from the vertex enters the brain, and then emerges to descend at the nape of the neck, where the meridian splits into two branches. The first branch runs downwards along the medial border of the scapular region parallel to the vertebral column, reaching the lumbar region, and then entering the body cavity via the paravertebral muscle to connect with the kidney and end at the bladder. Another branch separates into the lumbar region, descends via the hip, and enters the popliteal fossa of the knee. The branch separates at the nape of the neck and descends along the medial aspect of the scapular region, crosses the hip joint, and then descends along the posterio – lateral aspect of the thigh to meet with the previous branch of the channel in the popliteal fossa. From there, it descends through the gastrocnemius muscle, emerges posterior to the lateral malleolus, and follows along the 5th metatarsal bone to the lateral side of the tip of the little toe, where it communicates with the kidney meridian of foot – shaoyin (Fig 9 – 1).

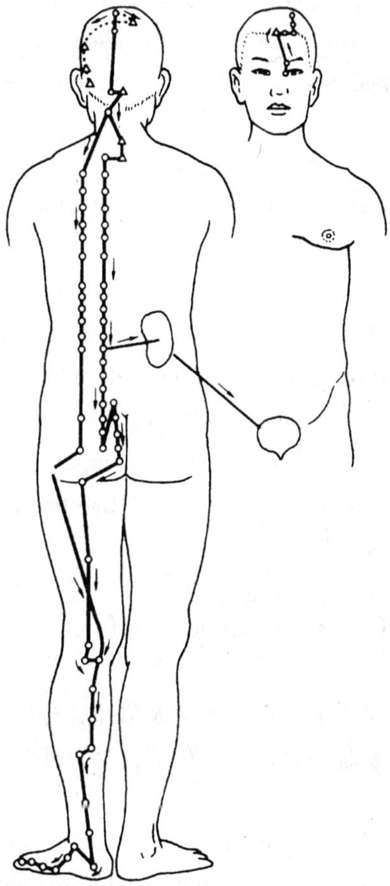

图例 ——本经有穴通路 ……本经无穴通路

Note ——Pathway with points

……Pathway without points

图 9 – 1 足太阳经脉、络脉循行示意图

Fig 9 – 1 The course of the meridian and collateral of foot – taiyang

(二) 经脉病候 The Syndromes of Meridian

本经异常就表现为下列病症：头重痛，眼睛要脱出，后项像被牵引，脊背痛，腰好像要折断，股关节不能弯曲，腘窝好像凝结，腓肠肌像要裂开；还可发生外踝部的气血阻逆，如厥冷、麻木、酸痛等。

本经穴主治“筋”方面所发生的病症：痔，疟疾，躁狂、癫病，头囟后项痛，眼睛昏黄，流泪，鼻塞、多涕或出血，后项、腰背部、骶尾部、腘窝、腓肠肌、脚都可发生病痛，小趾功能障碍。

Disorders of the meridian are manifested as: heaviness and pain in the head with a feeling of qi rushing upwards, pain in the eyes as if it would prolapse, pain in the back of the neck as if it's tractive, pain in the spine and lumbus as if it's broken, acampsia of the thigh, rigidity of the tendons in the popliteal fossa as if knotted, pain in the musculus gastrocnemius as if split; and coldness, numbness and aching pain in the external malleolus caused by qi and blood stagnation and reversing.

The syndromes caused by tendon trouble due to urinary bladder disorder shows: hemorrhoid, malaria, insanity, epilepsy, icteric sclera, lacrimation, nasal obstruction, poly - nasal discharge or epistaxis, pains in the fontanel and other parts such as back of the neck, lumbus, sacroiliac, popliteal fossa, gastrocnemius, and foot, and dysfunction of the small toe.

二、足太阳络脉 Collateral of Foot - Taiyang

足太阳络脉，名飞扬，在外踝上 7 寸处分出，走向足少阴经脉（图 9 - 1）。

实证，见鼻塞，头痛，背痛；虚证，见鼻流清涕，鼻出血。可取足太阳络穴治疗。

It arises from Feiyang (BL 58), seven cun above the external malleolus, it connects with the kidney meridian (Fig 9 - 1).

Its repletion disorders are nasal congestion and painful head and back. Its vacuity disorder is nasal congestion and nosebleed. Use this point.

三、足太阳经别 Divergent Meridian of Foot - Taiyang

足太阳经别，从足太阳经脉分出，进入腘窝中，一支在骶骨下 5 寸处分出，进入肛门，属于膀胱，散布联络肾脏，沿脊柱两旁的肌肉，到心脏部进入散布开；直行的一支，循脊部两旁的肌肉上行，进入项部，仍归属于足太阳经（图 9 - 2）。

After deriving from the bladder meridian in the popliteal fossa, it proceeds to a point 5 cun below the sacrum. Winding round to the anal region, it connects with the bladder and disperses in the kidneys. Then it follows the spine and disperses in the cardiac region and finally emerges at the neck and converges with the bladder meridian of foot - taiyang (Fig 9 - 2).

四、足太阳经筋 Muscular Region of Foot - Taiyang

足太阳经筋，起始于足小趾，上结于外踝；斜上结于膝部；下方沿足外侧结于足跟，向上沿跟腱结于腘部；其分支结于小腿肚（腨内），上向腘内侧，与腘部一支并行上结臀部；向上夹脊旁，上后项；分支入结于舌根。直行者结于枕骨，上向头项，由头的前方下行到颜面，结于鼻部。分支形成"目上纲"，下边结于鼻旁。背部的分支，从腋后外侧结于肩髃部位；一支进入腋下，向上出缺盆，上方结于完骨（耳后乳突）；再有分支从缺盆出来，斜上结于鼻旁部（图 9 - 3）。

其病症，可见足小趾僵滞不适和足跟部掣引酸痛，腘窝部挛急，脊背反张，项筋拘急，肩不能抬举，腋部僵滞不适，缺盆中牵掣样疼痛，不能左右活动。

It starts from the tip of the small finger, knots at the dorsum of the wrist, and proceeds up along the forearm to knot at the medial condyle of the humerus in the elbow. Then it continues up along the arm and knots below the axilla. A branch runs behind the axilla, curves around the scapula and emerges in front of the foot – taiyang (bladder) on the neck, knotting behind the ear. A branch separates behind the auricle and enters the ear. Emerging above the auricle, the straight branch descends across the face and knots beneath the mandible, then continues upwards to link the outer canthus. Another branch starts at the mandible, ascends around the teeth and in front of the ear, connects the outer canthus and knots at the angle of the forehead (Fig 9 – 3).

The main symptoms of this muscular region are: uncomfortable sensation in the little toe, pulling pain of the heel, spasm in the popliteal space, opisthotonus, contracture of the neck, dysfunction of the shoulder.

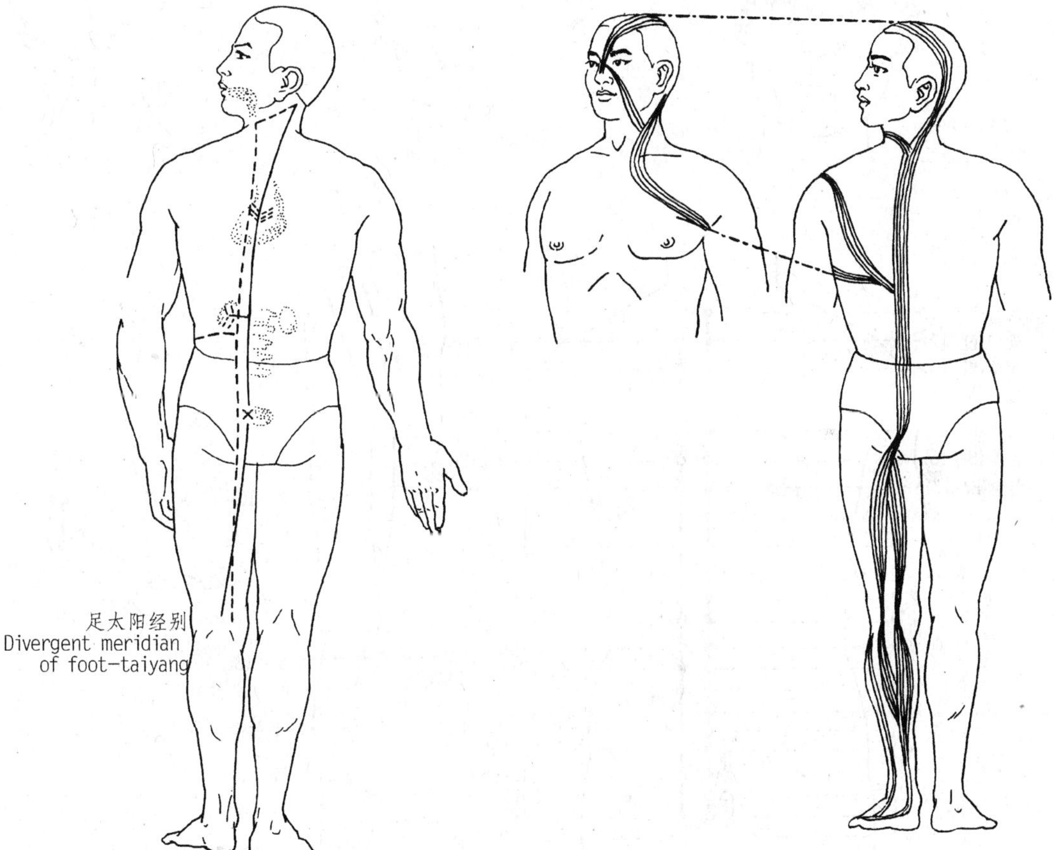

图9 – 2 足太阳经别循行示意图

Fig 9 – 2 The course of the divergent meridian of foot – taiyang

图9 – 3 足太阳经筋分布示意图

Fig 9 – 3 The course of the muscular region of foot – taiyang

第二节 足太阳腧穴
Acupoints of Foot - Taiyang

本经左右各67个穴位，首穴为睛明，末穴为至阴（图9-4）。

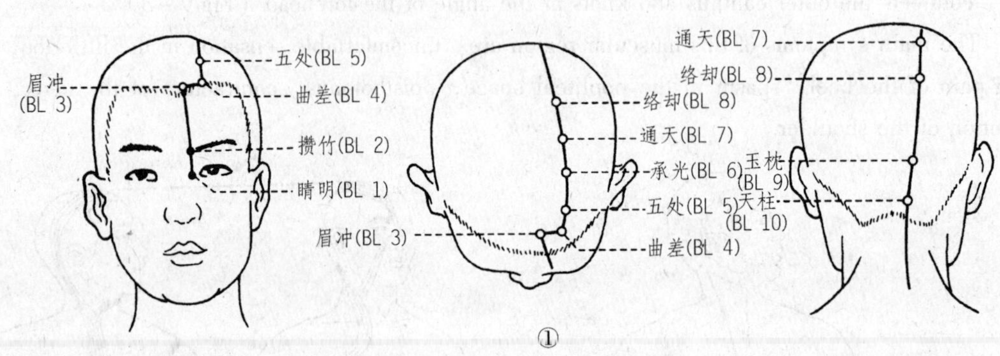

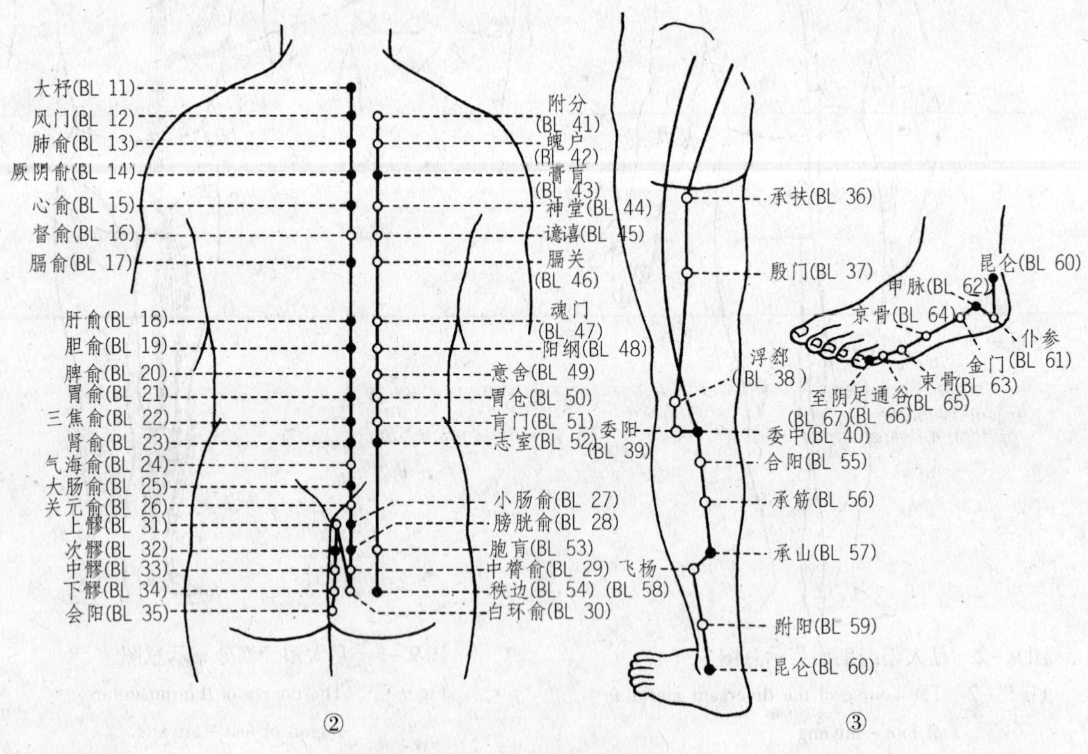

图例 ● 常用腧穴 ○ 一般腧穴

Note ● Main point ○ Common point

图9-4 足太阳膀胱经腧穴总图

Fig 9-4 Points of the bladder meridian of foot - taiyang

1. 睛明（BL 1），手、足太阳，足阳明经，阴跻脉，阳跻脉交会穴 Jingming（BL 1），Crossing Point of the Meridians of Hand - Taiyang，Foot - Taiyang，Foot - Yangming，Yin and Yang Heel Vessels

【释义】睛，眼睛；明，明亮。穴在眼区，有明目之功。

【定位】在面部，目内眦角稍上方凹陷处（图9－5）。

【解剖】皮肤→皮下组织→眼轮匝肌→上泪小管上方→内直肌与筛骨眶板之间。浅层布有三叉神经眼支的滑车上神经，内眦动、静脉的分支或属支。深层有眼动、静脉的分支或属支，眼神经的分支和动眼神经的分支。

【功用】通睛，明目。

【主治】①目赤肿痛，流泪，近视，视物不明，目眩，夜盲，色盲。②急性腰痛。

【操作】患者闭目，医者押手轻推眼球向外侧固定，刺手持针，紧靠眶缘缓慢直刺0.3～0.5寸，不宜提插和大幅度捻转，出针按压，以防出血，禁灸。

【Meaning】Jing, eye; ming, brightness. The point is located near the eye; its function is to clear the eye.

【Location】On the face, in the depression slightly superior to the inner canthus (Fig 9－4).

【Regional anatomy】Skin→subcutaneous tissue→the orbicularis oculi→upper side of superior lacrimal duct→between internus muscle of the eye and orbital lamina of ethmoid bone. Superficial layer, the distribution of the supratrochlear nerve derived from the ophthalmic branch of the trigeminal nerve, the branches or the subordinate ramus of the angular artery and vein. Deep layer, the branches or the subordinate ramus of the ophthalmic artery and vein, the branch of the ophthalmic nerve, and the branch of the oculomotor nerve.

【Properties】Improve eyesight.

【Indications】①Redness, pain and swelling of the eyes, lacrimation, myopia, blurred vision, dizziness, night blindness, color blindness. ②Acute lumbar pain.

【Needling method】Keeping the eyes closed, the practitioner gently pushes the eyeball to the lateral side. Puncture slowly perpendicularly along the orbital wall for 0.3～0.5 cun. The needle is not to be rotated, lifted and thrusted. When withdrawing the needle, use a dry cotton ball to press the puncture site to avoid bleeding. This point is contraindicated for moxibustion.

2. 攒竹 Cuanzhu（BL 2）

【释义】攒，簇聚；竹，竹子。穴在眉头，眉毛戢生，犹如竹子簇聚。

【定位】在面部，当眉头凹陷中，眶上切迹处（图9－5）。

【解剖】皮肤→皮下组织→眼轮匝肌。浅层布有额神经的滑车上神经，眶上动、静脉的分支或属支。深层有面神经的颞支和颧支。

【功用】祛风，明目，止痛。

【主治】①目视不明，目赤肿痛，流泪，眼睑瞤动。②头痛，眉棱骨痛，面瘫。③呃逆。

【操作】向下或向外平刺或斜刺0.3~0.5寸；禁灸。

【Meaning】Cuan，to assemble；zhu，bamboo. The point is at the end of the eyebrow，which appears like a luxuriant bamboo plant.

【Location】On the face，in the depression of the medial end of the eyebrow，on the supraorbital notch（Fig 9－5）.

【Regional anatomy】Skin→subcutaneous tissue→the orbicularis oculi. supratrochlear nerve of frontal nerve on superficial layer，branches of arteries and veins on eye sockets. temple branch and cheek branch of facial nerve on deeper layer.

【Properties】Expel pathogenic－wind，improve eyesight and relieve pain.

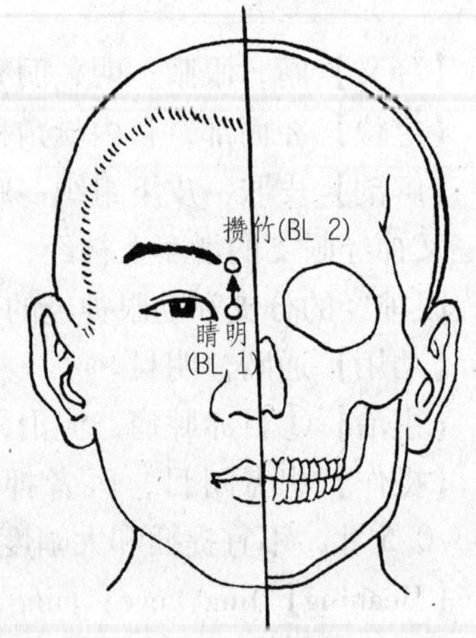

图9－5

Fig 9－5

【Indications】①Blurred vision，redness，pain and swelling of the eyes，lacrimation，twitching of the eyelid. ②Headache，pain in the supraorbital region，facial paralysis. ③Hiccups.

【Needling method】Puncture transversely or obliquely downward or outward 0.3～0.5 cun. This point is contraindicated to use moxibustion.

3. 眉冲 Meichong（BL 3）

【释义】眉，眉毛；冲，直上。穴在前发际，眉头的直上方。

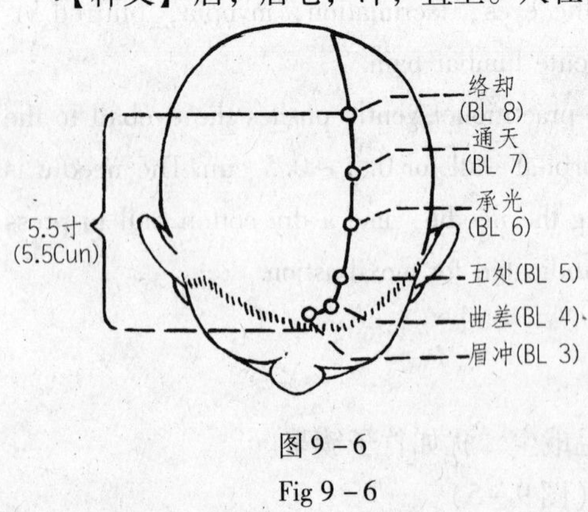

图9－6

Fig 9－6

【定位】在头部，当攒竹直上入发际0.5寸，神庭与曲差连线之间（图9－6）。

【解剖】皮肤→皮下组织→枕额肌额腹。浅层布有滑车上神经和滑车上动、静脉。深层有腱膜下疏松组织和颅骨外膜。

【功用】散风清热，镇痉宁神。

【主治】①头痛，眩晕，鼻塞。②癫痫。

【操作】平刺0.3~0.5寸。

【Meaning】Mei，eyebrow；chong，upward. The point is at the anterior hairline directly above the eyebrow.

【Location】On the scalp，directly above Cuanzhu（BL 2），0.5 cun within the anterior hairline，between Shenting（DU 24）and Qucha（BL 4）（Fig 9－6）.

【Regional anatomy】Skin→subcutaneous tissue→frontal belly of occipital of frontal muscle. In the superficial layer, there are the supratrochlear nerve and the supratrochlear artery and vein. In the deep layer, there are the subaponeurotic loose connective tissue and the pericranium.

【Properties】Dispel wind and clear heat, relieve spasm by tranquillization.

【Indications】①Headache, dizziness, nasal congestion. ②Epilepsy.

【Needling method】Puncture transversely 0. 3 ~0. 5 cun.

4. 曲差 Qucha（BL 4）

【释义】曲，弯曲；差，不齐。本脉自眉冲曲而向外，至此穴又曲而向后，表现为参差不齐。

【定位】在头部，当发际正中直上0. 5 寸，旁开 1. 5 寸，即神庭与头维连线的内 1/3 与中 1/3 的交点上（图 9 -6）。

【解剖】皮肤→皮下组织→枕额肌额腹。浅层布有滑车上神经和滑车上动、静脉。深层有腱膜下疏松组织和颅骨外膜。

【功用】清热明目，安神利窍。

【主治】①头痛，目眩，视物不明。②鼻塞，鼻衄。

【操作】平刺 0. 3 ~0. 5 寸。

【Meaning】Qu, crooked or curve; cha, unevenness. This meridian curves laterally from Meichong（BL 3）and then runs posteriorly from this point, becoming uneven.

【Location】On the scalp, 0. 5 cun within the anterior hairline, 1. 5 cun lateral to the midline, at the junction of the medial 1/3 and lateral 2/3 of the distance from Shenting（DU 24）and Touwei（ST 8）（Fig 9 -6）.

【Regional anatomy】Skin→subcutaneous tissue→frontal belly of occipital of frontal muscle. In the superficial layer, there are the supratrochlear nerve and the supratrochlear artery and vein. In the deep layer, there are the subaponeurotic loose connective tissue and the pericranium.

【Properties】Improve eyesight by clearing heat, calm heart for resuscitation.

【Indications】①Headache, dizziness, blurred vision. ②Nasal congestion, epistaxis.

【Needling method】Puncture transversely 0. 3 ~0. 5 cun.

5. 五处 Wuchu（BL 5）

【释义】五，第五；处，处所。此为足太阳脉之第五穴所在之处。

【定位】在头部，当前发际正中直上 1 寸，旁开 1. 5 寸（图 9 -6）。

【解剖】皮肤→皮下组织→枕额肌额腹。浅层布有滑车上神经和滑车上动、静脉。深层有腱膜下疏松组织和颅骨外膜。

【功用】清热散风，明目镇痉。

【主治】①头痛，目眩，目视不明。②癫痫。

【操作】平刺0.3～0.5寸。

【Meaning】Wu, fifth; chu, place. This is the 5th point of the bladder meridian of foot－taiyang.

【Location】On the scalp, 1 cun within the anterior hairline, 1.5 cun lateral to the midline (Fig 9－6).

【Regional anatomy】Skin→subcutaneous tissue→frontal belly of occipital of frontal muscle. In the superficial layer, there are the supratrochlear nerve and the supratrochlear artery and vein. In the deep layer, there are the subaponeurotic loose connective tissue and the pericranium.

【Properties】Dispel wind and clear heat, improve eyesight and relieve spasm.

【Indications】①Headache, dizziness, blurred vision. ②Epilepsy.

【Needling method】Puncture transversely 0.3～0.5 cun.

6. 承光 Chengguang (BL 6)

【释义】承，承受；光，光明。穴居头顶部，容易承受光线。

【定位】在头部，当前发际正中直上2.5寸，旁开1.5寸（图9－6）。

【解剖】皮肤→皮下组织→帽状腱膜。浅层布有眶上神经和眶上动、静脉。深层有腱膜下疏松组织和颅骨外膜。

【功用】清热明目，祛风通窍。

【主治】①头痛，目眩，目视不明。②鼻塞。③热病。

【操作】平刺0.3～0.5寸。

【Meaning】Cheng, to receive; guang, brightness. The point is at the vertex of the head, where brightness is easily received.

【Location】On the scalp, 2.5 cun within the anterior hairline, 1.5 cun lateral to the midline (Fig 9－6).

【Regional anatomy】Skin→subcutaneous tissue→epicranial aponeurosis. In the superficial layer, there are the supraorbital nerve and the supraorbital artery and vein. In the deep layer, there are the subaponeurotic loose connective tissue and the pericranium.

【Properties】Improve eyesight by clearing heat.

【Indications】①Headache, dizziness, blurred vision. ②Nasal congestion. ③Febrile diseases.

【Needling method】Puncture transversely 0.3～0.5 cun.

7. 通天 Tongtian (BL 7)

【释义】通，通达；天，天空。上为天。穴在头部，上通头顶。

【定位】在头部，当前发际正中直上4寸，旁开1.5寸（图9－6）

【解剖】皮肤→皮下组织→帽状腱膜。浅层布有眶上神经，眶上动、静脉和枕大神经，枕动、静脉与耳颞神经，颞浅动、静脉的神经间吻合和血管间的吻合网。深层有腱膜下疏松组织和颅骨外膜。

【功用】清热祛风，通利鼻窍。

【主治】①鼻塞，鼻渊，鼻衄。②头痛，眩晕。

【操作】平刺0.3~0.5寸。

【Meaning】Tong, reaching; tian, heaven. The upper part of the head is considered as heaven. The point is at the head and connects upward with the vertex.

【Location】On the scalp, 4 cun within the anterior hairline, 1.5 cun lateral to the midline (Fig 9-6).

【Regional anatomy】Skin→subcutaneous tissue→epicranial aponeurosis. In the superficial layer, there are the supraorbital nerve and the supraorbital artery and vein, the interneural and intervascular anastomotic network of the greater occipital nerve, the occipital artery and vein, the auriculotemporal nerve and the superficial temporal artery and vein. In the deep layer, there are the subaponeurotic loose connective tissue and the pericranium.

【Properties】Dispel wind and clear heat, relieve stuffy nose.

【Indications】①Nasal congestion, nasosinusitis, epistaxis. ②Headache, dizziness.

【Needling method】Puncture transversely 0.3~0.5 cun.

8. 络却 Luoque (BL 8)

【释义】络，联络，却，返回。本经脉气由此入颅内络于脑，然后返回体表。

【定位】在头部，当前发际正中直上5.5寸，旁开1.5寸（图9-6）。

【解剖】皮肤→皮下组织→帽状腱膜。浅层布有枕大神经和枕动、静脉。深层有腱膜下疏松组织和颅骨外膜。

【功用】清热安神，平肝息风。

【主治】①头晕。③耳鸣，目视不明。③癫狂痫。

【操作】平刺0.3~0.5寸。

【Meaning】Luo, linking; que, return. The collateral of bladder meridian returns to the body surface from this point after linking with the brain.

【Location】On the scalp, 5.5 cun within the anterior hairline, 1.5 cun lateral to the midline (Fig 9-6).

【Regional anatomy】Skin→subcutaneous tissue→epicranial aponeurosis. In the superficial layer, there are the greater occipital nerve and the occipital artery and vein. In the deep layer, there are the subaponeurotic loose connective tissue and the pericranium.

【Properties】Clear heat for tranquillization, calming liver wind.

【Indications】①Dizziness. ②Tinnitus, blurred vision. ③Psychosis, epilepsy.

【Needling method】Puncture transversely 0.3~0.5 cun.

9. 玉枕 Yuzhen（BL 9）

【释义】玉，玉石；枕，枕头；古称枕骨为“玉枕骨”，穴在其上。

【定位】在后头部，当后发际正中直上 2.5 寸，旁开 1.3 寸，平枕外隆凸上缘的凹陷处（图 9－7）。

【解剖】皮肤→皮下组织→枕额肌枕腹。浅层布有枕大神经和枕动、静脉。深层有腱膜下疏松组织和颅骨外膜。

【功用】清热明目，通经活络。

【主治】①头、项痛。②目痛，鼻塞。

【操作】平刺 0.3～0.5 寸。

【Meaning】Yu，jade；zhen，pillow. The ancient name of the occipital bone is Yuzhengu（jade pillow bone）. The point is on it.

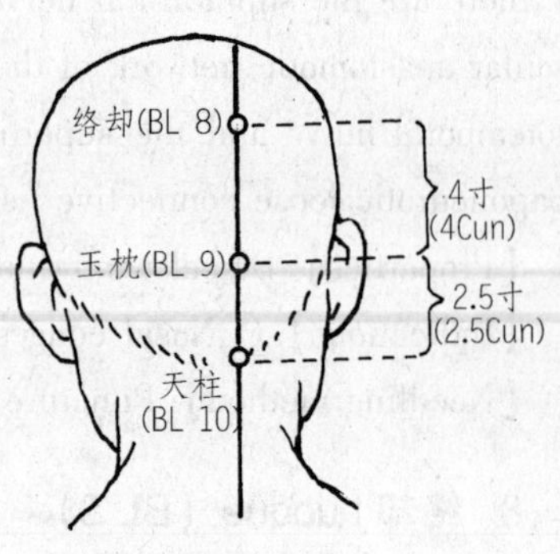

图 9－7
Fig 9－7

【Location】On the posterior aspect of the head，2.5 cun superior to the posterior hairline，1.3 cun lateral to the midline and level with the depression on the superior border of the external occipital protuberance（Fig 9－7）.

【Regional anatomy】Skin→subcutaneous tissue→occipital belly of occipital of frontal muscle. In the superficial layer，there are the greater occipital nerve and the occipital artery and vein. In the deep layer，there are the subaponeurotic loose connective tissue and the pericranium.

【Properties】Improve eyesight by clearing heat，dredge the meridian.

【Indications】①Headache and nape of the neck pain. ②Eye pain，nasal congestion.

【Needling method】Puncture transversely 0.3～0.5 cun.

10. 天柱 Tianzhu（BL 10）

【释义】天，天空；柱，支柱。上部为天。颈椎古称“柱骨”，穴在其旁。

【定位】正坐，在颈部，大筋（斜方肌）外缘之后发际凹陷中，约当后发际正中旁开 1.3 寸（图 9－7）。

【解剖】皮肤→皮下组织→斜方肌→头夹肌的内侧头→半棘肌。浅层有第 3 颈神经后支的内侧支和皮下静脉。深层有枕大神经。

【功用】清头明目，强筋骨。

【主治】①头痛，眩晕。②目视不明，鼻塞。③项强，肩背痛。

【操作】直刺或斜刺 0.5～0.8 寸，不可向内上方深刺，以免伤及延髓。

【Meaning】Tian，heaven；zhu，pillar. Upper is considered as heaven. The cervical spine was called Zhugu (pillar bone) in ancient times, the point is lateral to it.

【Location】On the nape of the neck, in the depression on the lateral border of the trapezius muscle, 1.3 cun lateral to the midpoint of the posterior hairline (Fig 9 – 7).

【Regional anatomy】Skin→subcutaneous tissue→the trapezius→medial border of splenius muscle of head→semispinalis muscle. Superficial layer, the distribution of the medial branch of the posterior branch of the 3rd carotid nerve and the subcutaneous vein. Deep layer, the greater occipital nerve.

【Properties】Refresh the mind and improve vision, strengthen the muscles and joints.

【Indications】①Headache, dizziness. ②Blurred vision, nasal congestion. ③Stiff neck, pain in the upper back and shoulder.

【Needling method】Puncture perpendicularly or obliquely 0.5 ~ 0.8 cun, a deep puncture is contraindicated to avoid damaging the medulla.

11. 大杼(BL 11),八会穴(骨会),手、足太阳经交会穴
Dazhu (BL 11), One of the Eight Influential Points (Bone Convergence), Crossing Point of the Meridians of Hand - Taiyang and Foot - Taiyang

【释义】大,大小之大;杼,即梭。第1胸椎较大,棘突如梭,穴在其旁。

【定位】在背部,当第1胸椎棘突下,旁开1.5寸(图9-8)。

【解剖】皮肤→皮下组织→斜方肌→菱形肌→上后锯肌→颈夹肌→竖脊肌。浅层布有第1、2胸神经后支的内侧皮支和伴行的肋间后动、静脉背侧支的内侧皮支。深层有第1、2胸神经后支的肌支和相应的肋间后动、静脉背侧支的分支等结构。

【功用】祛风除湿,通利关节。

【主治】①肩背痛,项强。②咳嗽。

【操作】斜刺0.5~0.8寸。本经背部诸穴不宜深刺,以免伤及内脏。

【Meaning】Da, large; zhu, shuttle. The 1st thoracic vertebra is bigger than the others, the spinous process is like a shuttle, and the point is lateral to it.

【Location】On the back, level with the lower border of the spinous process of the 1st thoracic vertebra, 1.5 cun lateral to the posterior midline (Fig 9 – 8).

【Regional anatomy】Skin→subcutaneous tissue→trapezius muscle→rhomboid muscle→superior posterior serratus muscle→splenius muscle of the neck→erector spinal muscle. In the superficial layer, there are the medial cutaneous branches of the posterior branches of the 1st and 2nd thoracic nerves and the medial cutaneous branches of the accompanying posterior branches of the 1st and 2nd thoracic nerves and the branches of the dorsal branches of the related posterior intercostal arteries and veins.

【Properties】Dispell pathogenic – wind and remove dampness from the joints to treat arthralgia.

【Indications】①Pain in the back and shoulder, stiff neck. ②Cough.

【Needling method】Puncture obliquely 0. 5 ~0. 8 cun. All points of the channel on the upper back are not to be punctured deeply to avoid damaging the internal organs.

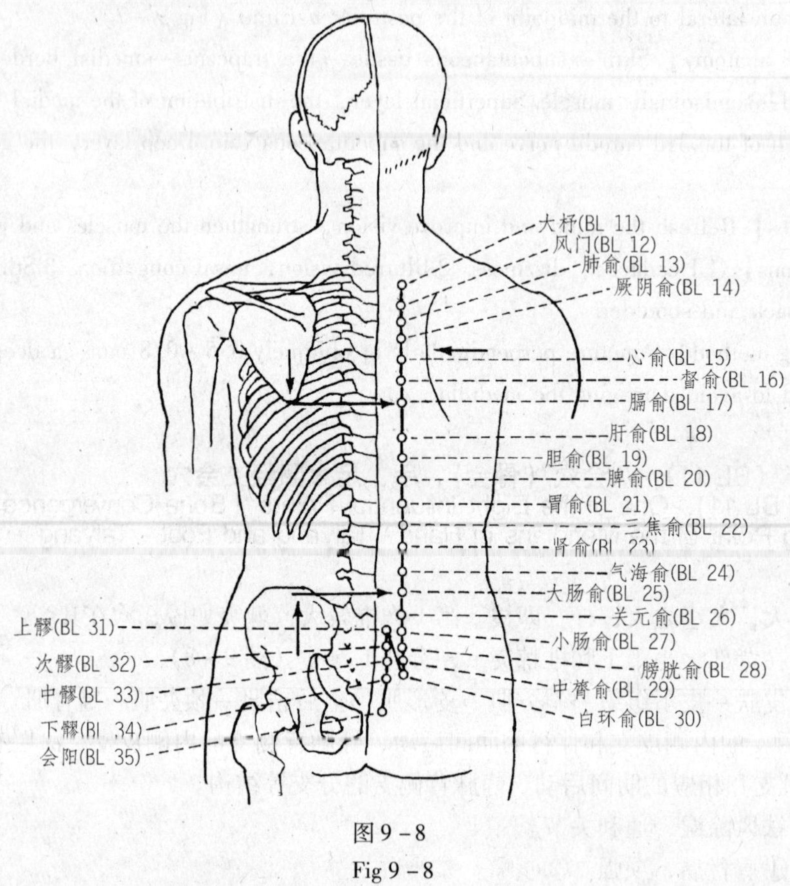

图 9 – 8

Fig 9 – 8

12. 风门（BL 12），足太阳经、督脉交会穴
Fengmen（BL 12），Crossing Point of the Foot - Taiyang Meridian and Governor Vessel

【释义】风，风邪；门，门户。穴居易为风邪侵入之处，并善治风邪之为病，故被认为是风邪出入之门户。

【定位】在背部，当第 2 胸椎棘突下，旁开 1.5 寸（图 9 –8）。

【解剖】皮肤→皮下组织→斜方肌→菱形肌→上后锯肌→颈夹肌→竖脊肌。浅层布有第 2、3 胸神经后支的内侧皮支和伴行的肋间后动、静脉背侧支的内侧皮支。深层有第 2、3 胸神经后支的肌支和相应的肋间后动、静脉背侧支的分支等。

【功用】祛风，散寒，温阳止痛。

【主治】①感冒，咳嗽，发热，头痛。②项强，胸背痛。

【操作】斜刺 0. 5 ~0. 8 寸。

【Meaning】Feng, pathogenic wind; men, door. The point is located where it is easily invaded by pathogenic wind and so is useful in treating diseases caused by pathogenic wind. The point is therefore considered as the door of pathogenic wind.

【Location】On the back, level with the lower border of the spinous process of the 2nd thoracic vertebra, 1.5 cun lateral to the posterior midline (Fig 9 – 8).

【Regional anatomy】Skin→subcutaneous tissue→trapezius muscle→rhomboid muscle→superior posterior serratus muscle→splenius muscle of the neck→erector spinae muscle. In the superficial layer there are the medial cutaneous branches of the posterior branches of the 2nd and 3rd thoracic nerves and the medial cutaneous branches of the dorsal branches of the accompanying posterior intercostal arteries and veins. In the deep layer, there are the muscular branches of the posterior branches of the 2nd and 3rd thoracic nerves and the branches of the dorsal branches of the related posterior intercostal arteries and veins.

【Properties】Dispel wind and dissipate cold, warming yang for relieving pain.

【Indications】①Common cold, cough, fever, headache. ②Stiff neck, pain in the back and chest.

【Needling method】Puncture obliquely 0.5 ~0.8 cun.

13. 肺俞（BL 13），肺之背俞穴
Feishu (BL 13), Back - Shu Point of the Lung

【释义】肺，肺脏；俞，输注。本穴是肺气转输于后背体表的部位。

【定位】在背部，当第3胸椎棘突下，旁开1.5寸（图9－8）。

【解剖】皮肤→皮下组织→斜方肌→菱形肌→上后锯肌→竖脊肌。浅层布有第3、4胸神经后支的内侧皮支和伴行的肋间后动、静脉背侧支的内侧皮支。深层有第3、4胸神经后支的肌支和相应的肋间后动、静脉背侧支的分支或属支。

【功用】清肺止咳，祛风散寒。

【主治】①咳喘，感冒，鼻塞。②骨蒸潮热，盗汗。③皮肤瘙痒，瘾疹。

【操作】斜刺0.5～0.8寸。

【Meaning】Fei, lung; shu, point. This point is where the qi of lung is infused into the back.

【Location】On the back, level with the lower border of the spinous process of the 3rd thoracic vertebra, 1.5 cun lateral to the posterior midline (Fig 9 – 8).

【Regional anatomy】Skin→subcutaneous tissue→trapezius muscle→rhomboid muscle→superior posterior serratus muscle→erector spinae muscle. Superficial layer, the distribution of the medial cutaneous branches of the posterior rami of the 3rd and 4th thoracic nerves, and the medial cutaneous branches of the dorsal branches of the posterior intercostal artery and vein along with them; deep layer, the muscular branch of the posterior rami of the 3rd and 4th thoracic nerves and the branches or the subordinate ramus of the dorsal branches of the relevant posterior intercostal artery and vein.

【Properties】Clear lung – heat for arresting cough, dispel wind and dissipate cold.

【Indications】①Cough with asthma, common cold, nasal congestion. ②High fever, night sweats. ③Itching of the skin, urticaria.

【Needling method】Puncture obliquely 0. 5 ~ 0. 8 cun.

14. 厥阴俞（BL 14），心包之背俞穴
Jueyinshu（BL 14），Back - Shu Point of the Pericardium

【释义】厥阴，两阴交尽之意，在此指心包络；俞，输注。本穴是心包络之气于后背体表的部位。

【定位】在背部，当第4胸椎棘突下，旁开1.5寸（图9－8）。

【解剖】皮肤→皮下组织→斜方肌→菱形肌→竖脊肌。浅层布有第4、5胸神经后支的内侧皮支和伴行的肋间后动、静脉背侧支。深层有第4、5胸神经后支的肌支和相应的肋间后动、静脉背侧支的分支或属支。

【功用】宽胸理气，活血止痛。

【主治】①心痛，心悸。②咳嗽，胸闷。③呕吐。

【操作】斜刺0.5~0.8寸。

【Meaning】Jueyin, the end of the two yin meridians, here referring to the pericardium shu point. This point is where the qi of pericardium is infused into the back.

【Location】On the back, level with the lower border of the spinous process of the 4th thoracic vertebra, 1. 5 cun lateral to the posterior midline（Fig 9 –8）.

【Regional anatomy】Skin→subcutaneous tissue→trapezius muscle→rhomboid muscle→erector spinal muscle. In the superficial layer, there are the medial cutaneous branches of the posterior branches of the 4th and 5th thoracic nerves and the medial cutaneous branches of the dorsal branches of the accompanying posterior intercostal arteries and veins. In the deep layer, there are the muscular branches of the posterior branches of the 4th and 5th thoracic nerves and the branches or tributaries of the dorsal branches of the related posterior intercostal arteries and veins.

【Properties】Move qi to soothe the chest, activate blood to relieve pain.

【Indications】①Cardiac pain, palpitations. ②Cough, tightness in the chest. ③Vomiting.

【Needling method】Puncture obliquely 0. 5 ~0. 8 cun.

15. 心俞（BL 15），心之背俞穴
Xinshu（BL 15), Back - Shu Point of the Heart

【释义】心，心脏；俞，输注。本穴是心气转输于后背体表的部位。

【定位】在背部，当第5胸椎棘突下，旁开1.5寸（图9－8）。

【解剖】皮肤→皮下组织→斜方肌→菱形肌下缘→竖脊肌。浅层布有第5、6胸神经后支的内侧皮支及伴行的动、静脉。深层有第5、6胸神经后支的肌支和相应的肋间后动、静

脉背侧支的分支或属支。

【功用】安神镇静，解痉止痛。

【主治】①心痛，心悸，失眠，健忘，癫痫。②咳嗽，吐血。③梦遗，盗汗。

【操作】斜刺0.5~0.8寸。

【Meaning】Xin, heart; shu, point. This point is where the qi of heart is infused into the back.

【Location】On the back, level with the lower border of the spinous process of the 5th thoracic vertebra, 1.5 cun lateral to the posterior midline (Fig 9-8).

【Regional anatomy】Skin→subcutaneous tissue→trapezius muscle→the inferior of the rhomboidmuscle→erector spinal muscle. Superficial layer, the distribution of the medial cutaneous branches of the posterior rami of the 5th and 6th thoracic nerves, and the artery and vein along with them; deep layer, the muscular branch of the posterior rami of the 5th and 6th thoracic nerves and the branches or the subordinate ramus of the dorsal branches of the relevant posterior intercostal artery and vein.

【Properties】Tranquilization and sedation, relax the muscular spasm and stop pain.

【Indications】①Cardiac pain, palpitations, insomnia, forgetfulness, epilepsy. ②Cough, hematemesis. ③Nocturnal emission, night sweats.

【Needling method】Puncture obliquely 0.5~0.8 cun.

16. 督俞 Dushu (BL 16)

【释义】督，督脉；俞，输注。本穴是督脉之气转输于后背体表的部位。

【定位】在背部，当第6胸椎棘突下，旁开1.5寸（图9-8）。

【解剖】皮肤→皮下组织→斜方肌→竖脊肌。浅层布有第6、7胸神经后支的内侧皮支和伴行的动、静脉。深层有第6、7胸神经后支的肌支和相应的肋间后动、静脉背侧支的分支或属支。

【功用】理气止痛，强心通脉。

【主治】①心痛，胸闷。②气喘。③胃痛，腹胀，呃逆。

【操作】斜刺0.5~0.8寸。

【Meaning】Du, governor vessel meridian; shu, point. This point is where the qi of governor vessel meridian is infused into the back.

【Location】On the back, level with the lower border of the spinous process of the 6th thoracic vertebra, 1.5 cun lateral to the posterior midline (Fig 9-8).

【Regional anatomy】Skin→subcutaneous tissue→trapezius muscle→erector spinal muscle. In the superficial layer, there are the medial cutaneous branches of the posterior branches of the 6th and 7th thoracic nerves and the medial cutaneous branches of the dorsal branches of the accompanying arteries and veins. In the deep layer, there are the muscular branches of the posterior branches of the 6th and 7th thoracic nerves and the branches or tributaries of the dorsal branches of the related posterior intercostal arteries and veins.

【Properties】Regulate qi - flowing for relieving pain, nourish the heart for smoothing channel.

【Indications】①Cardiac pain, tightness in the chest. ②Asthma. ③Stomachache, abdominal distention, hiccups.

【Needling method】Puncture obliquely 0.5 ~ 0.8 cun.

17. 膈俞（BL 17），八会穴（血会）
Geshu（BL 17），One of the Eight Influential Points（Blood Convergence）

【释义】膈，横隔；俞，输注。本穴是膈气转输于后背体表的部位。

【定位】在背部，当第7胸椎棘突下，旁开1.5寸（图9-8）。

【解剖】皮肤→皮下组织→斜方肌→背阔肌→竖脊肌。浅层布有第7、8胸神经后支的内侧皮支和伴行的动、静脉。深层有第7、8胸神经后支的肌支和相应肋间后动、静脉背侧支的分支或属支。

【功用】解痉止呃，补血益气。

【主治】①胃痛，呕吐，呃逆。②咳喘，吐血，潮热，盗汗。③瘾疹。

【操作】斜刺0.5～0.8寸。

【Meaning】Ge, diaphragm; shu, point. This point is where the qi of diaphragm is infused into the back.

【Location】On the back, level with the lower border of the spinous process of the 7th thoracic vertebra, 1.5 cun lateral to the posterior midline（Fig 9-8）.

【Regional anatomy】Skin→subcutaneous tissue→trapezius muscle→the latissimus dorsi→erector spinal muscle. Superficial layer, the distribution of the medial cutaneous branches of the posterior rami of the 7th and 8th thoracic nerves, and the artery and vein along with them. Deep layer, the muscular branch of the posterior rami of the 7th and 8th thoracic nerves and the branches or the subordinate ramus of the dorsal branches of the relevant posterior intercostal artery and vein.

【Properties】Relax the muscular spasm, stop hiccup, enrich the blood and benefit vital energy.

【Indications】①Stomachache, vomiting, hiccups. ②Cough with asthma, hematemesis, tidal fever, night sweats. ③Urticaria.

【Needling method】Puncture obliquely 0.5 ~ 0.8 cun.

18. 肝俞（BL 18），肝之背俞穴
Ganshu（BL 18），Back - Shu Point of the Liver

【释义】肝，肝脏；俞，输注。本穴是肝气转输于后背体表的部位。

【定位】在背部，当第9胸椎棘突下，旁开1.5寸（图9-8）。

【解剖】皮肤→皮下组织→斜方肌→背阔肌→下后锯肌→竖脊肌。浅层布有第9、10胸

神经后支的皮支和伴行的动、静脉。深层有第 9、10 胸神经后支的肌支和相应的肋间后动、静脉的分支或属支。

【功用】调理肝脾。

【主治】①黄疸，胁痛。②目赤，目视不明，夜盲。③吐血，衄血。④眩晕，癫狂痫。

【操作】斜刺 0.5 ~0.8 寸。

【Meaning】Gan, liver; shu, point. This point is where the qi of liver is infused into the back.

【Location】Level with the lower border of the spinous process of the 9th thoracic vertebra, 1.5 cun lateral to the posterior midline (Fig 9 –8).

【Regional anatomy】Skin→subcutaneous tissue→trapezius muscle→the latissimus dorsi→inferior posterior serratus muscle→erector spinal muscle. Superficial layer, the distribution of the cutaneous branches of the posterior rami of the 9th and 10th thoracic nerves, and the artery and vein along with them. Deep layer, the muscular branch of the posterior rami of the 9th and 10th thoracic nerves and the branches or the subordinate ramus of the relevant posterior intercostal artery and vein.

【Properties】Regulate the function of the liver and the spleen.

【Indications】①Jaundice, hypochondriac pain. ②Red eyes, blurred vision, night blindness. ③Hematemesis, epistaxis. ④Dizziness, depression and psychosis, mania, epilepsy.

【Needling method】Puncture obliquely 0.5 ~0.8 cun.

19. 胆俞（BL 19），胆之背俞穴
Danshu (BL 19), Back - Shu Point of the Gallbladder

【释义】胆，胆腑；俞，输注。本穴是胆腑之气转输于后背体表的部位。

【定位】在背部，当第 10 胸椎棘突下，旁开 1.5 寸（图 9 –8）。

【解剖】皮肤→皮下组织→斜方肌→背阔肌→下后锯肌→竖脊肌。浅层布有第 10、11 胸神经后支的皮支和伴行的动、静脉。深层有第 10、11 胸神经后支的肌支和相应的肋间后动、静脉的分支或属支。

【功用】行气消胀。

【主治】①黄疸，口苦，胁痛。②肺痨，潮热。

【操作】斜刺 0.5 ~0.8 寸。

【Meaning】Dan, gallbladder; shu, point. This point is where the qi of gallbladder is infused into the back.

【Location】On the back, level with the lower border of the spinous process of the 10th thoracic vertebra, 1.5 cun lateral to the posterior midline (Fig 9 –8).

【Regional anatomy】Skin→subcutaneous tissue→trapezius muscle→the latissimus dorsi→inferior posterior serratus muscle→erector spinal muscle. Superficial layer. the distribution of the cutaneous branches of the posterior rami of the 10th and 11th thoracic nerves, and the artery and vein along with them. Deep layer, the muscular branch of the posterior rami of the 10th and 11th thoracic nerves and the branches or the subordinate ramus of the relevant posterior intercostal artery and vein.

【Properties】Promote the circulation of vital energy, relieve abdominal distension.

【Indications】①Jaundice, bitter taste in mouth, hypochondriac pain. ②Pulmonary phthisis, high fever.

【Needling method】Puncture obliquely 0.5 ~ 0.8 cun.

20. 脾俞（BL 20），脾之背俞穴
Pishu (BL 20), Back - Shu Point of the Spleen

【释义】脾，脾脏；俞，输注。本穴是脾气转输于后背体表的部位。

【定位】在背部，当第11胸椎棘突下，旁开1.5寸（图9-8）。

【解剖】皮肤→皮下组织→背阔肌→下后锯肌→竖脊肌。浅层布有第11、12胸神经后支的皮支和伴行的动、静脉。深层有第11、12胸神经后支的肌支和相应的肋间、肋下动、静脉的分支或属支。

【功用】健脾补血。

【主治】①腹胀，泄泻，痢疾，便血，纳呆。②水肿，黄疸。

【操作】斜刺0.5~0.8寸。

【Meaning】Pi, spleen; shu, point. This point is where the qi of spleen is infused into the back.

【Location】On the back, level with the lower border of the spinous process of the 11th thoracic vertebra, 1.5 cun lateral to the posterior midline (Fig 9-8).

【Regional anatomy】Skin→subcutaneous tissue→the latissimus dorsi→the inferior serratus posterior→erector spinal muscle. Superficial layer, the distribution of the cutaneous branches of the posterior rami of the 11th and 12th thoracic nerves, and the artery and vein along with them. Deep layer, there are the muscular branch of the posterior branches or the 11th and 12th thoracic nerve and the branches or tributaries of the related intercostal and infracostal arteries and veins.

【Properties】Invigorate the spleen and enrich the blood.

【Indications】①Abdominal distension, diarrhea, dysentery, hematochezia, anorexia. ②Edema, jaundice.

【Needling method】Puncture obliquely 0.5 ~ 0.8 cun.

21. 胃俞（BL 21），胃之背俞穴
Weishu (BL 21), Back - Shu Point of the Stomach

【释义】胃，胃腑；俞，输注。本穴是胃气转输于后背体表的部位。

【定位】在背部，当第12胸椎棘突下，旁开1.5寸（图9-8）。

【解剖】皮肤→皮下组织→胸腰筋膜浅层和背阔肌腱膜→竖脊肌。浅层布有第 12 胸神经和第 1 腰神经后支的皮支和伴行的动、静脉。深层有第 12 胸神经和第 1 腰神经后支的肌支和相应的动、静脉的分支或属支。

【功用】健胃止呕。

【主治】①胃脘痛，呕吐，腹胀，肠鸣。②胸胁痛。

【操作】斜刺 0.5～0.8 寸。

【Meaning】Wei，stomach；shu，point. This point is where the Qi of Stomach is infused into the back.

【Location】On the back，level with the lower border of the spinous process of the 12th thoracic vertebra，1.5 cun lateral to the posterior midline（Fig 9－8）.

【Regional anatomy】Skin→subcutaneous tissue→the superficial layer of the thoracolumbar fascia and the aponeurosis of the latissimus dorsi→erector spinal muscle. Superficial layer，the distribution of the cutaneous branches of the posterior rami of the 12th thoracic nerve and the 1st lumbar nerve，and the artery and vein along with them. Deep layer，the muscular branch of the posterior rami of the 12th thoracic nerve and the 1st lumbar nerve and the branches or the subordinate ramus of the relevant artery and vein.

【Properties】Strengthen the stomach and stop vomiting.

【Indications】①Epigastric pain，vomiting，abdominal distension，borborygmus. ②Chest and hypochondriac pain.

【Needling method】Puncture obliquely 0.5～0.8 cun.

22. 三焦俞（BL 22），三焦之背俞穴
Sanjiaoshu（BL 22），Back - Shu Point of the Triple Energizer

【释义】三焦，三焦腑；俞，输注。本穴是三焦之气转输于后背体表的部位。

【定位】在腰部，当第 1 腰椎棘突下，旁开 1.5 寸（图 9－8）。

【解剖】皮肤→皮下组织→背阔肌腱膜和胸腰筋膜浅层→竖脊肌。浅层布有第 1、2 腰神经后支的皮支及伴行的动、静脉。深层有第 1、2 腰神经后支的肌支及相应腰动、静脉背侧支分支或属支。

【功用】调理三焦，利水强腰。

【主治】①水肿，小便不利。②腹胀，肠鸣，泄泻，痢疾。③腰背强痛。

【操作】直刺 0.5～1.0 寸。

【Meaning】Sanjiao，three regions of the body cavity；shu，point. This point is where the qi of Sanjiao is infused into the back.

【Location】Level with the lower border of the spinous process of the 1st lumbar vertebra，1.5 cun lateral to the posterior midline（Fig 9－8）.

【Regional anatomy】Skin→subcutaneous tissue→the aponeurosis of latissimus muscle of the back and superficial layer of thoracolumbar fascia→erector spinal muscle. In the superficial layer， there are the cutaneous branches of the posterior branches of the 1st and 2nd lumbar nerves and the medial cutaneous branches of the dorsal branches of the accompanying arteries and veins. In the deep layer, there are the muscular branches of the posterior branches of the 1st and 2nd lumbar nerves and the branches or tributaries of the dorsal branches of the related lumbar arteries and veins.

【Properties】Regulate the Triple Energizers, eliminating dampness and diuresis, strengthen the loins.

【Indications】①Edema, difficulty in urination. ②Abdominal distension, borborygmus, diarrhea, dysentery. ③Stiffness and pain in the back and lumbar region.

【Needling method】Puncture perpendicularly 0.5 ~ 1.0 cun.

23. 肾俞（BL 23），肾之背俞穴
Shenshu (BL 23), Back - Shu Point of the Kidney

【释义】肾，肾脏；俞，输注。本穴是肾气转输于后背体表的部位。

【定位】在腰部，当第2腰椎棘突下，旁开1.5寸（图9-8）。

【解剖】皮肤→皮下组织→背阔肌腱膜和胸腰筋膜浅层→竖脊肌。浅层布有第2、3腰神经后支的皮支及伴行动、静脉。深层有第2、3腰神经后支的肌支和相应腰动、静脉背侧支分支或属支。

【功用】补肾益精。

【主治】①耳鸣，耳聋。②遗精，阳痿，月经不调，带下，遗尿，小便不利，水肿。③腰痛。④咳喘少气。

【操作】直刺0.5~1.0寸。

【Meaning】Shen, kidney; shu, point. This point is where qi of the kidney is infused into the back.

【Location】Level with the lower border of the spinous process of the 2nd lumbar vertebra, 1.5 cun lateral to the posterior midline (Fig 9-8).

【Regional anatomy】Skin→subcutaneous tissue→the aponeurosis of latissimus muscle of the back and the superficial layer of the thoracolumbar fascia→erector spinal muscle. Superficial layer, the distribution of the cutaneous branches of the posterior rami of the 2nd and 3rd lumbar nerves. and the artery and vein along with them. Deep layer, the muscular branch of the posterior rami of the 2nd and 3rd lumbar nerves and the branches or the subordinate ramus of the dorsal branches of the relevant lumbar artery and vein.

【Properties】Invigorate the kidney and supplement semen.

【Indications】①Tinnitus, deafness. ②Seminal emission, impotence, irregular menstruation, morbid leucorrhea, enuresis, difficulty in urination, edema. ③Lumbar pain. ④Cough, asthma, asthenic breathing.

【Needling method】Puncture perpendicularly 0.5 ~ 1.0 cun.

24. 气海俞 Qihaishu（BL 24）

【释义】气海，元气之海；俞，输注。本穴前应气海，是元气转输于后背体表的部位。

【定位】在腰部，当第3腰椎棘突下，旁开1.5寸（图9-8）。

【解剖】皮肤→皮下组织→背阔肌腱膜和胸腰筋膜浅层→竖脊肌。浅层布有第3、4腰神经后支的皮支及伴行动、静脉。深层有第3、4腰神经后支的肌支和相应腰动、静脉分支或属支。

【功用】益肾壮阳，调经止痛。

【主治】①腰痛。②痛经。③腹胀，肠鸣，痔疾。

【操作】直刺0.5~1.0寸。

【Meaning】Qihai, sea or primary qi; shu, point. This point is opposite Qihai, where primary qi is infused into the back.

【Location】Level with the lower border of the spinous process of the 3rd lumbar vertebra, 1.5 cun lateral to the posterior midline（Fig 9-8）.

【Regional anatomy】Skin→subcutaneous tissue→the aponeurosis of latissimus muscle of the back and superficial layer of thoracolumbar fascia→erector spinal muscle. In the superficial layer, there are the cutaneous branches of the posterior branches of the 3rd and 4th lumbar nerves and the medial cutaneous branches of the dorsal branches of the accompanying arteries and veins. In the deep layer, there are the muscular branches of the posterior branches of the 3rd and 4th lumbar nerves and the branches or tributaries of the related lumbar arteries and veins.

【Properties】Warm and recuperate kidney yang, regulate menstruation for relieving the pain.

【Indications】①Lumbar pain. ②Dysmenorrhea. ③Abdominal distension, borborygmus, hemorrhoids.

【Needling method】Puncture perpendicularly 0.5~1.0 cun.

25. 大肠俞（BL 25），大肠之背俞穴 Dachangshu（BL 25），Back - Shu Point of the Large Intestine

【释义】大肠，大肠腑；俞，输注。本穴是大肠腑气转输于后背体表的部位。

【定位】在腰部，当第4腰椎棘突下，旁开1.5寸（图9-8）。

【解剖】皮肤→皮下组织→背阔肌腱膜和胸腰筋膜浅层→竖脊肌。浅层有第4、5腰神经后支的皮支及伴行动、静脉。深层有第4、5腰神经后支的肌支和有关动、静脉的分支或属支。

【功用】行气止痛。

【主治】①腰痛。②腹胀，泄泻，便秘，痢疾，痔疾。

【操作】直刺0.8~1.2寸。

【Meaning】Dachang, large intestine; shu, point. This point is where qi of the large intestine is infused into the back.

【Location】Level with the lower border of the spinous process of the 4th lumbar vertebra, 1. 5 cun lateral to the posterior midline (Fig 9 – 8).

【Regional anatomy】Skin→subcutaneous tissue→the aponeurosis of latissimus muscle of the back and the superficial layer of the thoracolumbar fascia→erector spinal muscle. Superficial layer, the distribution of the cutaneous branches of the posterior rami of the 4th and 5th lumbar nerves, and the artery and vein along with them. Deep layer, the muscular branch of the posterior rami of the 4th and 5th lumbar nerves and the branches or the subordinate ramus of the relevant artery and vein.

【Properties】Promote the circulation of vital energy.

【Indications】①Pain of the lumbar region and lower limbs。②Abdominal pain, diarrhea, constipation, dysentery, hemorrhoids.

【Needling method】Puncture perpendicularly 0. 8 ~ 1. 2 cun.

26. 关元俞 Guanyuanshu (BL 26)

【释义】关，关藏；元，元气；俞，输注。本穴前应关元，是关藏的元阴元阳之气转输于后背体表的部位。

【定位】在腰部，当第5腰椎棘突下，旁开1.5寸（图9–8）。

【解剖】皮肤→皮下组织→胸腰筋膜浅层→竖脊肌。浅层布有第5腰神经和第1骶神经后支的皮支及伴行的动、静脉。深层有第5腰神经后支的肌支。

【功用】培补元气，调理下焦。

【主治】①腰腿痛。②腹胀，泄泻。③小便频数或不利，遗尿。

【操作】直刺0.8~1.2寸。

【Meaning】Guan, storage; yuan, primary qi; shu, point. This point is opposite Guanyuan, where the stored qi of primary yin and primary yang is infused into the back.

【Location】Level with the lower border of the spinous process of the 5th lumbar vertebra, 1. 5 cun lateral to the posterior midline (Fig 9 – 8).

【Regional anatomy】Skin→subcutaneous tissue→superficial layer of thoracolumbar fascia→erector spinal muscle. In the superficial layer, there are the cutaneous branches of the posterior branches of the 5th lumbar and 1st sacral nerves and the accompanying arteries and veins. In the deep layer, there are the muscular branches of the posterior branches of the 5th lumbar nerves.

【Properties】Invigorate yuan – qi for regulating the lower energizer.

【Indications】①Pain of the lumbar region and lower limbs. ②Abdominal distension, diarrhea. ③Frequent urination or difficulty in urination, enuresis.

【Needling method】Puncture perpendicularly 0. 8 ~ 1. 2 cun.

27. 小肠俞（BL 27），小肠之背俞穴
Xiaochangshu（BL 27），Back - Shu Point of the Small Intestine

【释义】小肠，小肠腑；俞，转输。本穴是小肠之气转输于后背体表的部位。

【定位】在骶部，当骶正中嵴旁1.5寸，平第1骶后孔（图9-8）。

【解剖】皮肤→皮下组织→臀大肌内侧缘→竖脊肌腱。浅层布有臀中皮神经。深层布有臀下神经的属支和相应脊神经后支的肌支。

【功用】通调二便，清热利湿。

【主治】①腰骶痛。②小腹胀痛，泄泻，痢疾。③遗精，带下。④遗尿，尿血。

【操作】直刺或斜刺0.8~1.2寸。

【Meaning】Xiaochang, small intestine; shu, point. This is where qi of the small intestine is infused into the back.

【Location】Level with the 1st posterior sacral foramen, 1.5 cun lateral to the medial sacral crest（Fig 9-8）.

【Regional anatomy】Skin→subcutaneous tissue→medial border of the greater gluteal muscle→the erector spinal muscle tendon. In the superficial layer, there are the middle gluteal nerves. In the deep layer, there are the branches of the inferior gluteal nerve and the muscular branches of the posterior branches of the related spinal nerves.

【Properties】Regulate the difficulty in urination and defecation, clear heat and promote diuresis.

【Indications】①Lumbar pain, sacral pain. ②Lower abdominal pain and distention, diarrhea, dysentery. ③Seminal emission, morbid leucorrhea. ④Enuresis, hematuria.

【Needling method】Puncture perpendicularly or obliquely 0.8~1.2 cun.

28. 膀胱俞（BL 28），膀胱之背俞穴
Pangguangshu（BL 28），Back - Shu Point of the Bladder

【释义】膀胱，膀胱腑；俞，输注。本穴是膀胱之气转输于后背体表的部位。

【定位】在骶部，当骶正中嵴旁1.5寸，平第2骶后孔（图9-8）。

【解剖】皮肤→皮下组织→臀大肌→竖脊肌腱。浅层布有臀中皮神经。深层有臀下神经的属支和相应脊神经后支的肌支。

【功用】清热利湿，通经活络。

【主治】①小便不利，尿频，遗尿。②泄泻，便秘。③腰脊强痛。

【操作】直刺或斜刺0.8~1.2寸。

【Meaning】Pangguang, bladder; shu, point. This is where the qi of bladder is infused into the back.

【Location】Level with the 2nd posterior sacral foramen, 1.5 cun lateral to the medial sacral crest (Fig 9 – 8).

【Regional anatomy】Skin→subcutaneous tissue→the greatest gluteal muscle→erector spinal muscle tendon. In the superficial layer, there are the middle gluteal nerves. In the deep layer, there are the branches of the inferior gluteal nerve and the muscular branches of the posterior branches of the related spinal nerves.

【Properties】Clear heat and promote diuresis, dredge the meridian.

【Indications】①Difficulty in urination, frequent urination, enuresis. ②Diarrhea, constipation. ③Stiffness and pain in the lower back.

【Needling method】Puncture perpendicularly or obliquely 0.8 ~ 1.2 cun.

29. 中膂俞 Zhonglushu (BL 29)

【释义】中，中间；膂，夹脊肌肉；俞，输注。本穴位约居人身之中部，是夹脊肌肉之气转输于后背体表的部位。

【定位】在骶部，当骶正中嵴旁1.5寸，平第3骶后孔（图9－8）。

【解剖】皮肤→皮下组织→臀大肌→骶结节韧带。浅层布有臀中皮神经。深层有臀上、下动、静脉的分支或属支及臀下神经的属支。

【功用】益肾温阳，调理下焦。

【主治】①泄泻。②腰脊强痛。③疝气。

【操作】直刺1.0~1.5寸。

【Meaning】Zhong, center; lu, muscles on both sides of the spine; shu, point. This point is in the center of the body, where qi of the muscles on both sides of the spine is infused into the back.

【Location】Level with the 3rd posterior sacral foramen, 1.5 cun lateral to the medial sacral crest (Fig 9 – 8).

【Regional anatomy】Skin→subcutaneous tissue→greater gluteal muscle→sacrotuberous ligament. In the superficial layer, there are the middle gluteal nerves. In the deep layer, there are the branches or tributaries of the superior and inferior gluteal arteries and veins and the branches of the inferior gluteal nerve.

【Properties】Warm and recuperate kidney yang for regulating the lower energizer.

【Indications】①Diarrhea. ②Stiffness and pain in the lower back. ③Hernia.

【Needling method】Puncture perpendicularly 1.0 ~ 1.5 cun.

30. 白环俞 Baihuanshu (BL 30)

【释义】白，白色；环，物名；俞，穴。此穴可治妇女白带等症。

【定位】在骶部，当骶正中嵴旁1.5寸，平第4骶后孔（图9－8）。

【解剖】皮肤→皮下组织→臀大肌→骶结节韧带→梨状肌。浅层布有臀中和臀下皮神经。深层有臀上、下动、静脉的分支或属支，骶神经丛和骶静脉丛。

【功用】益肾固精，调理经带。

【主治】①遗精，遗尿，带下，月经不调，疝气。②腰骶疼痛。

【操作】直刺1.0~1.5寸。

【Meaning】Bai, white; huan, ring; shu, point. This point is indicated in leucorrhea.

【Location】Level with the 4th posterior sacral foramen, 1.5 cun lateral to the medial sacral crest (Fig 9-8).

【Regional anatomy】Skin→subcutaneous tissue→the greater gluteal muscle→sacrotuberous ligament→piriform muscle. In the superficial layer, there are the middle and inferior gluteal nerves. In the deep layer, there are the branches or tributaries of the superior and inferior gluteal arteries and veins and the sacral nervous and venous plexus.

【Properties】Invigorate the kidney and secure essence, regulate menstruation and vaginal discharge.

【Indications】①Seminal emission, enuresis, morbid leucorrhea, irregular menstruation, hernia. ②Pain in the lower back.

【Needling method】Puncture perpendicularly 1.0~1.5 cun.

31. 上髎 Shangliao (BL 31)

【释义】上，上下之上；髎，骨隙。本穴位当最上骶后孔。

【定位】在骶部，当骶后上棘与后正中线之间，适对第1骶后孔处（图9-8）。

【解剖】皮肤→皮下组织→胸腰筋膜浅层→竖脊肌→第1骶后孔。浅层布有臀中皮神经。深层有第1骶神经和骶外侧动、静脉的后支。

【功用】调理下焦，通经活络。

【主治】①月经不调，带下，阴挺，遗精，阳痿。②二便不利。③腰脊痛。

【操作】直刺1.0~1.5寸。

【Meaning】Shang, upper; liao, foramen. This point is at the first dorsal sacral foramen.

【Location】In the region of the sacrum, between the posterio-superior iliac spine and the posterior midline, in the 1st posterior sacral foramen (Fig 9-8).

【Regional anatomy】Skin→subcutaneous tissue→the superficial layer of the thoracolumbar fascia→erector spinal muscle→the first posterior sacral foramen. Superficial layer, the distribution of the intermediate gluteal cutaneous nerve. Deep layer, the first sacral nerve, the posterior branches of the lateral sacral artery and vein.

【Properties】Regulate the lower energizer and dredge the meridian.

【Indications】①Irregular menstruation, morbid leucorrhea, prolapsed uterus, seminal emission, impotency. ②Difficulty in urination and defecation. ③Pain in the lower back.

【Needling method】Puncture perpendicularly 1.0~1.5 cun.

32. 次髎 Ciliao (BL 32)

【释义】次，第二；髎，骨隙。本穴位当第2骶后孔。

【定位】在骶部，当髂后上棘内下方，适对第2骶后孔处（图9-8）。

【解剖】皮肤→皮下组织→竖脊肌→第2骶后孔。浅层布有臀中皮神经。深层有第2骶神经和骶外侧动、静脉的后支。

【功用】补益下焦，强腰利湿。

【主治】①月经不调，痛经，带下，遗精，阳痿，小便不利，遗尿。②腰骶痛，下肢痿痹。

【操作】直刺1.0~1.5寸。

【Meaning】Ci, 2nd; liao, foramen. This point is at the 2nd posterior sacral foramen.

【Location】In the region of the sacrum, medial and inferior to the posterio – superior iliac spine, in the 2nd posterior sacral foramen (Fig 9-8).

【Regional anatomy】Skin→subcutaneous tissue→erector spinal muscle→the 2nd posterior sacral foramen. Superficial layer, the distribution of the intermediate gluteal cutaneous nerve; deep layer, the 2nd sacral nerve, the posterior branches of the lateral sacral artery and vein.

【Properties】Invigorate the lower energizer for strengthening the loins, promote diuresis.

【Indications】①Irregular menstruation, dysmenorrhea, morbid leucorrhea, seminal emission, impotency, difficulty in urination, enuresis. ②Lumbosacral pain, weakness or paralysis in the lower limbs.

【Needling method】Puncture perpendicularly 1.0~1.5 cun.

33. 中髎 Zhongliao (BL 33)

【释义】中，中间；髎，骨隙。本穴位当第3骶后孔。

【定位】在骶部，当次髎下内方，适对第3骶后孔处（图9-8）。

【解剖】皮肤→皮下组织→臀大肌→竖脊肌。浅层布有臀中皮神经。深层有第3骶神经和骶外侧动、静脉的后支。

【功用】补益下焦，强腰利湿。

【主治】①月经不调，带下，小便不利。②便秘，泄泻。③腰骶痛。

【操作】直刺1.0~1.5寸。

【Meaning】Zhong, center; liao, foramen. This point is at the 3rd sacral foramen, approximately at the middle part.

【Location】In the region of the sacrum, medial and inferior to Ciliao (BL 32), in the 3rd posterior sacral foramen (Fig 9-8).

【Regional anatomy】Skin→subcutaneous tissue→the gluteus maximus→erector spinal muscle. Superficial layer, the distribution of the intermediate gluteal cutaneous nerve. Deep layer, the

3rd sacral nerve, the posterior branches of the lateral sacral artery and vein.

【Properties】Invigorate the lower energizer for strengthening the loins. promote diuresis.

【Indications】①Irregular menstruation, morbid leucorrhea, difficulty in urination. ②Constipation, diarrhea. ③Lumbosacral pain.

【Needling method】Puncture perpendicularly 1.0~1.5 cun.

34. 下髎 Xialiao（BL 34）

【释义】下，上下之下；髎，骨隙。本穴位当最下骶后孔。

【定位】在骶部，当中髎下内方，适对第4骶后孔处（图9-8）。

【解剖】皮肤→皮下组织→臀大肌→竖脊肌。浅层布有臀中皮神经。深层有臀上、下动、静脉的分支或属支，臀下神经，第4骶神经和骶外侧动、静脉的后支。

【功用】补益下焦，强腰利湿。

【主治】①小腹痛，腰骶痛。②二便不利，带下。

【操作】直刺1.0~1.5寸。

【Meaning】Xia, lower; liao, foramen. This point is at the lowest posterior sacral foramen.

【Location】In the region of the sacrum, medial and inferior to Zhongliao（BL 33）, in the 4th posterior sacral foramen（Fig 9-8）.

【Regional anatomy】Skin→subcutaneous tissue→the gluteus maximus→erector spinal muscle. Superficial layer, the distribution of the intermediate gluteal cutaneous nerve. Deep layer, the branches or the subordinate ramus of the superior and inferior gluteal arteries and veins, inferior gluteal nerve, the 4th sacral nerve, and the posterior branches of the lateral sacral artery and vein.

【Properties】Invigorate the lower energizer for strengthening the loins, promote diuresis.

【Indications】①Lower abdominal pain, lumbosacral pain. ②Difficulty in urination and defecation, morbid leucorrhea.

【Needling method】Puncture perpendicularly 1.0~1.5 cun.

35. 会阳 Huiyang（BL 35）

【释义】会，交会；阳，阴阳之阳。穴属阳经，与阳脉之海的督脉相交。

【定位】在骶部尾骨端旁开0.5寸（图9-8）。

【解剖】皮肤→皮下组织→臀大肌→提肛肌腱。浅层布有臀中皮神经。深层有臀下动、静脉的分支或属支和臀下神经。

【功用】清热利湿，益肾固带。

【主治】①泄泻，痢疾，便血，痔疾。②阳痿，带下。

【操作】直刺1.0~1.5寸。

【Meaning】Hui, crossing; yang, yang of yin-yang. This point pertains to yang meridian and is crossed with the governor vessel which is considered as the sea of the yang meridians.

【Location】In the region of the sacrum, 0.5 cun lateral to the tip of the coccyx (Fig 9 – 8).

【Regional anatomy】Skin→subcutaneous tissue→the gluteus maximus→the tendon of the levator ani, Superficial layer, the distribution of the intermediate gluteal cutaneous nerve. Deep layer, the branches or the. subordinate ramus of the inferior gluteal artery and vein, and inferior gluteal nerve.

【Propertics】Clear heat and remove dampness, invigorate the kidney and stanch vaginal discharge.

【Indications】① Diarrhea, dysentery, hematochezia, hemorrhoids. ② Impotency, morbid leucorrhea.

【Needling method】Puncture perpendicularly 1.0 ~ 1.5 cun.

36. 承扶 Chengfu (BL 36)

【释义】承，承受；扶，佐助。本穴位于股部上段，当肢体分界的臀沟中点，有佐助下肢承受头身重量的作用。

【定位】在大腿后面，臀下横纹的中点（图 9 – 9）。

【解剖】皮肤→皮下组织→臀大肌→股二头肌长头及半腱肌。浅层布有股后皮神经及臀下皮神经的分支。深层有股后皮神经本干，坐骨神经及并行动、静脉。

【功用】通便消痔，舒筋活络。

【主治】①腰腿痛，下肢痿痹。②痔疾。

【操作】直刺 1.5 ~ 2.0 寸。

【Meaning】Cheng, sustaining; fu, support. This point is on the upper part of the femur at the midpoint of the gluteofemoral crease. Its function is to support the lower limbs and sustain the body weight.

【Location】Posterior to the thigh, at the midpoint of the transverse gluteal crease (Fig 9 – 9).

【Regional anatomy】Skin→subcutaneous tissue→the gluteus maximus→the long head of the biceps muscle of the thigh and semitendinous muscle. In the superficial layer, there are the branches of the posterior femoral cutaneous nerve and the inferior gluteal nerve. In the deep layer, there are the trunk of the posterior femoral cutaneous nerve, the sciatic nerve and the accompanying arteries and veins.

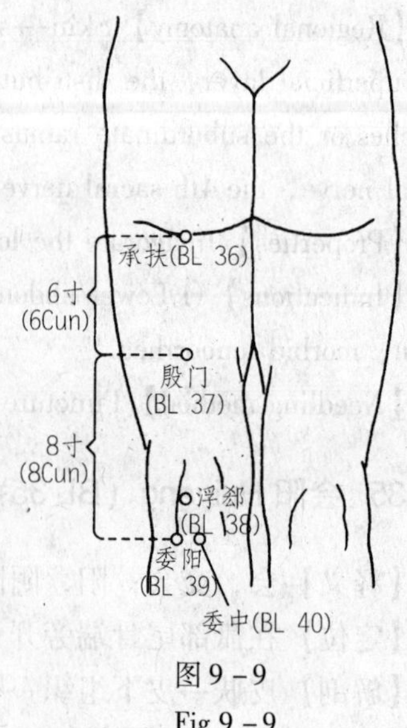

图 9 – 9
Fig 9 – 9

【Properties】Relax the bowels and dispel hemorrhoid, relieve the rigidity of muscles and activate collaterals.

【Indications】①Pain in the lumbar area and legs, weakness or paralysis in the lower limbs. ②Hemorrhoids.

【Needling method】Puncture perpendicularly 1. 5 ~ 2. 0 cun.

37. 殷门 Yinmen (BL 37)

【释义】殷，深厚，正中；门，门户。穴位局部肌肉深厚，为膀胱经气通过之门户。

【定位】在大腿后面，当承扶与委中的连线上，承扶下6寸（图9－9）。

【解剖】皮肤→皮下组织→股二头肌长头及半腱肌。浅层布有股后皮神经。深层有坐骨神经及并行动、静脉，股深动脉穿支等。

【功用】行气，和血，止痛。

【主治】腰腿痛，下肢痿痹。

【操作】直刺1.0~2.0寸。

【Meaning】Yin, thickness; men, door. The local muscle of the point is thick, and the point is a door where qi of the bladder meridian passes.

【Location】On the posterior aspect of the thigh, 6 cun below Chengfu (BL 36), on the line connecting Chengfu (BL 36) and Weizhong (BL 40) (Fig 9－9).

【Regional anatomy】Skin→subcutaneous tissue→the long head of biceps femoris muscle of thigh and semitendinous muscle. In the superficial layer, there is the posterior femoral cutaneous nerve. In the deep layer, there are the sciatic nerve, the accompanying artery and vein, the perforating branches of the deep femoral artery.

【Properties】Move qi, regulate and harmonize the blood for relieving pain.

【Indications】Pain in the lumbar area and legs, weakness or paralysis in the lower limbs.

【Needling method】Puncture perpendicularly 1. 0 ~ 2. 0 cun.

38. 浮郄 Fuxi (BL 38)

【释义】浮，顺流；郄，孔隙。本经之气从股后顺流下入的穴隙。

【定位】在腘横纹外侧端，委阳上1寸，股二头肌腱的内侧（图9－9）。

【解剖】皮肤→皮下组织→股二头肌腱内侧→腓肠肌外侧头。浅层布有股后皮神经。深层有腓总神经，腓肠外侧皮神经和膝上外动、静脉。

【功用】舒筋通络，润肠通便。

【主治】①膝腘痛麻挛急。②便秘。

【操作】直刺1.0~1.5寸。

【Meaning】Fu, floating; xi, seam. This point is on the upper border of the popliteus.

【Location】On the lateral end of the transverse crease of the popliteal fossa, 1 cun above Weiyang (BL 39) on the medial side of the tendon of the biceps femoris (Fig 9－9).

【Regional anatomy】Skin→subcutaneous tissue→medial border of the tendon of biceps femoris muscle of thigh→lateral head of gastrocnemius muscle. In the superficial layer, there is the posterior femoral cutaneous nerve. In the deep layer, there are the common peroneal nerve, the lateral cutaneous nerve of the calf, the lateral superior genicular artery and vein.

【Properties】Relieve the rigidity of muscles and activate collaterals, moisten the intestines and relax the bowels.

【Indications】①Pain, numbness and spasm in the popliteal fossa and knee. ②Constipation.

【Needling method】Puncture perpendicularly 1.0 ~1.5 cun.

39. 委阳（BL 39），三焦下合穴
Weiyang (BL 39), Lower He - Sea Point of the Triple Energizer

【释义】委，弯曲；阳，阴阳之阳。外属阳，穴在腘窝横纹委中穴外侧。

【定位】在腘横纹外侧端，当股二头肌腱的内侧（图9-9）。

【解剖】皮肤→皮下组织→股二头肌→腓肠肌外侧头→腘肌起始腱和腘肌，浅层有股后皮神经。深层有腓总神经和腓肠外侧皮神经。

【功用】舒筋活络，通利水湿。

【主治】①腹满，水肿，小便不利。②腰脊强痛，腿足挛痛。

【操作】直刺1.0~1.5寸。

【Meaning】Wei, crooked; yang, yang of yin - yang. The exterior pertains to yang. The point is lateral to Weizhong (BL 40) on the transverse crease of the popliteal fossa.

【Location】On the lateral end of the transverse crease of the popliteal fossa, on the medial border of the tendon of the biceps femoris (Fig 9-9).

【Regional anatomy】Skin→subcutaneous tissue→biceps femoris muscle of thigh→lateral head of the gastrocnemius muscle→origin of the popliteal muscle and plantar muscle. In the superficial layer, there is the posterior femoral cutaneous nerve. In the deep layer, there are the common peroneal nerve and the lateral cutaneous nerve of the calf.

【Properties】Relieve the rigidity of muscles, eliminating dampness and diuresis.

【Indications】①Abdominal distension, edema, difficulty in urination. ②Pain and stiffness in the back, spasm of the lower limbs.

【Needling method】Puncture perpendicularly 1.0 ~1.5 cun.

40. 委中（BL 40），合穴，膀胱下合穴
Weizhong (BL 40), He - Sea Point, Lower He - Sea Point of the Bladder

【释义】委，弯曲；中，中间。穴在腘窝横纹中点。

【定位】在腘横纹中点，当股二头肌腱与半腱肌肌腱的中间（图9-9）。

【解剖】皮肤→皮下组织→腓肠肌内、外侧头。浅层布有股后皮神经和小隐静脉。深层有胫神经，腘动、静脉和腓肠动脉等。

【功用】舒筋活络，泄热清暑，凉血解毒。

【主治】①腰痛，腘筋挛急，下肢痿痹。②小便不利，遗尿。③丹毒，瘾疹，疔疮。

【操作】直刺1.0～1.5寸或三棱针点刺出血。

【Meaning】Wei, crooked; zhong, center. This point is at the midpoint of the transverse crease of the popliteal fossa.

【Location】On the midpoint of the transverse crease of the popliteal fossa, between the tendons of the biceps femoris and semitendinous (Fig 9-9).

【Regional anatomy】Skin→subcutaneous tissue→between the medial and lateral heads of the gastrocnemius. Superficial layer, the distribution of the posterior femoral cutaneous nerve, and the small saphenous vein. Deep layer, the tibial nerve, the popliteal artery and vein, the sural artery.

【Properties】Relieve the rigidity of muscles and activate collaterals, clearing summer heat, cooling blood and remove toxic substance.

【Indications】①Lumbar pain, spasm of the popliteal tendons, weakness or paralysis in the lower limbs. ②Difficulty in urination, enuresis. ③Erysipelas, urticaria, furuncles.

【Needling method】Puncture perpendicularly 1.0～1.5 cun; or prick with a three-edged needle to induce bleeding.

41. 附分（BL 41），手、足太阳经交会穴
Fufen (BL 41), Crossing Point of the Meridians of Hand-Taiyang and Foot-Taiyang

【释义】附，依附；分，分离。膀胱自项而下，分为两行；本穴为第二行之首穴，附于第一之旁。

【定位】在背部，当第2胸椎棘突下，旁开3寸（图9-10）。

【解剖】皮肤→皮下组织→斜方肌→菱形肌→上后锯肌→竖脊肌。浅层布有第2、3胸神经后支的皮支和伴行的动、静脉。深层有肩胛背神经，肩胛背动、静脉，第2、3胸神经后支的肌支和相应的肋间后动、静脉背侧支的分支或属支。

【功用】舒筋活络，疏风散邪。

【主治】颈项强痛，肩背拘急，肘臂麻木。

【操作】斜刺0.5～0.8寸。

【Meaning】Fu, attached; fen, separation. The bladder meridian runs downward bilaterally from the neck. This point is at the beginning of the 2nd line attached to the first line.

【Location】On the back, level with the lower border of the spinous process of the 2nd thoracic vertebra, 3 cun lateral to the posterior midline (Fig 9-10).

【Regional anatomy】Skin→subcutaneous tissue→trapezius muscle→rhomboid muscle→superior posterior serratus muscle→erector spinal muscle. In the superficial layer, there are the cutaneous branches of the posterior branches of the 2nd and 3rd thoracic nerves and the accompanying arteries and veins. In the deep layer, there are the dorsal scapular nerve, the dorsal scapular artery and vein, the muscular branches of the posterior branches of the 2nd and 3rd thoracic nerves, the branches or tributaries of the dorsal branches of the related posterior intercostal arteries and veins.

【Properties】Relieve the rigidity of muscles and activate collaterals, relieve exterior syndrome by dispelling wind.

【Indications】Stiffness and pain of the neck and back, spasm of the shoulder and back, numbness of the elbow and arm.

【Needling method】Puncture obliquely 0.5~0.8 cun.

42. 魄户 Pohu (BL 42)

【释义】魄，气之灵；户，门户。肺藏魄；穴与肺俞平列，如肺气出入之门户。

【定位】在背部，当第3胸椎棘突下，旁开3寸（图9-10）。

【解剖】皮肤→皮下组织→斜方肌→菱形肌→上后锯肌→竖脊肌。浅层布有第3、4胸神经后支的皮支和伴行的动、静脉。深层有肩胛背神经，肩胛背动、静脉，第3、4胸神经后支的肌支和相应的肋间后动、静脉背侧支的分支或属支。

【功用】理气降逆，舒筋活络。

【主治】①咳嗽，气喘，肺痨。③项强，肩背痛。

【操作】斜刺0.5~0.8寸。

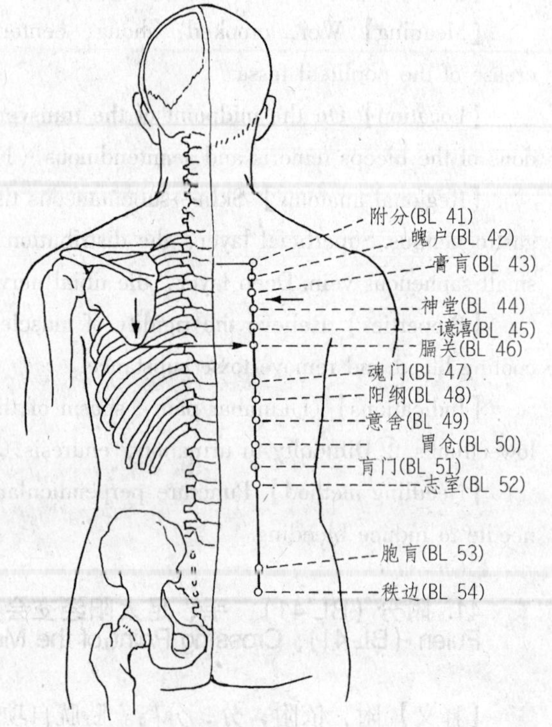

图9-10

Fig 9-10

【Meaning】Po, spirit; hu, door. The lung stores the spirit. The point is at the level of Feishu (BL 13), like a door for qi of the lung.

【Location】On the back, level with the lower border of the spinous process of the 3rd thoracic vertebra, 3 cun lateral to the posterior midline (Fig 9-10).

【Regional anatomy】Skin→subcutaneous tissue→trapezius muscle→rhomboid muscle→superior posterior serratus muscle→erector spinal muscle. In the superficial layer, there are the cutaneous branches of the posterior branches of the 3rd and 4th thoracic nerves, the accompanying arteries and veins. In the deep layer, there are the dorsal scapular nerve, the dorsal scapular artery and vein, the muscular branches of the posterior branches of the 3rd and 4th thoracic nerves, the branches or tributaries of the dorsal branches of the related posterior intercostal arteries and veins.

【Properties】Regulate qi-flowing and lower adverse qi, relieve the rigidity of muscles and activate collaterals.

【Indications】①Cough, asthma, pulmonary phthisis. ②Stiff neck, pain of the shoulder and back.

【Needling method】Puncture obliquely 0.5~0.8 cun.

43. 膏肓 Gaohuang（BL 43）

【释义】膏，膏脂；肓，肓膜。在此指心下膈上的膏脂肓膜；因近于心包故被看做心包组成部分，穴与厥阴俞平列，因名膏肓。

【定位】在背部，当第4胸椎棘突下，旁开3寸（图9－10）。

【解剖】皮肤→皮下组织→斜方肌→菱形肌→竖脊肌。浅层布有第4、5胸神经后支的皮支和伴行的动、静脉。深层有肩胛背神经，肩胛背动、静脉，第4、5胸神经后支的肌支和相应的肋间后动、静脉背侧支的分支或属支。

【功用】补虚益损，调理肺气。

【主治】①咳喘，肺痨。②健忘，遗精，盗汗，虚劳。③肩胛背痛。

【操作】斜刺0.5～0.8寸。

【Meaning】Gao, far; huang, membrane. Gaohuang refers to the far and membrane be low the heart and above the diaphragm. Since this part is close to the pericardium, it is taken as the component of the pericardium. The point is at the level of Jueyinshu（BL 14）point.

【Location】On the back, level with the lower border of the spinous process of the 4th thoracic vertebra, 3 cun lateral to the posterior midline（Fig 9－10）.

【Regional anatomy】Skin→subcutaneous tissue→trapezius muscle→rhomboid muscle→erector spinal muscle. In the superficial layer, there are the cutaneous branches of the posterior branches of the 4th and 5th thoracic nerves, the accompanying arteries and veins. In the deep layer, there are the dorsal scapular nerve, the dorsal scapular artery and vein, the muscular branches of the posterior branches of the 4th and 5th thoracic nerves, the branches or tributaries of the dorsal branches of the related posterior intercostal arteries and veins.

【Properties】Treat deficiency syndrome with tonifying method, regulate lung qi.

【Indications】①Cough, asthma, pulmonary phthisis. ②Forgetfulness, seminal emission, night sweats, consumptive disease. ③Pain of the shoulder and back.

【Needling method】Puncture obliquely 0.5～0.8 cun.

44. 神堂 Shentang（BL 44）

【释义】神，神灵；堂，殿堂。心藏神；穴与心俞平列，如心神所居之殿堂。

【定位】在背部，当第5胸椎棘突下，旁开3寸（图9－10）。

【解剖】皮肤→皮下组织→斜方肌→菱形肌→竖脊肌。浅层布有第5、6胸神经后支的皮支和伴行的动、静脉。深层有肩胛背神经，肩胛背动、静脉，第5、6胸神经后支的肌支和相应的肋间后动、静脉背侧支的分支或属支。

【功用】宽胸理气，宁心安神。

【主治】①心痛，心悸。②咳嗽，气喘，胸闷。③背痛。

【操作】斜刺0.5～0.8寸。

【Meaning】Shen, ming; tang, hall. The heart houses the mind. The point is at the level of Xinshu (BL 15), like a hall where the mind is housed.

【Location】On the back, level with the lower border of the spinous process of the 5th thoracic vertebra, 3 cun lateral to the posterior midline (Fig 9 – 10).

【Regional anatomy】Skin→subcutaneous tissue→trapezius muscle→rhomboid muscle→erector spinal muscle. In the superficial layer, there are the cutaneous branches of the posterior branches of the 5th and 6th thoracic nerves, the accompanying arteries and veins. In the deep layer, there are the dorsal scapular nerve, the dorsal scapular artery and vein, the muscular branches of the posterior branches of the 5th and 6th thoracic nerves, the branches or tributaries of the dorsal branches of the related posterior intercostal arteries and veins.

【Properties】Move qi to soothe the chest and clam the heart to tranquilize.

【Indications】①Cardiac pain, palpitations. ②Cough, asthma, tightness in the chest. ③Back pain.

【Needling method】Puncture obliquely 0.5 ~0.8 cun.

45 譩譆 Yixi (BL 45)

【释义】譩譆，叹息声。取穴时，令病人发譩譆声，穴位局部能够动应手指。

【定位】在背部，当第6胸椎棘突下，旁开3寸（图9－10）。

【解剖】皮肤→皮下组织→斜方肌→菱形肌→竖脊肌。浅层布有第6、7胸神经后支的皮支和伴行的动、静脉。深层有肩胛背神经，肩胛背动、静脉，第6胸神经后支的肌支和相应的肋间后动、静脉背侧支的分支或属支。

【功用】宣肺理气，通络止痛。

【主治】①咳嗽，气喘。②疟疾，热病。③肩背痛。

【操作】斜刺0.5~0.8寸。

【Meaning】Yixi, the sighing sound. If the patient is asked to say "YiXi" when the point is being located, the doctor's fingers may feel the vocal fremitus.

【Location】On the back, level with the lower border of the spinous process of the 6th thoracic vertebra, 3 cun lateral to the posterior midline (Fig 9 – 10).

【Regional anatomy】Skin→subcutaneous tissue→trapezius muscle→rhomboid muscle→erector spinal muscle. In the superficial layer, there are the cutaneous branches of the posterior branches of the 6th and 7th thoracic nerves and the accompanying arteries and veins. In the deep layer, there are the dorsal scapular nerve, the dorsal scapular artery and vein, the muscular branches of the posterior branches of the 6th thoracic nerve and the branches or tributaries of the dorsal branches of the related posterior intercostal arteries and veins.

【Properties】Diffuse the lung and regulate qi – flowing, free the collateral vessels for relieving the pain.

【Indications】①Cough, asthma. ②Malaria, febrile diseases. ③Pain of the shoulder and back.

【Needling method】Puncture obliquely 0. 5 ~0. 8 cun.

46. 膈关 Geguan（BL 46）

【释义】膈，横隔；关，关隘。本穴与膈俞平列，喻之为治疗横隔疾患的关隘。

【定位】在背部，当第7胸椎棘突下，旁开3寸（图9－10）。

【解剖】皮肤→皮下组织→斜方肌→菱形肌→竖脊肌。浅层布有第7、8胸神经后支的皮支和伴行的动、静脉。深层有肩胛背神经，肩胛背动、静脉，第7、8胸神经后支的肌支和相应的肋间后动、静脉背侧支的分支或属支。

【功用】宽胸理气，和胃降逆。

【主治】①呕吐，呃逆，嗳气，食不下，胸闷。②脊背强痛。

【操作】斜刺0. 5 ~0. 8 寸。

【Meaning】Ge, diaphragm; guan, pass. The point is at the level of Geshu（BL 17）and therefore is likened to the pass for treating disorders of the diaphragm.

【Location】On the back, level with the lower border of the spinous process of the 7th thoracic vertebra, 3 cun lateral to the posterior midline（Fig 9－10）.

【Regional anatomy】Skin→subcutaneous tissue→trapezius muscle→rhomboid muscle→erector spinal muscle. In the superficial layer, there are the cutaneous branches of the posterior branches of the 7th and 8th thoracic nerves, the accompanying arteries and veins. In the deep layer, there are the dorsal scapular nerve, the dorsal scapular artery and vein, the muscular branches of the posterior branches of the 7th and 8th thoracic nerves, the branches or tributaries of the dorsal branches of the related posterior intercostal arteries and veins.

【Properties】Move qi to soothe the chest, regulate stomach for lowering adverse qi.

【Indications】①Vomiting, hiccups, belching, dysphagia, tightness in the chest. ②Stiffness and pain of the back.

【Needling method】Puncture obliquely 0. 5 ~0. 8 cun.

47. 魂门 Hunmen（BL 47）

【释义】魂，灵魂；门，门户。肝藏魂；穴与肝俞平列，如肝气出入之门户。

【定位】在背部，当第9胸椎棘突下，旁开3寸（图9－10）。

【解剖】皮肤→皮下组织→背阔肌→下后锯肌→竖脊肌。浅层布有第9、10胸神经后支的外侧皮支和伴行的动、静脉。深层有第9、10胸神经后支的肌支和相应的肋间后动、静脉背侧支的分支或属支。

【功用】疏肝理气，降逆和胃。

【主治】①胸胁胀痛，呕吐，泄泻。②背痛。

【操作】斜刺0. 5 ~0. 8寸。

【Meaning】Hun, soul; men, door. The liver stores the soul. The point is at the level of Ganshu (BL 18), like a door for the qi of liver.

【Location】On the back, level with the lower border of the spinous process of the 9th thoracic vertebra, 3 cun lateral to the posterior midline (Fig 9 – 10).

【Regional anatomy】Skin→subcutaneous tissue→latissimus muscle of the back→inferior posterior serratus muscle→erector spinal muscle. In the superficial layer, there are the lateral cutaneous branches of the posterior branches of the 9th and 10th thoracic nerves, the accompanying arteries and veins. In the deep layer, there are the muscular branches of the posterior branches of the 9th and 10th thoracic nerves, the branches of the dorsal branches of the related posterior intercostal arteries and veins.

【Properties】Soothe the liver and regulate qi, regulate stomach for lowering adverse qi.

【Indications】①Distending pain in the chest and hypochondrium, vomiting, diarrhea. ②Back pain.

【Needling method】Puncture obliquely 0.5 ~0.8 cun.

48. 阳纲 Yanggang (BL 48)

【释义】阳，阴阳之阳；纲，纲要。胆属阳；穴与胆俞平列，为治疗胆病的要穴。

【定位】在背部，当第10胸椎棘突下，旁开3寸（图9－10）。

【解剖】皮肤→皮下组织→背阔肌→下后锯肌→竖脊肌。浅层布有第10、11胸神经后支的外侧皮支和伴行的动、静脉。深层有第10、11胸神经后支的肌支和相应的肋间后动、静脉背侧支的分支或属支。

【功用】疏肝利胆，健脾和中。

【主治】①肠鸣，腹痛，泄泻。②黄疸，消渴。

【操作】斜刺0.5 ~0.8寸。

【Meaning】Yang, yang of yin – yang; gang, key link. The gallbladder pertains to yang, the point is at the level of Danshu (BL 19) and is important in treating gallbladder diseases.

【Location】On the back, level with the lower border of the spinous process of the 10th thoracic vertebra, 3 cun lateral to the posterior midline (Fig 9 – 10).

【Regional anatomy】Skin→subcutaneous tissue→latissimus muscle of the back→inferior posterior serratus muscle→erector spinal muscle. In the superficial layer, there are the lateral cutaneous branches of the posterior branches of the 10th and 11th thoracic nerves, the accompanying arteries and veins. In the deep layer, there are the muscular branches of the posterior branches of the 10th and 11th thoracic nerves, the branches or tributaries of the dorsal branches of the related posterior intercostal arteries and veins.

【Properties】Disperse stagnated liver qi for promoting bile flow, strengthen spleen and harmonize stomach.

【Indications】①Borborygmus, abdominal pain, diarrhea. ②Jaundice, diabetes.

【Needling method】Puncture obliquely 0. 5 ~0. 8 cun.

49. 意舍 Yishe（BL 49）

【释义】意，意念；舍，宅舍。脾藏意；穴与脾俞平列，如脾气之宅舍。

【定位】在背部，当第 11 胸椎棘突下，旁开 3 寸（图 9 –10）。

【解剖】皮肤→皮下组织→背阔肌→下后锯肌→竖脊肌。浅层布有第 11、12 胸神经后支的外侧皮支和伴行的动、静脉。深层有第 11、12 胸神经后支的肌支和相应的肋间后动、静脉背侧支的分支或属支。

【功用】健脾和胃，利胆化湿。

【主治】腹胀，肠鸣，泄泻，呕吐。

【操作】斜刺 0. 5 ~0. 8 寸。

【Meaning】Yi，ideas；she，residence. The spleen stores ideas. The point is at the level of Pishu（BL 20），like a residence of the qi of spleen.

【Location】On the back，level with the lower border of the spinous process of the 11th thoracic vertebra，3 cun lateral to the posterior midline（Fig 9 –10）.

【Regional anatomy】Skin→subcutaneous tissue→latissimus muscle of the back→inferior posterior serratus muscle→erector spinal muscle. In the superficial layer，there are the lateral cutaneous branches of the posterior branches of the 11th and 12th thoracic nerves，the accompanying arteries and veins. In the deep layer，there are the muscular branches of the posterior branches of the 11th and 12th thoracic nerves，the branches or tributaries of the dorsal branches of the related posterior intercostal arteries and veins.

【Properties】Strengthen spleen and harmonize stomach，promote bile flow and resolving of dampness.

【Indications】Abdominal distension，borborygmus，diarrhea，vomiting.

【Needling method】Puncture obliquely 0. 5 ~0. 8 cun.

50. 胃仓 Weicang（BL 50）

【释义】胃，胃腑；仓，粮食。穴与胃俞平列，胃主纳气，犹如粮仓。

【定位】在背部，当第 12 胸椎棘突下，旁开 3 寸（图 9 –10）。

【解剖】皮肤→皮下组织→背阔肌→下后锯肌→竖脊肌→腰方肌。浅层布有第 12 胸神经和第 1 腰神经后支的外侧皮支和伴行的动、静脉。深层有第 12 胸神经和第 1 腰神经后支的肌支和相应的动、静脉背侧支的分支或属支。

【功用】和胃健脾，消食导滞。

【主治】①胃脘痛，腹胀，小儿食积。②水肿。

【操作】斜刺 0. 5 ~0. 8 寸。

【Meaning】Wei，stomach；cang，storehouse. The point is at the level of Weishu（BL 21）.

The stomach receives food, acting like a storehouse.

【Location】On the back, level with the lower border of the spinous process of the 12th thoracic vertebra, 3 cun lateral to the posterior midline (Fig 9 – 10).

【Regional anatomy】Skin→subcutaneous tissue→latissimus muscle of the back→inferior posterior serratus muscle→erector spinal muscle→lumbar quadrate muscle. In the superficial layer, there are the lateral cutaneous branches of the posterior branches of the posterior branches of the 12th thoracic and 1st lumbar nerves, the accompanying arteries and veins. In the deep layer, there are the muscular branches of the posterior branches of the 12th thoracic and the 1st lumbar nerves, the branches or tributaries of the dorsal branches of the related posterior intercostal arteries and veins.

【Properties】Strengthen spleen and harmonize stomach, resolve food stagnation.

【Indications】①Epigastric pain, abdominal distension, indigestion. ②Edema.

【Needling method】Puncture obliquely 0.5 ~0.8 cun.

51. 肓门 Huangmen (BL 51)

【释义】肓，肓膜；门，门户。穴与三焦俞平列，如肓膜之气出入的门户。

【定位】在腰部，当第1腰椎棘突下，旁开3寸（图9－10）。

【解剖】皮肤→皮下组织→背阔肌腱膜→竖脊肌→腰方肌。浅层布有第1、2腰神经后支的外侧皮支和伴行的动、静脉。深层有第1、2腰神经后支的肌支和第1腰背动、静脉背侧支的分支或属支。

【功用】理气和胃，清热消肿。

【主治】①腹痛，痞块。②便秘。

【操作】斜刺0.5~0.8寸。

【Meaning】Huang, membrane; men, door. The point is at the level of Sanjiaoshu (BL 22), like a door of the qi of triple energizer.

【Location】Level with the lower border of the spinous process of the 1st lumbar vertebra, 3 cun lateral to the posterior midline (Fig 9 – 10).

【Regional anatomy】Skin→subcutaneous tissue→aponeurosis of latissimus muscle of the back→erector spinal muscle→lumbar quadrate muscle. In the superficial layer, there are the lateral cutaneous branches of the posterior branches of the 1st and 2nd lumbar nerves, the accompanying arteries and veins. In the deep layer, there are the muscular branches of the posterior branches of the 1st and 2nd lumbar nerves, the branches or tributaries of the dorsal branches of the 1st lumbar artery and vein.

【Properties】Move qi to harmonize stomach, clear heat for detumescence.

【Indications】①Abdominal pain, abdominal masses. ②Constipation.

【Needling method】Puncture obliquely 0.5 ~0.8 cun.

52. 志室 Zhishi（BL 52）

【释义】志，意志；室，房室。肾藏志；穴与肾俞平列，如肾气聚集之房室。

【定位】在腰部，当第2腰椎棘突下，旁开3寸（图9－10）。

【解剖】皮肤→皮下组织→背阔肌腱膜→竖脊肌→腰方肌。浅层布有第1、2腰神经后支的外侧皮支和伴行的动、静脉。深层有第1、2腰神经后支的肌支和相应的腰背动、静脉背侧支的分支或属支。

【功用】益肾固精，清热利湿，强壮腰膝。

【主治】①遗精，阳痿。②小便不利，水肿。③腰脊强痛。

【操作】斜刺0.5～0.8寸。

【Meaning】Zhi, will; shi, chamber. The kidney stores the will. The point is at the level of Shenshu（BL 23）, like a chamber where qi of the kidney gathers.

【Location】Level with the lower border of the spinous process of the 2nd lumbar vertebra, 3 cun lateral to the posterior midline（Fig 9－10）.

【Regional anatomy】Skin→subcutaneous tissue→aponeurosis of latissimus muscle of the back→erector spinal muscle→lumbar quadrate muscle. Superficial layer, the distribution of the cutaneous branches of the posterior rami of the 1st and 2nd lumbar nerves, the artery and vein along with them. Deep layer, the muscular branch of the posterior rami of the 1st and 2nd lumbar nerves, the branches or the subordinate ramus of the dorsal branches of the relevant lumbar artery and vein.

【Properties】Invigorate the kidney and secure essence, clear heat and promote diuresis, strengthen the loins and knees.

【Indications】①Seminal emission, impotence. ②Difficulty in urination, edema. ③Stiffness and pain in the back.

【Needling method】Puncture obliquely 0.5～0.8 cun.

53. 胞肓 Baohuang（BL 53）

【释义】胞，囊袋；肓，肓膜。胞，在此主要指膀胱；穴与膀胱俞平列，故名。

【定位】在臀部，平第2骶后孔，骶正中嵴旁开3寸（图9－10）。

【解剖】皮肤→皮下组织→臀大肌→臀中肌。浅层布有臀上皮神经和臀中皮神经。深层有臀上动、静脉，臀上神经。

【功用】补肾强腰，通利二便。

【主治】①小便不利，阴肿。②腹胀，便秘。③腰脊痛。

【操作】直刺0.8～1.2寸。

【Meaning】Bao, cystic bag; huang, membrane. Bao refers to the bladder. The point is at the level of Pangguangshu（BL 28）.

【Location】Level with the 2nd posterior sacral foramen, 3 cun lateral to the median sacral crest（Fig 9 – 10）.

【Regional anatomy】Skin→subcutaneous tissue→the gluteus maximus→the gluteus medius muscle. In the superficial layer，there are the superior and middle gluteal nerves. In the deep layer，there are the superior gluteal artery and vein，the superior gluteal nerve.

【Properties】Invigorate the kidney and strengthen the loins，regulate the difficulty in urination and defecation.

【Indications】①Difficulty in urination，swelling of the vulva. ②Abdominal distension，constipation. ③Lumbar vertebral pain.

【Needling method】Puncture perpendicularly 0. 8 ~1. 2 cun.

54. 秩边 Zhibian（BL 54）

【释义】秩，秩序；边，边缘。膀胱经背部诸穴，排列有序；本穴居其最下边。

【定位】在臀部，平第 4 骶后孔，骶正中嵴旁开 3 寸（图 9 – 10）。

【解剖】皮肤→皮下组织→臀大肌→臀中肌→臀小肌。浅层布有臀中皮神经和臀下皮神经。深层有臀上、下动脉，臀上、下静脉，臀上、下神经。

【功用】舒筋活络，强壮腰膝，调理下焦。

【主治】①腰腿痛，下肢痿痹。③痔疾，便秘，小便不利。

【操作】直刺 1. 5 ~2. 0 寸。

【Meaning】Zhi，order；bian，edge. The back – shu point of the bladder meridian are arranged in order. This point is at the lowest among them.

【Location】Level with the 4th posterior sacral foramen，3 cun lateral to the median sacral crest（Fig 9 – 10）.

【Regional anatomy】Skin→subcutancous tissuc →thc glutcus maximus →the gluteus medius→the gluteus minimus. Superficial layer，the distribution of the intermediate and inferior gluteal cutaneous nerves. Deep layer，the superior and inferior gluteal arteries and veins，nerves.

【Properties】Relieve the rigidity of muscles and activate collaterals，strengthen the loins and knees，regulate the lower energizer.

【Indications】①Pain in the lumbar area and legs，atrophy or paralysis in the lower limbs. ②Hemorrhoids，constipation，difficulty in urination.

【Needling method】Puncture perpendicularly 1. 5 ~2. 0 cun.

55. 合阳 Heyang（BL 55）

【释义】合，汇合；阳，阴阳之阳。本经自项而下分为两支，行至委中与本穴则合而下行；高而为阳。

【定位】在小腿后面，当委中与承山的连线上，委中下 2 寸（图 9 – 11）。

【解剖】皮肤→皮下组织→腓肠肌→腘肌。浅层布有小隐静脉，股后皮神经和腓肠内侧皮神经。深层有胫动、静脉和胫神经。

【功用】舒筋通络，调经止带，强健腰膝。

【主治】①腰脊强痛，下肢痿痹。②疝气，崩漏。

【操作】直刺 1.0～2.0 寸。

【Meaning】He, confluence; yang, yang of yin－yang. The meridian runs downward from the neck, from where it branches out into two lines. After meeting at Weizhong (BL 40), it travels downward and gradually ascends along the muscle. The higher point is considered as yang.

【Location】On the posterior aspect of the lower leg, 2 cun below Weizhong (BL 40), on the line connecting Weizhong (BL 40) and Chengshan (BL 57) (Fig 9－11).

【Regional anatomy】Skin→subcutaneous tissue→gastrocnemius muscle→the plantar muscle. In the superficial layer, there are the small saphenous vein, the posterior cutaneous nerve of the thigh and the medial cutaneous nerve of the calf. In the deep layer, there are the popliteal artery and vein and the tibial nerve.

【Properties】Relieve the rigidity of muscles and activate collaterals, regulate menstruation and stanch vaginal discharge.

【Indications】①Lumbar stiffness and pain, atrophy or paralysis in the lower limbs. ②Hernia, uterine bleeding.

【Needling method】Puncture perpendicularly 1.0～2.0 cun.

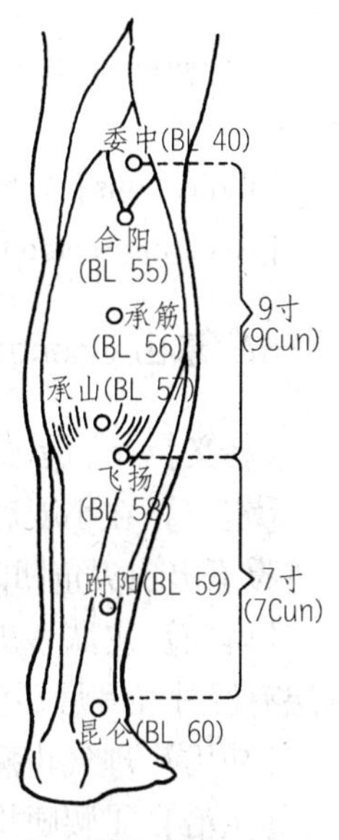

图 9－11

Fig 9－11

56. 承筋 Chengjin (BL 56)

【释义】承，承受；筋，筋肉。穴在腓肠肌处；这是小腿以下承受其以上部位的主要筋肉。

【定位】在小腿后面，当委中与承山的连线上，腓肠肌肌腹中央，委中下 5 寸（图 9－11）。

【解剖】皮肤→皮下组织→腓肠肌→比目鱼肌。浅层布有小隐静脉，腓肠内侧皮神经。深层有胫后动、静脉，膝动、静脉和胫神经。

【功用】舒筋活络，强健腰膝，清泄肠热。

【主治】①腰腿拘急疼痛。②痔疾。

【操作】直刺 1.0～1.5 寸。

【Meaning】Cheng, sustain; jin, tendon and muscle. The point is on the gastrocnemius, an important muscle of the leg for sustaining the upper part of the body.

【Location】On the posterior aspect of the lower leg, 5 cun below Weizhong (BL 40), on the line connecting Weizhong (BL 40) and Chengshan (BL 57), in the center of the belly of the gastrocnemius muscle（Fig 9－11）.

【Regional anatomy】Skin→subcutaneous tissue→the gastrocnemius→soleus muscle. In the superficial layer，there are the small saphenous vein and the medial cutaneous nerve of the calf. In the deep layer，there are the posterior tibial artery and vein，the peroneal artery and vein and the tibial nerve.

【Properties】Relieve the rigidity of muscles and activate collaterals，strengthen the loins and knees.

【Indications】①Spasm and pain of the lumbar area and legs. ②Hemorrhoids.

【Needling method】Puncture perpendicularly 1. 0～1. 5 cun.

57. 承山 Chengshan（BL 57）

【释义】承，承受；山，山岭。腓肠肌之二腹肌高突如山，穴在其下，有承受之势。

【定位】在小腿后面正中，委中与昆仑之间，当伸直小腿或足跟上提时，腓肠肌肌腹下出现尖角凹陷处（图9－11）。

【解剖】皮肤→皮下组织→腓肠肌→比目鱼肌。浅层布有小隐静脉和腓肠内侧皮神经。深层有胫神经和胫后动、静脉。

【功用】理气止痛，舒筋活络，消痔。

【主治】①腰腿拘急疼痛。②痔疾，便秘。

【操作】直刺1.0～2.0寸。

【Meaning】Cheng，sustain；shan，mountain. The two bellies of the gastrocnemius muscle are as prominent as a mountain. The point is below them，as though holding up a mountain.

【Location】In the center of the posterior aspect of the lower leg，between Weizhong（BL 40）and Kunlun（BL 60），in the triangle depression formed below the bellies of the gastrocnemius muscle when the foot is stretched（Fig 9－11）.

【Regional anatomy】Skin → subcutaneous tissue → the gastrocnemius → soleus muscle. Superficial layer，the distribution of the small saphenous vein and the medial sural cutaneous nerve. Deep layer，the tibial nerve，the posterior tibial artery and vein.

【Properties】Relax the muscular spasm and stop pain，relieve the rigidity of muscles and activate collaterals，dispel hemorrhoid.

【Indications】①Pain and spasm in the lumbar region and legs. ②Hemorrhoids，constipation.

【Needling method】Puncture perpendicularly 1. 0～2. 0 cun.

58. 飞扬（BL 58），络穴
Feiyang（BL 58），Luo－Connecting Point

【释义】飞，飞翔；扬，向上扬。外为阳，穴在小腿外侧，本经络脉从此飞离而去络肾经。

【定位】在小腿后面，当外踝后，昆仑穴直上7寸，承山外下方1寸处（图9-11）。

【解剖】皮肤→皮下组织→小腿三头肌→拇长屈肌。浅层布有腓肠外侧皮神经。深层有胫神经和胫后动、静脉。

【功用】清热安神，舒筋活络。

【主治】①腰腿疼痛。②头痛，目眩，鼻衄。③痔疾。

【操作】直刺1.0~1.5寸。

【Meaning】Fei, to fly; yang, lifting. The exterior is yang. The point is a luo-xue connecting point at the lateral aspect of the leg. And the collateral of this meridian flies out from this point to the kidney meridian.

【Location】On the posterior aspect of the lower leg, behind the external malleolus, 7 cun above Kunlun (BL 60), 1 cun posterior and inferior to Chengshan (BL 57) (Fig 9-11).

【Regional anatomy】Skin→subcutaneous tissue→triceps muscle of the calf→the long flexor muscle of the great toe. In the superficial layer, there is the lateral cutaneous nerve of the calf. In the deep layer, there are the tibial nerve, the posterior tibial artery and vein.

【Properties】Clear the heat for tranquillization, relieve the rigidity of muscles and activate collaterals.

【Indications】①Pain of the lumbar region and leg. ②Headache, dizziness, epistaxis. ③Hemorrhoids.

【Needling method】Puncture perpendicularly 1.0~1.5 cun.

59. 跗阳（BL 59），阳跻郄穴
Fuyang (BL 59), Xi-Cleft Point of Yang Heel Vessel

【释义】跗，足背；阳，阴阳之阳。外为阳，上为阳；穴在小腿外侧足背外上方。

【定位】在小腿后面，外踝后，昆仑穴直上3寸（图9-11）。

【解剖】皮肤→皮下组织→腓骨短肌→拇长屈肌。浅层布有腓肠神经和小隐静脉。深层有胫神经的分支和胫后动、静脉的肌支。

【功用】舒筋活络，退热散风。

【主治】①头痛，头重。②腰腿痛，下肢痿痹，外踝肿痛。

【操作】直刺0.8~1.2寸。

【Meaning】Fu, tarsus; yang, yang of yin-yang. The exterior and superior are yang, the point is at the superior aspect of the tarsus and at the lateral aspect of the leg.

【Location】On the posterior aspect of the lower leg, behind the external malleolus, 3 cun directly above Kunlun (BL 60) (Fig 9-11).

【Regional anatomy】Skin→subcutaneous tissue→the short peroneal muscle→the long flexor muscle of the great toe. In the superficial layer, there are the sural nerve and the small saphenous vein. In the deep layer, there are the branches of the tibial nerve, the muscular branches of the posterior tibial artery and vein.

【Properties】Relieve the rigidity of muscles and activate collaterals，disperse wind－heat.

【Indications】①Headache，heaviness of the head. ②Pain of the lumbar region and legs，atrophy or paralysis in the lower limbs，swelling and pain of the external malleolus.

【Needling method】Puncture perpendicularly 0.8～1.2 cun.

60. 昆仑（BL 60），经穴
Kunlun（BL 60），Jing－River Point

【释义】昆仑，山名。外踝高突，比作昆仑，穴在其后。

【定位】在足部外踝后方，当外踝尖与跟腱之间的凹陷处（图 9－12）。

【解剖】皮肤→皮下组织→跟腱前方的疏松结缔组织中。浅层布有腓肠神经和小隐静脉。深层有腓动、静脉的分支和属支。

【功用】安神清热，舒筋活络。

【主治】①头痛，项强。②腰痛，足跟痛。③滞产。④癫痫。

【操作】直刺 0.5～0.8 寸。孕妇禁用。

【Meaning】Kunlun，the name of mountains in West China. The lateral malleolus is shaped like a mountain，and the point is located next to it.

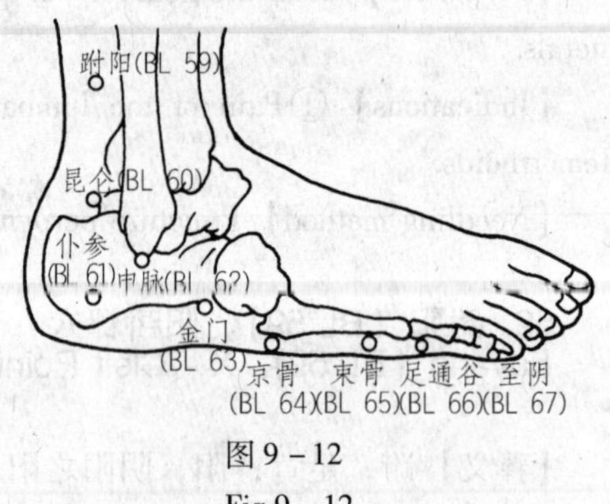

图 9－12
Fig 9－12

【Location】Posterior to the external malleolus，in the depression between the prominence of the external malleolus and the Achilles tendon（Fig 9－12）.

【Regional anatomy】Skin → subcutaneous tissue→in loose connective tissue of achilles tendon in anterior. There are sural nerve and short saphenous vein in superficial layer，branches of fibular artery and vein in deeper layer.

【Properties】Clear the heat for tranquillization，relax the muscular spasm and stop pain.

【Indications】①Headache，stiff neck. ②Lumbar pain，heel pain. ③Delayed labour. ④Epilepsy.

【Needling method】Puncture perpendicularly 0.5～0.8 cun. It is contraindicated in pregnant women.

61. 仆参 Pucan（BL 61）

【释义】仆，仆从；参，参拜。穴在足跟外侧，参拜时此处易显露。

【定位】在足外侧部，外踝后下方，昆仑穴直下，跟骨外侧，赤白肉际处（图 9－12）。

【解剖】皮肤→皮下组织→跟骨。布有小隐静脉的属支、腓肠神经跟外侧支腓动、静脉的跟支。

【功用】舒筋活络，强壮腰膝。

【主治】①下肢痿痹，足跟痛。②癫痫。

【操作】直刺0.3~0.5寸。

【Meaning】Pu, servant; can, paying respects. The point is at the lateral aspect of the heel and therefore was exposed when a servant paid respects.

【Location】On the lateral side of the foot, posterior and inferior to the external malleolus, directly below Kunlun (BL 60), lateral to the calcaneus at the junction of the red and white skin (Fig 9-12).

【Regional anatomy】Skin→subcutaneous tissue→calcaneus. There are the tributaries of the small saphenous vein, the lateral calcaneal branches of the sural nerve and the calcaneal branches of the peroneal artery and vein in this area.

【Properties】Relieve the rigidity of muscles and activate collaterals, strengthen the loins and knees.

【Indications】①Atrophy or paralysis in the lower limbs, heel pain. ②Epilepsy.

【Needling method】Puncture perpendicularly 0.3~0.5 cun.

62. 申脉（BL 62），八脉交会穴（通阳跻脉）
Shenmai (BL 62), One of the Eight Confluent Points Associating with Yang Heel Vessel

【释义】申，伸展的意思；脉，经脉。穴属膀胱经，又是发出阳跻脉处。

【定位】在足外侧部，外踝直下方凹陷中（图9-12）。

【解剖】皮肤→皮下组织→腓骨长肌腱→腓骨短肌腱→距跟外侧韧带。布有小隐静脉、腓肠神经的分支和外踝前动、静脉。

【功用】清热安神，利腰膝。

【主治】①失眠，癫狂痫。②头痛，项强，腰腿痛。③眼睑下垂，嗜卧。

【操作】直刺0.3~0.5寸。

【Meaning】Shen, to extend; mai, meridian. The point portains to the bladder meridian, from where the meridian extends to yang heel vessel.

【Location】On the lateral side of the foot, in the depression directly below the external malleolus (Fig 9-12).

【Regional anatomy】Skin→subcutaneous tissue→tendon of the long peroneal muscle→the tendon of the short peroneal muscle→lateral talocalcaneal ligament. There are the branches of the small saphenous vein, the sural nerve, the lateral anterior malleolus artery and vein in this area.

【Properties】Clear the heat for tranquillization, strengthen the loins and knees.

【Indications】①Insomnia, psychosis, epilepsy. ②Headache, stiff neck, pain of the lumbar region and legs. ③Blepharoptosis, somnolence.

【Needling method】Puncture perpendicularly 0.3~0.5 cun.

63. 金门（BL 63），郄穴
Jinmen（BL 63），Xi - Cleft Point

【释义】金，阳之维；门，门户。穴属于足太阳经，又是阳维脉的始发站，故比喻进入阳维脉的门户。

【定位】在足外侧，当外踝前缘直下，骰骨下缘处（图9－12）。

【解剖】皮肤→皮下组织→腓骨长肌腱及小趾展肌。布有足背外侧皮神经，足外侧缘静脉（小隐静脉）。

【功用】安神开窍，通经活络。

【主治】①头痛。②癫痫，小儿惊风。③腰痛，下肢痹痛，外踝肿痛。

【操作】直刺0.3～0.5寸。

【Meaning】Jin, gold; men, door. The point pertains to the bladder meridian of foot－taiyang and is the starting point of yang link vessel, as a door to enter the yang link vessel.

【Location】On the lateral side of the foot, directly below the anterior border of the external malleolus and below the border of the cuboid（Fig 9－12）.

【Regional anatomy】Skin→subcutaneous tissue→the tendon of the long peroneal muscle and abductor muscle of the little toe. There are the lateral dorsal cutaneous nerve of the foot and the lateral vein of the foot（the small saphenous vein）in this area.

【Properties】Tranquillize for resuscitation, unblock the meridian and activate collaterals.

【Indications】①Headache. ②Epilepsy, infantile convulsions. ③Lumbar pain, pain in the lower limbs, pain and swelling in the external malleolus.

【Needling method】Puncture perpendicularly 0.3～0.5 cun.

64. 京骨（BL 64），原穴
Jinggu（BL 64），Yuan - Source Point

【释义】京骨，是第5跖骨粗隆的古称。穴在第5跖骨粗隆外侧。

【定位】在足外侧，第5跖骨粗隆下方，赤白肉际处（图9－12）。

【解剖】皮肤→皮下组织→小趾展肌。布有足背外侧皮神经，足外侧缘静脉。

【功用】清热止痉，明目舒筋。

【主治】①头痛，项强，目翳。②腰腿痛。③癫痫。

【操作】直刺0.3～0.5寸。

【Meaning】Jinggu is an ancient name for the tuberosity of the 5th metatarsus. The point is at the lateral aspect of the tuberosity of the 5th metatarsus.

【Location】On the lateral side of the foot, below the tuberosity of the bone, at the junction of the red and white skin（Fig 9－12）.

【Regional anatomy】Skin→subcutaneous tissue→abductor muscle of the little toe. There are the lateral dorsal cutaneous nerve of the foot and the lateral vein of the foot in this area.

【Properties】Clear the heat to arrest convulsions, improve vision and relieve the rigidity of muscles.

【Indications】①Headache, stiff neck, superficial visual obstruction. ②lumbar and lower limbs. ③Epilepsy.

【Needling method】Puncture perpendicularly 0. 3 ~0. 5 cun.

65. 束骨（BL 65），输穴
Shugu（BL 65），Shu - Stream Point

【释义】束骨，为第5跖骨小头之古称。穴在第5跖骨小头外下方。

【定位】在足外侧，足小趾本节（第5跖趾关节）的后方，赤白肉际处（图9－12）。

【解剖】皮肤→皮下组织→小趾展肌→小趾对蹠肌腱→小趾短屈肌。浅层布有足背外侧皮神经，足背静脉弓的属支。深层有趾足底固有神经和趾底固有动、静脉。

【功用】通经活络，清头明目。

【主治】①头痛，项强，目眩。②腰腿痛。③癫狂。

【操作】直刺0. 3 ~0. 5寸。

【Meaning】Shugu is an ancient name for the head of the 5th metatarsus. The point is at the lateral and inferior aspect of the head of the 5th metatarsus.

【Location】On the lateral side of the foot, posterior to the head of the 5th metatarsal bone, at the junction of the red and white skin（Fig 9 – 12）.

【Regional anatomy】Skin→subcutaneous tissue→abductor muscle of the little toe→tendon of opponens muscle of the little toe→short flexor muscle of the little toe. In the superficial layer, there are the lateral dorsal cutaneous nerve of the foot and the tributaries of the arch of the dorsal venous arch of the foot. In the deep layer, there are the proper digital plantar nerve, the proper digital plantar arteries and veins.

【Properties】Unblock the meridian and activate collaterals, refresh the mind and improve vision.

【Indications】①Headache, stiff neck, dizziness. ②Pain in the lumbar area and 5th metatarsal. ③Psychosis.

【Needling method】Puncture perpendicularly 0. 3 ~0. 5 cun.

66. 足通谷（BL 66），荥穴
Zutonggu（BL 66），Ying - Spring Point

【释义】足，足部；通，通过；谷，山谷。穴在足部，该处凹陷如谷，脉气由此通过。

【定位】在足外侧部，足小趾本节（第5跖趾关节）的前方，赤白肉际处（图9－12）。

【解剖】皮肤→皮下组织→小趾近节趾骨底的跖侧面。布有足背外侧皮神经，足背静脉

弓的属支，趾足底固有动、静脉。

【功用】清热安神，清头明目。

【主治】①头痛，项强，目眩，鼻衄。②癫狂。

【操作】直刺0.2~0.3寸。

【Meaning】Zu, foot; tong, passing; gu, valley. The point is in the depression of the foot, which is likened to a valley through which the qi of meridian passes.

【Location】On the lateral side of the foot, anterior to the fifth metatarsophalangeal joint, at the junction of the red and white skin (Fig 9 – 12).

【Regional anatomy】Skin→subcutaneous tissue→plantar surface of the proximal end of the little toe. There are the lateral dorsal cutaneous nerve of the foot, the tributaries of the arch of the dorsal veins of the foot, the proper digital plantar arteries and veins in this area.

【Properties】Clear the heat for tranquillization, refresh the mind and improve vision.

【Indications】①Headache, stiff neck, dizziness, epistaxis. ②Psychosis.

【Needling method】Puncture perpendicularly 0.2 ~ 0.3 cun.

67. 至阴（BL 67），井穴
Zhiyin (BL 67), Jing - Well Point

【释义】至，到达；阴，阴阳之阴。阴，在此指足少阴经。此系足太阳膀胱经末穴。

【定位】在足小趾末节外侧，距趾甲角0.1寸（图9–12）。

【解剖】皮肤→皮下组织→甲根。布有足背外侧皮神经的趾背神经和趾背动、静脉网。

【功用】正胎催产，理气活血，清头明目。

【主治】①胎位不正，滞产。②头痛，目痛，鼻塞，鼻衄。

【操作】浅刺0.1寸。胎位不正用灸法。

【Meaning】Zhi, reaching; yin, yin of yin – yang. Yin refers to the foot – shaoyin meridian. This is the end point of the bladder meridian of foot – taiyang, from where it reaches to the foot – shaoyin meridian.

【Location】On the lateral side of the little toe, approximately 0.1 cun lateral from the corner of the nail (Fig 9 – 12).

【Regional anatomy】Skin→subcutaneous tissue→the base of nail. The distribution of the dorsal digital nerve derived from the lateral dorsal cutaneous nerve of foot, the dorsal digital artery and vein of foot.

【Properties】Regulate the malposition of foetus and Induce labour, move qi and promote blood circulation, refresh the mind and improve vision.

【Indications】①Breech presentation, delayed labour. ②Headache, eye pain, nasal congestion, epistaxis.

【Needling method】Puncture superficially 0.1 cun, or use moxibustion only for malposition of foetus.

复习思考题
Review Questions

1. 通读全文，然后用你自己的语言描述出足太阳膀胱经的正确循行路线，并在同伴身上比划出来。

Read the whole context and show the accurate course of this meridian with your partner as you retell it by your own words.

2. 请与你的同伴相互总结出足太阳膀胱经的主治概要。

Talk with your partner about what is the summary of indication of this meridian.

3. 牢记足太阳膀胱经上穴位的定位、主治和操作方法，并两两之间进行相互练习、复述。

Remember the location, indications and needling method of the points on this meridian and retell them with your partner each other.

第十章 足少阴经络与腧穴
Meridian and Collateral and Its Acupoints of Foot – Shaoyin

第一节 足少阴经络
Meridian and Collateral of Foot – Shaoyin

一、足少阴经脉
Meridian of Foot - Shaoyin

(一) 经脉循行
The Course of Meridian

足少阴肾经，起始于足小趾之下，斜向足心（涌泉），出于舟骨粗隆下，沿内踝之后，分支进入脚跟中（大钟），上向小腿内（复溜、交信；会三阴交），出腘窝内侧（筑宾、阴谷），上大腿内后侧，通过脊柱（会长强），属于肾，络于膀胱（肓俞、中注、四满、气穴、大赫、横骨；会关元、中极）。

上行主干，从肾向上（商曲、石关、阴都、通谷、幽门），通过肝、膈，进入肺中（步廊、神封、灵墟、神藏、彧中、俞府），沿着喉咙，夹舌根旁（通廉泉）。

其支脉，从肺出来，络于心，流注于胸中，接手厥阴心包经（图 10－1）。

《灵枢·经脉》原文：肾足少阴之脉，起于小指之下，邪走足心，出于然骨之下，循内踝之后，别入跟中，以上腨内，出腘内廉，上股内后廉，贯脊属肾，络膀胱。其直者，从肾上贯肝膈，入肺中，循喉咙，夹舌本。其支者，从肺出，络心，注胸中。

The kidney meridian of foot – shaoyin starts from the inferior aspect of the small toe and runs obliquely towards the sole（Yongquan，KI 1）. Emerging from the lower aspect of the tuberosity of the navicular bone and running behind the medial malleolus，it enters the hell. Then it ascends along the medial side of the leg to the medial side of the popliteal fossa and goes further upward along the posteromedial aspect of the thigh towards the vertebral column (Changqiang, DU 1), where it enters the kidney, its pertaining organ, and connects with the bladder.

The straight portion of the channel reemerges from the kidney. Ascending and passing through the liver and diaphragm, it enters the lung, runs along the throat, and terminates at the root of the tongue.

A branch springs from the lung, joins the heart and runs into the chest to link with the pericardium meridian of hand – jueyin. (Fig 10 – 1)

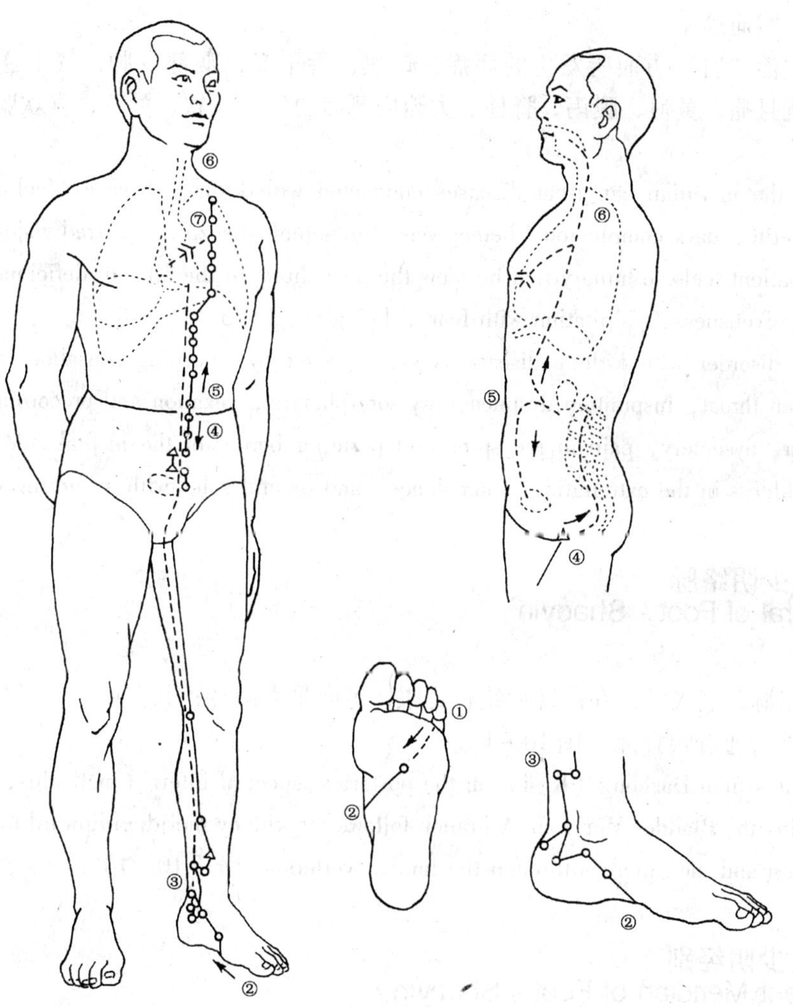

图例 ——本经有穴通路 ……本经无穴通路

Note ——Pathway with points ……Pathway without points

图 10 – 1 足少阴经脉、络脉循行示意图

Fig 10 – 1 The course of the meridian and collateral of foot – shaoyin

（二）经脉病候
The Syndromes of Meridian

本经异常就表现为下列病症：饥饿而不想进食，面色黯黑像漆炭，咳嗽痰唾带血，气急，坐着想起来时，感到两眼昏花视物模糊不清，心像悬空而不安，有似饥饿感；肾气虚者容易发生恐惧，心中怦怦跳动，好像有人要捉捕他；还可发生“骨”方面的深部的气血阻逆，如厥冷、酸痛等。

本经穴主治“肾”方面所发生的病症：口热，舌干燥，咽部发肿，气上逆，咽发干而痛，心内烦扰且痛，黄疸，腹泻，脊柱、大腿内侧后边痛，痿软、厥冷，喜欢躺着，脚心发热而痛。

Points of the meridian can treat diseases connected with kidney disease：feeling hungry yet having no appetite，dark complexion，hemoptysis，bronchial wheezing，blurred vision when standing up，the patient feels so hungry that he feels the heart hung in the air，qi deficiency in this meridian shows nervousness，palpitation with fear of being caught.

Meridian disorder with kidney disease is symptomized by：burning sensation of mouth，dry tongue，swollen throat，inspiratory dyspnea，dry sore pharynx，vexation and precordial pain，jaundice，diarrhea，dysentery，pain in the spine and posterior border of the medial side of the thigh，flaccidity，coldness in the extremities，somnolence，and painful soles with a burning sensation.

二、足少阴络脉
Collateral of Foot - Shaoyin

足少阴络脉，名大钟，在内踝后绕行足跟，走向足太阳经；其支脉与本经相并上行，走到心包下，外行通过腰脊部（图 10－1）。

It originates from Dazhong（KI 4）on the posterior aspect of internal malleolus，it crosses the heel，and joins the Bladder Meridian. A branch follows the kidney meridian upward to a point below the pericardium and then pierces through the lumbar vertebrae（Fig 10－1）.

三、足少阴经别
Divergent Meridian of Foot - Shaoyin

足少阴经别，在腘窝部分出后，与足太阳经别相合并行，上至肾脏，在十四椎（第 2 腰椎）处分出来，归属于带脉；其直行的继续上行，联系于舌根，再出来到项部，会合于足太阳经（图 10－2）。

After deriving from the kidney meridian in the popliteal fossa，it intersects the divergent meridian of the bladder meridian on the thigh. it then runs upward，connecting with the kidney and crossing belt vessel at about the level of the 2nd lumbar vertebra. further it ascends to the root of the tongue and finally, emerges at the nape to join the bladder meridian of foot – taiyang (fig 10 – 2).

四、足少阴经筋
Muscular Region of Foot - Shaoyin

足少阴经筋，起于足小趾下边，入足心部，同足太阴经筋斜走内踝下方，结于足跟，与足太阳经筋会合；向上结于胫骨内髁下，同足太阴经筋一起向上行，沿大腿内侧，结于阴部，沿膂（脊旁肌肉）里夹脊，上后项结于枕骨，与足太阳经筋会合（图 10 –3）。

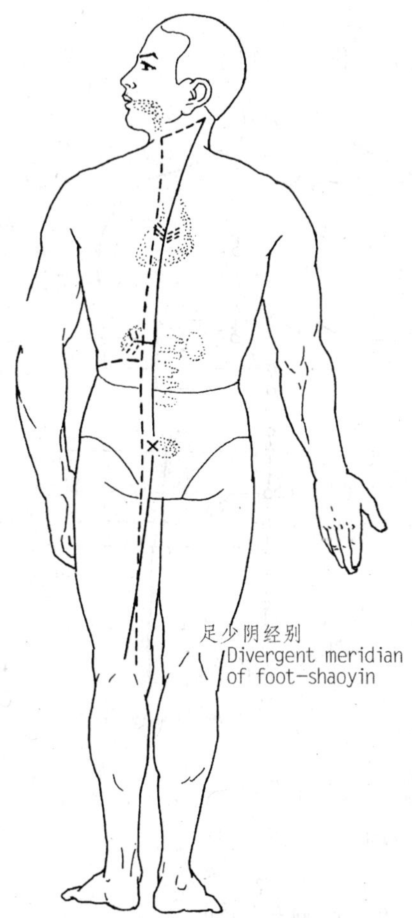

图 10 –2 足少阴经别循行示意图

Fig 10 – 2 The course of the divergent meridian of foot – shaoyin

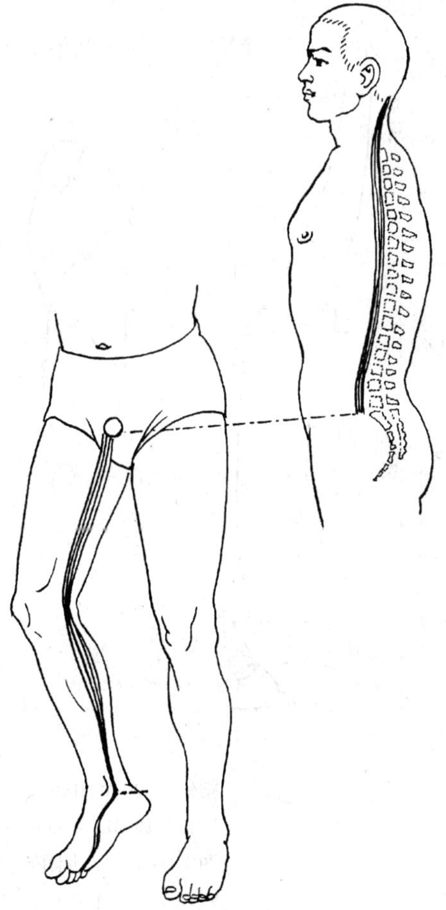

图 10 –3 足少阴经筋循行示意图

Fig 10 – 3 The course of the muscular region of foot – shaoyin

It begins beneath the little toe. together with the muscle region of foot – taiyin, it runs obliquely below the internal malleolus and knots at the heel, converging with muscle region of foot – taiyang (bladder), knotting at the lower, medial aspect of the knee, it joins with muscle region of foot – taiyin (spleen) and ascends along the medial aspect of the thigh to knot at the genital region. a branch proceeds upward along the side of the spine to the nape and knots with the occipital bone, converging with the muscle region of foot – taiyang (bladder) (Fig 10 – 3).

第二节 足少阴腧穴
Acupoints of Foot – Shaoyin

本经左右各 27 个穴位，首穴为涌泉，末穴为俞府（图 10 – 4）。

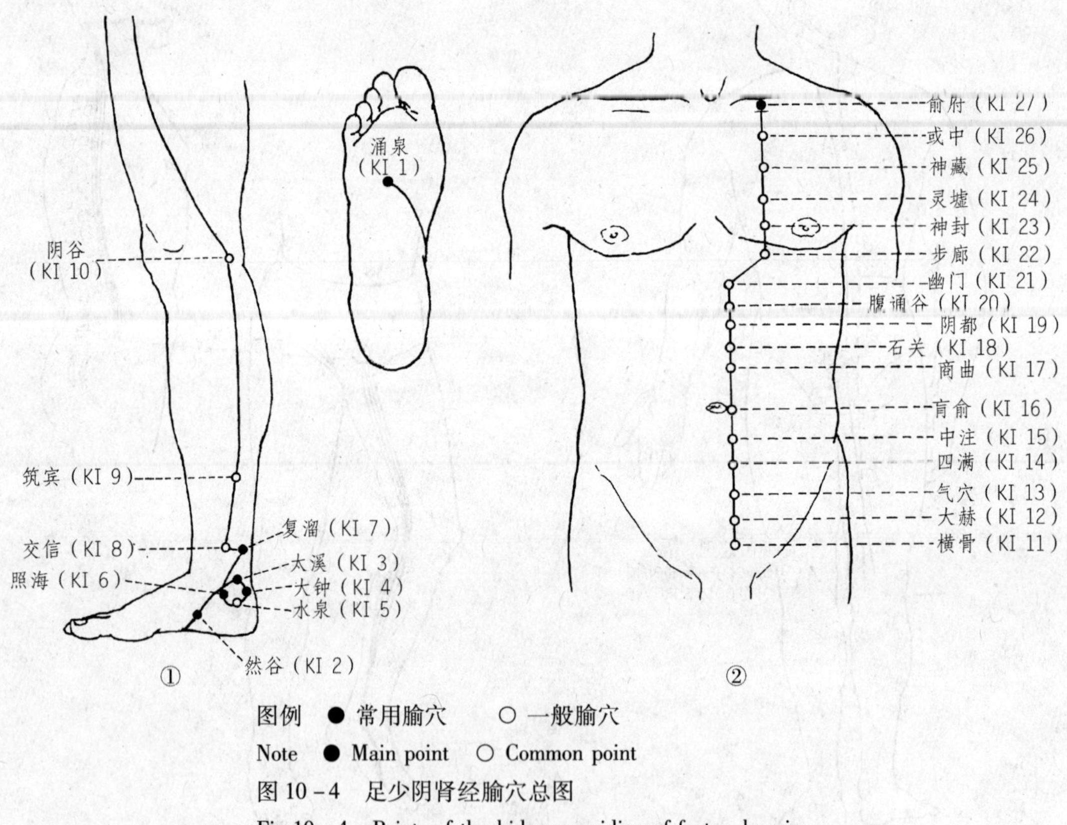

图例 ● 常用腧穴 ○ 一般腧穴

Note ● Main point ○ Common point

图 10 – 4 足少阴肾经腧穴总图

Fig 10 – 4 Points of the kidney meridian of foot – shaoyin

1. 涌泉 Yongquan (KI 1)，井穴
Yongquan (KI 1), Jing - Well Point

【释义】涌，涌出；泉，水泉。水上出为涌泉。穴居足心陷中，经气自下而上，如涌出

之水泉。

【定位】在足底部，卷足时足前部凹陷处，约当足底 2、3 趾趾缝纹头端与足跟连线的前 1/3 与后 2/3 交点上（图 10－5）。

【解剖】血管：深层为足底动脉弓；神经：第 2 趾足底总神经。

【功用】镇静潜阳，回阳救逆，醒神。

【主治】顶心头痛，眩晕，癫狂，咽喉肿痛，舌干，失音，小儿惊风，失眠，便秘，小便不利，足心热，昏厥。

【操作】直刺 0. 3 ~0. 5 寸，可灸。

【Meaning】Yong, to gush; quan, spring. Welled – up water is called gushing spring. The point is on the depression of the sole; the qi of meridian flows upwards as a gushing spring.

【Location】On the sole, in the depression when the foot is in plantar flexion, approximately at the junction of the anterior 1/3 and posterior 2/3 of the line connecting the base of the 2nd and 3rd toes and the heel (Fig 10 – 5).

【Regional anatomy】Vasculature: Deeper, the plantar arterial arch. Innervation: The 2nd common plantar digital nerve.

【Properties】Descend excess from the head, Calm the spirit, Revive consciousness and rescue yang.

【Indications】Headache, blurring of vision, dizziness, sore throat, dryness of the tongue, loss of voice, dysuria, infantile, convulsions, feverish sensation in the sole, loss of consciousness.

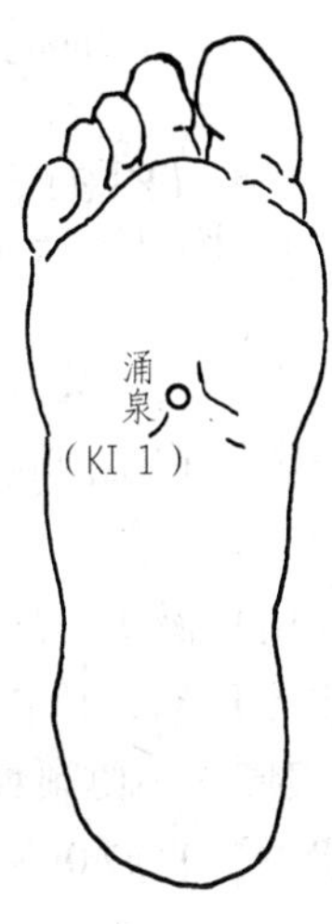

图 10 – 5

Fig 10 – 5

【Needling method】Puncture perpendicularly 0. 3 ~0. 5 cun. Moxibustion is applicable.

2. 然谷（KI 2），荥穴
Rangu (KI 2), Ying - Spring Point

【释义】然，然骨；谷，山谷。穴在然骨（舟骨粗隆）下陷中，如居山谷。

【定位】在足内侧缘，足舟骨粗隆下方，赤白肉际（图 10－6）。

【解剖】血管：深层为足底内侧动脉；神经：浅层布有隐神经的小腿内侧皮支及足底内侧神经皮支。

【功用】清虚热，益肾，利三焦。

【主治】阴挺，阴痒，月经不调，遗精，咳血，小便不利，消渴，泄泻，咽喉肿痛，口噤，小儿脐风。

【操作】直刺 0. 3 ~0. 5 寸，可灸。

【Meaning】Ran, tuberosity of the navicular bone; gu, valley. The point is in the depression below the tuberosity of the navicular bone, as in a valley.

【Location】Anterior and inferior to the medial malleolus, in the depression on the lower border of the tuberosity of the navicular bone（Fig 10 –6）.

【Regional anatomy】Vasculature：The branches of the medial plantar and medial tarsal arteries. Innervation：The terminal branch of the medial crural cutaneous nerve，the medial plantar nerve.

【Properties】Clear deficiency heat，regulates the Kidneys and the lower energizer.

【Indications】Pruritus vulvae，prolapse of uterus，irregular menstruation，nocturnal emission，hemoptysis，thirst，diarrhea，swelling and pain of the dorsum of foot，acute infantile omphalitis.

【Needling method】Puncture perpendicularly 0. 3 ~0. 5 cun. Moxibustion is applicable.

3. 太溪（KI 3），输穴，原穴
Taixi（KI 3），Shu - Stream Point，Yuan - Source Point

【释义】太，甚大；溪，沟溪。穴在内踝与跟腱之间凹陷中，如大的沟溪。

【定位】在足内侧，内踝后方，当内踝尖与跟腱之间的凹陷处（图 10 –6）。

【解剖】血管：深层有胫后动、静脉。神经：浅层布有隐神经的小腿内侧皮支。

【功用】滋阴清热，补益肾阳，补肺纳气，强腰膝。

【主治】咽喉肿痛，齿痛，耳聋，耳鸣，目眩，咳血，咳喘，消渴，遗精，失眠，月经不调，阳痿，小便频数，腰痛。

【操作】直刺 0. 3 ~0. 5 寸，可灸。

【Meaning】Tai，great ；xi，canyon. The point is in the depression between the medial malleolus and Achille's tendon，as in a vast canyon.

【Location】In the depression between the tip of the medial malleolus and Achilles' tendon（Fig 10 –6）.

【Regional anatomy】Vasculature：Anteriorly，the posterior tibial artery and vein. Innervation：The medial crural cutaneous nerve，on the course of the tibial nerve.

【Properties】Nourish Kidney yin and clear deficiency heat，tonifies kidney yang，anchors the qi and benefits the lung，strengthens the lumbar spine.

【Indications】Sore throat，toothache，deafness，tinnitus，dizziness，spitting of blood，asthma，thirst，irregular menstruation，insomnia，nocturnal emission，impotence，frequency of micturition，pain in the lower back.

【Needling method】Puncture perpendicularly 0. 3 ~0. 5 cun. Moxibustion is applicable.

4. 大钟（KI 4），络穴
Dazhong（KI 4），Luo - Connecting Point

【释义】大，大小之大；钟，如“踵”，即足跟。穴在足跟，其骨较大，故名大钟。

【定位】在足内侧，内踝后下方，当跟腱附着部的内侧前方凹陷处（图 10 –6）。

【解剖】血管：深层有胫后动脉的内踝支。神经：浅层布有隐神经的小腿内侧皮支。

【功用】益肾纳气，定志。

【主治】咳血，气喘，腰痛，癃闭，遗尿，足跟痛，便秘，痴呆，嗜卧。

【操作】直刺0.3～0.5寸，可灸。

【Meaning】Da, large; zhong, heel. The point is at the heel. Since the calcaneus bone is large, it is called.

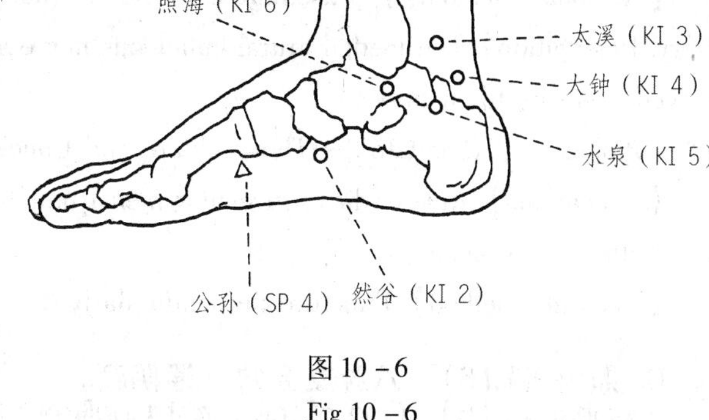

图 10－6

Fig 10－6

【Location】Posterior and inferior to the medial malleolus, in the depression anterior to the medial side of the attachment of Achilles' tendon (Fig 10－6).

【Regional anatomy】Vasculature: The medial calcaneal branch of the posterior tibial artery. Innervation: The medial crural cutaneous nerve, on the course of the medial calcaneal ramus derived from the tibial nerve.

【Properties】Reinforce the kidneys, anchors the qi and benefits the lung, strengthens the will and dispels fear.

【Indications】Spitting of blood, asthma, stiffness and pain of the lower back, dysuria, constipation, pain in the heel, dementia.

【Needling method】Puncture perpendicularly 0.3～0.5 cun. Moxibustion is applicable.

5. 水泉（KI 5），郄穴
Shuiquan (KI 5), Xi－Cleft Point

【释义】水，水液；泉，水泉。水泉有水源之意，肾主水，穴属本经郄穴，能治小便淋漓。

【定位】在足内侧，内踝后下方，当太溪穴直下1寸（指寸），跟骨结节的内侧凹陷处。(图 10－6)

【解剖】血管：深层有胫后动脉。神经：浅层布有隐神经的小腿内侧皮支及足底内侧神经（为胫神经的分支）。

【功用】调经，溢蓄诸经。

【主治】闭经，月经不调，痛经，阴挺，小便不利，子宫内膜炎。

【操作】直刺0.3～0.5寸，可灸。

【Meaning】Shui, water; quan, spring. The water spring means water source. The kidney dominates water clearance. This point is a Xi－Cleft point of the Kidney Meridian and indicated in case of dribbling urine.

【Location】1 cun directly below Taixi (KI 3), in the depression of the medial side of the tuberosity of the calcaneum (Fig 10 –6).

【Regional anatomy】Vasculature: The medial calcaneal branch of the posterior tibial artery. Innervation: The medial crural cutaneous nerve, on the course of the medial calcaneal ramus derived from the tibial nerve.

【Properties】Regulate the Thoroughfare and Conception vessels and regulate menstruation.

【Indications】Amenorrhea, irregular menstruation, dysmenorrhea, prolapse of uterus, dysuria, blurring of vision.

【Needling method】Puncture perpendicularly 0. 3 ~0. 5 cun. Moxibustion is applicable.

6. 照海（KI 6），八脉交会穴（通阴跻）
Zhaohai (KI 6), One of the Eight Confluent Points associated with Yin Heel Vessel

【释义】照，光照；海，海洋。穴属肾经，气盛如海，意为肾中真阳，可光照周身。

【定位】在足内侧，内踝尖下方凹陷处（图 10 –6）。

【解剖】血管：深层有跗内侧动、静脉。神经：浅层布有隐神经的小腿内侧皮支。

【功用】利咽喉，滋阴清热，安神，利下焦。

【主治】月经不调，阴痒，痛经，阴挺，带下，小便频数，癃闭，目赤肿痛，痫证，失眠，咽喉干痛，哮喘。

【操作】直刺 0. 3 ~0. 5 寸，可灸。

【Meaning】Zhao, to shine; hai, sea. The point pertains to the kidney meridian and the qi is abundant as the sea. It means that the real yang of the kidney may illuminate the whole body.

【Location】In the depression below the tip of the medial malleolus (Fig 10 –6).

【Regional anatomy】Vasculature: The posterior tibial artery and vein. Innervation: The medial crural cutaneous nerve.

【Properties】Eliminate the heat from the throat, nourish the Kidneys and clears deficiency heat, regulates the Yin Link vessel, calm the spirit, regulate the lower energizer.

【Indications】Irregular menstruation, morbid leukorrhea, prolapse of uterus, pruritus vulvae, frequency of micturition, retention of urine, constipation, epilepsy, insomnia, sore throat, asthma.

【Needling method】Puncture Perpendicularly 0. 3 ~ 0. 5 cun. Moxibustion is applicable.

7. 复溜（KI 7），经穴
Fuliu (KI 7), Jing - River Point

【释义】复，同“伏”，深伏；溜，流动。穴居照海之上，在此指经气至“海”入而复出并继续流注之意。

【定位】在小腿内侧，太溪直上 2 寸，跟腱的前方（图 10 –7）。

【解剖】血管：深层有胫后动、静脉。神经：浅层布有隐神经的小腿内侧皮支。

【功用】通调水道，利水消肿，补肾强腰膝。

【主治】水肿，腹胀，泄泻，下肢痿痹，自汗，盗汗，热病无汗或汗出不止。

【操作】直刺0.5～0.7寸，可灸。

【Meaning】Fu, continuing; liu, flowing; The point is above Zhaohai and refers to the qi of meridian flowing into the "sea", re-emerging and continuing to flow.

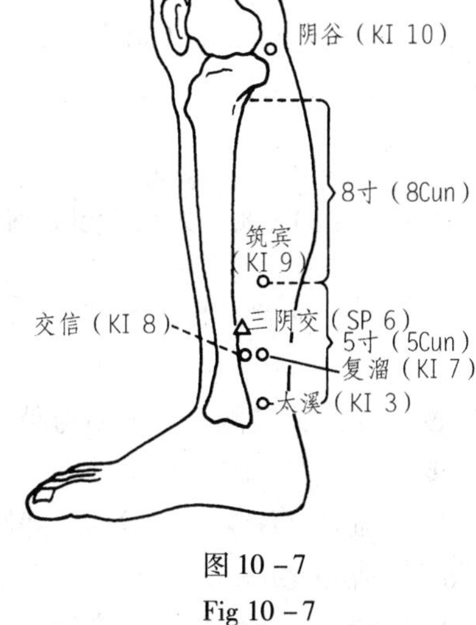

图 10－7

Fig 10－7

【Location】2 cun directly above Taixi (KI 3), on the anterior border of Achilles' tendon (Fig 10－7).

【Regional anatomy】Vasculature: The posterior tibial artery and vein. Innervation: The medial sural and medial crural cutaneous nerves.

【Properties】Invigorate the kidneys, regulate the water passages and treat edema, regulates sweating, eliminate dampness and dampness－heat, strengthen the lumbar region.

【Indications】Edema, abdominal distension, diarrhea, borborygmus, muscular atrophy of the leg, night sweating, spontaneous sweating, febrile diseases without sweating.

【Needling method】Puncture perpendicularly 0.5～0.7 cun. Moxibustion is applicable.

8. 交信（KI 8），阴跻脉之郄穴
Jiaoxin (KI 8), Xi-Cleft Point of Yin Heel Vessel

【释义】交，交会；信，信用。信，五常（仁、义、礼、智、信）之一，属土，指脾。本经脉气在此穴交会脾经。

【定位】在小腿内侧，当太溪直上2寸，复溜前0.5寸，胫骨内侧缘的后方（图10－7）。

【解剖】血管：深层有胫后动、静脉。神经：浅层布有隐神经的小腿内侧皮支。

【功用】调理冲任，清利三焦湿热，调经止血。

【主治】月经不调，痛经，阴挺，崩漏，泄泻，便秘，阴囊肿痛。

【操作】直刺1.0～1.5寸。

【Meaning】Jiao, crossing; xin, belief. Xin is one of the Five Moralities (benevolence, loyalty, courtesy, intelligence and belief), pertaining to earth and referring to the spleen. The qi of meridian is crossed by the spleen meridian at this point.

【Location】0.5 cun anterior to Fuliu (KI 7), 2 cun above Taixi (KI 3) posterior to the medial border of tibia (Fig 10－7).

【Regional anatomy】Vasculature: The posterior tibial artery and vein. Innervation: The medial crural cutaneous nerve.

【Properties】Regulate the Conception and Thoroughfare vessels and adjust menstruation, stop uterine bleeding, clear away heat and dampness from the lower energizer.

【Indications】Irregular menstruation, dysmenorrhea, uterine bleeding, prolapse of uterus, diarrhea, constipation, pain and swelling of testis.

【Needling method】Puncture perpendicularly 1.0~1.5 cun.

9. 筑宾（KI 9），阴维脉之郄穴
Zhubin (KI 9), Xi - Cleft Point of Yin Link Vessel

【释义】筑，强健；宾，通"膑"，泛指膝和小腿。穴在小腿内侧，有使腿膝强健的作用。

【定位】在小腿内侧，当太溪与阴谷的连线上，太溪上5寸，腓肠肌肌腹的内下方（图10-7）。

【解剖】血管：深层有胫后动、静脉。神经：浅层布有隐神经的小腿内侧皮支。

【功用】清心化痰，理气止痛。

【主治】癫狂，小腿疼痛，疝气，呕吐。

【操作】直刺0.5~0.7寸，可灸。

【Meaning】Zhu, strong; bin, knee and leg. The point is on the medial side of the leg. It has the function of strengthening the knee and leg.

【Location】5 cun directly above Taixi (KI 3) at the lower end of the belly of musculus gastrocnemius, on the line drawn from Taixi (KI 3) to Yingu (KI 10) (Fig 10-7).

【Regional anatomy】Vasculature: The posterior tibial artery and vein. Innervation: The medial sural and medial crural cutaneous nerves.

【Properties】Clear the Heart and transform phlegm, regulate qi and alleviate pain.

【Indications】Mental disorders, pain in the foot and lower leg, hernia, vomiting.

【Needling method】Puncture perpendicularly 0.5~0.7 cun. Moxibustion is applicable.

10. 阴谷（KI 10），合穴
Yingu (KI 10), He - Sea Point

【释义】阴，阴阳之阴；谷，山谷。内为阴，穴在膝关节内侧，局部凹陷如谷。

【定位】在腘窝内侧，屈膝时，当半腱肌腱与半膜肌腱之间（图10-8）。

【解剖】血管：深层有膝上内侧动、静脉。神经：浅层布有股后皮神经。

【功用】清利湿热，通经止痛。

【主治】阳痿，疝气，崩漏，癃闭，膝股痛，癫狂。

【操作】直刺0.8~1.0寸，可灸。

【Meaning】Yin, yin of yin – yang; gu, valley. The interior is yin. The point is at the medial side of the knee joint; the local depression is like a valley.

【Location】When the knee is flexed, the point is on the medial side of the popliteal fossa, between the tendons of m. semitendinosus and semimembranosus (Fig 10 – 8).

【Regional anatomy】Vasculature: The medial superior genicular artery and vein. Innervation: The medial femoral cutaneous nerve.

【Properties】Clear dampness – heat from the lower energizer, benefit the Kidneys, activate the channel and alleviates pain.

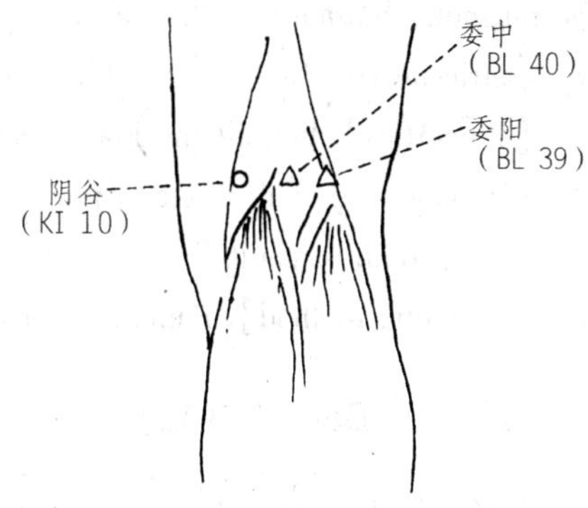

图 10 – 8
Fig 10 – 8

【Indications】Impotence, hernia, uterine bleeding, dysuria, pain in the knee and popliteal fossa, mental disorders.

【Needling method】Puncture perpendicularly 0. 8 ~ 1. 0 cun. Moxibustion is applicable.

11. 横骨 Henggu (KI 11)

【释义】横骨，为耻骨之古称。穴在耻骨上缘上方，故称横骨。

【定位】在下腹部，当脐中下 5 寸，前正中线旁开 0. 5 寸（图 10 – 9）。

【解剖】血管：深层有腹壁下动、静脉；神经：浅层布有髂腹下神经前皮支。

【功用】利三焦。

【主治】少腹胀痛，小便不利，遗尿，阳痿，阴痛，疝气，遗精。

【操作】直刺 1. 0 ~ 1. 5 寸，可灸。

【Meaning】Henggu is the ancient name of the pubis. The point is on the superior border of the pubis.

【Location】5 cun below the umbilicus, on the superior border of symphysis pubis, 0. 5 cun lateral to the anterior midline of the chest (Fig 10 – 9).

【Regional anatomy】Vasculature:

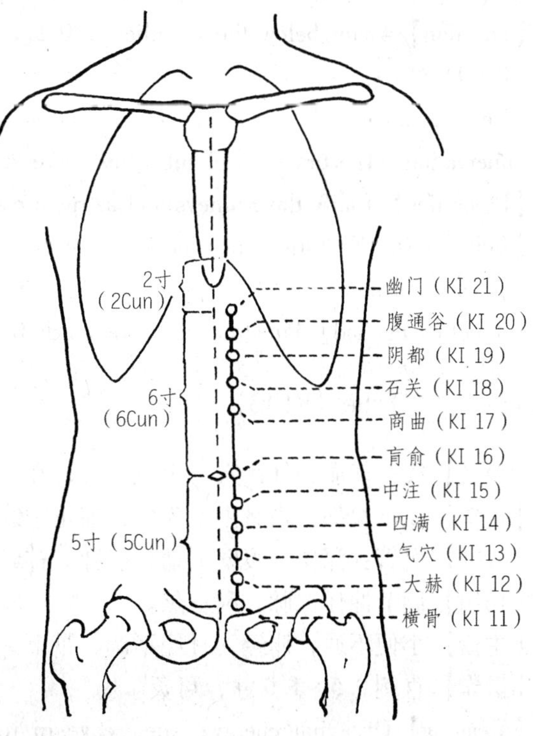

图 10 – 9
Fig 10 – 9

The muscular branches of the inferior epigastric artery and vein. Innervation: The branch of the iliohypogastric nerve.

【Properties】Benefit the lower energizer.

【Indications】Fullness and pain of the lower abdomen, dysuria enuresis, nocturnal emission, impotence, pain of genitalia.

【Needling method】Puncture perpendicularly 1.0～1.5 cun. Moxibustion is applicable.

12. 大赫 Dahe (KI 12)

【释义】大，大小之大；赫，显赫。显赫有盛大之意。此穴为足少阴、冲脉之会，下焦元气充盛之处。

【定位】在下腹部，当脐中下4寸，前正中线旁开0.5寸（图10-9）。

【解剖】血管：深层有腹壁下动、静脉。神经：胸神经和腰神经前支的分支。

【功用】补肾益精。

【主治】遗精，阳痿，不孕，阴痛，阴挺，带下。

【操作】直刺0.5～1.0寸，可灸。

【Meaning】Da, great; he, plentiful. This point is the confluence of the kidney meridian and Chongmai, where the primary qi of the lower jiao is plentiful.

【Location】4 cun below the umbilicus, 0.5 cun lateral to the anterior midline of the chest (Fig 10-9).

【Regional anatomy】Vasculature: The muscular branches of the inferior epigastric artery and vein. Innervation: The branches of subcostal nerve and the iliohypogastric nerve.

【Properties】Tonify the Kidneys and astringe essence.

【Indications】Nocturnal emission, impotence, morbid leukorrhea, pain in the external genitalia, prolapse of uterus.

【Needling method】Puncture perpendicularly 0.5～1.0 cun. Moxibustion is applicable.

13. 气穴 Qixue (KI 13)

【释义】气，气血的气；穴，土室。气，在此指肾气。穴在关元旁，为肾气藏聚之室。

【定位】在下腹部，当脐中下3寸，前正中线旁开0.5寸（图10-9）。

【解剖】血管：深层有腹壁下动、静脉。神经：胸神经和腰神经前支的分支。

【功用】调节冲任二脉，利三焦。

【主治】小便不通，痛经，月经不调，带下，经闭，崩漏，腹痛，泄泻。

【操作】直刺0.5～1.0寸，可灸。

【Meaning】Qi, vital energy; xue, cave. qi refers to the qi of kidney. The point is beside Guanyuan (RN 4) like a cave where the kidney qi is stored.

【Location】3 cun below the umbilicus, 0.5 cun lateral to the anterior midline of the chest

(Fig 10 -9).

【Regional anatomy】Vasculature: The muscular branches of the inferior epigastric artery and vein. Innervation: The branches of subcostal nerve and the iliohypogastric nerve.

【Properties】Regulate the thoroughfare vessel and conception vessel, regulate the lower energizer.

【Indications】Irregular menstruation, dysmenorrhea, dysuria, abdominal pain, diarrhea.

【Needling method】Puncture perpendicularly 0.5 ~ 1.0 cun. Moxibustion is applicable.

14. 四满 Siman (KI 14)

【释义】四，第四；满，充满。此为足少阴肾经入腹的第4穴，可治腹部胀满。

【定位】仰卧。在下腹部，当脐中下2寸，前正中线旁开0.5寸（图10-9）。

【解剖】血管：深层有腹壁下动、静脉，神经：胸神经和腰神经前支的分支。

【功用】通调下焦，理气活血止痛，利尿。

【主治】腹痛腹胀，腹泻，遗精，遗尿，月经不调，带下，疝气，便秘，产后腹痛。

【操作】直刺0.5~1.0寸，可灸。

【Meaning】Si, the 4th; man, fullness. This is the 4th point of the kidney meridian to the abdomen, and is indicated in abdominal distension.

【Location】2 cun below the umbilicus, 0.5 cun lateral to the anterior midline of the chest (Fig 10 -9).

【Regional anatomy】Vasculature: The muscular branches of the inferior epigastric artery and vein. Innervation: The branches of subcostal nerve and the iliohypogastric nerve.

【Properties】Benefit the lower energizer and alleviate pain, regulates qi to resolve blood stasis, regulates the water passages and promote urination.

【Indications】Abdominal pain and distension, diarrhea, nocturnal emission, irregular menstruation, dysmenorrhea, constipation, postpartum abdominal pain

【Needling method】Puncture perpendicularly 0.5 ~ 1.0 cun. Moxibustion is applicable.

15. 中注 Zhongzhu (KI 15)

【释义】中，中间；注，灌注。肾经之气由此灌注中焦。

【定位】在下腹部，当脐中下1寸，前正中线旁开0.5寸（图10-9）。

【解剖】血管：深层有腹壁下动、静脉，神经：胸神经和腰神经前支的分支。

【功用】通肠，调理下焦。

【主治】月经不调，痛经，腹痛，便秘，泄泻。

【操作】直刺0.5~1.0寸，可灸。

【Meaning】Zhong, middle; zhu, to pour. The qi of kidney meridian pours from this point into the middle jiao.

【Location】1 cun below the umbilicus, 0.5 cun lateral to the anterior midline of the chest (Fig 10－9).

【Regional anatomy】Vasculature: The muscular branches of the inferior epigastric artery and vein. Innervation: The branches of subcostal nerve and the iliohypogastric nerve.

【Properties】Regulates the intestines, adjust the lower energizer.

【Indications】Irregular menstruation, abdominal pain, constipation.

【Needling method】Puncture perpendicularly 0.5～1.0 cun. Moxibustion is applicable.

16. 肓俞 Huangshu (KI 16)

【释义】肓，肓膜；俞，输注。肾经之气由此输注肓膜。

【定位】仰卧。在中腹部，当脐中旁开0.5寸（图10－9）。

【解剖】血管：深层有腹壁下动、静脉，神经：胸神经和腰神经前支的分支。

【功用】理气止痛，温通肠腑。

【主治】腹痛，腹胀，呕吐，便秘，泄泻，月经不调，疝气，腰脊痛。

【操作】直刺0.5～1.0寸，可灸。

【Meaning】Huang, Huang－membrane; shu, to transport. The qi of kidney infuses from this point into the Huang－membrane.

【Location】0.5 cun lateral to the umbilicus (Fig 10－9).

【Regional anatomy】Vasculature: The muscular branches of the inferior epigastric artery and vein. Innervation: The branches of subcostal nerve and the iliohypogastric nerve.

【Properties】Regulate qi and alleviate pain, adjust and warm the intestines.

【Indications】Abdominal pain and distension, vomiting, constipation, diarrhea, hernia.

【Needling method】Puncture perpendicularly 0.5～1.0 cun. Moxibustion is applicable

17. 商曲 Shangqu (KI 17)

【释义】商，五音之一，属金；曲，弯曲。商为金音，大肠属金；此穴内对大肠弯曲处。

【定位】在上腹部，当脐中上2寸，前正中线旁开0.5寸（图10－9）。

【解剖】血管：深层有腹壁上动、静脉。神经：第9胸神经。

【功用】消积止痛。

【主治】腹痛，泄泻，便秘。

【操作】直刺0.5～1.0寸，可灸。

【Meaning】Shang, one of the Five Sounds, pertaining to metal; qu, twist. Shang is s sound pertaining to metal and the large intestine also pertains to metal. This point corresponds to the twisting of intestines.

【Location】2 cun above the umbilicus, 0.5 cun lateral to the anterior midline of the chest

(Fig 10 –9).

【Regional anatomy】Vasculature: The branches of the superior and inferior epigastric arteries and veins. Innervation: The 9th intercostal nerves.

【Properties】Dispel accumulation and alleviate pain.

【Indications】Abdominal pain, diarrhea, constipation.

【Needling method】Puncture perpendicularly 0.5 ~1.0 cun. Moxibustion is applicable.

18. 石关 Shiguan (KI 18)

【释义】石，石头；关，重要。石头有坚实之意，此穴为治腹部坚实病症的要穴。

【定位】在上腹部，当脐中上3寸，前正中线旁开0.5寸（图10 –9）。

【解剖】血管：深层有腹壁上动、静脉。神经：第8胸神经。

【功用】和胃缓急止痛，理气化瘀。

【主治】呕吐，腹痛，便秘，产后腹痛，不孕。

【操作】直刺0.5 ~1.0寸，可灸。

【Meaning】Shi, stone; guan, importance. Shi here means hard in consistency. This is an important point in treating abdominal diseases of hard consistency.

【Location】3 cun above the umbilicus, 0.5 cun lateral to the anterior midline of the chest (Fig 10 –9).

【Regional anatomy】Vasculature: The branches of the superior epigastric artery and vein. Innervation: The 8th intercostal nerves.

【Properties】Regulate the lower energizer and alleviate pain, regulates qi to resolve blood stasis, harmonize stomach.

【Indications】Vomiting, abdominal pain, constipation, postpartum abdominal pain, sterility.

【Needling method】Puncture perpendicularly 0.5 ~1.0 cun. Moxibustion is applicable.

19. 阴都 Yindu (KI 19)

【释义】阴，阴阳之阴；都，会聚。阴，指腹部，指阴经。穴在腹部，为水谷聚集之处。

【定位】在上腹部，当脐中上4寸，前正中线旁开0.5寸（图10 –9）。

【解剖】血管：深层有腹壁上动、静脉。神经：第8胸神经。

【功用】和胃理气，降逆止呃。

【主治】肠鸣腹痛，腹胀，便秘，呕吐，不孕。

【操作】直刺0.5 ~1.0寸，可灸。

【Meaning】Yin, yin of yin – yang; du, to gather. yin refers to the abdomen and the yin meridian. The point is in the abdomen where water and food meet.

【Location】4 cun above the umbilicus, 0.5 cun lateral to the anterior midline of the chest (Fig 10－9).

【Regional anatomy】Vasculature: The branches of the superior epigastric artery and vein. Innervation: The 8th intercostal nerves.

【Properties】Regulate qi and harmonize the Stomach, lower rebellion and alleviate cough and wheezing.

【Indications】Borborygmus, abdominal pain, epigastric distention, constipation, vomiting, sterility.

【Needling method】Puncture perpendicularly 0.5～1.0 cun. Moxibustion is applicable.

20. 腹通谷 Futonggu (KI 20)

【释义】腹，腹部；通，通过；谷，水谷。穴在腹部，为通过水谷之处。

【定位】在上腹部，当脐中上5寸，前正中线旁开0.5寸（图10－9）。

【解剖】血管：深层有腹壁上动、静脉。神经：第8胸神经。

【功用】斡旋中焦，宽胸理气化痰。

【主治】腹痛，腹胀，呕吐，消化不良，心痛，心悸。

【操作】直刺0.5～1.0寸，可灸。

【Meaning】Fu, abdomen; tong, passing; gu, water and food. The point is in the abdomen, where water and food pass.

【Location】5 cun above the umbilicus, 0.5 cun lateral to the anterior midline of the chest (Fig 10－9).

【Regional anatomy】Vasculature: The branches of the superior epigastric artery and vein. Innervation: The 8th intercostal nerves.

【Properties】Harmonize the middle energizer, smooth the chest and transform phlegm.

【Indications】Abdominal pain and distention, vomiting, indigestion.

【Needling method】Puncture perpendicularly 0.5～1.0 cun. Moxibustion is applicable.

21. 幽门 Youmen (KI 21)

【释义】幽，隐藏在腹部深处，门，门户。胃之下口称幽门。穴之深处，邻近幽门。

【定位】在上腹部，当脐中上6寸，前正中线旁开0.5寸（图10－9）。

【解剖】血管：深层有腹壁上动、静脉。神经：第8胸神经。

【功用】健脾和胃，疏肝理气止痛。

【主治】腹痛，腹胀，呕吐，泄泻，恶心，呕吐。

【操作】直刺0.3～0.7寸，内有肝脏，不可深刺，可灸。

【Meaning】You, hiding; men, door. The point pertains to kidney meridian and is located where the lower orifice of stomach is situated interiorly. It is hidden deep in the abdomen.

【Location】6 cun above the umbilicus, 0. 5 cun lateral to the anterior midline of the chest (Fig 10 –9).

【Regional anatomy】Vasculature: The branches of the superior epigastric artery and vein. Innervation: The 8th intercostal nerves.

【Properties】Invigorate spleen and harmonize stomach, disperse liver qi, benefit the chest and breast, alleviates pain.

【Indications】Abdominal pain and distension, indigestion, vomiting, diarrhea, nausea.

【Needling method】Puncture perpendicularly 0. 3 ~0. 7 cun. To avoid injuring the liver, deep insertion is not advisable. Moxibustion is applicable.

22. 步廊 Bulang (KI 22)

【释义】步，步行；廊，走廊。穴当中庭门旁；经气至此，如步行于庭堂之两廊。

【定位】在胸部，当第5肋间隙，前正中线旁开2寸（图10–10）。

【解剖】血管：胸廓内动、静脉。神经：浅层布有第5肋间神经的前皮支。

【功用】宽胸降气。

【主治】咳嗽，气喘，胸胁胀满，呕吐，食欲减退。

【操作】斜刺或平刺0. 3 ~0. 5寸，内为心脏，不可深刺，可灸。

【Meaning】Bu, step; lang, corridor. The point lies along the Zhongting (RN 16) epigastric region. When the qi of meridian flows here, it is like stepping into a corridor on either side of a courtyard.

【Location】In the 5th intercostal space, 2 cun lateral to the anterior midline of the chest (Fig 10 –10).

【Regional anatomy】Vasculature: The 5th intercostal artery and vein. Innervation: The anterior cutaneous branch of the 5th intercostals nerve.

【Properties】Unbind the chest, descend the adverse qi of the lung and stomach.

【Indications】Cough, asthma, distension and fullness in the chest and hypochondriac region, vomiting, anorexia.

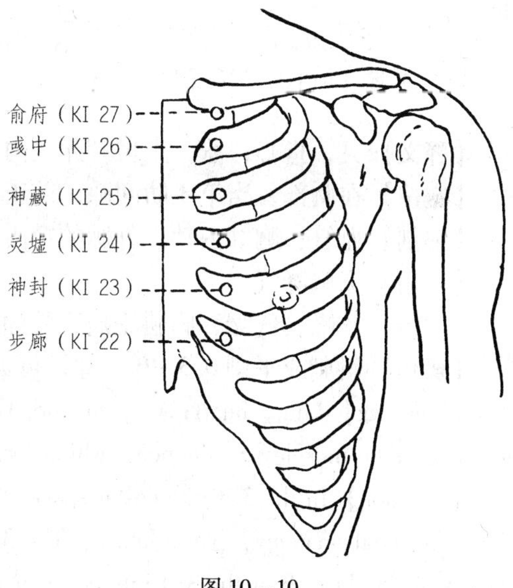

图10 –10

Fig 10 –10

【Needling method】Puncture obliquely or transversely 0. 3 ~0. 5 cun. To avoid injuring the heart, deep insertion is not advisable. Moxibustion is applicable.

23. 神封 Shenfeng（KI 23）

【释义】神，指心；封，领属。穴之所在为心之所属。

【定位】在胸部，当第4肋间隙，前正中线旁开2寸（图10－10）。

【解剖】血管：胸廓内动、静脉，神经：浅层布有第4肋间神经的前皮支。

【功用】宽胸降气。

【主治】咳嗽，气喘，胸胁胀满，乳痈，呕吐。

【操作】斜刺或平刺0.3～0.5寸，可灸。

【Meaning】Shen, heart; feng, manor. The region where the point is located pertains to the heart.

【Location】In the 4th intercostal space, 2 cun lateral to the anterior midline（Fig 10－10）.

【Regional anatomy】Vasculature: The 4th intercostal artery and vein. Innervation: The anterior cutaneous branch of the 4th intercostal nerves.

【Properties】Unbind the chest, descend the adverse qi.

【Indications】Cough, asthma, fullness in the chest and hypochondriac region, mastitis, vomiting.

【Needling method】Puncture obliquely or transversely 0.3～0.5 cun. Moxibustion is applicable.

24. 灵墟 Lingxu（KI 24）

【释义】灵，指心；墟，土堆。此穴内应心脏，外当肌肉隆起处，其隆起犹如土堆。

【定位】在胸部，当第3肋间隙，前正中线旁开2寸（图10－10）。

【解剖】血管：胸廓内动、静脉的穿支。神经：浅层布有第3肋间神经的前皮支。

【功用】宽胸降气。

【主治】咳嗽，气喘，胸胁胀痛，乳痈，呕吐。

【操作】斜刺或平刺0.3～0.5寸，可灸。

【Meaning】Ling, heart; wu, mound. The point internally corresponds to the heart; externally it is on thee muscle prominence, which looks like a mound.

【Location】In the 3rd intercostal space, 2 cun lateral to the anterior midline（Fig 10－10）.

【Regional anatomy】Vasculature: The 3rd intercostal artery and vein. Innervation: The anterior cutaneous branch of the 3rd intercostal nerves.

【Properties】Unbind the chest, descend the adverse qi.

【Indications】Cough, asthma, fullness in the chest and hypochondriac region, mastitis.

【Needling method】Puncture obliquely or transversely 0.3～0.5 cun. Moxibustion is applicable.

25. 神藏 Shencang（KI 25)

【释义】神，指心；藏，匿藏。穴当心神匿藏之处。

【定位】在胸部，当第2肋间隙，前正中线旁开2寸（图10-10)。

【解剖】血管：胸廓内动、静脉的穿支。神经：浅层布有第2肋间神经的前皮支。

【功用】宽胸降气。

【主治】咳嗽，气喘，胸痛，呕吐。

【操作】斜刺或平刺0.3~0.5寸，可灸。

【Meaning】Shen, heart; cang, concealment. The point is where the mind is concealed.

【Location】In the 2nd intercostal space, 2 cun lateral to the anterior midline (Fig 10-10).

【Regional anatomy】Vasculature: The 2nd intercostal artery and vein. Innervation: The anterior cutaneous branch of the 2nd intercostal nerves.

【Properties】Unbind the chest, descend the adverse qi.

【Indications】Cough, asthma, chest pain, vomiting.

【Needling method】Puncture obliquely or transversely 0.3~0.5 cun. Moxibustion is applicable.

26. 彧中 Yuzhong（KI 26)

【释义】彧，通郁；中，中间。郁，有茂盛之意，穴当肾气行于胸中大盛之处。

【定位】在胸部，当第1肋间隙，前正中线旁开2寸（图10-10)。

【解剖】血管：胸廓内动、静脉的穿支。神经：浅层布有第1肋间神经的前皮支。

【功用】宽胸降气，化痰止咳。

【主治】咳嗽，气喘，咳嗽痰多，胸胁胀满。

【操作】斜刺或平刺0.3~0.5寸，可灸。

【Meaning】Yu, luxuriance; zhong, middle. The point is where the qi of kidney is luxuriant when flowing into the chest.

【Location】In the 1st intercostal space, 2 cun lateral to the anterior midline (Fig 10-10).

【Regional anatomy】Vasculature: The 1st intercostal artery and vein. Innervation: The anterior cutaneous branch of the 1st intercostal nerves.

【Properties】Unbind the chest and descend the adverse qi, transforms phlegm and alleviates cough.

【Indications】Cough, asthma, accumulation of phlegm, fullness in the chest and hypochondriac region.

【Needling method】Puncture obliquely or transversely 0.3~0.5 cun. Moxibustion is applicable.

27. 俞府 Shufu（KI 27）

【释义】俞，输注；府，通“腑”。肾之经气由此输入内腑。

【定位】在胸部，当锁骨下缘，前正中线旁开2寸（图10－10）。

【解剖】血管：胸廓内动、静脉，神经：浅层布有锁骨上内侧神经。

【功用】宽胸化痰，降逆止呃。

【主治】咳嗽，气喘，胸痛，呕吐。

【操作】斜刺或平刺0.3～0.5寸，可灸。

【Meaning】Shu，point；fu，fu organ. The qi of kidney infuses from this point into the fu organs.

【Location】In the depression on the lower border of the clavicle，2 cun lateral to the anterior midline（Fig 10－10）.

【Regional anatomy】Vasculature：The anterior perforating branches of the internal mammary artery and vein. Innervation：The medial supraclavicular nerve.

【Properties】Unbind the chest，transforms phlegm and alleviate cough and wheezing，harmonizes stomach and descend the adverse qi.

【Indications】Cough，asthma，chest pain，vomiting.

【Needling method】Puncture obliquely or transversely 0.3～0.5 cun. Moxibustion is applicable.

复习思考题
Review Questions

1. 根据足少阴经脉循行，说明本经与肝、肺、心脏等的关系。

Discuss the relationship between the kidney and other zang－organs including the liver，lung and heart.

2. 归纳本经五输穴的定位。

List the location of the five－shu points in the kidney meridian.

3. 照海与申脉穴在主治上有何区别和联系？

Discuss the differences and relationships between Zhaohai（KI 6）and Shenmai（BL 62）?

4. 太溪穴的主治要点有哪些？

What are the indications of Taixi（KI 3）?

5. 步廊与俞府如何针刺？

How do you do acupuncture for points on the kidney Meridian from Bulang（KI 22）to Shufu（KI 27）?

第十一章 手厥阴经络与腧穴
Meridian and Collateral and Its Acupoints of Hand - Jueyin

第一节 手厥阴经络
Meridian and Collateral of Hand - Jueyin

一、手厥阴经脉
Meridian of Hand - Jueyin

(一) 经脉循行
The Course of Meridian

手厥阴心包经，从胸中开始，浅出属于心包，通过膈肌，经历胸部、上腹和下腹，络于上、中、下三焦。

胸中支脉，沿着胸内出胁部，当腋下3寸处（天池）向上到达腋下，沿上臂内侧（天泉），行于手太阴、手少阴之间，进入肘中（曲泽），下至前臂，走两筋（桡侧腕屈肌腱与掌长肌腱）之间（郄门、间使、内关、大陵），进入掌中（劳宫），沿中指桡侧出于末端。

掌中支脉，从掌中分出，沿无名指出于末端，接手少阳三焦经（图11-1）。

《灵枢·经脉》原文：心主手厥阴心包络之脉，起于胸中，出属心包，下膈，历络三焦。

其支者，循胸出胁，下腋三寸，上抵腋下，循臑内，行太阴、少阴之间，入肘中，下臂，行两筋之间，入掌中，循中指，出其端。

其支者，别掌中，循小指次指出其端。

The meridian of hand - jueyin originates from the chest. Emerging, it enters its pertaining organ, the pericardium. Then it descends through the diaphragm to connect successively with the upper, middle and lower jiao from the chest to the abdomen.

A branch arising from the chest runs inside the chest emerges from the costal region at the point 3 cun below the axilla (Tianchi, PC 1) and ascends to the axilla. Following the medial aspect of the upper arm, it runs between the lung meridian of hand - taiyin and the heart meridian of hand - shaoyin to the cubital fossa, further downwards to the forearm between the tendons of m. palmaris longus and m. flexor carpi radialis entering the palm. From there, it passes along the middle finger right down to its tip.

Another branch arising from the palm at Laogong (PC 8), runs along the ring finger to its tip and links with the triple energizer meridian of hand - shaoyang (Fig 11 - 1).

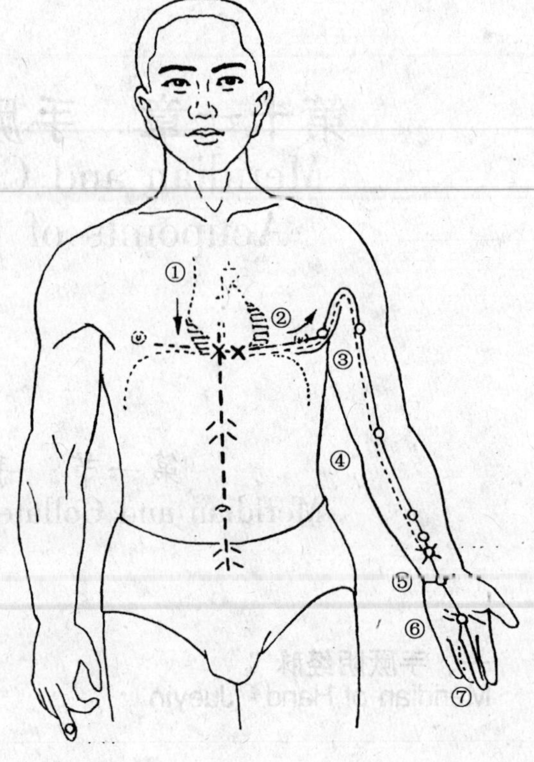

图 11 - 1 手厥阴经脉、络脉循环示意图

Fig 11 - 1 The course of the meridian and collateral of hand - jueyin

(二) 经脉病候
The Syndromes of Meridian

本经异常可表现为下列病症：心中热，前臂和肘部拘挛疼痛，腋窝部肿胀，甚至胸中满闷，心悸，面赤，眼睛昏黄，喜笑不止。

本经主治"脉"方面所发生的病症：心胸烦闷，心痛，掌心发热。

Disorder of the meridian is characterized by: feverish sensation, spasm and contraction of the arm and elbow, swelling in the axilla, chest and hypochondria congestion, violent palpitation with irritability, flushed face, icteric sclera, mania.

The main symptoms due to vessel's disorders are: irritability over the chest, cardiodynia, heat in the palm.

二、手厥阴络脉
Collateral of Hand - Jueyin

手厥阴络脉，名内关，在腕关节后 2 寸处，出于两筋之间，分支走向手少阳经脉，并沿经向上联系心包，散络于心系（图 11 - 1）。

It begins from Neiguan (PC 6). 2 cun above the wrist, disperses between the two tenders and runs along the Pericardium Meridian to the Pericardium, and finally connects with the heart (Fig 11 - 1).

三、手厥阴经别
Divergent Meridian of Hand - Jueyin

手厥阴经别，从腋下3寸处（天池）分出，进入胸腹，分别归属上、中、下三焦，上经喉咙，浅出于耳后，与手少阳经会合于完骨下方（图11－2）。

After deriving from the pericardium channel at a point three cun below the axilla, it enters the chest and communicates with the triple energizer. A branch ascends across the throat and emerges behind the ear and then converges with the triple energizer meridian (Fig 11－2).

四、手厥阴经筋
Muscular Region of Hand - Jueyin

手厥阴经筋，起于中指，与手太阴经筋并行，结于肘内侧；经上臂内侧，结于腋下，分散前后夹两胁。分支进入腋内，布散胸中，结于膈部（图11－3）。

It arises from the palmar aspect of the middle finger and follows the muscle region of hand－taiyin (lung) upward. It first knots at the medial aspect of the elbow, and afterwards below the axilla. Then it descends, dispersing at the front and back sides of the ribs. A branch enters the chest below the axilla and spreads over the diaphragm (Fig 11－3).

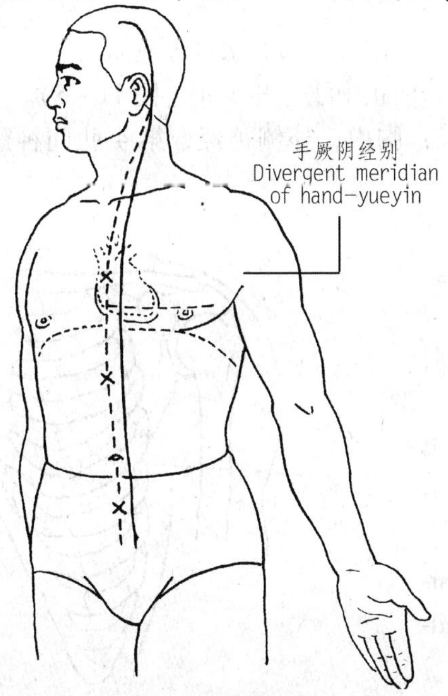

图11－2 手厥阴经别循行示意图

Fig 11－2 The course of the divergent meridian of hand－jueyin

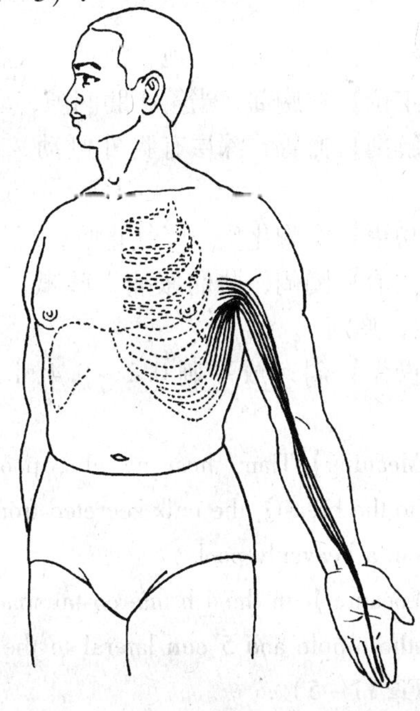

图11－3 手厥阴经筋循行示意图

Fig 11－3 The course of the muscular region of hand－jueyin

第二节 手厥阴腧穴
Acupoints of Hand – Jueyin

本经左右各 9 个穴位，首穴为天池，末穴为中冲（图 11 –4）。

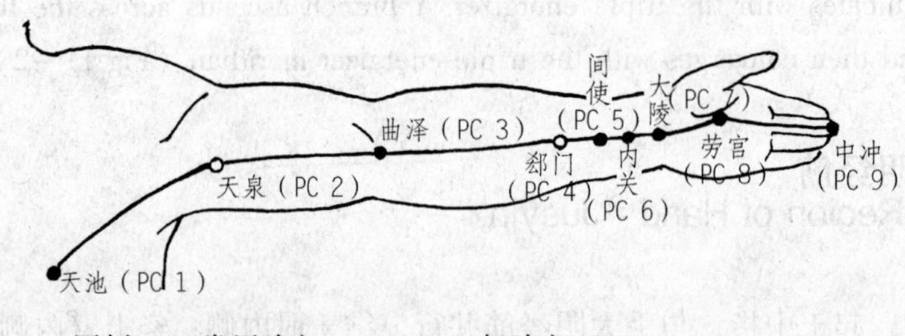

图 11 –4 手厥阴心包经腧穴总图

Fig 11 – 4 Points of the pericardium meridian of hand – jueyin

1. 天池 Tianchi (PC 1)

【释义】天，天空；池，池塘。穴在乳旁；乳房之泌乳，如有水自天池而出。

【定位】在胸部，当第 4 肋间隙，乳头外 1 寸，前正中线旁开 5 寸（图 11 –5）。

【解剖】血管：深层有胸外侧动、静脉，神经：胸内、外侧神经，第 4 肋间神经外侧皮支。

【功用】宽胸化痰，降气止呕，理气散结。

【主治】胸闷，胁肋胀痛，咳嗽，气喘，乳痈，乳汁少，瘰疬。

【操作】斜刺或平刺 0.2 ~ 0.4 寸，不可深刺，可灸。

【Meaning】Tian, heaven; chi, pool. The point is lateral to the breast; the milk secreted from the breast is as if from a heavenly pool.

【Location】In the 4th intercostal space, 1 cun lateral to the nipple and 5 cun lateral to the anterior midline (Fig 11 –5).

【Regional anatomy】Vasculature: The branchs of the lateral thoracic artery and vein. Innervation: The

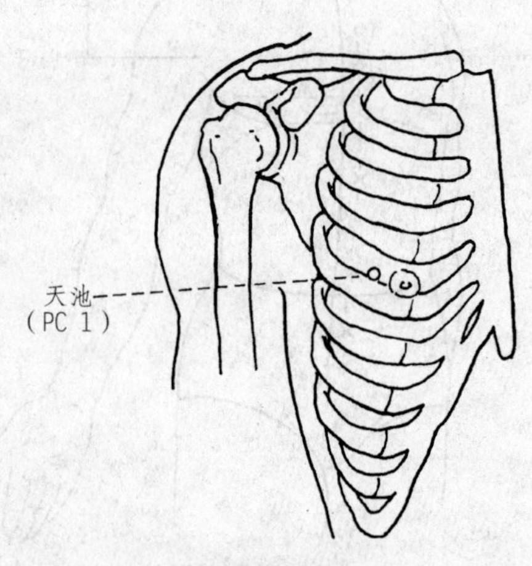

图 11 –5

Fig 11 –5

muscular branch of the anterior thoracic nerve, the 4th intercostal nerves.

【Properties】Unbind the chest, transform phlegm and descend rebellion, regulates qi and dissipates nodules, benefit the breasts.

【Indications】Suffocating sensation in the chest, pain in the hypochondriac region, swelling and pain of the axillary region, cough, asthma.

【Needling method】Puncture obliquely or transversely 0. 2 ~0. 4 cun. Deep puncture is not advisable. Moxibustion is applicable.

2. 天泉 Tianquan (PC 2)

【释义】天，天空；泉，泉水。源于天池的经气由此而下，如泉水从天而降。

【定位】在臂内侧，当腋前纹头下 2 寸，肱二头肌的长、短头之间（图 11 -6）。

【解剖】血管：肱动、静脉的肌支。神经：浅层分布着臂内侧皮神经的分支。

【功用】宽胸理气，活血止痛。

【主治】心痛，咳嗽，胸胁胀痛，背痛，侧臂痛。

【操作】直刺 0. 5 ~0. 7 寸，可灸。

【Meaning】Tian, heaven; quan, spring. The qi of meridian originating from Tianchi flows downward as spring water from heaven.

【Location】2 cun below the level of the anterior axillary fold, between the two heads of m. biceps brachii. (Fig 11 -6)

【Regional anatomy】Vasculature: The muscular branches of the branchial artery and vein. Innervation: The branch of medial brachial cutaneous nerve.

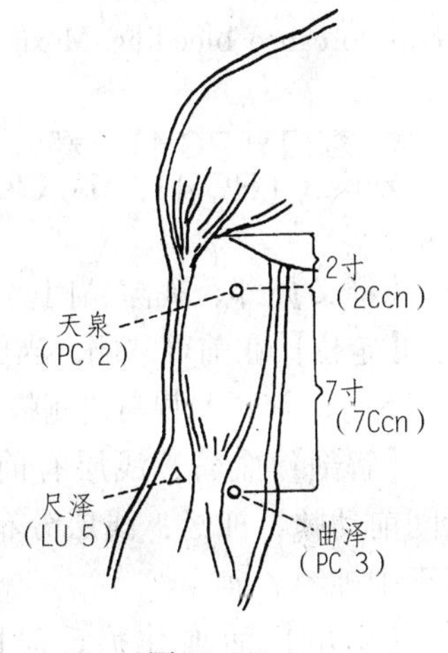

图 11 -6
Fig 11 -6

【Properties】Disperse the depressed qi in the chest, invigorate blood and alleviate pain.

【Indications】Cardiac pain, cough, distension of the hypochondriac region, pain in the chest, back and the medial aspect of the arm.

【Needling method】Puncture perpendicularly 0. 5 ~0. 7 cun. Moxibustion is applicable.

3. 曲泽 (PC 3), 合穴
Quze (PC 3), He - Sea Point

【释义】曲，弯曲；泽，沼泽。经气流注至此，入屈肘浅凹处，犹如水进沼泽。

【定位】在肘横纹中，当肱二头肌腱的尺侧缘（图 11 -6）。

【解剖】血管：深层有肱动、静脉，神经：正中神经的本干。

【功用】清气分热，养血和胃止呕，通经止痛。

【主治】心痛，心悸，热病，中暑，胃痛，呕吐，泄泻，肘臂疼痛，肢颤。

【操作】直刺0.5~0.7寸，或用三棱针点刺出血，可灸。

【Meaning】Qu，curve；ze，marsh. The qi of meridian infuses into the shallow depression of the elbow like water flowing into a marsh.

【Location】On the transverse cubital crease，at the ulnar side of the tendon of m. biceps brachii（Fig 11－6）.

【Regional anatomy】Vasculature：On the pathway of the branchial artery and vein. Innervation：The median nerve.

【Properties】Clear away the excessive heat at qi phase，enrich the blood，harmonize the stomach and intestines and stops vomiting，promote the qi and blood circulation in the meridians and alleviate pain.

【Indications】Cardiac pain，palpitation，febrile diseases，irritability，stomachache，vomiting，pain in the elbow and arm，tremor of the hand and arm.

【Needling method】Puncture perpendicularly 0.5～0.7 cun，or prick with a three－edged needle to cause bleeding. Moxibustion is applicable.

4. 郄门（PC 4），郄穴 Ximen（PC 4），Xi－Cleft Point

【释义】郄，孔隙；门，门户。此为本经郄穴，本经经气出入之门户。

【定位】在前臂掌侧，当曲泽与大陵的连线上，腕横纹上5寸。掌长肌腱与桡侧腕屈肌腱之间（图11－7）。

【解剖】血管：浅层有前臂正中动、静脉；深层有骨间前动脉。神经：浅层分布有前臂外侧皮神经，深层有正中神经。

【功用】活血化瘀，凉血止血，镇静安神，缓急止痛。

【主治】心痛，心悸，呕血，咳血，咯血胸痛，疔疮，癫痫。

【操作】直刺0.5~1.0寸，可灸。

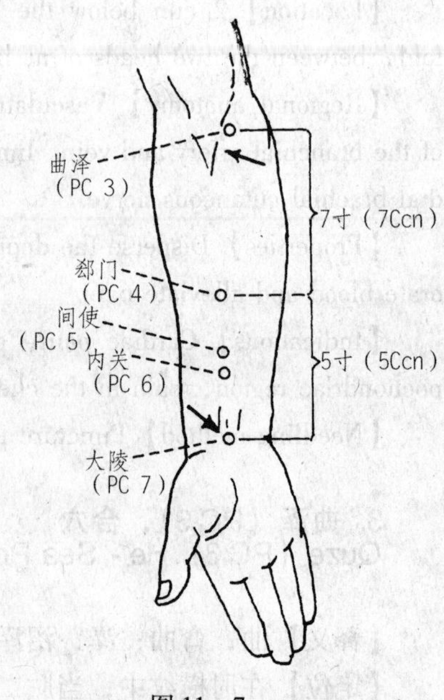

图11－7
Fig 11－7

【Meaning】Xi，cleft，men，door. This is xi－cleft point of the pericardium meridian，also a door where the qi of this meridian enters and exits.

【Location】5 cun above the transverse crease of the wrist，on the line connecting Quze（PC 3）and Daling（PC 7），between the tendons of m. palmaris longus and m. flexor carpi radialis（Fig 11－7）.

【Regional anatomy】Vasculature：The median artery and vein，the anterior interosseous artery in deep layer. Innervation：The medial antebrachial cutaneous nerve，the median nerve in deep layer.

【Properties】Invigorate the blood and dissipate blood stasis, cool blood to stops bleeding, calm the mind, moderate the acute conditions.

【Indications】Cardiac pain, palpitation, epistaxis, hematemesis, haemoptysis chest pain, furuncle, epilepsy.

【Needling method】Puncture perpendicularly 0.5 ~1.0 cun. Moxibustion is applicable.

5. 间使（PC 5），经穴
Jianshi（PC 5），Jing - River Point

【释义】间，间隙；使，臣使。穴属心包经，位于两筋之间隙，心包为臣使之官，故名。

【定位】在前臂掌侧，当曲泽与大陵的连线上，腕横纹上3寸。掌长肌腱与桡侧腕屈肌腱之间（图11－7）。

【解剖】血管：浅层有前臂正中动、静脉，深层分布有正中神经伴行动、静脉。神经：浅层分布有前臂内、外侧皮神经分支，深层有正中神经。

【功用】化痰安神。

【主治】心痛，心悸，胃痛，呕吐，热病，烦躁，疟疾，癫狂痫，腋肿，肘臂痛。

【操作】直刺0.5 ~1.0 寸，可灸。

【Meaning】Jian, space; shi, minister of a monarchy. The point pertains to the pericardium meridian and is in the space between the two tendons. It is so named because the pericardium is the minister of the heart.

【Location】3 cun above the transverse crease of the wrist, between the tendons of m. palmaris longus and m. flexor carpi radialis（Fig 11 –7）.

【Regional anatomy】Vasculature: The median artery and vein, the anterior interosseous artery and vein in deep layer. Innervation: The medial and lateral antebrachial cutaneous nerves, median nerve in deep layer.

【Properties】Transform phlegm, settle and calm the mind.

【Indications】Cardiac pain, palpitation, stomachache, vomiting, febrile diseases, irritability, malaria, mental disorders, epilepsy, swelling of the axilla, contracture of the elbow and arm.

【Needling method】Puncture perpendicularly 0.5 ~1.0 cun. Moxibustion is applicable.

6. 内关（PC 6），络穴，八脉交会穴（通阴维脉）
Neiguan（PC 6），Luo - Connecting Point，One of the Eight Confluent Points Associating with Yin Link Vessel

【释义】内，内外之内；关，关隘。

【定位】在前臂掌侧，当曲泽与大陵的连线上，腕横纹上2寸，掌长肌腱与桡侧腕屈肌腱之间（图 11 -7）。

【解剖】血管：浅层有前臂正中动、静脉，深层分布有骨间前动、静脉。神经：浅层分布着前臂内侧皮神经，深层有正中神经。

【功用】宽胸理气，宁心安神，和胃降逆止呕。

【主治】心痛，心悸，胸闷，胸胁胀痛，胃痛，眩晕，恶心，呕吐，呃逆，癫痫，失眠，热病，烦躁，疟疾，偏头痛，肘臂挛痛。

【操作】直刺 0.5 ~0.8 寸，可灸。

【Meaning】Nei，medial；guan，pass. The point is at an important site at the medial aspect of the forearm，like a pass.

【Location】2 cun above the transverse crease of the wrist，between the tendons of m. palmaris longus and m. flexor radialis（Fig 11 –7）.

【Regional anatomy】Vasculature：The median artery and vein，the anterior interosseous artery and vein in deep layer. Innervation：The medial and lateral antebrachial cutaneous nerves，median nerve in deep layer.

【Properties】Regulate and disperse the depressed – qi in the chest，adjust the mind and calm the spirit，harmonize the stomach and alleviate nausea and vomiting.

【Indications】Cardiac pain，palpitation，stuffy chest，pain in the hypochondriac region，stomachache，dizzy，nausea，vomiting，hiccup，mental disorders epilepsy，insomnia，febrile diseases，irritability，malaria，contracture and pain of the elbow and arm.

【Needling method】Puncture perpendicularly 0. 5 ~0. 8 cun. Moxibustion is applicable.

7. 大陵（PC 7），输穴，原穴
Daling（PC 7），Shu - Stream Point，Yuan - Source Point

【释义】大，大小之大；陵，丘陵。掌根突起部如同丘陵，穴在其腕侧陷中。

【定位】在腕掌横纹的中点处，当掌长肌腱与桡侧腕屈肌腱之间（图 11 –7）。

【解剖】血管：掌侧腕部动、静脉网。神经：深层正中神经。

【功用】安神清心热，宽胸和胃，凉血通络。

【主治】心痛，心悸，胃痛，呕吐，癫狂，胸闷，胸胁胀痛，失眠，烦躁，口臭，疮疡，手腕麻痛。

【操作】直刺 0.3 ~0.5 寸，可灸。

【Meaning】Da，large；ling，mound. The protrusion of the palmar root is large，like a mound. The point is in the depression of the wrist proximal to it.

【Location】In the middle of the transverse crease of the wrist，between the tendons of m. palmaris longus and m. flexor carpi radialis（Fig 11 –7）.

【Regional anatomy】Vasculature：The palmar arterial and venous network of the wrist. Innervation：the median nerve in deep layer.

【Properties】Clear away heat from the heart and calm the spirit，harmonize the stomach and intestines, disperse the depressed – qi in the chest, cool blood.

【Indications】Cardiac pain, palpitation, stomach ache, vomiting, mental disorders, epilepsy, stuffy chest, pain in the hypochondriac region, convulsion, insomnia, irritability, foul breath.

【Needling method】Puncture perpendicularly 0.3 ~ 0.5 cun. Moxibustion is applicable.

8. 劳宫（PC 8），荥穴
Laogong (PC 8), Ying - Spring Point

【释义】劳，劳动；宫，中央。手司劳动，劳指手。穴在掌中央。

【定位】在手掌心，当第2、3掌骨之间偏于第3掌骨，握拳屈指时中指尖处（图11－8）。

【解剖】血管：深层有指掌侧总动脉，神经：正中神经的指掌侧固有神经。

【功用】清心除烦宁神，醒神，和胃凉血通络。

【主治】心痛，痫狂，口疮，口臭，胃炎，手足癣，鼻衄，中暑，呕吐，恶心，中风昏迷。

【操作】直刺0.3～0.5寸，可灸。

【Meaning】Lao, labor; gong, center. The hand is for labor, and lao refers to the hand. The point is in the center of the palm.

【Location】At the center of the palm, between the 2nd and 3rd metacarpal bones, but close to the latter, and in the part touching the tip of the middle finger when a fist is made (Fig 11 – 8).

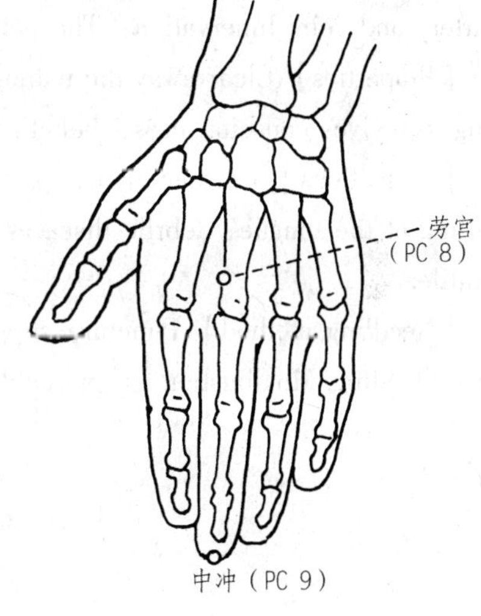

图 11 – 8
Fig 11 – 8

【Regional anatomy】Vasculature: The common palmar digital artery. Innervation: The 2nd common palmar digital nerve of the median nerve.

【Properties】Eliminate heat from the pericardium and revive consciousness, clear away heat from the heart and the middle energizer, harmonize the stomach, cool blood and calm the mind.

【Indications】Cardiac pain, mental disorder, epilepsy, gastritis, foul breath, fungus infection of the hand and foot, vomiting, nausea, loss of consciousness.

【Needling method】Puncture perpendicularly 0.3 ~ 0.5 cun. Moxibustion is applicable.

9. 中冲（PC 9），井穴
Zhongchong（PC 9），Jing - Well Point

【释义】中，中间。冲，冲动，涌出。穴在中指端，心包经之井穴，经气由此涌出，沿经脉上行。

【定位】在手中指末节尖端中央（图 11 - 8）。

【解剖】血管：指掌侧动、静脉网。神经：正中神经的指掌侧固有神经末梢。

【功用】清心醒神，利言语，清暑热。

【主治】心痛，昏迷，舌强肿痛，热病，中风，心烦，心痛，手心热，中暑，小儿惊风。

【操作】浅刺 0.1 寸；或用三棱针点刺出血，可灸。

【Meaning】Zhong，middle；chong，gushing. The point is at the tip of the middle finger and is the jing - well point of pericardium meridian，where the qi of meridian originates and gushes upward along the meridian.

【Location】In the centre of the tip of the middle finger（Fig 11 - 8）.

【Regional anatomy】Vasculature：The arterial and venous network formed by the palmar digital artery and vein. Innervation：The palmar digital nerve of the median nerve.

【Properties】Clear away the pathogenic - heat from the pericardium the heart fire and tranquillizing to revives consciousness，benefit the tongue，eliminate summer - heat.

【Indications】Cardiac pain，palpitation，loss of consciousness，aphasia with stiffness and swelling of the tongue，febrile diseases，heat stroke，convulsion，feverish sensation in the palm，infantile.

【Needling method】Puncture superficially 0.1 cun or prick with a three - edged needle to cause bleeding. Moxibustion is applicable.

复习思考题
Review Questions

1. 手厥阴心包经主治哪些病症？

What are the indications for points on the pericardium meridian of hand - jueyin?

2. 曲泽与尺泽穴有哪些异同点？

What are the differences and similarities of Quze（PC 3）and Chize（LU 5）?

3. 详述内关穴的定位、操作和主治。

Describe the location，needling method and indications of Neiguan（PC 6）.

4. 简述中冲穴的定位、操作和主治。

Describe the location，needling method and indications of Zhongchong（PC 9）.

第十二章 手少阳经络与腧穴
Meridian and Collateral and Its Acupoints of Hand – Shaoyang

第一节 手少阳经络
Meridian and Collateral of Hand – Shaoyang

一、手少阳经脉
Meridian of Hand - Shaoyang

(一) 经脉循行
The Course of Meridian

手少阳三焦经，起始于无名指末端（关冲），上行小指与无名指之间（液门），沿着手背至腕部（中渚、阳池），出于前臂伸侧两骨（尺骨、桡骨）之间（外关、支沟、会宗、三阳络、四渎），向上通过肘尖（天井），沿上臂外侧（清冷渊、消泺），向上通过肩部（臑会、肩髎），交出足少阳经的后面（天髎，会秉风、肩井、大椎），进入缺盆，分布于膻中，散络心包，通过膈肌，遍及上、中、下三焦。

胸中支脉，从膻中上行，出锁骨上窝，循项上行，联系耳后（天牖、翳风、瘈脉、颅息），直上出耳上方（角孙，会颔厌、悬厘、上关），弯下行于面颊，至目眶下（颧髎）。

耳后支脉，从耳后进入耳中，出走耳前（耳和髎、耳门，交听会），经过上关前，交面颊，行至外眼角（丝竹空，会瞳子髎），接足少阳胆经（图12－1）。

《灵枢·经脉》原文：三焦手少阳之脉，起于小指次指之端，上出两指之间，循手表腕，出臂外两骨之间，上贯肘，循臑外上肩，而交出足少阳之后，入缺盆，布膻中，散络心包，下膈，遍属三焦。

其支者，从膻中，上出缺盆，上项，系耳后，直上出耳上角，以屈下颊至䪼。

其支者，从耳后入耳中，出走耳前，过客主人，前交颊，至目锐眦。

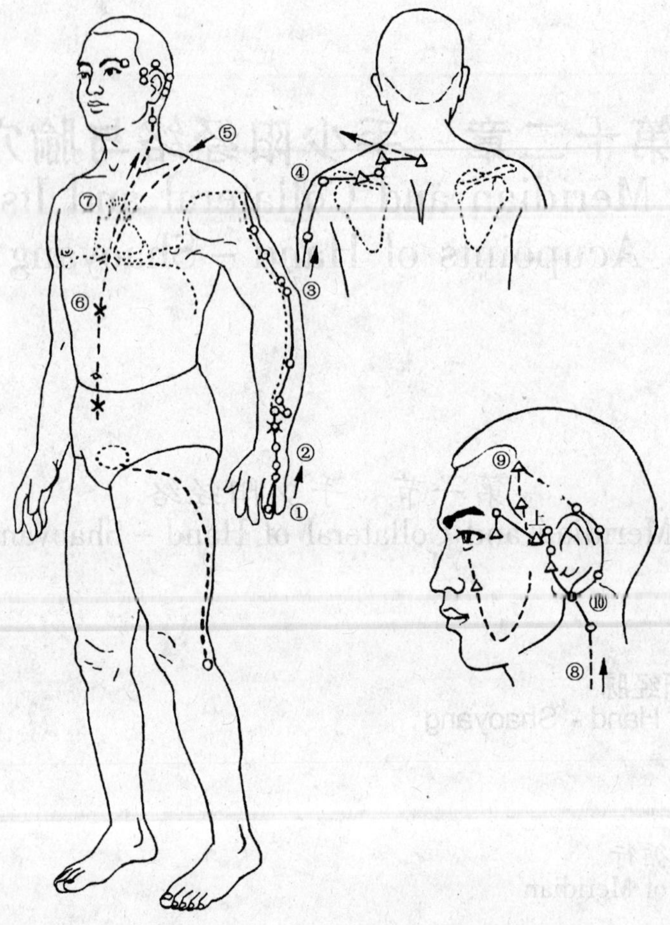

图例 ——本经有穴通路 ……本经无穴通路

Note ——Pathway with points ……Pathway without points

图 12 – 1 手少阳经脉、络脉循行示意图

Fig 12 – 1 The course of the meridian and collateral of hand – shaoyang

The triple energizer meridian of hand – shaoyang originates from the tip of the ring finger (Guanchong, SJ 1), running up – wards between the 4th and 5th metacarpal bones along the dorsal aspect of the wrist to the lateral aspect of the forearm between the radius and ulna. Ascending through the olecranon and going along the lateral aspect of the upper arm, it reaches the shoulder region, where it goes across and passes behind the gallbladder meridian of foot – shaoyang. Winding over to the supraclavicular fossa, it spreads in the chest to connect with the pericardium. It then descends through the diaphragm to the abdomen, and joins its pertaining organ, the upper, middle and lower jiao (i. e. sanjao, triple energizer).

A branch originates from the chest. Runing upwards, it emerges from the supraclavicular fossa. From there, it ascends to the neck, running along the posterior border of the ear, and further to the corner of the anterior hairline. Then it runs downwards to the cheek and terminates in the infraorbital region.

The auricular branch arises from the retroauricular region and enters the ear. Then it emerges in front of the ear, crosses the previous branch at the cheek and reaches the outer canthus to link with the gallbladder meridian of foot – shaoyang (Fig 12 – 1).

(二) 经脉病候
The Syndromes of Meridian

本经异常可表现为下列病症：耳聋，耳鸣，咽喉肿痛。

本经主治“气”方面所发生的病症：自汗出，眼外眦痛，面颊肿，耳后、肩臂、肘部、前臂外侧均可发生疼痛，小指、无名指功能障碍。

Symptoms of disorder of the meridian include: deafness, tinnitus, swelling of the pharynx, sore throat.

Indications include diseases caused by qi disorder that manifested as: spontaneous perspiration, pain in the outer canthus of the eye, swelling of the cheek, pain in the posterior border of the ear and along the lateral side of the shoulder, upper arm, elbow and forearm, dysfunction of the ring finger.

二、手少阳络脉
Collateral of Hand - Shaoyang

手少阳络脉：名外关，在腕关节后2寸处分出，绕行于臂膊的外侧，进入胸中，会合于心包（图12－1）。

It arises from waiguan (SJ 5), 2 cun above the dorsum of the wrist, it travels up the dorsum of the wrist, it travels up the posterior aspect of the arm and over the shoulder, disperses in the chest, converging with the Pericardium Meridian (Fig 12 – 1).

三、手少阳经别
Divergent Meridian of Hand - Shaoyang

在头部从手少阳经分出，向下进入缺盆，经过上中下三焦，散布于胸中（图12－2）。

After deriving from the triple energizer meridian at the vertex, it descends into the supraclavicular fossa crosses the upper jiao, middle jiao and lower jiao and finally disperses in the chest. (Fig 12 – 2)

四、手少阳经筋
Muscular Region of Hand - Shaoyang

手少阳经筋，起于第四指末端，结于腕背；上沿前臂外侧，结于肘尖；向上绕行于上臂外侧，上肩部，走向颈部，会合手太阳经筋。其分支当下颌角部进入，联系舌根；一支上至下颌关节处，沿着耳前，连接目外眦，上达颞部，结于额角（图 12－3）。

It starts at the end of the fourth fingers, knots in the wrist back, forwards into the lateral forearm, arrives at the elbow department of bypass in the upper arm up the outside, keeps on through the shoulder, reaches neck and the sun to join hands The tendon. When the mandibular angle of its branch entry, contact the base of the tongue; an office on the lower jaw along the front of the ear, outer canthus is present, the temporal reach, end on forehead（Fig 12－3）.

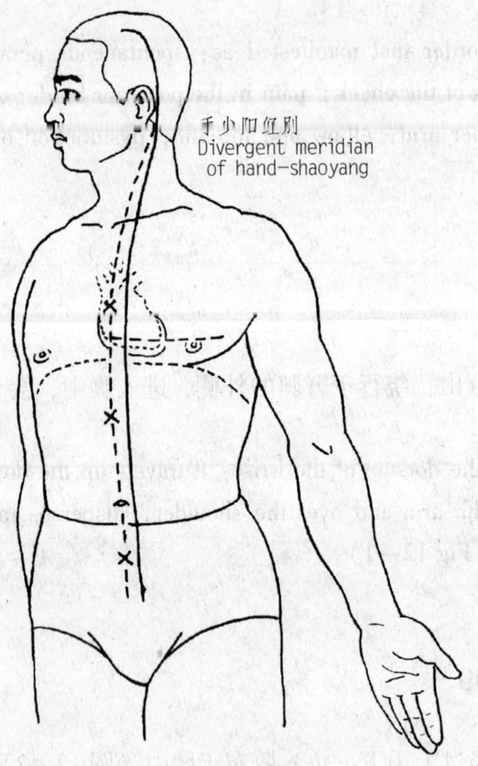

图 12－2 手少阳经别循行示意图
Fig 12－2 The course of the divergent meridians of hand－shaoyang

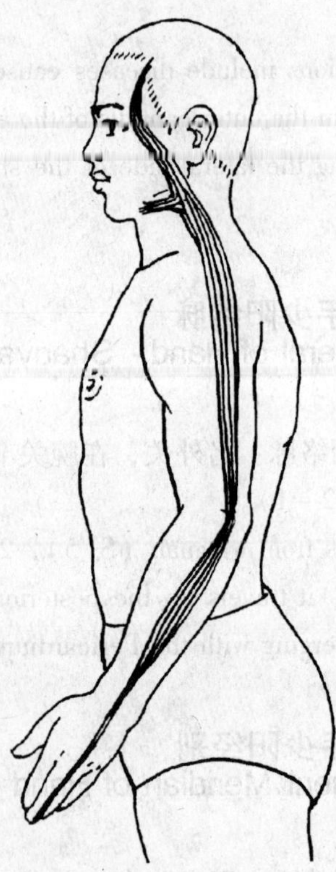

图 12－3 手少阳经筋循行示意图
Fig 12－3 The course of the muscular region of hand－shaoyang

第二节 手少阳腧穴
Acupoints of Hand – Shaoyang

本经左右各23个穴位，首穴为关冲，末穴为丝竹空（图12-4）。

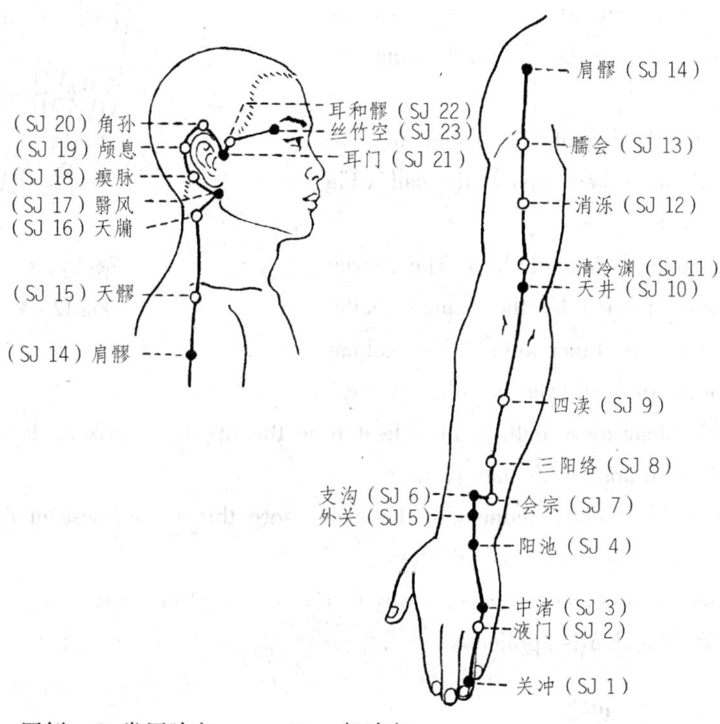

图12-4 手少阳三焦经腧穴总图

Fig 12-4 Points of the triple energizer meridian of hand – shaoyang

1. 关冲（SJ 1），井穴
Guanchong（SJ 1），Jing - Well Point

【释义】关，通弯；冲，冲要。无名指不能单独伸直，关（通弯字）在此代表无名指。穴在无名指端，系三焦经井穴，经气由此涌出，沿经脉上行。

【定位】在手环指末节尺侧，距指甲角0.1寸（图12-5）。

【解剖】血管：指掌侧固有动、静脉网。神经：尺神经指掌侧固有神经的指背支的分支。

【功用】清上焦热，明目利言语，通经止痛。

【主治】头痛，目赤，咽喉肿痛，舌强不语，热病，烦躁，昏厥，中暑，耳聋。

【操作】浅刺0.1寸，或用三棱针点刺出血，可灸。

【Meaning】Guan, same as bend; chong, gushing. As the ring finger cannot be stretched out alone, guan here refers to the ring finger. The point is at the tip of the ring finger and is the jing – well point of triple energizer meridian, where the qi of meridian originates and gushes upward along the meridian.

【Location】On the lateral side of the ring finger, about 0.1 cun from the corner of the nail (Fig 12 – 5).

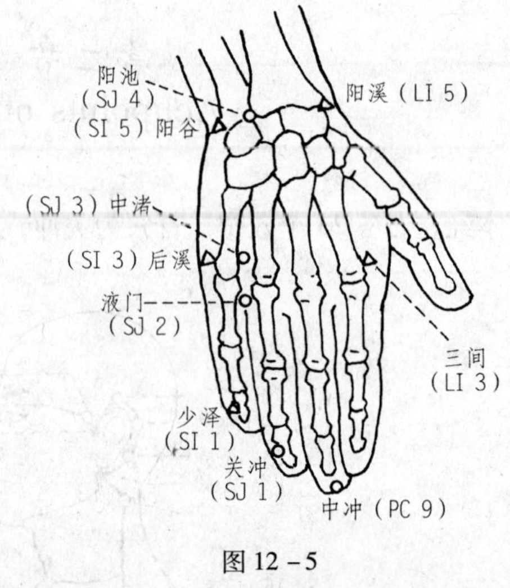

图 12 – 5
Fig 12 – 5

【Regional anatomy】Vasculature: The arterial and venous network formed by the palmar digital proprial artery and vein. Innervation: The palmar digital proprial nerve derived from the ulnar nerve.

【Properties】Clear away pathogenic – heat from the upper energizer, benefits the ears and tongue, activate meridians to alleviate pain.

【Indications】Headache, redness of the eyes, sore throat, stiffness of the tongue, febrile diseases, irritability, loss conscious, deafness.

【Needling method】Puncture superficially 0.1 cun, or prick with a three – edged needle to cause bleeding. Moxibustion is applicable.

2. 液门(SJ 2)，荥穴
Yemen (SJ 2), Ying - Spring Point

【释义】液，水液；门，门户。此为本经荥穴，属水，有通调水道之功，犹如水汽出入之门户。

【定位】在手背部，当第4、5指间，指蹼缘后方赤白肉际处(图12 – 5)。

【解剖】血管：指背动、静脉，神经：尺神经的指背神经。

【功用】清上焦热，聪耳宁神，通络止痛。

【主治】头痛，目赤，暴聋，咽喉肿痛，疟疾，手臂痛。

【操作】直刺0.3 ~0.5寸，可灸。

【Meaning】Ye, water; men, door. This is a ying – spring point of this meridian, pertaining to water. It has a function of regulating water passage like a door.

【Location】When the fist is clenched, the point is located in the depression proximal to the margin of the web between the ring and small fingers, at the junction of the red and white skin. (Fig 12 – 5)

【Regional anatomy】Vasculature: The dorsal digital artery and vein. Innervation: The dorsal branch of the ulnar nerve.

【Properties】Disperse heat from the upper energizer and benefit the ears, calm the mind, activate the meridians to alleviate pain.

【Indications】Headache, redness of the eyes, sudden deafness, sore throat, malaria, pain in the arm.

【Needling method】Puncture perpendicularly 0.3 ~0.5 cun. Moxibustion is applicable.

3. 中渚（SJ 3），输穴
Zhongzhu（SJ 3），Shu - Stream Point

【释义】中，中间；渚，水中之小块陆地。穴在五输流注穴之中间，经气如水循渚而行。

【定位】在手背部，当环指本节（掌指关节）的后方，第4、5掌骨间凹陷处（图12－5）。

【解剖】血管：深层有第4掌背动脉，神经：浅层布有尺神经的指背神经。

【功用】清热，聪耳明目，通络止痛。

【主治】头痛，目赤，耳鸣，耳聋，消渴，咽喉肿痛，热病，疟疾，肘臂肩背疼痛，手指屈伸不利。

【操作】直刺0.3～0.5寸，可灸。

【Meaning】Zhong, middle; zhu, a plot of small land in water. The point is in the middle of the five - shu points and the qi of meridian flows like water along the water margin.

【Location】When the fist is clenched, the point is on dorsum of the hand between the 4th and 5th metacarpal bones, in the depression proximal to the 4th metacarpophalangeal joint (Fig 12 5).

【Regional anatomy】Vasculature: The 4th dorsal metacarpal artery. Innervation: The dorsal branch of the ulnar nerve.

【Properties】Eliminate heat, benefit the ears, activate the meridians to alleviate pain.

【Indications】Headache, redness of the eyes, tinnitus, deafness, sore throat, febrile diseases, pain in the elbow and arm, motor impairment of fingers.

【Needling method】Puncture perpendicularly 0.3 ~0.5 cun. Moxibustion is applicable.

4. 阳池（SJ 4），原穴
Yangchi（SJ 4），Yuan - Source Point

【释义】阳，阴阳之阳；池，池塘。穴在腕背陷中，经气至此如水入池塘。

【定位】在腕背横纹中，当指伸肌腱的尺侧缘凹陷处（图12－5）。

【解剖】血管：深层有尺动脉腕背支，神经：浅层分布着尺神经手背支及前臂后皮神经。

【功用】舒筋止痛，清热。

【主治】腕、臂、肩痛，疟疾，耳聋，目赤肿痛，消渴。

【操作】直刺 0.3~0.5 寸，可灸。

【Meaning】Yang，yang of yin - yang；chi，pool. The point is in the depression on the back of the wrist，the qi of meridian flows like water into a pool.

【Location】On the transverse crease of the dorsum of wrist，in the depression lateral to the tendon of m. extensor digitorum communis（Fig 12 - 5）.

【Regional anatomy】Vasculature：The dorsal carpal branch of ulnar artery. Innervation：The terminal branch of the posterior antebrachial cutaneous nerve and the dorsal branch of the ulnar nerve.

【Properties】Relax the sinews and alleviate pain，clear away heat.

【Indications】Pain in the arm，shoulder and wrist，malaria，deafness，redness of the eyes，thirst.

【Needling method】Puncture perpendicularly 0. 3 ~ 0. 5 cun. Moxibustion is applicable.

5. 外关（SJ 5），络穴，八脉交会穴（通阳维脉）
Waiguan（SJ 5），Luo - Connecting Point，One of the Eight Confluent Points Associating with Yang Link Vessel

【释义】外，内外之外；关，关隘。穴在前臂外侧要处，犹如关隘。

【定位】在前臂背侧，当阳池与肘尖的连线上，腕背横纹上 2 寸，尺骨与桡骨之间（图 12 - 6）。

【解剖】血管：深层有骨间后动、静脉，神经：浅层布有前臂后皮神经，深层有骨间后神经。

【功用】疏风解表，清热利头，通阳活络止痛。

【主治】热病，头痛，面痛，项强，耳鸣，耳聋，目赤肿痛，胸胁痛，上肢运动神经损伤，手指痛，上肢痿痹。

【操作】直刺 0.5 ~ 1.0 寸，可灸。

【Meaning】Wai，lateral；guan，pass. The point is at the vital site on the lateral aspect of the forearm，like a pass.

【Location】2 cun proximal to the dorsal crease of the wrist，on the line connecting

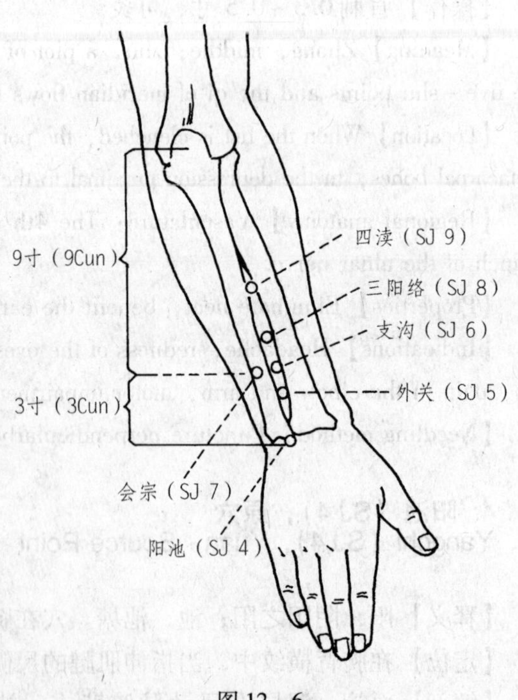

图 12 - 6

Fig 12 - 6

Yangchi (SJ 4) and the tip of olecranon, between the radius and ulna (Fig 12 –6).

【Regional anatomy】Vasculature: the posterior antebrachial interosseous arteries and veins on deep layer. Innervation: The posterior antebrachial cutaneous nerve, the posterior interosseous nerve in deep layer.

【Properties】Expel wind and release the exterior, benefits the head and ears, clear away heat, activate the meridians to alleviate pain.

【Indications】Febrile diseases, headache, pain in the cheek, strained neck, deafness, tinnitus, redness of the eyes, pain in the hypochondriac region, motor impairment of the elbow and arm, pain of the fingers, hand tremor.

【Needling method】Puncture perpendicularly 0.5 ~1.0 cun. Moxibustion is applicable.

6. 支沟 (SJ 6), 经穴
Zhigou (SJ 6), Jing - River Point

【释义】支，通“肢”；沟，沟渠。支，在此指上肢，穴在上肢尺桡骨间沟中。

【定位】在前臂背侧，当阳池与肘尖的连线上，腕背横纹上3寸，尺骨与桡骨之间（图12 –6）。

【解剖】血管：深层有骨间后动、静脉，神经：浅层分布有前臂后皮神经和骨间后神经。

【功用】清热理气，利胸胁，润肠通便，活络止痛。

【主治】耳鸣，耳聋，胁肋痛，呕吐，便秘，热病，项背强，落枕，暴喑。

【操作】直刺0.8 ~1.2 寸，可灸。

【Meaning】Zhi, limbs; gou, ditch. Zhi here refers to the upper limb. The point is located between the radius and the ulna.

【Location】3 cun proximal to the dorsal crease of the wrist, on the line connecting Yangchi (SJ 4) and the tip of olecranon, between the radius and ulna, on the radial side of m. extensor digitorum (Fig 12 –6).

【Regional anatomy】Vasculature: The posterior antebrachial interosseous arteries and veins in deep layer. Innervation: The posterior antebrachial cutaneous nerve and the posterior interosseous nerve.

【Properties】Regulate qi and clear away heat in the triple energizer, benefits the chest and lateral costal region, promote moving of the stool, activate the meridians to alleviate pain.

【Indications】Tinnitus, deafness, pain in the hypochondriac region, vomiting, constipation, febrile diseases, aching and heavy sensation of the shoulder and back, sudden hoarseness of voice.

【Needling method】Puncture perpendicularly 0.8 ~1.2 cun. Moxibustion is applicable.

7. 会宗（SJ 7），郄穴
Huizong（SJ 7），Xi - Cleft Point

【释义】会，会合；宗，集聚。此为本经郄穴，是经气会聚之处。

【定位】在前臂背侧，当腕背横纹上3寸，支沟尺侧，尺骨的桡侧缘（图12－6）。

【解剖】血管：深层有前臂骨间后动、静脉，神经：浅层有前臂后皮神经，深层有骨间后神经。

【功用】清利三焦，聪耳。

【主治】耳鸣，耳聋，耳痛，癫痫，上肢痹痛。

【操作】直刺0.5～1.0寸，可灸。

【Meaning】Hui，meeting；zong，gathering. This is a xi－cleft point of this meridian，a place where the qi of meridian gathers.

【Location】At the level with Zhigou（SJ 6），on the ulnar side of Zhigou（SJ 6），on the radial border of the ulna（Fig 12－6）.

【Regional anatomy】Vasculature：The posterior antebrachial interosseous artery and vein. Innervation：The posterior antebrachial cutaneous nerves，the posterior interosseous nerves in deep layer.

【Properties】Clear away the pathogen from the triple energizer meridian and benefit the ears.

【Indications】Deafness，pain in the ear，epilepsy，pain of the arm.

【Needling method】Puncture perpendicularly 0.5～1.0 cun. Moxibustion is applicable.

8. 三阳络 Sanyangluo（SJ 8）

【释义】三阳，指手三阳经；络，联络。此穴联络手之三条阳经。

【定位】在前臂背侧，腕背横纹上4寸，尺骨与桡骨之间（图12－6）。

【解剖】血管：深层有前臂骨间后动、静脉，神经：浅层分布有前臂后皮神经，深层有前臂骨间后神经。

【功用】清利三焦，通经止痛。

【主治】耳聋，暴喑，胸胁痛，上肢痹痛，齿痛。

【操作】直刺0.5～1.0寸，可灸。

【Meaning】Sanyang，three yang meridians of hand；luo，connection. This point connects the three yang meridians of hand.

【Location】4 cun proximal to the dorsal crease of the wrist，between the radius and ulna（Fig 12－6）.

【Regional anatomy】Vasculature：The posterior antebrachial interosseous artery and vein. Innervation：The posterior antebrachial cutaneous nerves，the posterior interosseous nerves in deep layer.

【Properties】 Clear away the pathogen from the triple energizer meridian to alleviate pain.

【Indications】 Deafness, sudden hoarseness of voice, pain in the chest and hypochondriac region, pain in the hand and arm, toothache.

【Needling method】 Puncture perpendicularly 0.5~1.0 cun. Moxibustion is applicable.

9. 四渎 Sidu (SJ 9)

【释义】四，四个，渎，河流。古称长江、黄河、淮河、济水为四渎，经气至此，渗灌更广，故喻称四渎。

【定位】在前臂背侧，当阳池与肘尖的连线上，肘尖下5寸，尺骨与桡骨之间（图12-6）。

【解剖】血管：深层有骨间后动、静脉，神经：前臂后皮神经。

【功用】利咽聪耳。

【主治】耳聋，齿痛，暴喑，咽喉肿痛，偏头痛，上肢痹痛。

【操作】直刺0.5~1.0寸，可灸。

【Meaning】 Si, four; du, river. The Yangtze, the Yellow, the Huaihe and the Jishui Rivers were called Sidu in ancient times. The qi of meridian is able to irrigate more regions when it reaches this point.

【Location】 On the lateral side of the forearm, 5 cun below the olecranon, between the radius and ulna (Fig 12-6).

【Regional anatomy】 Vasculature: The posterior antebrachial interosseous artery and vein. Innervation: The posterior antebrachial cutaneous nerves.

【Properties】 Benefit the throat and ears.

【Indications】 Deafness, toothache, migraine, sudden hoarseness of voice, pain in the forearm.

【Needling method】 Puncture perpendicularly 0.5~1.0 cun. Moxibustion is applicable.

10. 天井（SJ 10），合穴
Tianjing (SJ 10), He - Sea Point

【释义】天，天空；井，水井。喻上为天，穴在上肢鹰嘴窝，其陷如井。

【定位】在臂外侧，屈肘时，当肘尖直上1寸凹陷处（图12-7）。

【解剖】血管：深层有肘关节动、静脉网，神经：臂后皮神经及桡神经肌支。

【功用】化痰散结，理气降逆，宁神，清三焦热，通络止痛。

【主治】偏头痛，项痛，肘臂痛，癫痫，耳聋，瘰疬。

【操作】直刺0.3~0.5寸，可灸。

【Meaning】 Tian, heaven; jing, well. Upper is indicated as heaven. The point is in the depression by the olecranon of the upper limb, which is likened to a well.

【Location】When the elbow is flexed, the point is in the depression about 1 cun superior to the olecranon (Fig 12 – 7).

【Regional anatomy】Vasculature: The arterial and venous network of the elbow. Innervation: The posterior brachial cutaneous nerve and the muscular branch of the radial nerve.

【Properties】Transform phlegm and dissipates nodules, regulates qi and descend rebellion, calm the mind, clear away the pathogen from the triple energizer meridian to alleviate pain.

【Indications】Migraine, pain in the neck, shoulder and arm, epilepsy, deafness, scrofula.

【Needling method】Puncture perpendicularly 0.3 ~ 0.5 cun. Moxibustion is applicable.

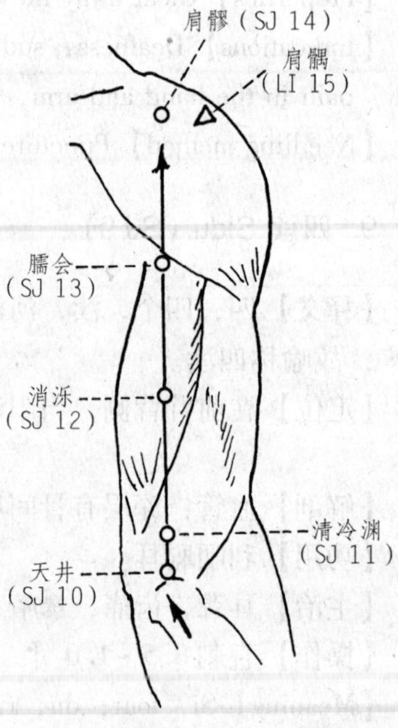

图 12 – 7

Fig 12 – 7

11. 清冷渊 Qinglengyuan (SJ 11)

【释义】清，清凉；冷，寒冷；渊，深水。此穴具有清三焦之热的作用，犹如入清凉之深水之中。

【定位】在臂外侧，屈肘，当肘尖直上 2 寸，即天井上 1 寸（图 12 – 7）。

【解剖】血管：深层有正中动、静脉，神经：浅层分布有臂后皮神经及桡神经肌支等。

【功用】通经活络，祛风湿，清湿热。

【主治】肩臂痛，偏头痛，目痛，胁痛。

【操作】直刺 0.3 ~ 0.5 寸，可灸。

【Meaning】Qing, cool; leng, cold; yuan, deep water. The function of this point is to eliminate the heat of triple energizer as if the patient were in cool deep water.

【Location】1 cun above Tianjing (SJ 10) when the elbow is flexed (Fig 12 – 7).

【Regional anatomy】Vasculature: The terminal branches of the median collateral artery and vein. Innervation: The posterior brachial cutaneous nerve and the muscular branch of the radial nerve.

【Properties】Activate the meridian and dispel the pathogenic wind – dampness.

【Indications】Motor impairment and pain of the shoulder and arm, migraine.

【Needling method】Puncture perpendicularly 0.3 ~ 0.5 cun. Moxibustion is applicable.

12. 消泺 Xiaoluo (SJ 12)

【释义】消，消除；泺，小水，沼泽。本穴属三焦经，具有通调水道的作用。

【定位】在臂外侧，当清冷渊与臑会连线的中点处（图 12 –7）。

【解剖】血管：深层有中副动、静脉，神经：浅层分布着臂后皮神经和桡神经的肌支。

【功用】通络止痛。

【主治】头痛，项强，齿痛，肩臂痛，运动障碍。

【操作】直刺 0.5 ~0.7 寸，可灸。

【Meaning】Xiao, to eliminate; luo, marsh. This point pertains to triple energizer meridian and functions to regulate water passage (water metabolism).

【Location】On the line joining the olecranon and Jianliao (SJ 14), midway between Qinglengyuan (SJ 11) and Naohui (SJ 13) (Fig 12 –7).

【Regional anatomy】Vasculature: The median collateral artery and vein. Innervation: The posterior brachial cutaneous nerve and the muscular branch of the radial nerve.

【Properties】Activate the meridian to alleviate pain.

【Indications】Headache, neck rigidity, motor impairment and pain of the arm.

【Needling method】Puncture perpendicularly 0.5 ~0.7 cun. Moxibustion is applicable.

13. 臑会 Naohui (SJ 13)

【释义】臑，上臂肌肉隆起处；会，交会。穴在上臂肌肉隆起处，为本经与阳维脉交会处。

【定位】在臂外侧，当肘尖与肩髎的连线上，肩髎下 3 寸，三角肌的后下缘（图 12 –7）。

【解剖】血管：正中动、静脉。神经：浅层有臂后皮神经，深层有桡神经。

【功用】理气化痰，通络止痛。

【主治】瘿气，瘰疬，上肢痿痹。

【操作】直刺 0.5 ~0.8 寸，可灸。

【Meaning】Nao, muscle prominence of the upper arm; hui, confluence. The point is at the muscle prominence of the upper arm and is a confluence of this meridian with yang link vessel.

【Location】On the line joining Jianliao (SJ 14) and the olecranon, on the posterior border of m. Deltoideus (Fig 12 –7).

【Regional anatomy】Vasculature: The median collateral artery and vein. Innervation: The posterior brachial cutaneous nerve, the radial nerve in deep layer.

【Properties】Regulate qi and transform phlegm, activates the channel and alleviates pain.

【Indications】Goiter, pain in the shoulder and arm.

【Needling method】Puncture perpendicularly 0.5 ~0.8 cun. Moxibustion is applicable.

14. 肩髎 Jianliao (SJ 14)

【释义】肩，肩部；髎，骨隙。穴在肩部骨隙中。

【定位】在肩部，肩髃后方，当臂外展时，于肩峰后下方呈现凹陷处（图 12－7）。

【解剖】血管：旋肱后动、静脉的肌支。神经：浅层分布着锁骨上外侧神经，深层有腋神经。

【功用】祛风湿，利关节，止痛。

【主治】肩臂挛痛不遂。

【操作】直刺 0.7～1.0 寸。

【Meaning】Jian, shoulder; liao, foramen. The point is in a foramen in the shoulder.

【Location】On the shoulder, posterior to Jianyu (LI 15), in the depression inferior and posterior to the acromion when the arm is abducted (Fig 12－7).

【Regional anatomy】Vasculature: The muscular branch of the posterior circumflex humeral artery and vein. Innervation: lateral supraclavicular nerves, axillary nerve in deep layer.

【Properties】Dispel wind－dampness, alleviate pain and benefit the shoulder joint.

【Indications】Pain and motor impairment of the shoulder and upper arm.

【Needling method】Puncture perpendicularly 0.7～1.0 cun.

15. 天髎 Tianliao (SJ 15)

【释义】天，天空；髎，骨隙。上为天，穴在肩胛岗上方之骨隙中。

【定位】在肩胛部，肩井与曲垣的中间，当肩胛骨上角处（图 12－8）。

【解剖】血管：肩胛上动、静脉的肌支，神经：分布着锁骨上神经及副神经。

【功用】祛风湿，活血通络，宽胸理气。

【主治】肩臂痛，颈项强痛。

【操作】直刺 0.3～0.5 寸，可灸。

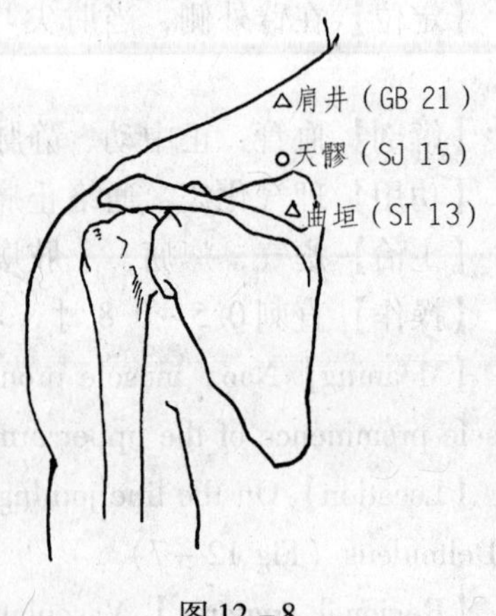

图 12－8

Fig 12－8

【Meaning】Tian, heaven; liao, foramen. Upper is referred to as heaven. The point is in a foramen above the shoulder blade.

【Location】Midway between Jianjing (GB 21) and Quyuan (SI 13), on the superior angle of the scapula (Fig 12－8).

【Regional anatomy】Vasculature: The muscular branch of the suprascapular artery and vein. Innervation: The accessory nerve and the branch of the suprascapular nerve.

【Properties】Dispel wind－dampness, activate the meridian to alleviates pain, disperse the depressed qi in the chest.

【Indications】Pain in the shoulder and elbow, stiffness of the neck.

【Needling method】Puncture perpendicularly 0.3～0.5 cun. Moxibustion is applicable.

16. 天牖 Tianyou (SJ 16)

【释义】天，天空；牖，窗。上为天，牖有天窗之意。穴在侧颈部上方，本穴能开上窍，故喻为天窗。

【定位】在颈侧部，当乳突的后方直下，平下颌角，胸锁乳突肌的后缘（图 12－9）。

【解剖】血管：深层有颈外动脉，神经：枕小神经。

【功用】利头目五官。

【主治】头痛，项强，目痛，耳聋，瘰疬，面肿。

【操作】直刺 0.3～0.5 寸，可灸。

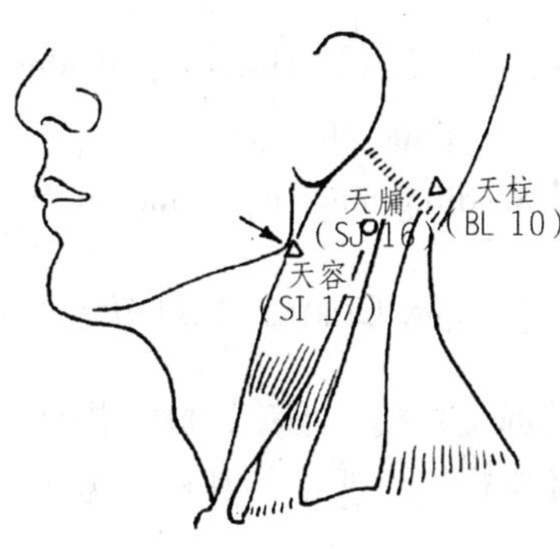

图 12－9
Fig 12－9

【Meaning】Tian, heaven; you, window. Upper is referred to as heaven. Tianyou means heavenly window. The point is on thee upper part of the lateral aspect of the neck and good to "open the upper aperture". It is therefore likened to a heavenly window.

【Location】On the lateral side of the neck, directly below the posterior border of mastoid process, on the level of the mandibular angle, and on the posterior border of sternocleidomastoid muscle (Fig 12－9).

【Regional anatomy】Vasculature: The posterior auricular artery. Innervation: The lesser occipital nerve.

【Properties】Benefit the head and sense organs.

【Indications】Headache, neck rigidity, facial swelling, blurring of vision, sudden deafness.

【Needling method】Puncture perpendicularly 0.3～0.5 cun. Moxibustion is applicable.

17. 翳风 Yifeng (SJ 17)

【释义】翳，遮蔽；风，风邪。穴当耳垂后方，为遮蔽风邪之处。

【定位】在耳垂后方，当乳突与下颌角之间的凹陷处（图 12－10）。

【解剖】血管：深层有颈外动脉、耳后动脉，神经：浅层分布有耳大神经、面神经等。

【功用】聪耳，疏风清热，活络止痛。

【主治】耳鸣，耳聋，聤耳，口㖞，牙关紧闭，齿痛，颊肿，呃逆，瘰疬。

【操作】直刺 0.5～1.0 寸，可灸。

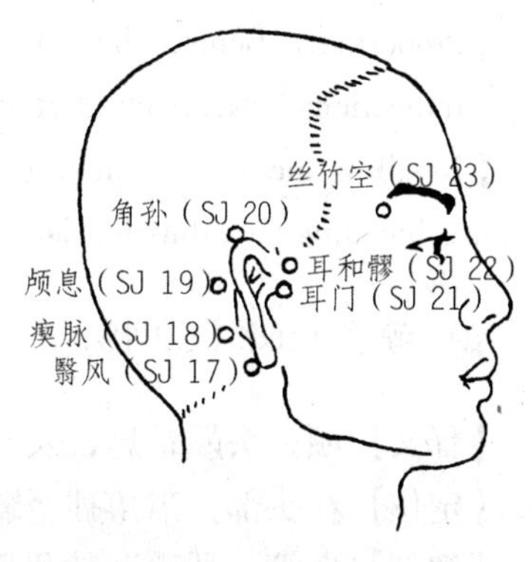

图 12－10
Fig 12－10

【Meaning】Yi, shielding; feng, pathogenic

wind. The point is behind the earlobe and is the place for shielding off pathogenic wind.

【Location】Posterior to the lobule of the ear, in the depression between the mandible and mastoid process (Fig 12－10).

【Regional anatomy】Vasculature: The posterior auricular artery, the external jugular artery. Innervation: The great auricular nerve and the facial nerve.

【Properties】Benefit the ears, eliminate wind and heat, activate the meridian to alleviate pain.

【Indications】Tinnitus, deafness, otorrhea, facial paralysis, toothache, swelling of the cheek, scrofula, trismus.

【Needling method】Puncture perpendicularly 0.5～1.0 cun. Moxibustion is applicable.

18. 瘈脉 Chimai (SJ 18)

【释义】瘈，瘈疭；脉，指络脉。穴在耳后，布有络脉，有治瘈疭的作用。

【定位】在头部，耳后乳突中央，当角孙至翳风之间，沿耳轮连线的中、下1/3的交点处（图12－10）。

【解剖】血管：耳后动脉和静脉。神经：耳大神经的耳后支。

【功用】聪耳，镇惊息风。

【主治】头痛，耳鸣，耳聋，小儿惊风。

【操作】平刺0.3～0.5寸，或点刺出血，可灸。

【Meaning】Chi, convulsion; ami, collateral. The point is behind the ear where the collaterals are distributed. It is useful therefore in treating convulsion.

【Location】In the centre of the mastoid process, at the junction of the middle and lower third of the curve formed by Yifeng (SJ 17) and Jiaosun (SJ 20) posterior to the helix (Fig 12－10).

【Regional anatomy】Vasculature: The posterior auricular artery and vein. Innervation: The posterior auricular branch of the great auricular nerve.

【Properties】Benefit the ears, calm the frightened and eliminate wind.

【Indications】Headache, tinnitus, deafness, infantile convulsion.

【Needling method】Puncture transversely 0.3～0.5 cun, or prick with a three－edged needle to cause bleeding. Moxibustion is applicable.

19. 颅息 Luxi (SJ 19)

【释义】颅，头颅；息，安宁。穴在头颅部，可安脑宁神。

【定位】在头部，当角孙至翳风之间，沿耳轮连线的上、中1/3的交点处（图12－10）。

【解剖】血管：耳后动脉和静脉。神经：耳大神经，枕小神经，面神经耳后支。

【功用】聪耳，清热镇惊止痉。

【主治】头痛，耳鸣，耳聋，耳痛，小儿惊风。

【操作】平刺0.3~0.5寸，可灸。

【Meaning】Lu, skull; xi, tranquility. The point is on the skull and is used to calm the mind.

【Location】Posterior to the ear, at the junction of the upper and middle third of the curve formed by Yifeng (SJ 17) and Jiaosun (SJ 20) behind the helix (Fig 12–10).

【Regional anatomy】Vasculature: The posterior auricular artery and vein. Innervation: the great auricular nerve and the lesser occipital nerve, the posterior auricular branch of facial nerve.

【Properties】Benefit the ears and clear heat, calm the frightened and relieve tinnitus.

【Indications】Headache, tinnitus, deafness, pain in the ear, infantile convulsion.

【Needling method】Puncture transversely 0.3~0.5 cun. Moxibustion is applicable.

20. 角孙 Jiaosun (SJ 20)

【释义】角，角隅；孙，孙络。穴在颞颥部，相当于耳上角对应部，布有孙络。

【定位】在头部，折耳廓向前，当耳尖直上入发际处（图12–10）。

【解剖】血管：颞浅动、静脉耳前支。神经：耳颞神经的分支。

【功用】清热聪耳，利齿益关节。

【主治】耳鸣，目翳，齿痛，偏头痛，牙龈肿，痄腮。

【操作】平刺0.3~0.5寸，可灸。

【Meaning】Jiao, corner; sun, tertiary collateral. The point is on the temporal region, corresponding to the ear apex, where the reticular meridians are distributed.

【Location】Directly above the ear apex, within the hair line (Fig 12–10).

【Regional anatomy】Vasculature: The branches of the superficial temporal artery and vein. Innervation: The branches of the auriculotemporal nerve.

【Properties】Benefit the ears, benefit the teeth, gums and lips, clear heat.

【Indications】Tinnitus, redness, pain and swelling of the eye, swelling of gum, toothache, migraine, parotitis.

【Needling method】Puncture transversely 0.3~0.5 cun. Moxibustion is applicable.

21. 耳门 Ermen (SJ 21)

【释义】耳，耳窍；门，门户。穴在耳前，犹如耳之门户。

【定位】在面部，当耳屏上切迹的前方，下颌骨髁状突后缘，张口有凹陷处（图12–10）。

【解剖】血管：颞浅动、静脉耳前支。神经：耳颞神经的分支。

【功用】聪耳清热。

【主治】耳鸣，耳聋，聤耳，齿痛，口㖞。

【操作】微张口，直刺0.5~1.0寸。

【Meaning】Er, ear; men, door. The point is in front of the ear, like a door to the ear.

【Location】In the depression anterior to the supratragic notch and behind the posterior border of the condyloid process of the mandible. The point is located with the mouth open (Fig 12 – 10).

【Regional anatomy】Vasculature: The superficial temporal artery and vein. Innervation: The branches of the auriculotemporal nerve.

【Properties】Benefit the ears, clear heat.

【Indications】Tinnitus, deafness, otorrhea, toothache, stiffness of the lip.

【Needling method】Puncture perpendicularly 0.5 ~ 1.0 cun.

22. 耳和髎 Erheliao (SJ 22)

【释义】耳，耳窍；和，调和；髎，骨隙。穴当耳前骨的浅表陷隙中，可调耳和声。

【定位】在头侧部，当鬓发后缘，平耳廓根之前方，颞浅动脉的后缘（图 12 – 10）。

【解剖】血管：颞浅动、静脉耳前支，神经：浅层分布有耳颞神经，面神经颞支。

【功用】祛风止痛。

【主治】偏头痛，耳鸣，牙关紧闭，口㖞。

【操作】避开动脉，斜刺或平刺 0.3 ~ 0.5 寸，可灸。

【Meaning】Er, ear; he, harmony; liao, foramen. The point is in the depression in front of tragicus and is used to improve hearing.

【Location】Anterior and superior to Ermen (SJ 21), at the level with the root of the auricle, on the posterior border of the hairline of the temple where the superficial temporal artery passes (Fig 12 – 10).

【Regional anatomy】Vasculature: The superficial temporal artery and vein. Innervation: The branch of the auriculotemporal nerve, on the course of the temporal branch of the facial nerve.

【Properties】Expel pathogenic – wind to alleviate pain.

【Indications】Migraine, tinnitus, lockjaw.

【Needling method】Avoid puncturing the artery, puncture obliquely or transversely 0.3 ~ 0.5 cun. Moxibustion is applicable.

23. 丝竹空 Sizhukong (SJ 23)

【释义】丝竹，即细竹；空，空隙。眉毛，状如细竹。穴在眉梢之凹陷处。

【定位】在面部，当眉梢凹陷处（图 12 – 10）。

【解剖】血管：颞浅动、静脉额支，神经：分布有眶上神经，面神经颞支和颧支。

【功用】息风止痛，明目。

【主治】头痛，目赤肿痛，目眩，目翳，眼睑瞤动，牙痛，面瘫。

【操作】平刺 0.3 ~ 0.5 寸。不灸。

【Meaning】Sizhu, slender bamboo; kong, space. The point is at the lateral end of the eyebrow, which looks like a slender bamboo. The local region of the point has a shallow depression.

【Location】 In the depression at the lateral end of the eyebrow (Fig 12 - 10).

【Regional anatomy】 Vasculature: The frontal branches of the superficial temporal artery and vein. Innervation: The zygomatic and temporal branch of the facial nerve, supraorbital nerve.

【Properties】 Eliminate wind to alleviate pain, benefits the eyes.

【Indications】 Headache, redness and pain of the eye, blurring of vision, twitching of the eyelid, toothache, facial paralysis.

【Needling method】 Puncture transversely 0.3 ~ 0.5 cun.

复习思考题
Review Questions

1. 手少阳三焦经联系哪些内脏和器官?

What are the organs and tissues connected with the triple energizer meridian of hand - shaoyang?

2. 手少阳三焦经穴位总数是多少?说出其起止穴位。

How many points are there on the meridian of triple energizer? What are the first and the last points?

3. 外关与内关有哪些异同点?

Discuss the differences and similarities of Neiguan (PC 6) and Waiguan (SJ 5).

4. 简述支沟穴的定位、操作和主治。

Describe the location, needling method and indications of Zhigou (SJ 6).

5. 耳门穴与听宫、听会的定位关系如何?

What are the locations of Ermen (SJ 21), Tingong (SI 19) and Tinghui (GB 2)?

第十三章 足少阳经络与腧穴
Meridian and Collateral and Its Acupoints of Foot – Shaoyang

第一节 足少阳经络
Meridian and Collateral of Foot – Shaoyang

一、足少阳经脉
Meridian of Foot - Shaoyang

（一）经脉循行
The Course of Meridian

足少阳胆经起于目外眦，上行额角部，下行至耳后，沿颈项部至肩上，下入缺盆。

耳部支脉，从耳后入耳中，经耳前，到目外眦后方；目外眦支脉，从目外眦下走大迎，再向上到达目眶下，下行经颊车，至颈部会合前脉于缺盆，内行进入胸中，通过横膈，联络肝，属于胆，沿胁肋内，下达腹股沟动脉部，经过外阴部毛际，横入髋关节部。直行主脉从缺盆下经腋部、侧胸、胁肋部，下合前脉于髋关节部，再向下沿着大腿外侧、膝外缘、腓骨之前，达外踝之前，循足背部，止于足第4趾外侧端。

足背部支脉，从足背上分出，沿第1、2跖骨之间，止于大趾端，接足厥阴肝经（图13-1）。

《灵枢·经脉》原文：胆足少阳之脉，起于目锐眦，上抵头角，下耳后，循颈，行手少阳之前，至肩上，却交出手少阳之后，入缺盆。

其支者，从耳后入耳中，出走耳前，至目锐眦后。

其支者，别锐眦，下大迎，合于手少阳，抵于䪼，下加颊车，下颈，合缺盆。以下胸中，贯膈，络肝，属胆，循胁里，出气街，绕毛际，横入髀厌中。

其直者，从缺盆下腋，循胸，过季胁，下合髀厌中。以下循髀阳，出膝外廉，下外辅骨之前，直下抵绝骨之端，下出外踝之前，循足跗上，入小指次指之间。

其支者，别跗上，入大指之间，循大指歧骨内，出其端，还贯爪甲，出三毛。

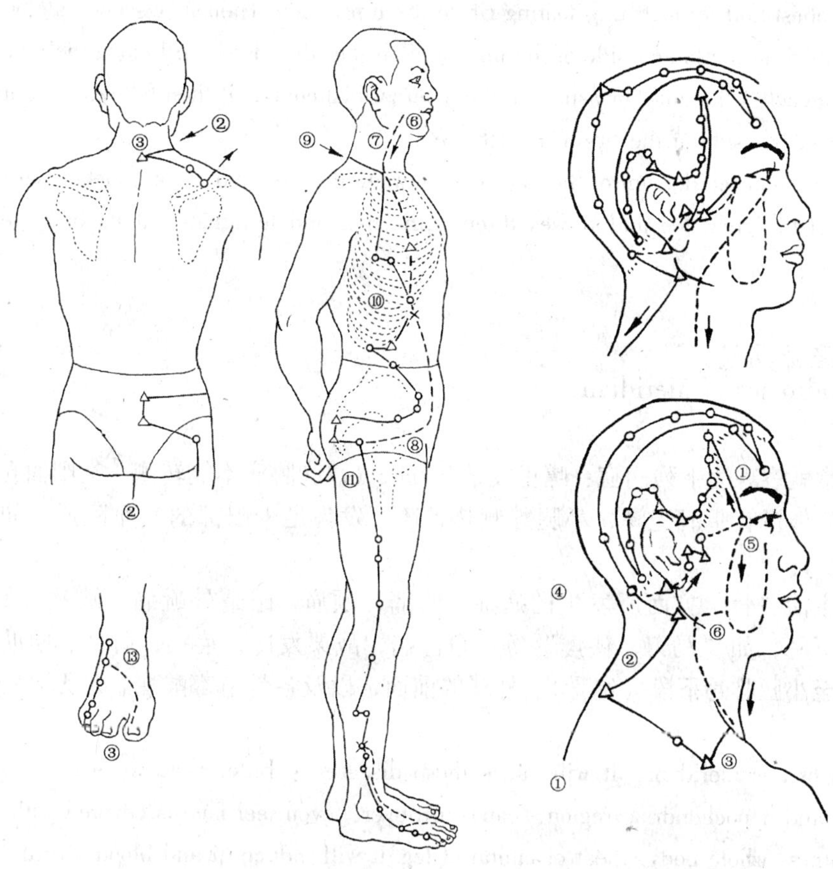

图例 ——本经有穴通路 ……本经无穴通路

Note ——Pathway with points ……Pathway without points

图 13－1 足少阳经脉、络脉循行示意图

Fig 13－1 The course of the meridian and collateral of foot－shaoyang

The gallbladder meridian starts from the outer canthus, ascends to the corner of the forehead, then curves downward to the retroauricular region, descending further along the neck to the shoulder, it enters the supraclavicular fossa.

One branch arises from the retroauricular region and enters into the ear. It comes out and passes the preauricular region to the posterior aspect of the outer canthus. Another branch arising from the outer canthus, runs downward to Daying (ST 5) and ascends to the infraorbital region, then passes near Jiache (ST 6), descends to the neck where it joins the previous branch at the supraclavicular fossa, then further descends into the chest, passes through the diaphragm to connect with the liver and pertain to the gallbladder. Then it runs inside the hypochondriac region, comes out from the lateral side of the lower abdomen, from there, runs superficially along the region of the pubic hair and goes transversely into the hip region.

The straight branch from the supraclavicular fossa runs downward to the axilla , along the lateral side of the chest and through the floating rib to the hip region. Then it descends along the lateral aspect of the thigh to the lateral side of the knee and goes further downward along the anterior aspect of the fibula, reaches the anterior aspect of the external malleolus, it then follows the dorsum of the foot to end on lateral side of the tip of the 4th toe.

The branch from the dorsum of the foot runs between the first and second metatarsal bone to the distal portion of the great toe and passes through the nail and terminates at its hairy region (Fig 13 – 1).

(二) 经脉病候
The Syndromes of Meridian

本经异常就表现为下列病症：嘴里发苦，好叹气，胸胁痛不能转侧，甚则面孔像蒙着微薄的灰尘，身体没有脂润光泽，小腿外侧热，还可发为足少阳部的气血阻逆，如厥冷、麻木、酸痛等。

本经穴主治“骨”方面所发生的病症：头痛，颞痛，眼睛外眦痛，缺盆（锁骨上窝）中肿痛，腋下肿，如“马刀、侠瘿”等。自汗出，战栗发冷，疟疾，脚部、胁肋、大腿及膝部外侧以至小腿腓骨下段（绝骨）、外踝的前面，以及各骨节都酸痛、足无名趾功能活动受限。

Disorder of this meridian, it will cause these diseases : bitter taste in mouth , often sigh, pain of chest and hypochondriac region, can't turn over, even feel face is covered with little dust, without brightness whole body, heat of lateral of leg. It will induce qi and blood obstruction of gallbladder meridian, cold, numbness, soreness and pain.

Points of the meridian can treat diseases connected with bone disorders: headache, temporal pain, pain of outer canthus, pain and swelling of supraclavicular fossa, swelling of axilla, scrofula, sweating, shiver and shaking, malaria, soreness and pain of chest, hepochondriac region and thigh, from external aspect of knee to lower of fibula, the anterior aspect of the external malleolus, all joints are soreness and pain, function of the 4th toe is limited.

二、足少阳络脉
Collateral of Foot - Shaoyang

足少阳之别，名曰光明。去踝五寸，别走厥阴，下络足跗（图 13 – 1）。

实则厥；虚则痿躄，坐不能起。取之所别也。

It begins from Guangming (GB 37), 5 cun above exterior malleolus, it joins the liver meridian and then runs downward and disperse over the dorsum of foot (Fig 13 – 1).

The points in this meridian can be used for treating the excess syndrome, which appears cold of foot, and the deficiency syndrome which shows atrophy or paralysis in the lower limbs.

三、足少阳经别 Divergent Meridian of Foot - Shaoyang

足少阳之正，绕髀，入毛际，合于厥阴；别者入季胁之间，循胸里，属胆，散之肝，上贯心，以上夹咽，出颐颔中，散于面，系目系，合少阳于外眦也（图 13 –2）。

After deriving from the gallbladder meridian on the thigh, it crosses over the hip joint and enters the lower abdomen in the pelvic region and converges with the divergent meridian of the liver Meridian. Then, it crosses between the lower ribs, connects with the gallbladder and spreads through the liver. Proceeding further upward. It crosses the heart and esophagus and disperses in the face. It then connects with the eye and rejoins the gallbladder meridian of foot – shaoyang at the outer canthus（Fig 13 –2）.

四、足少阳经筋 Muscular Region of Foot - Shaoyang

足少阳之筋，起于小指（趾）次指（趾），上结外踝，上循胫外廉，结于膝外廉。其支者别起外辅骨，上走髀，前者结于伏兔之上，后者结于尻。其直者，上乘眇、季胁，上走腋前廉，系于膺乳，结于缺盆。直者上出腋，贯缺盆，出太阳之前，循耳后，上额角，交巅上，下走颔，上结于頄。支者结于目外眦，为外维（图 13 –3）。

其病：小指（趾）次指（趾）支转筋，引膝外转筋，膝不可屈伸，腘筋急，前引髀，后引尻，即上乘眇季胁痛，上引缺盆、膺乳、颈维筋急，从左之右，右目不开，上过右角，并跻脉而行，左络于右，故伤左角，右足不用，命曰维筋相交。

It originates from the fourth toe, knots with the external malleolus. Then it ascends along the lateral side of the tibia where it knots with the knee. A branch begins at the upper part of the fibula and continues upward along the thigh. One of its subbranch runs anteriorly, knotting above Futu（ST 32）. Another subbranch runs posteriorly and knots with the sacrum. The straight branch ascends across the ribs, dispersing around and anterior to the axilla , connecting first at the breast region and then knotting at the Quepen（ST 12）. Another branch extends from the axilla upward across the clavicle, emerging in front of the foot – taiyang（bladder）muscle region where it continues upward behind the ear to the temple. Then, it proceeds up to the vertex to join its bilateral counterpart. A branch descends from the temple across the cheek and then knots beside the bridge of the nose. A subbranch knots with the outer canthus（Fig 13 –3）.

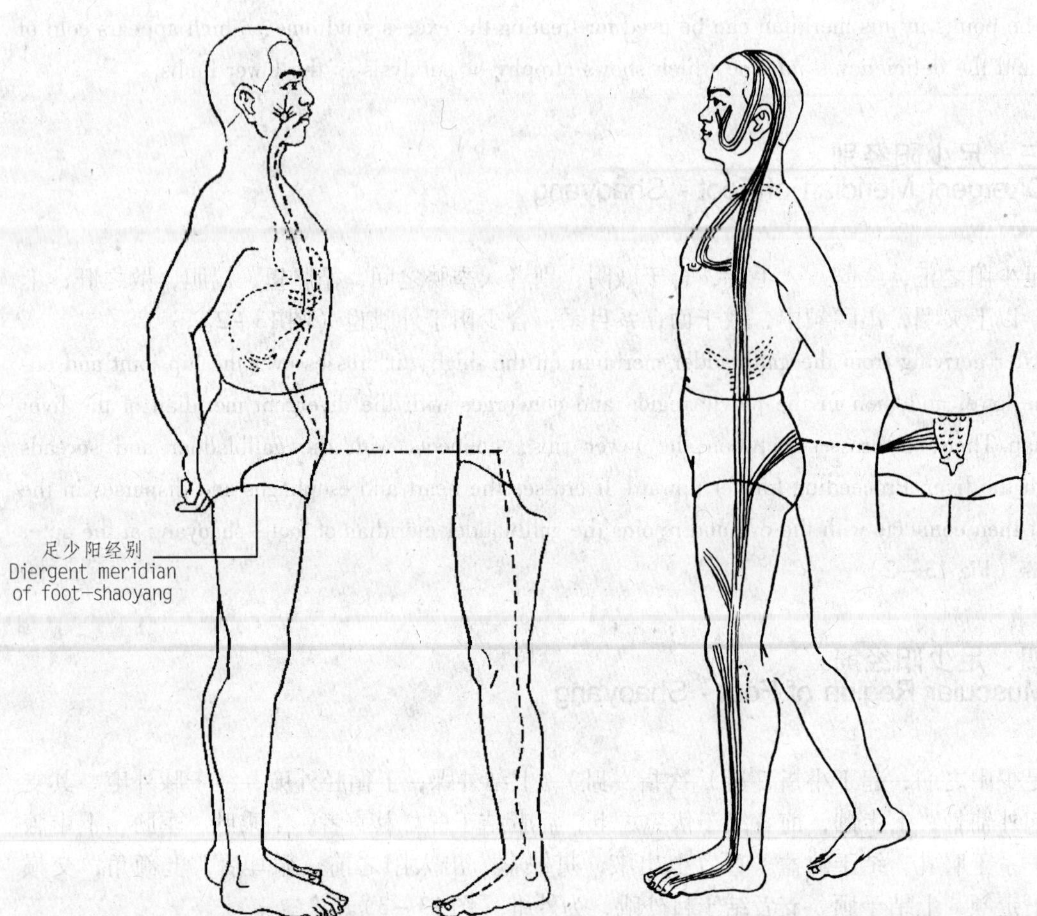

图 13－2 足少阳经别循行示意图
Fig 13－2 The course of the divergent meridian of foot－shaoyang

图 13－3 足少阳经筋分布示意图
Fig 13－3 The course of the muscular region of foot－shaoyang

第二节 足少阳腧穴
Acupoints of Foot－Shaoyang

本经左右各 44 个穴位，起穴瞳子髎，止穴足窍阴（图 13－4）。

1. 瞳子髎（GB 1），手太阳、手足少阳经交会穴
Tongziliao （GB 1)，Crossing Point of the Meridians of Hand－Taiyang，Hand－Shaoyang and Foot－Shaoyang

【释义】瞳子，即瞳孔；髎，骨隙。穴在小眼角外方骨隙中，横对瞳孔。

【定位】在面部，目外眦旁，当眶外侧缘处（图 13－5）。

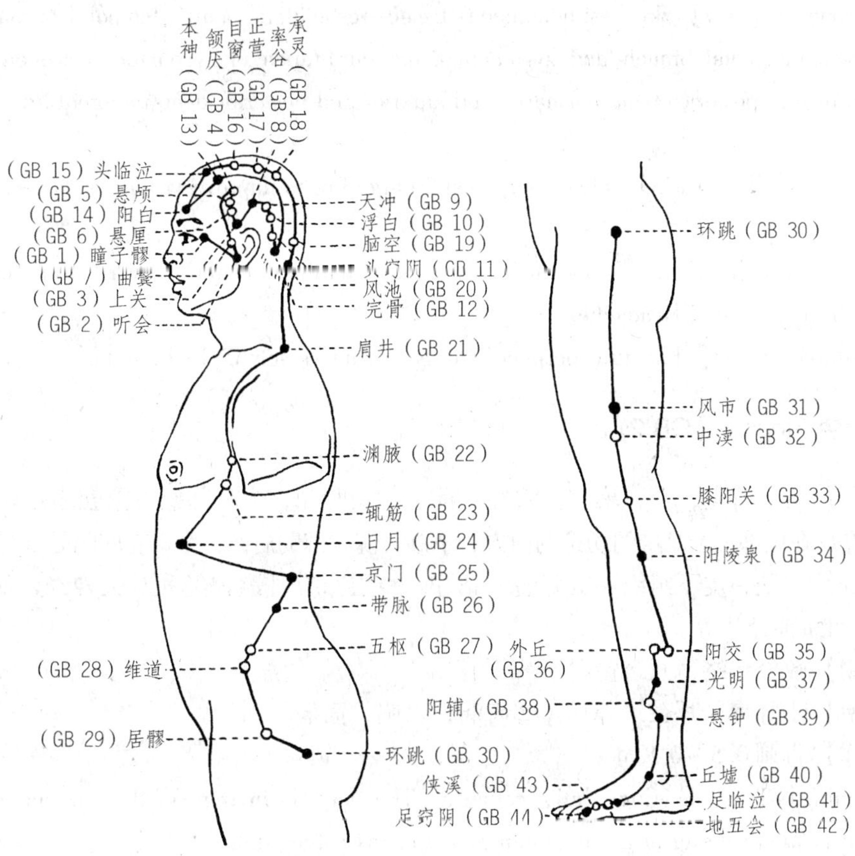

图例 ● 常用腧穴 ○ 一般腧穴

Note ● Main point ○ Common point

图 13－4 足少阳胆经腧穴总图

Fig 13－4 Points of the gallbladder meridian of foot－shaoyang

【解剖】皮肤→皮下组织→眼轮匝肌→颞筋膜→颞肌。浅层布有颧神经的颧面支与颧颞支。深层有颞深前、后神经和颞深前、后动脉的分支。

【功用】疏风散热，清头明目，消肿止痛。

【主治】①目赤肿痛，目翳，青盲，口㖞。②头痛。

【操作】直刺或平刺 0.3～0.5 寸。

【Meaning】Tongzi, pupil; liao, foramen. The point is in a foramen lateral to the outer canthus and at the level of the pupil.

【Location】Lateral to outer canthus, in the depression on the lateral aspect of the orbit（Fig 13－5）.

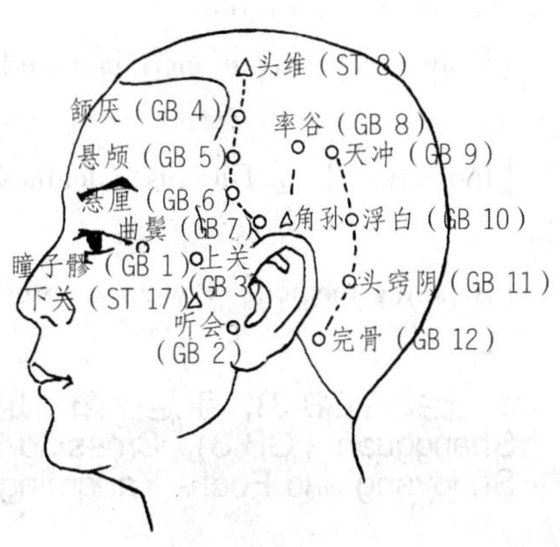

图 13－5

Fig 13－5

【Regional anatomy】Skin→subcutaneous tissue→orbicularis oculi→temporal fascia→temporal muscle. zygomaticofacial branch and zygomaticotemporal branch of zygomatic nerve on superficial layer. anterior and posterior temproal nerve and anterior and posterior deep temproal artery branch in deep layer.

【Properties】Expel wind, clear away heat, purge fire to improve vision, subdue swelling and relieve pain.

【Indications】①Redness and pain in the eyes, cloudiness of the cornea, optic atrophy, deviated mouth and eyes. ②Headache.

【Needling method】Puncture perpendicularly or transversely 0. 3 ~0. 5cun.

2. 听会 Tinghui (GB 2)

【释义】听，听觉；会，聚会。穴在耳前，功司听闻，为耳部经气聚会之处。

【定位】在面部，当耳屏间切迹的前方，下颌骨髁状突的后缘，张口有凹陷处（图13－5）。

【解剖】皮肤→皮下组织→腮腺囊→腮腺。浅层布有耳颞神经和耳大神经。深层有颞浅动、静脉和面神经丛等。

【功用】疏经活络，开窍益聪。

【主治】①耳鸣，耳聋，聤耳。②齿痛，口㖞，面痛。

【操作】直刺0. 5 ~0. 8寸。

【Meaning】Ting, hearing; hui, gathering. The point is in front of the ear and functions in hearing; it is whcre thc qi of the meridian at the ear is gathered.

【Location】In front of the intertragic notch, on the posterior border of the condyloid of the mandible, in the depression appearing when open mouth (Fig 13－5).

【Regional anatomy】Skin→subcutaneous tissue→parotid capsule→parotid. Auricular temporal nerve and great auricular nerve on superficial layer. superficial temporal vein and artery, the facial nerve plexus in deep layer.

【Properties】Dredge meridians and activate collaterals, induce resuscitation and benefit intelligence.

【Indications】①Tinnitus, deafness, otitis. ②Toothache, deviated mouth and eyes, facial pain.

【Needling method】Puncture perpendicularly 0. 5 ~0. 8cun.

3. 上关（GB 3)，手足少阳、足阳明经交会穴
Shangguan (GB 3), Crossing Point of the Meridians of Hand - Shaoyang, Foot - Shaoyang and Foot - Yangming

【释义】上，上方；关，关界。关，指颧骨弓，穴当其上缘。

【定位】在耳前，下关直上，当颧弓的上缘凹陷处（图13－5）。

【解剖】皮肤→皮下组织→颞浅筋膜→颞深筋膜→颞筋膜下结缔组织→颞肌。浅层布有耳颞神经，面神经颞支和颞浅动、静脉。深层有颞深前、后神经分支。

【功用】通经活络，开窍益聪。

【主治】①耳鸣，耳聋，聤耳。②偏头痛，口㖞，口噤，齿痛，面痛，癫狂痫。

【操作】直刺0.5～1.0寸。

【Meaning】Shang, upper; guan, border of gate. Guan refer to the zygomatic arch. The point is at the upper margin of the zygomatic arch.

【Location】Anterior to the ear, directly above Xiaguan (ST 7), in the depression on the upper border of the zygomatic arch (Fig 13-5).

【Regional anatomy】Skin→subcutaneous tissue→superficial fascia temporalis→deep temporal fascia→areolar tissue below fascia temporalis→temporal muscle. Auricular temporal nerve, facial nerve temporalis branch, superficial temporal arteries and veins on superficial layer. anterior and posterior deep temproal nerve branch in deep layer.

【Properties】Dredge channels and activate collaterals, induce resuscitation and benefit intelligence.

【Indications】①Tinnitus, deafness, otitis. ②Migraine, deviated mouth and eyes, locked jaw, toothache, facial pain, and epilepsy.

【Needling method】Puncture perpendicularly 0.5～1.0cun.

4. 颔厌（GB 4)，手足少阳、足阳明经交会穴
Hanyan (GB 4), Crossing Point of the Meridians of Hand - Shaoyang, Foot - Shaoyang and Foot - Yangming

【释义】颔，下颌；厌，顺从。穴在颞颥部，随咀嚼顺从下颌运动。

【定位】头维与曲鬓弧形连线的上1/4与下3/4交点处（图13-5)。

【解剖】皮肤→皮下组织→耳上肌→颞筋膜→颞肌。浅层布有耳颞神经，颞浅动、静脉顶支。深层有颞深前、后神经分支。

【功用】疏风活络，止痛益聪。

【主治】①偏头痛，眩晕，癫痫。②齿痛，耳鸣，口㖞。

【操作】平刺0.5～0.8寸。

【Meaning】Han, mandible; yan, obedience. The point is at the temple and moves along with the motion of the mandible when chewing.

【Location】At the junction of the upper 1/4 and lower 3/4 of on the arc connecting Touwei (ST 8) and Qubin (GB 7) (Fig 13-5).

【Regional anatomy】Skin→subcutaneous tissue→musculus auricularis superior→temporal fascia→temporal muscle. Auricular temporal nerve, superficial temporal arteries and veins top branch on superficial layer. anterior and posterior deep temproal nerve branch in deep layer.

【Properties】Expel wind, activate blood flow in the collaterals, relieve pain and improve intelligence.

【Indications】①Migraine, dizziness, epilepsy. ②Toothache, deafness, deviated mouth and eyes.

【Needling method】Puncture transversely 0.5 ~0.8cun.

5. 悬颅 Xuanlu (GB 5)

【释义】悬，悬挂，颅，头颅。穴在头颅部，如悬挂在头颅之两侧。

【定位】在头部鬓发上，当头维与曲鬓弧形连线的中点处（图 13 -5）。

【解剖】同颔厌穴。

【功用】清热止痛，散风消肿。

【主治】①偏头痛。②目赤肿痛，齿痛，面肿，鼽衄。

【操作】平刺0.5 ~0.8 寸。

【Meaning】Xuan, hung; lu, skull. The points are at the temples as if hanging on both sides of the skull.

【Location】On the hair of head, on the midpoint on the arc connecting Touwei (ST 8) and Qubin (GB 7) (Fig 13 -5).

【Regional anatomy】It is similar with Hanyan (GB 4).

【Properties】Clear away heat to relieve pain, expel wind and subdue swelling.

【Indications】①Migraine. ②Redness, swelling and pain of the eyes, toothache, facial swelling, epistaxis.

【Needling method】Puncture transversely 0.5 ~0.8cun.

6. 悬厘 (GB 6)，手少阳、足少阳、足阳明经交会穴
Xuanli (GB 6), Crossing Point of the Meridians of Hand - Shaoyang, Foot - Shaoyang and Foot - Yangming

【释义】悬，悬垂；厘，同“氂”，指头发。穴在颞颥部，头维与曲鬓弧形连线的中点。

【定位】当头维与曲鬓弧形连线的上 3/4 与下 1/4 交点处（图 13 -5）。

【解剖】同颔厌穴。

【功用】清热止痛，散风消肿。

【主治】①偏头痛。②目赤肿痛，耳聋，齿痛，面痛。

【操作】平刺0.5 ~0.8 寸。

【Meaning】Xuan, hanging; li, hair. The point is at the temple beneath long hair.

【Location】At the junction of the upper 3/4 and lower 1/4 on the arc connecting Touwei (ST 8) and Qubin (GB 7) (Fig 13 -5).

【Regional anatomy】It is similar with Hanyan (GB 4).

【Properties】Clear away heat to relieve pain, expel wind and subdue swelling.

【Indications】①Migraine. ②Redness, swelling and pain of the eyes, tinnitus, toothache, facial pain.

【Needling method】Puncture transversely 0.5~0.8cun.

7. 曲鬓（GB 7），足少阳、足太阳经交会穴
Qubin (GB 7), Crossing Point of the Meridians of Foot - Shaoyang and Foot - Taiyang

【释义】曲，弯曲；鬓，鬓发。穴在耳上鬓发边际的弯曲处。

【定位】在头部，当耳前鬓角发际后缘的垂线与耳尖水平线交点处（图13-5）。

【解剖】同颔厌穴。

【功用】止痛消肿，祛风开噤。

【主治】①偏头痛，颔颊肿。②目赤肿痛，暴喑，牙关紧闭。

【操作】平刺0.5~0.8寸。

【Meaning】Qu, curve; bin, hair at the temple. The point is at the hairline at the temple above the ear.

【Location】On the head, on the junction of the vertical line on the posterior border of the preauricular hairline level with the apex of the ear (Fig 13-5).

【Regional anatomy】It is similar with Hanyan (GB 4).

【Properties】Relieve pain, subdue swelling, disperse wind and treat trismus.

【Indications】①Migraine, swelling of mandible and cheek. ②Redness, swelling and pain of the eyes, suddenly lose voice. trismus.

【Needling method】Puncture transversely 0.5~0.8cun.

8. 率谷（GB 8），足少阳、足太阳经交会穴
Shuaigu (GB 8), Crossing Point of the Meridians of Foot - Shaoyang and Foot - Taiyang

【释义】率，统率；谷，山谷。穴在耳上，为以“谷”命名诸穴的最高者，如诸谷之统率。

【定位】当耳尖直上入发际1.5寸（图13-5）。

【解剖】皮肤→皮下组织→耳上肌→颞筋膜→颞肌。布有耳神经和枕大神经会合支及颞浅动、静脉顶支。

【功用】疏泄肝胆，清热息风。

【主治】①偏头痛，眩晕，耳聋，耳鸣。②小儿急、慢惊风。

【操作】平刺0.5~0.8寸。

【Meaning】Shuai, command; gu, valley. The point is above the ear and is the highest among all the points named gu (valley), like a commander.

【Location】1. 5 cun from the apex of the ear straight into the hairline（Fig 13 –5）.

【Regional anatomy】Skin→subcutaneous tissue→musculus auricularis superior→temporal fascia→temporal muscle. Distribute connecting branch of auricular nerve and greater occipital nerve, superficial temporal arteries and veins top branch.

【Properties】Soothe the flow of the liver – qi, purge heat from the liver and gallbladder, clear away heat and calm wind.

【Indications】①Migraine, dizziness, tinnitus, deafness. ②infantile acute or chronic convulsion.

【Needling method】Puncture transversely 0. 5 ~0. 8cun.

9. 天冲（GB 9），足少阳、足太阳经交会穴 Tianchong（GB 9），Crossing Point of the Meridian of Foot - Shaoyang and Foot - Taiyang

【释义】天，天空；冲，冲出。天指头部，穴在其两侧，本经气血由该穴冲向巅顶。

【定位】当耳根后缘直上入发际2寸，率谷后0.5寸（图13 –5）。

【解剖】皮肤→皮下组织→耳上肌→颞筋膜→颞肌。布有耳神经和枕小神经以及枕大神经的会合支，颞浅动、静脉顶支和耳后动、静脉。

【功用】祛风定惊。

【主治】①头痛，耳聋，耳鸣，牙龈肿痛。②癫痫。

【操作】平刺0.5 ~0.8寸。

【Meaning】Tian, heaven; chong, gushing. Tian refer to the head, where the point is located. The qi and blood gush to the vertex of the head from this point.

【Location】2 cun from the posterior border of the ear straight into the hairline, 0. 5 cun posterior to Shuaigu（Fig 13 –5）.

【Regional anatomy】Skin→subcutaneous tissue→musculus auricularis superior→temporal fascia→temporal muscle. Distribute auricular nerve and connecting branch of lesser occipital nerve and greater occipital nerve, superficial temporal arteries and veins top branch, posterior auricular arteries and veins.

【Properties】Expel wind and relieve convulsion.

【Indications】①Headache, tinnitus, deafness, swelling and pain of the gingiva. ②epilepsy.

【Needling method】Puncture transversely 0. 5 ~0. 8cun.

10. 浮白（GB 10），足少阳、足太阳经交会穴 Fubai（GB 10），Crossing Point of the Meridian of Foot - Shaoyang and Foot - Taiyang

【释义】浮，浮浅；白，光明。穴位于体表浮浅部位，有清头明目之功。

【定位】当耳后乳突的后上方，天冲与完骨的弧形连线的中 1/3 与上 1/3 交点处（图 13－5）。

【解剖】皮肤→皮下组织→帽状腱膜。布有枕小神经和枕大神经的吻合支以及耳后动、静脉。

【功用】祛风解表，行瘀理气。

【主治】①头痛，耳聋，耳鸣，目痛。②瘿气。

【操作】平刺 0.5～0.8 寸。

【Meaning】Fu, floating; bai bright. The point is on the superficial portion of the body and functions in clearing the mind and brightening the eyes.

【Location】At the junction of the central 1/3 and upper 1/3 on the curved line connecting Tianchong (GB 9) and Wangu (GB 12) (Fig 13－5).

【Regional anatomy】Skin→subcutaneous tissue→epicranial aponeurosis. Distribute connecting branch of lesser occipital nerve and greater occipital nerve and posterior auricular arteries and veins.

【Properties】Expel wind, relieve exterior syndrome, remove blood stasis, regulate flow of qi.

【Indications】①Headache, tinnitus, deafness, pain of the eyes. ②Goiter.

【Needling method】Puncture transversely 0.5～0.8cun.

11. 头窍阴（GB 11），足少阳、足太阳经交会穴
Touqiaoyin (GB 11), Crossing Point of the Meridian of Foot - Shaoyang and Foot - Taiyang

【释义】头，头部；窍，孔窍；阴，阴阳之阴。肾肝属阴，开窍于耳目。穴在头部，治疗耳目之疾。

【定位】当耳后乳突的后上方，天冲与完骨的弧形连线的中 1/3 与下 1/3 交点处（图 13－5）。

【解剖】皮肤→皮下组织→帽状腱膜。布有枕小神经和枕大神经的吻合支以及耳后动、静脉。

【功用】清风散热，通关开窍。

【主治】①耳聋，耳鸣。②头痛，眩晕，颈项强痛。

【操作】平刺 0.5～0.8 寸。

【Meaning】Tou, head; qiao, opening; yin, yin of yin and yang. The kindey and the liver pertain to Yin and open to the ear and eye. The point is on the head and is indicated in ear and eye diseases.

【Location】At the junction of the middle 1/3 and lower 1/3 on the curved line connecting Tianchong (GB 9) and Wangu (GB 12) (Fig 13－5).

【Regional anatomy】Skin→subcutaneous tissue→epicranial aponeurosis. Distribute connecting branch of lesser occipital nerve and greater occipital nerve and posterior auricular arteries and veins.

【Properties】Expel wind，clear away heat，purge fire to improve vision，regulate joints，induce resuscitation.

【Indications】①tinnitus，deafness. ②Headache，dizziness，stiffness and pain in the neck.

【Needling method】Puncture transversely 0. 5 ~0. 8cun.

12. 完骨（GB 12），足少阳、足太阳经交会穴
Wangu（GB 12），Crossing Point of the Meridian of Foot - Shaoyang and Foot - Taiyang

【释义】穴在耳后颞骨乳突下缘。

【定位】当耳后乳突的后下方凹陷处（图 13 –5）。

【解剖】皮肤→皮下组织→胸锁乳突肌→头夹肌→头最长肌。浅层布有枕小神经，耳后动、静脉的分支或属支。深层有颈深动、静脉。如果深刺可能刺中椎动脉。

【功用】祛风清热，止痛明目。

【主治】①头痛，项强，失眠。②齿痛，口㖞，口噤不开，颊肿。③癫痫，疟疾。

【操作】直刺 0. 5 ~0. 8 寸。

【Meaning】The point is at the lower margin of the mastoid process of the temporal bone behind the ear.

【Location】In the depression posterior and inferior to the mastoid process（Fig 13 –5）.

【Regional anatomy】Skin→subcutaneous tissue→sternocleidomastoid→musculus splenius capitis→longissimus capitis. lesser occipital nerve，branch and subordinate branch of posterior auricular arteries and veins in superficial layer. Deep carotid and jugular vein in deep layer.

【Properties】Expel wind，clear away heat，relieve pain and improve vision.

【Indications】①Headache，stiffness in the neck，insomnia. ②Toothache，deviated mouth and eyes，locked jaw，swollen cheek. ③epilepsy，malaria.

【Needling method】Puncture perpendicularly 0. 5 ~0. 8cun. Don't puncture deeply avoid stabbing vertebral artery.

13. 本神（GB 13），足少阳、阳维脉交会穴
Benshen（GB 13），Crossing Point of the Meridian of Foot - Shaoyang and Yang Link Vessel

【释义】本，根本；神，神志。穴在前发际神庭旁，内为脑之所在；脑为元神之府，主神志，为人之根本。

【定位】当前发际上 0. 5 寸，神庭旁开 3 寸，神庭与头维连线的内 2/3 与外 1/3 交点处（图 13 –6）。

【解剖】皮肤→皮下组织→枕额肌额腹。布有眶上动、静脉和眶上神经以及颞浅动、静脉额支。

【功用】清热止痛，祛风解痉。

【主治】①头痛，眩晕，目赤肿痛。②癫痫，小儿惊风，中风昏迷。

【操作】平刺0.3～0.5寸。

【Meaning】Ben, essential; shen, mind. The point is lateral to Shenting (DU 24) along the anterior hairline. The point is in the region where the brain is located and is considered as the residence and governor of the mind. It is therefore essential to the human body.

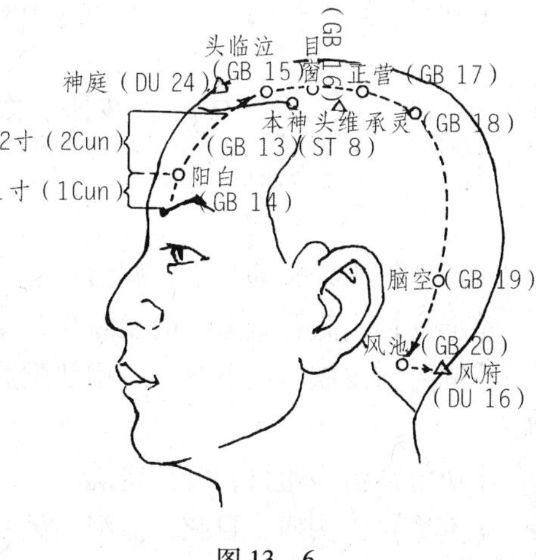

图 13－6

Fig 13－6

【Location】0.5 cun within the anterior hairline, 3 cun lateral to Shenting (DU 24) at the junction of the inner 2/3 and 1/3 of the curved connecting Shenting (DU 24) and Touwei (ST 8) (Fig 13－6).

【Regional anatomy】Skin→subcutaneous tissue→occipitofrontalis muscle belly. Distribute supraorbital artery and vein, supraorbital nerve and superficial temporal arteries and veins frontal branch.

【Properties】Clear away heat to relieve pain, expel wind and relieve convulsion.

【Indications】①Headache, dizziness, redness, swelling and pain of the eyes. ②Epilepsy, infantile convulsion, stoke coma.

【Needling method】Puncture transversely 0.3～0.5cun.

14. 阳白 (GB 14)，足少阳、阳维脉交会穴
Yangbai (GB 14), Crossing Point of the Meridian of Foot - Shaoyang and Yang Link Vessel

【释义】阳，阴阳之阳；白，光明。头为阳，穴在头面部，有明目之功。

【定位】在前额部，当瞳孔直上，眉上1寸（图13－6）。

【解剖】皮肤→皮下组织→枕额肌额腹。布有眶上神经外侧支和眶上动、静脉外侧支。

【功用】祛风泻火，清头明目。

【主治】①头痛，眩晕。②视物模糊，目痛，眼睑下垂，面瘫。

【操作】平刺0.3～0.5寸。

【Meaning】Yang, yang of yin－yang; bai, brightness. The head is yang. The point is at the head and its function is to brighten the eye.

【Location】On the forehead, directly above the pupils when the eyes are looking straightly ahead, 1 cun above the midpoint of the eyebrow (Fig 13－6).

【Regional anatomy】Skin→subcutaneous tissue→occipitofrontalis frontal belly. Distribute external branch of supraorbital nerve and external branch of supraorbital arteries and veins.

【Properties】Expel wind, purge fire, clear away heat from the head, improve vision.

【Indications】①Headache, dizziness. ②Blurred vision, pain of eyes, blepharoptosis, deviation of mouth and eyes.

【Needling method】Puncture transversely 0. 3 ~0. 5cun.

15. 头临泣（GB 15），足少阳、太阳、阳维脉交会穴 Toulinqi（GB 15），Crossing Point of the Meridian of Foot - Shaoyang，Foot - Taiyang and Yang Link Vessel

【释义】头，头部；临，调治；泣，流泪。穴在头部，可调治流泪等病。

【定位】当瞳孔直上入前发际0.5寸，神庭与头维连线的中点处（图13－6）。

【解剖】皮肤→皮下组织→帽状腱膜→腱膜下疏松结缔组织。布有眶上神经和眶上动、静脉。

【功用】清头明目，安神定志。

【主治】①头痛，目眩，流泪，鼻塞，鼻渊。② 小儿惊风，癫痫。

【操作】平刺0.3～0.5寸。

【Meaning】Tou，head；lin，regulation；qi，tears. The point is at the head and indicated in disorders of lacrimation.

【Location】Directly above the pupils when the eyes are looking straightly ahead，0. 5 cun within the anterior hairline，at the midpoint of the connecting Shenting（DU 24）and Touwei（ST 8）（Fig 13 －6）.

【Regional anatomy】Skin→subcutaneous tissue→epicranial aponeurosis→subaponeurotic loose connective tissue. Distribute supraorbital nerve and supraorbital artery and vein.

【Properties】Purge fire，improve vision，tranquilize mind and sedate emotional state.

【Indications】①Headache，dizziness，lacrimation，nasal congestion，nasosinusitis. ②infantile convulsion，epilepsy.

【Needling method】Puncture transversely 0. 3 ~0. 5cun.

16. 目窗（GB 16），足少阳经、阳维脉交会穴 Muchuang（GB 16），Crossing Point of the Meridians of Foot - Shaoyang and Yang Link Vessel

【释义】目，眼睛；窗，窗户。穴在眼的上方，善治眼疾，犹如眼目之窗。

【定位】在头部，当前发际上1.5寸，头正中线旁开2.25寸（图13－6）。

【解剖】皮肤→皮下组织→帽状腱膜→腱膜下疏松结缔组织。布有眶上神经和颞浅动、静脉额支。

【功用】祛风消肿，清头明目。

【主治】①目赤肿痛，青盲，视物模糊，鼻塞。② 头痛，眩晕，小儿惊痫。

【操作】平刺0.3~0.5寸。

【Meaning】Mu, eye; chuang, window. The point is above the eye and indicated in eye disorders, like a window of the eye.

【Location】On the head, 1.5cun within the anterior hairline, 2.25 cun lateral to the midline of the head (Fig 13-6).

【Regional anatomy】Skin→subcutaneous tissue→epicranial aponeurosis→subaponeurotic loose connective tissue. Distribute supraorbital nerve and superficial temporal artery and vein frontal branch.

【Properties】Disperse wind and subdue swelling, purge fire, improve vision.

【Indications】①Swelling and pain of the eyes, optic atrophy, blurred vision, nasal congestion. ②Headache, dizziness, infantile convulsion and epilepsy.

【Needling method】Puncture transversely 0.3~0.5cun.

17. 正营(GB 17),足少阳经、阳维脉交会穴
Zhengying (GB 17), Crossing Point of the Meridian of Foot - Shaoyang and Yang Link Vessel

【释义】正,正当;营,同荣。正营,惶恐不安的意思。本穴有主治惶恐不安等神志病的作用。

【定位】当前发际上2.5寸,头正中线旁开2.25寸(图13-6)。

【解剖】皮肤→皮下组织→帽状腱膜→腱膜下疏松结缔组织。布有眶上神经和枕大神经的吻合支,颞浅动、静脉的顶支,枕大神经和枕动、静脉的分支。

【功用】疏风,活络,止痛。

【主治】①头痛,眩晕,项强。②齿痛,唇吻急强。

【操作】平刺0.3~0.5寸。

【Meaning】Zhengying, fright and fear. This point is indicated in treating such mental states as fright and fear.

【Location】2.5 cun within the anterior hairline, 2.25 cun lateral to the midline of the head (Fig 13-6).

【Regional anatomy】Skin→subcutaneous tissue→epicranial aponeurosis→subaponeurotic loose connective tissue. Distribute connecting branch of supraorbital nerve and greater occipital nerve, superficial temporal artery and vein top branch, branch of greater occipital nerve and occipital artery and vein.

【Properties】Disperse wind, activate flow of qi and blood in the channels and collaterals, relieve pain.

【Indications】①Headache, dizziness, stiffness of neck. ②Toothache, stiffness of lip.

【Needling method】Puncture transversely 0.3~0.5cun.

18. 承灵（GB 18），足少阳经、阳维脉交会穴
Chengling（GB 18），Crossing Point of the Meridian of Foot - Shaoyang and Yang Link Vessel

【释义】承，承受；灵，神灵。脑主神灵，故脑上顶骨又称天灵骨；穴就在其外下方。

【定位】当前发际上4寸，头正中线旁开2.25寸（图13－6）。

【解剖】皮肤→皮下组织→帽状腱膜→腱膜下疏松结缔组织。布有枕大神经和枕动、静脉的分支。

【功用】清热散风。

【主治】①头痛，眩晕。②目痛，鼻塞，鼻衄。

【操作】平刺0.3～0.5寸。

【Meaning】Cheng，support；ling，spirit. The brain dominates the mind，so the parietal bone is also called the Tianling bone and the point is just lateral and inferior to it.

【Location】4 cun within the anterior hairline，2.25 cun lateral to the midline of the head（Fig 13－6）.

【Regional anatomy】Skin→subcutaneous tissue→epicranial aponeurosis→subaponeurotic loose connective tissue. Distribute greater occipital nerve and branch of occipital artery and vein.

【Properties】Clear away heat，disperse wind.

【Indications】①Headache，dizziness. ②Pain of the eyes，nasal congestion，epistaxis.

【Needling method】Puncture transversely 0.3～0.5cun.

19. 脑空（GB 19），足少阳经、阳维脉交会穴
Naokong（GB 19），Crossing Point of the Meridian of Foot - Shaoyang and Yang Link Vessel

【释义】脑，脑髓；空，孔窍。穴在枕骨外侧，内通脑窍，主治脑病。

【定位】当枕外隆凸的上缘外侧，头正中线旁开2.25寸（图13－6）。

【解剖】皮肤→皮下组织→枕额肌枕腹。布有枕大神经和枕动、静脉，面神经耳后支。

【功用】祛风，开窍。

【主治】①头痛，目眩，颈项强痛。②癫狂痫，惊悸。

【操作】平刺0.3～0.5寸。

【Meaning】Nao，brain；kong，cavity. The point is lateral to the occipital bone and internally related to the cranial cavity. It is indicated in treating neurological diseases.

【Location】On the lateral side of the superior border of the external occipital protuberance，2.25 cun lateral to the midline of the head（Fig 13－6）.

【Regional anatomy】Skin→subcutaneous tissue→occipitofrontalis muscle belly. Distribute greater occipital nerve and occipital artery and vein，posterior auricular branch of facial nerve.

【Properties】Expel wind, induce resuscitation.

【Indications】①Headache, dizziness, stiffness and pain of neck. ②Epilepsy, fright palpitations.

【Needling method】Puncture transversely 0. 3 ~0. 5cun.

20. 风池（GB 20)，足少阳经、阳维脉交会穴
Fengchi（GB 20)，Crossing Point of the Meridian of Foot - Shaoyang and Yang Link Vessel

【释义】风，风邪；池，池塘。穴在枕骨之下，局部凹陷如池，乃祛风之要穴。

【定位】在项部，当枕骨之下，与风府穴相平，胸锁乳突肌与斜方肌上端之间的凹陷处（图13－6）。

【解剖】皮肤→皮下组织→斜方肌和胸锁乳突肌之间→头夹肌→头半棘肌→头后大直肌与头上斜肌之间。浅层布有枕小神经和枕动、静脉的分支或属支。深层有枕大神经。

【功用】疏风解热，清头开窍，明目益聪。

【主治】①头痛，目眩，失眠，癫痫，中风。②目赤肿痛，视物不明，鼻塞，鼻衄，鼻渊，耳鸣，咽喉肿痛。③感冒，热病，颈项强痛。

【操作】向鼻尖方向斜刺0. 8 ~1. 2寸。

【Meaning】Feng, pathogenic wind; chi, pool. The point is below the occipital bone and the depression is like a pool. It is an important point in eliminating pathogenic wind.

【Location】Under the occipital, at the level of Fengfu（DU 16), in the depression between the upper portion of the sternocleidomastoid m. and trapezius m.（Fig 13 –6）.

【Regional anatomy】Skin→subcutaneous tissue→between the sternocleidomastoid m. and trapezius m. →m. splenius capitis. →m. semispinalis capitis→between m. rectus capitis posterior major and m. obliquus capitis superior. lesser occipital nerve and the branches of the occipital artery and vein in superficial layer. Greater occipital nerve in deep layer.

【Properties】Expel wind, clear away heat, purge fire, induce resuscitation, improve vision and intelligence.

【Indications】①Headache, dizziness, insomnia, epilepsy, stroke. ②Redness, welling and pain of the eyes, blurred vision, nasal congestion, epistaxis, nasosinusitis, tinnitus. ③Common cold, febrile diseases, stiffness and pain in the neck.

【Needling method】Puncture obliquely toward the tip of the nose for 0. 8 ~1. 2cun.

21. 肩井（GB 21)，手、足少阳、足阳明经、阳维脉交会穴
Jianjing（GB 21)，Crossing Point of the Meridian of Hand - Shaoyang, Foot - Shaoyang, Foot - Yangming and Yang Link Vessel

【释义】肩，肩部；井，水井。穴在肩上，局部凹陷如井。

【定位】在肩上，前直乳中，当大椎与肩峰端连线的中点（图 13－7）。

【解剖】皮肤→皮下组织→斜方肌→肩胛提肌。浅层布有锁骨上神经及颈浅动、静脉的分支或属支。深层有颈横动、静脉的分支或属支和肩胛背神经的分支。

【功用】通经理气，豁痰开郁。

【主治】①头痛，眩晕，颈项强痛，肩背疼痛，上肢不遂，瘰疬。②乳痈，乳汁少，难产，胞衣不下。

【操作】直刺 0.3 ~ 0.5 寸，切忌深刺，捣刺。孕妇禁用。

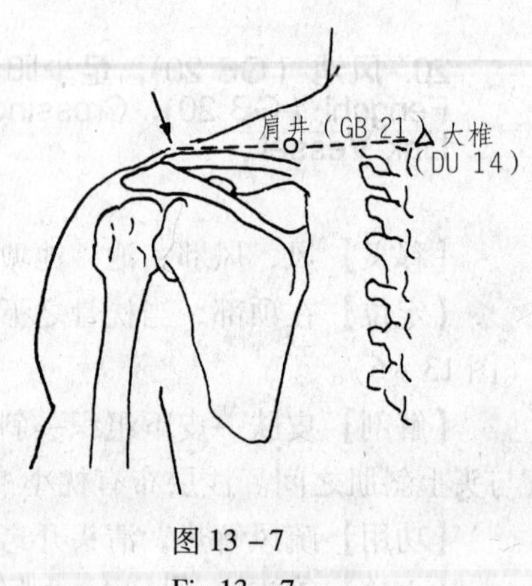

图 13－7

Fig 13－7

【Meaning】Jian，shoulder；jing，well. The point is on the shoulder and the depression is like a well.

【Location】On the shoulder，at the midpoint of the line joining Dazhui（DU 14） and the shoulder acromion（Fig 13－7）.

【Regional anatomy】Skin→subcutaneous tissue→the trapezius m. →m. levator scapulae. supraclavicular nerve，subordinate branch and branch of superficial cervical artery and vein in superficial layer. subordinate branch and branch of transverse cervical artery and vein，branch of dorsal scapular nerve in deep layer.

【Properties】Promote flow of blood in the channels，regulate flow of qi，dissolve phlegm and relieve depression.

【Indications】①Headache，dizziness，stiffness and pain in the neck，pain in the shoulder and upper back，paralysis of the upper extremities，scrofula. ②Mastitis，insufficient lactation，delayed labor，placenta stagnation.

【Needling method】Puncture perpendicularly 0. 3 ~ 0. 5cun，don't puncture deeply and puncture tamping. Prohibit for pregnant women.

22. 渊腋 Yuanye（GB 22）

【释义】渊，深潭；腋，腋部。腋深如渊，穴在腋下。

【定位】在侧胸部，当腋中线上，腋下 3 寸，第 4 肋间隙中（图 13－8）。

【解剖】皮肤→皮下组织→前锯肌→肋间外肌。浅层布有第 3、4、5 肋间神经外侧皮支，胸长神经和胸外侧动、静脉。深层有第 4 肋间神经和第 4 肋间后动、静脉。

【功用】理气行瘀。

【主治】①胸满，胁痛。②上肢痹痛。

【操作】平刺 0.5 ~0.8 寸。

【Meaning】The axilla is deep，like a pond，and the point is at the axilla.

【Location】On the lateral chest，on the axillary midline，3 cun below axilla，in the 4th intercostal space（Fig 13－8）.

【Regional anatomy】 Skin → subcutaneous tissue → m. serratus anterior → musculi intercostales externi. Lateral cutaneous branch intercostal nerve of 3rd、4th、5th, long thoracic nerve, lateral thoracic artery and vein in superficial layer. 4th intercostal nerve and 4th posterior intercostal artery and vein in deep layer.

【Properties】 Regulate flow of qi, remove blood stasis.

【Indications】 ①Tightness in chest, pain in the hepochondriac region. ②Spasm and pain in the upper limbs.

【Needling method】 Puncture transversely 0. 5 ~0. 8cun.

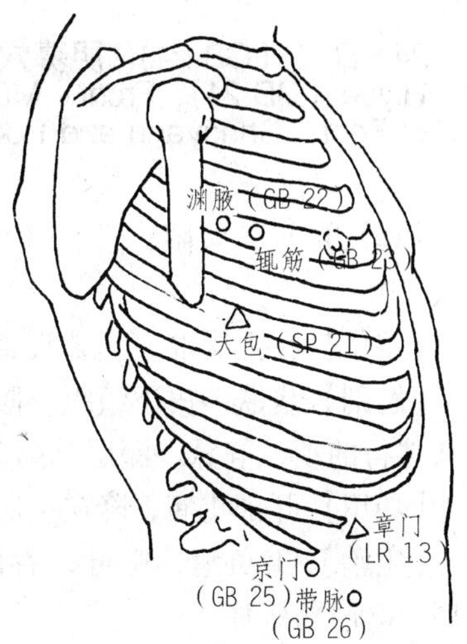

图 13 –8

Fig 13 –8

23. 辄筋 Zhejin（GB 23）

【释义】辄，车耳；筋，筋肉。车耳，即马车的护轮板。两侧胁肋筋肉隆起，形如车耳，穴在其处。

【定位】在侧胸部，渊腋前 1 寸，平乳头，第 4 肋间隙中（图 13 –8）。

【解剖】皮肤→皮下组织→前锯肌→肋间外肌。浅层布有第 3、4、5 肋间神经外侧皮支和胸外侧动、静脉的分支或属支。深层有第 4 肋间神经和第 4 肋间后动、静脉。

【功用】理气平喘，活血止痛。

【主治】①胸满，胁痛，腋肿。②呕叶，吞酸。③气喘。

【操作】平刺 0. 3 ~0. 5 寸。

【Meaning】 Zhe, ear of the cart; jin, muscle. The ear of the cart is the wheel protection plate of the cart. The muscle on both sides of the flanks are prominent as the ear of the cart, where the point is located.

【Location】 On the lateral chest, 1 cun anterior to Yuanye, at the level of the nipple, in the 4th intercostal space（Fig 13 –8）.

【Regional anatomy】 Skin→subcutaneous tissue→m. serratus anterior→musculi intercostales externi. Lateral cutaneous branch intercostal nerve of 3rd、4th、5th long thoracic nerve, lateral thoracic artery and vein in superficial layer. 4th intercostal nerve and 4th posterior intercostal artery an vein in deep layer.

【Properties】 Facilitate flow of the lung qi, relieve asthma, activate blood flow, relieve pain.

【Indications】 ①Tightness in chest, pain in the hepochondriac region, swelling of axilla. ②Vomiting, acid regurgitation. ③Asthma.

【Needling method】 Puncture transversely 0. 3 ~0. 5cun.

24. 日月（GB 24），胆募穴，足少阳、足太阴经交会穴
Riyue（GB 24），Front - Mu Point of the Gallbladder；Crossing Point of the Meridian of Foot - Shaoyang and Foot - Taiyin

【释义】日，太阳；月，月亮。日为阳，指胆；月为阴，指肝。此为治疗肝胆疾病的要穴。

【定位】在上腹部，当乳头直下，第7肋间隙，前正中线旁开4寸（图13－9）。

【解剖】皮肤→皮下组织→腹外斜肌→肋间外肌。浅层布有第6、7、8肋间神经外侧皮支和伴行的动、静脉。深层有第7肋间神经和第7肋间后动、静脉。

【功用】开郁止痛，降逆利胆。

【主治】①黄疸，呕吐，吞酸，呃逆，胃脘痛。②胁肋胀痛。

【操作】斜刺或平刺0.3～0.5寸。

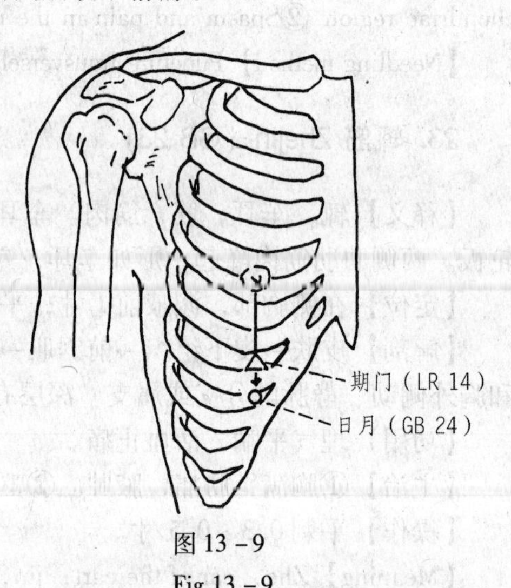

图13－9
Fig 13－9

【Meaning】Ri，sun；yue，moon. Ri is Yang，indicating the gallbladder，while yue is Yin，indicating the liver. This is an important point in treating liver and gallbladder diseases.

【Location】On the abdomen，directly below the nipple，in the 7th intercostal space，4cun lateral to the anterior midline（Fig 13－9）.

【Regional anatomy】Skin→subcutaneous tissue→external oblique muscle of abdomen→musculi intercostales externi. Lateral cutaneous branch intercostal nerve of 6th、7th、8th and accompanying vein and artery in superficial layer. 7th intercostal nerve and 7th posterior intercostal artery and vein in deep layer.

【Properties】Relieve liver depression and pain，lower upward adverse flow of qi and benefit gallbladder.

【Indications】①Jaundice，vomiting，acid regurgitation，hiccup，pain in the epigastrium and stomach. ②Pain in the hypochondrium and chest.

【Needling method】Puncture obliquely or transversely 0.3～0.5cun.

25. 京门（GB 25），肾募穴
Jingmen（GB 25），Front - Mu Point of the Kidney

【释义】京，同"原"字；门，门户。此为肾之募穴。肾主一身之元气，穴之所在为肾气出入之门户。

【定位】在侧腰部，章门后1.8寸，当12肋骨游离端的下方（图13－8）。

【解剖】皮肤→皮下组织→腹外斜肌→腹内斜肌→腹横肌。浅层布有第 11、12 胸神经的外侧皮支和伴行的动、静脉。深层有第 11、12 胸神经前支的肌支和相应的肋间、肋下动、静脉。

【功用】益肾利水。

【主治】①小便不利，水肿。②腹胀，泄泻，肠鸣，呕吐。③腰痛，胁痛。

【操作】直刺 0.5 ~1.0 寸。

【Meaning】Jing，primary；men，door. This is a mu - front point of the kidney meridian which dominates the primary qi of the general body. The point is the door where the pi of kidney enters and exits.

【Location】On the lateral waist，1.8 cun posterior to Zhangmen（LR 13），on the inferior free end of the 12th rib（Fig 13 -8）.

【Regional anatomy】Skin→subcutaneous tissue→external oblique muscle of abdomen→musculus obliquus internus abdominis→m. transversus abdominis. Lateral cutaneous branch thoracic nerve of 11th、12th and accompanying vein and artery in superficial layer. anterior muscular branches of 11th、12th thoracic nerve and accompanying intercostal and subcostal vein and artery in deep layer.

【Properties】Benefit the kidney and induce diuresis.

【Indications】①Difficulty in urination，edema. ②Abdominal distention，diarrhea，borborygmus，vomiting. ③Lumbar pain，pain in the hypochondriac region.

【Needling method】Puncture perpendicularly 0.5 ~1.0cun.

26. 带脉（GB 26），足少阳经、带脉交会穴
Daimai（GB 26），Crossing Point of the Meridian of Foot - Shaoyang and Belt Vessel

【释义】带，腰带；脉，经脉。穴属胆经，交会在带脉上。

【定位】在侧腹部，章门下 1.8 寸，当第 11 肋骨游离端下方垂线与脐水平线的交点上（图 13 -8）。

【解剖】皮肤→皮下组织→腹外斜肌→腹内斜肌→腹横肌。浅层布有第 9、10、11 胸神经前支的外侧皮支及伴行的动、静脉。深层有第 9、10、11 胸神经前支的肌支和相应的动、静脉。

【功用】调经，利胆。

【主治】①带下，月经不调，阴挺，经闭，疝气，小腹痛。②胁痛，腰痛。

【操作】直刺 0.8 ~1.0 寸。

【Meaning】Dai，belt；mai，meridian. The point pertains to the Gallbladder Meridian and meets at the Belt Vessel.

【Location】On the lateral abdomen，1.8 cun posterior to Zhangmen（LR 13），at the junction of the vertical line of the free end of the 11th rib and horizontal line of the umbilicus（Fig 13 -8）.

【Regional anatomy】Skin→subcutaneous tissue→external oblique muscle of abdomen→musculus obliquus internus abdominis→m. transversus abdominis. Lateral cutaneous branch thoracic nerve of 9th、10th、11th and accompanying vein and artery in superficial layer. 9th、10th、11th anterior muscular branches of thoracic nerve and accompanying intercostal and subcostal vein and artery in deep layer.

【Properties】Regulate the menstruation, promote gallbladder.

【Indications】①Morbid leucorrhea, irregular menstruation, prolapsed uterus, amenorrhea, hernia, lower abdominal pain. ②Pain in the hypochondriac region, lumbar pain.

【Needling method】Puncture perpendicularly 0. 8～1. 0cun.

27. 五枢（GB 27），足少阳经、带脉交会穴
Daimai（GB 27），Crossing Point of the Meridian of Foot - Shaoyang and Belt Vessel

【释义】五，五个；枢，枢纽。五为中数，少阳主枢；穴在人身的中部的枢要之处。

【定位】在侧腹部，当髂前上棘的前方，横平脐下3寸处（图13－10）。

【解剖】皮肤→皮下组织→腹外斜肌→腹内斜肌→腹横肌。浅层布有第11、12胸神经前支和第1腰神经前支的外侧皮支及伴行的动、静脉。深层有旋髂深动静、脉，第11、12胸神经，第1腰神经前支的肌支及相应的动、静脉。

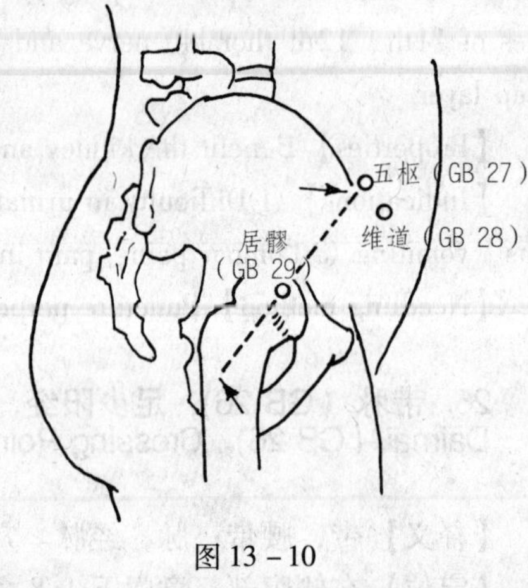

图13－10

Fig 13－10

【功用】调理经带。

【主治】①腹痛，便秘。②带下，月经不调，阴挺，疝气。

【操作】直刺1.0～1.5寸。

【Meaning】Wu, five; shu, pivot. The numeral 5 is a middle number and shaoyang governs the point between the surface and the interior of the body. The point is in a vital place at the middle of the body.

【Location】On the lateral abdomen, anterior to the superior iliac spine, level with 3 cun below the umbilicus（Fig 13－10）.

【Regional anatomy】Skin→subcutaneous tissue→external oblique muscle of abdomen→musculus obliquus internus abdominis→m. transversus abdominis. anterior branch thoracic nerve of 11th、12th and anterior lateral cutaneous branch of 1st lumbar nerve and accompanying vein and artery in superficial layer. deep iliac circumflex artery and vein and thoracic nerve of 11th、12th, anterior muscular branch of 1st lumbar nerve and accompanying vein and artery in deep layer.

【Properties】Regulate menstruation and leukorrhea.

【Indications】①Abdominal pain, constipation. ②Morbid leucorrhea, irregular menstruation, prolapsed uterus, hernia.

【Needling method】Puncture perpendicularly 1. 0～1. 5cun.

28. 维道（GB 28），足少阳经、带脉交会穴
Weidao (GB 28), Crossing Point of the Meridian of Foot - Shaoyang and Belt Vessel

【释义】维，维系；道，通道。此穴为胆经与带脉之会，带脉维系诸经。

【定位】当髂前上棘的前下方，五枢前下 0.5 寸（图 13 – 10）。

【解剖】皮肤→皮下组织→腹外斜肌→腹内斜肌→腹横肌→髂腰肌。浅层布有旋髂浅动、静脉，第 11、12 胸神经前支和第 1 腰神经前支的外侧皮支及伴行的动、静脉。深层有旋髂深动静、脉，第 11、12 胸神经前支和第 1 腰神经前支的肌支及相应的动、静脉。

【功用】调经固冲，理肠通便。

【主治】①少腹痛，便秘，肠痈。②阴挺，带下，疝气，月经不调。

【操作】直刺 1.0 ~ 1.5 寸。

【Meaning】Wei, maintain; dao, passage. This point is the meeting point of the gallbladder meridian and belt vessel, which maintain all the meridians.

【Location】Anterior and inferior to the superior iliac spine, 0. 5 cun anterior and inferior to Wushu (GB 27) (Fig 13 – 10).

【Regional anatomy】Skin→subcutaneous tissue→external oblique muscle of abdomen→musculus obliquus internus abdominis→m. transversus abdominis→m. iliopsoas. superficial iliac circumflex artery and vein, anterior branch thoracic nerve of 11th、12th and lateral cutaneous branch of 1st lumbar nerve and accompanying vein and artery in superficial layer, deep iliac circumflex artery and vein and anterior branch thoracic nerve of 11th、12th, anterior muscular branch of 1st lumbar nerve and accompanying vein and artery in deep layer.

【Properties】Regulate menstruation, consolidate the Thoroughfare Meridian, regulate the bowel movement and relax the bowel.

【Indications】①Lower abdominal pain, constipation, appendicitis. ②Prolapsed uterus, morbid leucorrhea, hernia, irregular menstruation.

【Needling method】Puncture perpendicularly 1. 0 ~ 1. 5cun.

29. 居髎（GB 29），足少阳经、阳跻脉交会穴
Juliao (GB 29), Crossing Point of the Meridian of Foot - Shaoyang and Yang Heel Vessel

【释义】居，居处；髎，近骨之凹陷处。穴居髋骨上凹陷处。

【定位】在髋部，当髂前上棘与股骨大转子最凸点连线的中点处（图 13 – 10）。

【解剖】皮肤→皮下组织→阔筋膜→臀中肌→臀小肌。浅层布有臀上皮神经和髂腹下神经外侧皮支。深层有臀上动、静脉的分支或属支和臀上神经。

【功用】舒筋活络，强健腰腿。

【主治】①腰痛，下肢痿痹。②疝气。

【操作】直刺1.0～1.5寸。

【Meaning】Ju, reside; liao, foramen. The point is in the depression on the hipbone.

【Location】On the hipbone, on the midpoint of the line linking the anterior superior iliac spine and the prominence of the greater trochanter (Fig 13－10).

【Regional anatomy】Skin→subcutaneous tissue→fascial lata→musculus gluteus medius→gluteus minimus. superior clunial nerves and lateral cutaneous branch of iliohypogastric nerve in superficial layer. subordinate branch and branch of superior gluteal artery and vein, superior gluteal nerve in deep layer.

【Properties】Relax muscles and tendons and activate flow of qi and blood in the channels and collaterals, strengthen the loins and the legs.

【Indications】①Lumbar pain, atrophy or pain in the lower limbs. ②Hernia.

【Needling method】Puncture perpendicularly 1. 0～1. 5cun.

30. 环跳（GB 30），足少阳、足太阳经交会穴 Huantiao（GB 30），Crossing Point of the Meridian of Foot - Shaoyang and Foot - Taiyang

【释义】环，环曲；跳，跳跃。穴在髀枢中，髀枢为环曲跳跃之枢纽。

【定位】在股外侧部，侧卧屈股，当股骨大转子最凸点与骶管裂孔连线的外1/3与内2/3交点处（图13－11）。

【解剖】皮肤→皮下组织→臀大肌→坐骨神经→股方肌。浅层布有臀上皮神经。深层有坐骨神经，臀下神经，股后皮神经和臀下动、静脉等。

【功用】通经活络，祛风散寒，强健腰腿。

【主治】下肢痿痹，半身不遂，腰腿痛。

【操作】直刺2.0～3.0寸。

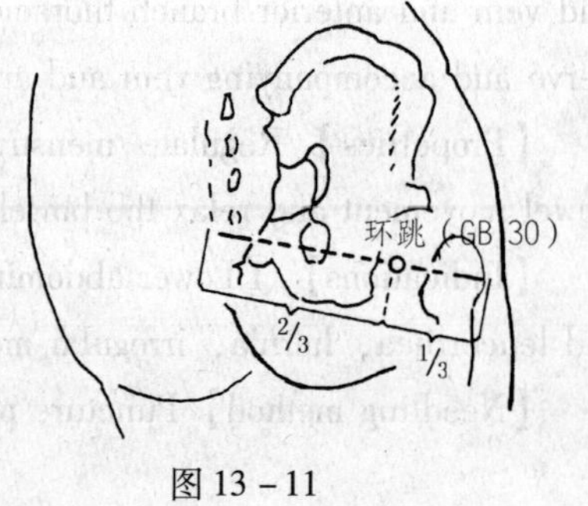

图13－11

Fig 13－11

【Meaning】Huan, a ring; tiao, jump. The point is at the hip joint, which is the pivot for jumping.

【Location】On the external hip, with the patient lying on the side with the upper hip and knee bent, point is at the junction of the medial 2/3 and lateral 1/3 of the line joining the prominence of the greater trochanter and the sacro－coccygeal hiatus (Fig 13－11).

【Regional anatomy】Skin→subcutaneous tissue→the gluteus maximus→the sciatic nerve→quadratus femoris. superior clunial nerves on superficial layer. the sciatic nerve, posterior femoral cutaneous nerve and inferior gluteal artery and vein on deep layer.

【Properties】Promote flow of qi and blood in the meridians and collaterals, expel wind and cold, strengthen the loins and legs.

【Indications】Atrophy or paralysis in the lower limbs, pain of leg and waist.

【Needling method】 Puncture perpendicularly 2.0 ~ 3.0 cun.

31. 风市 Fengshi (GB 31)

【释义】风，风邪；市，集市。集市有聚集之意，此为疏散风邪之要穴。

【定位】在大腿外侧部的中线上，当腘横纹上 7 寸（图 13 – 12）。

【解剖】皮肤→皮下组织→髂胫束→股外侧肌→股中间肌。浅层布有股外侧皮神经。深层有旋股外侧动脉降支的肌支和股神经的肌支。

【功用】通经活络，疏风除湿。

【主治】①下肢痿痹。②遍身瘙痒，脚气。

【操作】直刺 1.0 ~ 2.0 寸。

【Meaning】 Feng, pathogenic wind; shi, market. Market means gathering and dispersing. This is an important point for removing pathogenic wind.

【Location】 On the midline of the lateral aspect of the thigh, 7 cun superior to the popliteal crease (Fig 13 – 12).

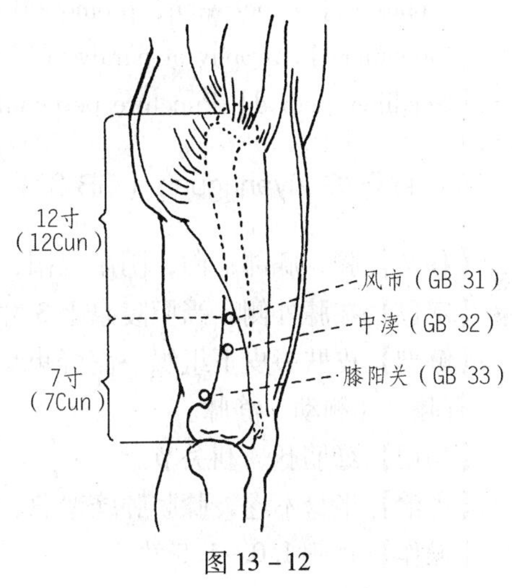

图 13 – 12
Fig 13 – 12

【Regional anatomy】 Skin→subcutaneous tissue→tractus iliotibialis→musculus vastus lateralis→musculus vastus intermedius. lateral femoral cutaneous nerve in superficial layer. descending muscular branch of lateral femoral circumflex artery and muscular branch femoral nerve in deep layer.

【Properties】 Promote flow of qi and blood in the channels and collaterals, expel wind and remove dampness.

【Indications】 ①Atrophy or paralysis in the lower limbs. ②Itching of the entire body, beriberi.

【Needling method】 Puncture perpendicularly 1.0 ~ 2.0cun.

32. 中渎 zhongdu (GB 32)

【释义】中，中间；渎，小的沟渠。穴在股外侧两筋之间，如在沟渠之中。

【定位】在大腿外侧，当风市下 2 寸，或腘横纹上 5 寸，股外侧肌与股二头肌之间（图 13 – 12）。

【解剖】皮肤→皮下组织→髂胫束→股外侧肌→股中间肌。浅层布有股外侧皮神经。深层有旋股外侧动、静脉降支的肌支和股神经的肌支。

【功用】祛风活络。

【主治】下肢痿痹，半身不遂，脚气。

【操作】直刺 1.0 ~ 2.0 寸。

【Meaning】Zhong, middle; du, small ditch. This point is between the tendons at the lateral aspect of the thigh , as if in a ditch.

【Location】2 cun inferior to Fengshi（GB 31）, 5 cun superior to the popliteal crease between the vastus lateralis and biceps femoris（Fig 13 – 12）.

【Regional anatomy】Skin→subcutaneous tissue→tractus iliotibialis→musculus vastus lateralis→musculus vastus intermedius. lateral femoral cutaneous nerve in superficial layer. descending muscular branch of lateral femoral circumflex artery and vein, muscular branch femoral nerve in deep layer.

【Properties】Expel wind, promote flow of qi and blood in the collaterals.

【Indications】Atrophy or paralysis in the lower limbs, hemiplegia, beriberi.

【Needling method】Puncture perpendicularly 1. 0 ~ 2. 0cun.

33. 膝阳关 Xiyangguan（GB 33）

【释义】膝，膝部；阳，阴阳之阳；关，机关。外为阳，穴在膝关节外侧。

【定位】在膝外侧，当阳陵泉上 3 寸，股骨外上髁上方的凹陷处（图 13 – 12）。

【解剖】皮肤→皮下组织→髂胫束后缘→腓肠肌外侧头前方。浅层布有股外侧皮神经。深层有膝上外侧动、静脉。

【功用】舒筋脉，利关节。

【主治】半身不遂，膝膑肿痛挛急，小腿麻木，脚气。

【操作】直刺 1. 0 ~ 1. 5 寸。

【Meaning】Xi, knee; yang, yang of yin – yang; guan, joint. The exterior is yang, The point is at the lateral aspect of the knee joint.

【Location】On the external knee, 3 cun superior to Yanglingquan（GB 34）, in the depression supcrior to the lateral epicondyle of the femur（Fig 13 – 12）.

【Regional anatomy】Skin→subcutaneous tissue→fasciculus posterior tractus iliotibialis→frontage of lateral head of musculus gastrocnemius. lateral cutaneous femoral nerve in superficial layer. lateral superior genicular artery and vein in deep layer.

【Properties】Relax muscles and tendons and benefit joints.

【Indications】Hemiplegia, swelling, pain and spasm in the knee, numbness of the lower leg, beriberi.

【Needling method】Puncture perpendicularly 1. 0 ~ 1. 5cun.

34. 阳陵泉（GB 34），合穴，胆经下合穴，八会穴（筋会）
Yanglingquan（GB 34）, He - Sea Point; Lower He - Sea Point of Gallbladder; One of the Eight Influential Points（Tendon Convergence）

【释义】阳，阴阳之阳；陵，丘陵；泉，水泉。外为阳，膝外侧腓骨小头隆起如陵，穴在其下陷中，犹如水泉。

【定位】在小腿外侧，当腓骨小头前下方凹陷处（图 13－13）。

【解剖】皮肤→皮下组织→腓骨长肌→趾长伸肌。浅层布有腓肠外侧皮神经。深层有胫前返动、静脉，膝下外侧动、静脉的分支或属支和腓总神经分支。

【功用】疏肝利胆，清泄湿热，舒筋活络。

【主治】①黄疸，口苦，呕吐，胁肋疼痛。②下肢痿痹，膝膑肿痛，脚气，肩痛。③小儿惊风。

【操作】直刺 1.0～1.5 寸。

【Meaning】 Yang, yang of yin － yang; ling, mound; quan, spring. The exterior is yang. The small head of the fibula at the lateral aspect of the knee is prominent as a mound, below which in the depression the point is located, like a spring.

【Location】 On the external leg, in the depression anterior and inferior to the small head of the fibula (Fig 13 － 13).

【Regional anatomy】 Skin→subcutaneous tissue→musculus peroneus longus → extensor digitorum longus. lateral cutaneous sural nerve in superficial layer. anterior tibial recurrent artery and vein, subordinate branch and branch of lateral inferior genicular artery and vein and branch of common peroneal nerve in deep layer.

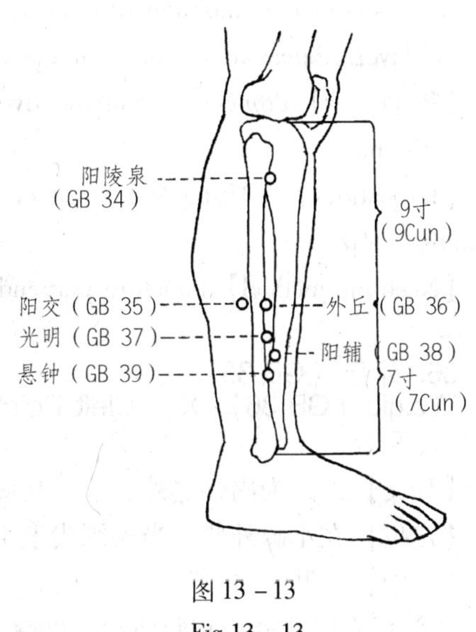

图 13 － 13

Fig 13 － 13

【Properties】 Promote flow of the liver － qi, normalize functioning of gallbladder, purge dampness － heat, relax muscles and tendons and activate flow of qi and blood in the meridians and collaterals.

【Indications】 ①Jaundice, vomiting, bitter taste in mouth, pain in the hypochondriac region and chest. ②Atrophy or paralysis in the lower limbs, swelling and pain in the knee, beriberi, pain of shoulder. ③Infantile convulsion.

【Needling method】 Puncture perpendicularly 1.0～1.5cun.

35. 阳交（GB 35），阳维脉之郄穴
Yangjiao (GB 35), Xi - Cleft Point of Yang Link Vessel

【释义】阳，阴阳之阳；交，交会。外为阳，穴在小腿外侧，与膀胱经交会。

【定位】在小腿外侧，当外踝尖上 7 寸，腓骨后缘（图 13－13）。

【解剖】皮肤→皮下组织→小腿三头肌→腓骨长肌→后肌间隔→腓长屈肌。浅层布有腓肠外侧皮神经。深层有腓动、静脉，胫后动、静脉和胫神经。

【功用】疏肝利胆，定惊安神。

【主治】①胸胁胀满。②下肢痿痹。③癫狂。

【操作】直刺 1.0 ~1.5 寸。

【Meaning】Yang, yang of yin – yang; jiao, crossing. The exterior is yang. The point is at the lateral aspect of the leg, where it crosses with the bladder meridian.

【Location】On the external leg, 7 cun superior the tip of the lateral malleolus, on the posterior border of the fibula (Fig 13 – 13).

【Regional anatomy】Skin→subcutaneous tissue→musculus triceps surae→musculus peroneus longus→posterior intermuscular septum→peroneus longus flexor. lateral cutaneous sural nerve in superficial layer. fibular artery and vein, posterior tibial artery and vein, tibial nerve in deep layer.

【Properties】Promote flow of the liver – qi, normalize functioning of gallbladder, and tranquilize the mind.

【Indications】①Distending in the chest and hypochondrium. ②Atrophy or paralysis in the lower limbs. ③Epilepsy.

【Needling method】Puncture perpendicularly 1.0 ~ 1.5cun.

36. 外丘(GB 36),郄穴
Waiqiu (GB 36), Xi - Cleft Point

【释义】外,为内外之外;丘,丘陵。穴在外踝上方,局部肌肉隆起如丘。

【定位】在小腿外侧,当外踝尖上 7 寸,腓骨前缘,平阳交(图 13 – 13)。

【解剖】皮肤→皮下组织→腓骨长、短肌→前肌间隔→趾长伸肌。浅层布有腓肠外侧皮神经。深层有腓浅神经和胫前动、静脉。

【功用】疏肝利胆,清热利湿。

【主治】①胸胁胀痛。②颈项强痛,下肢痿痹。③癫狂。④狂犬伤毒不出。

【操作】直刺 1.0 ~1.5 寸。

【Meaning】Wai, lateral; qiu, mound. The point is above the lateral malleolus and the local muscle is prominent as a mound.

【Location】On the external leg, 7 cun superior the tip of the lateral malleolus, on the anterior border of the fibula, level with Yangjiao (Fig 13 – 13).

【Regional anatomy】Skin→subcutaneous tissue→musculus peroneus longus and brevis→anterior intermuscular septum→extensor digitorum longus. lateral cutaneous sural nerve in superficial layer. superficial peroneal nerve and anterior tibial artery and vein in deep layer.

【Properties】Promote flow of the liver – qi, normalize functions of gallbladder, clear away heat and remove dampness.

【Indications】①Distending and pain in the chest and hypochondrium. ②Stiffness and pain in the neck, atrophy or paralysis in the lower limbs. ③Epilepsy. ④No discharging of rabies virus.

【Needling method】Puncture perpendicularly 1.0 ~ 1.5cun.

37. 光明（GB 37），络穴
Guangming（GB 37），Luo - Connecting Point

【释义】光明，即明亮的意思。为胆经络穴，主治眼病，使之重见光明。

【定位】在小腿外侧，当外踝尖上 5 寸，腓骨前缘（图 13－13）。

【解剖】皮肤→皮下组织→腓骨短肌→前肌间隔→趾长伸肌→拇长伸肌→小腿骨间膜→胫骨后肌。浅层布有腓浅神经和腓肠外侧皮神经。深层有腓深神经和胫前动、静脉。

【功用】通经活络，调肝明目。

【主治】①目痛，夜盲，目视不明。②乳房胀痛，乳汁少。

【操作】直刺 1.0～1.5 寸。

【Meaning】Guangming, brightness. This is a luo－connecting point of the gallbladder meridian and is indicated in eye diseases to regain brightness.

【Location】On the external leg, 5 cun superior the tip of the lateral malleolus, on the anterior border of the fibula（Fig 13－13）.

【Regional anatomy】Skin→subcutaneous tissue→musculus peroneus brevis→anterior intermuscular septum →extensor digitorum longus→ extensor pollicis longus→crural interosseous membrane→musculus tibialis posterior. superficial peroneal nerve and lateral cutaneous sural nerve in superficial layer. deep peroneal nerve and anterior tibial artery and vein in deep layer.

【Properties】Activate flow of qi and blood in the meridians and collaterals, regulate functions of the liver and improve vision.

【Indications】①Pain in the eyes, night blindness, blurred vision. ②Distension and pain in the breasts, deficiency of lactation.

【Needling method】Puncture perpendicularly 1.0－1.5cun.

38. 阳辅（GB 38），经穴
Yangfu（GB 38），Jing - River Point

【释义】阳，阴阳之阳；辅，辅助。外为阳。辅，指辅骨，即腓骨。穴在小腿外侧腓骨前。

【定位】在小腿外侧，当外踝尖上 4 寸，腓骨前缘（图 13－13）。

【解剖】皮肤→皮下组织→趾长伸肌→拇长伸肌→小腿骨间膜→胫骨后肌。浅层布有腓肠外侧皮神经和腓浅神经。深层有腓动、静脉。

【功用】清肝利胆，行气开郁。

【主治】①偏头痛，目外眦痛，咽喉肿痛。②腋下肿痛，胸胁胀痛，瘰疬。③下肢痿痹，脚气。

【操作】直刺 0.8～1.2 寸。

【Meaning】Yang, yang of yin－yang; fu, auxiliary. The exterior is yang and fu is fibula,

The point is anterior to the fibula on the lateral aspect of the leg.

【Location】On the external leg, 4cun superior the tip of the lateral malleolus, on the anterior border of the fibula (Fig 13 – 13).

【Regional anatomy】Skin→subcutaneous tissue→musculus extensor digitorum longus→musculus extensor pollicis longus→crural interosseous membrane→musculus tibialis posterior. lateral cutaneous sural nerve and superficial peroneal nerve in superficial layer. fibular artery and vein in deep layer.

【Properties】Clear away heat from the liver, normalize the functions of gallbladder, promote flow of qi and relieve stagnation.

【Indications】①Migraine, pain of outer cantus, swollen and pain in the throat. ②Swollen and pain in the axil, distension and pain in the chest and hypochondrium, scrofula. ③Atrophy or paralysis in the lower limbs, beriberi.

【Needling method】Puncture perpendicularly 0. 8 ~ 1. 2cun.

39. 悬钟（GB 39），八会穴（髓会）
Xuanzhong（GB 39），One of the Eight Influential Points（Marrow Convergence）

【释义】悬，悬挂；钟，钟铃。穴当外踝上，是古时候小儿悬挂脚铃处。

【定位】在小腿外侧，当外踝尖上 3 寸，腓骨前缘（图 13 – 13）。

【解剖】皮肤→皮下组织→趾长伸肌→小腿骨间膜。浅层布有腓肠外侧皮神经。深层有腓深神经的分支。如穿透小腿骨间膜可刺中腓动、静脉。

【功用】通经活络，坚筋壮骨。

【主治】①颈项强痛，偏头痛，咽喉肿痛。②胸胁胀痛。③痔疾，便秘。④下肢痿痹，脚气。

【操作】直刺 0. 5 ~0. 8 寸。

【Meaning】Xuan, hanging; zhong, bell. The point is above the lateral malleolus, where the children in ancient times used to hang a bell.

【Location】On the external leg, 3 cun above the tip of the lateral malleolus, anterior to the fibula (Fig 13 – 13).

【Regional anatomy】Skin→subcutaneous tissue→musculus extensor digitorum longus→crural interosseous membrane. lateral cutaneous sural nerve on superficial layer. branch of deep peroneal nerve on deep layer. puncturing through crural interosseous membrane will stick fibular artery and vein.

【Properties】Promote flow of qi and blood in the channels and collaterals, strengthen the tendons and bones.

【Indications】①Stiffness and pain in the neck, migraine, swollen and pain in the throat. ② Distension and pain in the chest and hypochondrium. ③Hemorrhoid, constipation. ④Atrophy or paralysis in the lower limbs, beriberi.

【Needling method】Puncture perpendicularly 0.5 ~0.8cun.

40. 丘墟（GB 40），原穴
Qiuxu（GB 40），Yuan - Source Point

【释义】丘，小土堆；墟，大土堆。此穴在外踝（如丘墟）与跟骨滑车突（如丘）之间。

【定位】在足外踝的前下方，当趾长伸肌腱的外侧凹陷处（图 13－14）。

【解剖】皮肤→皮下组织→趾长伸肌→距跟外侧韧带→跗骨窦。布有足背浅静脉，足背外侧皮神经，足背中间皮神经，外踝前动、静脉。

【功用】活络化瘀，疏肝利胆。

【主治】①胸胁胀痛。②下肢痿痹，外踝肿痛，脚气。③疟疾。

【操作】直刺 0.5 ~0.8 寸。

【Meaning】Qiu，mound；xu，large mound. The point is between the lateral malleolus（like a mound）and the peroneal trochlea of calcaneus（like a large mound）.

【Location】Anterior and inferior to the lateral malleolus，in the depression lateral to the tendon of the long extensor of toes（Fig 13－14）.

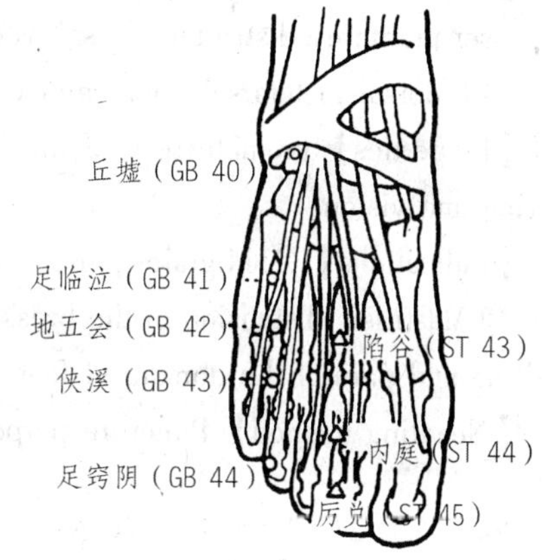

图 13－14
Fig 13－14

【Regional anatomy】Skin→subcutaneous tissue→musculus extensor digitorum longus→lateral talocalcaneal ligament→tarsal sinus. Distribute dorsal superficial vein，lateral dorsal cutaneous nerve of foot，intermediate dorsal cutaneous nerve of foot，lateral anterior malleolar artery and vein.

【Properties】Activate flow of qi and blood in the channels and collaterals，remove blood stasis，promote flow of the liver－qi and normalize functions of the gallbladder.

【Indications】①Distension and pain in the chest and hypochondrium. ②Atrophy or paralysis in the lower limbs，swollen and pain of external malleolus，beriberi. ③Malaria.

【Needling method】Puncture perpendicularly 0.5 ~0.8cun.

41. 足临泣（GB 41），输穴，八脉交会穴（通带脉）
Zulinqi（GB 41），Shu - Stream Point；One of the Eight Confluent Points Associating with Belt Vessel

【释义】足，足部；临，调治；泣，流泪。穴在足部，可调治流泪等眼病。

【定位】当足 4、5 跖骨结合部前方，小趾伸肌腱的外侧凹陷处（图 13－14）。

【解剖】皮肤→皮下组织→第 4 骨间背侧肌→第 3 骨间足底肌（第 4 与第 5 跖骨之间）。布有足背静脉网，足背中间皮神经，第 4 跖背动、静脉和足底外侧神经的分支。

【功用】疏肝利胆，聪耳明目。

【主治】①偏头痛，目赤肿痛，目眩，目涩。②乳痈，乳胀，月经不调。③胁肋疼痛，足跗肿痛。④瘰疬，疟疾。

【操作】直刺 0.3 ~0.5 寸。

【Meaning】Zu, foot; lin, regulation; qi, tears. The point is at the foot and indicated in lacrimation and other eye disorders.

【Location】In the depression distal to the junction of the 4th and 5th metatarsal bones, on the lateral side of the tendon of the extensor digital minimi of the foot（Fig 13 –14）.

【Regional anatomy】Skin→subcutaneous tissue→4th musculi interossei dorsales→3rd musculi interossei plantares. distribute dorsal venous rete of foot, intermediate dorsal cutaneous nerve of foot, 4th dorsal metatarsal artery and vein and branch of lateral plantar nerve.

【Properties】Promote flow of the liver – qi, normalize functions of the gallbladder, improve hearing and vision.

【Indications】①Migraine, redness, swollen and pain in the eyes, dizziness, dry in the eyes. ②Mastitis, distension in the breasts, irregular menstruation. ③Pain in the hypochondriac rib, swelling and pain of the dorsum of foot. ④scrofula, malaria.

【Needling method】Puncture perpendicularly 0. 3 ~0. 5cun.

42. 地五会 Diwuhui（GB 42）

【释义】地，土地；五，五个；会，会合。地在下，指足部。足部胆经穴有五，此穴居其中，为上下脉气会合之处。

【定位】第 4、5 跖骨之间，小趾伸肌腱的内侧缘（图 13 –14）。

【解剖】皮肤→皮下组织→趾长伸肌腱→趾短伸肌腱外侧→第 4 骨间背侧肌→第 3 骨间足底肌。浅层布有足背中间皮神经，足背静脉网和跖背动、静脉。深层有趾足底总神经和趾底总动、静脉。

【功用】行气开窍。

【主治】①头痛，目赤，耳鸣。②乳痈，乳胀。③胁肋胀痛，足跗肿痛。

【操作】直刺 0.3 ~0.5 寸。

【Meaning】Di, ground; wu, five; hui, confluence. The ground is inferior, indicating the foot. There are five points of the gallbladder meridian on the foot. This point is among them and is a confluence of qi of meridian upper and lower.

【Location】Between the 4th and 5th metatarsal bones, on the medial side of the tendon of the long extensor of toes（Fig 13 –14）.

【Regional anatomy】Skin→subcutaneous tissue→tendon of extensor digitorum longus→external aspect of tendon of extensor digitorum brevis→4th musculi interossei dorsales→3rd musculi interossei plantares. intermediate dorsal cutaneous nerve of foot, dorsal venous rete of foot and dorsal metatarsal artery and vein in superficial layer. common plantar digital nerves and common plantar digital artery and vein in deep layer.

【Properties】 Promote the circulation of vital energy and open aperture.

【Indications】 ①Headache, redness in the eyes, tinnitus. ②Mastitis, distension in the breasts. ③Distension and pain in the hypochondriac rib, swelling and pain of the dorsum of foot.

【Needling method】 Puncture perpendicularly 0. 3 ~0. 5cun.

43. 侠溪（GB 43），荥穴
Xiaxi（GB 43），Yin - Spring Point

【释义】侠，通“夹”；溪，溪谷。穴在第4、5趾的夹缝间，局部犹如溪谷。

【定位】在足背外侧，当第4、5趾间，趾蹼缘后方赤白肉际处（图13－14）。

【解剖】皮肤→皮下组织→第4趾的趾长、短伸肌腱与第5趾的趾长、短伸肌腱之间→第4、第5趾的近节趾骨底之间。布有足背中间皮神经的趾背神经和趾背动、静脉。

【功用】清头明目，息风通络。

【主治】①头痛，眩晕，目赤肿痛，耳聋，耳鸣。②胁肋疼痛，乳痈。③热病。

【操作】直刺0.3～0.5寸。

【Meaning】 Xia, to press from both sides; xi, stream. The point is in the space between the 4th and 5th toes. The space is like a stream.

【Location】 On the aspect of dorsum of foot, between the 4th and 5th toes, posterior to the margin of the web, at the junction of the red and white skin (Fig 13 – 14).

【Regional anatomy】 Skin→subcutaneous tissue→between 4th tendon of extensor digitorum longus and brevis and 5th tendon of extensor digitorum longus and brevis→between proximal base of phalanx of 4th and 5th toes. Distribute dorsal digital nerves of foot of intermediate dorsal cutaneous nerve of foot, dorsal digital artery and vein.

【Properties】 Clear away heat from head, improve vision, calm wind and promote flow of qi and blood in the collaterals.

【Indications】 ①Headache, dizziness, redness, swelling and pain in the eyes, deafness, tinnitus. ②Pain in the chest and hypochondrium, mastitis. ③Febrile diseases.

【Needling method】 Puncture perpendicularly 0. 3 ~0. 5cun.

44. 足窍阴（GB 44），井穴
Zuqiaoyin（GB 44），Jing - Well Point

【释义】足，足部；窍，孔窍；阴，阴阳之会。肾肝属阴，开窍于耳目。穴在头部，治疗耳目之疾。

【定位】在第4趾末节外侧，距趾甲角0.1寸（图13－14）。

【解剖】皮肤→皮下组织→甲根。布有足背中间皮神经的趾背神经和趾背动、静脉和趾底固有动、静脉构成的动、静脉网。

【功用】开窍泄热，聪利耳目。

【主治】①目赤肿痛，耳聋，耳鸣，咽喉肿痛。②头痛，失眠，多梦。③胁痛，足跗肿痛；④热病。

【操作】浅刺0.1～0.2寸，或点刺出血。

【Meaning】Zu，foot；qiao，opening；yin，yin of yin－yang. The kindey and the liver pertain to yin and open into the ear and the eye. The point is on the foot and is indicated in treating ear and eye disorders.

【Location】On the lateral aspect of the 4th toe，0.1 cun lateral to the corner of the toenail (Fig 13－14).

【Regional anatomy】Skin→subcutaneous tissue→nail root. Distribute dorsal digital nerves of foot of intermediate dorsal cutaneous nerve of foot，dorsal digital artery and vein，arterial and veins rete of composing proper plantar digital arteries and veins.

【Properties】Induce resuscitation，purge heat，improve hearing and vision

【Indications】①Redness，swelling and pain in the eyes，deafness，tinnitus，swelling and pain in the throat. ②Headache，insomnia，dreams. ③Pain in the hypochondriac region，swelling and pain of the dorsum of foot. ④Febrile diseases.

【Needling method】Puncture superficially 0.1～0.2cun，or prink to cause bleeding.

复习思考题
Review Questions

1. 和足少阳胆经相联系的组织、器官是什么？

What the organs and tissues connected with the gallbladder meridian?

2. 足少阳胆经有多少个腧穴？起点和终点的腧穴是什么？

How many points are there on the gallbladder meridian? What are the first and last points?

3. 说出悬钟穴的定位、功用、主治及针刺方法。

Discuss in detail the location，properties，needling method and indications of Xuanzhong (GB 39).

第十四章 足厥阴经络与腧穴
Meridian and Collateral and Its Acupoints of Foot – Jueyin

第一节 足厥阴经络
Meridian and Collateral of Foot – Jueyin

一、足厥阴经脉
Meridian of Foot - Jueyin

（一）经脉循行
The Course of Meridian

足厥阴肝经，从大趾背毫毛部开始，向上沿着足背内侧，至距内踝1寸处，上循小腿内侧，在内踝上8寸处交出足太阴脾经之后，上膝腘内侧，沿着大腿内侧，进入阴毛中，环绕阴部，至小腹，夹胃旁边，属于肝，络于胆；向上通过膈肌，分布胁肋部，沿气管之后，向上入颃颡，连接目系，上行出于额部，与督脉交会于头顶。目部支脉，从“目系”下向颊里，环绕唇内。肝部支脉，从肝分出，通过膈肌，向上流注于肺，接手太阴肺经（图14－1）。

《灵枢·经脉》原文：肝足厥阴之脉，起于大指丛毛之际，上循足跗上廉，去内踝一寸，上踝八寸，交出太阴之后，上腘内廉，循股阴，入毛中，环阴器，抵小腹，夹胃，属肝，络胆，上贯膈，布胁肋，循喉咙之后，上入颃颡，连目系，上出额，与督脉会于巅。

其支者，从目系下颊里，环唇内。其支者，复从肝别贯膈，上注肺。

The chapter “Discussion on the Meridians” in *Miraculous Pivot* says: The liver meridian starts from the dorsal hair of the great toe, runs upward along the dorsum of the foot anterior to the medial malleolus. It then ascends to the area 8 cun above the medial malleolus where it crosses and runs behind the spleen meridian of foot – taiyin. Then it runs further upward to the medial side of the knee, and along the medial aspect of the thigh and enters the pubic hair region, where it curves around the external genitalia and goes up to the lower abdomen. It then runs upward and curves around the stomach, where it pertains to the liver and connects with the gallbladder. It then ascends through the diaphragm, branching out in the costal and hypochondriac region. From here it ascends along the posterior aspect of the throat, entering the nasopharynx and connects with the "eye system". It then runs upward and comes out from the forehead and meets governor vessel at the vertex.

One branch arising from the eye runs downward into the cheek and curves around the inner surface of the lips. Another branch splits from the liver, passes through the diaphragm and runs upward into the lung (Fig 14 – 1).

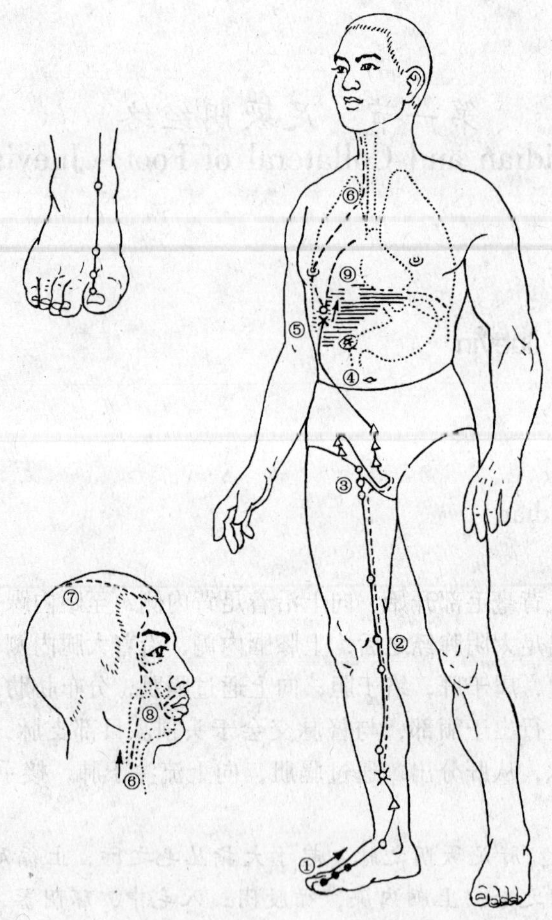

图例 ——本经有穴通路 ……本经无穴通路

Note ——Pathway with points ……Pathway without points

图 14 – 1 足厥阴经脉、络脉循行示意图

Fig 14 – 1 The course of the meridian and collateral of foot – jueyin

（二）经脉病候
The Syndromes of Meridian

本经有了异常就表现为下列病症：腰痛得不好前俯后仰，男人可出现小肠疝气，女人可出现小腹部肿胀，严重的见咽喉干，面部像有灰尘，脱了血色。

本经穴能主治有关肝方面所发生的病症，如胸闷，恶心呕吐，大便溏泄，疝气，遗尿或癃闭。

Disorder of the meridian will cause the following diseases: waist too pain to extend and bent, men will show intestinal hernia, women will cause abdominal distention, even throat feel dry, faces have dust and complexion exhaustion.

Points of the meridian can treat disease connected with liver, chest obstruction, hiccup and vomiting, loose bowels, hernia, enuresis, urinary retention.

二、足厥阴络脉
Collateral of Foot - Jueyin

足厥阴之别，名曰蠡沟，去内踝五寸，别走少阳；其别者，循经上睾，结于茎（图14－1）。

其病：气逆则睾肿卒疝。实则挺长；虚则暴痒。取之所别也。

It starts from Ligou (LR 5), five cun above the internal malleolus and connects with the gallbladder meridian. A branch runs up the leg to the genitals (Fig 14－1).

Its disorder: reversing flow of qi will cause testis swelling and sudden hernia. Excess syndrome will induce postcoital protrusion; deficiency syndrome will induce itching of pubic region. Selecting this point to treat.

三、足厥阴经别
Divergent Meridian of Foot - Jueyin

足厥阴之正，别跗上，上至毛际，合于少阳，与别俱行（图14－2）。

After deriving from the liver meridian on the instep, it duns upward to the pubic region, and converges with the gallbladder meridian of foot－shaoyang (Fig 14－2).

四、足厥阴经筋
Muscular Region of Foot - Jueyin

足厥阴之筋，起于大指（趾）之上，上结于内踝之前，上循胫，结内辅骨之下，上循阴股，结于阴器，络诸筋（图 14－3）。

其病：足大指支，内踝之前痛，内辅痛，阴股痛，转筋，阴器不用。伤于内则不起，伤于寒则阴缩入，伤于热则纵挺不收。

It originates from the dorsum of the big toe and knots anterior to the internal malleolus. Then it runs upward along the medial side of the tibia and knots at the lower. medial aspect of the knee. From there, it runs upward along the medial aspect of the thigh to the genital region, where it converges with other muscle regions（Fig 14－3）.

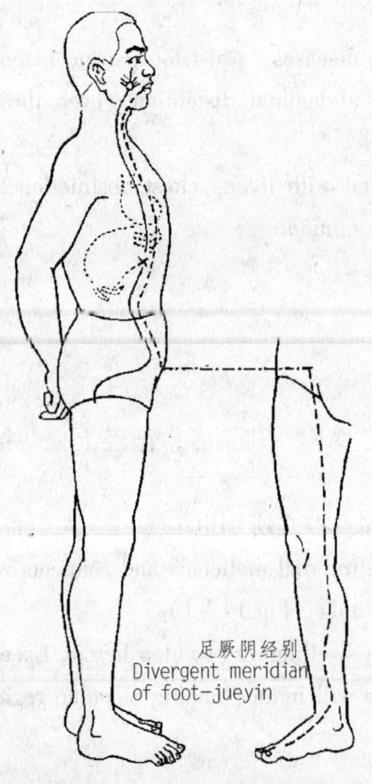

图 14－2 足厥阴经别循行示意图

Fig 14－2 The course of the divergent meridian of foot－jueyin

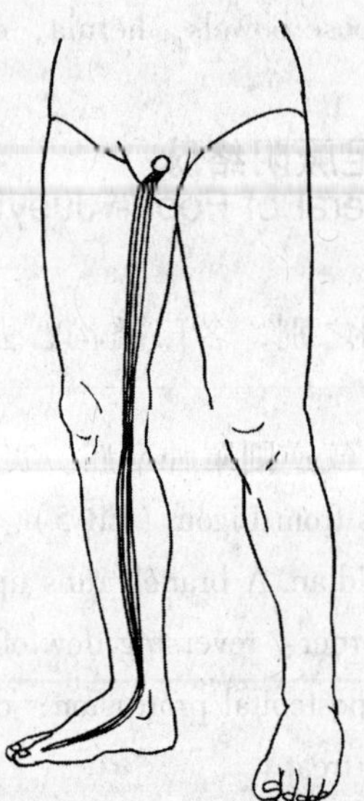

图 14－3 足厥阴经筋分布示意图

Fig 14－3 The course of the muscular region of foot－jueyin

第二节 足厥阴腧穴
Acupoints of Foot－Jueyin

本经腧穴始于大敦，止于期门，共有 14 个腧穴（图 14－4）。

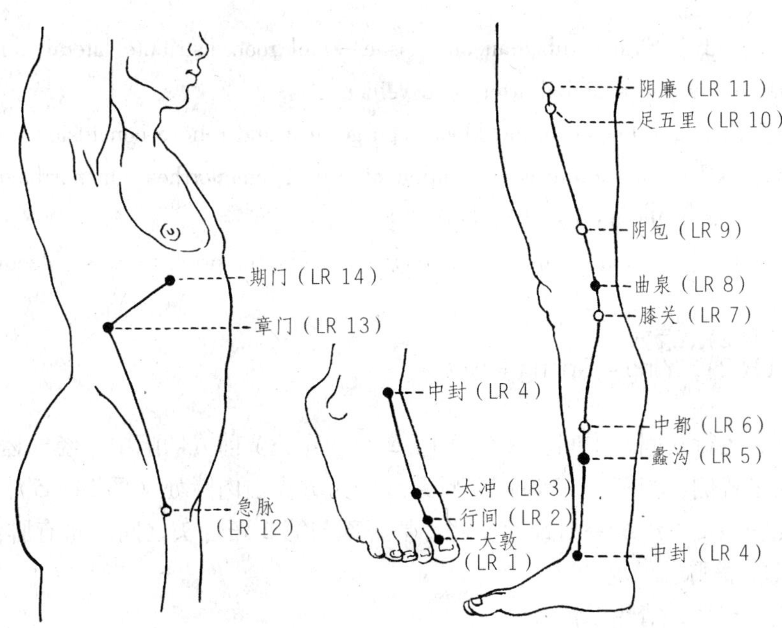

图例 ● 常用腧穴 ○ 一般腧穴

Note ● Main point ○ Common point

图 14－4 足厥阴肝经腧穴总图

Fig 14－4 Points of the liver meridian of foot－jueyin

1. 大敦（LR 1），井穴
Dadun（LR 1），Jing－Well Point

【释义】大，大小之大；敦，敦厚。大，指大趾。穴在大趾内侧，肌肉敦厚。

【定位】在足大指末节外侧，距趾甲角 0.1 寸（图 14－5）。

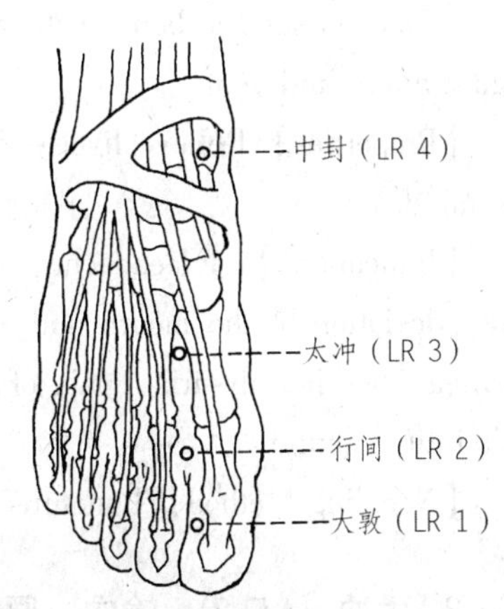

图 14－5

Fig 14－5

【解剖】皮肤→皮下组织→甲根。布有腓深神经的背外侧神经和趾背动、静脉。

【功用】理气调血，泄热解痉。

【主治】①疝气，遗尿，癃闭，经闭，崩漏，月经不调，阴挺。②癫痫。

【操作】浅刺 0.1～0.2 寸，或点刺出血。

【Meaning】Da, large; dun, thickness. Da refer to the big toe, The point is at the medial aspect of the big toe, where the muscle is thick.

【Location】On the lateral aspect of the distal segment of the great toe, 0.1 cun lateral to the corner of the toenail（Fig

14 –5）.

【Regional anatomy】Skin→subcutaneous tissue→nail root. distribute lateral dorsal nerve of deep peroneal nerve and dorsal digital artery and vein.

【Properties】Regulate flow of qi and blood，purge heat and relieve convulsion.

【Indications】①Hernia，enuresis，retention of urine，amenorrhea，menorrhagia，irregular menstruation，prolapse of the uterus. ②Epilepsy.

【Needling method】Puncture superficially 0. 1 ~0. 2cun，or prink to cause bleeding.

2. 行间（LR 2），荥穴
Xingjian（LR 2），Ying - Spring Point

【释义】行，运行；间，中间。穴在第 1、2 跖趾间关节前方凹陷中，经气运行其间。

【定位】在足背侧，当第 1、2 趾间，趾蹼缘的后方赤白肉际处（图 14 –5）。

【解剖】皮肤→皮下组织→拇趾近节趾骨基底部与第 2 跖骨头之间。布有腓深神经的趾背神经和趾背动、静脉。

【功用】疏肝理气，清热镇惊。

【主治】①头痛，目晕，目赤肿痛，青盲，口㖞。②月经过多，痛经，经闭，带下，疝气，小便不利，尿痛。③中风，癫痫。④胁肋疼痛，急躁易怒，黄疸。

【操作】直刺 0. 5 ~0. 8 寸。

【Meaning】Xing，walking；jian，middle. The point is in the depression anterior to the 1st and 2nd metatarsophalangeal joins. The qi of meridian runs between them.

【Location】On the dorsum of the foot，on the web margin between the 1st and 2nd toes，at the junction of the red and white skin（Fig 14 –5）.

【Regional anatomy】Skin→subcutaneous tissue→between hallux proximal base of phalanx and head of metatarsal 2nd bone. distribute dorsal digital nerves of foot of deep peroneal nerve and dorsal digital artery and vein.

【Properties】Relieve liver – depression，regulate flow of qi，clear away heat and tranquilize the mind.

【Indications】①Headache，dizziness，redness，swelling and pain in the eyes，optic atrophy，deviation of the mouth and eyes. ②Menorrhagia，dysmenorrhea，amenorrhea，morbid leucorrhea，hernia，dysuria，pain of urination. ③Stroke，epilepsy. ④Pain in the hypochondriac rib，irritability，jaundice.

【Needling Method】Puncture perpendicularly 0. 5 ~0. 8cun.

3. 太冲（LR 3），输穴，原穴
Taichong（LR 3），Shu - Stream Point，Yuan - Source Point

【释义】太，大；冲，重要位置。穴在足背，脉气盛大，为本经之要穴之处。

【定位】在足背侧，当第 1、2 跖骨结合部之前凹陷中（图 14－5）。

【解剖】皮肤→皮下组织→拇长伸肌腱与趾长伸肌腱之间→第 1 骨间背侧肌。浅层布有足背静脉网，足背内侧皮神经。深层布有腓深神经和第 1 趾背动、静脉。

【功用】疏肝理气，泄热镇惊。

【主治】①头痛，眩晕，目赤肿痛，口㖞，青盲，咽喉肿痛，耳聋，耳鸣。②月经不调，崩漏，疝气，遗尿。③癫痫，小儿惊风，中风。④胁痛，郁闷，急躁易怒。⑤下肢痿痹。

【操作】直刺 0.5～1.0 寸。

【Meaning】Tai，big；chong，important pass. The point is on the foot，where the qi of meridian is abundant. This an important pass of this meridian.

【Location】On the dorsum of the foot，in the depression distal to the junction of the 1st and 2nd metatarsal bones（Fig 14－5）.

【Regional anatomy】Skin→subcutaneous tissue→between tendon of extensor pollicis longus and tendon extensor digitorum longus→1st musculi interossei dorsales. dorsal venous rete of foot，medial dorsal cutaneous nerve of foot in superficial layer. deep peroneal nerve and 1st dorsal digital artery and vein in deep layer.

【Properties】Promote flow of the liver－qi，regulate flow of qi，purge heat and relieve convulsion.

【Indications】①Headache，dizziness，redness，swelling and pain in the eyes，deviation of the mouth and eyes，optic atrophy，swelling and pain in the throat，tinnitus，deafness. ②Irregular menstruation，menorrhagia，hernia，enuresis. ③Epilepsy，infantile convulsion，stroke. ④Pain in the hypochondriac region，depression，irritability. ⑤Atrophy or paralysis of the lower extremities.

【Needling method】Puncture perpendicularly 0.5～1.0cun.

4. 中封（LR 4），经穴
Zhongfeng（LR 4），Jing－River Point

【释义】中，中间；封，聚土成堆。穴在两踝之间，如土堆之中。

【定位】在足背侧，当足内踝前，商丘与解溪连线之间，胫骨前肌腱的内侧凹陷处（图 14－5）。

【解剖】皮肤→皮下组织→胫骨前肌腱内侧→距骨和胫骨内踝之间。布有足背内侧皮神经的分支，内踝前动脉，足背浅静脉。

【功用】疏肝通络。

【主治】①疝气，腹痛，小便不利，遗精。②下肢痿痹，足踝肿痛。

【操作】直刺 0.5～0.8 寸。

【Meaning】Zhong，middle；feng，earth heaped into a mound. The point is between the two malleolus as if between the mounds.

【Location】On the dorsum of the foot，anterior to the medial malleolus，on the line joining

Shangqiu（SP 5）and Jiexi（ST 41）, in the depression of the medial border of the tendon of the anterior tibial m.（Fig 14 –5）.

【Regional anatomy】Skin→subcutaneous tissue→medial tendon of tibialis anterior→between talus and medial malleolus. Distribute branch of medial dorsal cutaneous nerve of foot, medial anterior malleolar artery, dorsal superficial vein of foot.

【Properties】Promote flow of the liver – qi and remove obstruction from the collaterals.

【Indications】①Hernia, pain of abdomen, seminal emission, dysuria. ②Atrophy or paralysis of the lower extremities, swelling and pain of foot and malleolus.

【Needling method】Puncture perpendicularly 0. 5 ~0. 8cun.

5. 蠡沟（LR 5），络穴
Ligou（LR 5），Luo - Connecting Point

【释义】蠡，贝壳；沟，水沟。腓肠肌外形酷似贝壳，穴在其内前方沟中。

【定位】在小腿内侧，当足内踝尖上 5 寸，胫骨内侧面的中央（图 14 –6）。

【解剖】皮肤→皮下组织→胫骨骨面。浅层布有隐神经的小腿内侧皮支和大隐静脉。

【功用】疏肝理气，调经活络。

【主治】①睾丸肿痛，阳强挺长，外阴瘙痒，小便不利，遗尿，月经不调，带下。②足胫疼痛。

【操作】平刺 0. 5 ~0. 8 寸。

【Meaning】Li, shell; gou, groove. The external shape of the gastrocnemius muscle looks a shell and the point is in the groove medial and anterior to it.

【Location】On the medial leg, in the center of the medial aspect of the tibia, 5 cun above the tip of the medial malleolus（Fig 14 –6）.

【Regional anatomy】Skin→subcutaneous tissue→surface of tibia. medial crural cutaneous branches of saphenous nerve and great saphenous vein in superficial layer.

【Properties】Soothe flow of the liver – qi, regulate flow of qi, activate collaterals to treat menstrual disorders.

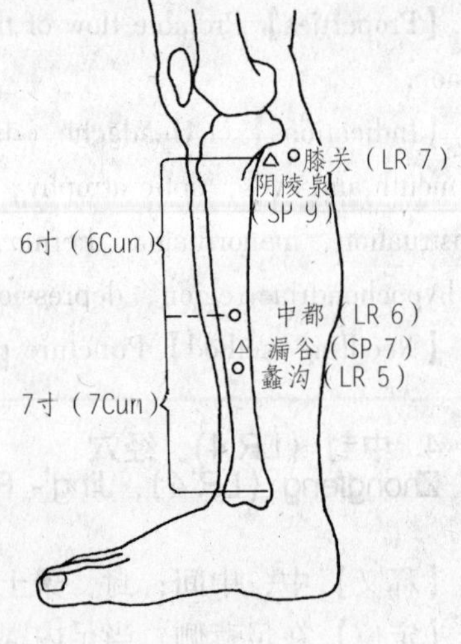

图 14 –6
Fig 14 –6

【Indications】①Swelling and pain in the testis, postcoital protrusion, pruritus vulvae, difficulty in urination, enuresis, irregular menstruation, morbid leucorrhea. ②Pain of the tibia.

【Needling method】Puncture transversely 0. 5 ~0. 8cun.

6. 中都（LR 6），郄穴
Zhongdu（LR 6），Xi - Cleft Point

【释义】中，中间；都，会聚。穴在小腿内侧中间，为肝经之气深聚之处。

【定位】在小腿内侧，当足内踝尖上 7 寸，胫骨内侧面的中央（图 14 –6）。

【解剖】皮肤→皮下组织→胫骨骨面。浅层布有隐神经的小腿内侧皮支和大隐静脉。

【功用】调肝理血。

【主治】①疝气，崩漏，恶露不尽。②腹痛，泄泻。③胁痛，下肢痿痹。

【操作】平刺 0. 5 ~0. 8 寸。

【Meaning】Zhong, middle; du, confluence. The point is on the medial aspect of the leg and at midpoint of the leg. It is a confluence of the qi of the liver meridian.

【Location】On the medial leg, in the center of the medial aspect of the tibia, 7 cun above the tip of the medial malleolus（Fig 14 –6）.

【Regional anatomy】Skin → subcutaneous tissue → surface of tibia. medial crural cutaneous branches of saphenous nerve and great saphenous vein on superficial layer.

【Properties】Regulate flow of liver – qi and blood.

【Indications】① Hernia, menorrhagia, lochia discharge. ② Abdominal pain, diarrhea. ③ Pain in the hypochondriac region, atrophy or paralysis of the lower extremities.

【Needling method】Puncture transversely 0. 5 ~0. 8cun.

7. 膝关 Xiguan（LR 7）

【释义】膝，膝部；关，关节。穴在膝关节附近。

【定位】在小腿内侧，当胫骨内上髁的后下方，阴陵泉后 1 寸（图 14 –6）。

【解剖】皮肤→皮下组织→腓肠肌。浅层布有隐神经的小腿内侧皮支，大隐静脉的属支。深层有腘动、静脉，胫神经等结构。

【功用】散寒除湿，通经利节。

【主治】膝股疼痛，下肢痿痹。

【操作】直刺 1. 0 ~1. 5 寸。

【Meaning】Xi, knee; guan, joint. The point is in the vicinity of the knee joint.

【Location】On the medial leg, posterior inferior to the medial epicondyle of the tibia, 1cun posterior to Yinlingquan（SP 9）（Fig 14 –6）.

【Regional anatomy】Skin→subcutaneous tissue→musculus gastrocnemius. medial crural cutaneous branches of saphenous nerve, subordinate branch of great saphenous vein in superficial layer. popliteal artery and vein, tibial nerve and other structures in deep layer.

【Properties】Expel wind, remove dampness, promote flow of qi and blood in the channels and collaterals, and benefit the joins.

【Indications】Pain in the knee and leg, atrophy or paralysis of the lower extremities.

【Needling method】Puncture perpendicularly 1.0 ~ 1.5cun.

8. 曲泉（LR 8），合穴 Ququan（LR 8），He - Sea Point

【释义】曲，弯曲；泉，水泉。穴在腘窝横纹内侧端，屈膝时局部呈凹陷如泉。

【定位】屈膝，当膝关节内侧端，股骨内侧髁的后缘，半腱肌、半膜肌止端的前缘凹陷处（图 14－7）。

【解剖】皮肤→皮下组织→缝匠肌后缘→股薄肌腱后缘→半膜肌腱→腓肠肌内侧头。浅层有隐神经，大隐静脉。深层有膝上内侧动、静脉的分支或属支。

【功用】舒筋活络，清湿热，利下焦。

【主治】①小腹痛，小便不利，癃闭。②月经不调，痛经，带下，阴挺，阴痒，遗精，阳痿。③膝股疼痛。

【操作】直刺 0.8 ~ 1.0 寸。

【Meaning】Qu, crooked; quan, spring. The point is at the medial end of the transverse crease of the popliteal fossa. With the knee flexed, the local depression is like a spring.

【Location】When the knee is flexed, superior to the medial end of the transverse popliteal crease, posterior to the medial epicondyle of the tibia, anterior superior to the junction of the semitendinous m. and semimembranosus m. (Fig 14 – 7).

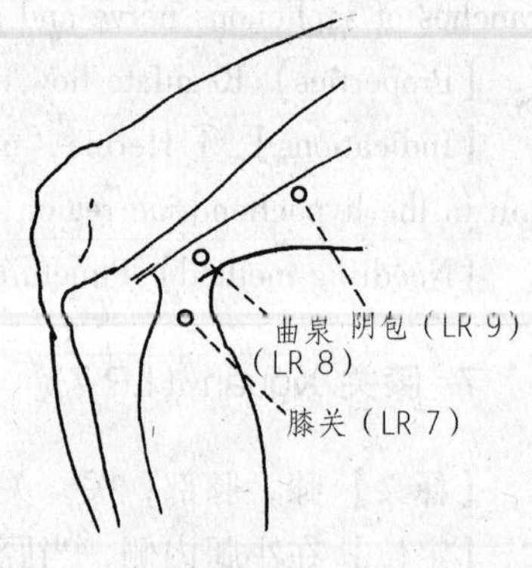

图 14 – 7
Fig 14 – 7

【Regional anatomy】Skin→subcutaneous tissue→posterior of sartorius→posterior of tendon of musculus gracilis→tendon of m. semimembranosus→medial head of musculus gastrocnemius. saphenous nerve and great saphenous vein in superficial layer. subordinate branch and branch of medial superior genicular artery and vein in deep layer.

【Properties】Relax muscles and tendons, promote flow of qi and blood in the meridian and collaterals, clear away dampness – heat, and benefit the lower – jiao.

【Indications】①Lower abdominal pain, difficulty in urination, urinary retention. ②Irregular menstruation, dysmenorrheal, morbid leucorrhea, prolonged uterus, itching of pubic region, nocturnal emission, impotence. ③Pain in the knee and leg.

【Needling method】Puncture perpendicularly 0.8 ~ 1.0cun.

9. 阴包 Yinbao（LR 9）

【释义】阴，阴阳之阴；包，通“胞”字。内为阴。包，在此指子宫。穴在大腿内侧，主治子宫疾病。

【定位】在大腿内侧，当股骨内上髁上4寸，股内肌与缝匠肌之间（图14－7）。

【解剖】皮肤→皮下组织→缝匠肌与股薄肌腱之间→大收肌。浅层有闭孔神经的皮支，大隐静脉的属支。深层有股神经的肌支，隐神经，股动、静脉等结构。

【功用】调经血，理下焦。

【主治】①月经不调，遗尿，小便不利。②腰骶痛。

【操作】直刺1.0～2.0寸。

【Meaning】Yin, yin of yin－yang; bao, womb. The interior is yin. Bao refer to the uterus. The point is at the medial aspect of the thigh and is indicated in disorders of the uterus.

【Location】On the medial leg, 4 cun above the medial epicondyle of the femur, between the sartorius m and vastus medialis.（Fig 14－7）.

【Regional anatomy】Skin→subcutaneous tissue→between tendon of sartorius and tendon of musculus gracilis→m. adductor magnus. cutaneous branches of obturator nerve, subordinate branch of great saphenous vein in superficial layer. muscular branches of femoral nerve, saphenous nerve, femoral artery and vein and other structures in deep layer.

【Properties】Treat menstrual disorders, regulate the lower－jiao.

【Indications】①Irregular menstruation, enuresis, difficulty in urination. ②Pain in the lumbar and sacral region.

【Needling method】Puncture perpendicularly 1.0～2.0cun.

10. 足五里 Zuwuli（LR 10）

【释义】足，下肢；五，数词；里，古代有以里为寸之说。穴在下肢，约当箕门穴上5寸。

【定位】在大腿内侧，当气冲直下3寸，大腿根部，耻骨结节的下方（图14－8）。

【解剖】皮肤→皮下组织→长收肌→短收肌→大收肌。浅层布有股神经的前皮支，大隐静脉。深层有闭孔神经的前支和后支，股动、静脉的肌支，旋股内侧动、静脉的肌支。

【功用】清热利湿，活络止痛。

【主治】小便不利，小腹胀痛，遗尿，带下，阴囊湿痒，阴挺，睾丸肿痛。

【操作】直刺1.0～1.5寸。

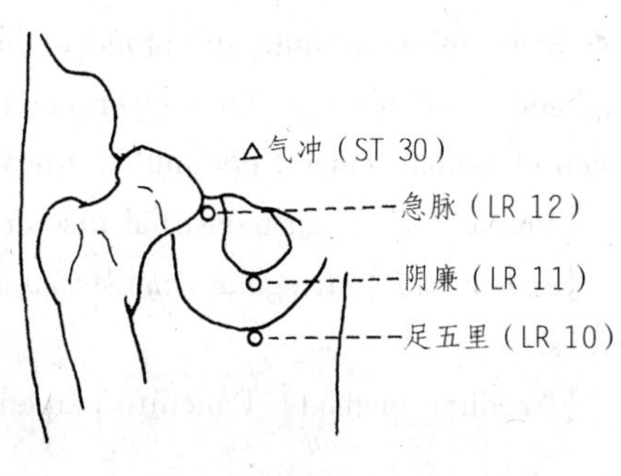

图14－8

Fig 14－8

【Meaning】Zu, lower limbs; wu, five; li, used as cun in ancient times. The point is in the lower limbs, 5 cun above Qimen.

【Location】On the medial thigh, 3 cun directly below Qichong (ST 30), at the end of the thigh, below the pubic tubercle (Fig 14 – 8).

【Regional anatomy】Skin→subcutaneous tissue→m. adductor longus→m. adductor brevis→m. adductor magnus. anterior cutaneous branch of femoral nerve, great saphenous vein in superficial layer. anterior and posterior branches of obturator nerve, muscular branch of femoral artery and vein, muscular branch of medial femoral circumflex artery and vein in deep layer.

【Properties】Clear away dampness – heat, promote flow of qi and blood in the collaterals, relieve pain.

【Indications】Difficulty in urination, lower abdominal pain and distention, enuresis, morbid leucorrhea, dampness and itching of scrotum, prolonged uterus, swelling and pain in the testis.

【Needling method】Puncture perpendicularly 1. 0 ~ 1. 5cun.

11. 阴廉 Yinlian (LR 11)

【释义】阴，阴阳之阴；廉，边缘。内为阴。穴在大腿内侧阴器的边缘。

【定位】在大腿内侧，当气冲直下2寸，大腿根部，耻骨结节的下方（图14-8）。

【解剖】皮肤→皮下组织→长收肌→短收肌→小收肌。浅层布有股神经的前皮支，大隐静脉和腹股沟淋巴结。深层有闭孔神经的前支和后支，旋股内侧动、静脉的肌支。

【功用】调经血，理下焦。

【主治】月经不调，小腹胀痛，带下。

【操作】直刺1.0~2.0寸。

【Meaning】Yin, yin of yin – yang; lian, edge. The inferior is yin. The point is on the medial aspect of the thigh, near the genitalia.

【Location】On the medial thigh, 2 cun directly below Qichong (ST 30), at the end of the thigh, below the pubic tubercle (Fig 14 – 8).

【Regional anatomy】Skin→subcutaneous tissue→m. adductor longus→m. adductor brevis→m. adductor minimus. anterior cutaneous branch of femoral nerve, great saphenous vein and inguinal lymphatic gland in superficial layer. anterior and posterior branches of obturator nerve, muscular branch of medial femoral circumflex artery and vein in deep layer.

【Properties】Treat menstrual disorders, regulate the lower – jiao.

【Indications】Irregular menstruation, lower abdominal pain and distention, morbid leucorrhea.

【Needling method】Puncture perpendicularly 1. 0 ~ 2. 0cun.

12. 急脉 Jimai (LR 12)

【释义】急，急促；脉，动脉。穴在大腿根部内侧，局部动脉应手处。

【定位】当气冲外下方腹股沟股动脉搏动处，前正中线旁开2.5寸（图14-8）。

【解剖】皮肤→皮下组织→耻骨肌→闭孔外肌。浅层布有股神经的前皮支，大隐静脉和腹股沟淋巴结。深层有阴部外动、静脉，旋股内侧动、静脉的分支或属支，闭孔神经前支等结构。

【功用】疏肝理气，止痛。

【主治】疝气，小腹痛，阴挺，阴茎痛，外阴肿痛。

【操作】避开动脉，直刺0.5~0.8寸。

【Meaning】Ji, urgent; mai, artery. The point is at the medial aspect of the thigh, where the artery is felt.

【Location】Lateral and inferior to Qichong (ST 30), in the crease of the groin where the femoral artery pulsates, 2.5 cun lateral to the midpoint of the pubic tubercle (Fig 14-8).

【Regional anatomy】Skin→subcutaneous tissue→musculi pectineus→musculi obturator externus. anterior cutaneous branch of femoral nerve, great saphenous vein and inguinal lymphatic gland in superficial layer. external pudendal artery and vein, subordinate branch and branch of medial femoral circumflex artery and vein, anterior branches of obturator nerve and other structures in deep layer.

【Properties】Soothe flow of the liver-qi, regulate flow of qi, relieve pain.

【Indications】Hernia, lower abdominal pain, prolonged uterus, phallalgia, swelling and pain in vulva.

【Needling method】Puncture perpendicularly 0.5~0.8cun, avoid penetrating the femoral artery.

13. 章门（LR 13），脾募，八会穴（脏会），足厥阴、足少阳经交会穴 Zhangmen (LR 13), Front-Mu Point of the Spleen; One of the Eight Influential Points (Zang-Organs Convergence); Crossing Point of the Meridian of Foot-Jueyin and Foot-Shaoyang

【释义】章，同“障”，门，门户。穴在季胁下，如同屏障内脏之门户。

【定位】在侧腹部，当第11肋游离端的下方（图14-9）。

【解剖】皮肤→皮下组织→腹外斜肌→腹内斜肌→腹横肌。浅层布有第10、11胸神经前支的外侧皮支，胸腹壁浅静脉的属支。深层有第10、11胸神经和肋间后动、静脉的分支或属支。

【功用】疏肝理气，活血化瘀。

【主治】①腹胀，泄泻，痞块。②胁痛，黄疸。

【操作】直刺0.8~1.0寸。

【Meaning】Zhang, screen; men, door. The point is below the hypochondrium, which is like a screen for the internal organs.

【Location】On the lateral abdomen, on the lower border of the free end of the 11th floating rib

(Fig 14 –9).

【Regional anatomy】Skin→subcutaneous tissue→external oblique muscle of abdomen→musculus obliquus internus abdominis→m. transversus abdominis. Lateral cutaneous branch of 10th、11th thoracic nerve and subordinate branch of superficial thoracoepigastric vein in superficial layer. 10th、11th thoracic nerve, subordinate branch and branch of posterior intercostal arteries and veins in deep layer.

【Properties】Soothe flow of the liver – qi, activate blood flow and remove blood stasis.

【Indications】①Abdominal distention, diarrhea, abdominal masses. ②Pain in the hypochondriac region, jaundice.

【Needling method】Puncture perpendicularly 0.8 –1.0cun.

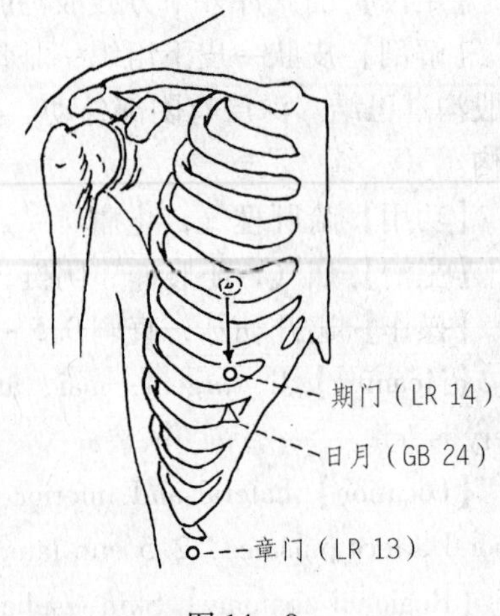

图 14 –9

Fig 14 –9

14. 期门（LR 14），肝募穴，足厥阴、太阴经、阴维脉交会穴 Qimen（LR 14），Front - Mu Point of the Liver；Crossing Point of the Meridian of Foot - Jueyin，Foot - taiyin and the Yin Link Vessel

【释义】期，周期；门，门户。两侧胁肋如敞开之门户。穴在胁肋部，经气运行至此为一周期，故称期门。

【定位】在胸部，当乳头直下，第6肋间隙，前正中线旁开4寸（图14–9）。

【解剖】皮肤→皮下组织→胸大肌下缘→腹外斜肌→肋间外肌→肋间内肌。浅层布有第6肋间神经的外侧皮支，胸腹壁静脉的属支。深层有第6肋间神经和第6肋间后动、静脉的分支或属支。

【功用】疏肝理气、活血化瘀。

【主治】①胸胁胀痛。②腹胀，呃逆，吐酸。③乳痈，郁闷。

【操作】斜刺0.5~0.8寸。

【Meaning】Qi, cycle; men, door. The flanks on both sides are like an open door, where the point is located. When the qi of meridian circulates here, it is considered as one cycle. The point is therefore named Qimen.

【Location】On the chest, directly below the nipple, at the 6th intercostal space, 4 cun lateral to the anterior midline (Fig 14 –9).

【Regional anatomy】Skin→subcutaneous tissue→inferior border of pectoralis major→external oblique muscle of abdomen→m. intercostales externi→m. intercostales interni. Lateral cutaneous branch of 6th intercostal nerve, subordinate branch of superficial thoracoepigastric vein in superficial layer. The 6th intercostal nerve, subordinate branch and branch of the 6th posterior intercostal artery and vein in deep layer.

【Properties】Soothe flow of the liver – qi, activate blood flow and remove blood stasis.

【Indications】①Pain and distension in the chest and hypochondriac region. ②hiccups, singultus, acid regurgitation. ③Mastitis, depression.

【Needling method】Puncture obliquely 0.5 ~ 0.8cun.

复习思考题
Review Questions

1. 为什么足厥阴肝经能治疗巅顶痛?

Why can the liver meridian of foot – jueyin treat headaches on the vertex?

2. 复述足厥阴肝经起始穴和终止穴的定位、主治及功用。

Describe the location, properties, indications of the first and last points of the liver meridian of foot – jueyin.

3. 复述足厥阴肝经的主治范围。

Describe the general indications of the liver meridian of foot – jueyin.

第十五章 奇经八脉
Eight Extra Meridians and Its Acupoints

第一节 督 脉
Governor Vessel and Its Acupoints

一、循行分布
The Course of Governor Vessel

起于少腹，以下骨中央（胞中），下出会阴，经长强，行于后背止中，上至风府，入属于脑，上巅，循额，至鼻柱，经素髎、水沟，会手足阳明，至兑端，入龈交。

分支：其少腹直上者，贯脐中央，上贯心，入喉，上颐，环唇，上系两目之下中央（《素问·骨空论》）。

络脉：督脉之别，名曰长强，夹膂上项，散头上，下当肩胛左右，别走太阳，入贯膂（《灵枢·经脉》）（图15－1）。

The course of the Vessel: It arises from the lower abdomen and comes out from the perineum. It runs posteriorly along the interior side of the spinal column to Fengfu (DU16) at the nape where it enters the brain. It further ascends to the vertex and goes down along the forehead to the nasal column. It passes through Suliao, Shuigou, and runs together with the Yangming Vessels of the hand and foot. Then it

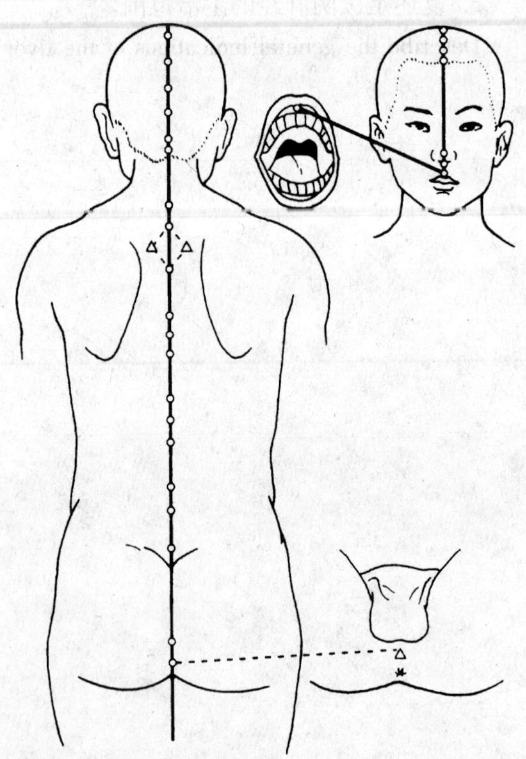

图例 ——本经有穴通路 ……本经无穴通路

Note ——Pathway with points

……Pathway without points

图15－1 督脉循行示意图

Fig. 15－1 The course of governor vessel

arrives at Duiduan (DU 27), which finally enters Yinjiao (DU 28) (Fig 15 - 1).

二、功能与病候
Properties and Syndromes

督脉的功能可以概括为“总督全身的阳气”，为“阳脉之海”。督脉具有督领全身阳气，统率诸阳经的作用。

督脉病候主要表现为腰脊强痛，头重头痛和神志病。此外，有髓海不足的症候表现，如头晕，耳鸣，眩晕，目无所见，懈怠，嗜睡等。

The properties of governor vessel can be summarized as "governing all yang qi of the whole body", "being the sea of yang meridians", which mean Governor vessel leading and commanding all the yang qi and yang meridians.

The principal symptoms of governor vessel are: stiffness and pain in the waist and spine, feel heaviness in the head, headache and mental diseases. In addition, the symptoms due to deficiency of marrow sea (Suihai) are also caused by the dificiency of governor vessel, such as dizziness, tinnitus, vertigo, dim eyesight, sluggishness, somnolence, etc.

三、督脉腧穴
Acupoints of Governor Vessel

本经总共28个穴位，始于长强，终于龈交（图15-2）。

1. 长强（DU 1），络穴，督脉、足少阳、足少阴经交会穴
Changqiang (PU 1), Luo - Connecting Point of Governor vessel; Crossing Point of the meridians of Foot - Shaoyang and Foot - Shaoyin and Governor Vessel

【释义】长，长短之长；强，强弱之强。脊柱长而强韧，穴在其下端。

【定位】在尾骨端下，当尾骨端与肛门连线的中点处（图15-3）。

【解剖】皮肤→皮下组织→肛尾韧带。浅层主要布有尾神经的后支。深层有阴部神经的分支，肛神经，阴部内动、静脉的分支或属支，肛动、静脉。

【功用】温阳除湿。

【主治】①痔疾，脱肛，泄泻，便秘。②癫狂痫，瘈疭。③腰痛，尾骶骨痛。

【操作】斜刺，针尖向上与骶骨平行刺入0.5~1.0寸。不得刺穿直肠，以防感染。

【Meaning】Chang, long; qiang, strong. The spinal column is long and strong. The point is at the lower end of the spinal column.

【Location】Below the tip of the coccyx, at the midpoint between the tip of the coccyx and anus (Fig 15 - 3).

【Regional anatomy】Skin → subcutaneous tissue → Anal tail ligaments. There are posterior

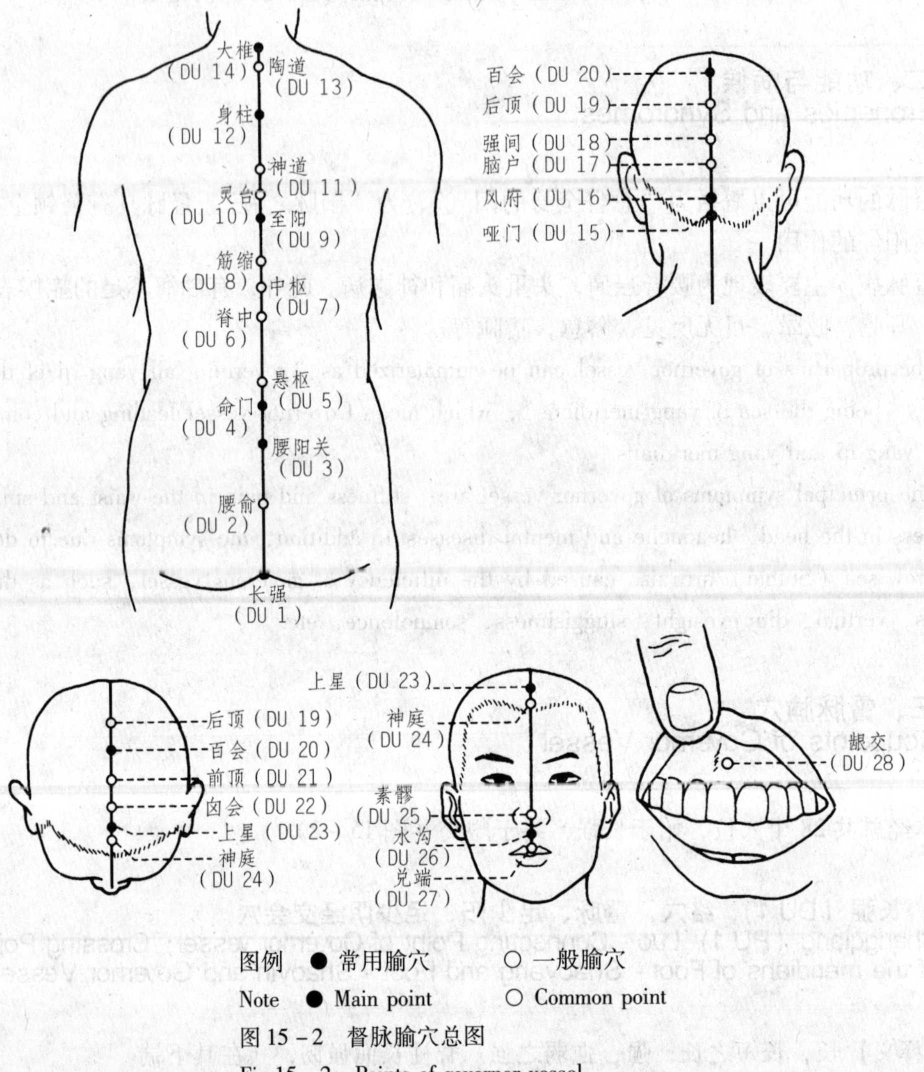

图 15-2 督脉腧穴总图

Fig 15-2 Points of governor vessel

branch of tail nerve in the superficial layer. In the deep layer, there are branches of pudendum nerve, anal nerve, branches of left and right pudendum arteries and veins, anal arteries and veins in the area.

【Properties】Warm yang and eliminate dampness.

【Indications】①Hemorrhoids, prolapse of the rectum, diarrhea, constipation. ②Psychosis and epilepsy, infantile convulsion. ③Backache, Pain in the coccyx.

【Needling method】Puncture obliquely, puncture transversely upward 0.5 ~ 1.0 cun along the anterior aspect of the coccyx. Not advisable to insert the needle through the rectum to prevent infection.

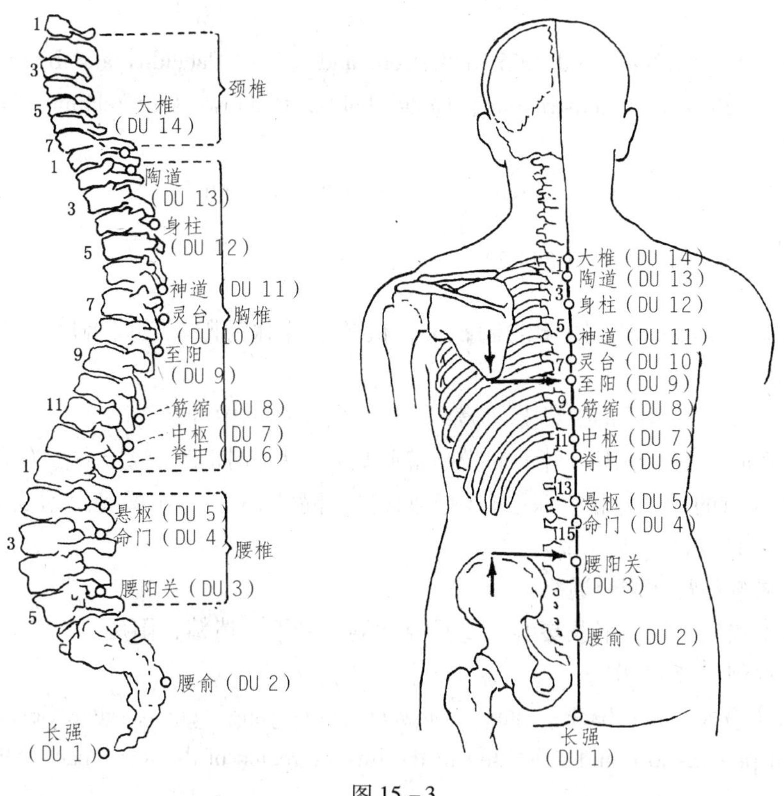

图 15－3

Fig 15－3

2. 腰俞 Yaoshu (DU 2)

【释义】腰，腰部；俞，输注。穴在腰部，是经气输注之处。

【定位】在骶部，当后正中线上，适对骶管裂孔（图 15－3）。

【解剖】皮肤→皮下组织→骶尾背侧韧带→骶管。浅层主要布有第 5 骶神经的后支。深层有尾丛。

【功用】调经通络，清热利湿。

【主治】①腰脊强痛，下肢痿痹。②月经不调，痔疾，脱肛，便秘。③癫痫。

【操作】向上斜刺 0.5～1.0 寸。

【Meaning】Yao, low back; shu, point. The point is on the lower back, where the qi of meridian is infused.

【Location】On the sacrum and on the posterior midline, just at the sacral hiatus (Fig 15－3).

【Regional anatomy】Skin → subcutaneous tissue → sacrococcygeal dorsal ligament → caudal. There are posterior branch of sacral nerve in the superficial layer. In the deep layer, there are sacrococcygeal plexus.

【Properties】Regulate menstruation and free the collateral vessel, clear heat and drain dampness.

【Indications】①Stiffness and pain in the loin and spine, flaccidity and bi syndrome in the lower extremities. ②Irregular menstruation, Hemorrhoids, Prolapse of the rectum, Constipation. ③Epilepsy.

【Needling method】Puncture obliquely upward 0.5 ~ 1.0 cun.

3. 腰阳关 Yaoyangguan（DU 3）

【释义】腰，腰部；阳，阴阳之阳；关，机关。督脉为阳。穴属督脉，位于腰部转动处，如腰之机关。

【定位】在腰部，当后正中线上，第4腰椎棘突下凹陷中（图15－3）。

【解剖】皮肤→皮下组织→棘上韧带→棘间韧带→弓间韧带。浅层主要布有第4腰神经后支的内侧和伴行的动、静脉。深层有棘突间的椎外静脉丛，第4腰神经后支的分支和第4腰动、静脉的背侧支的分支或属支。

【功用】强腰补肾，调经通络。

【主治】①腰骶疼痛，下肢痿痹。②月经不调，带下，遗精，阳痿。

【操作】直刺0.5～1.0寸。

【Meaning】Yao, low back; yang, yang of yin－yang; guan, gear. Governor vessel is yang. The point pertains to it and is located in the turning region of the lower back, like the gear of the lumbar joint.

【Location】On the low back and on the posterior midline, in the depression below the spinous process of the 4th lumbar vertebra（Fig 15－3）.

【Regional anatomy】Skin→subcutaneous tissue→supraspinal ligaments→interspinal ligament→ligament flava. There are medial branch of posterior branch of the 4th lumbar nerve, following arteries and veins in the superficial layer. In the deep layer there are posterior external vertebral venous plexus, branches of posterior branch of the 4th lumbar nerve, branches of dorsal branch of the 4th lumbar arteries and veins among spinous processes.

【Properties】Strengthen lower back and fortify the kidney, regulate menstruation and free the collateral vessel.

【Indications】①Pain in the lumbosacral region, flaccidity and bi syndrome in the lower extremities. ②Irregular menstruation, leukorrhea, nocturnal emission, impotence.

【Needling method】Puncture perpendicularly 0.5 ~ 1.0 cun.

4. 命门 Mingmen（DU 4）

【释义】命，生命；门，门户。肾为生命之源，穴在肾俞之间，相当于肾气出入之门户。

【定位】在腰部，当后正中线上，第2腰椎棘突下凹陷中（图15－3）。

【解剖】皮肤→皮下组织→棘上韧带→棘间韧带→弓间韧带。浅层主要布有第2腰神经后支的内侧支和伴行的动、静脉。深层有棘突间的椎外静脉丛，第2腰神经后支的分支和第2腰动、静脉背侧支的分支或属支。

【功用】补肾助阳，调经止泻。

【主治】①腰痛，下肢痿痹。②遗精，阳痿，早泄，月经不调，赤白带下，遗尿，尿频。③泄泻。

【操作】直刺0.5~1.0寸。

【Meaning】Ming, life; men, door. The Kidney is the source of life. The point is between Shengshu. like a door for the qi of the kidney.

【Location】On the low back and on the posterior midline, in the depression below the spinous process of the 2nd lumbar vertebra (Fig 15-3).

【Regional anatomy】Skin→subcutaneous tissue→supraspinal ligaments→interspinal ligament→ligament flava. There are medial branch of posterior branch of the 2nd lumbar, following arteries and veins in the superficial layer. In the deep layer there are posterior external vertebral venous plexus, branches of posterior branch of the 2nd lumbar nerve, branches of dorsal branch of the 2nd lumbar arteries and veins among spinous processes.

【Properties】Fortify the kidney and support yang, regulate menstruation and check diarrhea.

【Indications】①Lumbar pain, flaccidity and Bi syndrome in the lower extremities. ②Nocturnal emission, impotence, premature ejaculation, irregular menstruation, leukorrhea, enuresis enuresis, frequency of the urination. ③Diarrhea.

【Needling method】Puncture perpendicularly 0.5~1.0 cun.

5. 悬枢 Xuanshu (DU 5)

【释义】悬，悬挂；枢，枢纽。穴在腰部，仰卧时局部悬起，为腰部活动的枢纽。

【定位】在腰部，当后正中线，第1腰椎棘突下凹陷中（图15-3）。

【解剖】皮肤→皮下组织→棘上韧带→棘间韧带。浅层主要布有第1腰神经后支的内侧支和伴行的动、静脉。深层有棘突间的椎外静脉丛，第1腰神经后支的分支和第1腰动、静脉背侧支的分支或属支。

【功用】温肾健脾，强健腰脊。

【主治】①腰痛，泄泻，肠鸣。②腰脊强痛。

【操作】直刺0.5~1.0寸。

【Meaning】Xuan, suspended; shu, pivot. The point is on the lower back. When lying supine, the local region is suspended as a pivot for lumbar movement.

【Location】On the low back and on the posterior midline. in the depression below the spinous process of the 1st lumbar vertebra (Fig 15-3).

【Regional anatomy】Skin→subcutaneous tissue→supraspinal ligaments→interspinal ligament. There are medial branch of posterior branch of the 1st lumbar, following arteries and veins in the superficial layer. In the deep layer, there are posterior external vertebral venous plexus, branches of posterior branch of the 1st lumbar nerve, branches of dorsal branch of the 1st lumbar arteries and veins among spinous processes.

【Properties】Warm the kidney and fortify the spleen, strengthen the back and spine.

【Indications】①Lumbar pain, diarrhea, borborygmus. ②Stiffness and pain in the loin and spine.

【Needling method】Puncture perpendicularly0. 5 ~ 1. 0 cun.

6. 脊中 Jizhong (DU 6)

【释义】脊，脊柱；中，中间。脊柱古作二十一椎；穴在第 11 椎下，正当其中。

【定位】在背部，当后正中线上，第 11 胸椎棘突下凹陷中（图 15 - 3）。

【解剖】皮肤→皮下组织→棘上韧带→棘间韧带。浅层主要布有第 11 胸神经后支的内侧支和伴行的动、静脉。深层有棘突间的椎外静脉丛，第 11 胸神经后支的分支和第 11 肋间动、静脉背侧支的分支或属支。

【功用】祛风清热。

【主治】①泄泻，脱肛，痔疾，黄疸，小儿疳积。②癫痫。③腰脊强痛。

【操作】斜刺 0. 5 ~ 1. 0 寸。

【Meaning】Ji, spine; zhong, middle. The spine consists of 21vertebrae. The point is below the 11th vertebra at exactly the middle.

【Location】On the back and on the posterior midline, in the depression below the spinous process of the 11th thoracic vertebra (Fig 15 - 3).

【Regional anatomy】Skin → subcutaneous tissue → supraspinal ligaments → interspinal ligament. There are medial branch of posterior branch of the 11th chest nerve, following arteries and veins in the superficial layer. In the deep layer, there are posterior external vertebral venous plexus, branches of posterior branch of 11th chest nerve, branches of dorsal branch of the 11th intercostal arteries and veins among spinous processes.

【Properties】Dispel wind and clear heat.

【Indications】①Diarrhea, prolapse of the rectum, hemorrhoids, jaundice, infantile retention of food. ②Epilepsy. ③Stiffness and pain in the loin and spine.

【Needling method】Puncture obliquely 0. 5 ~ 1. 0 cun.

7. 中枢 Zhongshu (DU 7)

【释义】中，中间；枢，枢纽。穴在第 10 胸椎下，相当于脊柱中部之枢纽。

【定位】在背部，当后正中线上，第 10 胸椎棘突下凹陷中（图 15 - 3）。

【解剖】皮肤→皮下组织→棘上韧带→棘间韧带。浅层主要布有第 10 胸神经后支的内侧支和伴行的动、静脉。深层有棘突间的椎外静脉丛，第 10 胸神经后支的分支和第 10 肋间动、静脉背侧支的分支或属支。

【功用】祛风清热。

【主治】①胃病，呕吐，腹痛，黄疸。②腰背疼痛。

【操作】斜刺0.5～1.0寸。

【Meaning】Zhong, middle; shu, pivot. The point is below the 10th vertebra and is like a pivot in the middle of the spine.

【Location】On the back and on the posterior midline, in the depression below the spinous process of the 10th thoracic vertebra (Fig 15－3).

【Regional anatomy】Skin→subcutaneous tissue→supraspinal ligaments→interspinal ligament. There are medial branch of posterior branch of the 10th chest nerve, following arteries and veins in the superficial layer. In the deep layer, there are posterior external vertebral venous plexus, branches of posterior branch of the 10th chest nerve, branches of dorsal branch of the 10th intercostal arteries and veins among spinous processes.

【Properties】Dispel wind and clear heat.

【Indications】①Stomachache, vomiting, abdominal pain, Jaundice. ②Pain in the back.

【Needling method】Puncture obliquely 0.5～1.0cun.

8. 筋缩 Jinsuo (DU 8)

【释义】筋，筋肉；缩，挛缩。本穴能治筋肉挛缩诸病。

【定位】在背部，当后正中线上，第9胸椎棘突下凹陷中（图15－3）。

【解剖】皮肤→皮下组织→棘上韧带→棘间韧带。浅层主要布有第9胸神经后支的内侧支和伴行的动、静脉。深层有棘突间的椎外静脉丛，第9胸神经后支的分支和第9肋间动、静脉背侧支的分支或属支。

【功用】解痉止痛。

【主治】脊强，癫痫，抽搐，胃痛。

【操作】斜刺0.5～1.0寸。

【Meaning】Jin, muscle; suo, contracture. This point is useful in treating muscle contracture of all types.

【Location】On the back and on the posterior midline, in the depression below the spinous process of the 9th thoracic vertebra (Fig 15－3).

【Regional anatomy】Skin→subcutaneous tissue→supraspinal ligaments→interspinal ligament. There are medial branch of posterior branch of the 9th chest nerve, following arteries and veins in the superficial layer. In the deep layer, there are posterior external vertebral venous plexus, branches of posterior branch of the 9th chest nerve, branches of dorsal branch of the 9th intercostal arteries and veins among spinous processes.

【Properties】Relax the muscular spasm and stop pain.

【Indications】Stiffness of the spine, epilepsy, twitch, stomachache.

【Needling method】Puncture obliquely 0.5 ~ 1.0cun.

9. 至阳 Zhiyang (DU 9)

【释义】至，到达；阳，阴阳之阳。本穴与横膈平。经气至此从膈下的阳中之阴到达膈上的阳中之阳。

【定位】在背部，当后正中线上，第7胸椎棘突下凹陷中（图15-3）。

【解剖】皮肤→皮下组织→棘上韧带→棘间韧带。浅层主要布有第7胸神经后支的内侧支和伴行的动、静脉。深层有棘突间的椎外静脉丛，第7胸神经后支的分支和第7肋间动、静脉背侧支的分支或属支。

【功用】清热，解痉止痛。

【主治】①黄疸，胸胁胀痛，身热。②咳嗽，气喘。③胃痛，脊背强痛。

【操作】斜刺0.5~1.0寸。

【Meaning】Zhi, reaching; yang, yang of yin - yang. The point is at the level of the diaphragm. The qi of this meridian passes here and ascends, i. e. it reaches "yang within yang" above the diaphragm from "yin within yang" below the diaphragm.

【Location】On the back and on the posterior midline, in the depression below the spinous process of the 7th thoracic vertebra (Fig 15-3).

【Regional anatomy】Skin → subcutaneous tissue → supraspinal ligaments → interspinal ligament. There are medial branch of posterior branch of the 7th chest nerve, following arteries and veins in the superficial layer. In the deep layer, there are posterior external vertebral venous plexus, branches of posterior branch of the 7th chest nerve, branches of dorsal branch of the 7th intercostal arteries and veins among spinous processes.

【Properties】Clear heat, relax the muscular spasm and stop pain.

【Indications】①Jaundice, distension and pain in the chest and hypochondrium, feverish body. ②cough, asthma. ③Stomachache, pain and stiffness of the back.

【Needling method】Puncture obliquely 0.5 ~ 1.0cun.

10. 灵台 Lingtai (PU 10)

【释义】灵，神灵；台，亭台。穴在神道和心俞两穴之下，故喻为心灵之台。

【定位】在背部，当后正中线上，第6胸椎棘突下凹陷中（图15-3）。

【解剖】皮肤→皮下组织→棘上韧带→棘间韧带。浅层主要布有第6胸神经后支的内侧支和伴行的动、静脉。深层有棘突间的椎外静脉丛，第6胸神经后支的分支和第6肋间动、静脉背侧支的分支或属支。

【功用】清热，止痛。

【主治】①疔疮。②气喘，咳嗽。③胃痛，脊背强痛。

【操作】斜刺0.5~1.0寸。

【Meaning】Ling, spirit; tai, platform. The point is below Shengdao and Xinshu and is therefore likened to a platform for the Heart spirit.

【Location】On the back and on the posterior midline, in the depression below the spinous process of the 6th thoracic vertebra (Fig 15 –3).

【Regional anatomy】Skin → subcutaneous tissue → supraspinal ligaments → interspinal ligament. There are medial branch of posterior branch of the 6th chest nerve, following arteries and veins in the superficial layer. In the deep layer, there are posterior external vertebral venous plexus, branches of posterior branch of the 6th chest nerve, branches of dorsal branch of the 6th intercostal arteries and veins among spinous processes.

【Properties】Clear heat, stop pain.

【Indications】①Furuncle. ②Asthma, cough. ③Stomachache, pain and stiffness of the back.

【Needling method】Puncture obliquely 0.5 ~1.0 cun.

11. 神道 Shendao (DU 11)

【释义】神，心神；道，通道。心藏神，穴在心俞旁，如同心神之通道。

【定位】在背部，当后正中线上，第5胸椎棘突下凹陷中（图15 –3）。

【解剖】皮肤→皮下组织→棘上韧带→棘间韧带。浅层主要布有第5胸神经后支的内侧支和伴行的动、静脉。深层有棘突间的椎外静脉丛，第5胸神经后支的分支和第5肋间动、静脉背侧支的分支或属支。

【功用】养心宁神，清热息风，通络止痛。

【主治】①心悸，健忘，小儿惊痫。②咳喘，脊背强痛。

【操作】斜刺0.5 ~1.0寸。

【Meaning】Shen, mind; dao, pathway. The heart houses the mind and the point is lateral to Xinshu, like a pathway fo the mind.

【Location】On the back and on the posterior midline, in the depression below the spinous process of the 5th thoracic vertebra (Fig 15 –3).

【Regional anatomy】Skin → subcutaneous tissue → supraspinal ligaments → interspinal ligament. There are medial branch of posterior branch of the 5th chest nerve, following arteries and veins in the superficial layer. In the deep layer, there are posterior external vertebral venous plexus, branches of posterior branch of the 5th chest nerve, branches of dorsal branch of the 5th intercostal arteries and veins among spinous processes.

【Properties】Nourish the heart to tranquilize, clear heat and subdue wind, free the collateral vessel and stop pain.

【Indications】①Palpitations, forgetful, infantile convulsion. ②Cough and asthma, pain and stiffness of the back.

【Needling method】Puncture obliquely 0.5 ~1.0 cun.

12. 身柱 Shenzhu（DU 12）

【释义】身，身体；柱，支柱。穴在第 3 胸椎下，上连头项，下通背腰，如一身之支柱。

【定位】在背部，当后正中线上，第 3 胸椎棘突下凹陷中（图 15－3）。

【解剖】皮肤→皮下组织→棘上韧带→棘间韧带。浅层主要布有第 3 胸神经后支的内侧支和伴行的动、静脉。深层有棘突间的椎外静脉丛，第 3 胸神经后支的分支和第 3 肋间动、静脉背侧支的分支或属支。

【功用】宣肺止咳，祛风清热，宁心安神。

【主治】①咳嗽，气喘。②身热，癫痫。③脊背强痛。

【操作】斜刺 0.5～1.0 寸。

【Meaning】Shen，body；zhu，pillar. The point is below the 3rd thoracic vertebra and connects upward with the head and neck. then downward with the back and the lumbar vertebra，like a pillar of he body.

【Location】On the back and on the posterior midline，in the depression below the spinous process of the 3rd thoracic vertebra（Fig 15－3）.

【Regional anatomy】Skin → subcutaneous tissue → supraspinal ligaments → interspinal ligament. There are medial branch of posterior branch of the 3rd chest nerve，following arteries and veins in the superficial layer. In the deep layer，there are posterior external vertebral venous plexus，branches of posterior branch of the 3rd chest nerve，branches of dorsal branch of the 3rd intercostal arteries and veins among spinous processes.

【Properties】Diffuse the lung to suppress cough，dispel wind and clear heat，nourish the heart to tranquilize.

【Indications】①Cough，asthma. ②Feverish body，epilepsy. ③Pain and stiffness of the back.

【Needling method】Puncture obliquely 0.5～1.0 cun.

13. 陶道（DU 13），督脉、足太阳经交会穴 Taodao（DU 13），Crossing Point of Governor Vessel and the Foot－Taiyang Meridian

【释义】陶，陶冶；道，道路。比喻脏腑之气汇集于督脉，由此路上升。

【定位】在背部，当后正中线上，第 1 胸椎棘突下凹陷中（图 15－3）。

【解剖】皮肤→皮下组织→棘上韧带→棘间韧带。浅层主要布有第 1 胸神经后支的内侧支和伴行的动、静脉。深层有棘突间的椎外静脉丛，第 1 胸神经后支的分支和第 1 肋间动、静脉背侧支的分支或属支。

【功用】解表退热，镇惊安神。

【主治】①热病，骨蒸潮热，疟疾。②头痛，脊强。③癫狂痫。

【操作】斜刺 0.5～1.0 寸。

【Meaning】Tao, moulding; dao, pathway. Qi of zang – fu organs is gathered at governor vessel and ascends along this way.

【Location】On the back and on the posterior midline, in the depression below the spinous process of the 1st thoracic vertebra (Fig 15 –3).

【Regional anatomy】Skin → subcutaneous tissue → supraspinal ligaments → interspinal ligament. There are medial branch of posterior branch of the 1st chest nerve, following arteries and veins in the superficial layer. In the deep layer, there are posterior external vertebral venous plexus, branches of posterior branch of the 1st chest nerve, branches of dorsal branch of the 1st intercostal arteries and veins among spinous processes.

【Properties】Release the exterior and clear heat, settle fright and tranquilize.

【Indications】①Febrile disease, afternoon fever, malaria. ②Headache, Stiffness of the back. ③Psychosis and epilepsy.

【Needling method】Puncture obliquely 0.5 ~1.0 cun.

14. 大椎（DU 14），督脉、手足三阳经交会穴 Dazhui (DU 14), Crossing Point of Governor Vessel and Three Yang Meridians of Foot ang Hand

【释义】大，巨大；椎，椎骨。古称第7颈椎棘突为大椎，穴适在其下方，故名。

【定位】在后正中线上，第7颈椎棘突下凹陷中（图15－3）。

【解剖】皮肤→皮下组织→棘上韧带→棘间韧带。浅层主要布有第8颈神经后支的内侧支和棘突间皮下静脉丛。深层有棘突间的椎外静脉丛和第8颈神经后支的分支。

【功用】解表清热，安神镇静。

【主治】①热病，疟疾，骨蒸盗汗，咳嗽，气喘。②癫痫，小儿惊风。③感冒，畏寒，风疹，头项强痛。

【操作】斜刺0.5～1.0寸。

【Meaning】Da, large; zhui, vertebra. The point is below the prominence of the 7th cervical vertebra which is the largest of the vertebra.

【Location】On the posterior midline, in the depression below the 7th cervical vertebra (Fig 15 –3).

【Regional anatomy】Skin → subcutaneous tissue → supraspinal ligaments → interspinal ligaments. There are medial branch of posterior branch of the 8th cervical nerve and cutaneous venous plexus among spinous processes in the superficial layer. In the deep layer, there are posterior external vertebral venous plexus and branches of posterior branch of the 8th cervical verve among spinous processes.

【Properties】Release the exterior and clear heat, settle fright and tranquilize.

【Indications】①Febrile disease, malaria, afternoon fever, cough, asthma. ②Epilepsy, infantile convulsion. ③Cold, chills, rubella, pain and stiffness of the neck and head.

【Needling method】Puncture obliquely 0.5 ~1.0 cun.

15. 哑门（DU 15），督脉、阳维脉交会穴
Yamen（DU 15），Crossing Point of Governor Vessel and Yang Link Vessel

【释义】哑，音哑；门，门户。此穴深刺可以致哑，故比喻为音哑的门户。

【定位】在项部，当后发际正中直上0.5寸，第1颈椎下（图15－4）。

【解剖】皮肤→皮下组织→左、右斜方肌之间→项韧带（左、右头夹肌之间→左、右头半棘肌之间）。浅层有第3枕神经和皮下静脉。深层有第2、3颈神经后支的分支，椎外（后）静脉丛和枕动、静脉的分支或属支。

【功用】息风止痉，通络开窍，利咽开音。

【主治】①暴喑，舌强不语。②癫狂痫。③头痛，项强，中风。

【操作】伏案正坐位，使头微前倾，项肌放松，向下颌方向缓慢刺入0.5～1.0寸。

【Meaning】 Ya, mutism; men, door. This point may either cause or treat mutism, so it is likened to a two－way door to mutism.

【Location】On the nape, 0.5 cun directly above the midpoint of the posterior hairline, below the 1st cervical vertebra (Fig 15－4).

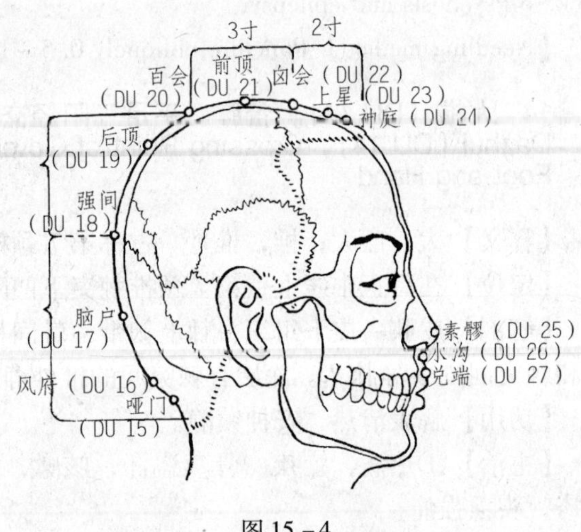

图15－4
Fig 15－4

【Regional anatomy】Skin→subcutaneous tissue → between left and right trapezius muscle→nuchal ligament (between left and right splenius muscle of head→between left and right semispinalis capitis muscle). There are the 3rd occipital nerve and cutaneous veins in the superficial layer. In the deep layer, there are branches of posterior branch of the 2nd and the 3rd cervical nerve, posterior external vertebral venous plexus, branches of occipital arteries and veins.

【Properties】Subdue wind and stop spasm, free the collateral vessel and open the orifices, soothe the throat and promote the pronunciation.

【Indications】①Sudden loss of voice, aphasia due to stiff tongue. ②Psychosis and epilepsy. ③Headache, neck rigidity, stroke.

【Needling method】Puncture slowly toward the mandible 0.5～1.0 cun in the erect sitting position with the head bowed.

16. 风府（DU 16），督脉、阳维脉交会穴
Fengfu（DU 16），Crossing Point of Governor Vessel and Yang Link Vessel

【释义】风，风邪；府，处所。本穴为治风邪之处。

【定位】在项部，当后发际正中直上1寸，枕外隆凸直下，两侧斜方肌之间凹陷中（图15－4）。

【解剖】皮肤→皮下组织→左、右斜方肌腱之间→项韧带（左、右头半棘肌之间）→左、右头后大、小直肌之间。浅层布有枕大神经和第3枕神经的分支及枕动、静脉的分支或属支。深层有枕下神经的分支。

【功用】清热散风，开窍。

【主治】①头痛，眩晕，项强，中风不语，半身不遂，癫狂痫。②目痛，鼻衄，咽喉肿痛。

【操作】伏案正坐，使头微前倾，项肌放松，向下颌方向缓慢刺入0.5～1.0寸。针尖不可向上，以免刺入枕骨大孔，误伤延髓。

【Meaning】Feng, pathogenic wind; fu, place. This is a point for eliminating pathogenic wind.

【Location】On the nape, 1 cun directly above the midpoint of the posterior hairline, directly below the external occipital protuberance, the depression between the trapezius muscle of both sides（Fig 15－4）.

【Regional anatomy】Skin→subcutaneous tissue→between the left and right tendon of trapezius muscle→nuchal ligament（between left and right semispinalis capitis muscle）→between left and right greater/lesser posterior straight occipital nerve. greater occipital nerve, the 3rd occipital verve, branches of occipital arteries and veins in the superficial layer. In the deep layer, there are branches of suboccipital nerve.

【Properties】Clear heat and dispel wind, open the orifices.

【Indications】①Headache, dizziness, neck rigidity, aphasia due to apoplexy, hemiplegia, psychosis and epilepsy. ②Pain in the eyes, epistaxis, sore throat.

【Needling method】Puncture slowly toward the mandible 0.5～1.0 cun in the erect sitting position with the head bowed. Not advisable to insert the needle deep upward to avoid pricking the medullary bulb through the great occipital foramen.

17. 脑户（DU 17），督脉、足太阳经交会穴
Naohu（DU 17），Crossing Point of Governor Vessel and the Foot - Taiyang Meridian

【释义】脑，脑髓；户，门户。督脉循脊上行入脑。穴在枕部，相当于脉气入脑的门户。

【定位】在头部，后发际正中直上2.5寸，风府上1.5寸，枕外隆凸的上缘凹陷处（图15－4）。

【解剖】皮肤→皮下组织→左、右枕额肌枕腹之间→腱膜下疏松组织。布有枕大神经的分支和枕动、静脉的分支或属支。

【功用】清头明目，通络开窍。

【主治】①头痛，项强，眩晕。②癫痫。

【操作】平刺 0.5 ~1.0 寸。

【Meaning】Nao, brain; hu, door. Governor vessel runs upward along the spine and enters the brain. The point is like a door on the occipital region for the qi of the meridian to the brain.

【Location】On the head, 2.5 cun directly above the midpoint of the posterior hairline, 1.5 cun above Fengfu, in the depression on the upper border of the external occipital protuberance（Fig 15 –4）.

【Regional anatomy】Skin→subcutaneous tissue→between the left and right tendon of pillow amount of muscle→porous tissue under aponeurosis. There are branches of greater occipital nerve, branches of occipital arteries and veins .

【Properties】Clear heat of head and improve vision, free the collateral vessel and open the orifices.

【Indications】①Headache, Neck rigidity, dizziness. ②Epilepsy.

【Needling method】Puncture transversely 0.5 ~1.0 cun.

18. 强间 Qiangjian（DU 18）

【释义】强，强硬；间，中间。穴当顶骨与枕骨结合之中间，能治头项强痛。

【定位】在头部，当后发际正中直上 4 寸（脑户上 1.5 寸）（图 15 –4）。

【解剖】皮肤→皮下组织→帽状腱膜→腱膜下疏松组织。布有枕大神经及左、右枕动脉与左、右枕静脉的吻合网。

【功用】清头散风，镇静安神。

【主治】①头痛，目眩，项强。②癫狂，失眠。

【操作】平刺 0.5 ~0.8 寸。

【Meaning】Qiang, stiffness; jian, middle. The point is between the parietal and occipital bones and is indicated in stiff neck and headache.

【Location】On the head, 4 cun directly above the midpoint of the posterior hairline（1.5 cun above Naohu）（Fig 15 –4）.

【Regional anatomy】Skin→subcutaneous tissue→galea aponeurotica→porous tissue under aponeurosis. There are branches of greater occipital nerve, rete composed of left and right occipital arteries and veins in the area.

【Properties】Clear heat and expel the wind, settle fright and tranquilize.

【Indications】①Headache, dizziness, neck rigidity. ②Psychosis, insomnia.

【Needling method】Puncture transversely 0.5 ~0.8 cun.

19. 后顶 Houding (DU 19)

【释义】后，后方；顶，头顶。穴在头顶之后方。

【定位】在头部，当后发际正中直上5.5寸（脑户上3寸）（图15-4）。

【解剖】皮肤→皮下组织→帽状腱膜→腱膜下疏松组织。布有枕大神经以及枕动、静脉和颞浅动、静脉的吻合网。

【功用】清头散风，健脑安神。

【主治】①头痛，项强，眩晕。②癫狂痫。

【操作】平刺0.5~1.0寸。

【Meaning】Hou, posterior; ding, vertex. The point is posterior to the vertex.

【Location】On the head, 5.5 cun directly above the midpoint of the posterior hairline (3 cun above Naohu) (Fig 15-4).

【Regional anatomy】Skin→subcutaneous tissue→galea aponeurotica→porous tissue under aponeurosis. There are branches of greater occipital nerve, rete composed of superficial temporal arteries and veins, occipital arteries and veins in the area.

【Properties】Clear heat and expel the wind, nourish the brain to tranquilize.

【Indications】①Headache, Neck rigidity, dizziness. ②Psychosis and epilepsy.

【Needling method】Puncture transversely 0.5~1.0 cun.

20. 百会（DU 20），督脉、足太阳经交会穴 Baihui (DU 20), Crossing Point of the Meridians of Foot-Taiyang and Governor Vessel

【释义】百，多的意思；会，交会。穴在巅顶部，是足三阳经、肝经和督脉等多经之交汇处。

【定位】在头部，当前发际正中直上5寸，或两耳尖连线的中点处（图15-4）。

【解剖】皮肤→皮下组织→帽状腱膜→腱膜下疏松组织。布有枕大神经、额神经的分支和左、右颞浅动脉与左、右颞浅静脉及枕动、静脉吻合网。

【功用】补气升阳，安神止痛。

【主治】①头痛，眩晕，中风失语，癫狂痫。②失眠，健忘。③脱肛，阴挺，久泻。

【操作】平刺0.5~1.0寸。

【Meaning】Bai, hundred; hui, meeting. The point is at the vertex and is a meeting place of the three yang meridians of foot, the liver meridian and governor vessel.

【Location】On the head, 5cun directly above the midpoint of the anterior hairline, at the midpoint of the line connecting the apexes of both ears (Fig 15-4).

【Regional anatomy】Skin→subcutaneous tissue→galea aponeurotica→porous tissue under aponeurosis. There are branches of greater occipital nerve and frontal nerve, rete composed of left and right superficial temporal arteries and veins in the areas.

【Properties】Tonify qi and support yang, tranquilize and stop pain.

【Indications】①Headache, dizziness, aphasia due to apoplexy, psychosis apoplexy. ②Insomnia, forgetful. ③Prolapse of the rectum, prolapse of uterus, chronic diarrhea.

【Needling method】Puncture transversely 0.5 ~1.0 cun.

21. 前顶 Qianding (DU 21)

【释义】前，前方；顶，头顶。穴在头顶之前方。

【定位】在头部，当前发际正中直上3.5寸（百会前1.5寸）（图15-4）。

【解剖】皮肤→皮下组织→帽状腱膜→腱膜下疏松组织。布有额神经，左、右颞浅动、静脉和额动、静脉的吻合网。

【功用】平肝潜阳，通络止痛。

【主治】①头痛，眩晕，中风偏瘫，癫痫。②目赤肿痛，鼻渊。

【操作】平刺0.3~0.5寸。

【Meaning】Qian, front; ding, vertex. The point is in front of the vertex.

【Location】On the head, 3.5 cun directly above the midpoint of the anterior hairline (1.5 cun anterior to Baihui) (Fig 15-4).

【Regional anatomy】Skin→subcutaneous tissue→galea aponeurotica→porous tissue under aponeurosis. There are frontal nerve, rete composed of left/right superficial temporal arteries and veins, left/right frontal arteries and veins in the area.

【Properties】Pacify the liver to subdue yang, free the collateral vessel and stop pain.

【Indications】①Headache, dizziness, hemiplegia, epilepsy. ②Swelling and pain in the eyes, rhinorrhea.

【Needling method】Puncture transversely 0.3 ~0.5 cun.

22. 囟会 Xinhui (DU 22)

【释义】囟，囟门；会，在此作开合讲。穴当大囟门的开合处。

【定位】在头部，当前发际正中直上2寸（百会前3寸）（图15-4）。

【解剖】皮肤→皮下组织→帽状腱膜→腱膜下疏松组织。布有额神经及左、右颞浅动、静脉和额动、静脉的吻合网。

【功用】清头散风，醒脑镇惊。

【主治】①头痛，眩晕，鼻渊，鼻衄。②癫痫。

【操作】平刺0.3~0.5寸，小儿禁刺。

【Meaning】Xin, fontanel; hui, closing. The point is located where the major fontanel closes.

【Location】On the head, 2 cun directly above the midpoint of the anterior hairline (3 cun anterior to Baihui) (Fig 15-4).

【Regional anatomy】Skin→subcutaneous tissue→galea aponeurotica→porous tissue under aponeurosis. There are frontal nerve, rete composed of left/right superficial temporal arteries and veins, left/righr frontal arteries and veins in the area.

【Properties】Clear heat and expel wind, wake up the head and settle fright.

【Indications】①Headache, dizziness, rhinorrhea, epistaxis. ②Epilepsy.

【Needling method】Puncture transversely 0.3 ~0.5cun, children is prohibited.

23. 上星 Shangxing (DU 23)

【释义】上，上方；星，星球。入头像天，穴在头上，如星在天。

【定位】在头部，当发际正中直上1寸（图15－4）。

【解剖】皮肤→皮下组织→帽状腱膜→腱膜下疏松组织。布有额神经的分支和额动、静脉的分支或属支。

【功用】清头散风，明目开窍。

【主治】①鼻渊，鼻衄，目痛，头痛，眩晕，癫狂。②热病，疟疾。

【操作】平刺0.5～0.8寸。

【Meaning】Shang, upper; xing, star. The head is considered as heaven. The point is at the head like a star in the sky.

【Location】On the head, 1 cun directly above the midpoint of the anterior hairline (Fig 15－4).

【Regional anatomy】Skin→subcutaneous tissue→galea aponeurotica→porous tissue under aponeurosis. There are branches of frontal nerve, branches of frontal arteries and veins in the area.

【Properties】Clear heat and expel wind, improve vision and open the orifices.

【Indications】①Rhinorrhea, epistaxis, pain in the eyes, headache, dizziness, psychosis. ②Febrile disease, malaria.

【Needling method】Puncture transversely 0.5 ~0.8 cun.

24. 神庭（DU 24），督脉、足太阳、足阳明经交会穴
Shenting (DU 24), Crossing Point of the Meridians of Foot - Taiyang and Foot - Yangming and Governor Vessel

【释义】神，神明；庭，前庭。"脑为元神之府"，神在此指脑。穴在前额部，如脑室之前庭。

【定位】在头部，当前发际正中直上0.5寸（图15－4）。

【解剖】皮肤→皮下组织→帽状腱膜→腱膜下疏松组织。布有额神经的滑车上神经和额动、静脉的分支或属支。

【功用】安神止痛。

【主治】①头痛，眩晕，失眠，癫痫。②鼻渊，流泪，目痛。

【操作】平刺0.3～0.5寸。

【Meaning】Shen, mind; thing, vestibule. "The brain is the mansion of the primordial mind". Shen here means brain. The point is on the forehead, like a vestibule of the brain.

【Location】On the head, 0.5 cun directly above the midpoint of the anterior hairline (Fig 15－4).

【Regional anatomy】Skin→subcutaneous tissue→galea aponeurotica→porous tissue under aponeurosis. There are branches of supratrochlear nerve of frontal nerve, branches of frontal arteries and veins in the area.

【Properties】Tranquilize and stop pain.

【Indications】① Headache, dizziness, palpitation, epilepsy. ② Rhinorrhea, lacrimation, pain in the eyes.

【Needling method】Puncture transversely 0.3～0.5 cun.

25. 素髎 Suliao (DU 25)

【释义】素，鼻软骨；髎，骨隙。穴在鼻软骨下端的骨隙中。

【定位】在面部，当鼻尖的正中央（图 15－4）。

【解剖】皮肤→皮下组织→鼻中隔软骨和鼻外侧软骨。布有筛前神经鼻外支及面动、静脉的鼻背支。

【功用】清热开窍。

【主治】①鼻塞，鼻渊，鼻衄，酒皶鼻，目痛。②惊厥，晕迷，窒息。

【操作】向上斜刺 0.3～0.5 寸，或点刺出血。一般不灸。

【Meaning】Su, nasal cartilage; liao, foramen. The point is in a foramen at the lower end of the nasal cartilage.

【Location】On the face, at the center of the nose apex (Fig 15－4).

【Regional anatomy】Skin→subcutaneous tissue→cartilage of nasal septum and lateral nasal cartilage. There are lateral nasal branches of anterior ethmoidal nerve, lateral (dorsal) branch of nose of facial arteries and veins in this area.

【Properties】Clear heat and open the orifices.

【Indications】①Nasal obstruction, rhinorrhea, epistaxis, rosacea, pain in the eyes. ②Convulsions, coma, asphyxia.

【Needling method】Puncture obliquely upward 0.3～0.5 cun; or prick to cause bleeding. Moxibustion is prohibited.

26. 水沟（DU 26），督脉、手、足阳明经交会穴 Shuigou (DU 26), Crossing Point of the Meridians of Hand - Yangming and Foot - Yangming and Governor Vessel

【释义】水，水液；沟，沟渠。穴在人中沟中，人中沟形似水沟。

【定位】在面部，当人中沟上 1/3 与中 1/3 交点处（图 15－4）。

【解剖】皮肤→皮下组织→口轮匝肌。布有眶下神经的分支和上唇动、静脉。

【功用】祛风，解痉，补气开窍。

【主治】①昏迷，晕厥，中风，癫狂痫，抽搐。②口㖞，唇肿，齿痛，鼻塞，鼻衄，牙关紧闭。③闪挫腰痛，脊膂强痛。④消渴，黄疸，遍身水肿。

【操作】向上斜刺0.3～0.5寸（或用指甲按掐）。一般不灸。

【Meaning】Shui，water；gou，groove. The point is in the philtrum which looks like a water groove.

【Location】On the face，at the junction of the upper 1/3 and middle 1/3 of the philtrum（Fig 15－4）.

【Regional anatomy】Skin→subcutaneous tissue→orbicular muscle of mouth. There are branches of infraorbital nerve，superior labial artery and vein in this area.

【Properties】Dispel wind，relax the muscular spasm，tonify qi and open the orifices.

【Indications】①Coma，faintness，apoplexy，psychosis and epilepsy，convulsion. ②Facial paralysis，swelling of the lip，toothache，nasal obstruction，epistaxis，lockjaw. ③Lumbago due to sprain and contusion，pain and stiffness of the spine. ④Diabetes，jaundice，edema.

【Needling method】Puncture obliquely upward 0.3 ～ 0.5 cun，or pinch with fingernail. Moxibustion is prohibited.

27. 兑端 Duiduan（DU 27）

【释义】兑，指口；端，尖端。穴在口的上唇尖端。

【定位】在面部，当上唇的尖端，人中沟下端的皮肤与唇的移行部（图15－4）。

【解剖】皮肤→皮下组织→口轮匝肌。布有眶下神经的分支和上唇动、静脉。

【功用】清泄胃热，定惊止痛。

【主治】①口㖞，齿龈肿痛，鼻塞，鼻衄。②癫疾，晕厥。

【操作】斜刺0.2～0.3寸。一般不灸。

【Meaning】Dui，mouth；duan，tip. The point is at the tip of the upper lip.

【Location】On the face，on the labial tubercle of the upper lip，on the vermilion border between the philtrum and upper lip（Fig 15－4）.

【Regional anatomy】Skin→subcutaneous tissue→orbicular muscle of mouth. There are branches of infraorbital nerve，superior labial artery and vein in this area.

【Properties】Clear stomach heat，arrest convulsion and stop pain.

【Indications】①Facial paralysis，swelling and pain in the gum，nasal obstruction，epistaxis. ②Psychosis，faintness.

【Needling method】Puncture obliquely 0.2～0.3 cun；moxibustion is prohibited.

28. 龈交 Yinjiao（DU 28）

【释义】龈，齿龈；交，交会。穴在上齿龈中缝，为督脉和任脉的交汇处。

【定位】在上唇内，唇系带和上齿龈的相接处（图15－5）。

【解剖】上唇系带与牙龈之移行处→口轮匝肌深面与上颌骨牙槽弓之间。布有上颌神经的上唇支以及眶下神经与面神经分支交叉形成的眶下丛和上唇动、静脉。

【功用】清热开窍，通络醒脑。

【主治】①牙龈肿痛，鼻渊，鼻衄。②癫狂痫。③腰痛，项强。④痔疾。

【操作】向上斜刺0.2～0.3寸。不灸。

【Meaning】Yin，gum；jiao，meet. The point is on the incisive suture of the upper gum where governor vessel and conception vessel meet.

【Location】Inside of the upper lip，at the junction of the labial frenum and upper gum（Fig 15－5）.

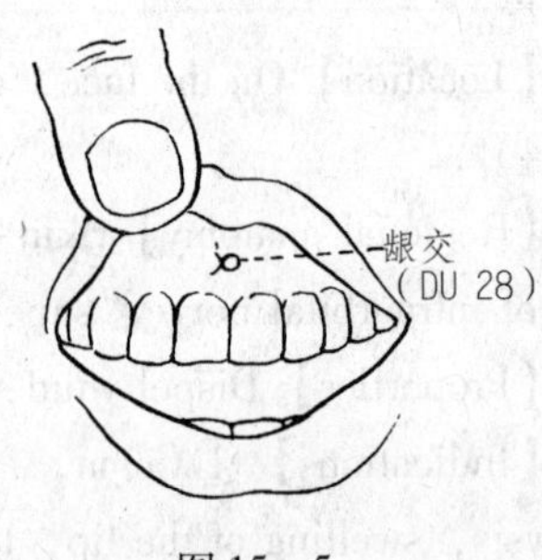

图15－5
Fig 15－5

【Regional anatomy】Between the lace upper lip and the gum → between the orbicular muscle of mouth and the maxillary's alveolar arch. There are superior branch of maxillary nerve，rete composed of infraorbital nerve and facial nerve，superior labial artery and vein in this area.

【Properties】Clear away pathogenic－heat and open the orifices，promote the circulation in the collaterals and restore consciousness.

【Indications】①Swelling and pain in the gum，nasal obstruction，epistaxis. ②Psychosis and epilepsy. ③Pain in the lower back，Neck rigidity. ④Hemorrhoids.

【Needling method】Puncture obliquely upward 0.2～0.3 cun；moxibustion is prohibited.

复习思考题
Review Questions

1. 为什么督脉的穴位大都可以治疗脑部的疾病？

Why can most of the points on governor vessel be used to treat brain diseases？

2. 督脉的起始穴是什么？其定位及主治如何？

What is the first acupoint of governor vessel？What are its location and indications？

3. 命门的定位是什么？可以治疗哪些病症？

What are the location and indications of Mingmen（DU 4）？

4. 百会的定位、主治是什么？操作方法有什么具体要求？

Discuss the location，indications and needling method of Baihui（DU 20）？

5. 水沟穴可以治疗哪些病症？如何正确操作？

What are the indications of Shuigou（DU 26）？How do you manipulate needling and moxibustion correctly at this point？

第二节 任 脉
Conception Vessel and Its Acupoints

一、循行分布
The Course of Conception Vessel

起于胞中，出于会阴，上循毛际，循腹里，上关元，至咽喉，上颐循面入目。

络脉：任脉之别，名曰尾翳，下鸠尾，散于腹（《灵枢·经脉》）（图 15 -6）。

It originates from the inferior of the lower abdomen and emerges from the perineum. It goes anteriorly to the pubic region and ascends along the interior of the abdomen, passes through Guanyuan (RN 4) and the other points to the throat. Ascending further, it curves around the lips, passes through the cheek and enters the infraorbital region Chengqi (ST 1) (Fig 15 -6).

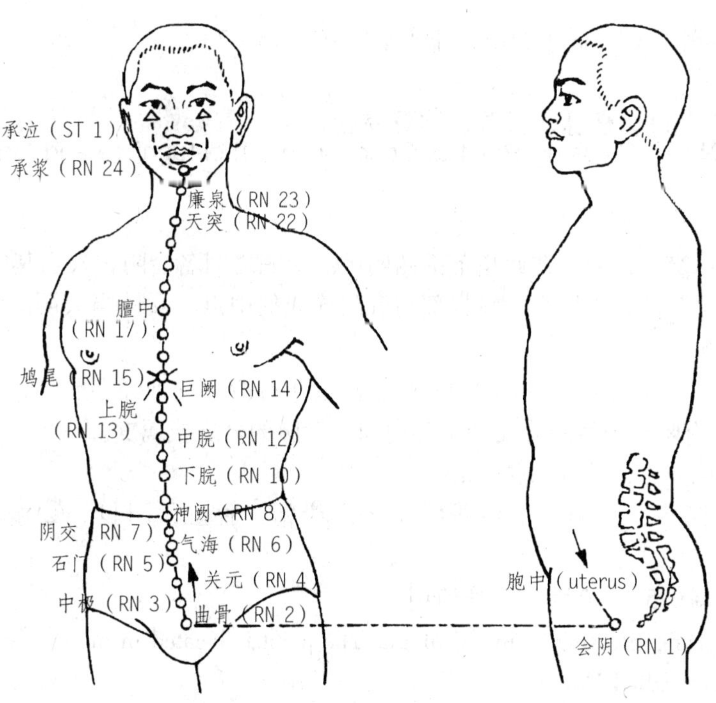

图例 ——本经有穴通路 ……本经无穴通路

Note ——Pathway with points ……Pathway without points

图 15 -6 任脉循行示意图

Fig 15 -6 The course of the conception vessel

二、功能与病候
Properties and Syndromes

任脉的功能主要可以概括为“阴脉之海”，任脉可以统率诸阴经，主胞胎。

任脉病候主要表现为泌尿生殖系统病症和下腹部病痛，如带下，不孕，少腹疼痛，月经不调，阳痿，早泄，遗精，遗尿，男子疝气，女子盆腔肿块等。

The properties of conception vessel can be summarized as “being the sea of yin meridian”, which means commanding all the yin meridians, dominating pregnancy.

The principal symptoms of conception vessel are disorder of genitourinary system and ache of lower abdomen. e. g. morbid leucorrhea, sterility, ache of lower abdomen, irregular menstruation, impotence, prospermia, spermatorrhea, enuresis, hernia in males, pelvic lump in females, etc.

三、任脉腧穴
Acupoints of Conception Vessel

本经总共24个穴位，起于会阴，止于承浆（图15－7）。

1. 会阴（RN 1），任脉、督脉、冲脉交会穴
Huiyin（RN 1），Crossing Point of Conception，Thoroughfare and Governor Vessels

【释义】会，交会；阴，在此指下部两阴区。两阴之间名会阴，穴当其中。

【定位】在会阴部，男性当阴囊根部与肛门连线的中点。女性当大阴唇后联合与肛门连线的中点（图15－7）。

【解剖】皮肤→皮下组织→会阴中心腱。浅层布有股后皮神经会阴支，阴部神经的会阴神经分支。深层有阴部神经的分支和阴部内动、静脉的分支或属支。

【功用】回阳升压，补肾固脱。

【主治】①阴痒，阴痛，小便难，闭经，遗精，脱肛，阴挺。②溺水，产后昏迷，癫狂。

【操作】直刺0.5～1.0寸，孕妇慎用。

【Meaning】Hui, crossing; yin, genitalia. The point is located in the space between the genitalia and the anus, called Huiyin.

【Location】On the perineum, at the midpoint between the posterior border of scrotum and anus in male, and between the posterior commissure of large labia and anus in female（Fig 15－7）.

【Regional anatomy】Skin→subcutaneous tissue→central tendon of perineum. There are perineum branch of posterior cutaneous nerve of thigh, and perineum branches of pudendal nerve in the superficial layer. In the deep layer, there are branches of pudendal nerve, branches of pudendal artery and vein in this area.

【Properties】Support yang, increase pressure, fortify the kidney and stop the prolapse.

【Indications】①Pruritus vulvae, pain in the external genitalia, dysuria, amenorrhea, emission, prolapse of the rectum, prolapse of the uterus. ②drowning, postpartum coma, and mania.

【Needling method】Puncture perpendicularly 0. 5 ~ 1. 0 cun. Pregnant women with caution.

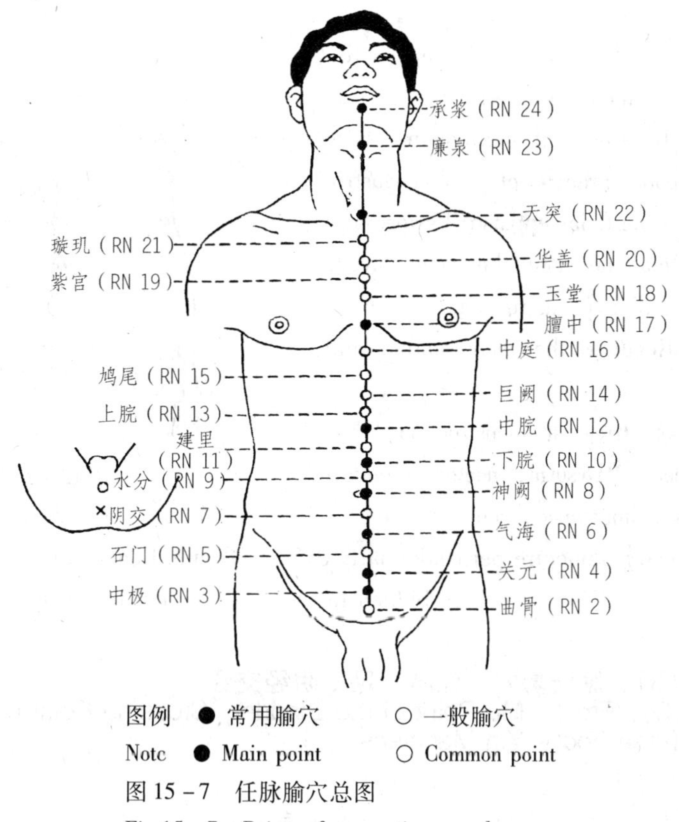

图例 ● 常用腧穴 ○ 一般腧穴

Notc ● Main point ○ Common point

图 15 – 7 任脉腧穴总图

Fig 15 – 7 Points of conception vessel

2. 曲骨（RN 2），任脉、足厥阴经交会穴
Qugu（RN 2）, Crossing Point of Conception Vessel and Foot - Jueyin Meridian

【释义】曲，弯曲；骨，骨头。曲骨，指耻骨，穴在耻骨联合上缘。

【定位】在前正中线上，耻骨联合上缘的中点处（图 15 – 8）。

【解剖】皮肤→皮下组织→腹白线→腹横筋膜→腹膜外脂肪→壁腹膜。浅层主要布有髂腹下神经的前皮支和腹壁浅静脉的属支。深层主要有髂腹下神经的分支。

【功用】调经止痛。

【主治】①月经不调，痛经，带下。②小便不利，遗尿，遗精，阳痿，阴囊湿疹。

【操作】直刺0. 5 ~ 1. 0 寸，本穴深部为膀胱，故应在排尿后进行针刺。孕妇禁针。

【Meaning】Qu, crooked; gu, bone. Qugu refers to the pubic bone, and the point is at the superior margin of the pubic symphysis.

【Location】on the anterior midline, at he midpoint of the upper border of pubic symphysis (Fig 15－8).

【Regional anatomy】Skin→subcutaneous tissue→linea alba of abdomen→transverse fascia→extraperitoneal adiposity→parietal peritoneum. There are anterior cutaneous branch of iliohypogastric nerve, branches of superficial epigastric artery and vein in the superficial layer. In the deep layer, there are branches of iliohypogastric nerve.

【Properties】Regulate the menstruation and stop pain.

【Indications】① Irregular menstruation, dysmenorrhea, leucorrhea. ② Dysuria, nocturnal enuresis, seminal emission, impotence, scrotum eczema.

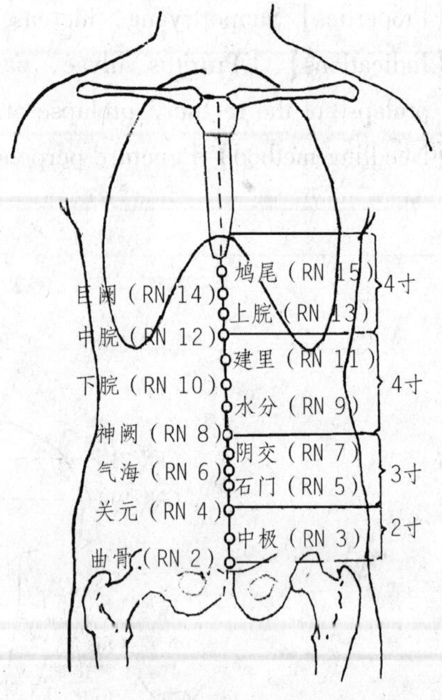

图 15－8
Fig 15－8

【Needling method】Puncture perpendicularly 0.5～1.0 cun. Behind this point is bladder, so after the patient passing his water. It is forbidden to use this acupoint in pregnant women.

3. 中极（RN 3），膀胱募穴，任脉、足三阴经交会
Zhongji (RN 3), Front - Mu Point of the Bladder, Crossing Point of Conception Vesset and Three Foot - Yin Meridians

【释义】中，中间；极，正是。穴位正是在人身上下左右之中间。

【定位】在下腹部，前正中线上，当脐中下 4 寸（图 15－8）。

【解剖】皮肤→皮下组织→腹白线→腹横筋膜→腹膜外脂肪→壁腹膜。浅层主要布有髂腹下神经的前皮支和腹壁浅动、静脉的分支或属支。深层主要有髂腹下神经的分支。

【功用】调经利水，理气止痛。

【主治】①癃闭，遗尿，尿频。②月经不调，带下，痛经，崩漏，阴挺，遗精，阳痿，疝气。

【操作】直刺 1.0～1.5 寸，需在排尿后进行针刺。孕妇禁针。

【Meaning】Zhong, center; ji, exactly. The point is exactly "at the center" of the body.

【Location】On the lower abdomen and on the anterior midline, 4 cun below the center of the umbilicus (Fig 15－8).

【Regional anatomy】Skin→subcutaneous tissue→linea alba of abdomen→transverse fascia→extraperitoneal adiposity→parietal peritoneum. There are anterior cutaneous branch of iliohypogastric nerve, branches of superficial epigastric artery and vein in the superficial layer. In the deep layer, there are branches of iliohypogastric nerve.

【Properties】Regulate the menstruation and induce diuresis, regulate qi and stop pain.

【Indications】①Dysuria, nocturnal enuresis, frequency of micturition. ② Irregular menstruation, leucorrhea, dysmenorrhea, prolapse of uterus, seminal emission, Impotence.

【Needling method】Puncture perpendicularly 1.0 ~ 1.5 cun. After the patient passing his water. It is forbidden to use this acupoint in pregnant women.

4. 关元（RN 4），小肠募穴，任脉、足三阴经交会穴
Guanyuan（RN 4）, Front - Mu Point of the Small Intestine, Crossing Point of three foot - yin meridians and Conception Vessel

【释义】关，关藏；元，元气。此穴位关藏人身元气之处。

【定位】在下腹部，前正中线上，当脐中下3寸（图15－8）。

【解剖】皮肤→皮下组织→腹白线→腹横筋膜→腹膜外脂肪→壁腹膜。浅层主要有第12胸神经前皮支和腹壁浅动、静脉的分支或属支。深层主要有第12胸神经前支的分支。

【功用】补气壮阳。

【主治】①少腹痛，吐泻，带下，遗精，阳痿，痛经，尿频，尿闭。②中风脱证。

【操作】直刺1.0～2.0寸，需在排尿后进行针刺。孕妇慎用。

【Meaning】Guan, storage; yuan, primordial qi. The point is a storage place for the primordial qi of the body.

【Location】On the lower abdomen and on the anterior midline, 3 cun below the center of the umbilicus（Fig 15－8）.

【Regional anatomy】Skin→Subcutaneous tissue→linea alba of abdomen→transverse fascia→extraperitoneal adiposity → parietal peritoneum. There are anterior cutaneous branch of anterior branch of the 12th thoracic nerve, branches of superficial epigastric artery and vein in the superficial layer. In the deep layer, there are branches of anterior branch of the 12th thoracic nerve.

【Properties】Tonify qi and invigorate yang.

【Indications】②Lower abdominal pain, vomiting and diarrhea, leucorrhea, nocturnal emission, impotence, dysmenorrheal, frequent urination, retention of urine. ② Collapse syndrome due to apoplexy.

【Needling method】Puncture perpendicularly1.0 ~ 2.0 cun. After the patient passing his water. Pregnant women with caution.

5. 石门（RN 5），三焦募穴
Shimen（RN 5）, Front - Mu Point of the Triple Energizer

【释义】石，岩石；门，门户。石有坚实之意，本穴能治下腹坚实之证。

【定位】在下腹部，前正中线上，当脐中下2寸（图15-8）。

【解剖】皮肤→皮下组织→腹白线→腹横筋膜→腹膜外脂肪→壁腹膜。浅层主要布有第11胸神经前皮支和腹壁浅静脉的属支。深层主要有第11胸神经前支的分支。

【功用】调经利水，活血祛瘀。

【主治】①少腹痛，小便不利，水肿。②泻痢，阴缩，遗精，阳痿。

【操作】直刺1.0~2.0寸。孕妇慎用。

【Meaning】Shi, stone; men, door. Stone here means "hard", the point is indicated in treating lumps in the lower abdomen.

【Location】On the lower abdomen and on the anterior midline, 2 cun below the center of the umbilicus (Fig 15-8).

【Regional anatomy】Skin→subcutaneous tissue→linea alba of abdomen→transverse fascia→extraperitoneal adiposity→parietal peritoneum. There are anterior cutaneous branch of anterior branch of the 11th thoracic nerve, branches of superficial epigastric vein in the superficial layer. In the deep layer, there are branches of anterior branch of the 11th thoracic nerve.

【Properties】Regulate the menstruation and induce diuresis, activate blood and resolve stasis.

【Indications】①Lower abdominal pain, dysuria, edema. ② Diarrhea, shrinkage of external genitals, nocturnal emission, impotence.

【Needling method】Puncture perpendicularly1.0~2.0 cun. Pregnant women with caution.

6. 气海 Qihai (RN 6)

【释义】气，元气；海，海洋。穴在脐下，为人身元气之海。

【定位】在下腹部，前正中线上，当脐中下1.5寸（图15-8）。

【解剖】皮肤→皮下组织→腹白线→腹横筋膜→腹膜外脂肪→壁腹膜。浅层主要布有第11胸神经前支的前皮支和脐周静脉网。深层主要有第11胸神经前支的分支。

【功用】理气宽肠，调经利水。

【主治】①下腹痛，大便不通，泻痢不止。②癃淋，遗尿，遗精，阳痿，闭经，崩漏。③中风脱证，气喘。

【操作】直刺1.0~2.0寸。

【Meaning】Qi, primary qi; hai, sea. The point is below the navel, is the sea of the primary qi of the whole body.

【Location】On the lower abdomen and on the anterior midline, 1.5 cun below the center of the umbilicus (Fig 15-8).

【Regional anatomy】Skin→subcutaneous tissue→linea alba of abdomen→transverse fascia→extraperitoneal adiposity→parietal peritoneum. there are anterior cutaneous branch of anterior branch of the 11th thoracic nerve, rete of umbilical vein in the superficial layer. In the deep layer, there are branches of anterior branch of the 11th thoracic nerve.

【Properties】Regulate qi and relax the bowels, regulate menstruation and promote diuresis.

【Indications】①Lower abdominal pain, constipation, diarrhea. ②Anuria and stranguria, enuresis, nocturnal emission, impotence, amenorrhea, menorrhagia. ③Collapse syndrome due to apoplexy, asthma.

【Needling method】Puncture perpendicularly 1.0 ~ 2.0 cun.

7. 阴交（RN 7），任脉、冲脉交会穴 Yinjiao (RN 7), Crossing Point of Conception Vessel and Thoroughfare Vessel

【释义】阴，阴阳之阴；交，交会。此穴为任脉、冲脉和肾经交会处。

【定位】在下腹部，前正中线上，当脐中下 1 寸（图 15 – 8）。

【解剖】皮肤→皮下组织→腹白线→腹横筋膜→腹膜外脂肪→壁腹膜。浅层主要布有第 11 胸神经前支的前皮支，脐周静脉网。深层主要有第 11 胸神经前支的分支。

【功用】补肾益气，调理冲任。

【主治】①绕脐冷痛，腹满水肿，泄泻。②奔豚，疝气，血崩。

【操作】直刺 1.0 ~ 2.0 寸。

【Meaning】Yin, yin of yin – yang; jiao, crossing. The point is the crossing point of conception vessel, thoroughfare Vessel and the kidney meridian.

【Location】On the lower abdomen and on the anterior midline, 1 cun below the center of the umbilicus (Fig 15 – 8).

【Regional anatomy】Skin→subcutaneous tissue→linea alba of abdomen→transverse fascia→extraperitoneal adiposity→parietal peritoneum. There are anterior cutaneous branch of anterior branch of the 11th thoracic nerve, rete of umbilical vein in the superficial layer. In the deep layer, there are branches of anterior branch of the 11th thoracic nerve.

【Properties】Tonify the kidney and replenish qi, regulate the conception vessel and thoroughfare vessel.

【Indications】①Cold abdominal pain around the umbilicus, fullness in the abdomen and edema, diarrhea. ②globus hystericus, hernia, metrorrhagia and metrostaxis.

【Needling Method】Puncture perpendicularly 1.0 ~ 2.0 cun.

8. 神阙 Shenque (RN 8)

【释义】神，神气；阙，宫门。穴在脐中。脐为胎儿气血运行之要道，如神气出入之宫门。

【定位】在腹中部，脐中央（图 15 – 8）。

【解剖】皮肤→结缔组织→壁腹膜。浅层主要布有第 10 胸神经前支的前皮支和腹壁脐周静脉网。深层主要有第 10 胸神经前支的分支。

【功用】补气开窍。

【主治】①绕脐冷痛，泄泻，脱肛，五淋。②中风脱证，尸厥，风痫。③水肿鼓胀。

【操作】禁刺，宜灸。

【Meaning】Shen, spirit; que, palace gate. The point is at the center of the navel which is an important for the circulation of fetal qi and blood, like a palace gate of the qi of spirit.

【Location】On the middle abdomen and at the center of the umbilicus (Fig 15 – 8).

【Regional anatomy】Skin→connective tissue→parietal peritoneum. There are anterior cutaneous branch of anterior branch of the 10th thoracic nerve, rete of umbilical vein in the superficial layer. In the deep layer, there are branches of anterior branch of the 10th thoracic nerve.

【Properties】Tonify qi and open the orifices.

【Indications】①Abdominal pain around the umbilicus, diarrhea, proctoptosis, five types of stranguria. ② Apoplectic depletion syndrome, dead syncope, wind – epilepsy. ③edema and tympany.

【Needling method】Prohibit acupuncture, moxibustion is applicable.

9. 水分 Shuifen (RN 9)

【释义】水，水饮；分，分别。穴在脐上 1 寸，内应小肠，水饮至此分别清浊。

【定位】在上腹部，前正中线上，当脐中上 1 寸（图 15 – 8）。

【解剖】皮肤→皮下组织→腹白线→腹横筋膜→腹膜外脂肪→壁腹膜。浅层主要布有第 9 胸神经前支的前皮支及腹壁浅静脉的属支。深层主要有第 9 胸神经前支的分支。

【功用】健脾利湿，利水消肿。

【主治】①绕脐痛，腹胀，肠鸣，泄泻。②水肿，反胃。

【操作】直刺 1.0~2.0 寸。宜灸。

【Meaning】Shui, water and food; fen, separation. The point is 1 cun above the naval and corresponds internally to the small intestine, where water and food are separated into turbid and clear.

【Location】On the upper abdomen and on the anterior midline, 1 cun above the center of the umbilicus (Fig 15 – 8).

【Regional anatomy】Skin→subcutaneous tissue→linea alba of abdomen→transverse fascia→extraperitoneal adiposity → parietal peritoneum. There are anterior cutaneous branch of anterior branch of the 9th thoracic nerve and branches of superficial epigastric vein in the superficial layer. In the deep layer, there are branches of anterior branch of the 9th thoracic nerve.

【Properties】Fortify the spleen and drain dampness, induce diuresis to alleviate edema.

【Indications】①Abdominal pain around the umbilicus, abdominal distension, borborygmus, diarrhea. ②Edema, regurgitation.

【Needling method】Puncture perpendicularly 1.0 ~ 2.0 cun; moxibustion is applicable.

10. 下脘 (RN 10)，任脉、足太阴经交会穴
Xiawan (RN 10), Crossing Point of Conception Vessel and the Meridian of Foot - Taiyin

【释义】下，下方；脘，胃脘。穴当胃脘之下部。

【定位】在上腹部，前正中线上，当脐中上2寸（图15－8）。

【解剖】皮肤→皮下组织→腹白线→腹横筋膜→腹膜外脂肪→壁腹膜。浅层主要布有第9胸神经前支的前皮支和腹壁浅静脉的属支。深层主要有第9胸神经前支的分支。

【功用】健脾和胃，消积导滞。

【主治】①腹痛，腹胀，食不化，泄泻。②虚肿，痞块。

【操作】直刺1.0～2.0寸。可灸。

【Meaning】Xia, inferior; wan, stomach. The point is at the inferior portion of the stomach.

【Location】On the upper abdomen and on the anterior midline, 2 cun above the center of the umbilicus (Fig 15－8).

【Regional anatomy】Skin→subcutaneous tissue→linea alba of abdomen→transverse fascia→extraperitoneal adiposity→parietal peritoneum. There are anterior cutaneous branch of anterior branch of the 9th thoracic nerve and branches of superficial epigastric vein in the superficial layer. In the deep layer, there are branches of anterior branch of the 9th thoracic nerve.

【Properties】Fortify the spleen and harmonize the stomach, promote digestion and remove food stagnation.

【Indications】①Abdominal pain and distension, indigestion, diarrhea. ②Deficient edema, abdominal masses.

【Needling method】Puncture perpendicularly 1.0～2.0 cun; moxibustion is applicable.

11. 建里 Jianli (RN 11)

【释义】建，建立；里，里部。穴当胃脘部，有助于建立中焦里气。

【定位】在上腹部，前正中线上，当脐中上3寸（图15－8）。

【解剖】皮肤→皮下组织→腹白线→腹横筋膜→腹膜外脂肪→壁腹膜。浅层主要布有第8胸神经前支的前皮支和腹壁浅静脉的属支。深层主要有第8胸神经前支的分支。

【功用】健脾和胃，消食化滞。

【主治】①胃痛，腹痛，腹胀，呕逆。②水肿。

【操作】直刺1.0～1.5寸。

【Meaning】Jian, establishing; li, interior. The point located in the epigastric region, aids in establishing the qi of the middle jiao.

【Location】On the upper abdomen and on the anterior midline, 3 cun above the center of the umbilicus (Fig 15－8).

【Regional anatomy】Skin→subcutaneous tissue→linea alba of abdomen→transverse fascia→extraperitoneal adiposity→parietal peritoneum. There are anterior cutaneous branch of anterior branch of the 8th thoracic nerve and branches of superficial epigastric vein in the superficial layer. In the deep layer, there are branches of anterior branch of the 8th thoracic nerve.

【Properties】Fortify the spleen and harmonize the stomach, promote digestion and resolve food stagnation.

【Indications】①Stomachache, abdominal distension, borborygmus, vomiting, poor appetite. ②Edema.

【Needling method】Puncture perpendicularly 1.0～1.5 cun.

12. 中脘（RN 12），胃募穴，腑会，任脉、手太阳、足阳明经交会穴
Zhongwan（RN 12），Front - Mu Point of the Stomach; One of the Eight Influential Points（Fu - Organs Convergence）; Crossing Point of the Meridians of Hand - Taiyang and Foot - Yangming and Conception Vessel

【释义】中，中间；脘，胃脘。穴当胃脘之中部。

【定位】在上腹部，前正中线上，当脐中上4寸（图15－8）。

【解剖】皮肤→皮下组织→腹白线→腹横筋膜→腹膜外脂肪→壁腹膜。浅层主要布有第8胸神经前支的前皮支和腹壁浅静脉的属支。深层主要有第8胸神经前支的分支。

【功用】健脾和胃，理气止痛。

【主治】胃痛，腹痛，腹胀，呕逆，食不化，泄泻，便秘；癫痫。

【操作】直刺1.0～1.5寸。

【Meaning】Zhong, middle; wan, stomach. The point is at the middle of the stomach.

【Location】On the upper abdomen and on the anterior midline, 4 cun above the center of the umbilicus（Fig 15－8）.

【Regional anatomy】Skin→subcutaneous tissue→linea alba of abdomen→transverse fascia→extraperitoneal adiposity→parietal peritoneum. There are anterior cutaneous branch of anterior branch of the 8th thoracic nerve and branches of superficial epigastric vein in the superficial layer. In the deep layer, there are branches of anterior branch of the 8th thoracic nerve.

【Properties】Fortify the spleen and harmonize the stomach, regulate qi to stop pain.

【Indications】Stomachache, abdominal distension, borborygmus, vomiting, indigestion, astriction, diarrheal; epilepsy.

【Needling method】Puncture perpendicularly 1.0～1.5 cun.

13. 上脘（RN 13），任脉、手太阳、足阳明经交会穴
Shangwan（RN 13），Crossing Point of the Meridians of Hand - Taiyang and Foot - Yangming and Conception Vessel

【释义】上，上方；脘，胃脘。穴当胃脘之上部。

【定位】在上腹部，前正中线上，当脐中上5寸（图15－8）。

【解剖】皮肤→皮下组织→腹白线→腹横筋膜→腹膜外脂肪→壁腹膜。浅层主要布有第7胸神经前支的前皮支和腹壁浅静脉的属支。深层主要有第7胸神经前支的分支。

【功用】健胃补气。

【主治】胃痛，呕吐，腹胀，吞酸，食不化，吐血，黄疸；癫痫。

【操作】直刺1.0~1.5寸。

【Meaning】Shang, superior; wan, stomach. The point is at the upper portion of the stomach.

【Location】On the upper abdomen and on the anterior midline, 5 cun above the center of the umbilicus (Fig 15-8).

【Regional anatomy】Skin→subcutaneous tissue→linea alba of abdomen→transverse fascia→extraperitoneal adiposity→parietal peritoneum. There are anterior cutaneous branch of anterior branch of the 7th thoracic nerve and branches of superficial epigastric vein in the superficial layer. In the deep layer, there are branches of anterior branch of the 7th thoracic nerve.

【Properties】Fortify the stomach and tonify qi.

【Indications】Stomachache, vomiting, abdominal distension, indigestion, vomiting of blood, jaundice; epilepsy.

【Needling method】Puncture perpendicularly 1.0~1.5 cun.

14. 巨阙 (RN 14) 心募穴
Juque (RN 14), Front - Mu Point of the Heart

【释义】巨，巨大；阙，宫门。此为心之募穴，如心气出入的大门。

【定位】在上腹部，前正中线上，当脐中上6寸（图15-8）。

【解剖】皮肤→皮下组织→腹白线→腹横筋膜→腹膜外脂肪→壁腹膜。浅层主要布有第7胸神经前支的前皮支和腹壁浅静脉的属支。深层主要有第7胸神经前支的分支。

【功用】和中降逆，宽胸化痰，宁心安神。

【主治】胃痛，吞酸，呕吐，胸痛，心悸。

【操作】直刺0.3~0.6寸。

【Meaning】Ju, great; que, palace gate. This is a front-mu Point of the Heart, like a door for the qi of the heart.

【Locations】On the upper abdomen and on the anterior midline, 6 cun above the center of the umbilicus (Fig 15-8).

【Regional anatomy】Skin→subcutaneous tissue→linea alba of abdomen→transverse fascia→extraperitoneal adiposity→parietal peritoneum. There are anterior cutaneous branch of anterior branch of the 7th thoracic nerve and branches of superficial epigastric vein in the superficial layer. In the deep layer, there are branches of anterior branch of the 7th thoracic nerve.

【Properties】Harmonize the middle to relieve hiccup, relax the chest and resolve phlegm, nourish the heart to tranquilize.

【Indication】Stomachache, acid regurgitation, vomiting, chest pain, palpitation.

【Needling Method】Puncture perpendicularly 0.3~0.6 cun.

15. 鸠尾（RN 15），络穴 Jiuwei（RN 15），Luo - Connecting Point

【释义】鸠，鸠鸟；尾，尾巴。胸骨剑突形如鸠鸟之尾，穴在其下。

【定位】在上腹部，前正中线上，当胸剑结合部下1寸（图15－8）。

【解剖】皮肤→皮下组织→腹白线→腹横筋膜→腹膜外脂肪→壁腹膜。浅层主要布有第7胸神经前支的前皮支和腹壁浅静脉的属支。深层主要有第7胸神经前支的分支。

【功用】和中降逆，清心安神。

【主治】胸闷，心悸；噎嗝，呕吐，癫狂痫。

【操作】直刺0.3～0.6寸。

【Meaning】Jiu，turtledove；wei，tail. The point is below the xiphoid process of the sternum，which resembles a turtledove's tail.

【Location】On the upper abdomen and on the anterior midline，1 cun below the xiphosternal synchondrosis（Fig 15－8）.

【Regional anatomy】Skin→subcutaneous tissue→linea alba of abdomen→transverse fascia→extraperitoneal adiposity→parietal peritoneum. There are anterior cutaneous branch of anterior branch of the 7th thoracic nerve and branches of superficial epigastric vein in the superficial layer. In the deep layer，there are branches of anterior branch of the 7th thoracic nerve.

【Properties】Harmonize the middle to relieve hiccup，clear the heart to tranquilize.

【Indications】Stuffy chest，palpitation；hiccup，vomiting；psychosis and epilepsy.

【Needling method】Puncture perpendicularly 0.3～0.6 cun.

16. 中庭 Zhongting（RN 16）

【释义】中，中间；庭，庭院。穴在心下，犹如在宫殿前的庭院之中。

【定位】在胸部，前正中线上，平第5肋间，即胸剑结合部（图15－9）。

【解剖】皮肤→皮下组织→胸肋辐状韧带和肋剑突韧带→胸剑结合部。布有第6肋间神经的前皮支和胸廓内动、静脉的穿支。

【功用】宽胸理气，降逆止呕。

【主治】胸胁胀满；呕吐，小儿吐乳。

【操作】直刺0.3～0.5寸。

【Meaning】Zhong，middle；ting，courtyard. The point is below the heart，as if in the courtyard in front of the palace.

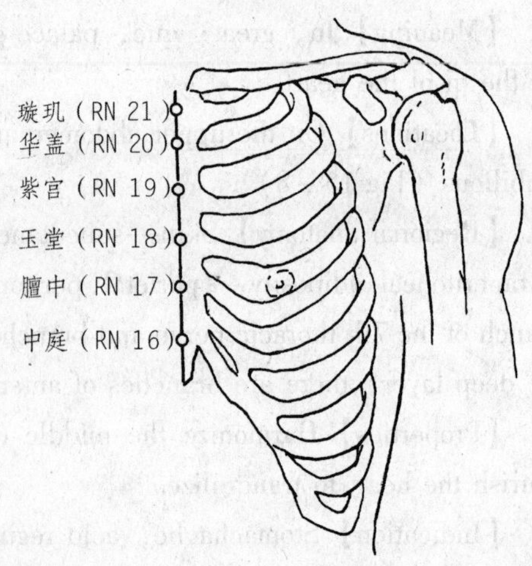

图15－9

Fig 15－9

【Location】 On the chest and on the anterior midline, on the level of the 5th intercostal space, on the xiphosternal synchondrosis（Fig 15 –9）.

【Regional anatomy】 Skin→subcutaneous tissue→between the sternocostal rotate ligament and the xiphoid rib ligament→the department of thoracic and sword combination. There are anterior cutaneous branch of the 6th intercostal nerve, perforating branches of internal thoracic arteries and veins in this area.

【Properties】 Relax the chest and regulate qi, relieve hiccup to stop vomiting.

【Indications】 Distension and fullness in the chest and abdomen, vomiting, vomiting of milk in baby.

【Needling method】 Puncture perpendicularly 0. 3 ~0. 5 cun.

17. 膻中（RN 17），心包募穴，气会
Danzhong（RN 17), Front - Mu Point of the Pericardium, One of the Eight Influential Points（Qi Convergence)

【释义】膻，袒露；中，中间。胸部袒露出的中间部位古称膻中，穴当其处。

【定位】在胸部，当前正中线上，平第4肋间，两乳头连线的中点（图15 –9)。

【解剖】皮肤→皮下组织→胸骨体。主要布有第4肋间神经前皮支和胸廓内动、静脉的穿支。

【功用】补气止痛，降逆。

【主治】①胸闷，气短，胸痛，心悸，咳嗽，气喘。②乳汁少，乳痈。

【操作】直刺0. 3 ~0. 5 寸，或平刺。

【Meaning】 Dan, exposure; zhong, middle. The point is located at the exposed middle part of the chest, called danzhong in ancient times.

【Location】 On the chest and on the anterior midline, on the level of the 4th intercostal space, at the midpoint of the line connecting both nipples（Fig 15 –9）.

【Regional anatomy】 Skin→subcutaneous tissue→body of sternum. There are anterior cutaneous branch of the 4th intercostal nerve, perforating branches of internal thoracic arteries and veins in this area.

【Properties】 Tonify qi to stop pain, relieve hiccup.

【Indications】 ①Stuffy chest, short breath, chest pain, palpitation, cough, asthma. ②Lactation insufficiency, acute mastitis.

【Needling method】 Puncture perpendicularly 0. 3 ~0. 5 cun, or puncture transversely.

18. 玉堂 Yutang（RN 18)

【释义】玉，玉石；堂，殿堂。玉有贵重之意。穴位所在相当于心的部位，因其重要，故比之为玉堂。

【定位】在胸部，当前正中线上，平第3肋间（图15－9）。

【解剖】皮肤→皮下组织→胸骨体。主要布有第3肋间神经前皮支和胸廓内动、静脉的穿支。

【功用】宽胸理气，止咳化痰。

【主治】胸痛，胸闷，咳嗽，气喘，呕吐。

【操作】直刺0.3～0.5寸。

【Meaning】Yu，jade；tang，palace. The point is located at the site of the heart，and since jade is valuable，it is considered a jade palace.

【Location】On the chest and on the anterior midline，on the level of the 3rd intercostal space（Fig 15－9）.

【Regional anatomy】Skin→subcutaneous tissue→body of sternal. There are anterior cutaneous branch of the 3rd intercostal nerve，perforating branches of internal thoracic arteries and veins in this area.

【Properties】Relax the chest and regulate qi，suppress cough and resolve phlegm.

【Indications】Chest pain，stuffy chest，cough，asthma，vomiting.

【Needling method】Puncture perpendicularly 0.3～0.5 cun.

19. 紫宫 Zigong（RN 19）

【释义】紫，紫色；宫，宫殿。紫宫，星名，代表帝王所居之处。穴对心的部位，心为君主之官，故名。

【定位】在胸部，当前正中线上，平第2肋间（图15－9）。

【解剖】皮肤→皮下组织→胸大肌起始腱→胸骨体。主要布有第2肋间神经前皮支和胸廓内动、静脉的穿支。

【功用】宽胸理气，清肺利咽。

【主治】咳嗽，气喘，胸痛，胸闷。

【操作】直刺0.3～0.5寸。

【Meaning】Zi，purple；gong，palace. Zigong is the name of a star and refers to the emperor's residence. The point corresponds to the heart which is the organ of the monarch，and is therefore called Zigong.

【Location】On the chest and on the anterior midline，on the level of the 2nd intercostal space（Fig 15－9）.

【Regional anatomy】Skin→subcutaneous tissue→the original tendon of greater pectoral muscle→body of sternal. There are anterior cutaneous branch of the 2nd intercostal nerve，perforating branches of internal thoracic arteries and veins in this area.

【Properties】Relax the chest and regulate qi，clear lung fire to soothe the throat.

【Indications】Cough，asthma，chest pain，stuffy chest.

【Needling method】Puncture perpendicularly 0.3～0.5 cun.

20. 华盖 Huagai（RN 20）

【释义】华盖在此指帝王所用盖伞。穴位所在相当于肺脏部位；肺处心君之上，犹如心之华盖。

【定位】在胸部，当前正中线上，平第1肋间（图15－9）。

【解剖】皮肤→皮下组织→胸大肌起始腱→胸骨柄与胸骨体之间（胸骨角）。主要布有第1肋间神经前皮支和胸廓内动、静脉的穿支。

【功用】行气宽胸，清肺化痰。

【主治】咳嗽，气喘，胸痛，咽喉肿痛。

【操作】直刺0.3～0.5寸。

【Meaning】Huagai refers to the emperor's umbrella. The location of the point corresponds to the lung，which is above the heart and like an umbrella over it.

【Location】On the chest and on the anterior midline，on the level of the 1st intercostal space（Fig 15－9）.

【Regional anatomy】Skin→subcutaneous tissue→the original tendon of greater pectoral muscle→between the sternal and body of sternal. There are anterior cutaneous branch of the 1st intercostal nerve，perforating branches of internal thoracic arteries and veins in this area.

【Properties】Move qi to soothe the chest，clear lung fire to resolve phlegm.

【Indications】Cough，asthma，chest pain，sore throat.

【Needling method】Puncture perpendicularly 0.3～0.5 cun.

21. 漩玑 Xuanji（RN 21）

【释义】璇，同"旋"；玑，同"机"。璇玑，为北斗星的第二至第三星，与紫宫星相对，故名。

【定位】在胸部，当前正中线上，胸骨上窝中央下1寸（图15－9）。

【解剖】皮肤→皮下组织→胸大肌起始腱→胸骨柄。主要布有锁骨上内侧神经和胸廓内动、静脉的穿支。

【功用】行气宽胸，清肺利咽。

【主治】咳嗽，气喘，胸痛，咽喉肿痛，胃中积滞。

【操作】直刺0.3～0.5寸。

【Meaning】Xuan，rotation；ji，axis. Xuanji is the name of the 2nd and the 3rd stars of the Big Dipper，opposite the Zigong star. This point is also opposite the Zigong point and therefore named Xuanji.

【Location】On the chest and on the anterior midline，1 cun below Tiantu（RN 22）（Fig 15－9）.

【Regional anatomy】Skin→subcutaneous tissue→the original tendon of greater pectoral muscle→

sternal. There are medial supraclavicular nerves, perforating branches of internal thoracic arteries and veins in this area.

【Properties】Move qi to soothe the chest, clear lung fire to soothe the throat.

【Indications】Cough, asthma, chest pain, sore throat, retention of food in the stomach.

【Needling method】Puncture perpendicularly 0.3 ~0.5 cun.

22. 天突（RN 22），任脉、阴维脉交会穴
Tiantu（RN 22），Crossing Point of Conception Vesset and Yin Link Vessel

【释义】天，天空；突，突出。穴位于气管上段，喻为肺气上通于天的部位。

【定位】仰靠坐位，在颈部，当前正中线上，胸骨上窝中央（图15－10）。

【解剖】皮肤→皮下组织→左、右胸锁乳突肌腱（两胸骨头）之间→胸骨柄颈静脉切迹上方→左、右胸骨甲状肌→气管前间隙。浅层布有锁骨上内侧神经，皮下组织内有颈阔肌和颈静脉弓。深层有头臂干、左颈总动脉、主动脉弓和头臂静脉等重要结构。

【功用】宣肺化痰，利咽。

【主治】咳嗽，哮喘，胸痛，咽喉肿痛，暴喑，瘿气，噎膈。

【操作】先直刺0.2寸，当针尖超过胸骨柄内缘后，即向下沿胸骨柄后缘、气管前缘缓慢向下刺入0.5～1.0寸。

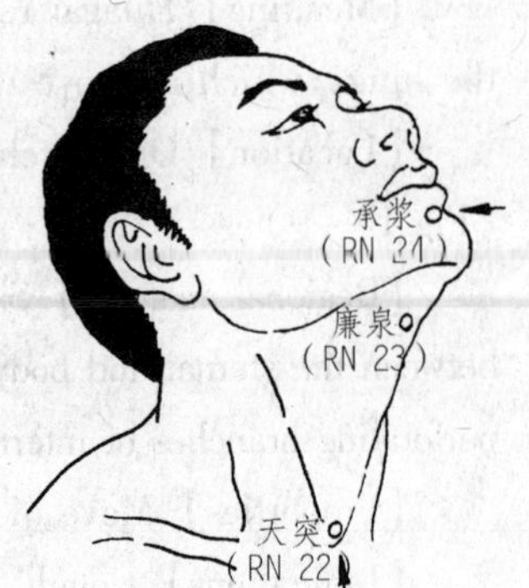

图15－10
Fig 15－10

【Meaning】Tian, heaven; tu, chimney. The location of the point corresponds to the upper end of the trachea, like the chimney for the qi of the lung.

【Location】On the neck and on the anterior midline, at the center of suprasternal fossa（see Fig. 15－9）.

【Regional anatomy】Skin→subcutaneous tissue→between the left and right tendon of sternocleidomastoid muscle→up the jugular notch of manubrium sterni→left and right sternothyroid muscle→pretracheal space. There are medial supraclavicular nerves, platysma and jugular venous arch in the superficial layer. In the deep layer, there are brachiocephalic trunk, left common carotid artery, arch of aorta and brachiocephalic vein.

【Properties】Diffuse the lung to resolve phlegm, soothe the throat.

【Indications】Cough, asthma, chest pain, sore throat, sudden loss of voice, simple goiter, hiccup.

【Needling method】First puncture perpendicularly 0.2 cun and then insert the needle downward along the posterior aspect of the sternum and the anterior aspect of the trachea slowly 0.5 ~1.0 cun.

23. 廉泉（RN 23），任脉、阴维脉交会穴
Lianquan（RN 23）, Crossing Point of Conception Vessel and Yin Link Vessel

【释义】廉，清；泉，水泉。舌下两脉古名为廉泉。穴在喉结上缘，靠近此脉。

【定位】仰靠坐位。在颈部，当前正中线上，喉结上方，舌骨上缘凹陷处（图15－10）。

【解剖】皮肤→皮下组织→颈阔肌→左、右二腹肌前腹之间→下颌骨肌→颏舌骨肌→颏舌肌。浅层布有面神经颈支和颈横神经上支的分支。深层有舌动、静脉的分支或属支，舌下神经的分支和下颌舌骨肌神经等。

【功用】清咽开音。

【主治】舌强不语，舌下肿痛，舌纵涎出，舌本挛急，暴喑，吞咽困难，口舌生疮，咽喉肿痛。

【操作】针尖向咽喉部刺入0.5～0.8寸。

【Meaning】Lian, clear; quan, spring. In ancient times the two blood vessels below the tongue were called Lianquan. The point is at the superior margin of the laryngeal prominence, close to the Lianquan vessels.

【Location】On the neck and on the anterior midline, above the laryngeal protuberance, in the depression above the upper border of hyoid bone（Fig 15－10）.

【Regional anatomy】Skin→subcutaneous tissue→between right and left digastric muscle→mylohyoid muscle→geniohyoid muscle→genioglossus. There are branches of cervical branch of facial nerve and superior branchcs of transverse nerve of neck. In the deep layer, there are branches of lingual artery and vein, branches of hypoglossal nerve and mylohyoid nerve.

【Properties】Soothe the throat to promote pronunciation.

【Indications】Aphasia with stiff tonguc, swelling and pain of the subglossal region, retracted tongue, sudden loss of voice, difficulty in swallowing, sore of tongue and mouth, sore throat.

【Needling method】Puncture perpendicularly toward throat 0.5～0.8 cun.

24. 承浆（RN 24），任脉、足阳明经交会穴
Chengjiang（RN 24）, Crossing Point of Conception Vessel and Meridian of Foot - Yangming

【释义】承，承受；浆，水浆。穴在颏唇沟正中的凹陷中，为承受从口流出的水浆之处。

【定位】仰靠坐位。在面部，当颏唇沟的正中凹陷处（图15－10）。

【解剖】皮肤→皮下组织→口轮匝肌→降下唇肌→颏肌。布有下牙槽神经的终支颏神经和颏动、静脉。

【功用】祛风通络，生津敛液。

【主治】口㖞，唇紧，齿龈肿痛，流涎，暴喑，口舌生疮；消渴，癫痫。

【操作】斜刺 0.3 ~0.5 寸。

【Meaning】Cheng, receiving; jiang, fluid. The point is in the depression at the midpoint of the chin, is where excessive saliva is received.

【Location】On the face, in the depression at the midpoint of mentolabial sulcus (Fig 15 – 10).

【Regional anatomy】Skin→subcutaneous tissue→orbicular muscle of mouth→depressor muscle of lower lip→mental muscle. There are mental nerve (the last branch of inferior alveolar nerve), mental artery and vein in this area.

【Properties】Dispel wind to free the collateral vessels, engender fluid and constrain spittle.

【Indications】Facial paralysis, trismus, swelling and pain in the gum, salivation, sudden loss of voice, sore of tongue and mouth, diabetes, epilepsy.

【Needling method】Puncture obliquely 0.3 ~0.5 cun.

复习思考题
Review Questions

1. 任脉的络穴是什么？其定位及主治如何？

What is the luo – connecting point of conception vessel? What are its location and indications?

2. 胃的募穴是什么？其定位及主治如何？

What is the front – mu point of the stomach ? What are its location and indications?

3. 关元的定位是什么？可以治疗哪些病症？

What are the location and indications of Guanyuan (NR 4)?

4. 神阙的定位、主治是什么？操作方法有什么具体要求？

Discuss the locations, indications and needling method of Shenque (NR 8)?

5. 承浆穴可以治疗哪些病症？如何正确操作？

What are the indications of Chengjiang (NR 24)? How do you manipulate needling and moxibustion correctly at this point?

第三节　冲　脉
Thoroughfare Vessel

一、循行分布
The Course of Thoroughfare Vessel

起于胞中，下出会阴后，从气街部起与足少阴经相并，夹脐上行，散布于胸中，再向上行，经喉，环绕口唇，到目眶下。

分支：从气街部浅出体表，沿大腿内侧进入腘窝，再沿胫骨内缘，下行到足底；又有支脉从内踝后分出，向前斜入足背，进入足大趾。

分支：从胞中分出，向后与督脉相通，上行于脊柱内（图 15－11）。

Thoroughfare vessel originates from the interior of the lower abdomen（womb）. Descending, it emerges at the perineum. Then it superficially bifurcates to reach the inguinal regions. Then it joins the meridian of foot－shaoyin，ascends by the umbilicus，and spreads in the chest. Then it runs up through the throat and curving round the lips，terminating at the infraorbital region.

Branch 1：Comes out superficially at the inguinal regions，it runs down along the medial aspect of the thigh to the popliteal. Then it further descends along the medial side of the tibia to the sole. The branch of the area posterior to the medial malleolus runs forward and obliquely passes the dorsum of the foot，and enters the big toe.

Branch 2：Starting from the interior of the lower abdomen，it runs backward and connects governor vessel，running up in front of the spinal column（Fig 15－11）.

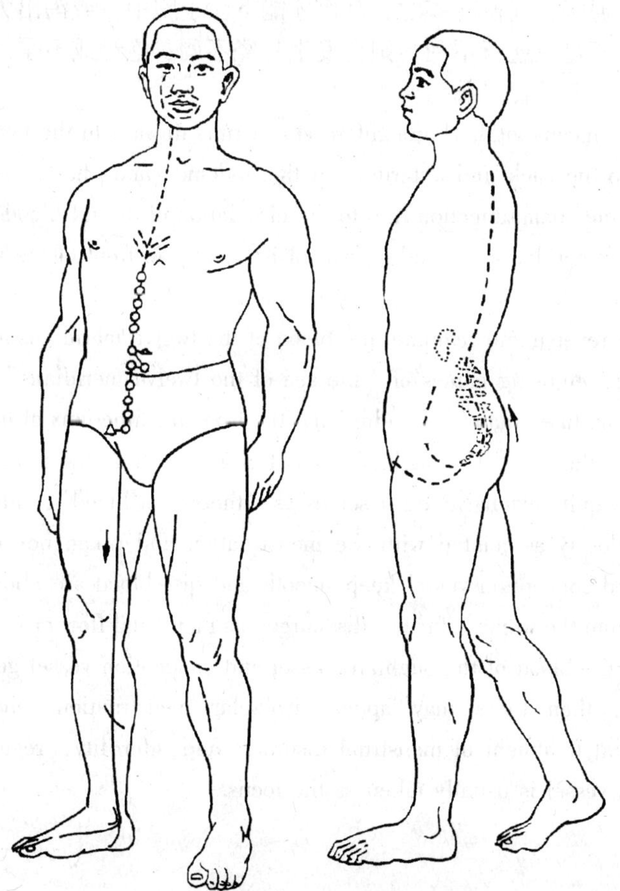

图 15－11 冲脉循环示意图

Fig 15－11 The course of thoroughfare vessel

二、功能和病候
Properties and Syndromes

（一）功能
Properties

冲脉的“冲”字，含有要冲、要道的意思。冲脉上至于头，下至于足，后行于背，前布于胸腹，贯穿全身，成为气血的要冲，能调节十二经气血。且上行者，行于脊内，渗之于阳；下行者，行于下肢，渗之于阴，能容纳和调节十二经脉及五脏六腑之气血，故有“十二经脉之海”和“五脏六腑之海”之称。另一方面，女子月经来潮及孕育功能，皆以血为基础。冲脉起于胞中，分布广泛，为“血海”，因此女子月经来潮及妊娠与冲脉盛衰密切相关。只有当冲任二脉通畅、气血旺盛时，其血才能下注于胞中，或泻出为月经，或妊娠时以养胚胎。若冲任气血不足或通行不利，则会发生月经不调、绝经或不孕。因此，临床上治月经病及不孕症，多以调理冲任二脉为要。

Thoroughfare here means vital. Thoroughfare vessel runs upward to the head, and downward to the foot, posteriorly in the back and anteriorly in the abdomen and chest, running throughout the whole body. So, it is the communication hub to the circulation of qi and blood, and can regulate qi and blood of the twelve meridians. Ascending part of it runs up in front of the spinal column, opening into yang meridians; the descending part of it runs in the lower limb, opening into yin meridians. Therefore, it can receive and regulate qi – blood of the twelve meridians and the five zang – organ and six fu – organ, enjoying names of “the sea of the twelve meridians” and “the sea of the five zang – organ and six fu – organ” . In addition, the women’s functions of menstruation and pregnancy all take blood as the basis. Thoroughfare Vessel originates from the interior of the lower abdomen; its attribution is quite extensive. So it serves as “the sea of blood”, and whether it functions powerfully or not is closely associated with the menstruation and pregnancy of women. Only when thoroughfare vessel and conception vessel keep smooth and qi – blood are abundant, can the blood be poured downward into the womb, further discharged as menstrual flow or to nourish the fetus during the pregnancy. If qi – blood of thoroughfare vessel and conception vessel get deficient or the meridians get impeded, then there may appear irregular menstruation, menopause or infertility. Therefore in clinical treatment of menstrual disorders and infertility, regulation of thoroughfare vessel and conception vessel is usually taken as the focus.

（二）病候
Syndromes

本经病候主要表现在两方面：一是逆气上冲，表现为心痛，心烦，胸闷胁胀，腹痛里急；二是生殖、泌尿系统病症，如男女不育，月经不调，遗尿等。叶天士的《临证指南》说：“不孕，经不调，冲脉病也。”

The pathological symptoms of thoroughfare vessel lie in two aspects: one is diseases caused by adverse qi, such as cardiac pain, hypochondriac and costal pain; the other is diseases of urogenital system, such as infertility, irregular menstruation, enuresis and so on.

第四节　带　脉
Belt Vessel

一、循行分布
The Course of Belt Vessel

起于季胁，斜向下行到带脉穴，绕身一周。在腹面的带脉下垂到少腹（图 15－12）。

Belt vessel originates at the site inferior to the free end of the 12th rib, runs obliquely downward to Daimai points, and then runs transversely around the body. Belt vessel in the surface of the abdomen runs down to the lateral aspects of the lower abdomen (Fig 15－12).

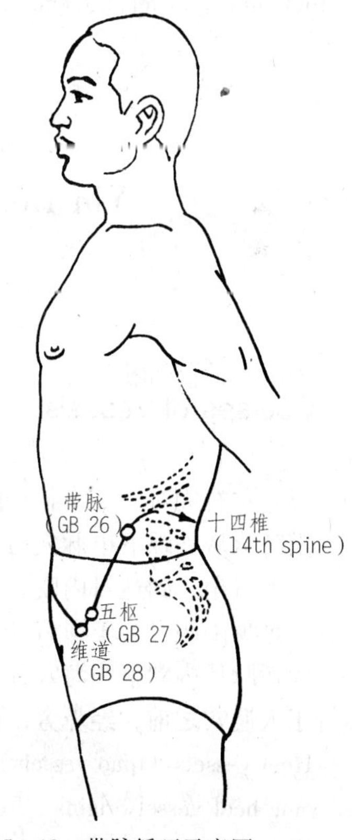

图 15－12　带脉循环示意图
Fig 15－12　The course of belt vessel

二、功能和病候
Properties and Syndromes

（一）功能
Properties

带脉的“带”字，含有束带的意思。因其横行于腰腹之间，统束经过腰腹间的纵行经脉，状如束带，故称带脉。十二正经与奇经八脉多为上下纵行，唯有带脉环腰一周，有总束诸脉的功能。带脉约束相关经脉，以调节脉气，使之通畅。另一方面，带脉又主司妇女带下，因带脉亏虚，不能约束经脉，多见妇女带下量多、腰酸无力等症。

Belt vessel (dai vessel), “dai” here means belt. Because

Dai Vessel runs transversely around the waist and the abdomen, binds and controls the meridians, which run vertically, like a belt, hence the name of Dai (Belt). The twelve regular and extra meridians mostly run vertically, only Belt Vessel runs around the waist so as to have the function of binding the dependent meridians. It binds and controls the relative meridians to regulate qi of the meridians to keep it free from obstruction. In addition, Belt Vessel can control the white in women. So if Belt Vessel gets insufficient and fails to control the meridians, there often appear leukorrhagia, soreness and weakness of the waist in women.

(二) 病候
Syndromes

带脉约束无力导致各种弛缓、痿废诸症，如腰部酸软，腹痛引腰脊，下肢不利，以及男女生殖器官病症，包括阳痿，遗精，月经不调，崩漏，带下，少腹拘急，疝气下坠等。

The main pathological symptoms of belt vessel are all paralysis caused by belt vessel failing to control the meridians, such as soreness and weakness of the waist, abdominal distention and pain radiating to the waist, flaccidity of the foot and its inability to move and diseases of reproductive organ including impotence, emission, irregular menstruation, uterine bleeding, leukorrhagia, hernia, etc.

第五节 阴跻、阳跻脉
Yin Heel Vessel and Yang Heel Vessel

一、循行分布
Courses of Vessels

跻脉左右成对。阴跻脉、阳跻脉均起于足踝下。

阳跻脉从外踝下申脉穴分出，沿外踝后上行，经腹部，沿胸部后外侧，经肩部、颈外侧，上夹口角，到达目内眦，与手足太阳经、阴跻脉会合，再上行进入发际，向下到达耳后，与足少阳胆经会于项后（图 15－13）。

阴跻脉从内踝下照海穴分出，沿内踝后直上下肢内侧，经过前阴，沿腹、胸进入缺盆，出行于人迎穴之前，经鼻旁，到目内眦，与手足太阳经、阳跻脉会合（图 15－14）。

Heel vessels (qiao vessels) exist in pair on the left and right sides of the body. yin heel vessel and yang heel vessel originate from the site inferior to the malleolus.

Yang heel vessel originates from Shenmai point inferior to the external malleolus, and runs upward via the posterior side of the external malleolus and along the posterior border of the fibular aspect of the thigh. Passing through the abdomen and along the posterolateral aspect of the chest, it runs up via the shoulder and lateral side of the neck to the angle of the mouth, reaching the inner canthus where it meets with meridians of hand – taiyang and foot – taiyang, and yin heel vessel. Then it further ascends through the anterior hairline, turns down to the retroauricular region, and finally meets gallbladder meridian of foot – shaoyang at the nape (Fengchi, GB 20) (Fig 15 – 13).

Yin heel vessel originates from Zhaohai point inferior to the medial malleolus and runs upward, via the posterior side of the medial malleolus and along the medial aspect of the lower limb, passing the external genitalia, ascending along the abdomen and chest to Quepen. Running further upward by the area anterior to Renying, it runs by the bridge of the nose to the inner canthus and meets with meridians of hand – taiyang and foot – taiyang, and yang link vessel (Fig 15 – 14).

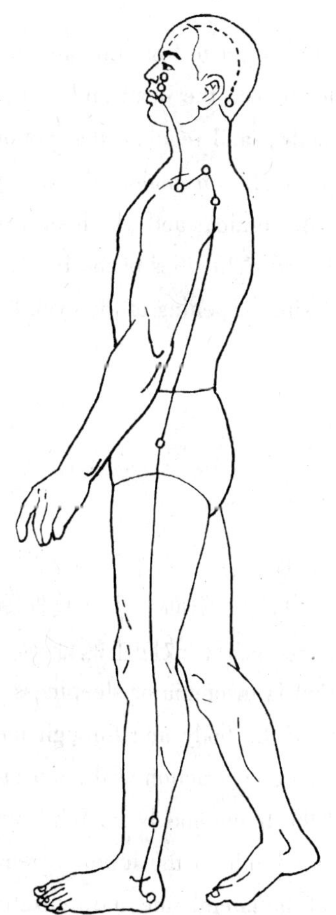

图 15 – 13 阳跻脉循行示意图

Fig 15 – 13 The course of yang heel vessel

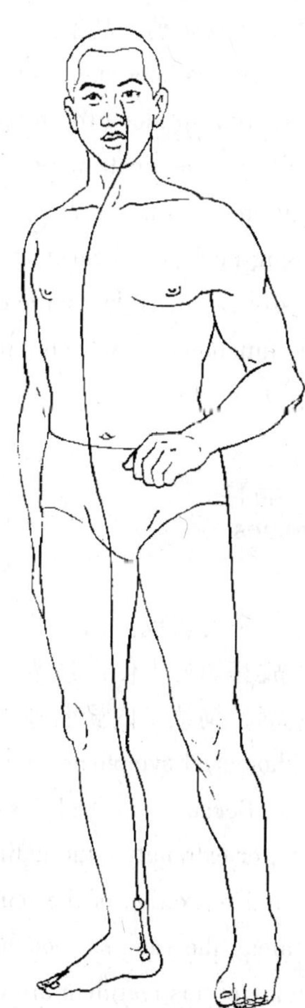

图 15 – 14 阴跻脉循行示意图

Fig 15 – 14 The course of yin heel vessel

二、功能和病候
Properties and Syndromes

（一）功能
Properties

跻脉的“跻”字有足跟和矫捷的含意。因跻脉起于足踝下，从下肢内、外侧上行头面，具有交通一身阴阳之气和调节肢体肌肉运动的功能，故能使下肢灵活矫捷。又由于阴阳跻脉交会于目内眦，入属于脑，阳跻主一身左右之阳，阴跻主一身左右之阴，故还有濡养眼目，司眼睑开合和下肢运动的功能。

Qiao here means heel and, forceful and nimble. Heel vessels originate from the sites inferior to the malleolus, run up along the medial and lateral sides of the limb to the head and face, having the functions to communicate yin qi and yang qi of the whole body, and regulate the motion of the limbs and muscles; so that it can make lower limbs forceful and nimble in motion. Because yin heel vessel and yang heel vessel meet at the inner canthus, enter the brain, and yin heel vessel and yang heel vessel respectively dominate yin and yang on both left and right sides of the body, so they also have the function of moistening the eyes, controlling the closing – opening of the eyelids and the motion of the lower limb.

（二）病候
Syndromes

跻脉病候主要表现为两方面，一是失眠或嗜睡；二是下肢拘急。因阴跻循行于阴面，经下肢内侧，故其病见内侧面痉挛、拘急，外侧面弛缓；阳跻循行于阳面，经下肢外侧，故其病外侧面痉挛、拘急，内侧面弛缓。这些征象可见于癫痫一类病中，故同主痫证。

The pathological symptoms sign mainly in two aspects: First is insomnia or sleepiness; second is limb spasm. Because yin heel vessel runs along the yin side of the body and through the medial side of the lower extremity, the main symptoms of this meridian are contraction of the muscles of the medial side and relaxation of the muscles of the lateral side of the limbs and body. While yang heel vessel runs along the yang side of the body and through the lateral side of the lower extremity, the main symptoms of this meridian are contraction of the muscles of the lateral side and relaxation of the muscles of the medial side of the limbs and body. These signs can be seen in epilepsy patients, so the two vessels is related with epilepsy.

第六节 阴维、阳维脉
Yin Link Vessel and Yang Link Vessel

一、循行分布
Courses of Vessels

阳维脉起于外踝下，与足少阳胆经并行，沿下肢外侧向上，经躯干部后外侧，从腋后上肩，经颈部、耳后，前行到额部，分布于头侧及项后，与督脉会合（图 15－15）。

阴维脉起于小腿内侧足三阴经交会之处，沿下肢内侧上行，至腹部，与足太阴脾经同行，到胁部，与足厥阴经相合，然后上行至咽喉，与任脉相会（图 15－16）。

Yang link vessel originates from the site inferior to the external malleolus. Coinciding with the gallbladder meridian of foot－shaoyang, it runs up along the lateral side of the lower limb, and posterolateral aspect of the trunk, passing through the posterior of the axilla to the shoulder. It further ascends via the neck and retroauricular region, and forward to the forehead, and then turns backward to the lateral side of the head and the back of the nape, where it communicates with governor vessel (Fig 15－15).

Yin link vessel originates from the site at the medial side of the leg where the three yin meridians of foot meet, runs up along the medial side of the lower limb to the abdomen, then coinciding with the spleen meridian of foot－taiyin; arriving at the hypochondrium, it meets with the liver meridian of foot－jueyin. Then it ascends to the throat to meet with conception vessel (Fig 15－16).

二、功能和病候
Properties and Syndromes

（一）功能
Properties

维脉的“维”字，含有维系、维络的意思。维脉的主要功能是维系全身经脉。由于阴维脉在循行过程中与足三阴经相交会，并最后合于任脉，故有维系、联络全身阴经的作用；阳维脉在循行过程中与手足三阳经相交，并最后合于督脉，故有维系、联络全身阳经的作用。在正常情况下，阴维脉、阳维脉互相维系，对气血盛衰起调节溢蓄的作用，但不参与环流。

Link vessels (wei vessels), “wei” here means regulating and connecting. The major functions of link vessels are to regulate all the meridians of the body. yin link vessel in its course meets three yin meridians of foot and finally joins conception vessel, so it is of the function to regulate and connect with yin meridians of the whole body. While yang link vessel in its course meets three yang meridians of foot and hand, finally joins governor vessel, so it is of the function to regulate and connect with yang meridians of the whole body. Under the normal conditions, Yin link vessel and yang link vessel regulate commonly to play the role of importing and exporting qi - blood, but not to participate their circulation.

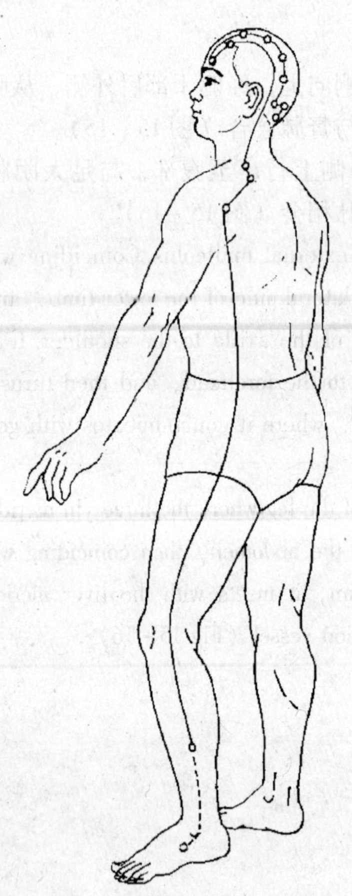

图 15 - 15 阳维脉循环示意图

Fig 15 - 15 The course of yang link vessel

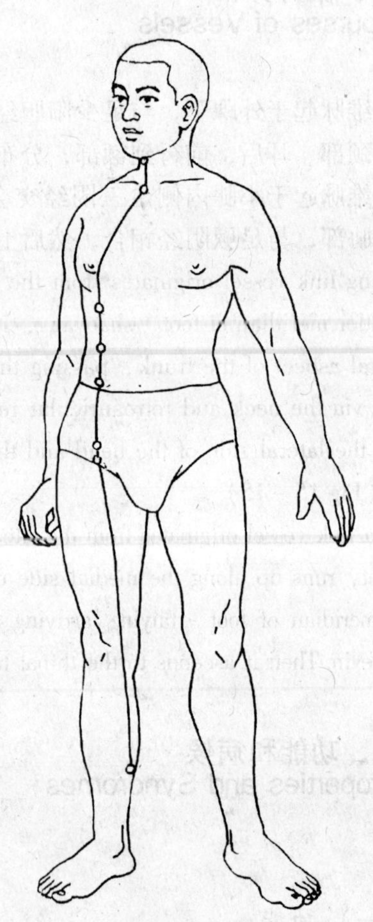

图 15 - 16 阴维脉循环示意图

Fig 15 - 16 The course of yin link vessel

(二) 病候
Symptoms

阳维失去维络，就出现阳证、表证，见寒热、头痛、目眩等；阴维失去维络，就出现阴证、里证，见心腹痛，胸胁痛等。

If yang link Vessel can't maintain and connect with other yang meridians of hand and foot, it will manifest yang syndromes and superficial syndromes such as chills and fever, headache, dizzy, etc. If yin link vessel can't maintain and connect with other yin meridians of foot, it will manifest yin syndromes and interior syndromes such as abdominal pain and thoraxico – hypochondriac pain.

第七节 奇经八脉的综合作用
The Comprehensive Properties of Eight Extra Meridians

一、统领、联络作用
Superintending and Connecting All the Parts of the Body

八脉中的督、任、冲脉都称为“海”，意指其功能之大，联系之广。督脉为“阳脉之海”；任脉为“阴脉之海”；冲脉总领、调节十二经脉气血，为“十二经脉之海”、“血海”。任脉主一身之阴气；督脉主一身之阳气。冲、任、督脉又相互交通，下起于胞中，上及于头脑；前贯心，后贯脊。可见，这三条经脉对全身经络系统的统率、联络作用十分广泛。

Among the eight extra meridians, governor vessel, conception vessel and thoroughfare vessel are all named “sea”, which means in China “strong power and contacting extensively”. Governor vessel is called “the sea of all the yang meridians”. Conception vessel is called “the sea of all the yin meridians”; While thoroughfare vessel controls and regulates the qi and blood inside the twelve regular meridians, it named “the sea of the twelve meridians” or “the sea of blood”. Conception vessel controls and regulates the yin qi of the whole body and governor vessel controls and regulates the yang qi of the whole body. Thoroughfare vessel, conception vessel and Governor Vessel connect with each other, and all originate from Baozhong (womb), rising upward head and brain inside, running through the heart and along the spine. So, these three meridians superintend and connect the channel system of the whole body widely.

奇经八脉在循行分布过程中，不但与十二经脉交叉相接，加强十二经脉间的联系，补充十二经脉在循行分布上的不足，而且对十二经脉的联系还起到分类组合的作用。如督脉与手足六阳经交会于大椎穴而称“阳脉之海”；任脉与足三阴经交会于关元穴，而足三阴又接手三阴经，故任脉因联系手足六阴经而称“阴脉之海”；冲脉通行上下前后，渗灌三阴三阳，有“十二经脉之海”之称；带脉约束纵行诸经，沟通腰腹部的经脉；阳维脉维络诸阳，联络所有阳经而与督脉相合，阴维脉维络诸阴，联络所有阴经而与任脉相会；阳跻脉与阴跻脉左右成对，有“分主一身左右阴阳”之说。

In the running and distributing process, eight extra meridians not only criss – cross with the twelve meridians so as to strengthen the communication among the twelve meridians and supplement the shortage of them in distribution, but also play a classifying or grouping role. For example, governor vessel meets with the six yang meridians of both hand and foot at Dazhui (DU 14), thus is called "the sea of yang meridians"; thoroughfare vessel meets the three yin meridians of foot at Guanyuan (RN 4), and the three yin meridians of foot connect with the three yin meridians of hand, so thoroughfare vessel is called "the sea of yin meridians"; thoroughfare vessel runs superiorly, inferiorly, anteriorly and posteriorly, communicating with three yin and three yang meridians, thus it is called "the sea of the twelve meridians"; belt vessel binds all the meridians vertically, communicates with the meridians run through the waist and abdomen; yang link vessel regulates all the yang meridians to link them with governor vessel; yin link vessel regulates all the yin meridians to link them with conception vessel; and yin heel and yang heel vessels are in pair on the right and left, dominate yin and yang on both the right and left sides of the body respectively.

二、溢蓄、调节作用
Storing and Regulating Qi - Blood of the Twelve Meridians

奇经八脉虽然除任脉、督脉外，不参与气血循环，但具有溢蓄和调节十二经气血的功能。当十二经脉气血满溢时，就会流入奇经八脉，蓄以备用；当十二经脉气血不足时，奇经中所蓄积的气血则溢出给予补充，以保持十二经脉气血的相对恒定状态，有利于维持机体生理功能的需要。这正是古人将正经比作"沟渠"，将奇经比作"湖泽"的含义。可见，奇经八脉对十二经气血的蓄积和调节是双向性的，既能蓄入也能溢出。

Eight extra meridians, except for conception vessel and governor vessel, do not join the circulation of qi – blood, but they possess the function to store and regulate qi – blood of the twelve meridians. When qi – blood of the twelve meridians gets over abundant, it will flow into eight extra meridians for storage; as qi – blood of the twelve meridians gets deficient, the qi – blood stored in eight extra meridians will flow out for compensation so as to keep a relatively constant state of qi – blood within the twelve meridians, being conducive to the demand for maintaining the physiological function of the body. This is the very meaning that ancient people compared the twelve meridians with "rivers" and eight extra meridians with "lakes" It can be thus seen that the functions of eight extra meridians for the qi – blood of the twelve meridians are dual, or importation and exportation.

第十六章 经外奇穴
Extra Points

第一节 头颈部穴位
Extra Points of the Head and Neck

1. 四神聪 Sishencong (EX-HN 1)

【释义】四，基数词四；神，神志；聪，聪明。此穴一名四穴，能主治神志失调，耳目不聪等病症，故名四神聪。

【定位】在头顶部，当百会穴前后左右各 1 寸，共 4 穴（图 16－1）。

【解剖】皮肤→皮下组织→帽状腱膜→腱膜下疏松结缔组织。布有枕动、静脉，颞浅动、静脉顶支和眶上动、静脉的吻合网，有枕大神经，耳颞神经及眶上神经分支。

【功用】安神聪脑，疏通经络。

【主治】头痛，眩晕，失眠，健忘，癫痫。

【操作】平刺 0.5～0.8 寸。

【Meaning】Si, number four; shen, consciousness; cong, intelligent. One name is four points. Indication: unconsciousness, disease of ears and eyes, so it was named Sishencong.

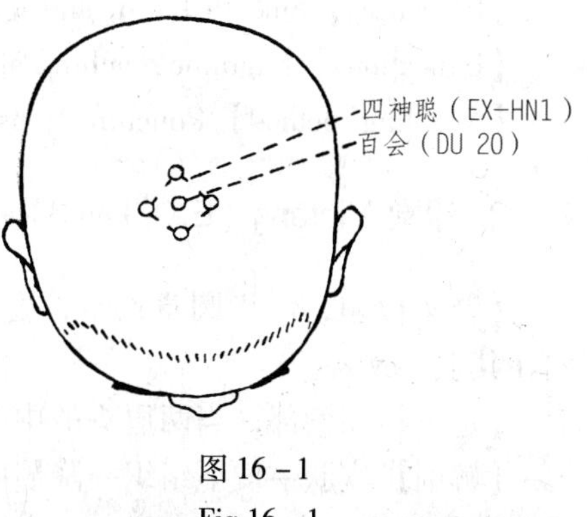

图 16－1

Fig 16－1

【Location】This name refers to four points located on the vertex, 1 cun anterior, posterior and lateral to Baihui (DU 20) respectively (Fig 16－1).

【Regional anatomy】Skin→subcutaneous tissue→galea aponeurosis→subaponeurotic loose connective tissue. Distributed occipital artery and vein, rete of parietal branch of superficial temporal artery and vein, supraorbital artery and vein, greater occipital nerve, auriculotemporal nerve and supraorbital nerve.

【Properties】Tranquilize the mind, improve mentality, remove obstructions in the meridians and collaterals.

【Indications】Headache, vertigo, insomnia, forgetfulness, epilepsy.

【Needling method】Puncture transversely 0.5 ~0.8 cun.

2. 当阳 Dangyang (EX-HN 2)

【释义】当，向着；阳，阴阳之阳。穴在头前部，头前部为阳，故名。

【定位】在前头部，当瞳孔直上，前发际上1寸（图16-2）。

【解剖】皮肤→皮下组织→枕额肌额腹或帽状腱膜→腱膜下疏松结缔组织。布有眶上神经和眶上动、静脉的分支或属支。

【功用】疏风通络，清头明目。

【主治】偏、正头痛，眩晕，目赤肿痛。

【操作】沿皮向上刺0.5~0.8寸。

【Meaning】Dang, face; yang, yang of yin-yang. The point is on the anterior of head, where was called yang, so this point name was called Dangyang.

【Location】At the frontal past of the head, directly above the pupil, 1cun above the anterior hairline. (Fig 16-2)

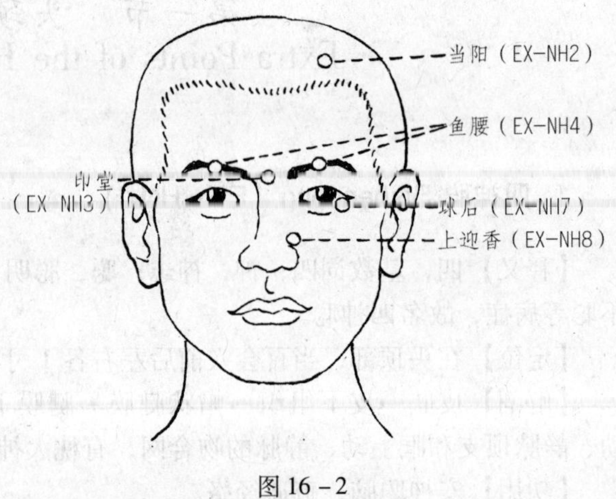

图16-2

Fig 16-2

【Regional anatomy】Skin→subcutaneous tissue→occipitofrontalis or galea aponeurotica → subaponeurotic loose connective tissue. Distributed nerves supraorbitalis, branch of suprorbital artery and vein.

【Properties】Smooth the qi and the veins, clear head and improve vision.

【Indications】Migraine, aching all over the head, dizziness, swelling and pain of the eyes.

【Needling method】Puncture transversely upward 0.5 ~0.8 cun.

3. 印堂 Yintang (EX-HN 3)

【释义】印，泛指圆章；堂，庭堂。古代指额部两眉头之间为“阙”，星相家称印堂，穴在其上，故名。

【定位】在额部，当两眉头的中间（图16-2）。

【解剖】皮肤→皮下组织→降眉间肌。布有额神经的分支滑车上神经、眼动脉的分支额动脉及伴行的静脉。

【功用】活络疏风，镇痉安神。

【主治】①头痛，眩晕，失眠，小儿惊风。②鼻塞，鼻渊、鼻衄，眉棱骨痛，目痛。

【操作】平刺0.5~1.0寸。

【Meaning】Yin, generally refers to the seal; tang, hall. The place that between the medial ends of the eyebrows was called "Que" in ancient time and was called Yintang by astrologers, the point is on that place, so it was called Yintang.

【Location】Midway between the two medial ends of the two eyebrow (Fig 16-2).

【Regional anatomy】Skin→subcutaneous tissue→procerus muscle. Distributed frontal nerve supratrochlear nerve, ophthalmic artery frontal artery and accompanied vein.

【Properties】Activate flow of qi and blood in the collaterals, expel wind, relieve convulsion and tranquilize the mind.

【Indications】①Headache, vertigo, insomnia, infantile convulsion. ②Forgetfulness, epilepsy, sinusitis, epistaxis, pain in the supraorbital region.

【Needling method】Puncture transversely 0.5~1.0 cun.

4. 鱼腰 Yuyao (EX-HN 4)

【释义】鱼，生活在水中的脊椎动物，如鲤鱼等；腰，泛指物体中部。

【定位】在额部，瞳孔直上，眉毛中（图16-2）。

【解剖】皮肤→皮下组织→眼轮匝肌→枕额肌额腹。布有眶上神经的外侧支，面神经的分支和眶上动、静脉的外侧支。

【功用】祛风清热，清头明目。

【主治】目赤肿痛，目翳，眼睑瞤动，眼睑下垂，眉棱骨痛。

【操作】平刺0.3~0.5寸。

【Meaning】Yu, fish living in water; yao, generally refers to the middle of the body. Eyebrow of mankind likes fish, this point is on the middle of the eyebrow, so called it as Yuyao.

【Location】In the center of the eyebrow, in the depression directly above the pupil where the eyes looking straight forwards (Fig 16-2).

【Regional anatomy】Skin→subcutaneous tissue→orbicularis oculi→frontal belly of occipitofrontal muscle. Distributed lateral branch of supraorbital nerve, branches of facial nerve and ramus lateralis of supraorbital artery and vein

【Properties】Expel wind, clear away heat, clear away heat from the head and improve vision.

【Indications】Red and painful eyes, cataract, twitching of swelling and pain of the eye, ptosis of the eyelid pain in the supraorbital region.

【Needling Method】Puncture transversely 0.3~0.5 cun.

5. 太阳 Taiyang (EX-HN 5)

【释义】太，形容词；高、大、极、最；阳，阴阳之阳。头颞部之微凹陷处，俗称太阳穴，穴在其上，故名。

【定位】在颞部，眉梢和目外眦之间，向后约1横指的凹陷处（图16－3）。

【解剖】皮肤→皮下组织→眼轮匝肌→颞筋膜→颞肌。布有颧神经的分支颧面神经，面神经的颞支和颧支，下颌神经的颞神经和颞浅动、静脉的分支或属支。

【功用】疏风散热，清头明目。

【主治】头痛，目疾，齿痛，面痛。

【操作】直刺或斜刺0.3～0.5寸，或用三棱针点刺放血。

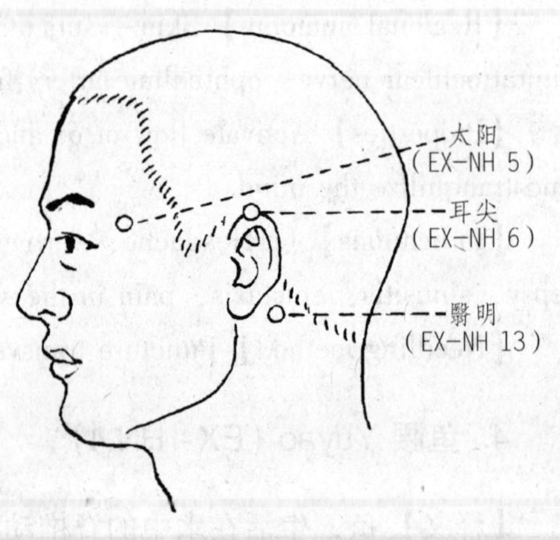

图16－3
Fig 16－3

【Meaning】Tai, adjective, such as high, big, extremely; yang, yang of yin－yang.

【Location】In the depression about one finger－breadth posterior to the midpoint between the lateral end of the eyebrow and the outer canthus（Fig 16－3）.

【Rogional anatomy】Skin→subcutaneous tissue→orbicularis oculi → temporal fascia → temporal muscle. Distributed zygomaticofacial nerve which is branch of zygomatic nerve, zygomatic branch and temporal branch of facial nerve, temporal nerve of inferior maxillary nerve, and branches of superficial temporal artery and vein.

【Properties】Expel wind, clear away heat from head and improve vision.

【Indications】Headache, disease of the eye, toothache, facial pain.

【Needling method】Puncture transversely or obliquely 0.3～0.5 cun, or prick with a three－edged needle to induce bleeding.

6. 耳尖 Erjian（EX－HN 6）

【释义】耳，耳廓；尖，顶端、顶点。耳廓之顶端称耳尖，穴在其上，故名。

【定位】在耳廓的上方，当折耳向前，耳廓上方的尖端处（图16－3）。

【解剖】皮肤→皮下组织→耳廓软骨。布有颞浅动、静脉的耳前支，耳后动、静脉的耳后支，耳颞神经耳前支、枕小神经耳后支和面神经耳支等。

【功用】清热消肿，明目利咽。

【主治】目赤肿痛，目翳，麦粒肿，咽喉肿痛。

【操作】直刺0.1～0.2寸，或点刺出血。

【Meaning】Er, auricle; jian, tip. The tip of auricle was called "Erjian", The point is on it.

【Location】On the top region of the ear, fold the ear forward, the point is at the apex of the ear（Fig 16－3）.

【Regional anatomy】Skin→subcutaneous tissue→auricular cartilage. Distributed anterior auricular branches of superficial temporal artery and vein, posterior auricular artery and vein, auriculotemporal nerve, lesser occipital nerve and auricular branch of facial nerve.

【Properties】Relieve heat, anti – inflammatory, improve eyesight and benefit the throat.

【Indications】Swelling and pain of the eye, cataract, hordeolum, swelling and pain of throat.

【Needling method】Puncture perpendicularly 0. 1 ~0. 2cun, or prick to cause bleeding.

7. 球后 Qiuhou (EX- HN 7)

【释义】球，眼球；后，前后之后。此穴位置较深，在眼球后部，故名。

【定位】当眶下缘外 1/4 与内 3/4 交界处（图 16 –2）。

【解剖】皮肤→皮下组织→眼轮匝肌→眶脂体→下斜肌与眶下壁之间。浅层布有眶下神经，面神经的分支和眶下动、静脉的分支或属支。深层有动眼神经下支，眼动、静脉的分支或属支和眶下动、静脉。

【功用】活血明目。

【主治】目疾。

【操作】用押手将眼球推向上方，针尖沿眶下缘刺入 0. 5 ~1. 0 寸，不宜捻转提插。

【Meaning】Qiu, eyeball; hou, posterior, The location of this point is deep and at the posterior site of eyeball. So It was named "Qiuhou".

【Location】At the junction of the lateral 1/4 and the medial 3/4 of the infraorbital margin (Fig 16 –2).

【Regional anatomy】Skin→subcutaneous tissue→orbicularis oculi→adipose body of orbit→between inferior obliquus and paries inferior orbitae. The superficial layer, there are infraorbital nerve, branch of facial nerve, branches of infraorbital artery and vein. In the deep layer, there are inferior branch of oculomotor nerve, branches of ophthalmic artery and vein, branches of infraorbital artery and vein.

【Properties】Activate blood flow and improve vision.

【Indications】Eye diseases.

【Needling method】Gently push the eye ball upward, insert the needle slightly downward towards the orbital margin for 0. 5 ~1. 0 cun without lifting and thrusting.

8. 上迎香 Shangyingxiang (EX- HN 8)

【释义】上，上下之上；迎，迎接；香，香味，泛指气味。穴在鼻部，大肠经迎香穴之上方，故名上迎香。

【定位】在面部，当鼻翼软骨与鼻甲的交界处，近鼻唇沟上端处（图 16 –2）。

【解剖】皮肤→皮下组织→提上唇鼻翼肌。布有眶下神经，滑车下神经的分支，面神经的颊支和内眦动、静脉。

【功用】清热散风，明目通鼻。

【主治】鼻塞，鼻渊，目赤肿痛，迎风流泪，头痛。

【操作】向内上方斜刺0.3～0.5寸。

【Meaning】Shang, upper; ying, receiving; xiang, fragrant or flavours. This point located at the nose and above Yingxiang (LI 20). So, it was named "Shangyingxiang".

【Location】On the region of the face, at the junction of the cartilage of the alae nasi and the nasal concha, near the upper end of the nasolabial groove (Fig 16–2).

【Regional anatomy】skin→subcutaneous tissue→levator labii superioris alae nasi. Distributed infraorbital nerve, branches of infratrochlear nerve, buccal branch of facial nerve, and angular artery and vein.

【Properties】Relieve heat, expel wind, improve vision and open nasal passages.

【Indications】Nasal obstruction, sinusitis, swelling and pain in the eyes, headache.

【Needling method】Puncture obliquely and centrally upward 0.3～0.5 cun.

9. 内迎香 Neiyingxiang (EX-HN 9)

【释义】内，内外之内；迎，迎接，迎来；香，香味，泛指气味，穴在鼻腔内，与迎香穴隔鼻翼相对，故名内迎香。

【定位】在鼻孔，当鼻翼软骨与鼻甲的黏膜处（图16–4）。

【解剖】鼻黏膜→黏膜下疏松组织。布有面动、静脉的鼻背支之动、静脉和筛前神经的鼻外支。

【功用】清热明目，消肿通窍。

【主治】鼻疾，目赤肿痛。

【操作】用三棱针点刺出血。有出血体质的人忌用。

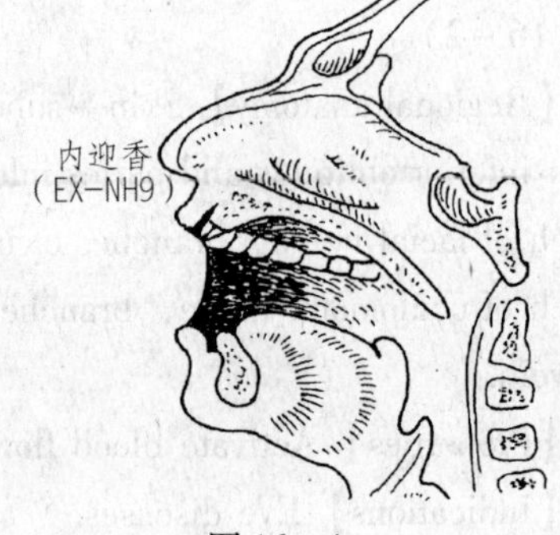

图16–4
Fig 16–4

【Meaning】Nei, interior; ying, meet; xiang, fragrance. This point is in the nasal cavity, opposite to Yingxiang (LI 20) separate by nasal ala, so called it "Neiyingxiang".

【Location】Inside of the nostrils, on the mucous menbrane at the junction of the cartilage of the alae nasi and the nasal concha (Fig 16–4).

【Regional anatomy】Nasal mucous menbrane→loose tissue under mucosa. Distributed rete formed of external nasal branch of facial artery and vein, and external nasal branch of anterior ethmoid nerve.

【Properties】Relieve heat, improve vision anti–inflammatory and promoting the restoration consciousness.

【Indications】Diseases of the nose, swelling and pain in the eyes.

【Needling method】Prink to induce bleeding using three – edged needle, this method is contraindicated in patients with a bleeding disorder.

10. 聚泉 Juquan（EX- HN 10）

【释义】聚，聚集；泉，泉水。穴在舌背中缝之中点处，古人认为口腔内之津液出自此处，如泉水之汇聚，故名。

【定位】在口腔内，当舌背正中缝的中点处（图 16 –5）。

【解剖】舌黏膜→黏膜下疏松结缔组织→舌肌。布有下颌神经的舌神经，舌下神经和鼓索的神经纤维及舌动、静脉的动、静脉网。

【功用】清散风热，祛邪开窍。

【主治】①舌强，舌缓，食不知味。②消渴。

【操作】直刺 0. 1 ~0. 2 寸，或用三棱针点刺出血。

【Meaning】Ju, accumulate; quan, spring water. This point is on the middle of the dorsal of the tongue. The ancients considered the saliva in mouth accumulated on the place like spring water, so called "Juquan".

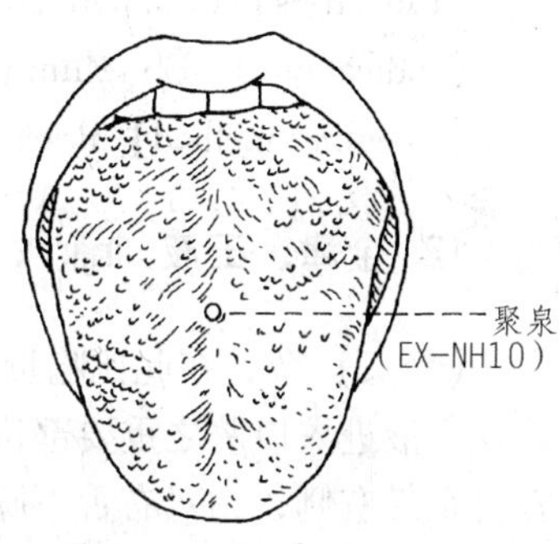

图 16 –5

Fig 16 –5

【Location】In the mouth, at the midpoint of the dorsal midline of the tongue. (Fig 16 –5)

【Regional anatomy】Lingual mucous membrane → loose connective tissue under mucosa → lingual muscle. Distributed nerve lingual never of inferior maxillary, hypoglossal nerve, chorda tympani nerve fiber, lingual artery and vein.

【Properties】Dispel wind and clear heat, eliminating evil qi, induce resuscitation.

【Indications】①Stiff tongue, flaccidity of the tongue, hypogeusesthesia. ②Diabetes.

【Needling method】Puncture perpendicularly 0. 1 ~ 0. 2 cun, or prick with a three – edged needle to induce bleeding.

11. 海泉 Haiquan（EX- HN 11）

【释义】海，大洋靠近陆地的部分，海洋之海；泉，泉水。穴在口腔内舌系带中点上。古人认为，口腔内津液由此出来，状如海水、泉水，永不间断。

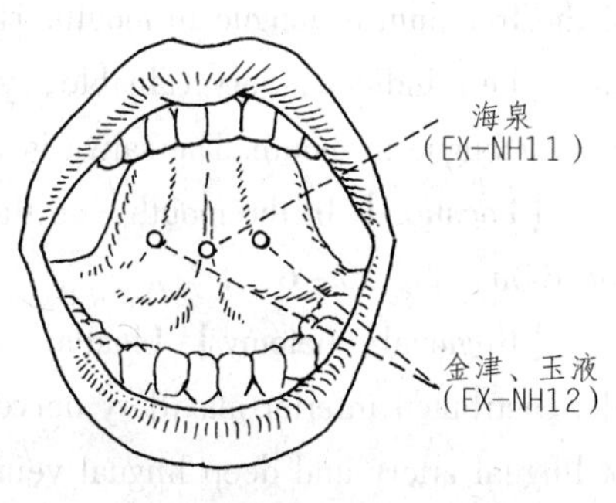

图 16 –6

Fig 16 –6

【定位】在口腔内，当舌下系带中点处（图 16 –6）。

【解剖】舌黏膜→黏膜下组织→舌肌。布有下颌神经的舌神经，舌下神经和面神经鼓索的神经纤维及舌动脉的分支舌深动脉和舌静脉的属支舌深静脉。

【功用】祛邪开窍，生津止渴。

【主治】①舌体肿胀，舌缓不收。②消渴。

【操作】用三棱针点刺出血。

【Meaning】Hai, the part of nearly land of ocean, sea; quan, spring water. This point is on the median of frenulum of tongue in mouth. The ancients considered saliva in mouth run from this place like sea water are constantly emerging.

【Location】In the mouth, at the midpoint of the frenulum of the tongue (Fig 16－6).

【Regional anatomy】Lingual mucous membrance → submucous tissue → lingual muscle. Distributed lingual nerve of inferior maxillary nerve, hypoglossal nerve, chorda tympani nerve fiber, deep lingual artery of lingual artery and deep lingual vein of lingual vein.

【Properties】Eliminating evil qi, induce resuscitation, invite body fluid and pacify thirst.

【Indications】①Swelling of the tongue, flaccidity of the tongue. ②Diabetes.

【Needling method】Prick with a three－edged needle to induce bleeding.

12. 金津、玉液 Jinjin、Yuye (EX-HN 12)

【释义】金，在此比喻贵重；津，唾液。穴在口腔舌系带左侧，约对左舌下腺管开口处，唾液进入口腔之重要部位，故取名金津。玉，玉石，在此比喻贵重；液，津液。穴在口腔舌系带右侧，约对右舌下腺管开口处，口腔内唾液是津液之精华，故名津液。

【定位】张口，舌卷向后方，于舌面下，舌系带两旁之静脉上取穴。左为金津，右为玉液（图 16－6）。

【解剖】舌黏膜→黏膜下组织→颏舌肌。布有下颌神经的颌神经，舌下神经和面神经鼓索的神经纤维及舌动脉的分支舌深动脉，舌静脉的属支色深静脉。

【功用】清热开窍。

【主治】①舌强不语，舌肿，口疮。②呕吐，消渴。

【操作】点刺出血。

【Meaning】Jin, here it means valuable; jin, saliva. This point is on the vein on the left side of the frenulum of tongue in mouth. The saliva is very valuable liquid, so called it "Jinjin". Yu, jade, here indicates very valuable; ye, liquid. This point is on the vein of right side of the frenulum of tongue in mouth. The saliva is very valuable liquid, in the mouth, so called it as "Yuye".

【Location】In the mouth, on the two veins under the tongue, Jinjin is on the left, Yuye is on the right (Fig 16－6).

【Regional anatomy】Lingual mucous membrane → submucous tissue → genioglossus muscle. Distrbuted inferior maxillary nerve, hypoglossal nerve, cord of tympanum, deep lingual artery of lingual artery and deep lingual vein of lingual vein.

【Properties】Clear away heat and induce resuscitation.

【Indications】①Aphasia with a stiff tongue, swelling of the tongue, sore mouth. ②Vomiting and diabetes.

【Needling method】Prick to induce bleeding.

13. 翳明 Yiming (EX-HN 13)

【释义】翳，遮蔽，白翳；明，光明。此穴能治眼目病症，如揭开云雾见光明，故名。

【定位】在项部，当翳风后1寸（图16－3）。

【解剖】皮肤→皮下组织→胸锁乳突肌→头夹肌。浅层布有耳大神经的分支。深层有颈深动、静脉。

【功用】明目聪耳。

【主治】目疾，耳鸣，失眠，头痛。

【操作】直刺0.5～1.0寸。

【Meaning】Yi, cover or cloud－like; ming, light. The point can treat the diseases of eye, with it just like dispelling the clouds and seeing the light. So it was named "Yiming".

【Location】On the neck, 1 cun posterior to Yifeng (SJ 17) (Fig 16－3).

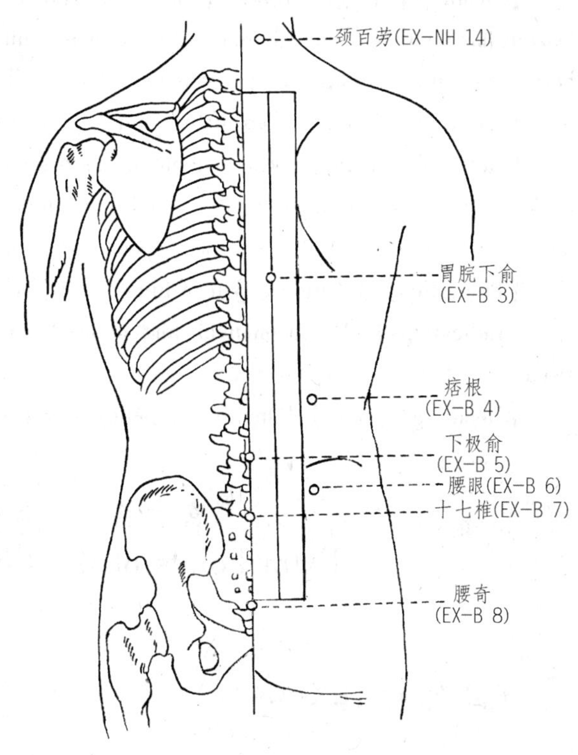

图16－7

Fig 16－7

【Regional anatomy】skin→subcutaneous tissue→sternocleidomastoid→splenius capitis. The superficial layer has greater auricular nerve, the deep layer has deep cervical artery and vein.

【Properties】Improve vision and hearing.

【Indications】Eye disease, tinnitus, insomnia, headache.

【Needling method】Puncture perpendicularly 0.5～1.0 cun.

14. 颈百劳 Jingbailao (EX-HN 14)

【释义】颈，颈部；百，基数词百；劳，劳伤、劳瘵。大椎穴又名百劳，此穴在颈部大椎穴上，能治疗劳瘵（肺结核）、颈淋巴结核，故名颈百劳。

【定位】在颈部，当大椎直上2寸，后正中线旁开1寸（图16－7）。

【解剖】皮肤→皮下组织→斜方肌→上后锯肌→头颈夹肌→头半棘肌→多裂肌。浅层布有第4、5神经后支的分支。深层有第4、5颈神经后支的分支。

【功用】滋补肺阴，舒筋活络。

【主治】①颈项强痛。②咳嗽，气喘，骨蒸潮热，盗汗。

【操作】直刺0.5~1.0寸。

【Meaning】Jing, means neck; Bai, hundred; Lao, impairment caused by overstrain. Dazhui has another name – Bailao, this point is right up Dazhui, can be used to cure pulmonary tuberculosis, neck scrofula. Soit was named "Jingbailao".

【Location】2 cun up Dazhui, 1 cun lateral to the posterior middle line (Fig 16 –7).

【Regional anatomy】Skin→subcutaneous tissue→trapezius muscle→serratus posterior superior→neck splenius→semispinalis capitis→multifidus muscle. The 4th and 5th nerve branch in superficial layer, and the 4th and 5th neck nerve posterior branch in deeper layer.

【Properties】nutrition to yin of lung, relaxing muscles and tendons.

【Indications】①acid on neck and nape. ②cough, asthma, steaming bone tidal heat, night sweat.

【Needling method】Puncture perpendicularly 0.5 ~1.0 cun.

第二节 胸腹部穴位 Extra Points of the Chest and Abdomen

子宫 Zigong (EX- CA 1)

【释义】子，古代指儿女；宫，宫室，古代房屋的通称。子宫是现代解剖学名词，中医学称胞宫，是女子孕育胎儿的器官。因此穴能治子宫下垂，故名。

【定位】在下腹部，当脐中下4寸，中极旁开3寸（图16-8）。

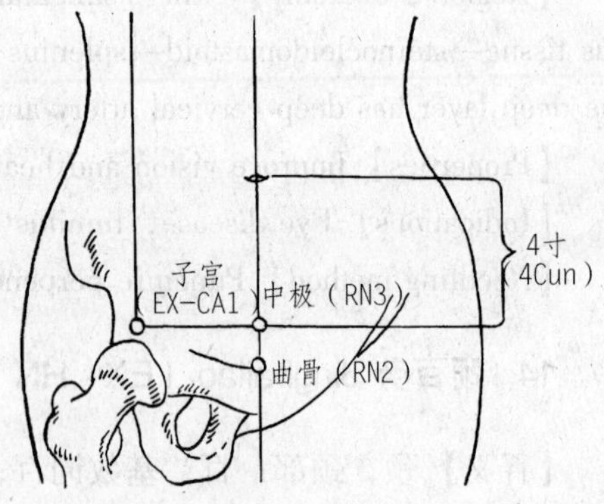

图16-8
Fig 16-8

【解剖】皮肤→皮下组织→腹外斜肌腱膜→腹内斜肌→腹横肌→腹横筋膜。浅层主要布有髂腹下神经的外侧皮支和腹壁浅静脉。深层主要有髂腹下神经的分支和腹壁下动、静脉的分支或属支。

【功用】升阳举陷，调经止痛。

【主治】阴挺，不孕，月经不调，痛经，崩漏。

【操作】直刺0.8~1.2寸；可灸。

【Meaning】Zi, indicated sons and daughters in ancient times; gong, palace. Houses was commonly called gong (palace) in ancient times. Zigong is an anatomy term, it was called "Baogong" in TCM. It is organ for embryo pregnancy. The point can be treated on hysteroptosis, so it was named.

【Location】On the lower abdomen, 4 cun below the center of umbilicus, 3 cun lateral to Zhongji (RN 3) (Fig 16 –8).

【Regional anatomy】Skin→subcutaneous tissue→tendinous membrance of external oblique muscle of abdomen→interal oblique muscle of abdomen→transversal abdominal muscle→transversalis fascia. There are lateral cutaneous branches of iliohypogastric nerve and superficial epigastric vein in the superficial deep, The deep layer has branch of iliohypogastric nerve, branches of inferior epigastric artery and vein.

【Properties】Lift yang and treat prolapse, regulate menstruation and relieve pain.

【Indications】Prolapse of uterus, infertility, irregular menstruation, dysmenorrheal, uterine bleeding.

【Needling method】Puncture perpendicularly 0. 8 ~ 1. 2 cun. Moxibustion is applicable.

第三节 背部穴位
Extra Points of the Back

1. 定喘 Dingchuan (EX- B 1)

【释义】定，平定；喘，哮喘。本穴有平定哮喘发作的作用，故名。

【定位】在背部，当第7颈椎棘突下，旁开0.5寸（图16－9）。

【解剖】皮肤→皮下组织→斜方肌→菱形肌→上后锯肌→颈夹肌→竖脊肌。浅层主要布有第8颈神经后支的内侧皮支。深层有颈横动、静脉的分支或属支及第8颈神经，第1胸神经后支的肌支。

【功用】宣肺定喘，祛风活血。

【主治】哮喘，咳嗽，落枕，肩背痛，上肢疼痛不举。

【操作】直刺0.5～1.0寸。

【Meaning】Ding, calm down; chuan, asthma. The point has been applied for calming down the attack of asthma. So, it was named "Dingchuan".

【Location】Below the spinous process of the 7th cervical vertebra, 0.5 cun lateral to the posterior midline (Fig 16－9).

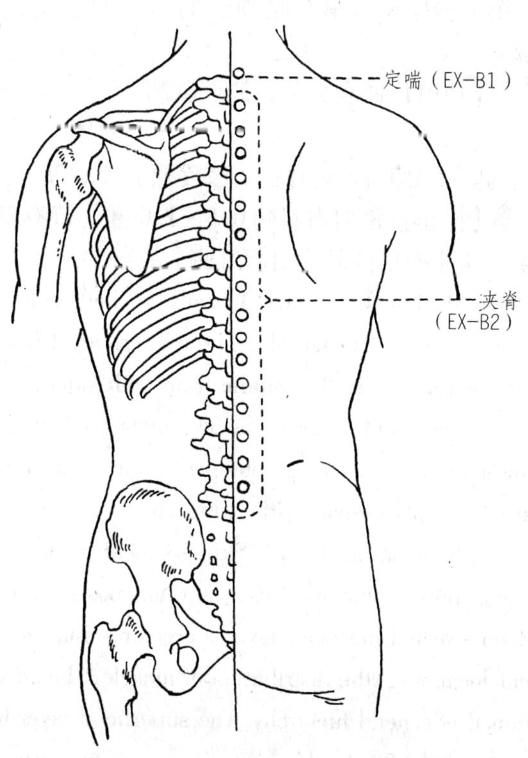

图16－9
Fig 16－9

【Regional anatomy】Skin→subcutaneous tissue→trapezius→rhomboideus→serratus posterior superior→slpenius cervicis→arector spinal muscle. The superficial layer has medial cutaneous branch of the 8th posterior branch of cervical nerve, the deep layer has transverse cervical artery and vein, the 8th cervical nerve, and posterior branch of the 1st thoracic nerve.

【Properties】Facilitate flow of the lung qi, expel wind and activate flow of blood.

【Indications】Asthma, cough, stiff neck, painful shoulder and back, upper limb pain.

【Needling method】Puncture perpendicularly 0.5 ~1.0cun.

2. 夹脊 Jiaji (EX- B 2)

【释义】夹，从两个相对的方向固定不动；脊，脊柱。穴在脊柱两侧共计 34 穴，从两旁将脊柱夹于其中，故名。

【定位】在背腰部，当第 1 胸椎至第 5 腰椎棘突下两侧，后正中线旁开 0.5 寸，一侧 17 穴（图 16 –9）。

【解剖】因各穴位置不同，其肌肉、血管、神经也各不同。一般的层次结构是，皮肤→皮下组织→浅肌层（斜方肌、背阔肌、菱形肌、上后锯肌、下后锯肌）→深层肌（竖脊肌、横突棘肌）。浅层内分别有第 1 胸神经至第 5 腰神经的内侧皮支和伴行的动、静脉。深层布有第 1 胸神经至第 5 腰神经的后支的肌支，肋间后动、静脉或腰动、静脉背侧的分支或属支。

【功用】通利关节，调理脏腑。

【主治】①胸 1 ~5 夹脊：心肺、胸部及上肢疾病。②胸 6 ~12 夹脊：胃肠、脾、肝、胆疾病。③腰 1 ~5 夹脊：下肢疼痛，腰、骶、小腹部疾病。

【操作】稍向内斜刺 0.5 ~1.0 寸，待有麻胀感即停止进针，严格掌握进针的角度及深度，防止损伤内脏或引起气胸。

【Meaning】Jia, fixed firmly on both side; ji, vertebral column. The points are respectively on both sides of vertebral column. There are 17 points on each side. It seemed that these points might fix the vertebra in the middle from both sides, so the points were named "Jiaji".

【Location】A group of 34 points on both sides of the spinal column, 0.5 cun lateral to the lower border of each spinous process from the 1st thoracic vertebra to the 5th lumbar vertebra. There are 17 points on each side (Fig 16 –9).

【Regional anatomy】Skin→subcutaneous tissue→superficial muscular layer (trapezius, latissimus dorsi, rhomboideus, serratus posterior superior, musculus serratus posterior inferior)→deep – seated muscular layer (erector spinal muscle, transversospinal muscle). Because of different locations, the distribution of muscle, blood vessel and nerve are different, too. The above mentioned is general hierarchy. The superficial layer has medial cutaneous branches from the 1st thoracic nerve to the 5th lumbar nerve, concomitant artery and vein. The deep layer has the posterior muscular branches from the 1st thoracic nerve to the 5th lumbar nerve, posterior intercostal artery and vein, dorsal branches of lumbar artery and vein.

【Properties】Smooth the articulations, regulate functions of zang－fu organ.

【Indications】There are many indications for the use of these points. the indications of different parts of the spine are as follow.

①The points on the upper portion of the thorax are used to treat diseases/disorders of the throat, chest, heart, lung, and upper extremities (thoracic vertebra T1～T5). ②The points on the lower portion of the thorax are used to treat diseases/disorders of the liver, gallbladder, spleen, stomach and intestine (thoracic vertebra T6～T12). ③The points on the lumbar region are used to treat diseases of the lumbar, scrum, lower abdomen and lower extremities (lumbar vertebra L1～L5).

【Needling method】Puncture obliquely 0.5～1.0cun, use caution when inserting the needing to prevent damaging the viscera or causing pneumothorax. The plum－needling technique can be utilized instead.

3. 胃脘下俞 Weiwanxiashu (EX-B 3)

【释义】胃脘，中医学名词，泛指肋弓以下之腹上部；下，上下之下；俞，气血转输之处。此穴能治胃部疼痛（胃神经痛、胰腺炎引起的疼痛等），故名。

【定位】在背部，当第8胸椎棘突下，旁开1.5寸（图16－7）。

【解剖】皮肤→皮下组织→斜方肌→背阔肌→竖脊肌。浅层主要布有第8胸神经后支的皮支和伴行的动、静脉。深层有第8胸神经后支的肌支和第8肋间后动、静脉背侧的分支或属支。

【功用】宽胸理气，和中降逆。

【主治】消渴，胰腺炎，胃痛，腹痛，胸胁痛。

【操作】向内斜刺0.3～0.5寸。

【Meaning】Weiwan, a term of TCM, here means the part of the body at the upper abdomen under the costal arch; Xia means the inferior; Shu, the point of transferring and transporting qi and blood. The point can treat the pain on the epigastric area (such as the gastricneuralgia, pancreatitis, etc). so it was called "Weiwanxiashu".

【Location】1.5 cun lateral to the lower border of the spinous process of the 8th thoracic vertebra (Fig 16－7).

【Regional anatomy】Skin→subcutaneous tissue→trapezius→latissimus dorsi→erector spinal muscle. The superficial layer has posterior cutaneous branch of the 8th thoracic nerve, concomitant artery and vein. The deep layer has posterior muscular branch of the 8th thoracic nerve, posterior branches of the 8th intercostal artery and vein

【Properties】Soothe flow of qi in the chest, regulate functions of the middle－energizer, lower down upward adverse flow of qi.

【Indications】Diabetes, pancreatitis stomachache, pain in the abdomen, chest and hypochondriac region.

【Needling method】Puncture obliquely 0.3 ~ 0.5 cun.

4. 痞根 Pigen (EX-B 4)

【释义】痞，痞块；根，根部。腹内肿大的器官，如肝肿大、脾肿大，泛称痞块。此穴有治疗肝脾肿大的作用，有如截断痞块根部的作用，因而取名。

【定位】在腰部，当第1腰椎棘突下，旁开3.5寸（图16-7）。

【解剖】皮肤→皮下组织→背阔肌→下后锯肌→髂肋肌。浅层主要布有第12胸神经后支的外侧支和伴行的动、静脉。深层主要有第12胸神经后支的肌支。

【功用】健脾和胃，理气止痛。

【主治】①腰痛。②痞块，癥瘕。

【操作】直刺0.5~1.0寸。

【Meaning】Pi, mass; gen, part of root. The hyperplasia of organs in abdomen such as the hepatomegaly and splenomegaly were called "Pi" (mass). This point is applied on treating hepato-splenomegaly just like to cut off the root of the mass. So it was named "Pigen".

【Location】On the lower back, below the spinous process of the 1st lumbar vertebra, 3.5 cun lateral to the posterior mid line. (Fig 16-7)

【Regional anatomy】Skin→subcutaneous tissue→latissimus dorsi→serratus posterior inferior→iliocostalis muscle. The superficial layer have posterior branch of the 12th thoracic nerve and accompanying artery and vein, the deep layer have posterior muscular branch of the 12th thoracic nerve.

【Properties】Strengthen the spleen and stomach, regulate and alleviate pain

【Indications】①Lumbago. ②Lump glomus.

【Needling method】Puncture perpendicularly 0.5 ~ 1.0 cun.

5. 下极俞 Xiajishu (EX-B 5)

【释义】下，上下之下；极，顶端，尽头处；俞，输注气血的穴位。下极，意指脊柱下部，气血输注之处，故名。

【定位】在腰部，当后正中线上，第3腰椎棘突下（图16-7）。

【解剖】皮肤→皮下组织→棘上韧带→棘间韧带。浅层有第4腰神经后支的内侧支和伴行的动、静脉。深层有棘突间的椎外静脉丛，第4腰神经的后支的分支和第4腰动、静脉背侧支的分支和属支。

【功用】强腰健肾。

【主治】①腰痛。②小便不利，遗尿。

【操作】直刺0.5~1.0寸。

【Meaning】Xia, lower; ji, extreme, pole; shu, point. Xiaji, means the lower part of the trunk of the body, where is qi and blood is transfused into.

【Location】On the midline of the lower back, below the spinous process of the 3rd lumbar vertebra (Fig 16 –7).

【Regional anatomy】Skin → subcutaneous tissue → supraspinal ligament → interspinal ligament. The superficial layer has posterior cutaneous branch of the 4th lumbar nerve, accompanying artery and vein. The deep layer has external venous plexus, posterior branch of the 4th lumbar nerve, dorsal branch of lumbar artery and vein.

【Properties】Strengthening waist and tonifying the kidney

【Indications】①Lumbago. ②Difficulty in urination, nocturnal enuresis.

【Needling method】Puncture perpendicularly 0.5 ~1.0 cun.

6. 腰眼 Yaoyan (EX-B 6)

【释义】腰，腰部；眼，眼窝。穴在腰部脊柱与髂后上嵴构成的凹陷处俗称腰眼，故名。

【定位】在腰部，当第4腰椎棘突下旁开约3.5寸凹陷中（图16－7）。

【解剖】皮肤→皮下组织→胸腰筋膜浅层和背阔肌腱膜→髂肋肌→胸腰筋膜深层→腰方肌。浅层主要有臀上皮神经和第4腰神经后支的分支。深层主要布有第4腰神经后支的肌支和第4腰动、静脉的分支或属支。

【功用】补肾壮腰，活血祛瘀。

【主治】腰痛，月经不调，带下，尿频。

【操作】直刺0.5～1.0寸。

【Meaning】Yao, lumbar part; yan, socket of eyeball. In general, "Yaoyan" is the depression, located within the lumbar vertebra column and the posterior, superior iliac spine. The name is called just as.

【Location】In the depression on the lower border of the 4th lumbar vertebra, 3.5 cun lateral to the posterior midline (Fig 16 –7).

【Regional anatomy】Skin→subcutaneous tissue→superficial layer of thoracolumbar fascia and tendinous membrance of latissimus dorsi→iliocostalis muscle→deep layer of thoracolumbar fascia→lumbar quadrate muscle. The superficial layer has posterior branch of the 4th lumbar nerves and superior clunial nerve. The deep layer has posterior muscular branch of the 4th lumbar nerve, branches of the 4th lumbar artery and vein.

【Properties】Tonify the kidney, strengthen the loins, activate blood flow and remove blood stasis.

【Indications】Lumbago, irregular menstruation, morbid leucorrhea and frequency of urination.

【Needling method】Puncture perpendicularly 0.5 ~1.0 cun.

7. 十七椎 Shiqizhui (EX-B 7)

【释义】十七，基数词；椎，椎骨。中医学称第1胸椎为1椎。穴在第5腰椎棘突下，故称十七椎，是以解剖部位命名的。

【定位】在腰部，当后正中线上，第5腰椎棘突下（图16－7）。

【解剖】皮肤→皮下组织→棘上韧带→棘间韧带。浅层主要布有第5腰神经后支的皮支和伴行的动、静脉。深层主要有第5腰神经后支的分支和棘突间的椎外（后）静脉。

【功用】补肾壮腰。

【主治】腰骶痛，痛经，崩漏，月经不调，遗尿。

【操作】直刺0.5~1.0寸。

【Meaning】Shiqi，number seventeen，zhui，vertebra. The 1st thoracic vertebra was called "first vertebra" in TCM. On account of location on the lower border of the spinous process of the 5th lumbar vertebra，this point was named "Shiqizhui"（the 17th Vertebra），according to the anatomy of Traditional Chinese Medicine.

【Location】On the posterior midline，in the depression below the spinous process of the 5th lumbar vertebra（Fig 16－7）.

【Regional anatomy】Skin → subcutaneous tissue → supraspinal ligament → interspinal ligament. The superficial layer has posterior cutaneous branch of the 5th lumbar nerve and accompanying artery and vein. The deep layer has posterior branches of the 5th lumbar nerve and interspinal（posterior）external vertebral veins.

【Properties】Tonify the kidney，strengthen the loin.

【Indications】Lumbago and sacrocoxalgia，dysmenorrhea，uterine bleeding，irregular menstruation，enuresis.

【Needling method】Puncture perpendicularly 0.5 ~1.0 cun.

8. 腰奇 Yaoqi（EX- B 8）

【释义】腰，腰部；奇，奇特的，非常的。穴在腰之最下部，治疗便秘、头痛、癫痫有明显效果，因而取名。

【定位】在骶部，当尾骨端直上2寸，骶角之间凹陷中（图16－7）。

【解剖】皮肤→皮下组织→棘上韧带。布有第2、3骶神经后支的分支及伴行的动、静脉。

【功用】宁神通络。

【主治】癫痫，头痛，失眠，便秘。

【操作】向上平刺1.0~1.5寸。

【Meaning】Yao，lumbar part；qi，special or extraordinary. The point is at the lower spot of the lumbar part. It was named on the outstanding effectiveness on treating constipation，headache and epilepsy.

【Location】On the low back，2 cun directly above the tip of coccyx，in the depression of the sacral horn（Fig 16－7）.

【Regional anatomy】Skin→subcutaneous tissue→supraspinal ligament. Distributed the posterior branches of the 2nd and 3rd sacral nerves and accompanying artery and vein.

【Properties】Tranquilize the mind, promote flow of qi and blood in the collateral.

【Indications】Epilepsy, headache, insomnia, constipation.

【Needling method】Puncture transversely 1.0 ~ 1.5 cun.

第四节 上肢部穴位
Extra Points of the Upper Extremities

1. 肘尖 Zhoujian (EX-UE 1)

【释义】肘，肘部；尖，尖端，顶点。肘尖是中医解剖学名词，指尺骨鹰嘴之突出部分，穴在其上，故名。

【定位】屈肘90°，在肘后部，屈肘当尺骨鹰嘴的尖端（图16－10）。

【解剖】皮肤→皮下组织→鹰嘴皮下囊→肱三头肌腱。布有前臂背侧皮神经和肘关节周围动、静脉网。

【功用】化痰散结，清热解毒。

【主治】瘰疬，痈疽，疔疮。

【操作】灸。

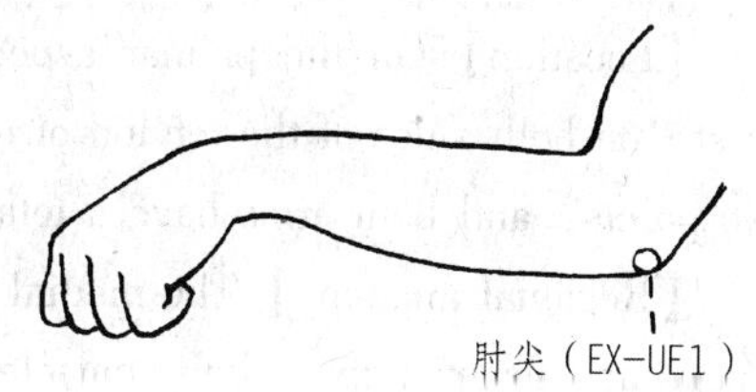

图16－10
Fig 16－10

【Meaning】Zhou, elbow; jian, tip or apex. Zhoujian (tip of elbow) is an anatomical term of Traditional Chinese Medicine; which is the process of the ulnar olecranon. Because the point is on it, the name was called it.

【Location】When the elbow flexed, the point is on the tip of ulnar olecranon (Fig 16－10).

【Regional anatomy】Skin→subcutaneous tissue→subcutaneous bursa of olecranon→tendon of triceps brachii. Distributes posterior antebrachial cutaneous nerve, rete formed of arteries and veins around cubital articulation.

【Properties】Reduce phlegm, resolve masses, clearing away heat and toxic material.

【Indications】Scrofula, superficial infections, furuncle.

【Needling method】Moxibustion is applicable.

2. 二白 Erbai (EX-UE 2)

【释义】二，基数词；白，白色。穴在前臂掌面腕上，桡侧腕屈肌腱内外侧各一，在外侧的临近肺经。肺在色为白，故名二白。

【定位】伸腕仰掌。在前臂掌侧，腕横纹上4寸，桡侧腕屈肌腱的两侧，一侧各1穴，一臂2穴，左右两臂共4穴（图16－11）。

【解剖】臂内侧穴：皮肤→皮下组织→掌长肌腱与桡侧腕屈肌腱之间→指浅屈肌→正中神经→拇长屈肌→前臂骨间膜。浅层布有前臂外侧皮神经和前臂正中静脉的属支。深层布有正中神经、正中动脉。

臂外侧穴：皮肤→皮下组织→桡侧腕屈肌与肱桡肌腱之间→指浅屈肌→拇长屈肌。浅层布有前臂外侧皮神经和头静脉的属支。深层有桡动、静脉。

【功用】活血通经。

【主治】痔疾，脱肛，前臂痛，胸肋痛。

【操作】直刺0.5～0.8寸。

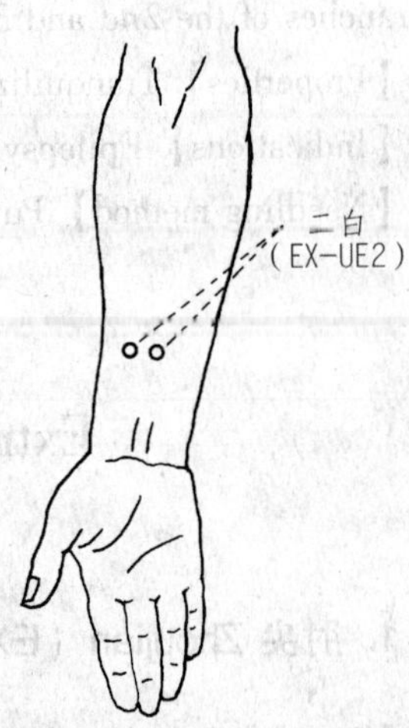

图16－11

Fig 16－11

【Meaning】Er，number two；bai，white. The point are located above the transverse wrist crease at the palmar aspect of forearm and on the medial and lateral sides of the tendon of flexor carpi radialis. The lateral one is close to lung meridian. Because the corresponding color of Lung is white，the points were called "Erbai".

【Location】On the palmar aspect of the forearm，4 cun above the transverse crease of the wrist，on both sides of the tendon of m. flexor carpi radialis. Each side has one point，each arm has two points，and both arms have a total of four points（Fig 16－11）.

【Regional anatomy】The medial one：skin→subcutaneous tissue→between tendon of palmaris longus and flexor carpi radialis muscle→musculus flexor digitorum superficial→median nerve→flexor pollicis longus→interosseous membrane of forearm. The superficial layer has lateral antebrachial cutaneous nerve and branches of median vein of forearm. The deep layer has median nerve and median artery.

The lateral one：skin→subcutaneous tissue→between flexor carpi radialis muscle and tendon of brachioradialis→musculus flexor digitorum superficial→flexor pollicis longus. The superficial layer has lateral antebrachial cutaneous nerve and branches of cephalic vein. The deep layer has radial artery and vein.

【Properties】Activate flow of blood in the meridians and collaterals.

【Indications】Hemorrhoids，prolapse，pain in the arm，chest and hypochondriac region.

【Needling method】Puncture perpendicularly 0.5～0.8cun.

3. 中泉 Zhongquan（EX-UE 3）

【释义】中，中间；泉，泉眼，在此指体表之凹陷处。穴在腕背面中央，当阳溪与阳池之间的凹陷处，故名。

【定位】伏掌，在腕背侧横纹中，当指总伸肌腱桡侧的凹陷处（图16－12）。

【解剖】皮肤→皮下组织→指伸肌腱与桡侧腕短伸肌腱之间。布有前臂后皮神经和桡神经浅支的分支，手背静脉网，桡动脉腕背支的分支。

【功用】理气宽胸，调和气血。

【主治】①胸胁胀满，咳嗽，气喘，心痛。②胃脘疼痛。③掌中热。

【操作】直刺0.3～0.5寸。

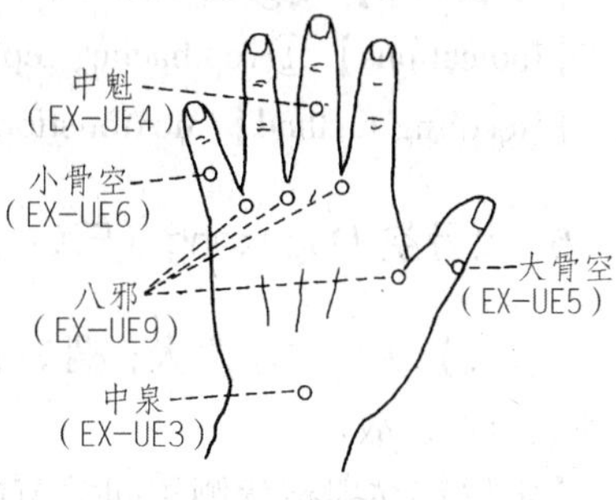

图 16－12

Fig 16－12

【Meaning】Zhong, middle; quan, the hole of spring, here it means the depression of the body surface. The point is on the middle of the wrist dorsum and in the depression between Yangxi (LI 5) and Yangchi (SJ 4). So, the point was named.

【Location】On the dorsal crease of the wrist, in the depression on the radial side of the tendon of common extensor muscle of fingers (Fig 16－12).

【Regional anatomy】Skin→subcutaneous tissue→between tendon of extensor digitorum and tendon of extensor carpi radialis brevis. Distributed posterior antebrachial cutaneous nerve, superficial radial nerve, dorsal vein rete of hand and dorsal carpal branch of radial artery.

【Properties】Regulating vital energy, coordinating qi and blood.

【Indications】①Fullness chest and hypochondrium, cough, asthma, heartache. ②Stomachache. ③Feverish palms.

【Needling method】Puncture perpendicularly 0.3～0.5cun.

4. 中魁 Zhongkui (EX- UE 4)

【释义】中，中指；魁，为首的，突出的。握拳时，手中指第1指间关节较为突出，穴在其上，故名。

【定位】握拳，掌心向下。在中指背侧近侧指间关节的中点处（图16－12）。

【解剖】皮肤→皮下组织→指背筋膜。布有指背神经，其桡侧支来自桡神经，其尺侧支来自尺神经。血管有来自掌背动脉的指背动脉和掌背静脉网的属支指背静脉。

【功用】和胃降逆。

【主治】①牙痛，鼻衄。②噎膈，翻胃，呕吐。

【操作】灸。

【Meaning】Zhong, here means middle finger; kui, first and protrusive. When the fist was made, the proximal interphalangeal joint of the middle finger is the most protrusive. So, the point was named.

【Location】In the midpoint of the proximal interphalangeal joint of the dorsum of the middle finger (Fig 16－12).

【Regional anatomy】skin→subcutaneous tissue→dorsal aponeurosis. Distributed dorsal digital nerves, which radial branch comes from radial nerve and ulnar branch comes from ulnar nerve. Blood vessels comes from dorsal metacarpal arteries dorsal digital arteries and dorsal digital vein of volardorsal vein rete.

【Properties】Regulate the function of the stomach and lower down upward adverse flow of qi.

【Indications】①Toothache, epistaxis. ② dysphagia, regurgitation and vomiting.

【Needling method】Moxibustion.

5. 大骨空 Dagukong（EX- UE 5)

【释义】大，大小之大；骨，骨头；空，空隙。穴在大拇指背面，第1指骨与第2指骨之间关节处，故名。

【定位】在拇指背侧指间关节的中点处（图16－12）。

【解剖】皮肤→皮下组织→拇长伸肌腱。布有桡神经的指背神经，指背动脉和指背静脉。

【功用】退翳明目。

【主治】①目痛，目翳。②吐泻，衄血。

【操作】灸。

【Meaning】Da, big; gu, bone; kong, space. The point is on the dorsum of thumb (big finger in chinese) and the joint between the 1st and 2nd phalangeal bone. So it was called "Dagukong".

【Location】On the dorsal side of the thumb, at the center of the interphalangeal joint. (Fig 16－12)

【Regional anatomy】Skin → subcutaneous tissue → tendon of extensor pollicis longus. Distributed dorsal digital nerves of radial nerve, dorsal digital arteries and veins.

【Properties】Improve acuity of vision and remove nebula.

【Indications】①Eye pain, conjunctivitis. ②Vomiting and diarrhea, apostaxis.

【Needling method】Moxibustion.

6. 小骨空 Xiaogukong（EX- UE 6)

【释义】小，大小之小；骨，骨头；空，空隙。穴在小指背面，第1指骨与第2指骨之间关节处，故名。

【定位】在小指背侧近端指间关节中点处（图16－12）。

【解剖】皮肤→皮下组织→指背腱膜。布有指背动、静脉的分支及属支和尺神经的指背神经的分支。

【功用】明目止痛。

【主治】目赤肿痛，目翳，咽喉肿痛。

【操作】灸。

【Meaning】Xiao, small; gu, bone; kong, space. The point is on the dorsum of small finger, the joint between the 1st and 2nd phalangeal bone. So it was called "Xiaogukong".

【Location】On the dorsal side of the litter finger, at the center of the proximal interphalangeal joint (Fig 16 – 12).

【Regional anatomy】Skin→subcutaneous tissue→dorsal aponeurosis. Distributed dorsal digital arteries and veins, dorsal digital nerve of ulnar nerve.

【Properties】Improve eyesight and relieve pain.

【Indications】Red swollen and painful eye, conjunctivitis, sore throat.

【Needling method】Moxibustion.

7. 腰痛点 Yaotongdian (EX- UE 7)

【释义】腰，腰部；痛，疼痛；点，很小的部位。此穴能治疗腰痛，故名。

【定位】在手背侧，当第2、3掌骨及第4、5掌骨之间，当腕横纹与掌指关节中点处。一侧2穴，左右共4个穴位（图16－13）。

【解剖】一穴：皮肤→皮下组织→指伸肌腱和桡侧腕短伸肌腱。另一穴：皮肤→皮下组织→小指伸肌腱与第4指伸肌腱之间。此二穴处布有手背静脉网和掌背动脉，有桡神经的浅支和布有尺神经的手背支。

【功用】理气消肿，通络止痛。

【主治】急性腰扭伤。

【操作】直刺0.3～0.5寸。

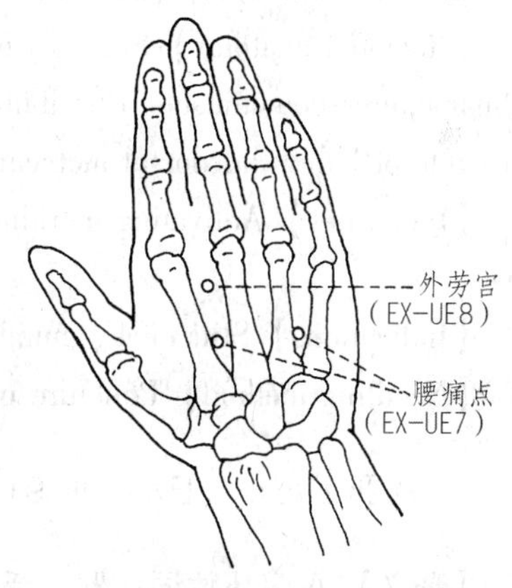

图16－13
Fig 16－13

【Meaning】Yao, lumbar; tong, pain; dian, point or very small portion. It is a effective point for treating the lumbago. So, it was named.

【Location】On the dorsum of the hand, between the 2nd and 3rd, 4th and 5th metacarpal bones, at the midpoint from the line through the metacarpophalangeal joint to the transverse crease of the wrist. One hand has two points, a total of four points on both hands (Fig 16 – 13).

【Regional anatomy】The one point: skin→subcutaneous tissue→between tendon of extensor digitorum and tendon of extensor carpi radialis brevis. The other point: skin→subcutaneous tissue→between tendon of extensor digiti minimi and the forth tendon of extensor digitorum. Distributed dorsal metacarpal venous rete and dorsal metacarpal arteries, superficial radial nerve and volardorsal branch of ulnar nerve.

【Properties】Regulating vital energy and detumescence, activating meridians and stop pain.

【Indications】Acute lumbar muscle sprain.

【Needling method】Puncture perpendicularly 0.3～0.5 cun.

8. 外劳宫 Wailaogong (EX- UE 8)

【释义】外，内外之外；劳，劳动；宫，宫室。手为劳动器官，手心有穴名劳宫。此穴在手背面，与劳宫相对，故名。

【定位】在手背侧，当第2、3掌骨间，指掌关节后约0.5寸（图16－13）。

【解剖】皮肤→皮下组织→第2骨间背侧肌→第1骨间掌侧肌。布有桡神经浅支的指背神经，手背静脉网和掌背动脉。

【功用】通络止痛，健脾消积。

【主治】落枕，手指麻木，手指屈伸不利。

【操作】直刺0.5～0.8寸。

【Meaning】Wai，lateral or outer；lao，work；gong，palace or room. The hand is a working organ and there is an other point named Laogong（PC 8）on the palmar center. But this point is on the dorsum and opposite to Laogong（PC 8）. So，it was named Wailaogong.

【Location】On the dorsum of the hand，between the 2nd and 3rd metacarpal bones，0.5 cun posterior to the metacarpophalangeal joint（Fig 16－13）.

【Regional anatomy】Skin→subcutaneous tissue→the and dorsal interosseous muscle→the 1st palmar interosseous muscle. Distributed of dorsal digital nerves of superficial radial nerve，dorsal venous rete of hand and dorsal metacarpal arteries.

【Properties】Activating meridians and stop pain，strengthening the spleen and rids of blood stasis.

【Indications】Stiff neck，numbness of the fingers.

【Needling method】Puncture perpendicularly 0.5～0.8 cun.

9. 八邪 Baxie（EX- UE 9）

【释义】八，基数词；邪，泛指引起疾病的因素。一名八穴，能治疗因受邪气所致病症，故名。

【定位】微握拳，在手背侧，第1～5指间，指蹼缘后方赤白肉际处，左右共8个穴位（图16－12）。

【解剖】皮肤→皮下组织→骨间背侧肌→骨间掌侧肌→蚓状肌。浅层布有掌背动、静脉或指背动、静脉和指背神经。深层有指掌侧总动、静脉或指掌侧固有动、静脉和指掌侧固有神经。

【功用】祛瘀通络，清热解毒。

【主治】①烦热，目痛。②毒蛇咬伤，手背肿痛，手指麻木。

【操作】向下斜刺0.5～0.8寸，或点刺出血。

【Meaning】Ba，number eight；xie，in general sense，it means any pathogenic factor. It includes 8 points with one name and can be used to treat the disease caused by any exogenous pathogenic factor. So it was named.

【Location】When a loose fist is made，the points are on the dorsum of the hand，proximal to the margins of the webbing between all five fingers，at the junction of the red and white skin. Both hands altogether have a total of eight points（Fig 16－12）.

【Regional anatomy】Skin→subcutaneous tissue→dorsal interossei→palmar interossei→ lumbrical. The superficial layer has dorsal metacarpal arteries and vein, dorsal digital arteries and vein, dorsal digital nerves. the deep layer has common palmar digital artery and vein, proper palmar digital artery and vein, proper palmar digital nerve.

【Properties】Remove blood stasis, activate flow of qi and blood in the channels and collaterals, clear away heat, remove toxic materials.

【Indications】①Vexation, fever, eye pain. ② Venomous snake - bite, swelling and pain of the dorsum of the hand, numbness of the fingers.

【Needling method】Puncture obliquely 0.5 ~ 0.8 cun, or prick to induce bleeding.

10. 四缝 Sifeng (EX- UE 10)

【释义】四，基数词；缝，缝隙。穴在手尺侧四指掌面，一手4穴，故名。

【定位】仰掌伸指。在第2~5指掌面侧，近端指关节的中点，一侧4穴（图16-14）。

【解剖】皮肤→皮下组织→指深屈肌腱。各穴的血管：指掌侧固有动、静脉的分支或属支和指皮下静脉。各穴的神经：浅层有掌侧固有神经，深层有正中神经肌支和尺神经肌支。

【功用】消积化痰，和中健脾。

【主治】小儿疳积，百日咳。

【操作】直刺0.1~0.2寸，挤出少量黄白色透明样黏液或出血。

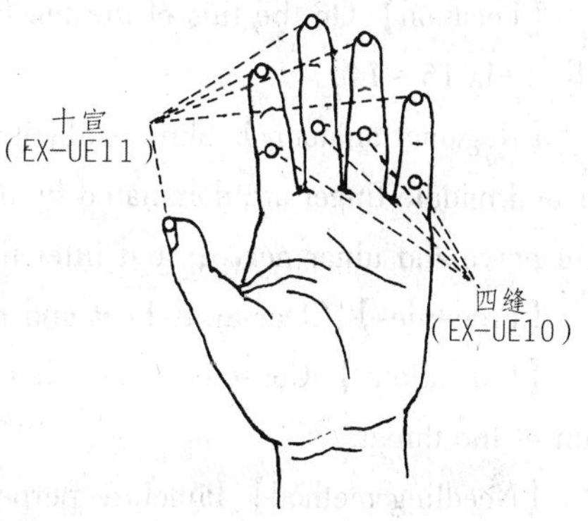

图16-14

Fig 16-14

【Meaning】Si, number four; feng, crevice, The point is located on the ulnar palmar aspect of the index, middle, ring and little fingers. Four points on each hand. So it was called "Sifeng".

【Location】On the palmar surface, midpoint of the transverse crease of the proximal interphalangeal joints of the index, middle, ring and little fingers. 4 points on one side, with a total of 8 points on both bands (Fig 16-14).

【Regional anatomy】Skin→subcutaneous tissue→tendon of flexor digitorum profundus. Blood vessels of each point: branches of proper palmar digital artery and vein, digital subcutaneous veins. Nerves of each point: the superficial layer has proper palmar digital nerves, the deep layer has muscular branches of median nerve and ulnar nerve.

【Properties】Promote digestion, dissolve phlegm, regulate function of the middle energizer and strengthen the spleen.

【Indications】Infantile malnutrition, whooping cough.

【Needling method】Puncture perpendicularly 0.1 ~ 0.2 cun, Prick to induce bleeding or squeeze out a small amount of yellowish viscous fluid from the crease.

11. 十宣 Shixuan (EX-UE 11)

【释义】十，基数词；宣，宣泄。穴在两手指端，有宣泄因邪气引起的高热、头痛、咽喉肿痛等病症的作用，故名。

【定位】在手十指尖端，距指甲游离缘0.1寸，左右共10穴（图16-14）。

【解剖】皮肤→皮下组织。各穴的神经：拇指到中指的十宣穴由正中神经支配；无名指的十宣由桡侧的正中神经和尺神经双重支配；小指的十宣穴由尺神经支配。

【功用】清热，开窍醒神。

【主治】昏迷，高热，晕厥，中暑，癫痫，咽喉肿痛。

【操作】直刺0.1~0.2寸，或用三棱针点刺出血。

【Meaning】Shi, number ten; xuan, expel. The points are located at the tips of ten fingers of both hands and it can be used to expel the exogenous pathogenic factors to treat the disease such as the high fever, headache, sore - throat and so on. So it was named.

【Location】On the tips of the ten fingers, about 0.1 cun distal to the nails, 10 acupoints totally (Fig 16-14).

【Regional anatomy】Skin→subcutaneous tissue. Innervation of each point: thumb, index finger and middle finger are dominated by median nerve, ring finger is doubly dominated by radial median nerve and ulnar nerve, and litter finger is dominated by ulnar nerve.

【Properties】Clear away heat and restore resuscitation.

【Indications】Consciousness, high fever, dizziness, heat stroke, epilepsy, swelling and pain of the throat.

【Needling method】Puncture perpendicularly 0.1~0.2 cun, or prick to with a three - edged needle to reduce bleeding.

第五节 下肢部穴位
Extra Points of the Lower Extremities

1. 髋骨 Kuangu (EX-LE 1)

【释义】髋，有髂骨组成骨盆之大骨；骨，骨头。这是以中医学名词命名的穴名。

【定位】仰卧。在大腿前面下部，当梁丘两旁各1.5寸，一侧2穴，左右共4个穴位（图16-15）。

【解剖】外侧髋骨穴：皮肤→皮下组织→股外侧肌。浅层布有股神经前皮支和股外侧皮神经，深层有旋股外侧动、静脉降支的分支或属支。内侧髋骨穴：皮肤→皮下组织→股内侧肌。浅层布有股神经前皮支，深层有股深动脉的肌支等。

【功用】疏风祛邪，舒筋通络。

【主治】鹤膝风，下肢痿痹。

【操作】直刺0.5～1.0寸。

【Meaning】Kuan，ilium，a big bone，constructing a component of the pelvis；gu，bone. The point was named with the term of Traditional Chinese Medicine.

【Location】Two points on each thigh，in the lower part of the anterior surface of the thigh at the superior of the lateral condyle of the distal femur，1.5 cun lateral and medial to ST 34.（Fig 16－15）

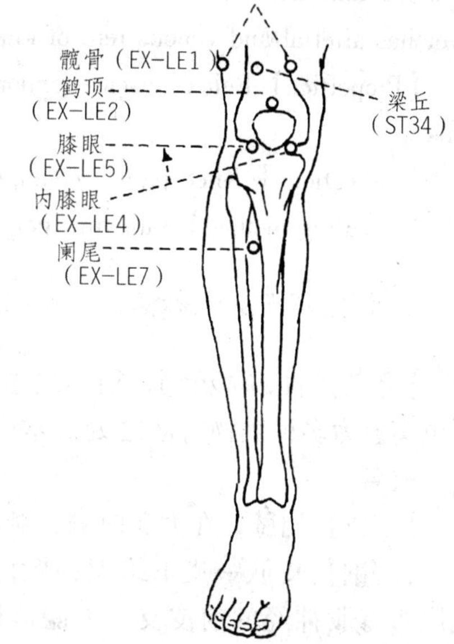

图16－15

Fig 16－15

【Regional anatomy】The lateral one：Skin→subcutaneous tissue→vastus lateralis. The superficial layer has anterior cutaneous branch of femoral nerve and lateral femoral cutaneous nerve. The deep layer has branch of lateral femoral circumflex artery and vein.

The medial one：Skin→subcutaneous tissue→vastus medialis. The superficial layer has anterior cutaneous branches of femoral nerve. The deep layer has muscular branch of profunda femoris artery.

【Properties】Expel wind，eliminate pathogens and relax muscle and tendons.

【Indications】Paralysis of knee and lower extremities.

【Needling method】Puncture perpendicularly 0.5～1.0 cun.

2. 鹤顶 Heding（EX-LE 2）

【释义】鹤，鸟类的一种，俗称仙鹤；顶，人或物体上最高的部分，如头顶。膝关节状如头顶，故名鹤顶。

【定位】在膝上部，髌底的中点上方凹陷处（图16－15）。

【解剖】皮肤→皮下组织→股四头肌腱。浅层布有股神经前皮支和大隐静脉的属支。深层有膝关节的动、静脉网。

【功用】舒筋活络，通利关节。

【主治】膝关节酸痛，腿足无力，鹤膝风。

【操作】直刺0.5～0.8寸。

【Meaning】He，a genus of the birds，crane in general name；ding，the highest point of human body or object such as the vertex. The knee joint looks like a crane's head. So，it was called "Heding".

【Location】Above the knee，in the depression of the midpoint of the superior patellar border（Fig 16－15）.

【Regional anatomy】Skin→subcutaneous tissue→tendon of quadriceps femoris. The superficial layer has anterior cutaneous branch of femoral nerve and branches of great saphenous vein. the deep layer has arterial and venous rete of knee joint.

【Properties】Relax muscles tendons, activate flow of qi and blood in the meridians and collaterals.

【Indications】Knee pain, weakness of the leg and foot, palsy.

【Needling method】Puncture perpendicularly 0.5～0.8cun.

3. 百虫窝 Baichongwo（EX-LE 3）

【释义】百，基数词，很多之意；虫，虫类，引起疾病的微生物等；窝，动物的巢窝。百虫窝意为多种生物寄居之处，常引起皮肤瘙痒、荨麻疹等病症。针灸此穴能治疗这些病症，故名。

【定位】屈膝，在大腿内侧，髌底内侧端上 3 寸，即血海上 1 寸（图 16－16）。

【解剖】皮肤→皮下组织→股内侧肌。浅层布有股神经的前皮支，大隐静脉的属支。深层有股动、静脉的肌支和股神经的分支。

【功用】解毒杀虫，祛风止痒。

【主治】皮肤瘙痒，风疹，湿疹，疮疡，蛔虫病。

【操作】直刺 0.5～1.0 寸。

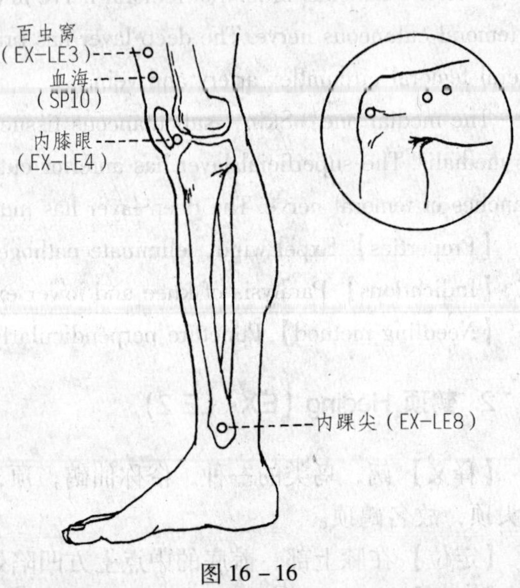

图 16－16

Fig 16－16

【Meaning】Bai, hundred, lots of; chong, insect, microorganism; wo, nest. The point name means the place where is the nest of lots of microorganism caused diseases like pruritus and urticaria, It can be use to treat these diseases.

【Location】When the knee is flexed, the point is on the medial aspect of the thigh, 3 cun superior to the medial end of the patella, 1 cun above Xuehai（SP 10）（Fig 16－16）.

【Regional anatomy】Skin→subcutaneous tissue→vastus medialis. The superficial layer has anterior cutaneous branch of femoral nerve and branch of great saphenous vein. The deep layer has muscular banches of femoral artery and vein, femoral nerve.

【Properties】Detoxicate, destroy parasites, expel wind and relieve itching.

【Indications】Itching of the skin, skin ulcers on the lower portion of the body, rubella, eczema, ascariasis.

【Needling method】Puncture perpendicularly 0.5～1.0 cun.

4. 内膝眼 Neixiyan（EX-LE 4）

【释义】内，内外之内；膝，膝部；眼，眼窝。穴在膝眼之内侧，故名。

【定位】屈膝，在髌韧带内侧凹陷处（图 16－16）。

【解剖】皮肤→皮下组织→髌韧带与髌内侧支持带之间→膝关节囊、翼状皱襞。浅层布有隐神经的髌下支和股神经的前皮支。深层有膝关节的动、静脉网。

【功用】祛风湿，利关节。

【主治】膝肿痛。

【操作】向膝关节中心成45°角斜刺0.5～1.0寸。

【Meaning】nei, medial; xi, knee; yan, the socket of eyeball. The points were in the depressions which located on the medial side of patella ligament on the knee joint look like the socket of eyeball in shape. So, it was called the name.

【Location】In the depression medial to patellar ligament when the knee is flexed（Fig 16－16）.

【Regional anatomy】Skin→subcutaneous tissue→between patellar ligament and medial patellar retinaculum→capsula articularis genus, plica alares. The superficial layer has infrapatellar branch of saphenous nerve and anterior cutaneous branch of femoral nerve. The deep layer has kneed arterial and venous rete.

【Properties】Expel wind－dampness, benefit articulations.

【Indications】Swelling and pain in the knee.

【Needling method】Puncture obliquely 0.5～1.0cun towards the center of the knee on 45°.

5. 膝眼 Xiyan（EX-LE 5）

【释义】膝，膝部；眼，眼窝。膝关节髌韧带两侧之凹陷处，状如眼窝，穴在其上，故名。

【定位】屈膝，在髌韧带两侧凹陷处。在内侧的称膝眼（图 16－15）。

【解剖】皮肤→皮下组织→髌韧带与髌外侧支持带之间→膝关节囊、翼状皱襞。浅层布有腓肠外侧皮神经，股神经前皮支，隐神经的髌下支和膝关节动、静脉网。深层有膝关节腔。

【功用】祛风湿，利关节。

【主治】膝肿痛，脚气。

【操作】向膝关节中心成45°角斜刺0.5～1.0寸。

【Meaning】Xi, knee; yan, the socket of eyeball. The points were in the depressions which located on the lateral side of patella ligament on the knee joint look like the socket of eyeball in shape. So, it was called the name.

【Location】In the depression medial and lateral to patellar ligament when the knee is flexed. The lateral side is called Xiyan (Fig 16 – 15).

【Regional anatomy】Skin→subcutaneous tissue→between patellar ligament and lateral patellar retinaculum→capsula articularis genus, plica alares. The superficial layer has lateral sural cutaneous nerve, anterior cutaneous branches of femoral nerve, the infrapatellar branch of the saphenous nerve, kneed arterial and venous rete. the deep layer has keen joint cavity.

【Properties】Expel wind – dampness, benefit articulations.

【Indications】Swelling and pain in the knee, beriberi.

【Needling method】Puncture obliquely 0.5 ~ 1.0cun towards the center of the knee on 45°.

6. 胆囊 Dannang (EX- LE 6)

【释义】胆，胆腑之胆；囊，中空之袋状物。

【定位】在小腿外侧上部，当腓骨小头前下方凹陷处直下2寸（图16 – 17）。

【解剖】皮肤→皮下组织→腓骨长肌。浅层布有腓肠外侧皮神经分布。深层有腓浅神经、腓深神经干和胫前动、静脉。

【功用】利胆通络。

【主治】急、慢性胆囊炎，胆石症，胆道蛔虫症，胆绞痛。

【操作】直刺1.0 ~ 1.5寸。

【Meaning】Dan, gallbladder; nang, a hollow bag – like object.

【Location】On the superior lateral aspect of the lower leg, 2 cun directly below the depression anterior and inferior to the small head of the fibula (Fig 16 – 17).

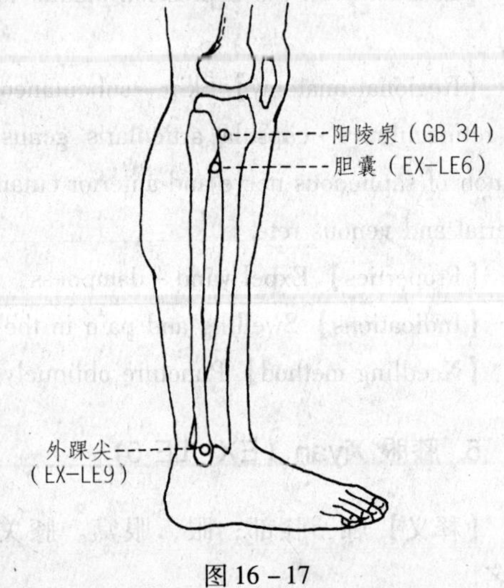

图 16 – 17
Fig 16 – 17

【Regional anatomy】Skin→subcutaneous tissue→fibularis longus. The superficial layer has lateral sural cutaneous nerve. the deep layer has superficial fibular nerve, deep fibular nerve trunk, anterior tibial artery and vein.

【Properties】Benefit gallbladder and activate flow of blood and qi in the meridians and collaterals.

【Indications】Acute and chronic cholecystitis, cholelithiasis, biliary ascariasis, gallbladder colic.

【Needling method】Puncture perpendicularly 1.0 ~ 1.5 cun.

7. 阑尾 Lanwei (EX-LE 7)

【释义】阑，将尽之意；尾，尾部。阑尾是解剖学名词，盲肠下端蚯蚓状的突起。阑尾发炎时，常在小腿足三里与上巨虚之间出现明显压痛点，有助于诊治阑尾炎，故名。

【定位】在小腿前侧上部，当犊鼻下5寸，胫骨前缘旁开1横指（图16-15）。

【解剖】皮肤→皮下组织→胫骨前肌→小腿骨间膜→胫骨后肌。浅层布有腓肠外侧皮神经和浅静脉。深层有腓深神经和胫前动、静脉。

【功用】调肠止痛，通经活络。

【主治】急、慢性阑尾炎。

【操作】直刺1.0~1.5寸。

【Meaning】Lan, will end soon; wei, tail. Lanwei (appendix) is an anatomical term which is an earthworm like process on the lower end of cecum. There is an apparent tender point between Zusanli (ST 36) and Shangjuxu (ST 37) on the shank. It is helpful for diagnosing the appendicitis. So, it was also named Lanwei (appendix point).

【Location】On the superior anterior aspect of the lower leg, 5 cun below Dubi (ST 35), one finger-breadth from the anterior crest of the tibia (Fig 16-15).

【Regional anatomy】Skin→subcutaneous tissue→tibialis anterior→crural interosseous membrance→tibialis posterior. The superficial layer has lateral sural cutaneous nerve and superficial vein. The deep layer has deep fibular nerve, anterior tibial artery and vein.

【Properties】Regulate the movement of the bowel to relieve pain, promote blood flow in the meridians and collaterals.

【Indications】Acute and chronic appendicitis.

【Needling method】Puncture perpendicularly 1.0~1.5cun.

8. 内踝尖 Neihuaijian (EX-LE 8)

【释义】内，内外之内；踝，踝关节部；尖，骨之突出部。胫骨下端之膨大部叫内踝，内踝之最突出点叫做内踝尖，穴在其上，故名。

【定位】正坐位或仰卧位。在足内侧面，内踝凸起处（图16-16）。

【解剖】皮肤→皮下组织→内踝。布有隐神经的小腿内侧皮支的分支，胫前动脉的内踝网，内踝前动脉的分支和胫后动脉的内踝支。

【功用】舒筋通络。

【主治】乳蛾，齿痛，小儿不语，霍乱转筋。

【操作】禁刺，可灸。

【Meaning】Nei, medial; huai, malleolus; jian, tip. The medial malleolus is a process of the lower end of tibia, the highest point of the malleolus was called "Neihuaijian" (tip of medial malleolus), so it was named.

【Location】 On the medial surface of the foot, on the top of the medial malleolus (Fig 16－16).

【Regional anatomy】 Skin → subcutaneous tissue → medial malleolus. Distributed saphenous nerve medial crural cutaneous branches, medial malleolar rete of anterior tibial artery, branches of anterior malleolar artery and medial malleolar branches of posterior tibial artery.

【Properties】 Relax tendons and activate collaterals.

【Indications】 Toothache, swelling and pain of the throat, infantile mute, cholera muscle spasms.

【Needling method】 Acupuncture is contraindicated, moxibustion is applicable.

9. 外踝尖 Waihuaijian (EX－LE 9)

【释义】外，内外之外；踝，踝关节部；尖，骨之突出部。腓骨下端之膨大部叫外踝，其向外方之最突出点叫外踝尖，穴在其上，故名。

【定位】正坐位或仰卧位。在足外侧面，外踝凸起处（图 16－17）。

【解剖】皮肤→皮下组织→外踝。布有胫前动脉的内踝网，腓动脉的外踝支和腓肠神经及腓浅神经的分支。

【功用】舒筋通络。

【主治】①十趾拘急，脚外廉转筋，脚气。②齿痛，重舌。

【操作】禁刺，可灸。

【Meaning】Wai, lateral; huai, malleolus; jian, tip. The lateral malleolus is a process of the lower end of fibula. The highest point of the lateral malleolus was called "Waihuaijian" (tip of lateral malleolus). The point is named anatomically.

【Location】 On the lateral surface of the foot, on the top of the external malleolus (Fig 16－17).

【Regional anatomy】 Skin→subcutaneous tissue→lateral malleolar. Distributed anterior tibial artery lateral malleolar rete, lateral malleolar branches of fibular artery, branches of sural nerve and superficial fibular nerve.

【Properties】 Relax tendons and activate collaterals.

【Indications】 ①Spasm of the toes, muscle spasms of the foot on the lateral margin, beriberi. ② Toothache, double tongue.

【Needling method】 Acupuncture is contraindicated, moxibustion is applicable.

10. 八风 Bafeng (EX－LE 10)

【释义】八，基数词；风，风寒之风，致病因素之一。一名八穴，在足五趾之趾间缝纹头处，故名八风。

【定位】在足背侧，第 1～5 趾间，趾蹼缘后方赤白肉际处，一侧 4 穴，共 8 穴（图16－

18）。

【解剖】第1趾与第2趾之间的八风穴，层次解剖同行间穴。第2趾与第3趾之间的八风穴，层次解剖同内庭穴。第4趾与小趾之间的八风穴，层次解剖同侠溪穴。第3趾与第4趾之间的八风穴的层次解剖：皮肤→皮下组织→第3、4趾的趾长、短伸肌腱之间→第3、4跖骨头之间。浅层布有足背中间皮神经的趾背神经和足背浅静脉网。深层有跖背动脉，跖背静脉的属支趾背静脉。

【功用】活血祛瘀，清热解毒。

【主治】趾痛，毒蛇咬伤，足跗肿痛，脚气。

【操作】斜刺0.5～0.8寸，或点刺出血。

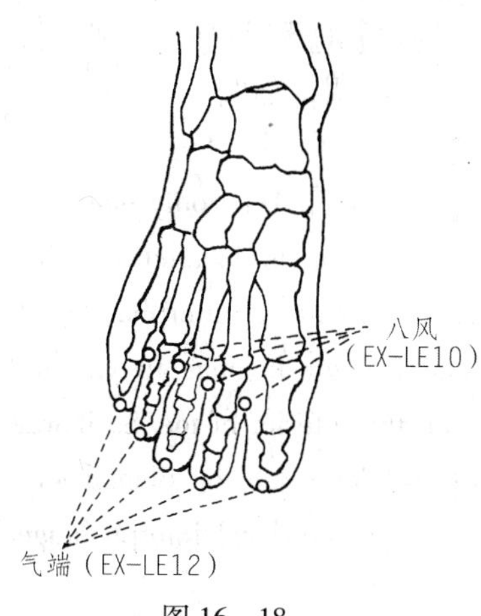

图16－18

Fig 16－18

【Meaning】Ba, number eight; feng, wind, a kind of the pathogenic factors. Eight points are called by one name, they are located at the webs between toes on the dorsum of foot. Eight points in a group are include, so it was called "Bafeng".

【Location】On the dorsum of foot, in the depression between the webbing of the toes, at the junction of the red and white skin. proximal to the web margin. One foot has four points, both feet have a total of eight points (Fig 16－18).

【Regional anatomy】Layered anatomy of the point between the big toe and the and toe is similar to Xingjian (LR 2). Layered anatomy of the point between the 2nd toe and the 3rd toe is similar to Neiting (ST 44). Layered anatomy of the point between the 4th toe and the little toe is similar to Xiaxi (GB 43). Layered anatomy of the point between the 3rd toe and the 4th toe: skin→subcutaneous tissue→between basilar part of the 3rd caput phalangis digitorum pedis and the 4th caput phalangis digitorum pedis→between the 3rd and 4th caput phalangis digitorum pedis. The superficial layer has dorsal digital nerve of foot of intermediate dorsal cutaneous nerve of foot and dorsal pedal vein rete. the deep layer has dorsal metatarsal artery and dorsal digital vein.

【Properties】Activate blood flow and remove blood stasis, clear away heat and remove toxic material.

【Indications】Venomous snake－bite, swelling and pain of the dorsum of the foot, beriberi.

【Needling method】Puncture obliquely 0.5～0.8 cun; or prick to reduce bleeding.

11. 独阴 Duyin（EX－LE 11）

【释义】独，一个；阴，阴阳之阴。穴在足第2趾下面之第2趾间关节横纹上，下为阴，而足趾下面只有此一穴，故名独阴。

【定位】在足第2趾的趾侧远侧趾间关节的中点（图16－19）。

【解剖】皮肤→皮下组织→趾短、长屈肌腱。布有趾足底固有神经，趾底固有动、静脉的分支或属支。

【功用】调理冲任。

【主治】①胸胁痛，卒心痛，呕吐；②胞衣不下，月经不调，疝气。

【操作】直刺 0.1～0.2 寸。孕妇禁用。

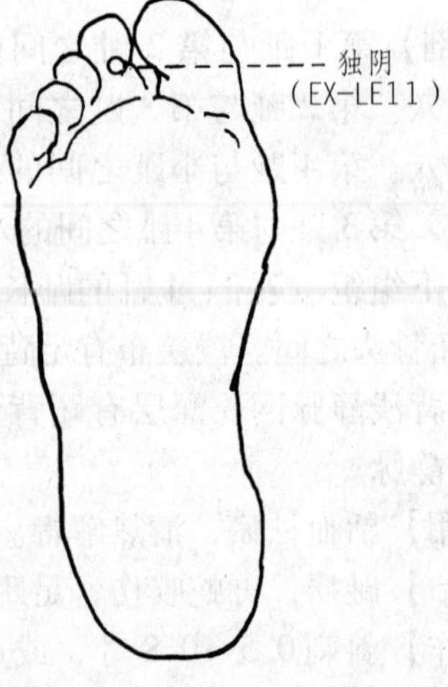

图 16－19

Fig 16－19

【Meaning】Du，only one，yin，the yin of yin－yang. The point is located on the inferior transverse crease of proximal interphalangeal joint of the 2nd toe. The inferior belongs to yin and there is only one point on the inferior of toe. So it was named "Duyin".

【Location】On the plantar side of the 2nd toe，at the center of the distal interphalangeal joint.（Fig 16－19）

【Regional anatomy】Skin→subcutaneous tissue→tendon of flexor digitorum brevis and tendon of flexor digitorum longus. Distributed proper plantar digital nerves，branch of proper plantar digital arteries and veins.

【Properties】Regulate thoroughfare vessel and conception vessel.

【Indications】①Pain in the hypochondrium，heartache，vomiting. ②Fetal death，irregular menstruation，hernia.

【Needling method】Puncture perpendicularly 0. 1～0. 2 cun. Pregnant is forbidden.

12. 气端 Qiduan（EX-LE12）

【释义】气，经脉之气；端，趾端。足十趾端是经脉之气所出之处。穴在其上，故名。

【定位】在足十趾尖端，距趾甲游离缘 0.1 寸（指寸），左右共 10 个穴位（图 16－18）。

【解剖】皮肤→皮下组织。神经支配是：拇趾和第 2 趾由来自腓浅神经的趾背神经、腓深神经的趾背神经和胫神经的趾足底固有神经支配；第 3、4 趾由来自腓浅神经的趾背神经和胫神经的趾足底固有神经支配；小趾由来自腓肠神经的趾背神经、腓浅神经的趾背神经和胫神经的趾足底固有神经支配。血管供应是来源于足底内、外动脉的趾底固有动脉和足背动脉的趾背动脉。

【功用】通络开窍。

【主治】足趾麻木，足背红肿疼痛，卒中。

【操作】直刺 0.1～0.2 寸。

【Meaning】Qi，here it means qi（energy）of meridian；duan，the end or tip of toe. The end of the 10 toes are the stating points of the qi flowing out of meridian qi. The points are locates on them respectively. Therefore，it was called "Qiduan".

【Location】 The point at the tips of the toes of both feet, 0. 1cun from the free margin of each toenail (Fig 16 – 18).

【Regional anatomy】 Skin→subcutaneous tissue. The big and 2nd toes are controlled by superficial fibular nerve dorsal digital nerve of foot, deep fibular nerve dorsal digital nerve of foot and tibial nerve proper plantar digital nerve. The 3rd and 4th toes are controlled by superficial fibular nerve dorsal digital nerve of foot and tibial nerve proper plantar digital nerves. The small toe sural nerve dorsal digital nerve of foot, superficial fibular nerve dorsal digital nerve of foot and tibial nerve proper plantar digital nerves. Supplied blood comes from arteria plantaris medialis and lateralis proper plantar digital artery.

【Properties】 Dredge meridians and restore resuscitation.

【Indications】 Numbness of the toes, swelling and pain of the instep of the foot, apoplexy.

【Needling method】 Puncture perpendicularly 0. 1 ~0. 2 cun.

复习思考题
Review Questions

1. 举例说明头颈部奇穴的主治。

Using examples explain the indications of extra points on the head and neck.

2. 哪些奇穴可以用来治疗下肢痛?

What extra point can be applied for the lower extremities pain?

3. 请说明夹脊穴的定位、主治和操作。

What are the location, indications and needling method of Jiaji (EX – B 2).

4. 印堂穴的定位、主治和针刺操作是什么?

What are the location, indications and needling method of Yintang (EX – HN 3)?

5. 膝周围有哪些奇穴? 它们的作用机制是什么?

What are the extra points located around the knee? What are their effects?

附篇　经络腧穴现代研究
Appendix　Modern Research on Meridians and Acupoints

第一节　经络现代研究
Modern Research on Meridians and Collaterals

一、经络现象
The Meridian Phenomenon

经络现象是指沿古典经络路线出现的一些特殊的感觉传导和感觉障碍以及可见的皮肤色泽和组织形态变化等现象。"循经性"是各种经络现象的共同特征。经络现象一般是针刺、艾灸、推拿及电脉冲等刺激作用于经穴后而产生的，也可在机体某种病理状态下自发地出现，有时还可经入静诱导和意守丹田等气功锻炼而被诱发出现。经络现象的出现机理非常复杂，但各种经络现象从感觉到形态的多个侧面，反映出古代记载的经络路线的客观存在。特别是可见的经络现象，持续时间长，客观性强，"看得见，摸得着"，形象、直观、生动地显示着人体"活的经络图"。"现象是本质的显现"，经络现象亦应是经络本质的显现，从经络现象入手开展经络实质的研究无疑是人体生命科学的重要研究内容。

The meridian phenomena are some especial sensory conductions, disturbances and visible changing of color and tissue on the skin on the routes of meridians according to the classical theory. "meridian - like" characters are the various phenomena in common, which generally generate after stimulating acupoints by acupuncture, moxibustion, massage and electric impulse, and also emerge spontaneously under certain pathological condition, sometimes could be provocative by qigong through brooding or omphaloskepsis etc. The formation of the meridian phenomena is very complicated, but the objective reality of the meridian system recorded by ancient books could be deduced from various aspects of sensations and its morphology. Visible meridians is a special case which could be seen and touched, last long and has strong objectivity, and is a alive meridian graphic that is visualized and vivid. "Phenomenon is the essence of the show", meridian phenomena are also the show of the essence of the meridians within human body, so it is doubtless that the study on the substance of the meridians sourcing from meridian phenomena are the essential content of the human life science.

(一) 循经感传现象
Meridian - Route Sensory Transmission Phenomenon

循经感传现象，是指沿经络路线出现的感觉传导现象，在各类经络现象中最为多见，是经络现代研究的重要内容。

The phenomenon of propagated sensation along meridians (PSM) is the conduction of the sense travel along the route of the meridian, which is the most common in various meridian performances and also one of the most significant study areas.

1. 循经感传现象的发现与调查
Discovery and Investigation

循经感传是针灸临床最常见的一种经络现象，通常在针刺、脉冲电、按压等方法刺激人体穴位时产生。循经感传现象在古书中早有记载，只是没有这一明确的提法而已。20 世纪 50 年代，日本学者报道了循经感传现象后，国内外类似的报道日益增多，我国首先开展了大规模普查研究。1973 年卫生部颁布了全国循经感传现象调查统一方法和分型标准后，研究工作走上了规范化的科学轨道。从 1972 年至 1978 年，全国 20 多个省、市、自治区有关单位，按照统一标准对不同民族、性别、年龄和健康状况的人群进行了 6 万多人次的调查，结果发现感传出现率为 5.6% ~45.2%，大多在 12% ~24% 之间。对于感传显著者，即六条以上贯通一经全程的，出现率约为 4% ~13% 之间。大规模的调查结果表明，循经感传广泛存在于人群之中，基本上无种族、地域、年龄等方面的差别。

PSM is common in acupuncture and moxibustion clinical practice, often generated after stimulating the acupoints by needling, electrical impulse and pressing. It was recorded in ancient books thought not identify clearly as a definition. After the first report by Japanese scientists in 1950s, more and more similar reports appeared at home and abroad. A large - scale survey first started in China.

Research has been carried out on a standard track according to the style standard and survey criteria given by ministry of health in 1973. From 1972 to 1978, relevant departments from more than 20 regions carried out survey of more than 60, 000 people, according to different national, age and gender and health condition of the crowd, under the unified standards. Results is that sense and transmit rate is 5.6% to 45.2%, mostly 12% to 24%. To the remarkableness whose sense and conduction run through the whole meridian, the rate is around 4% to 13%. The large - scale survey results shows that PSM exist in people widely, and basically there is no differences in aspect of races, regions, ages, etc.

2. 循经感传现象的基本特征
Basic Feature

循经感传现象具有循经性、双向传导、回流性、慢速传导、可阻性、感传线宽度粗细不匀、感觉性质多样、趋病性和效应性等特征。

The phenomenon of PSM has some features like propagated sensation along meridians, bidirectional conduction, backflow, low speed conduction, resistibility, uneven width of the conduction route, variety senses, nidus tendency and effectivity.

（1）循经性：感传路线的循经性是感传被列为经络现象的首要条件。从大量的经络现象的调查结果来看，感传路线与古典的经络路线基本一致，而与神经、血管等已知结构的分布在总体上存在显著差异。一般而言，在四肢部，感传线与古典经络路线大体一致；在胸腹部常有偏离；头面部则变异较大。刺激经穴所引起的感传，除沿本经路线扩布外，有时还会窜入相邻或有关的经脉，或表现为超过、不及或另有旁支。

Propagated sensation along meridians: Propagated sensation along meridians is the conduction as the primary condition of meridian phenomenon. Observing from results of mass meridian phenomena survey, the conduction route is basically the same as the classical, and generally has significant variation of known structures like nervus, vessels.

Generally speaking, conduction line is almost the same as the classic on limbs, deviates on chest and belly partially, and differ on head and face. The conduction caused by stimulating the acupoint would turn into the adjacent or relevant channels, or passes by, not reach or has another branch except radiating along its own channel.

（2）双向传导：除经脉上的始穴和终穴外，刺激经脉线上的其他穴位所引发的感传多呈双向传导。例如，刺激曲池穴，感传可向肩髃传导，也可向合谷传导。

Bidirectionals conduction: The conduction caused by stimulating acupoints except for the first and last acupoint on the meridian, conduct double ways mostly. For example, stimulate Quchi（LI 11）, the conduction will conduct to Jianyu（LI 15）and also to Hegu（LI 4）.

（3）回流性：这是感传最奇特的现象之一。在感传延伸过程中，若突然中止穴位刺激，大多数感传者会出现感传沿原路向原刺激穴位回流的现象。回流的感传抵达原刺激穴位或其附近时，逐渐“淡化”后便自行消失。回流的感传多呈匀速传导。

Backflow: This is one of the most miraculous phenomena of the conduction. If terminate the stimulating during the conduction, most of the sensor would feel the conduction retracing to the origin. The retraced conduction is weaken little by little and then disappears spontaneously. The retraced are conducting in a uniform speed mostly.

（4）慢速传导：与刺中神经干时的触电样传导不同，感传是一种慢速传导，传导速度一般为每秒10cm左右。这一传导速度较自主神经慢，较躯体神经更慢。感传的延伸过程并非匀速进行，可出现时快时慢或间歇传导的现象。在经过肘、膝、肩、髋等关节时，感传常出现减速现象。

Low speed conduction：Meridian conduction is different from the electric shock when needling nerve trunk；it is low speed at 10cm per second. This speed is slower than automatic nerve's and much slower than the somatic nerve's. The extension is at non－uniform speed，sometimes faster，slower and intermittent. The conduction slows down while passing joints like elbow，knee，shoulder and hip.

（5）可阻性：在感传线上施加机械压迫，常可阻断感传自压迫点继续传导，而刺激点与压迫点之间的感传依然存在，并常有增强甚至出现憋胀的感觉。如刺激合谷出现向曲池方向的传导后，压迫手三里，则感传中止于手三里，不再向曲池传导，而合谷与手三里之间的感传依然存在，并有增强的现象，甚至可出现憋胀的感觉。阻滞感传的有效压力因人而异，一般为每平方厘米500g。在感传线上注射普鲁卡因或生理盐水，可部分或完全阻滞感传，这种阻滞效应可能是因液体注入而增加局部压力所致，与机械压迫阻滞感传的机理相似。在感传线上放置冰袋，降低局部温度也可阻滞感传，一般将穴位深部温度降至21.6℃±0.4℃时便可产生这一效应。用软毛刷在感传线上轻刷10～15分钟，也可使感传逐渐减弱直至消失。感传一旦被阻滞，它所引起的相应脏腑功能的变化即显著降低甚至消失。解除阻滞，感传常可继续延伸，脏腑功能的改变又重新出现。此外，感传扩布的前方如遇手术切口、疤痕、肿块或肿大的脏器时，感传常因此而被阻断。

Resistibility：To press mechanical pressure on the route of the conduction would block the further conduction right from the pressing point while the conduction between stimulating and pressing point still exists，and even be strengthen or bulging. As an example，to press the point Shousanli（LI 10）while there is a conduction of Hegu（LI 4）to Quchi（LI 11），the transmission stop at Shousanli（LI 10），at the mean while the conduction between Hegu（LI 4）and Shousanli（LI 10）still there and be strengthen，sometimes bulging. The effective pressure for blocking is different to groups，normally is 500g per square centimeter. The conduction could be block partially or completely when procaine or saline be injected on the route. The effect of block maybe because of local pressure caused by liquid injection，the forming reason is familiar with the mechanical pressure. Putting an ice bag on the route to decrease the local temperature would block the conduction either，the trigger temperature deep in the point range from 21.2℃ to 22℃. Using soft bristle brush to brush gently on the route for 10 to 15 minutes would reduce the conduction generally till disappeared totally. As long as the conduction is blocked，the accommodation of internal organs decline significantly and even extinction，if remove the block，conduction extends normally and accommodation appears again. Besides，incisions，scars，lumps or bulged organs would cut off conduction also.

（6）感传线宽度粗细不匀：多数感传显著者将感传线的粗细描述为线状、绳索状、琴弦或筷子状等。在感传过程中，感传线有保持不变的，也有线状和带状交替出现的。在带状感传中，感传带中间可有一条较两侧边缘更为清晰的中心线。一般感传线在四肢部较细，在0.2～2.0cm之间，到达胸、腹部或头面部常变宽至10cm以上，有时还出现较大面积的扩散现象。

Uneven width of the conduction route：Most of sensitive sensors describe the conduction route as thread，rope，string or chopstick. On conducting，some route remains it was，some change into thread and zone alternatively. There is a midline on the route which is more distinct than both edges in zone conduction. The width of the conduction route is slim on limbs，ranges from 0.2～2.0cm，could enlarges to 10cm on the chest，belly，head and face. Diffusing phenomenon in large range would appear sometimes.

（7）感觉性质多样：用不同刺激方法，在不同部位及在不同个体身上可诱发不同感觉性质的感传。常见的感觉性质有酸、胀、重、麻、水流、气流、虫行、冷、热等。一般针刺引发的感传，其性质较为多样；电针及穴位注射，以酸、胀、重感为多；电脉冲穴位表面刺激常为电麻、虫跳或蠕动感；艾灸为温热感；指压多为酸胀、麻胀或热感。

Variety senses：Different conduction could be evoked through varieties stimulations on different part of the body for each individual. Senses that commonly felt about are sore，expanding，heavy，numb，water flowing，air flowing，ant crawling，cold and heat，etc. The conduction evoked by needling involves multiple senses. The senses of the conduction of electric acupuncture and acupoint injection are mostly sore，expending and heavy. Adding electric impulse on the surface of the acupoints，it would be electric numb and insect jumping and worm wriggling. The senses of moxibustion are heat，and finger press is sore with expending，numb with expanding or just tepid.

（8）趋病性：在病理状态下，当感传邻近某一病灶时，常可偏离经脉，折向病灶部位，使局部症状即时缓解。这种“气至病所”的现象有重要的治疗学意义。

Nidus tendency：Under certain pathological conditions，the conduction deviate from the original route to the affected sites when it passes by which the local symptoms will be relieved. This phenomenon “qi extending affected parts” means a lot in therapeutics.

（9）效应性：感传不仅在经脉线上循行，还可抵达相应的脏腑器官，并改变其功能。如当心脏病患者的感传沿心包经上达胸部时，患者可觉心区舒畅，闷重感消失。

Effectivity：The conduction not only transmit on the route of the meridian，but also reaches the relevant organs，and alter its performance. Take cardiac patient’s experience as an example，when the conduction reaches the chest along the pericardium meridian，patient would feel unloaded and comfortable.

(二) 循经性感觉障碍现象
Disturbance Phenomenon of Propagated Sensation along Meridians

通常所说的感觉障碍，包括感觉麻痹、感觉异常和感觉过敏。感觉麻痹即感觉消失或减退；感觉异常是指在无外来刺激情况下机体出现的蚁行、虫爬、电麻等异常感觉；感觉过敏是指对刺激的异常敏感，如以棉花触及皮肤即引起不适，甚至疼痛等。这里所谓的循经性感觉障碍现象，是指沿经络路线自发出现的麻木、痛敏、异常感觉等感觉障碍现象。

So called sensory disturbance includes sensory numbness, sensory abnormality and sensory allergy. Sensory numbness is the decline or disappearing of the sense. Sensory abnormality means body got abnormal feelings such as ant crawl, worm creep, electric numb, etc. without any stimulating. Sensory allergy is excessive sensitivity, such as feeling uncomfortable or even pain with the touch of the cotton. The sensory disturbance phenomenon we talk about here is numb, pain or abnormal sense show up spontaneously along the meridian.

1. 感觉性质
Attributes of Conduction Senses

循经性感觉障碍的感觉性质可多种多样，如痛、麻、酸、冷、热、痒、胀、跳动、风吹、水流、虫行等。其中以循经性麻痛最为多见，临床上常表现为循经性的麻木反应带和痛敏反应带。

There are many attributes of the disturbance phenomenon of propagated sensation along meridians, like pain, numb, soreness, cold, heat, itch, expanding, twitch, air flow, water flow and worm creep, etc. Amount of all, numb is thc most common and in clinical practice, it performs as zones of numb and hyperalgesia along the meridians.

2. 分布路线
Distributions

循经性感觉障碍的分布路线与古典经络路线相吻合，而与神经、血管的走行路线不同，也不同于现代医学中的某些神经痛、感觉障碍及内脏病变所致的海特带。

1883 年，西方学者 Ross、Dana 等提出内脏病变可引起皮肤痛敏的观点，后经 Head 等人补充，形成 Head 痛敏带。这种痛敏带是指内脏发生病变时在相应部位皮肤的痛觉敏感性提高。海特带与循经性麻痛带相似，但两者不尽相同。海特带按外周神经皮节分布，而循经性麻痛带则按古典经络路线分布，常超出神经皮节分布范围。海特带只提及痛敏区，未提到麻木区，而这种麻木带在临床上很常见。循经性麻痛带的发现修正和丰富了海特带，提供了远远超越神经节段论的经络脏腑相关的理论依据和临床资料。

Distribution of the disturbance phenomenon of propagated sensation along meridians matches the classic meridian route, and differ from the nerves' and vessels' routes or Head's zones caused by nerve pain, sensory disturbance and pathological changes of organs.

In 1883, western scholars Ross and Dana concluded that pathological organs would lead to hyperalgesia of the skin, and finally come to the zones of hyperalgesia, after the complement work from Mr. Head. The zone of hyperalgesia means the pain sensitivity of the relevant skin arises when lesions occur in the organs. The head's zones are similar with the numbness zones but not the same. Head's zone distributes over peripheral nerve section while numbness zone distributes over classical meridian routes which out of peripheral nerve logtion range mostly. The Head's zones theory includes hyperalgesia only without zones of numbness which is common in clinical practice. The discovery of the pain – numb zone which is along the meridians modifies and enriches the Head's zone theory, and provides more theoretical basis and clinical data related with meridians and organs that way beyond the peripheral nerve section theory.

3. 与脏腑病变的关系
Relations with Pathological Organs

循经性感觉障碍，尤其是循经性麻痛反应带与脏腑、经络的关系呈一定的规律性。脏腑病变大多可以麻痛反应带的形式反应于相应的经脉上，主要在病变脏腑所属的本经，或其表里经、同名经及表里经的同名经，有时还可累及膀胱经和督脉。如心脏病，首先表现于心经或小肠经，进而表现于肾经和膀胱经，偶尔也可先表现于表里经或同名经。

The relation among the disturbance phenomenon, especially the numbness zone along the meridians, organs and meridians has a certain regular patterns. The pathological changes of the internal organs reflect on the relevant meridian which is the pertaining meridian to the pathological organ mainly, or the exterior – interior or homonymic meridian,, exterior – interior and homonymic meridians, sometimes governor vessel and the bladder meridian are involved, with the numb – pain sensitive zone. Take heart disease for instance, reflects are shown on the heart meridian and small intestine meridian first, and then on the kidney and bladder meridians, occasionally, shown on the exterior – interior or homonymic meridian of the heart.

循经性麻痛带与脏腑病变的程度常呈正相关关系，病变严重，反应带明显；病变轻，反应带亦轻；病变好转，反应带常变细、宽窄不匀、弯曲、断裂或消失；病变加重，反应带加宽，数目增多。麻木和痛敏在不同阶段可相互转化。发病初期或恢复期，以痛敏为主，或呈痛、麻相间之带状区；病变重或慢性期，以麻木带为主要表现形式。

The positive correlation exists among the numb – pain zone and the degree of the pathological organs. Serious changes with obvious reflecting zone and slight one with vague one. If it starts recovering, the zone changes into slim or uneven width of edges or banded or breaking one; the opposite situation is the lesion become worse, the zone widen, and the number of that increases. The numbness and pain would convert to each other at different stages. At the beginning and recovering period, pain sensitive zone is the major reflection while chronic and developing period, numbness zone is on top.

(三) 可见的经络现象 Visible Meridian Phenomenon

可见的经络现象主要为沿经络路线出现的线带状皮肤病以及类似表皮血管扩张或收缩所引成的红线、白线等，即循经性皮肤病和循经性皮肤显痕——循经性皮肤血管神经性反应。

Visible meridian phenomenon is thread or band shaped dermatosis and red or white lines caused by hemangiectasis or vasoconstriction of the superficial skin. Dermatosis and dominant marks on skin are neurological reaction of the capillary of the skin with on the meridian route.

1. 循经性皮肤病 Meridian - Route Dermatosis

自20世纪50年代后期，有关循经性皮肤病的案例在国内已有零星报道。至20世纪70年代，随着循经感传现象研究的大规模开展，对循经性皮肤病的研究也得到了重视，观察的病种和病例不断增多。北京第六医院等单位对此进行了长期有计划的临床观察，获取了一些珍贵的、颇有说服力的循经性皮肤病的临床资料。在国外，匈牙利、日本等国也有这方面的报道。从已有资料看，目前已在25个病种的346个病例中观察到了478条循经性皮肤病。但事实上，循经性皮肤病的例数应远远超过这个数字，因为掌握中医经络知识并能将皮肤病损与经络路线联系起来的皮肤科医师只是极少数。可以想象，很多这方面的资料未被记录、研究和报道。

A few cases of dermatosis along the channel have been reported in mainland since the late 1950s. Since the extensive study to the phenomenon expending, the research of dermatosis along the meridian is earn widespread respect, and more and more classes and cases have been investigated in 1970s. Departments like the sixth Hospital in Beijing have long - term plans in clinic over this subject, and obtain some rare and persuasive clinical data. Reports on this subject have also found in abroad such as Hungary and Japan, etc. Analyzing from the obtained data, 478 cases of the dermatosis have been recorded from the 25 diseases in 346 patients. But in fact, the cases should be far over the number for dermatologists who earned the TCM meridian knowledge and could connect dermatosis with meridian route is absolute minority. So the true picture is the majority of the data is unrecorded and ignored.

循经性皮肤病涉及的病种较多，常见的有神经性皮炎、扁平苔藓和贫血痣，尚可见疣状痣、色素痣、皮肤萎缩、色素沉着、白癜风、湿疹、银屑病、硬皮病、皮肤腺痣等。循经性皮肤病可分布于十四经和带脉上，其中以肾经、大肠经最为多见，肺经、心包经次之，分布范围可见于经脉的某一行程段或经脉的整个外行路线。有些皮肤病损，如贫血痣、色素痣等，边缘整齐，连续不断，宛若一条细带或细线，十分醒目。循经性皮肤病有时和相应脏腑病变有一定关系。发生于肾经的皮损常伴有肾（泌尿）、神经系统和精神方面的变化；出现于脾经的皮损常伴有消化不良和慢性泄泻；发生于心经的皮损多伴有心脏病。有些循经性皮肤病是先天性的，也有一些是在青春期前逐步形成的。这类循经性皮肤病是在个体发育过程中出现的，可能与遗传基因缺陷有关。人体皮肤发育的缺陷，或受某种外来因素的作用，或受脏腑病理变化的影响而出现的某种病损的分布与古典经络路线的一致性，看来并非偶然，应有某种内在的联系，值得研究。

There are varieties diseases related with the meridian dermatosis, such as neurodermatitis, lichen planus, nevus anemicus which of those are common in clinic, some of the others are warty mole, pigmented naevus, adermotrophia, pigmentation, leukoderma, eczema, psoriasis, scleroderma and dermal gland mole, etc. Meridian routing dermatosis distributes on the 14 main meridians and belt vessel, the kidney and the large intestine meridians are the majority, the lung and the pericardium meridians after that. A certain part of the route or the complete exterior route is the distribution range. Some pathological signs are unstopped and regular edged, looks like a slim stream or a thread, very impressively. There is a certain connection between meridian - route dermatosis and the relevant internal organs sometimes. The dermatosis appears on the kidney meridian usually comes with pathological changes on urinary system, nervous system and mental performance; on the spleen meridian always comes with dyspepsia and chronic diarrhea; on the heart meridian mostly comes with cardiopathy. Some meridian - route dermatosis are congenital, others are emerged gradually in adolescence. This kind of dermatosis emerges on the process of growth, probably related with genetic defect. It is worth to study in the inner mechanism of the uniformity between the classic meridian route and the distribution of the defects of the skin that maybe affected by external influence or by pathologic changes of internal organs.

2. 循经性皮肤血管神经性反应
Cutaneous Vascular Nervous Reaction of the Meridian - like

在临床针灸治疗中，有时在针刺后可出现沿相应经络路线的红线、白线、丘疹和皮下出血等皮肤血管神经性反应，这种皮肤反应又称“循经性皮肤显痕”。这些循经性皮肤血管神经性反应，有的细如丝线，有的宽达 1 ~2 cm，短的仅出现于相应经络的某一行程段，长的几乎可通达全程。这些皮肤反应是在刺激穴位后出现的，有的针刺后立即出现或发生于留针过程中，有的针刺后数小时甚或十余小时才出现。皮肤反应出现后一般可持续数分钟至数小时，少数患者可达十余小时，有的可多次重复出现。有人曾将循经性红线与皮肤划痕反应作比较，结果，在划痕反应完全消失之后，循经性红线仍可持续数小时至十余小时之久，表明两者有所不同。尽管不少研究者对循经性皮肤血管神经性反应的发生过程做了各种解释，但其形成机理至今尚未完全明了。

The cutaneous vascular nervous reaction of the meridian - like is the red line, white line, papule and subcutaneous hemorrhage that appear on the relevant meridian route after needling stimulation in the clinical treatment by acupuncture and moxibustion. This reaction is also called "visible cutaneous trace on meridian – like" . Some of these reactions are slim as a silk thread or wide to 1 to 2 centimeters or short as a certain section on the relevant meridian or long as a consistent line on total external meridian route. These reactions emerge after the stimulation on acupoints, some of them appears right after the needling or in the process of needle retaining, others become visible after hours or more than ten hours. It could last from several minutes to couple of hours; a few patients' reaction could be visible for more than ten hours and show up repeatedly. Someone took the meridian – route red line and skin scratch as a comparison, the result was the meridian – route red line could last for several hours or even more than ten hours after the scratch disappeared completely, that means they are dissimilar completely. Although a lot of researchers gave various explanations to the occurrence of the cutaneous vascular nervous reaction of the meridian – like, the formation is not totally clearly yet.

二、经络检测 Meridian Detection

大量的经络现象的观察、调查和研究资料表明，经络现象是客观存在的，但现象终究是现象，不能从根本上揭示经络的实质。因此，如能应用现代科学的技术手段将古人描述的经络路线客观地显示和检测出来，这是阐明和揭示经络实质的一个重要而有效的方法和途径。长期以来，国内外经络研究者们在这方面做了不懈的努力，对经络的声、光、电、热、磁、核等物理和化学特性做了大量深入的研究，取得了一些重要研究成果和进展。

Meridian phenomenon is existed objectively manifested by mass research data of observation, investigation. But the essence of the meridian can't be reveal fundamentally from phenomena. So it is a significant and effective way to explain and reveal the essence of the meridian that using modern technical means to detect and visualize the meridian route described by the ancients. Domestic and overseas researchers have contributed unremitting efforts on this subject, and some significant achievements and progress have gained on physical and chemical features of the meridian, such as sonic, light, electric, heat, magnetic, nuclear.

（一）皮肤电阻检测 Dermal Resistance Detection

皮肤电阻检测是在经络循行路线的客观检测中应用最早的方法之一。1950 年，日本中谷义雄在检测一名肾病患者的皮肤导电量时，发现患者下肢皮肤有许多导电量较其他部位高的位点，这些点的连线与足少阴肾经路线相似。此后，中谷义雄又在其他经上发现了类似的结果。这些皮肤导电量较高的点后来被命名为“良导点”，由良导点连成的线被称为“良导络”。良导点的位置与传统经穴的部位一致，而良导络则与经脉循行路线相符。继中谷义雄之后，国内许多研究人员开展了大量的经络电阻的检测研究工作，但其中绝大部分工作是从穴位皮肤电阻入手的，对经络循行路线皮肤电阻的测定工作开展的不多。由于方法上的缺陷，测定结果不是很稳定，各家报道差异较大，但总体上基本肯定了穴位和经络的低阻（高导电量）特性。

The dermal resistance detection is one of the earliest methods used in the objective detection to meridian route. In 1950, Ryodoraku in Japan found some points on the skin of the patient's lower limbs which are high conductive than others and the connecting lines of the points are consistent with the kidney meridian, when he was detecting the electric quantity on the skin of a nephrotic. After that, he found the similar results on other meridians. The higher charge passed points are named "Ryodoraku points" and the connecting lines "Ryodoraku lines". Ryodoraku points are very close or at the site of acupoints, Ryodoraku lines are comparable to meridians. Chinese mainland researchers started the study of the meridian resistance after that, but most of the work focused on the skin resistance, a little aimed at the resistance along the meridian route. Reports are in a large difference, detecting results are instability since the defect of the method, but the feature of low resistance on acupoints and meridians is basically accepted in general.

（二）放射性核素示踪 Radionuclide Tracer

在经络循行路线的客观显示和检测中，放射性核素示踪技术也是较早得到应用的一种方法。早在20世纪60年代初，我国学者即已开始应用放射性同位素示踪的方法检测经脉循行路线。在人体的穴位注入低于治疗剂量的^{32}P，以盖缪计数器记录，可以观察到相应经脉线上的放射性强度较其两侧旁开的对照部位高，所测试到的十二条同位素的示踪轨迹与传统的十二经脉的路线大体一致。在非经非穴部位注射，则观察不到同位素循经迁移的现象。随着同位素示踪技术的不断发展，20世纪80年代以来，罗马尼亚、法国和我国学者先后将γ闪烁照相技术应用于经络路线的检测中，发现穴位注射核素后出现循经性示踪轨迹。中国中医研究院针灸研究所、解放军总医院等单位的研究者将^{99m}Tc－高锝酸钠注入人体穴位，以大视野γ闪烁照相机记录其迁徙轨迹。

Radionuclide tracer is one of the earliest methods used in detecting the meridian route in an objective and visible way. In the early 1960s, researchers in china already took the advantage of this technology in to the detecting work. Injecting ^{32}P with lower dosage than therapeutic dose on the acupoints countered by Geiger－Muller counter, the recorded intensity of radioactivity showed that the intensity on meridian is higher than the flanks, and the detected traces match the classic in general, on the contrary, isotope transmission along the meridian can't be observed when injected on non－meridians or non－points. With the development of radionuclide tracer, the gamma scintillation camera used in detecting by researchers from Romania, France and China drew the meridian－route trace after the acupoint injection from1980s. Researchers from institute of acupuncture, China Academy of Chinese Medical Sciences and PLA general hospital, etc, injected ^{99m}Tc – sodium pertechnetate into acupoints and recorded its transmission trace by wide view gamma scintillation camera.

在腕踝部穴位皮下注入的核素可循经迁徙 30 ~ 110cm，其中迁移较远者可从四肢上达躯干。在躯干部穴位注入，同位素亦可在不同程度上循经上下迁移。同位素的示踪轨迹与古典十二经脉的路线基本一致，在四肢部吻合率达 78%。在同一肢体的两条经脉的穴位上同时注入核素，则可同时显示出两条相应的循经示踪轨迹。在经穴旁开的非经非穴对照点注入核素后，其迁移多呈淤积移行，在扩散过程中逐渐向邻近的经脉、合穴、郄穴或络穴靠移，进入经脉或穴位后即沿经向心迁移。若注射点远离经脉，则无循经轨迹出现。同位素的示踪轨迹主要在皮下。

The isotope injected in acupoints around wrist and ankle could transmit 30 ~ 110cm along the meridian, the farthest may reached trunk from limbs and injected on the trunk, it could travel up and down in various degrees. The isotope traces is much the same with the classic and about 78% of identity on limbs. Injecting isotope in acupoints on two meridians on the same limb at the meantime, it would porform two traces on each meridian. When isotope injected in the non – acupoints around acupoints and near the meridian, the transmission is alluvial move, and travelled to the neighbor meridian, he – sea point, xi – cleft point or luo – connecting point during its diffusion, and transmitted to the heart along meridians after accumulated in acupoints or meridians. If the injection points are far away from meridians, there will be no trace at all. The isotope traces distributed mainly under the superficial skin.

将同位素注入穴位后，一般要经过一定的潜伏期才出现迁移线，十二经的平均潜伏期为 37.28 ± 15.63mm/sec，示踪剂的迁移速度为 1.3 ~ 4.4mm/sec。迁移时快时慢，有时还会出现淤滞点，淤滞点与穴位的位置常吻合。核素迁移可呈双向性，但以向心性为主。

The transmission lines have an incubation period of up to 37.28 ± 15.63mm/sec for twelve meridians and the migration rate of tracer is 1.3 ~ 1.4mm/sec. It transmits slow and fast from time to time, and even sometimes accumulates on certain points which are acupoints mostly. The isotope transmission is double way, but the main direction is centrality.

穴位注射淋巴显影剂^{99m}Tc – 硫化锑和血管显影剂^{99m} Tcrbc 均未出现与穴位注射^{99m} Tc – 高锝酸钠相同的迁移规律；局部注射神经麻醉剂普鲁卡因和对神经毫无作用的生理盐水对迁移的阻断作用完全相同，说明核素循经迁移不是血管和淋巴管的直接显像，与神经亦无直接关系。用 Na^{131} I 作放射性自显影观察到，沿豚鼠“膀胱经”的迁移轨迹走行于组织间隙中，标记的银粒并未存在或附着于任何特殊的组织结构。

The law of transmission of ^{99m}Tc – sodium pertechnetate is different from injecting lymph contrast agent ^{99m}Tc – antimony sulfide and vessel contrast agent ^{99m}Tcrbc in acupoints. Locally injecting nerve blocking agent procaine and normal saline which is totally useless could block transmission. This phenomenon indicates that the meridian route isotope transmission is not the direct visualization of blood vessels and lymph - vessel and not related to nerves either. It is observed with $Na^{131}I$ as autoradiography that the route along cavia "the bladder meridian" transmits in tissue space, the silver grains used as marker do not exist in or attach to any specific tissues.

（三）低频声信号检测
Low Frequency Acoustic Signal Detection

1980年，辽宁中医学院首先以低频声信号（即低频机械振动波）为指标开展经络循行路线的检测工作。近年，这一检测技术有了进一步的提高，从单探头发展到6探头测试，并采用计算机采样处理系统从定性提高到定量分析阶段。在对大肠经的检测中观察到，在大肠经商阳穴输入定量低频声信号，沿大肠经均可检测到与输入声信号相同频率和波形的声波，与旁开对照点比较差异显著。声信号的传播轨迹与古典大肠经循行路线一致，大肠经循行路线中的弯曲、交叉及交会都得到了显示，并测出了与肺经、胃经的衔接。实验发现，循经性声波的出现必须有适宜的输声强度和频率。经络的传声速度仅为每秒10m左右，比周围组织缓慢许多，表明经络有自己的独特结构。根据低频声的循经性及其对相应脏腑具有调节作用的特点，经络输声疗法被应用于临床，并取得了满意疗效。尽管这些实验结果在其他经脉得到重复，但声波的传播规律与经络的关系及其传播的媒介有待进一步证实和探索。

In 1980, Liaoning Collage of TCM firstly took low frequency acoustic signal (LFAS) as index to detect meridian route. The detection technology has been developing for these years from one sensor to six sensors and from qualitative analysis to quantitative analysis with the help of sample processing system in computer. It is observed while detecting the Large Intestine Meridian that inputting quantitative LFAS on Shangyang (LI 1) point, the same frequency and waveform sonic wave could be detected along the whole Large Intestine Meridian which is different from both sides significantly. The transmission route of acoustic signal pretty matched the classic route and the bends, crossings and intersections were revealed, and even the joint points. It is found that proper input intensity and frequency is necessary for transmission. The acoustic velocity in meridians is merely about 10 m/sec, much slower than surrounding tissues. This phenomenon indicates that meridian has its own unique structure. Inputting acoustic signal therapy is applied in clinic for its meridian - route feature and accommodation to relevant organs and the efficacy is satisfactory. Although the experiment could be repeated in other meridians, it is worth further study on the law of transmission of acoustic signal, the relation with meridians and the medium.

（四）红外辐射成像
Infrared Radiation Imaging Detection

地球上的一切物体当温度高于绝对零度（即-273.15℃）时，其内部的分子就会因热运动而向外辐射红外线。不同的物体有不同的温度，辐射红外线的波长和强度也各不相同，利用灵敏的红外线探测器可察知被探测物体的特征。从量子生物学角度看，机体由细胞构成，而组成细胞的核酸、蛋白质和类脂质等化学物质的分子、原子又都与氢结合。由于热量子活动的原因，原子外周的电子层不断变化，表现为结合分离的新陈代谢变化，所产生的能量则使机体产生温度变化并向周围空间辐射红外线。将辐射信号转换为等效电信号，经电子装置处理后加以显示成像，这样"不可见的"红外线便可转换成可见的图像。因此，人体的红外辐射可反映人体脏器和全身各部的代谢变化。1970 年，法国 J. Borsarello 最早应用红外线热像图摄影术来显示人体经络穴位。此后，国内外研究者在这方面开展了许多研究。应用红外热成像技术在循经感传和针刺过程中可观察到循经高温带或低温带。中国中医研究院针灸研究所观察到，在无刺激的情况下，也有一定比例的循经高温线带出现，尤其在额部的两条太阳经上比较明显。面部膀胱经高温线带的宽度与四肢部的高低温线带相近，可稳定持续显示，针刺可使其出现率增加，温度升高，连续性和均匀度提高。自然状态下，健康人背部正中线和腹部正中线的纵向高温线带的出现率分别为 51.7% 和 7.7%，艾灸可使其温度升高，行程延长，连续性更明显。研究者推测，循躯干前后正中线分布的这两条高温线带似是督任二脉温度特性的显示，线带的形成可能与致密结缔组织或微循环的某种特异性调节机制有关。福建中医研究院在红外辐射成像的基础上，提取体表强度相同的瞬时红外辐射信号，并连续加以显示，在完全没有外加因素刺激或干扰的情况下显示出人体体表自然存在的红外辐射轨迹。这些轨迹呈线带状，其行程与古典十四经脉的路线基本一致或完全一致。长者可跨越多个体区，有的可通达经脉的全程。这种循经红外辐射轨迹始终处于动态变化之中，它与皮下或深部的大血管无明显的关系，也难以用热力学有关温度扩散的理论来解释，确是一种自然存在的生命现象。

All objects on earth whose temperature are above absolute zero (−273.15℃) emit infrared radiation for the inner molecules movement. The different intensity and wavelength could be detected by sensitive detector to identify features of objects for each matter has its own temperature. Observing from quantum biology, the chemicals like nucleic acid, protein and lipoid, etc. make up molecules and atoms which combine with hydrogen atoms to form organism. The vibrational electronic cell surrounded the atom for quantum heat movement performs changing metabolism, and the energy it generated changes body's temperature and emits infrared radiation in the space. "Invisible" infrared radiation could be imaged by electronic device which transform radioactive signal into equivalent electrical signal. Therefore human body's infrared radiation reflects metabolism from all parts of body and organs. In 1970, J. Borsarello from France firstly imaged the human acupoints and meridians by infrared imaging technology. Many researchers around the world started in this filed after that. Meridian – route high temp zone or low temp zone could be observed during the meridian – route transmission and needling by infrared imaging tech. in Acupuncture institute, China Academy of Chinese Medical Sciences, proportional meridian – route high temp zone could be revealed without any stimulation, especially on the Taiyang meridians on the forehead. The width of the high temp zone on the Bladder Meridian on face is similar with the limbs, and the zone is visualized stead-

y. Needling increases the proportion and higher temp raises the continuity and uniformity. In nature, the each proportion of the vertical high temp zone on back and belly middle lines is 51.7% and 7.7%, and moxibustion could raises its temperature, extends length and enhances continuity. The researchers presume that the two zones along the middle lines fore and back are the performance of the temperature feature of governor vessel and conception vessel. The formation of the zones probably related with dense connective tissues or special accommodation mechanism of microcirculation. Fujian Academy of TCM took the instant infrared radiation to display constantly on the basis of infrared radiation imaging tech. It revealed nature trace of infrared radiation on the surface of the human body without any external stimulation and disturbance. These traces are zonal, their routes are basically or completely matched the 14 classic meridian routes. The longer traces distribute on different parts of the body, some travel throughout the whole meridian. The meridian - route infrared radiation traces were vibrating all the time, it didn't correlated with subcutaneous or deep macro vascular, or hard to explain by the temperature diffusivity theory in thermodynamics. It is an existing nature life phenomenon.

（五）体表超微弱发光检测
Detection of Ultra - Weak Bioluminescence on Body Surface

目前已知的地球上的发光生物约上千种。人体活体体表也可向外发射超微弱冷光，但这种冷光很微弱，仅为蜡光的亿万分之一，不为肉眼所见，需用精密仪器方可显现。20 世纪 70 年代后期，我国学者开始人体经络穴位的发光研究，发现人体经穴能发出较强的冷光，发光波长为 3800～4200Å；健康大白鼠的“督脉”和“任脉”路线具有高发光特性；失血和死亡家兔的发光强度明显下降，而针刺得气可增加发光强度，有感传者发光强度的上升更为明显。研究者还发现，死亡不久的人体的某些部位仍在发光，这些发光的部位居然与人体的穴位一致。机体的发光强度在一定程度上反映了机体生命活动能力的强弱。从现有的这方面的研究资料看，有关经络体表超微弱发光的研究尚待进一步拓展和深入。

There are over one thousand known bioluminescent organisms on the earth and live human body emits ultra - weak bioluminescence too, though it is as weak as one of hundred million cents, only precise instrument detects but naked eyes. In the late 1970s, Chinese researchers started to study the lights on acupoints, revealed that stronger luminescence extracted from acupoints, its wavelength was 3800～4200Å. "governor vessel" and "conception vessel" of health sprague - dawley rats emit higher intensity bioluminescence. Bleeding and death rabbits' intensity of bioluminescence was declined, meanwhile the sensed needling enhanced the intensity of bioluminescence and the ascending was more significant if subject is sensitive. Researchers revealed that some parts of newly dead body emitted cold light still, and those parts matched acupoints. The intensity of bioluminescence represents the strength of life energy. Based on current situation, researches on meridian ultra - weak bioluminescence on surface of the body are still worth more attention.

（六）钙测定
Determination of Calcium

Ca^{2+}是生物机体内一种重要的信使物质，参与多种生理过程。钙在机体内主要分布于细胞外，骨组织是细胞外钙库。细胞内Ca^{2+}浓度是细胞外钙的万分之一，细胞内的某些细胞器如内质网等被认为是细胞内钙库。细胞内Ca^{2+}作为一种重要的第二信使物质参与多种生理活动，而细胞内的Ca^{2+}水平又受作为第一信使物质的细胞外Ca^{2+}的浓度的影响。近年来，在经络循行路线的客观检测中，细胞外钙逐渐受到研究人员的重视。天津中医学院等用离子选择性电极观察到，在经穴位和在经非穴的Ca^{2+}浓度均明显高于旁开的非经非穴；针刺穴位或在经非穴可使该经其他穴处的Ca^{2+}浓度显著增高；当家兔出现实验性心律失常时，其外周手厥阴心包经路线上的Ca^{2+}浓度降低，心律失常恢复后其Ca^{2+}浓度也得到恢复；当用EDTA络合手厥阴心包经路线几处的Ca^{2+}后，针刺对家兔实验性心律失常的治疗效应消失。复旦大学、上海中医药大学等采用质子激发X射线荧光发射（PIXE）技术发现，经脉线上的穴位有钙富集现象，其钙含量明显高于在经非穴和非经非穴，钙富集区的纵向连线呈一含量不均等的钙纵向富集带，与经脉路线相符。由于PIXE测定的是钙元素的含量，故穴区钙可有多种形式，如结合钙、亚稳态结合钙、游离钙等，其中亚稳态结合钙和游离钙最有可能参与经络穴位的功能活动，值得深入研究。

Ca^{2+} is an important messenger in organisms which participants many life processes. Calcium distributes outside of the cells, and the bone tissue is the storage of calcium out of the cell. The intensity of inside Ca^{2+} is one of ten thousand percent of outsider, some organelles in cells like endoplasmic reticulum are regarded as storage of calcium. Ca^{2+} inside is one of important secondary messengers participants various physiological activity meanwhile it affected by the intensity of Ca^{2+} as primary messenger from outside. More and more attention gives calcium outside of cell in the objective detection of meridian route in these years. Tianjin college of TCM, etc, observed by ion selective electrode that the intensity of Ca^{2+} in acupoints and non – acupoints on meridian is higher than other points which are not on meridian; and the intensity of other acupoints on the right meridian could be enhanced by needling on acupoints or non – acupoints on the meridian; when rabbits attacked by experimental arrhythmia, the intensity on pericardium meridian went up markedly, then it went back normal when rabbits recovered from arrhythmia; when Ca^{2+} on pericardium meridian was complexing with EDTA, the effectiveness of needling to rabbits' experimental arrhythmia disappeared. Fudan University and Shanghai University of TCM, etc, revealed calcium concentration on acupoints, its intensity is higher than non – acupoints on or outside meridian through particle induced X – ray emission (PIXE). The vertical connecting line of calcium concentration areas is unequal density calcium vertical zone which matches the meridian route. Since PIXE detects the contents of the calcium, calcium in acupoints area are in various formations like bound calcium, metastable bound calcium and ionized calcium, etc. It is worth to study deeper on the metastable bound calcium and ionized calcium which participant the functions of acupoints.

三、经络脏腑相关
The Relevance of Meridians and Zang - Fu Organs

《灵枢·海论》指出："夫十二经脉者，内属于腑脏，外络于支节。"中医学的观点很明确，体表与内脏之间的联系是靠经脉实现的。十二经脉是经络系统的主干，所以"经络脏腑相关"常被称作"经脉脏腑相关"。以往有关经络脏腑的研究多从经穴入手，故"经络脏腑相关"又常与"经穴脏腑相关"相混淆。事实上，经穴只是经络通道上的一个"驿站"，是经络的一个部分，它属于经络，但不等于经络。经络脏腑相关包括经穴脏腑相关的内容，而经穴脏腑相关不能替代经络脏腑相关。长期以来，经络脏腑相关的研究停留于经穴脏腑相关的阶段。近年来，这方面的工作逐渐从经穴一个点与脏腑的关系发展到经络一条线与脏腑关系的研究。经穴脏腑相关的研究已有大量报道，不再赘述。下面仅介绍近年经络脏腑相关研究的一些进展。

"The twelve meridians belong to zang – fu organs internally and connect limbs externally" quotes from the chapter 33, *Miraculous Pivot*. Standpoints from TCM are clear that the surface and interior connects through meridians. The twelve regular meridians are trunks of the meridian system, so it is "the relevance between meridians and zang – fu organs" instead of "the dependence between meridians, collaterals and zang – fu organs", which usually mixed up with the saying "the relation between acupoints and zang – fu organs" for the former researches for their work always started from acupoints; actually acupoints are just sites on meridian route, they belong to meridians, but not equal to meridians. The relevance of meridians and zang – fu organs contains the relevance of acupoints and zang – fu organs, but the latter cannot take the place of the former. In a long period, the study of the relevance of meridians and zang – fu organs have been sticking in the relevance of acupoints and zang – fu organs, and recently it develop from points to lines. The following materials are newly achievements in this field.

（一）脏腑病变在经络的反应
The Reflection of Pathological Organs on Meridians

脏腑病变可反应到经络，古人对此早有认识。《灵枢·九针十二原》指出："五脏有疾也，应出十二原，而原各有所出，明知其原，睹其应，而知五脏之害矣。"这是说，五脏有病，可反应到十二经原穴，各经原穴可反映相应脏腑的病变，分清五脏相应的原穴，审视原穴的反应情况，就能知道五脏的病变了。脏腑病变在经络的反应主要表现为经络路线的感觉、组织形态和生物物理特性等方面的变化。

The ancients realized that the pathological organs would reflect on meridians. "If five – zang organs sick, there will be reflects on twelve yuan – source points. Each yuan – source point has its own origin, so distinguish each yuan - source point and examine their changes; we will know the diseases suffering from certain five - zang organs." Quote from the chapter 1, *Miraculous Pivot*. The reflections of pathological organs are feelings, organization transformations and biophysical feature changes, etc. on the meridian route.

内脏病变可引起体表某一部分发生疼痛或感觉过敏，现代医学将这种现象称为牵涉痛。中医学在这方面的认识更为全面系统，脏腑发生病理变化时，相应的经络路线上常可出现压痛或疼痛、酸、麻、胀和知热感度等感觉变化。北京第六医院在对各系统疾病的体表感觉检查中发现，各种内脏病可在体表出现麻木或痛敏反应带。这种反应带除见于本经外，尚可见于表里经、同名经或表里经的同名经以及膀胱经等部位。这一发现与海特痛敏带单纯为神经皮节反应的论点不同，远较海特带规律、完整和系统。

Pathological changes in interior organs lead to pain or hyperesthesia on partial surface of the body, it is called referred pain in modern medicine. The knowledge in this field is much more comprehensive for TCM, senses changes on the route of relevant meridian such as pressing pain, or pain, sourness, numbness, distention and heat sensitive level, etc, when the organs get illnesses. It is noticed by the 6th hospital in Beijing that various interior organs diseases reflect numb zone or hyperalgesia zone on the surface of the body during the examine to all kinds of system diseases. These kinds of zones could be detected not only on the organ - related meridian but also on their exterior - interior meridians, homonymic meridians or exterior - interior homonymic meridians and urinary bladder meridian, etc. it is quite different from and far more regular, complete and systematic than Head's hyperalgesia.

通过触摸、按压、循捏、观视等方法常可发现经络循行路线上组织形态的异常变化，如可触及麦粒或黄豆大小的结节、条索状反应物和组织松弛，或可发现经络路线上的皮肤脱屑、凹陷、隆突、皱纹、丘疹、斑点和色泽改变等。经络路线上的这些组织形态的变化常可反映相应脏腑器官的病理变化。

Abnormal changing of tissues on the meridian route like kernel or soybean sized nodules, streak things, slack tissues, desquamation, sag, bump, wrinkle, papula, spots and changing in colour and lustre of skin could be detected through palpation, pressing, meridian - route pinch and observing, etc. These changes of the tissue on the meridian route normally reflect the pathological changes of the relevant organs inside.

脏腑发生病变时在相应经络路线上可出现生物物理特性的改变。利用红外热像技术在面部热像图上观察到，健康人面部膀胱经的高温线出现率为 21.6%，而面瘫患者为 17.7%。高温线均从睛明穴上行至前发际，但面瘫患者的该高温线出现不对称性，一般高于周围皮肤 0.5℃ ~1.0℃。

Biophysical features may change on the route of meridians when their relevant organs get diseases. Observing from infrared thermo gram, the occurrence ratio of high temp lines of urinary bladder meridian of healthy person on face is 21. 6% , meanwhile 17. 7% for facial paralysis. In most of the time, high temp lines start from Jingming (BL 1) to anterior hair line, but they are asymmetrical for facial paralysis and the temp is 0. 5℃ ~1. 0℃ higher than surroundings.

(二) 经络对脏腑的调治
The Therapeutic Efficacy on Interior Organs Based on Meridians

脏腑病变可反应于相应的经络上，而在经络路线上施行各种刺激也可调节相应脏腑的功能，二者的对应关系是一致的。

Pathological changes of interior organs would reflect on the relevant meridians, various stimulations on the route of meridian adjust the function of the relevant organs at the same time, they are synchronism.

采用逐点动态兴奋的方法在动物身上观察循经感传的模拟效应，结果在胃经经线上的模拟循经感传有明显加速胃排空的作用，而在经线内外侧的对照组作用较差。电针心包经内关、中冲、劳宫和大陵穴及经上非穴均可维持兔缺血心肌电活动的相对稳定，改善泵血功能，促进血压的恢复。福建中医药研究院对100名冠心病患者针刺心包经路线上的4个穴位和2个非穴位以及旁开1. 5cm的8个对照点。结果显示，在经线上针刺与在旁开对照点上针刺对患者心脏功能的影响有非常显著的差异，说明心包经作为一条经脉，与心脏的功能活动有密切关系。福建中医药研究院尚对170名冠心病患者针刺内关穴，观察有感传者和无感传者心电图ST段和T波变化的时间差异。针刺15分钟时，有感传者的心电图改善明显，而无感传者的心电图无明显变化，两者差异显著。针刺30分钟时，有感传者和无感传者的心电图都有明显改善，两者差异不再显著。从对部分患者针刺90分钟连续记录的动态心电图上看到，有感传组的针刺效应优于无感传组，出现显效的时间也比无感传组早。机械压迫心包经穴位和经上非穴可明显降低针刺对冠心病患者的效应，而压迫其两侧对照点对针效无明显影响。

Observing the analog effect of meridian – route transmission on animal through point to point dynamic excitation, the result is that analogical meridian – route transmission on stomach meridian accelerates the gastric emptying remarkably meanwhile less efficiency on bilateral areas. Electric acupuncture on Neiguan (PC 6), Zhongchong (PC 9), Laogong (PC 8), Daling (PC 7) and other non – acupoints on meridian stabilize the electrical activity of ischemic cardiac myocyte, and improve the function of cardiac pump, promote the blood pressure back to normal. Fujian Institute of TCM & Pharmacology needles four acupoints, two non – acupoints and eight controlled points deviate 1. 5 cm from meridian on 100 coronary diseases' patients, the result is that there are significant differences on cardiac function between needling on acupoints and on controlled points. It proves that pericardium meridian relates with cardiomotility closely. Fujian Institute of TCM & Pharmacology needles Neiguan（PC 6） on 170 coronary diseases' patients to study the ST section and the time difference of T wave variation of ECG between transmissible patients and un - transmissible ones. In 15 minutes, the transmissible's gram improves remarkably but the opposite's not; in 30 minutes, the grams of both improve remarkably, there is no significant difference. Results from records of 90 minutes continuous dynamic ECG on partial needled patients is that needling efficacy of the transmissible group is better than un - transmissible group, and the effective time is earlier. Mechanical pressure on acupoints of pericardium meridian and non - acupoints on meridian could reduce the efficacy of needling on coronary artery patients, meanwhile on the bilateral control points has no remarkable influence.

四、关于经络实质的假说
Hypothesis of Essence of the Meridian System

任何科学实验都必须建立假说，实验只是验证假说的途径而已，经络研究也是如此。为揭示经络的实质——经络的形态结构和物质基础，经络研究者们从不同的角度提出了各种关于经络实质的假说，并进行了相应的实验验证。这些假说可概括为以下三种观点：

第一，经络是一种已知结构及其已知功能的调控系统。

第二，经络是一种已知结构的未知功能或几种已知结构共同参与的未知的综合功能的调控系统。

第三，经络是一种未知的特殊结构及其功能的调控系统。

下面介绍的是其中有代表性的一些假说。

Hypothesis is the necessity for any science experiments, and experiments are the method to confirm hypothesis. Many hypotheses are given from multiple standing points for the structure and material basis of the meridians, and relevant experiments are taken. In conclusion, there are three viewpoints:

Firstly, the meridian system is a control system with known structures and functions.

Secondly, the meridian system is an integrated functional control system with unknown functions of known structures and several known structures.

Thirdly, the meridian system is a control system with unknown special structures and functions.

（一）脉管说
Vessel Hypothesis

在早期的中医文献中，“经脉”的概念常以“脉”的形式出现。如现存最早的经络学专著中国长沙马王堆汉墓出土的古帛书及竹简中记载的十一条经脉，都称为“脉”，而不称“经脉”。《内经》中，则“脉”、“经脉”混用。可见，古人对脉管和经络的关系早有认识。

古代有关这方面的记载还有很多。《素问·脉要精微论》认为："脉者，血之府也。"《灵枢·本脏》也说："经脉者，所以行血气而营阴阳，濡筋骨，利关节者也。"古人除对经脉和脉管的关系有所认识外，还认识到经脉中有动脉和静脉的区别。《灵枢·血络论》说："血气俱盛而阴气多者，其血滑，刺之则射。阳气蓄积，久留而不泻者，其血黑以浊，故不能射。"显然，前者描述的是动脉，后者描述的是静脉。《灵枢·动输》还说："经脉十二，而手太阴、足少阴、阳明独动不休。"这里所说的搏动不止，显然是指肺、肾、胃经上搏动的动脉，具体部位是肺经的太渊，肾经的太溪及胃经的人迎、冲阳穴等处。《难经》还明确指出："十二经皆有动脉。"所指更为广泛。可见，经脉应包括动脉。《内经》中还有许多有关络脉的描述，如，"诸脉之浮而常见者，皆络脉也"（《灵枢·经脉》）。这里所说的络脉，实际上是指皮肤小血管和微血管。络脉也可指黏膜表面的小血管，如"阳络伤则血外溢，血外溢则衄血；阴络伤则血内溢，血内溢则后血；肠胃之络伤，则血溢于肠外"（《灵枢·百病始生》）。在针灸临床上，有直接刺激血管的方法。如传统的"刺络"方法，即是刺破皮肤微血管及浅静脉的放血疗法；"脉刺"是在太渊穴处刺桡动脉的一种疗法；"窦刺"是刺颈动脉窦的一种针法。

The concept of "meridian" appears as the form of "vessel" in early papers. Mawangdui Silk Texts and bamboo slips called meridian vessels. *Yellow Emperor's Inner Canon* mixed the "vessel" and "meridian" up. Many records on this subject in ancient book show that the ancients cleared about the relations between "vessel" and "meridian". In the chapter 17, *Plain Question* it's recorded that vessels were the place where blood ran. In the chapter 47, *Miraculous Pivot*, it's a saying "meridians run blood and qi inside, and soft tendons and bones, lubricate joints". The ancients distinguished the difference between artery and vein. A record in the chapter 39, *Miraculous Pivot* said "people with abundant blood, qi and yin - qi have smooth blood, needle it then it would eject. With long stayed yang - qi, the people have dirty and black blood, there wouldn't be ejected". Obviously, the former is artery and latter is vein. In the chapter 62, *Miraculous Pivot*, it said that "hand - taiyin, foot - shaoyin, foot - yangming of twelve meridians bounce continuously". It means the arteries on the meridians of lung, kidney, stomach; the specific location is Taiyuan (LU 9), Taixi (KI 3) and Renyin (ST 9), Chongyang (ST 42). *Classic on Medical Problems* pointed it out specifically that "all twelve meridians had arteries". There is a mark in the chapter 10, *miraculous pivot* described that "the floating and vivid meridians were collaterals". The collaterals we mentioned is small vessels and capillaries on skin. The collaterals also means small vessels on mucosal surface. "If yang collaterals broke then blood would be extravasating; if yin collaterals broke then blood would floating inward and hematochezia would be taken; if collaterals broke on intestines and stomach then blood would spill out of intestines", quote from the chapter 66, *Miraculous Pivot.* In clinical practice, there is stimulations on vessels directly. Traditional "pricking collaterals" Method is a therapy for pricking to make bleeding on capillaries and shallow veins; "pricking vessels" is stabbing on the radial artery, the Taiyuan (LU 9); "pricking sinus" is stabbing on the carotid sinus.

在经络形态学的现代研究中也观察到经络与包括淋巴管在内的血管的关系。有些经脉的某些行程段与血管的分布相似。例如手太阴肺经沿头静脉分布；手少阴心经沿尺动脉和尺静脉分布等。在仅留股动脉及股静脉与躯体联系的动物下肢上，针刺“足三里”能引起与针刺正常动物类似的肠效应，表明针刺可以通过血管途经而产生相应内脏效应。Hilton 测得的每秒 10cm 的动脉壁平滑肌兴奋时的传导速度，与循经感传速度恰好一致，提示动脉壁平滑肌的兴奋传导可能也是一种循经感传。为观察经络与淋巴管的关系，上海中医药大学在胎儿尸体上注射碳素墨水以显示淋巴管，发现在少商穴处注入的墨水沿皮下淋巴管到第一掌骨内侧面后，经腕部桡侧，上行至肘部肱二头肌腱桡侧，再斜行至腋下淋巴结。其路线与手太阴肺经上肢部的循行一致。进一步的研究发现，十四经和带脉、冲脉都与淋巴管系的淋巴收集丛或淋巴管和淋巴结的分布基本一致。例如，不少穴位位于淋巴收集丛，尤其是任、督及带脉和相应淋巴收集丛的连接线颇为相似。有些经脉，如胃经、肺经、心经、脾经及下肢部的膀胱经等与穴位下深、浅淋巴管的走向也很相近。头面部的经脉到躯体的主要“中转站”——“缺盆”位于锁骨上淋巴结处；上肢部经脉到躯体的“中转站”是“缺盆”、“云门”、“中府”、“周荣”和“天池”，它们与锁骨上淋巴结、锁骨下淋巴结及腋淋巴结的部位相当；下肢部经脉到躯体的“中转站”是“维道”、“气冲”、“冲门”和“急脉”，它们和腹股沟淋巴结的部位相当。在功能观察的研究中还发现，牵拉或电刺激兔子小腿淋巴管和刺激股动脉、股神经及针刺“足三里”一样，也可引起肠运动效应。这些研究结果表明，淋巴管系在形态学上和功能上都与经络有关。

The relation of meridians and vessels including lymph – vessel is taken into account in modern study. Some sections on meridian is familiar with the vessel distribution, such as the lung meridian goes along cephalic vein, the heart meridian goes along artery and vein of ulnar. Needling Zusanli (ST 36) on the lower limbs of only femoral artery and vein connected with animal body lead to intestinal effect, this means that relevant interior organ effect could be evoked through vessels. Hilton measures the 10cm/sec on smooth muscle of artery which is the same as the speed of transmission. It indicates that conduction of excitation might be a kind of transmission. In order to observe the relation of meridians and lymph vessels, Shanghai University of TCM injects carbon ink in fetus corpse to display lymph vessel and find out that the ink injected in Shaoshang (LU 11) go along from first metacarpal bone to radial of wrist and radial of biceps brachii muscle and then armpit lymph nodes. Its route is the same as the lung meridian on upper limb. Further research find out that the fourteen meridians, belt vessel, thoroughfare vessel matches the distribution of lymph vessels and nodes. a lot of acupoints locates on lymph gathering bush, conception and governor vessels' routes are the same as the connection lines of bushes. Some meridians' route like stomach, lung, heart, spleen, urinary bladder is familiar with the deep and shallow lymph vessels under acupoints. Quepen (ST 12) which is the hub of meridians of head and body locates on supraclavicular lymph nodes; as well as the location of Quepen (ST 12), Yunmen (LU 2), Zhongfu (LU 1), Zhourong (SP 20) and Tianchi (PC 1) matches supraclavicular lymph nodes, intercostal lymph node, and axillary lymph node, and Weidao (GB 28), Qichong (ST 30), Chongmen (SP 12) and Jimai (LR 12) as the hub of lower limbs and body, their location matches the inguinal lymph nodes. On the observation of function study, draw off or electric stimulate the lymph vessel on rabbit's leg may evoke intestinal effect as well as stimulating femoral artery, femoral nerves and needling Zusanli (ST 36). All these results indicate that lymph vessel system relates with meridians.

（二）中枢兴奋扩散说 Central Excitation Spreading Hypothesis

持此种观点的学者认为，循经感传的基本过程是在中枢神经系统内部进行的，感传线是针刺穴位时产生的兴奋在中枢神经系统，特别是在大脑皮层内的定向扩散所形成，在外周不存在有关感传线的组织结构，即“感在中枢，传也在中枢”。中枢说的提出主要基于以下事实：

Researchers with this point of view regard that the basic process of meridian – route transmission is running in the central nervous system (CNS), the transmission lines are tissues of needling excitation on CNS, especially formed in cerebral cortex, without any transmission tissues around, it is "sensing in CNS, transfer in CNS too". This hypothesis is based on the following truths:

1. 幻肢存在感传 Transmission on Phantom Limbs

针刺截肢患者或先天性缺肢者的残端肢体，可以引发感传并通向并不存在的“肢体”。这种感传出现在已失去外周组织结构的缺肢中，说明其形成过程主要是中枢因素的作用。有人曾用低频脉冲电刺激55名截肢患者的残肢端的穴位，结果有34人（61.82%）出现幻肢感传。这些出现于幻肢的幻肢感传，同样具有循经性、可阻性及慢速传导等循经感传的基本特征。

Needling residual limbs on amputees or congenital disables would evoke transmission and transfer to the non – existed limbs. This transmission appears in the residual limbs indicates that the process is controlled by CNS. Someone stimulated acupoints on 55 amputees by low pulse frequency electric current, the result is 34 people (at 61.82%) felt the transmission on phantom limbs. These transmission on phantom limbs has basic features like meridian – rout, block – able, low speed transmit.

2. 气功可诱发感传 Qigong Induces Transmission

气功锻炼过程中，在无外周特定刺激的情况下，仅通过在穴位（丹田）的意念集注，便能引发循经感传现象。有关这方面的记载在古今气功文献中很多，并非偶然现象。气功锻炼过程中的入静沉思，实际上是大脑的一种特殊的功能状态。采用入静诱发感传的方法，在改变中枢机能状态的条件下，可大幅度地提高循经感传的出现率。这表明循经感传的产生与大脑的功能密切相关。

In the process of qigong exercise, only focus on Dantian point without any exterior stimulation, transmission appears. There are many records in ancient materials. The meditation is a special function state of the brain. The ratio of meridian - route transmission appearance could be raised remarkably by meditation under the condition of changing the state of central brain function.

3. 颅内病变患者可自发感传 Spontaneous Transmission for Encephalic Pathogenic Patient

颅内病变患者可自发出现循经感传，其性状与针刺等引发的感传并无区别。此外，直接电刺激大脑皮层的第一体感区，可引起身体对侧出现蚁行感。

There is no difference between needling transmission and spontaneous transmission for encephalic pathogenic patient. Electric stimulating on primary somatosensory area of the cerebral cortex could evoke the ants - crawling feeling on the other side of the body.

4. 感传以皮层感觉功能为基础 Cerebral Cortex Sensory Function Is the Basis of Transmission

循经感传是以大脑皮层感觉功能为基础的，一旦中枢神经系统遭受损害，循经感传现象便不能出现。例如，脊髓完全横断者损伤水平以下部位不能引出感传；腰麻后，刺激麻醉平面以上的穴位，多数受试者出现的感传能进入全部感觉机能消失的麻醉区，并直达足趾。麻醉后出现的这种感传的性状与麻醉前比较无明显变化。中枢论者认为，感传能“自由”地进入麻醉区而保持其性状不变，说明感传是中枢神经系统，特别是皮层躯体感觉区内的某种定向扩散形式，若是感传的基本过程在外周，则不可能出现这种感传能“自由”地进入麻醉区的现象。

Transmission is based on cerebral cortex sensory function, once the CNS is damaged, the transmission is gone. transmission cannot be evoked on the injury partial of the patient with complete transection of spinal cord; stimulating the acupoints above the anesthesia plane after lumbar anesthesia, most of the subjects' transmission reach the anesthesia area and to the toes. There is no difference on transmission between before and after anesthesia. The CNS hypothesis holder regards that transmission with unchanged features transmits into the anesthesia area, indicates that the transmission is some sort of directional diffusion on sensory area, if the process is in periphery, the phenomenon of transmission “freely” in anesthesia area won't happen.

5. 杰克逊癫痫与感传相似 Jacksonian Epilepsy Is Familiar with Transmission

在杰克逊（Jackson）癫痫中，发作性抽搐可从身体某部沿一定方向逐渐扩布。发作终了，抽搐停止的顺序，也像感传的“回流”一样，由抽搐扩布的终端向其起始部位返回。抽搐的扩布可被中途的重压及用绳索紧扎而中止，从而也中止了癫痫的进一步发展。这和循经感传的可阻断及针刺效应的因此而消失也有相似之处。

Paroxysmal spasm diffuses from one part of body to a certain direction in Jacksonian epilepsy. At the end of spasm, the tic “flow back” from end to start point like the sensory transmission. The diffusion could be blocked by pressing and thread tie, and this feature is familiar with the block - able meridian - route transmission.

（三）外周动因激发说 Peripheral Motivation Hypothesis

这里所说的“外周”，是指感传循行的躯体部位而言，不只指神经系统的外周部分。持这种观点的研究者认为，循经感传形成的根本环节在体表。针刺时产生的某种“动因”将外周神经感受装置“沿经传导”般地依次兴奋，这种兴奋冲动相继传入中枢神经系统，从而产生主观感受得到的循经感传，即“传在外周，感在中枢”。外周论者认为，经络可能是一种具有特殊结构的传导系统，故感传形成的主要过程应在外周，其主要依据有：

The exterior here is the outer part of body on which transmission transmits, not only peripheral part of nerve system. This hypothesis holder believe that the truly mechanism of transmission is on the surface of the body. Some “motivation” generated by needling excites the sensors along meridian. The excitation introduces in the CNS, and then subjective feelings transmit along meridians, that is saying “transmiting in the peripheral and responsing in CNS”. The peripheral motivation hypothesis holders believe that meridians might be a conductive system with specific structure, the process of generation is in periphery, evidence as below:

1. 感传可伴形态学改变 Transmission Alters with Morphological Changing

感传不只是一种主观感觉，有时还可继发产生循经的红线、白线、丘疹、水疱、线状出汗、皮下出血以及循经性皮肤病等可见的形态学变化。

Not only transmission is a subjective feeling, but also morphological changing like meridian - route red, white line, papule, blister, striation sweating, subcutaneous hemorrhage on skin, and other meridian - route dermatopathy.

2. 感传可被阻滞 Transmission Could Be Blocked

机械压迫、液体注射或局部冷冻等直接作用于外周的理化因素可阻滞循经感传过程的推进，并使针刺效应减弱或消失，但对周围神经动作电位及皮层诱发电位无明显影响。

Physical factors used on periphery directly such as mechanical pressing, liquid injection or local freeze would block the transmission and reduce the needling efficacy, but no remarkably effect on the potential of peripheral nerve action potential and cortical evoked potential.

3. 感传线与已知结构不同 Transmission Lines Are Different from Known Body Structure

循经感传的路线与已知的神经、血管、淋巴管的分布很不一致，感传的速度较周围神经的传导速度慢得多。

The route of transmission is quite different from the known distributions of nerves, vessels, lymph vessels, and the speed is much lower than that of peripheral nerve.

4. 在体表感觉缺失区感传会改变 Transmission Modifies on Anesthesia Zones

肌肉、肌腱手术后感传会改道，遇到创伤、疤痕或关节时感传会减速、受阻或绕道。截瘫患者会出现感传的"跨越式传导"。这些现象说明，在体表感觉缺失区内仍存在某种沿一定路线行进的传递过程。

The transmission would be rechanneled after operations on muscle and tendon, and slow down, be blocked or make a detour on injuries, scarves or joints. Over - partition transmission would appear on paraplegia patients. These phenomena indicate that there is a certain transmission on some route existed in anesthesia area on body surface.

5. 感传可干扰第一体感区 Transmission Disturbs the Primary Cortical Somatosensory Area

在循经感传者皮层体感诱发电位（SEP）的观察中未见与感传同步的中枢兴奋的有序扩散。10 名感传显著者 SEP 的 $C_4 - C_5$ 成分低于 16 名无感传者，表明感传过程中，第一体感区的功能受到了某种干扰。研究者认为，这种干扰可能是由外周感受装置被循经扩布的某种动因的依次激发所造成。

There is no ordered diffusion synchronized with transmission on the observation of somatosensory cortical evoked potential (SEP). The component of $C_4 - C_5$ of SEP from 10 sensitive transmitters is lower than 16 non - transmitters. It is indicated that the function of primary cortical somatosensory is disturbed during transmission. Researchers believe that the disturbance maybe caused by ordered, meridian - route excitation of peripheral sensors.

有人认为，中枢兴奋扩散说和外周动因激发说各有一定的事实依据，但在推论上走向两个极端。在循经感传过程中，外周和中枢是不可分割的统一体。经络如果作为一个实体存在，不应局限于身体的某一局部。作为一个完整的调节系统，经络不应是独立于中枢之外的一个孤立的外周系统，也不应是和外周隔离的一个孤立的中枢系统，而应有从外周到中枢，从低级到高级的谱系。外周有循经感传的实质过程，中枢则有循经感传的功能联系。感传在中枢内的某种特定联系，实际上是感传的外周实质过程的反映和投射，没有外周的循经性实质过程，也就不可能出现中枢的特定功能联系。在循经感传过程中的外周和中枢的协调活动中，起决定作用的是外周的实质过程。当然，外周的实质过程需有中枢的参与才能形成完整的循经感传过程。

Someone believe that central excitation spreading hypothesis and peripheral motivation hypothesis are based on evidences, though the conclusion is much of difference. The periphery and the CNS is an indivisible entity. The meridian system should not be limited in a narrow location but as an existing entity. As an integrated accommodation system, the meridian system should not be an isolated peripheral system independent with CNS, or isolated CNS independent with peripheral system either, but a pedigree from low level to high level, from periphery to CNS. The periphery has substance process of transmission; the CNS connects with functional relationship. The certain specific connection in the CNS is the reflection and reaction of process of peripheral substance. Without meridian－route peripheral substance process, there would be not existence of the specific functional connection of CNS. The process of peripheral substance is the key during the coordination of periphery and CNS in the transmission. Of course, the participation of CNS during peripheral substance process would complete the process of meridian－route transmission.

（四）周围神经说
Peripheral Nerves Hypothesis

经络的形态学研究结果表明，在穴位或其附近，常有神经干或较大的分支通过。显微镜观察也证明穴位处的各层组织中有丰富的神经末梢、神经丛和神经束。无论从穴位一个“点”的角度，还是从经脉一条“线”的角度，均可体现经络与周围神经的关系。

The result of the morphological study on meridians indicates that there are nerve trunk or some major branches go through the location of acupoints. The microscope observation proves that there are abundance of nerve endings, nerve plexus and nerve tract in each level tissue around acupoints. No matter from the view point of acupoints as “dots”, or meridians as “lines”, can all be reflected in the relations of meridian and surrounding nerves.

1. 经脉的某些行程段常与神经干及其主要分支的行程基本一致
Some Logtions of Meridians Matches the Route of Nerve Trunk and Its Main Branches

经脉的某些行程段，特别是四肢肘膝关节以下的经脉路线常和一根或几根神经干及其主要分支的行程基本一致。例如，手太阴肺经沿臂外侧皮神经、前臂外侧皮神经、肌皮神经及桡神经分布。手少阴心经沿臂内侧皮神经、前臂内侧皮神经及尺神经分布。手厥阴心包经沿正中神经分布。足太阳膀胱经沿腓肠神经、股后皮神经分布。足厥阴肝经沿腓深神经、腓浅神经和隐神经分布。

Some sections of meridians especially routes on limbs below joints matches the routes of one or more nerve trunks and its major branches. The lung meridian extends along the nervus cutaneous brachii laterals, lateral ante - brachial cutaneous nerve, muscular cutaneous nerve and radial nerve. The heart meridian extends along the medial brachial cutaneous nerve, medial ante - brachial cutaneous nerve and ulnar nerve. The pericardium meridian extends along the median nerve. The bladder meridian extends along the sural nerve, posterior femoral cutaneous nerve. The liver meridian extends along the deep peroneal nerve, superficial peroneal nerve and saphenous nerve.

2. 经脉弯曲部位常有相应神经结构分布
The Band Parts of Meridian Are Surrounded by Corresponding Nerve Structure

膀胱经在骶部有两个弯曲，其中由上髎至下髎穴的一个弯曲相当于骶神经后支外侧支的第一次神经袢，而从小肠俞到白环俞的一个弯曲相当于该神经的第二次神经袢。膀胱经在腘窝由浮郄经委阳到委中的这一弯曲，可从腓总神经与胫神经之间的关系来理解。

There are two bends on sacral bone on The bladder meridian; one of them from Shangliao（BL 31）to Xialiao（BL 34）is the first loop nerve of lateral posterior branch of sacral nerve, and the bending from Xiaochangshu（BL 27）to Baihuanshu（BL 30）is the 2nd loop nerve. The banding from Fuxi（BL 38）to Weiyang（BL 39）, Weizhong（BL 40）on popliteal fossa could be known from the relation of common peroneal nerve and tibial nerve.

3. 表里经络穴处常有相应神经分支吻合
Luo - Connecting Points of Exterior - Interior Meridians Matches the Distribution of Relevant Nerves

有些络脉从经脉分出到另一经的部位正好是有关神经分支吻合的部位。例如，前臂外侧皮神经的分支与桡神经浅支在列缺和偏历穴处吻合，前臂外侧皮神经和肺经有关，桡神经浅支和大肠经有关。前臂骨间掌侧神经与前臂骨间背侧神经在内关和外关穴处相互吻合，前臂骨间掌侧神经与心包经有关，前臂骨间背侧神经与三焦经有关。一般来说，表里两经的络穴都有相应神经分支的沟通。

Some points on collaterals are the meridian divarication matched the relevant nerve branches. The branch of lateral ante - brachial cutaneous nerve matches superficial branch of radial nerve on Lieque（LU 7）and Pianli（LI 6）, the lateral ante - brachial cutaneous nerve is related with the lung meridian, the superficial branch of radial nerve is related with the large intestine meridian. The inter - osseous ante - brachii volaris matches on Neiguan（PC 6）and Waiguan（SJ 5）, the inter - osseous ante - brachii volaris is related with the pericardium meridian, the posterior inter - osseous nerve is related with the triple energizer. Normally, there are relevant nerve branches connect luo - connecting point of the exterior - interior meridians.

4. 表里两经上常有相同神经或大致发自相同脊髓节段的神经分布 The Same Nerves or Nerves from the Same Segment of Spinal Cord Are on the Exterior - Interior Meridians

肺经和大肠经都与肌皮神经和桡神经有关，这两根神经均发自 $C_{5\sim8}$。心经和小肠经都与尺神经及前臂内侧皮神经有关，尺神经发自 $C_{7\sim8}$ 及 T_1，前臂内侧皮神经发自 C_8 和 T_1。脾经和胃经都有隐神经及腓浅神经分布。肾经和膀胱经都有胫神经分布。

The lung meridian and the large intestine meridian are related with muscular cutaneous nerve and radial nerve originated from $C_{5\sim8}$. The heart meridian and the small intestine meridian are related with the ulnar nerve and the medial ante - brachial cutaneous nerve, and the ulnar nerve starts from $C_{7\sim8}$ and T_1, the medial ante - brachial cutaneous nerve originates from C_8 and T_1. There are saphenous nerve and superficial peroneal nerve on the spleen meridian and the stomach meridian, tibial nerve on the kidney meridian and the bladder meridian.

5. 手足同名经的某些相应穴位处有类似的神经分布形式 Some Acupoints on Homonym Meridians of Foot and Hand Have Similar Nerve Distributions

前臂外侧皮神经与桡神经浅支在手太阴经列缺穴处吻合；小腿内侧皮神经与腓神经浅支在足太阴经公孙穴处吻合。在解剖学上，前臂外侧皮神经与小腿内侧皮神经相当，桡神经浅支和腓神经浅支相当，而列缺和公孙二穴亦相当，都是太阴经络穴。手三里穴处有桡神经深支分布，足三里穴处有腓深神经分布，两穴不仅同属阳明经穴，其名称、位置及神经分布亦相当。

The lateral ante - brachial cutaneous nerve meets the superficial branch of radial nerve at Lieque（LU 7）on the lung meridian and the medial ante - crural cutaneous nerve meets the cutaneous branch of superficial peroneal nerve at Gongsun（SP 4）on the spleen meridian. In anatomy, the lateral ante - brachial cutaneous nerve is corresponding with the superficial branch of radial nerve meanwhile Lieque（LU 7）is corresponding with Gongsun（SP 4）which is luo - connecting points on Taiyin meridians. There are deep branch of radial nerves on Shousanli（LI 10）and deep peroneal nerves on Zusanli（ST 36）, the two acupoints belong to the yangming meridians, their names, locations and nerve distributions are almost the same.

6. 手足三阴、三阳经的主治特点与相应脊神经和自主神经的联系有关 The Properties Characteristic in the Three Yin and Yang Meridians of Foot and Hand Relates with the Connection of Relevant Spinal Nerves and Automatic Nerves

手三阴经分布于上肢掌面，通过上肢部脊神经组成的颈丛和臂丛，在颈部和胸部与支配心肺的交感神经联系，主治胸部疾患。手三阳经分布于上肢背面，通过颈部脊神经和颈上交感神经节的联系，再经颈内动脉和脑神经与头部各器官联系，从而主治头部病症。足三阴经分布于下肢内侧，通过下肢脊神经组成的腰丛和骶丛，在腰骶部与分布于腹部的自主神经联系，故主治腹部病症。足三阳经分布于下肢外侧和后侧，通过腰骶部脊神经与交感神经相连，再上行与分布于背部和头部的神经联系，从而主治头部和五官病症。交感神经及其各交通支与脊神经联系点的体表投影，恰与背俞穴的位置重合或相近。有人采用荧光组织化学方法，在人和动物器官的结缔组织中的中细小阻力血管周围，找到绝大部分属于交感节后纤维的肾上腺素能和胆碱能神经末梢的双重支配，认为这种交感节后纤维与阻力血管的关系，和气血与经脉的关系有相似之处。可见，交感神经和经络也有重要关系。

Three yin meridians of hand are on the palm side of upper limb, go through brachial plexus and cervical plexus, connects with sympathetic nerves controlled heart and lung to cure chest diseases. Three yang meridians of hand are on the back side of upper limb, go through neck spinal nerve and ganglion sympathetic on neck, and connect with artery in neck and cranial nerve to cure head diseases. Three yin meridians of foot are on the inner side of lower limb, go through lumber plexus and sacral plexus consisted by spinal nerve on lower limb, connect with belly sympathetic nerve on lumbosacral portion to cure abdominal diseases. Three yang meridians of foot are on the outside and inner side of lower limb, and go up to connect with nerves on back and head to cure head and five sense organs disease. The surface reflection of the connection of sympathetic nerve and its crossing branches and spinal nerve matches the location of back - shu points. The fluorescence histochemical method is used on finding diplonomy of fibrous adrenergic belonged to ganglia and nerve ending of cholinergic at the surrounding of tiny resistance vessels in connective tissue on human and animal organs. It is believed that the relationship of fiber after ganglia and resistant vessel is the same as the qi - blood and meridians. So the sympathetic nerve relates with meridians.

此外，在针灸临床上，不少针刺方法和周围神经有关。如早期的电针疗法，主要是在神经干部位或皮神经分布区进行针刺通电治疗。再如，“节刺”即刺星状神经节；“傍神经刺”即刺在神经干旁边。这些针刺方法所产生的经气传导及其效应也体现出了经络与周围神经之间的关系。

In addition, in clinical practice, many needling methods are about peripheral nerves. in the early electric acupuncture therapy, electric stimulation were mainly focus on the nerve trunk or nerve cutaneous area. “puncturing jie methods” is stimulating the stellate ganglion; “puncturing bilateral nerves method” is needling on the side of nerve trunk. These transmissions and effects caused by needling methods reflect the relationship of meridians and peripheral nerves.

（五）神经节段说
Ganglion Hypothesis

在四肢部，经络与周围神经的分布有相似之处。但在躯干部，经络主要是纵向分布，而神经则主要是横向分布。躯干部这种纵行的经脉与横行的神经之间的关系如何？从躯干部腧穴及各经腧穴的主治特点来看，纵行的经脉也有前后的横向联系，经脉的这种联系与神经节段的划分也有相似之处。这种经络与神经节段相关假说的提出，主要有以下几方面的依据：

The istributions of meridians and peripheral nerves on the four limbs are familiar. The meridians on trunk are longitudinal meanwhile nerves are latitudinal. What is the relationship between longitudinal meridians and latitudinal nerves? The longitudinal meridian has the latitudinal connections and the connection of meridians is familiar with the division of nerve section. The following materials are the evidences for this hypothesis:

1. 经络腧穴与相关内脏在神经节段分布上的一致性
The Consistency of the Meridians and Acupoints and the Nerve Grafts' Distribution of the Relevant Organs

经络、腧穴的形态学研究表明，经穴在 0.5cm 的范围内，几乎都有脊神经或脑神经的支配。每一经穴的神经节段常位于相关脏腑的那个神经节段上，或在相关脏腑所属的神经节段范围内。也就是说，穴位与其所主治的脏腑在神经节段上具有相当的一致性。

The morphological study of meridians and acupoints shows that there is domination of spinal nerve and cranial nerve around acupoints in 0.5cm range. The nerve section of each acupoint locates on the nerve grafts belonged to the relevant organs. That means there is quite consistency of acupoints and relevant nerve grafts.

（1）躯干部经穴与相应脏腑的神经节段关系：俞募穴是躯干部最具代表性、最常用的腧穴，是脏腑之气向背腰和腹胸部输注通达的部位。俞募穴与相应脏腑之间的这种关系，在神经节段的划分上也得到了体现。形态学研究表明，绝大多数俞募穴的神经节段位于相应脏腑的神经节段范围内，或邻近这些节段。

The relationship between acupoints on body trunk and the nerve grafts' distribution of the relevant organs: The back – shu points and front – mu points are the most commonly used acupoints, are the collection points from the internal organs' qi on the back, wrist and chest, abdomen. This relationship is suitable for the division of the nerve grafts. The study of morphology indicates that the majority nerve grafts of locate in the range of relevant internal organs' nerve grafts.

除俞募穴以外，循行于躯干部的任、督、胃、肾、脾经穴及膀胱经的其他腧穴，与相应脏腑的神经节段之间也存在这种关系。例如：

膻中属 T_4，主治属 $T_{2\sim4}$的呼吸系及属 $T_{1\sim5}$的心脏病症。

中脘属 T_8，主治属 $T_{6\sim10}$的脾胃病症。

关元属 T_{12}，主治属 $T_{10}\sim L_1$ 的泌尿生殖系疾患。

魂门属 $T_{7\sim8}$，主治属 $T_{6\sim9}$的肝脏病症。

志室属 $T_{12}\sim L_1$，主治属 $T_{11}\sim L_1$ 的肾脏病症。

梁门属 T_8，主治属 $T_{6\sim10}$的脾胃病症。

水道属 T_{12}，主治属 $T_{10}\sim L_1$ 的泌尿生殖系疾患。

Except for Back – Shu points and Front – Shu points，there is the same relationship for other acupoints on meridians，such as：

Danzhong（RN 17）from T_4，treatment respiratory from $T_{2\sim4}$ and cardiopathy from $T_{1\sim5}$.

Zhongwan（RN 12）from T_8，treatment syndrome patterns of the spleen and stomach from $T_{6\sim10}$.

Guanyuan（RN 4）from T_{12}，treatment urogenital system diseases from $T_{10}\sim L_1$.

Hunmen（BL 47）from $T_{7\sim8}$，treatment liver diseases from $T_{6\sim9}$.

Zhishi（BL 52）from $T_{12}\sim L_1$，treatment kidney diseases from $T_{11}\sim L_1$.

Liangmen（ST 21）from T_8，treatment syndrome patterns of the spleen and stomach from $T_{6\sim10}$.

Shuidao（ST 28）from T_{12}，treatment urogenital system diseases from $T_{10}\sim L_1$.

通过对躯干部腧穴与相应脏腑的神经节段之间的关系的分析发现，同一经的穴位，可因所处神经节段的不同而具有不同的主治特点，而不同经脉的腧穴，可因所处神经节段的相同而具有相同的主治。如中脘、关元同属任脉，但因所属神经节段的不同，其主治也不相同；胃经的梁门、水道穴也是如此。而任脉的中脘和胃经的梁门，因同属一个神经节段，故具有相似的主治特征；关元和水道也是如此。

The Analysis on the relationship is that acupoints on the same meridian treat the different diseases since their various ganglion locations，and acupoints on different meridians treat the same diseases because the same ganglion location. Zhongwan，Guanyuan from ren meridian treat differently for the different ganglion locations，as well as Liangmen，Shuidao from stomach meridian. Zhongwan on Ren meridian，Liangmen on the stomach meridian treat the same just for their ganglions is one，as well as Guanyuan，Shuidao.

（2）四肢部经穴与相应脏腑的神经节段关系：躯干部腧穴的主治与神经节段之间的这种关系在四肢部经穴也是存在的。虽然四肢部皮节的分布是扭转的，从表面上很难辨认经穴与神经节段之间的关系，但若从皮节的感觉神经根的分布来分析，则不难看出它们之间的联系。一个皮节或一个感觉神经根的分布范围，可按脊髓的单个后根的传入神经纤维在体表皮区的分布来确定。当人体四肢向下时，神经节段是沿四肢纵行分布的。若将皮节的分布特征和有关经脉的循行路线加以比较，便可看出经脉按皮节分布的迹象。每条经脉沿 1 ~ 3 个神经节段分布。四肢部同经腧穴主治的一致性与经脉分布的神经节段性也是不无关系的。如手少阴心经循行于上肢内侧后缘，其部位正属胸髓上部节段（$T_{1\sim3}$），与心经循行部位相关的躯体神经进入上部胸髓节段后角，而支配心脏的内脏传入神经也进入上部胸髓节段（$T_{1\sim5}$）后角，两者在这些节段后角内发生汇聚。因此，心经各穴皆主治与心脏有关的病症，针刺心经各穴可通过上部胸髓节段而影响心脏功能，实现低位中枢的相关调整作用。

The relationship between acupoints on the limbs and the nerve grafts of relevant organ: The relationship mentioned above exists in acupoints on the limbs. Although the distribution of dermatomes is twisted, the relation between acupoints and nerve grafts is hard recognized, but on the distribution of roots of sensory nerve then the relation is clear. The distribution of dermatome and sensory nerve root is confirmed by the distribution of afferent neural fibers of single root on spinal cord on skin. The nerve grafts extend longitudinal when limbs are adown. The law that meridian extends along nerve grafts could be clear if comparing the features of dermatomes with routes of relevant meridians. Each meridian extends along 1 ~ 3 nerve grafts. The consistency of acupoints treatment on limbs is correspond with meridian - route nerve grafts. The heart meridian goes along lower part of inner side of upper limbs, its section belongs to upper thoracic spinal ($T_{1\sim3}$), and the somatic nerve related with the heart meridian section goes into the posterior cornu of the upper thoracic spinal cords and the visceral afferent nerve related with heart goes into posterior cornu of the upper thoracic spinal cords ($T_{1\sim5}$), they are getting together. So acupoints on the heart meridian treat heart diseases, and needling them could adjust heart function through the upper thoracic spinal cords to achieve the relevant regulation by the lower central.

四肢部其他经脉也有类似特征。同经腧穴的主治有其共性，而不同经脉腧穴则主治各异。

经穴与相应脏腑在神经节段分布上的这种关系，在近年的形态学研究中得到了证实。应用辣根过氧化物酶（HRP）等神经追踪显示法观察到，从经穴和相应内脏注入的 HRP 等标记物在若干脊髓节段有重叠标记的现象，提示经穴和相应内脏的初级传入神经在相关神经节段上确有会聚。

There are similar features on the other meridians of the four limbs. There are common indications of the acupoints in the same meridians and different properties of acupoints in different meridians.

The relationship between acupoints and relevant nerve grafts has been proved in the morphological study. Observing through nerve trace methods like Horse Radish Peroxidase (HRP), there is phenomenon of overlay marks on some sections of spinal cord when the HRP is injected from acupoints or relevant internal organs. This means acupoints meet the primary afferent nerve on relevant nerve grafts indeed.

（3）表里两经的神经节段关系：表里两经不仅常由相同的神经分布，在神经节段的分布上也有相同之处。例如，肺与大肠相表里，两经都有肌皮神经和桡神经的分布，同属 $C_{5\sim8}$；心与小肠相表里，两经的分布与前臂内侧皮神经和尺神经有关，前者属 $C_8 \sim T_1$，后者属 $C_{7\sim8} \sim T_1$。

The relationship of the exterior and interior meridians' nerve grafts: The same distributions of nerve and nerve grafts are on the exterior - interior meridians, e. g. the lung and the large intestine are the exterior and interior meridians in TCM, both of their meridians have muscular cutaneous nerve and radial nerve, belong to $C_{5\sim8}$; and the heart and the small intestine are the exterior and interior relation, the distributions of their meridians is related with medial ante – brachial cutaneous nerve and ulnar nerve, the former belongs to $C_8 \sim T_1$, and the latter belongs to $C_{7\sim8} \sim T_1$.

2. 牵涉痛与相应经络在神经节段分布上的相关性
The Relevance of Referred Pain and Its Relevant Meridians on Nerve Grafts

大量临床观察和研究资料表明，某些内脏器官病变引起的牵涉痛或某些神经痛的放射路线常与经络的循行路线相吻合，且具有明显的（神经）节段性。例如：

心绞痛常由心前区经左肩、沿上肢内侧后缘直向小指放射，所经部位与手少阴心经的循行路线相当，所属节段正是 $C_8 \sim T_1$ 交感性皮节。

哮喘、肺结核病患者常出现从颈肩沿上肢桡侧向拇指方向的放射痛。这是副交感性（迷走神经）内脏感觉传入 C_2 节段脊髓后扩散到 $C_{3\sim5}$ 的牵涉痛，与手太阴肺经的循行路线一致，说明肺经循行部位与肺脏确有联系，所以，对针刺孔最、尺泽等肺经穴位能治疗肺部疾患，也就不难理解了。

某些盆腔脏器的病变传入 S_2 形成牵涉痛，再向下肢后侧放射，其放射部位与膀胱经循行路线一致。这种放射痛的形成与沿膀胱经路线的肌紧张有关。因此，在治疗盆腔脏器及大肠下部疾病时，可考虑选用膀胱经的膀胱俞、白环俞等与骶髓节段有关的穴位。

肝脏和胆囊发生病变时所产生的放射痛的部位通常在右颈部和右肩部，相当于该部位肝经和胆经的循行路线。

Mass of research data and clinical observation indicates that the referred pain caused by pathological internal organs or radial route of neuralgia matches the meridian routes, and the feature of section (nervous) is significant, e. g. angina pectoris starts from precordium to left shoulder, passing upper inner side of up limb, the passing area is the route of the heart meridian of hand – shaoyin. This section is $C_8 \sim T_1$ sympathetic dermatomes.

Asthma and tuberculosis patients have the radial pain from neck and shoulder to radius side and thumb direction. This is the referred pain caused by vagus nerve visceral sense transfer to C_2 spinal cord and then spread to $C_{3\sim5}$. Its trace is the same with the lung meridian course. This phenomenon proves that the lung meridian is related with the lung, therefore needling Kongzui (LU 6), Chize (LU 5), etc, may cure lung diseases.

The referred pain from the afferent nerve S_2 caused by some pathological changes in the organs in the pelvic cavity radiates to the back side of lower limbs, the position is the same as the route of the bladder meridian. It is about muscular tension along the pathway of the bladder meridian. Therefore, Pangguangshu (BL 28) and Baihuanshu (BL 30), etc, are chosen to treat relevant diseases.

The radial pain caused by the liver and the gallbladder is usual on right neck and shoulder correspond with the distribution of the liver meridian and the gallbladder meridian.

3. 经络和神经节段相关的胚胎学基础
Embryology Basis about Meridians and Nerve Grafts

大约在受精后第 14 天的脊椎动物的早期胚胎，除头部不易识别外，躯干的节段性结构已经形成。胚胎的每一个节段性单位，称为体节。每个体节包括体壁部、内脏部和相应的神经节三个部分。人类早期胚胎结构的基本形式是沿身体纵轴从头到尾排列的，各节段的伸展是横列位。

The early embryo fertilized for 14 days already has the segmental structure of the body except head. Every segmental unit is called "somite", and every somite includes body well, visceral part and the relevant nerve grafts. The basic form of early embryo of human is arranged from head to end along the body vertical axis, the extension of each unit becomes a row long.

在胚胎发育过程中，包括肌节和皮节的体壁部演化成为未来的四肢和躯干；内脏部发生变形，形成束状、管状或实质性内脏器官；神经节逐渐变成保持节段状的脊髓，并向体壁部和内脏部分别发出躯体神经和内脏神经将两者联成一体。胚胎的每一脊髓节段所发出的传出神经纤维，经过相应的前根支配相应的肌节。同样，其传入纤维由相应的皮节经相应的后根，传入同一脊髓节段。随着胚胎的生长分化，体节各部分发生了很大的位移，肌节和皮节的节段性变得难以辨认，有些器官从原来的位置转移到别的部位。但不管肢芽如何伸长，皮节和肌节如何变位或转移，内脏形态如何演变，它们的神经支配如何重新排列组合，而神经系统与体壁和内脏之间仍保持着原始的联系。如发生于颈部肌节的膈，虽已转移到胸腹腔之间，而支配它的膈神经仍起于第 4 颈神经。神经系统与躯体和内脏之间的这种原始的节段性分布关系，不仅帮助我们根据不同体表部位的牵涉痛来判断相应内脏的病变，同时为经络与神经节段相关说也提供了理论依据。所谓的经络与神经节段相关的观点，就是用这种躯干四肢－神经节段－内脏联系来说明穴位－经络－内脏联系的一种假说。

In the development of embryo, the body well including sarcomere and dermatome develop to limbs and body trunk, the visceral part transforms into fasciculate, tubular shaped or substantial organs; ganglion turns into segment－like spinal cord, and send somatic nerve and visceral nerve to the body well and visceral part and connect them into one. The efferent nerve fiber send from every segment of spinal cord dominates relevant sarcomere by relevant anterior root. And the afferent fibers send into the same segment of spinal cord by the relevant posterior root of relevant dermatomes. Great movement take place for somite parts during the development, and it is hard to recognize the segments of sarcomere and dermatome, and some organs change places. The original connection between nerve system, body wall and organs remains, no matter what kind of changing on limb bud, sarcomere, dermatome, organs and the domination of nerves, e. g. the diaphragm generated from the 4th neck nerve dominates the phrenic which is generated from neck sarcomere, though it is in the middle of chest and abdomen. The relationship of original segment distribution of nerve system, body and internal organs helps us to judge the pathological changing on the different parts of referred pain and give the evidence for the consistency of meridians and nerve grafts. The so called point view of meridians and nerve grafts is the hypothesis using the relation of limb, nerve grafts and visceral organs to explain the connections of acupoint, meridians and internal organs.

4. 气街与神经节段的相似性 The Similarity of the Pathway of Qi and Nerve Grafts

《内经》中也有关于经络的横斜通路的记载。从《内经》的根结标本理论看，十二经脉气通行于四肢、头面和躯干。脉气从四肢汇聚到头面、躯干后，还要向四周扩散弥漫，以濡养周围的组织器官。脉气在头面、躯干部向四周扩散的径路，便是气街。人体有四气街，"胸气有街，腹气有街，头气有街，胫气有街。故气在头者，止之于脑；气在胸者，止之膺与背腧；气在腹者，止之背腧与冲脉于脐左右之动脉者；气在胫者，止之于气街与承山踝上以下"（《灵枢·卫气》）。由上可知，"四街者，气之通路也"（《灵枢·动输》）。头气街，内通于脑，外应于五官；胸气街，内通于肺、心，外应于胸膺和背俞；腹气街，内通于肝、脾和肾，外应于背俞及腹部冲脉之交会穴；胫气街，内通于胞中，外应于气冲穴及承山穴和踝部上下。四气街和神经节段在它们的划分及其与内脏器官和躯干四肢部的联系方面非常相似。

There is record about the horizontal and diagonal path way of meridians in *Huangdi Internal Classic*. Seeing from the view of the branch - foundation, tip - root theories, the qi of twelve meridians goes around the limbs, face, head and body trunk. The qi gathering from limbs to head, body trunk spreads and pervades to moistening and nourishing the tissue and organs surrounding. The pathway on head, body trunk diffusing to surrounding is the qi pathway. There are four qi thoroughfare, "the chest qi, abdomen qi, head qi, and shank qi have their own qi thoroughfare respectively. So qi in the head terminates at the brain; qi in the chest ends at the breast and back - shu points; qi in the abdomen terminates in the area between back - shu points, the thoroughfare vessel and around the pulsing arteries of the left and right side of the umbilicus; and qi in the shank ends at the region inferior to Qijie and Chengshan (BL 57) which are located above to the ankle", quote from the chapter 52, *Miraculous Pivot*. So the pathway on head connects brain inside and five senses organs outside; the pathway on chest connects lung, heart inside and breast, back - shu outside; the pathway on abdomen connects liver, spleen, and kidney inside and back - shu, crossing points of thoroughfare vessel outside; the pathway of shank connects uterus inside and Qichong (ST 30), Chengshan (BL 57) and around ankle outside. The division and relationship of four qi pathways on the internal organs and body limbs & trunk is the same as nerve grafts does.

（六）二重反射假说 Dual Reflex Hypothesis

关于经络实质的二重反射假说是汪桐于 1977 年提出的。汪氏认为，针刺穴位时，一方面可通过中枢神经系统引起通常的反射效应，即长反射；另一方面，由于针刺部位局部组织的损伤可产生一些酶化学物质，这些物质作用于游离神经末梢，便引起局部的短反射。这里所谓的双重反射，是指针刺过程中长、短两种反射的同时出现。汪氏认为，二重反射假说可比较完满地解释针刺穴位时出现的反射效应和各种循经出现的经络现象。

Wang tong suggested this hypothesis in 1977. He believed that there are, from one side, an usual reflection effect from the CNS, "a long spinal reflex", and from the other side, a local shot reflex caused by free nerve endings which was affected by enzyme generated by local tissue injury after puncturing. The dual reflex we talk about here is the long and short reflex appears at the same time during needling. Mr. Wang believed that this hypothesis could perfectly explain the reflex effect and various meridian phenomena.

1. 二重反射假说的主要依据和观点
Proofs and Viewpoints

二重反射假说的提出主要基于以下依据和观点：

The hypothesis is based on the following evidences:

（1）器官功能的神经调节可通过长、短两种反射形式实现：现代生理学认为，人和动物生理功能的调节是通过神经体液综合调节机制实现的，但其器官功能的神经调节可通过两种形式来实现。其一，是通过中枢神经系统的长反射。其二，是通过位于器官内部的局部神经丛而实现的短反射。消化系统功能活动的调节是这两种反射的典型例子，其他器官也有类似的情况。

The neuroregulation organs' functions could reach through long and short reflex: The modern physiology believes that the physiological accommodation of human and animal is neurohumor comprehensive accommodation, and the neuroregulation on functions of organs works in dual ways, one is long reflex based on the CNS, another one is short reflex with the help of local nerves of organs. The accommodation of digestive system is one of the typical examples, and other organs have the similar situation.

（2）经络线上有相对丰富的血管、淋巴管和神经丛或神经网：经络循行线上存在着相对丰富的血管和淋巴管，其分布可能有特殊的构型。经络循行线上的皮肤、皮下组织和血管周围有相对丰富的神经丛或神经网，它们主要由交感肾上腺素能和胆碱能纤维及传入神经组成。这些游离的神经末梢之间可相互影响。

Comparative abundant vessels, lymph vessels, nerve plexus and nerve net on meridian route: There are comparative abundant vessels and lymph vessels on the route of meridians, and their distributions are special structures. There are comparative abundant nerve plexus and nerve net around the skin, subcutaneous tissue and vessel surroundings, they were made up with sympathetic adrenergic, cholinergic fibers and afferent nerve. These free nerve ending affect each other.

（3）针刺可引起循经相继触发的短反射：针刺时，由于局部组织损伤而产生的一些酶化学物质可作用于游离神经末梢而引起局部短反射。通过神经丛或神经网的相互作用，一个局部短反射的效应可成为引起另一个短反射的动因。如此，短反射相继触发，向一定的方向推进，从而引起循经出现的各种经络现象。在一系列局部短反射相继激发的过程中，每一个反射环节所引起的兴奋，可经传入神经传入中枢，上升为意识。各个短反射在人脑皮层上的相应代表区依次连接，便可形成经络在大脑皮层上的投影图。在经脉线上，以神经和血管为基础的局部短反射效应，可以被认为是一种比较低级、比较古老的外周整合系统，是进化过程中遗留下来的一种比较原始的机能。

Sequential triggered short reflex along meridians could be evoked by needling: Some enzymes generated by local injured tissues affect free nerve ending and then evoke the local short reflex, which could be the motivation of another one caused by the mutual affection of nerve plexus and nerve net. In this way, the serious short reflex being evoked one after another like chain reaction in nuclear reaction, and head to a certain direction, perform various meridian phenomena. Every excitation evoked could transfer to the CNS, and then become the consciousness in the process of chain reaction. The connections of the cortical representations of short reflexes form the projection print of meridian on cerebral cortex. The local short reflex based on nerves and vessels could be recognized as a kind of low level, primitive peripheral integrated system, it is an original mechanism in evolution.

2. 二重反射假说的实验验证 Experimental Verification

要肯定二重反射假说的成立，首先必须证明外周神经末梢之间确有传递兴奋的可能性。早在 1950 年，Habgood 就曾报道，在只带有两根神经支配的蛙皮肤离体标本上，迷走神经和交感神经之间也可形成突触联系。为证明短反射的存在，汪氏也进行了一系列的实验：

The provability of the possibility that there is transmission between peripheral nerves is necessary. Back in 1950, Habgood reported that stimulating one of the breaking ends of nerves on an isolated preparation of a frog with only two nerves domination could evoke nerve discharge on another one. The synaptic connection could be formed between vagus nerve sympathetic nerves. Mr. Wang did serious experiments to prove the existence of the short reflex:

（1）外周神经末梢之间兴奋传递的实验研究：在大白鼠身上分离腓浅神经和腓深神经，并切断它们和中枢的联系，发现在通常情况下，电刺激腓浅神经的外周端，在腓深神经干上可引出动作电位（AP），其出现率为 7.14%。刺激腓深神经外周端，在腓浅神经干上记录不到动作电位。但是，如果电针足三里 30 分钟后再进行观察，则电刺激腓浅神经外周端时，在腓深神经干上可引出动作电位，其出现率为 44.44%；刺激腓深神经，在腓浅神经上也可引出动作电位，其出现率为 39.29%。电针足三里前后动作电位的出现率有非常显著的差异

（$P<0.005$）。如果同时刺激同侧下肢交感神经干的外周端，则动作电位的出现率显著降低（$P<0.01$）。进一步的研究表明，刺激一条神经干，可在邻近的另一条神经的单纤维上记录到动作电位。实验结果表明，在一定条件下，兴奋可以在外周神经末梢之间传递。这种传递又可被交感神经抑制。

Experiment of excitation delivery of free ending of peripheral nerve: Isolate the superficial peroneal nerve and deep peroneal nerve on mouse, and cut off the connection to the CNS, and then find out that normally electric stimulating the exterior end and the action potential (AP) on deep peroneal nerve, the radio is 7.14%. Operate oppositely, the AP could not be recorded on superficial peroneal nerve. If electro needling on Zusanli (ST 36) for 30 minutes first, and the radio on deep peroneal nerve is 44.44% and on superficial peroneal nerve is 39.29%. So the AP appearance radio is significant difference ($P<0.005$) in the condition of before and after electro needling Zusanli (ST 36). If stimulating the peripheral nerve of vagus nerve on the same lateral of low limbs synchronously, the radio of AP is remarkably low ($P<0.01$). Further research indicates that stimulating one nerve trunk and AP could be recorded on cell fiber on the adjacent nerve. The results tell that the excitation could be transferred between ends of peripheral nerves in certain condition and it could be block by vagus nerve.

（2）针刺切断脊髓前后根大鼠内关穴对急性心肌缺血心电图的影响：对大鼠静脉注射垂体后叶素引起实验性急性心肌缺血，并将大鼠分为四组。A 组：切断 $C_6 \sim T_2$ 前后根，针刺内关；B 组：不切断前后根，针刺内关；C 组：切断前后根，针刺非穴；D 组：切断前后根，不予针刺。结果显示，对 A、B 两组大鼠电针双侧内关穴半分钟左右，急性心肌缺血心电图各项指标迅速得到纠正，除逆转期外，两组心电图数值的改变和恢复的时间均无显著差异；而 C、D 两组心肌缺血心电图恢复时间显著延长，与 A、B 组相比，差异显著。这说明不依赖中枢的短反射确实存在，内关－心脏的联系有相对特异性。

The influence of needling Neiguan (PC 6) on rat with neurotomy of posterior and anterior roots of spinal cord to ECG of acute myocardial ischaemia: Inject hypophysin in mice to evoke experimental acute myocardial ischemia and divide them into four groups. A group, cut off anterior and posterior roots of $C_6 \sim T_2$, needling Neiguan (PC 6); B group retain anterior and posterior roots, needling Neiguan (PC 6); C group cut off anterior and posterior roots, needling non-acupoints; D group cut off anterior and posterior roots, no needling. The result is needling bilateral Neiguan (PC 6) on mice of A and B group for 30 secs, the indexes of acute myocardial ischemia on ECG is modified, the changing and recovery time is no significant difference except on reversion period, meanwhile the recovery time of C and D group is remarkably longer, and compare with A and B group, the difference is significant, this means the reflex, independent with the CNS, is existed and the connection of Neiguan (PC 6) and heart is relative specificity.

（3）刺激切断脊髓前后根大鼠正中神经对急性心肌缺血心电图的影响：切断大鼠右侧

脊髓 $C_6 \sim T_2$ 前后根，并将其造成急性心肌缺血，再分别刺激两侧正中神经、尺神经以及内关穴区的肌肉，观察其对心肌缺血的影响。在29只大鼠的实验中发现，刺激右侧正中神经对急性心肌缺血心电图也有明显的改善作用，进一步证明短反射的存在；而刺激尺神经作用较小，刺激内关穴区的肌肉则无作用，说明内关穴的主要神经通路是正中神经，尺神经也参与。

The influence of stimulating rat with neurotomy of median nerve of spinal cord mouse to ECG of acute myocardial ischaemia: Cutting off anterior and posterior roots on $C_6 \sim T_2$ on right side of spinal cord to evoke acute myocardial ischemia and then stimulating the bilateral median nerve, ulnar nerve and muscle on Neiguan (PC 6) separately to observe the influence on myocardial ischemia. Find in experiment with 29 rats that stimulating on right side of median nerve could modify the ECG significantly, this further proves the existence of short reflex. Stimulating ulnar nerve is less useful, muscle on Neiguan (PC 6) area is useless. This experiment indicates that the main access of Neiguan (PC 6) is median nerve; ulnar nerve also takes part in.

(4) 对切断前后根大鼠因急性心肌缺血引起的神经源性皮炎的研究：随着静脉注入垂体后叶素时间的延长，大鼠在出现急性心肌缺血心电改变的同时，两前肢皮肤逐渐出现局灶性蓝色斑点，其中，两侧内关穴区的蓝斑明显而又恒定。在切断和保留脊髓前后根的两侧内关穴区皮肤内染料的含量基本相同，无明显差异，表明内关－心脏确有相对特异的联系，这种联系除通过中枢的长反射外，还存在着通过脊神经节的短反射。

The study of neurodermatitis on rat with neurotomy of posterior and anterior roots of spinal cord: There are focal spots appear on the skin of two fore limbs of rat with ECG changing on acute myocardial ischemia during the extension of hypophysin injected in vein, and blue spots in Neiguan (PC 6) area are steady and clear. The contents of dye in bilateral skin area of Neiguan (PC 6) are the same when cut off or retain the anterior and posterior roots of spinal cord; this indicates that there is relative specificity between Neiguan (PC 6) and heart and short reflex through spinal cord except long reflex through the CNS.

(5) 经穴和相关内脏短反射的形态学研究：采用荧光双标记法，将快蓝和核黄两种荧光素，分别注入穴位和相关内脏。结果，在相应后根节内发现若干双标记细胞。双标记细胞主要是一些中小型细胞，其轴突的分支，一支支配体表，一支达到相关内脏，是短反射的形态学基础。

上述实验结果从几个侧面为验证经络实质的二重反射假说提供了必要的前提。

The morphology study of short reflex of acupoints and relevant internal organs: Inject fast blue and nuclear yellow into acupoints and relevant organs, and find several double－tagging cells in the relevant posterior roots. The double－tagging cells are small and medium size cells, one their branches of axon matches the surface of body, another to the relevant organs, this is the morphology basis for short reflex.

（七）轴索反射接力联动假说
Transmission of Relay Axonal Reflex Hypothesis

1980年，张保真根据经络路线皮肤反应和循经感传形态生理学等方面的大量文献资料，提出了轴索反射接力联动假说，试图从组织生理学的角度对经络现象的产生机理和经络的组织结构基础作出合理的解释。轴索反射接力联动假说和二重反射假说在总体观点上有类似之处，但前者对某些细节的解释较后者更详细具体些。

In 1980, Zhang baozhen suggested the hypothesis of transmission of relay axonal reflex based on mass materials of skin reaction on the route of meridians and meridian – route transmission in morphophysiology, and trying to give a reasonable explanation on the mechanism of production of meridian phenomena and structure of meridians on the viewpoint of histophysiology. The transmission of relay axonal reflex hypothesis is familiar with the dual reflex hypothesis generally, but the former gives more detail explanation than the latter.

轴索反射接力联动假说认为，穴位中的神经末梢属于某个感传神经元的周围轴索的一个分支。当穴位受到各种形式的刺激时，分布于穴位的感觉神经末梢产生兴奋，其冲动传到该轴索分支的分歧处，反转逆向，沿其另一分支传向皮肤，在此分支的终末处释放扩血管的或其他的效应物质，使皮肤的小动脉扩大，微血管通透性提高，接近此分支终末的肥大细胞进入活跃状态。小动脉扩张形成潮红，微血管通透性提高形成风团，由穴位刺激直接引起的和由轴索反射引起的肥大细胞活动改变了中间物质的成分和含量。这些中间物质可将信息从一个神经元的轴索终末传给下一个神经元的轴索终末。它们包括从上一轴索终末释放出的递质及存在于微环境中的各种生物活性物质或介质，也包括构成荷电基质的大分子物质和电解质。主要由于中间物质导电能力的增强，促使皮肤中按经络线特定排列的、与上一神经元末梢重叠分布的下一个神经元轴索终末产生兴奋，进行轴索反射。该轴索反射的结果同样形成相应区域的潮红或/和风团，同样增强中间物质的导电能力。轴索反射如此一个接一个地传下去，潮红或/和风团就从局部延长，成为跨过若干皮节的红线或皮丘带。

This hypothesis believes that nerve endings in acupoints belong to a branch of peripheral axon of a certain neuron. The sensory nerve ending on acupoints excites and passing the excitation to the parting of axon branch, and then roll back and transfer to the skin through another branch, releasing chemic materials like expand blood vessel thing to expand arteriole in the skin, enhancing the permeability of capillaries. Mast cells closed to the endings excites. Arteriole expands and forms the flushing, permeability of capillary enhances and forms wheal, the movement of mast cell caused by acupoint direct stimulation and axonal reflex changes the component and content of intermediates. These intermediates pass the information from one ending of axon to another ending. The information includes transmitter released from last axonal ending, various bio – activators existed in microenvironment, macromolecule the basic material of electric charge and electrolysis. The increased conductivity of intermediates evokes the excitation on nerve axonal endings which are lined in specific order along meridian route and overlay with the former nerve and then form the axonal reflex. The flushing and wheal formed in relevant region generated by axonal reflex enhances the conductivity of intermediates. The axonal reflex passing through one by one and the flushing and wheal extends to form the red lines or papule zone jumped over a number of dermatomes.

Habgood 的实验对轴索反射接力联动假说是一个支持。Habgood 认为，在皮肤内也许由于前一神经的刺激释放类似组胺的介质，这些介质降低了第 2 条神经兴奋的阈值。1983 年，Lembeck 提出的关于 Lewis 三联反应机理的解释与轴索反射接力联动假说相似。他认为，当皮肤受刺激后会产生许多化学物质和缓激肽、钾离子、组胺、前列腺素等。它们作用于感觉神经的外周轴突末梢，形成刺激。这不仅引起感觉神经末梢向中枢的冲动传递，也产生向周围释放的 P 物质（SP），造成血管扩张，血浆外渗。同时，经轴索反射在轴索分支末梢也释放 SP。这些 SP 诱发邻近的肥大细胞释放组胺。这些组胺再作用于下一节段的神经轴突末梢，使之兴奋。如此一连串的反应造成神经性炎症的扩散。

The Habgood' s experiment is a support to the hypothesis. Habgood believes there are some mediators similar to histamine released by the former nerve stimulation; these mediators reduce the latter nerve's excitability threshold. In1983, Lembeck suggested an explanation about triple response Lewis which was familiar with relay axonal reflex hypothesis. He believed that many chemical materials, bradykinin, potassium ion, histamine, prostaglandin, etc, would be released after stimulation. These things effect on the peripheral axonal endings of sensory nerve and produce stimulation. It evokes nerve impulse transmission from endings to the CNS and also releases substance P（SP）around to expand vessels and plasma, at the same time SP is released at the branch ending of axon through axonal reflex. These SP evoke the nearby mast cells to release histamine and the histamine effect on the next section of nerve axon endings to excite it. This is the chain reaction to diffuse the nervous phlogosis.

张氏在实验中发现，在人体足阳明胃经路线上的皮肤中确实存在两种不同的神经肥大细胞联接。其中一种为传出性神经肥大细胞联接，或称之为 A 型联接。此种联接建立于轴突终末和肥大细胞之间，而不是轴突在其行程中与肥大细胞单纯的联接。参与联接的轴突终末有薛旺细胞相伴并被其覆围。终末呈特殊膨大，内有囊泡、线粒体、神经丝和复合小体等。肥大细胞表面的皱褶可参与联接的形成。这种联接可能与轴突反射时感觉神经纤维的传出性分支有联系。与肥大细胞形成联接的轴突终末似属 C 类纤维。另一种联接称 B 型联接，在构造上与 A 型联接有很大的差异。它的轴索终末不膨大，也不含任何已知的细胞器，陷入或偃卧在肥大细胞的凹窝中。根据这一结构特点，B 型联接可能是属于传入性的。在小鼠的皮肤中也观察到了神经肥大细胞联接。电生理学方面的研究也证明了 Lembeck 于 1983 年提出的关于 SP 可能是感觉神经传递物的著名假设，并证明 SP 确实存在于初级细传入神经纤维，它既可从细纤维的中枢端向脊髓背角释放，也可从外周端向皮肤释放。中枢端 SP 的释放成为感觉信息的传递物，外周端的SP释放则参与伤害性保护反应，成为神经性炎症的介质。进一步的研究表明，SP和组胺均可在皮肤局部引起末梢神经的传入发放。这种化学物质对局部皮肤神经感觉末梢的直接兴奋作用，证明这些物质确能作为轴索反射接力联动的中间介质，并表明在经络路线皮肤反应和循经感传过程中，不仅有形态学方面的变化，沿经络路线的信息也可不断地传入中枢。神经肥大细胞联接是神经末梢释放SP进而诱发肥大细胞释放组胺的结构基础。微量SP和组胺都可引起外周感觉神经末梢的传入发放。SP可来自直接受刺激的感觉神经末梢，也可经轴索反射而在邻近的其他分支末端释放。组胺可由受刺激部位的细胞释放，也可由肥大细胞在SP的作用下释放。局部SP及组胺含量的增加，又可作用于邻近的感觉神经末梢和肥大细胞。如此一连串接力联动的不断扩展，便形成沿经络路线的皮肤反应，并引起外周神经末梢间跨节段的冲动传递而造成循经感传。张氏还通过在小白鼠皮肤内注射微量SP、组胺等化学物质，成功地制成循经出现的红线和皮丘带等皮肤反应，为轴索反射接力联动假说提供了依据。

Mr. Zhang found that there were two kinds of neuromastocytic junctions in the skin on the route of the Stomach Meridian. One of them is efferent neuromastocytic junction, we called it A junction. The A junction build up between axon endings and mast cells. The axon endings taken part in the junction are surrounded and covered by Schwann cell. The axon ending is inflated; there are vesica, mitochondrion, neurofilament and compound corpuscle, etc. Wrinkles on the surface of the mast cell take part in the production of junction. This junction may connect with efferent branch of sensory nerve fiber during the axon reflex. The axon ending connected with mast cells is similar with C type fiber. Another junction is B junction which is quite different from A junction in structure. Its axon ending is normal, not contain any organelle and sink into or lay in slot of mast cell. The B junction may be the afferent based on this structure feature. It is found neuromastocytic junctions in the mouse's skin. Studies in electrophysiology prove that famous hypothesis proposed by Lembeck in 1983 on the issue of SP might be sensory nerve transmitter, and SP exist in the primary afferent neurofilament, it could release from center to spinal dorsal horn and from periphery to skin. The SP from center becomes transmitter of sensory information, and the SP from periphery takes part in the harmful protective reaction and become the mediator of nervous phlogosis. Further research shows that the SP and histamine evoke afferent action of peripheral nerve on local skin. The direct excitation on sensory nerve ending of local skin caused by this chemical substance prove that these substances is the intermediates for relay of the transmission of relay axonal reflex, and there are morphological changes and information along the meridian routes transfer into the CNS during the process of meridian – route transmission and skin reaction on meridian route. The neuromastocytic junctions are the structure basis of nerve ending releasing SP and then evoking mast cell to release histamine. Micro scale SP and histamine could produce the afferent action of peripheral sensory nerve ending. The SP could come from direct stimulated sensory nerve ending or from nearby branch ending releasing through axon reflex. The histamine could come from stimulated cell releasing or SP affected mast cell releasing. The increase of local contend of SP and histamine could effects on the nearby sensory nerve ending and mast cell. The relay action is expending to the skin reaction on the meridian routes and evokes nerve impulse transmission between peripheral nerve endings to produce meridian – route transmission. Mr. Zhang made skin reaction such as red lines and papule to support his hypothesis by injecting micro chemical substances like SP, histamine in mice skin.

(八) 第三平衡系统假说
The Third Balance System Hypothesis

根据大量循经感传现象的研究资料，孟昭威于 1978 年提出了有关经络实质的第三平衡系统假说。孟氏认为，《内经》所指的经脉实际上是循经感传线。书本上的经线来自生理上的循经感传线，而不是来自解剖形态的观察。《灵枢·脉度》中描述的许多关于经脉长度的尺寸实际上是对经脉感传线的测量结果，而不是血管的长度。《内经》中所说的行于经脉中的“气”，应理解为感传。《灵枢·五十营》中所说的“呼吸定息，气行六寸”，指的是感传速度。这一速度合每秒 2. 8 ~3. 6cm，与循经感传的速度接近，而绝非血流速度。经络的主要作用是沟通体表和内脏之间的联系，调节两者间的相对平衡。据此，孟氏认为，经络应是一个平衡系统。这个系统在现代医学中是没有的。现代生理学中没有将人体按平衡作用进行系统分类的，故没有平衡系统的概念，而只有内环境稳定一词。然而，人体是一个完整的体系。人体生命活动的关键在于如何维持身体的动态平衡。内环境稳定只是人体平衡作用的一个方面，从人体的各种功能活动来看，人体应有数个平衡系统，以维持人体的生命活动。现代生理学中已知的具有调节功能的结构是神经系统和内分泌系统。经络系统必然和它们协作共同完成全身的平衡调节作用。这几个调节系统主要是根据各自不同的反应速度来划分的。不同的反应速度具有不同的调节速度（表18 –1）。

Meng Zhaowei proposed the third balance system hypothesis in 1978 based on amount of research materials about meridian – route transmission phenomena. Mr. Meng believes that the meridian mentioned in *Internal Classic* is the meridian – route transmission actually, on which the meridians come from meridian – route transmission but not from anatomic morphological observation. The length of meridians in the chapter 17, *Miraculous Pivot* is the measurement of actual transmission lines not the length of vessels. The “qi” mentioned in *Internal Classic* should be understood as transmission. “The qi walks six cun in a breath” quoted in the chapter 15, *Miraculous Pivot*, indicates the speed of transmission. The meridian speed is 2. 8 ~3. 6cm/s close to the speed of transmission, but not the speed of blood flowing definitely. The main function of meridian is communicating inside and outside of the body and accommodates its balance. Mr. Meng believes the meridian system is a balance system which is not existed in modern medicine concepts. There is only homeostasis in modern physiology. Human body is a complete system, and the key to the system is keeping dynamic balance. There should be several balance systems in human body to keep alive since the functions we have and the homeostasis is one of them. Nerve system and endocrine system are the structures with accommodating function in modern physiology, and the meridian system should work with them to keep body balance. These regulation systems are defined by their own respond speed. Different responding speed matches different accommodating speed（Tab 18－1）.

表 18－1 人体四种平衡系统

Tab 18－1 The Four Balance Systems

平衡系统 Balance system	调节及反应速度 Accommodating and responding speed	作用 Function
第一平衡系统（躯体神经） The first balance system（somatic system）	70～120 m/sec（传导） 70～120 m/sec（conduction）	快速姿势平衡 Rapid position balance
第二平衡系统（自主神经） The second balance system（automatic nerve system）	2～14 m/sec（传导） 2～14 m/sec（conduction）	内脏活动平衡 Visceral activities balance
第三平衡系统（经络系统） The third balance system（meridian system）	0.02～0.1 m/sec（感传） 0.02～0.1 m/sec（transmission）	体表内脏间平衡 Balance between surface and internal organs
第四平衡系统（内分泌系统） The fourth balance system（endocrine system）	以分钟计（效应作用） Count minimum minute（effect）	全身性慢平衡 Slow balance in the whole body

第一平衡系统是控制随意肌运动的躯体神经系统，进行各种快速平衡的调节，如打乒乓球、赛跑等体育运动之类的快速平衡，其传导速度约为每秒70～120m。第二平衡系统为控制内脏活动的自主神经系统，其传导速度约为每秒2～14m。它的平衡调节速度比躯体神经系统慢许多，主要调节内脏活动的较慢的平衡。第四平衡系统是内分泌系统，控制全身内分泌系统以及其他一切器官组织的慢平衡，如血糖平衡、血压平衡等，其调节速度以分钟计算，较自主神经还慢。第三平衡系统是经络系统，控制体表内脏间的协调平衡，其传导速度约为每秒2～10cm。

The first balance system is somatic system which controls voluntary muscle movement and various rapid balances such as playing ping pong, racing, etc. Its conduction velocity is 70～120 m/sec. The second balance system is automatic nerve system which controls visceral activities, its conduction velocity is 2～14 m/sec. Its balance adjusting speed is much lower than somatic system, mainly focus on the slow balance in visceral activities. The fourth balance system is endocrine system which controls slow balance in endocrine system and other organs such as sugar balance, stabilized blood pressure, etc. Its speed is slower than automatic nerve system, count minimum minutes. The third balance system is meridian system which control the balance between surface and internal organs, its speed is 2～10 cm/sec.

上述第一、二、四三个平衡系统是现代生理学中已知的结构，从它们的调节速度来看，自主神经系统和内分泌系统的调节速度相差甚大，这两个平衡系统之间似乎还有一个平衡系统。经络系统的调节速度刚好介乎于这两个平衡系统之间，故将它作为第三平衡系统置于第二、四平衡系统之间，正好填补两者之间的空缺。只是其他三个平衡系统的组织结构已经明了，而经络这个平衡系统的形态学基础尚未清楚。它既似神经，又不似神经，好像是一个类神经系统。

The above mentioned the first, second, fourth balance systems are the known systems in modern physiology, the adjusting speeds are quite different between automatic nerve system and endocrine system, it seems that there should be another one between them to fill the gap. And the meridian system speed is just between them, so it defined as the third balance system. Until now, the morphology basis of meridian system is not clear yet, it familiar with nerve and does not, seems like an analogical nerve system.

第三平衡系统的形态学实质，就其传导速度而言，其结构应较自主神经为细。英国学者皮尔斯 1980 年曾提出神经第三分支系统，即神经内分泌系统，或称 APUD 系统。APUD 是 Amine Precursor Uptake and Decarboxylation 的缩写，直译为胺的前体的摄取和脱羧。目前已知 APUD 系统包括分布于体内各器官的 40 余种细胞，可产生 35 种肽类物质和 7 种胺类物质。其中 23 种肽类物质既存在于神经系统，又可见于周围其他组织中。神经第三分支系统和已知的神经系统中的躯体神经和自主神经相比具有起动慢、作用时间长的特点。这和经络系统有相似之处。故孟氏认为，APUD 系统与经络这个平衡系统有遥相呼应之势，或许它属于经络的范围。

The morphological essence of the third balance system is that its structure should be thinner than automatic nerve for its conduction velocity. Pearse from England proposed the third division of nerve system in 1980 which is neuroendocrine system or named as amine precursor uptake and decarboxylation (APUD). The APUD system includes more than 40 kinds of cells in various organs, and may produce 35 peptides materials and 7 amino materials. Amount of them, 23 peptides materials exists in nerve system and other tissues around them. Compare with somatic nerve in nerve system and automatic nerve, the third division of nerve system has the features as low speed and long term effect. All these are familiar with the meridian system. So Mr. Meng believes that APUD system matches with meridian system, or maybe the APUD belongs to the meridian system.

第二节 腧穴现代研究
Modern Research on Acupoints

有关腧穴现代研究的资料非常丰富，本节根据本教材特点仅就腧穴特异性研究作一扼要介绍。腧穴特异性，起初是指腧穴的主治作用和反映病候的特异性，是人们在长期的针灸临床实验中总结提炼出来的。为了证实腧穴的这种特异性，国内外研究人员采用现代科技手段，从腧穴的形态结构、生物物理、病理反应、刺激效应等方面对腧穴的特异性进行了大量的实验研究，并取得了可喜的进展。

There are so many materials on modern study of acupoints; the following is the brief introduction. The specificities of acupoints were major functions and diseases reflections based on long term clinical practice experiences. Foreign researchers take the advantages of modern technology to prove the specificities through several aspects such as tissue structure, biophysics, pathological reaction, etc.

一、腧穴形态结构研究 Study of the Structure of Acupoints

（一）腧穴与感受器 Acupoints and Sensors

作为针灸治病时的一个刺激感受点，腧穴应和某些感受器密切相关。研究表明，腧穴所处部位的不同，其感受器的类别和数量亦不同。西安医科大学等采用组织形态学方法观察到：足三里、合谷、内关等肌肉丰厚处的穴位以肌梭为主；肌腱附近的曲泽、昆仑等穴多为环层小体；肌腱接头处的承山等穴的中心多为腱器官，周围为肌梭；头皮处的百会、印堂、攒竹、丝竹空等穴主要是游离神经末梢和包囊感受器；关节囊处的内、外膝眼等穴以露菲尼小体为主。在指尖部穴位观察到，其表皮基层细胞之间，有新月状或小环状游离神经末梢；棘层细胞间有更为纤细的、无特殊形态的游离神经末梢；真皮乳头层内有构造复杂而多样化的触觉小体；真皮网状层内有游离神经末梢、露菲尼小体和克氏终球；皮下组织与真皮交界处可见到大量环层小体；在血管周围有粗细两类纤维构成的神经束与血管伴行。足趾部的隐白、大敦等穴主要为触觉小体和游离神经末梢。在足三里、三阴交、内关等穴处还可见各种游离神经末梢、露菲尼小体、麦氏小体、克氏终球、环层小体和高尔基-马楚尼小体等无囊和有囊感受器。穴处血管周围尚有血管旁包囊感受器。上海生理研究所采用神经组织学方法在对人体皮肤的观察中发现，每 $1mm^2$ 皮肤内有 100 多个来源于许多不同的神经纤维的神经末梢，即使是极细的点状刺激也避免不了对神经末梢的刺激。所以，每个腧穴的相应皮肤上可能都有神经末梢的分布。奥地利组织学家 V. G. Keller 在 12000 张组织学连续切片中观察到，穴区神经末梢比周围非穴丰富，穴区由感觉神经末梢支配的皮肤表面积为 $2.8mm^2$，而非穴区为 $12.8mm^2$，穴位在直径 5～7mm 内的组织学结构与非穴明显不同；穴位是麦氏小体、克氏小体、巴西尼小体等感受器和效应器明显集中的部位。Keller 认为，穴位区域相当于皮肤的感觉区。还有研究显示，合谷、内关等穴区内肌梭密度远较周围非穴区大；足三里穴区内压力感受器密度也较非穴区大得多；穴位的分布部位与各种感受器在体表的聚集部位相一致。因此，虽然未见穴位中有什么普遍存在的穴位感受器和新的特殊结构，但穴处的感受器有相对密集的趋势，不同部位的腧穴，其感受器的类型亦不尽相同。感受器数量上的差别可能是穴位与周围非穴比较所具特异性的一种体现，而穴位与其他穴位比较所具的特异性可能体现在感受器类型上的不同。

Acupoints should connect with some sensors as stimulation receiver in treat. The study result is different location matches various sensors. Xi'an medical university studies in the point of view of histomorphology, and discovers that acupoints in thick muscle area like Zusanli (ST 36), Hegu (LI 4), Neiguan (PC 6), etc, its related sensors are muscular spindles; and lamellar corpuscles for muscle tendon area, like Quze (PC 3), Kunlun (BL 60), etc; and muscular spindles for the joints of tendon, such as Chengshan (BL 57); and free nerve endings, cystica sensors for scalp area like Baihui (DU 20), Yintang (EX – HN 3), Cuanzhu (BL 2), Sizhukong (SJ 23), etc; and ruffinis for capsular articularis area like interior and exterior knee eyes; and new moon shaped or small ring shaped free nerve ending for basic layer of epidermis areas; and much more thin, unshaped free nerve ending in spin layer cells; and tactile corpuscle in papillary layer; and free nerve endings, ruffinis, in reticular layer; and mass of lamellar corpuscles in the boundary of subcutaneous tissue and dermis; and nerve tract formed by thick and thin fibers around the vessels; and tactile corpuscles, free nerve endings for toe area like Yinbai (SP 1), Dadun (LR 1), etc. Various of free nerve endings, ruffinis, Meissner's corpuscles, Krauses end bulbs, lamellar corpuscles and golgi body are in the areas of Zusanli (ST 36), Sanyinjiao (SP 6), Neiguan (PC 6), etc. Cystica sensors beside vessels locate around vessels on acupoints. Shanghai institute of physiology reveals that more than 100 nerve endings originated from different nerve fibers are in each square millimeter. So the distribution of nerve ending might be on every inch skin on acupoints. V. G. Keller form Austria observed on 12000 pieces serial section tissue that more nerve endings in acupoint area, and the surface area on acupoints controlled by nerve endings is 2. 8 mm^2, rather than 12. 8mm^2 in non – acupoints area. The structures of acupoints in depth of 5 – 7mm are remarkably different from non – acupoints. Acupoints are the gathering place of Meissner's corpuscles, Krause's bulb, pacinian corpuscle. Keller regards acupoint area as sensory area on skin. Other researches explain that the density of acupoint area like Hegu (LI 4), Neiguan (PC 6), etc, is larger; the sensors gathering place matches the distribution of acupoints. Therefore, there are no new structures in acupoint, but sensors gather at acupoints. The numbers of sensors is the specificity of acupoints, and between acupoints different sensors is the key.

(二) 腧穴与神经
Acupoints and Nerves

有关腧穴形态结构特异性的研究，早期和主要的研究是从解剖学和组织学入手观察腧穴和神经的关系。上海第一医科大学在对经穴的尸体解剖中发现，所观察的 324 个穴位中有 323 个穴位与周围神经有关（占 99.6%）。其中与浅层皮神经有关者 304 穴（占 93.8%），与深部神经有关者 155 穴（占 47.8%），与浅层皮神经和深部神经均有关者 137 穴（占 42.3%）。徐州医学院对全身所有经穴做全面观察，结果 361 个经穴中 205 穴（占 56.8%）靠近神经干，其中靠近皮神经主干者 104 穴（占 38.8%），靠近深部神经主干者 122 穴（占 33.8%）。上海中医药大学对 309 个穴位的针刺解剖中观察到，直接刺中神经干者 152 穴

（占49.19%），针刺点旁0.5cm内有神经干者157穴（占50.81%）。有关腧穴和神经感受器关系的研究已在上面介绍。其他一些单位所做的大量的穴位解剖学和组织学观察均得到了类似的结果，表明穴位与周围神经的关系非常密切。大多数穴位位于神经干和神经分支周围，大部分穴位都有细小神经分支通过，而非穴区的神经干支均较穴区少。腧穴的组织穴研究还显示，穴区表皮、真皮、皮下组织、肌肉层及血管壁上都有丰富多样的神经末梢、神经束或神经丛，其神经纤维的类型多为有髓传入纤维、粗纤维和Ⅱ类纤维，而非穴区不具备穴区的这种结构特征。

The early research on acupoints started in anatomy and human histology. The first medical university in Shanghai reveals in anatomy that 323 acupoints out of 324 are related with surrounding nerve (at 99.6%), 304 points related with superficial cutaneous nerves (at 93.8%), 155 points related with deeper nerves (at 47.8%), and 137 points related with both (at 42.3%). Xuzhou medical college study all the acupoints and find out that 205 out of 361 acupoints near nerve trunk (at 56.8%), 104 points near cutaneous nerve trunk (at 38.8%), and 122 points near deep nerve trunk (at 33.8%). Shanghai university of TCM needling and anatomize the 309 acupoints, find out that 152 points were stabbed on nerve trunk (at 49.19%), and 157 points beside nerve trunks in 0.5cm (at 50.81%). Similar results were reported by other researchers; acupoints are close with surrounding nerves, most of acupoints site around nerve trunk and nervous ramification and went through by tiny nervous ramification. There are various nerves ending, nerve tract, nerve plexus in scarf skin, dermis, subcutaneous tissue, muscular layer and vascular wall in acupoint area, the types of nerve fiber are medullated fiber, crude fiber and secondary fibers, meanwhile non - acupoints are not.

（三）腧穴与脉管
Acupoints and Vessels

早期和近年的解剖学和组织学研究均表明，腧穴与血管的关系也很密切。上海中医药大学观察了309个经穴与动、静脉的关系，发现有286穴（占91.62%）正当动脉干或位于动、静脉干旁。尚有研究显示，穴区皮下组织内的小血管和毛细血管网非常丰富。有人以蓝点法对家兔足三里等7个穴位的组织结构做了形态学观察，发现蓝点中心的小血管出现次数较多，并由此向外逐渐减少。第二军医大学采用巨微解剖、组织切片、图像分析等方法观察到，在小腿骨间膜胆经和胃经穴位“地”区都有特定的血管分支，这些分支主要是胫前动脉特定的骨膜骨间膜支。它们在骨间膜上的分布区与胆经的外丘、光明、阳辅和悬钟穴及胃经的足三里、上巨虚、条口和下巨虚穴相对应。穴位区的血管以微动脉为主，管径在14～84um之间，主要分布于骨间膜前面的浅表位置。上海中医药大学以H.E染色组织切片法观察到足三里穴区的微小血管分支明显多于对照点。在对穴区血管观察的同时，有些研究者还观察了穴区的淋巴管分布，发现两者也有一定联系。哈尔滨医科大学报道，有些穴区有一条或数条淋巴管通过，一条淋巴管也可通过数穴。上海中医药大学用墨水和电泳法观察到，不少穴位位于淋巴收集丛的部位。缺盆、云门、中府、极泉、周荣和天池穴分别与锁骨上、锁骨下和腋淋巴结相应；维道、气冲、冲门和急脉与腹股沟淋巴结有关；秩边和承扶穴分别与臀上、臀下淋巴结一致；委中和委阳分别与腘窝淋巴结和腘窝处股四头肌上的淋巴结相一致；在三阴交穴处还见相互吻合的三条淋巴管。上述资料显示的穴区脉管的分布特征可能是腧穴形态结构特异性的一个方面。

Anatomy and histology studies prove that acupoints are related with vessels in these years. Shanghai university of TCM studies the relationship between 309 acupoints and artery, vein, the result is 286 points (at 91.62%) on or beside artery or vein. Other researchers believe that there are abundant of small vessel and capillary nets in subcutaneous tissue in acupoint area. Morphological observation on seven acupoints like Zusanli (ST 36) of rabbits through blue point method is that many small vessel in the middle of blue point, and declines generally outside. Second military medical university find out that there are specific branches of vessel on the "earth" points of the gallbladder meridian and the stomach meridian on inter osseous membrane of leg through methods like macro – micro – anatomy, tissue slice, image treatment, etc. These branches are specific inter osseous membrane branches on anterior tibial artery. Their distribution area on inter osseous membrane matches Waiqiu (GB 36), Guangming (GB 37), Yangfu (GB 38) and Xuanzhong (GB 39) of the gallbladder meridian and Zusanli (ST 36), Shangjuxu (ST 37), Tiaokou (ST 38), Xiajuxu (ST 39) of the stomach meridian. Arterioles are the major vessels on acupoint area, their diameter is 14 ~ 84μm, distributes on the surface of inter osseous membrane. Shanghai university of TCM observes that arteriole branches about Zusanli (ST 36) is more than contrast point remarkably through H. E tinct tissue slice. And the distribution of lymph obeys the same rule. One or more lymph vessels go across an acupoint region, and one lymph vessel might go through several acupoint regions reported by Haerbin medical university. Shanghai university of TCM use the method of ink & electrophoresis to come to a conclusion that many acupoints locate on plexus of lymph. Quepen (ST 12), Yunmen (LU 2), Zhongfu (LU 1), Jiquan (HT 1), Zhourong (SP 20) and Tianchi (PC 1) correspond with up and down sides of collarbone and plexus lymph in axillary; and Weidao (GB 28), Qichong (ST 30), Chongmen (SP 12) and Jimai (LR 12) correspond with inguinal lymph nodes; and Zhibian (BL 54) and Chengfu (BL 36) correspond with up and down sides of hip lymph nodes; and Weizhong (BL 40) to popliteal fossa lymph node, Weiyang (BL 39) to lymph node on quadriceps femoris muscle; and three lymph vessels meet at Sanyinjiao (SP 6). All above materials prove that the distribution of vessels on acupoint region is one of the specificity.

（四）腧穴与肌肉和肌腱
Acupoints and Muscle, Tendon

据统计，占经穴总数62.5%的穴位分布于“分肉之间”，其余37.5%的穴位则多位于肌肉、肌腱之中或其起止点上。加拿大 C. C. Gunn 等在对 70 个穴位的研究中发现，有 35 个穴位位于肌肉运动点上，这些部位正是肌肉神经最接近皮肤的位点，对电刺激最敏感；还有一些穴位位于肌－腱连接处。第二军医大学和上海中医药大学近年的研究表明，胆经、胃经在小腿的穴位均位于肌肉起点范围内。有关腧穴与肌肉和肌腱关系方面的研究开展的比较少，但这些已有资料也说明了腧穴与非穴在与肌肉和肌腱关系上的差别。

上述研究资料显示了腧穴在几种不同的、单一的组织结构上的特异性。但也有些研究人员认为腧穴与多种组织结构相关。

It is counted that 62.5% of acupoints are between muscles, 37.5% on muscle or start, ending, middle point tendon. C. C. Gunn, etc, from Canada research on 70 acupoints and find out that 35 of them are on the motor point nearest to the surface of the skin, and sensitive to electric stimulus; and some other on the joint of muscle and tendon. Recent research from the second military medical university and Shanghai university of TCM indicate that acupoints on legs on the gallbladder meridian, the stomach meridian are located on the region of starting point of muscles. Although studies on the relationship of acupoints, muscles and tendon are rare, the current data already prove the difference of acupoints and non－acupoints with muscle and tendon.

二、腧穴生物物理研究
Biophysical Features of Acupoints

（一）电阻特性
Resistance Features

继 1955 年日本学者发现穴位“良导点”之后，国内许多研究人员也开展了大量的穴位电阻的研究工作，尽管结果不是很稳定，各家报道差异较大，但总体上基本肯定了穴位的低阻（高导电量）特性。在 1700 余人身上检测到的 690 多个良导点的分布与经穴部位大致相符。应用皮肤电阻抗检测的微机系统对人体皮肤低阻点分布检测结果表明，皮肤低阻点基本上是循经分布的。对家兔“内关”穴皮肤电阻的测定及其影响因素的观察显示，穴区皮肤电阻明显低于非穴区，麻醉和死亡均不改变穴区低电阻特性，穴区局部皮肤状态的变化，如温度、湿度和损伤等，可使皮肤电阻降低。对排卵前后三阴交等穴电阻变化及雌激素对其影响的观察表明，穴位电阻的增高与排卵活动存在着一定关系，雌激素可降低穴位电阻。对妇女月经周期和妇科虚实证经穴电阻变化的研究显示，育龄妇女在月经周期各期中，经前与经后冲、任脉电阻有明显差异；在病理状态下，虚证组的电阻比正常组高，实证与正常组均较低。

Chinese researchers have been doing a lot of study on resistance of acupoints since the “ryodo points” was named by a scholar from Japan in 1955. Although results are vibrating, the low resistance （LR） feature is admitted. Over 690 LR points on 1700 volunteers distribute on meridian routes. The result from skin resistance detection computer system shows that the LR points are basically on meridian routes. The measurement of the Neiguan（PC 6） on rabbit and its effect factors indicates that the resistance on acupoints area is lower than non – acupoints area remarkably. Anesthesia and death wouldn't change the feature but the change of status of the skin like temperature, humidity and injury could reduce the resistance. Observing from the resistance variation on Sanyinjiao（SP 6） before or after ovulation and estrogen affection, the increase of resistance on acupoint correspond with ovulation, and estrogen reduces the resistance. The study on the resistance variation of menstrual period and women illnesses shows that there is remarkable difference on thoroughfare vessel's resistance and conception vessel's resistance on the each section of menstrual period of women of child – bearing age at the time of pre and post menstruation. Under pathological condition, the resistance of asthenia syndrome group is higher than normal group meanwhile sthenia group is lower.

（二）电位特性
Electric Potential Features

皮肤导电性能（电阻）测量，通常是指当外加一个电流于皮肤两点时皮肤导电量或皮肤电阻的变化。而穴位皮肤电位测量，一般是指在没有外加电流时从皮肤导出电流或皮肤电位的变化。1955 年，前苏联 Цодщибякий 发现人体体表有许多皮肤电位较周围皮肤高，它们能反映内脏活动的变化。这些被称为“皮肤活动点”的部位大多与传统经穴的位置相符。此后又有不少研究表明，穴位皮肤电位较非穴高。国内许多学者也应用高灵敏度检流计证实穴位确有较非穴为高的皮肤电位，并随机体不同机能状态而发生相应变化。国外许多学者研究结果也证实了这一点。Dumitrescu 等测得穴位的皮肤电位比周围非穴皮肤高 2 ~ 6mV。Brown 等发现在人体双侧上臂可测出分布于各经脉线上的 18 个穴位。尽管受试者身材不同，但各穴分布的位置相似，其皮肤电位值为 2 ~ 42mV。Wheeler 等分别用皮肤电阻和皮肤电位测定技术证实羊也有左右对称的穴位，且在同一个体不同日期测得穴位位置是固定的，并据此绘制出羊的针灸穴位图。中国中医研究院将多头探测电极分别固定于穴位和非穴上测试，结果有 70% 的穴位皮肤电位明显高于非穴位。尽管不少资料显示穴位皮肤电位与非穴比较具有特异性，但由于测试方法和测试条件方面存在一定问题，所以对结果的可靠性及其意义的评价尚有争议。因此，这方面的工作有待理论和实验上的进一步验证。

Electric potential measurement is the current of the skin without external current or skin potential variation. In 1955, Цодщибякий from the Soviet Union found that there were many points on surface of the body got higher potential than surrounding, these points reflected the changing inside. These “dermoactive points” matched the acupoint location. Many researchers in China proved the higher potential feature on acupoint through high sensitivity galvanometer, and the potential changed with health condition, and agreed with foreign results. Dumitrescu measured the potential was 2 ~ 6mV higher than non – acupoint skin. Brown found 18 acupoints on meridians on arms. The skin potential is 2 ~42 mV for all acupoints and the location is similar, though body sizes might different for each one. Wheeler proved goats had binate acupoints, and the position is fixed, and drew out the acupoint map for goat through technic of resistance and potential on skin. China Academy of Chinese Medical Sciences fixed multi – sensors exploring electrode on acupoints and non – acupoints to test, the result was 70% of potential on acupoints were higher. The importance and reliability of the skin potential test is still controversial because of the problems on measure methods and testing conditions. So this feature needs more efforts.

（三）伏安特性 Volt – Ampere Features

导体的电阻特性有线性和非线性之分。在线性导体上用欧姆定律计算的结果不受测试条件（测试电流或电压）改变的影响，其伏安曲线呈一直线。但人体是一个相当复杂的容积导体。上海中医药大学在正常人和患者穴位伏安曲线的检测中发现，人体这个容积导体的电阻特性是非线性的。电阻非线性是指电阻的伏安曲线不呈一直线，在这种情况下，用不同的电流或电压所测得的电阻值是不同的，当检测电流（△I）增大或减小时，被测穴处的电压（△V）并不相应的呈相同倍率地增大或减小，这时△I 和△V 的比值——相应电阻值可因检测电流的改变而出现变化。正常人穴位伏安曲线具有非线性和低惯性特征。

The resistance of conductor is separated into linearity and nonlinearity. The results calculated by Ohm's law on linear conductor wound not change by testing condition (testing electric current or voltage), the volt – ampere curve is a straight line. The radio of current intensity and voltage is a relative fix value. Human body is a complicated conductor. Shanghai university of TCM tests the volt – ampere curve of normal people and patients, and discovers that human as a conductor is nonlinear, which means the volt – ampere curve is not a straight line, and different current with different voltage would get different resistance. When the intensity of current (△I) goes up or down, the voltage (△V) on test point won't go up and down in the same scale, so the resistance, the ratio, is changing. The former resistance detections took a certain voltage or current intensity, so the result is merely a certain point on the volt – ampere curve of the test point. Those detections cannot reflect the whole picture of the volt – ampere curve of the acupoint. In conclusion, the root cause of chaos in detection experiments is using linear resistance detection to detect nonlinear resistance on human body. The normal volt – ampere curve of acupoints is nonlinear and low inertia.

（四）超微弱发光特性 Ultra – Weak Bioluminescence Features

人体活体体表可向外发射超微弱冷光。研究人体腧穴的超微弱发光特性，可从一个侧面探索腧穴的生物物理特异性。对 144 人的 139 个穴位和 278 个非穴的 10000 多次的超微弱发光测试显示，穴位的发光强度均明显高于非穴点；特定穴与非特定穴的发光强度也有差异，井、荥、输（原）、经、（下）合、络、郄穴等特定穴不但显著高于非穴，而且还明显高于非特定穴；不同类型特定穴的发光强度又有差别，井、输、原穴和下合穴的发光强度明显高于其他特定穴。健康人井穴的发光强度明显高于四肢部的其他经穴，上肢经穴的发光强度高于下肢，左右同名经穴的发光强度基本相同，三阳经和三阴经经穴的发光强度也基本相同。可见，腧穴与非穴及与不同腧穴比较在超微弱发光强度上具有特异性。

Human body's surface emits ultra - weak bioluminescence in the air. To explore the biophysical features of acupoints could study through the ultra - weak bioluminescence on the body points. More than 10000 times tests on 139 acupoints and 278 non - acupoints to 144 persons indicate that the luminous intensity on acupoints is higher than non - acupoints; the intensity of special acupoints is different from normal acupoints, jing - well point, ying - spring point, shu - stream (yuan - source) point, jing - river point, (lower) he - sea point, luo - connecting point, xi - cleft point are higher than non - acupoints and normal points. In special therapeutic points, jing - well point, shu - stream point, yuan - sourcing point and lower he - sea point's intensity on healthy person is remarkably high than other acupoints on limbs, upper limbs' intensity is higher than lower limbs, and bilateral same name acupoints' intensity are the same, the intensity of the three yang meridians is basically the same with the three yin meridians. So there is specificity on acupoints and between kinds of acupoints.

（五）红外辐射特性
Infrared Radiation Features

人体的红外辐射可反映人体脏器和全身各部的代谢变化。1970 年，法国 J. Borsarello 最早应用红外线热像图摄影术来显示人体经络穴位。此后，国内外研究者在这方面开展了许多研究。日本学者在 50 名 20 ~ 36 岁的健康男子的胸、腹、背、头等部位共拍摄全身红外热像图照片 2 万张，发现穴位部位的温度比其周围组织高约 0. 5℃ ~ 1. 0℃。在 8 名健康成年男子的胸、腹部发现有较周围高 0. 5℃ ~ 1. 0℃的高温点和高温线，其分布虽有个体差异，但与募穴部位相符。高温点的位置恒定，四季不变，其热传导率也较周围组织高。萩原挥章报道，应用红外线摄影技术通过温差可清楚地确定经穴部位，经穴在体表的直径为 2mm，美国学者在背部皮温图上见到沿脊柱两侧有与膀胱经穴位相应的小白点区，在头面部还可辨认出膀胱经的睛明、攒竹和眉冲等穴。体表存在着许多高温点和低温点，它们中一部分所在的部位与穴位的分布有关。从已有资料看，穴位的红外辐射特异性是客观存在的，但尚待进一步的证实。

Infrared radiation (IR) of the body reflects metabolism of all organs. In 1970, J. Borsarello in France was the first man who used IR thermal imaging to display human meridians and acupoints. More and more Chinese researchers do studies after that. Scholars in Japan took 20000 pictures of chest, belly, back and head on 50 healthy men aged from 20 ~ 36, found that the temperature on acupoint was 0.5℃ ~ 1℃ higher than surrounding tissues. A scholar revealed high temp dots and lines on health men's chest and abdomen which is 0.5℃ ~ 1℃ higher than surroundings, basically matched the distribution of front – mu points. The position of high temp dots is still in years round, and the thermal conductivity is greater than surrounding tissues. Acupoints' diameter is 2mm and its position could be confirmed by IR thermal imaging technic, reported by a Japanese scholar. A scientist from the U. S. finds white dots area on bilateral of the spin correlated with the bladder meridian from back skin temperature image, and Jingming (BL 1), Cuanzhu (BL 2), Meichong (BL 3), etc, on the face area. There are many high temp dots and low temp dots on the surface of body, some of their position is related with distribution of acupoints, after the analysis on thermal images of limbs, body trunk and face. Based on current data, the IR feature of acupoints is objective existing, but more confirmation is needed.

(六) 超声波特性
Ultrasonic Wave Features

日本学者在应用红外线摄像技术确定经穴后，又采用超声波诊断装置，对膀胱经肾俞、志室穴的横断反射进行摄影观察，发现穴位中央有液体性反射波，并可见到微小的心脏样搏动。前苏联 Новынский 认为，穴位组织不像周围组织那样致密，所以穴处组织的超声波吸收系数和声速与周围组织不同，这方面的研究有待进一步深入。

A scholar from Japan used ultrasonic wave appliance to observe the traverse reflect of Shenshu (BL 23), Zhishi (BL 52) on the bladder meridian after IR imaging. He found that there was liquid reflect wave in the middle of the acupoints, and slight hearted bump was detected. Новынский from the Soviet Union considered that the density of acupoint tissue was not dense as surroundings, so the ultrasonic waves could be reflected. More researches in this field are needed.

以上有关腧穴生物物理特异性的研究结果，从总体上讲是有意义的，但有些结论尚有争议，有待进一步证实。我们相信，随着现代科学的不断发展，我们将在中医理论的指导下，应用现代科学的高新技术手段，从根本上揭示腧穴的理化特性和物质基础。

The results all above about specificities of biophysics of acupoints are worthy, and more questions need to be answered. We truly believe, the material basis of acupoint will be clear in future, guided by Traditional Chinese Medicine theory and with the help of the modern technics.

三、腧穴病理反应研究
Study of Pathological Reaction of Acupoints

这里所说的腧穴的病理反应是指腧穴能反映相应脏腑器官的病理变化。古人对腧穴的这种特性早有认识。《灵枢·九针十二原》指出："五脏有疾也，应出十二原，而原各有所出，明知其原，睹其应，而知五脏之害矣。”腧穴的病理反应主要表现为穴处感觉、组织形态和生物物理特性三方面的变化。

The definition of pathological reaction of acupoints is acupoints would reflect the pathological changes in relevant organs inside. “If five - zang organs are sick, there will be reflects on twelve yuan - source points. each yuan - source point has its own root, so distinguish each yuan - source point and examine their changes. We will know the diseases from which five - zang organ suffered.” Quote from the chapter 1, *Miraculous Pivot*. The reactions are feelings on acupoints, morphology of tissues and biophysical features.

（一）穴位感觉变化
Senses Changing on Acupoints

穴位感觉变化主要表现为穴处的压痛或疼痛、酸、麻、胀和知热感度变化等。临床观察表明，膻中穴压痛可反映支气管炎；横骨穴压痛可反映月经不调和遗精；传染性肝炎患者可在中都穴出现敏感点；胰腺炎、阑尾炎、肾结核和肺癌患者可分别在左脾俞、右天枢、肾俞和肺俞穴出现明显压痛。穴位压痛有时还可反映疾病的证型，如阳明头痛可在阳白穴出现压痛，太阳头痛可在天柱穴出现压痛，期门穴压痛为肝火上亢头痛，京门穴压痛为肾亏头痛。

The senses changing on acupoints are pressing pain, pain, soreness, numbness, bloated and heat sensitiveness, etc. In clinic practices, pressing pain in Danzhong（RN 17）reflects bronchitis; Henggu（KI 11）pressing pain reflects irregular menses and spermatorrhoea; Zhongdu（LR 7）sensitive point reflects infectious hepatitis; and pancreatitis to left Pishu（BL 20）, appendicitis to right Tianshu（ST 25）, nephronophthisis to Shenshu（BL 23）, lung cancer to Feishu（BL 13）. Pressing pain reflects the syndromes of diseases, e. g. Yangbai（GB 14）reflects headache of yangming meridian, Tianzhu（BL 10）to taiyang meridian's headache, Qimen（LR 14）to the live - fire, Jingmen（GB 25）to kidney asthenia.

（二）穴位组织形态变化
Transformation on Acupoints' Tissue

通过触摸、按压、循捏、观视等方法常可发现穴处组织形态的异常变化，如可触及麦粒或黄豆大小的结节、条索状反应物和组织松弛，或可发现穴处皮肤脱屑、凹陷、隆突、皱纹、丘疹、斑点和色泽改变等。腧穴的这些组织形态的变化常可反映相应脏腑器官的病理变化。如胃癌患者可在胃俞穴出现条索状反应物，脾胃虚弱患者可出现脾俞、胃俞穴的松弛和凹陷，期门、太冲、曲泉穴处的结节常提示患者有严重肝病。

The tissue transformation on acupoints area could be checked by palpation, pressing, pinch and watch, e. g. kernel or soybean sized nodules, streak things, slack tissues, desquamation, sag, bump, wrinkle, papula, spots and color changing of skin could be detected through palpation, pressing, meridian – route pinch and observing, etc. These changes of the tissue on the meridian route normally reflect the pathological changes of the relevant organs inside. And streak things on Weishu (BL 21) reflect gastric cancer; slack and sag on Pishu (BL 20), Weishu (BL 21); nodes on Qimen (LR 14), Taichong (LR 3), Ququan (LR 8) reflect serious liver disease.

(三) 穴位生物物理特性变化 Biophysical Features Changing on Acupoints

这里所说的穴位生物物理特性变化，是指当脏腑器官发生病变时其相应穴位失去正常的生物物理特性。在电学特性方面主要表现为穴位皮肤电阻降低、电位增高或左右失衡等变化。北京医学院观察到消化性溃疡患者胃经穴位电阻左右失衡。北京针灸骨伤学院在对60名消化性溃疡患者的测试中发现其胃、脾、肾、肝和胆经井穴的导电量较正常人显著增高。河北医学院发现肺结核患者的神藏、中府和肺俞穴的电位常呈失衡态，肝硬化患者常在肝俞、行间穴出现电位失衡。Lahcehko发现中枢神经系统疾病患者头面部穴位的皮肤电位明显增高。近年，上海中医药大学观察到胃炎发作期患者所测足三里、冲阳、梁丘、公孙等穴伏安曲线的惯性面积均大于正常人；原发性高血压患者的肝俞、期门、太冲、太溪、鱼际等穴位的光谱值左右呈不对称性。有人对呈阳性病理反应的背俞穴做红外热像检测，发现背俞穴的温度异常与相应疾病有关，符合率达95.12%。

The definition of biophysical features changing is that normal biophysical features lacking on relevant acupoints reflects pathological changing on organs inside. The electrical properties changing are resistance decline, potential ascend, or lost bilateral balance. The Beijing College of Acupuncture – Moxibustion and Orthopedics – Traumatology found the quantity of conduction was higher than normal people on Jing – Well points on meridians of stomach, spleen, kidney, liver and gall bladder on the observation of 60 peptic ulcer patients. Hebei medical college found that potential unbalance on Shencang (KI 25), Zhongfu (LU 1), Feishu (BL 13) for lunger, and Ganshu (BL 18), Xingjian (LR 2) for liver cirrhosis. Lahcehko found skin potential on face was remarkably higher for central nervous system patients. Shanghai university of TCM find the inertia area of volt – ampere curves on Zusanli (ST 36), Chongyang (ST 42), Liangqiu (ST 34), Gongsun (SP 4), etc, are larger than normal for gastritis patients on stage of attack; the term value is unbalance on Ganshu (BL 18), Qimen (LR 14), Taichong (LR 3), Taixi (KI 3), Yuji (LU 10), etc, for essential hypertension. Someone uses IR imaging to detect the back – shu points on positive reaction, and find that the temperature abnormity is related with relevant diseases, the degree of accuracy is 95.12%.

腧穴的病理反应特异性并非绝对，而是相对的。这种相对性主要体现在两个方面。第一，一个穴位通常可反映多种疾病。如足三里主要反映胃的病症，包括胃溃疡、胃炎、胃癌等，尚可反映大肠、小肠和肝的病症。通常在生理病理上联系密切的脏腑的病变可在相同穴位上出现病理反应。第二，一个脏或腑的病症可反映在多个穴位上。如冠心病，除主要反应于心俞、神堂穴外，患者$T_{3\sim4}$左侧的皮肤还常出现皱纹和增厚等病理反应，有时小肠经或肾经的一些穴位也出现病理反应。

The specificity of pathological changing is conditional, and in two ways. The first one is an acupoint corresponds with multiple diseases, e. g. Zusanli (ST 36) reflects about stomach diseases, including gastric ulcer, gastritis, gastric cancer and also reflects diseases on large intestine, small intestine and liver. The second is a kind of disease reflects on multiple acupoints, e. g. Coronary heart disease not only reflects on Xinshu (BL 15), Shentang (BL 44), and wrinkles, thickness on $T_{3\sim4}$ left skin but also some reactions on the small intestine meridian and kidney meridian.

四、腧穴刺激效应研究
Study of the Effect of Stimulation on Acupoints

腧穴的刺激效应具有特异性，即刺激穴位可特异地对相应脏腑器官产生调治效应。腧穴刺激效应的这种特异性主要是与非穴和其他穴位比较而言的。

The specificity of stimulation on acupoint is the accommodation on relevant organs through stimulating on certain acupoints. This kind of effect is comparative for other acupoints and non - acupoints.

（一）对呼吸系统的调整作用
Accommodation on Respiratory System

针刺足三里捻针时，安静通气量、耗氧量均比针前增加，而针刺冲阳、厉兑、中脘等穴虽也可使呼吸和代谢机能有不同程度的加强，但均较针刺足三里效应为弱。针刺腹部穴位对呼吸机能有一定的抑制作用。针刺郄门、鱼际、太溪可使因开胸引起的纵膈摆动现象趋于平衡，其效果远比肺门周围神经封闭的古老方法优越。动物实验表明，针刺素髎、人中、会阴等穴均可引起呼吸即时性增强，对呼吸暂时停止皆有急救作用，但针刺不同穴位呼吸变化的阳性率不同，由高到低依次为素髎、人中、会阴，而非穴位点则无此效应。

The quiet ventilation and oxygen consumption goes up when needling on Zusanli (ST 36) and twirling, and needling Chongyang (ST 42), Lidui (ST 45), Zhongwan (RN 12), etc, enhance the metabolism also, but weaker. Needling acupoints on belly could restrain breathing. Mediastinum swing caused by thoracotomy could trend to peace by needling Ximen (PC 4), Yuji (LU 10), Taixi (KI 3), and the efficacy is better than traditional ways. Animal experiments show that breathing could be enhanced immediately by needling Suliao (DU 25), Renzhong (DU 26), Huiyin (RN 1), etc, can use it in emergency, the efficiency is different, from top to bottom is Suliao (DU 25), Renzhong (DU 26), Huiyin (RN 1).

(二) 针刺对心血管系统的调整作用
Accommodation on Cardio Vascular System

对冠心病患者针刺膻中、内关、足三里等穴，有三分之一的患者在针后20分钟内心电图出现明显好转。在以内关为主穴对急性心肌梗死合并心律失常的临床观察中发现，内关穴对心率、心律具有双向调节作用。对300例冠心病患者针刺内关、心俞等十穴后，患者左右心功能多呈良性变化，在改善指标的数量、程度、心肌氧耗量 MVO_2 和心电图疗效上，以内关、三阴交最为明显。另一项临床观察显示，针刺冠心病患者内关穴具有良好的调整心脏自主神经及改善变异性（HRV）作用。动物实验表明，针刺内关、郄门、神门等穴，可明显改善心肌缺血缺氧状态，降低由于缺血造成的心肌组织损伤的程度。

More than one third electric cardio gram of coronary disease patient improved in 20 minutes by needling Danzhong（RN 17）, Neiguan（PC 6）, Zusanli（ST 36）, etc. Neiguan（PC 6）adjusts heart rate and rhythm dual directional in the observation of cure on acute myocardial infarction, arrhythmia by Neiguan（PC 6）. The 300 coronary disease patients' heart function turns well after 10 acupoints like Neiguan（PC 6）, Xinshu（BL 15）, etc. Neiguan（PC 6）and Sanyinjiao（SP 6）have the best efficient on improving myocardium oxygen consumption（MVO_2）and other indices. Another clinical observation shows that needling Neiguan（PC 6）on coronary disease patient could adjust heart automatic nerve and heart rate variability. Animal experiments show that the injury of cardiac muscle and myocardial ischaemia and anoxia could be improved remarkably by needling Neiguan（PC 6）, Ximen（PC 4）, Shenmen（HT 7）, etc.

(三) 对消化系统的调节作用
Accommodation on Digestive System

针刺膻中、天突、合谷、巨阙穴，可使食道蠕动增强，管腔增宽，痉挛解除。不同穴位对胃蠕动具有不同的影响，针刺手三里后主要表现为胃蠕动增强，而针刺足三里后则主要表现为胃蠕动抑制。针刺肺俞、中府穴可使肝血流量明显增加，而针刺期门、肝俞穴则使肝血流量明显减少。在正常情况下，针刺足三里穴可明显促进葡萄糖的生成，并降低酮体、游离胆固醇和游离脂肪酸。针刺胆瘘患者的足三里、阳陵泉、承山等穴，可使胆汁流出量减少。对胆囊的收缩作用，穴位间的特异性表现也很突出，针刺足三里、胆囊、心俞、丘墟、阳陵泉等穴，可使胆囊明显收缩，其中正常人以阳陵泉最为明显，非胆经穴和非穴位无明显作用，而患者则以足三里最为明显，胆俞最弱。

Needling Danzhong（RN 17）, Tiantu（RN 22）, Hegu（LI 4）, Juque（RN 14）could enhance esophageal dysmotility, widen lumen, ease spasm. Different acupoints affect peristalsis differently, needling Shousanli（LI 10）enhance it but Zusanli（ST 36）reduce. Needling Feishu（BL 13）, Zhongfu（LU 1）increases the volume of blood in liver but Qimen（LR 14）, Ganshu（BL

18) decrease it. Normally, needling Zusanli (ST 36) promote the produce of glucose, decrease acetone bodies, free cholesterol and non – esterified fatty acid. The quantity of gall would be decreased by needling Zusanli (ST 36), Yanglingquan (GB 34), Chengshan (BL 57), etc, on the biliary fistulas. The usage on shrink of cholecyst is distinct between acupoints, needling Zusanli (ST 36), Dannang (EX – LE 6), Xinshu (BL 15), Qiuxu (GB 40), Yanglingquan (GB 34), etc, make the cholecyst shrink, and Yanglingquan (GB 34) is the most remarkable on normal people meanwhile acupoints out of the gallbladder meridian and non – acupoint are not significant; in patient, Zusanli (ST 36) is the most significant, and Danshu (BL 19) is the weakest.

(四) 对泌尿系统的调整作用 Accommodation on Urinary System

针刺肾炎患者的肾俞、气海或照海、列缺、太溪、飞扬等穴，可使患者肾脏泌尿功能明显增强，酚红排出量较针前增加，尿蛋白减少，高血压及浮肿亦有明显好转。针刺正常受试者的肾经复溜穴和膀胱经志室穴，多数于24小时内尿量、环磷酸腺苷及肌酐显著增高。针刺关元、三阴交等穴对功能性尿失禁的疗效非常显著。以肾俞、关元、阴陵泉为主穴，对泌尿系结石及由于结石梗阻所致的痉挛都有良好的调整作用，针刺次髎、曲骨、中极、关元穴可使膀胱内压升高者达80%，而针刺四肢部三阴交、阴陵泉、阳谷、列缺穴效应较差。

Needling Shenshu (BL 23), Qihai (RN 6) or Zhaohai (KI 6), Lieque (LU 7), Taixi (KI 3), Feiyang (BL 58), etc, enhance the urinary function, output of phenol red on the nephritis and decrease the urine protein, hypertension, and edema. Needling Fuliu (KI 7) on kidney meridian, Zhishi (BL 52) on the bladder meridian on healthy volunteer, the urine volume, cyclic adenosine monophosphate (CAMP), and creatinine increases remarkably in 24 hours. The efficacy to functional urinary incontinence is significant when needling Guanyuan (RN 4), Sanyinjiao (SP 6), etc. A fine accommodation of spasm caused by urinary stones, and stone blocking is cured by needling Shenshu (BL 23), Guanyuan (RN 4), Yinlingquan (SP 9) and 80% of subjects' urinary bladder pressure goes up caused by needling Ciliao (BL 32), Qugu (RN 2), Zhongji (RN 3), Guanyuan (RN 4), meanwhile low efficacy on Sanyinjiao (SP 6), Yinlingquan (SP 9), Yanggu (SI 5), Lieque (LU 7).

(五) 对神经-体液系统的调节作用 Accommodation on Nerve – Body Fluid System

针刺气舍、天突、合谷等穴，可使地方性甲状腺肿患者甲状腺缩小，症状减轻或消失，尿中排碘量明显降低，甲状腺对碘的吸聚和利用能力提高。针刺天突、廉泉、合谷等穴可使甲状腺功能亢进患者甲状腺缩小，症状消失，基础代谢明显降低。给正常人服用大量糖后，针刺合谷、肝俞、胃俞、膈俞和足三里穴，可得到三种耐糖曲线，即耐糖曲线原水平高者显著下降，而原水平低者略有升高，少数变化不定的，可能与个体差异及穴位的特异性有关。针刺空腹正常人合谷、内关和足三里穴或艾灸曲池、足三里等穴，空腹血糖大多上升，特别是原血糖较低者，上升尤为显著。选用关元、中极、三阴交等穴治疗不孕症或继发性闭经，可使患者的排卵过程与月经周期恢复正常。针刺中极、归来、血海、关元、三阴交等穴，可使继发性闭经患者出现激素撤退性出血现象。

Needling Qishe (ST 11), Tiantu (RN 22), Hegu (LI 4), etc, makes thyroid gland lessen, relieve or disappear symptom on the local goiters, decrease the quantity of iodine in urine, improve the absorb ability of thyroid gland. Needling Tiantu (RN 22), Lianquan (RN 23), Hegu (LI 4), etc, shrinks the thyroid gland on the hyperthyroidism, and ease the symptom, reduce the basic metabolism. Three sugar tolerance curves generates by needling Hegu (LI 4), Ganshu (BL 18), Weishu (BL 19), Geshu (BL 17), ZusanLi (ST 36) on normal people after mass sugar input, they are the much higher than normal, the little higher and the vibrating, maybe caused by individual difference. Needling Hegu (LI 4), Neiguan (PC 6) and Zusanli (ST 36) or moxa Quchi (LI 11), Zusanli (ST 36) on normal people with emptiness, the blood sugar index goes up mostly, especially for those lower level ones. Using Guanyuan (RN 4), Zhongji (RN 3), Sanyinjiao (SP 6), etc, to cure infertility or secondary amenorrhea could help the ovulation and menses recovery. Needling Zhongji (RN 3), Guilai (ST 29), Xuehai (SP 10), Guanyuan (RN 4), Sanyinjiao (SP 6), etc, could make internal hemorrhage caused by hormone withdrawal on the secondary amenorrhea.

和腧穴的病理反应具有特异性一样，腧穴刺激效应的特异性也是相对的。如内关穴除主要用于心脏病的治疗外，又可用来和胃止呕，有时还可用于头痛等脑部病变的治疗。合谷穴除对头面部相应器官和部位产生镇痛作用外，有时还可产生全身性的镇痛效应。

The effect of stimulation on acupoints is conditional, and the main efficacy is multiple directions for diseases. Take Neiguan (PC 6) as an example, it could cure heart disease, preventing vomiting and headache, and also Hegu (LI 4) could ease head analgesia and general analgesia.